Music in Western Civilization

VOLUME I: ANTIQUITY THROUGH THE BAROQUE

Music in Western Civilization

VOLUME I: ANTIQUITY THROUGH THE BAROQUE

Music in Western Civilization

VOLUME I: ANTIQUITY THROUGH THE BAROQUE

Craig Wright

Yale University

Bryan Simms

University of Southern California

SCHIRMER

CENGAGE Learning™

Australia • Brazil • Japan • Korea • Mexico • Singapore • Spain • United Kingdom • United States

SCHIRMER
CENGAGE Learning™

Music in Western Civilization
Volume I: Antiquity Through the Baroque
Craig Wright
Bryan Simms

Publisher: Clark Baxter

Senior Development Editor: Sue Gleason

Senior Assistant Editor: Julie Yardley

Editorial Assistant: Emily Perkins

Executive Technology Project Manager: Matt Dorsey

Executive Marketing Manager: Diane Wenckebach

Marketing Assistant: Rachel Bairstow

Marketing Communications Manager: Patrick Rooney

Project Manager, Editorial Production: Trudy Brown

Creative Director: Rob Hugel

Executive Art Director: Maria Epes

Print Buyer: Karen Hunt

Permissions Editor: Sarah Harkrader

Production Service: Johnstone Associates

Text and Cover Designer: Diane Beasley

Photo Researcher: Roberta Broyer

Copy Editor: Judith Johnstone

Autographer: Ernie Mansfield

Cover Image: Carlo Saraceni (1585–1620), *Saint Cecilia.*
   Galleria Nazionale d'Arte Antica, Rome, Italy. Scala/Art
   Resource, NY.

Compositor: Thompson Type

Text and Cover Printer: Quebecor World/Dubuque

For product information and technology assistance, contact us at
Cengage Learning Customer & Sales Support,
1-800-354-9706
For permission to use material from this text or product, submit all
requests online at **cengage.com/permissions**
Further permissions questions can be emailed to
permissionrequest@cengage.com

ExamView® and *ExamView Pro*® are registered trademarks of FSCreations,
Inc. Windows is a registered trademark of the Microsoft Corporation used
herein under license. Macintosh and Power Macintosh are registered
trademarks of Apple Computer, Inc. Used herein under license.

© 2006 Cengage Learning, Inc. All Rights Reserved. Cengage Learning
WebTutor™ is a trademark of Cengage Learning, Inc.

Student Edition
ISBN-13: 978-495-00865-6
ISBN-10: 0-495-00865-6

Wadsworth
10 Davis Drive
Belmont, CA 94002-3098
USA

Cengage Learning is a leading provider of customized learning solutions
with office locations around the globe, including Singapore, the United
Kingdom, Australia, Mexico, Brazil, and Japan. Locate your local office at:
international.cengage.com/region

Cengage Learning products are represented in Canada by Nelson
Education, Ltd.

For your course and learning solutions, visit **academic.cengage.com**

Purchase any of our products at your local college store or at our preferred
online store **www.ichapters.com**

Printed in China by China Translation & Printing Services Limited
4 5 6 7 11 10 09

BRIEF CONTENTS

ANTIQUITY AND THE MIDDLE AGES

1 Music in Ancient Greece   2

2 Antiquity to the Middle Ages: Music in Rome, Jerusalem, and the Early Christian World   12

3 Music in the Monastery and Convent   17

4 Music Theory in the Monastery: John of St. Gall and Guido of Arezzo   28

5 Later Medieval Chant: Tropes, Sequences, and the Liturgical Drama of Hildegard of Bingen   34

6 Troubadours and Trouvères   41

7 Early Polyphony   47

8 Music in Medieval Paris: Polyphony at Notre Dame   52

9 Music in the Cathedral Close and University: Conductus and Motet   61

10 In the Parisian Master's Study: Music Theory of the *Ars Antiqua* and *Ars Nova*   70

11 Music at the Court of the French Kings   75

12 Fourteenth-Century Music in Reims: Guillaume de Machaut   82

13 Avignon, Symbolic Scores, and the *Ars Subtilior*   89

Musical Interlude 1   From Medieval Manuscript to Modern Performance   95

THE LATE MIDDLE AGES AND EARLY RENAISSANCE

14 Music in Florence, 1350–1450   104

15 Music at the Cathedral of Florence   110

16 Music in England   115

17 Music at the Court of Burgundy   123

18 Music at the French Royal Court   131

19 Music in the Low Countries   140

THE LATE RENAISSANCE

Musical Interlude 2   Musical Humanism and
the Renaissance   148

20 Popular Music in Florence, 1475–1540: Carnival Song and Lauda,
Frottola, and Early Madrigal   150

21 Josquin des Prez and Music in Ferrara   158

Musical Interlude 3   Music Printing in the Renaissance   165

22 Music in Renaissance Paris   168

23 Renaissance Instruments and Instrumental Music   177

Musical Interlude 4   Music Theory in
the Renaissance   186

24 Music in Three German Cities: The Protestant-Catholic
Confrontation   190

25 Rome and the Music of the Counter-Reformation   203

26 Music in Elizabethan England: Early Vocal Music   210

27 Music in Elizabethan England: Instrumental Music and
Later Vocal Music   217

28 The Later Madrigal in Ferrara and Mantua: Gesualdo
and Monteverdi   222

BAROQUE MUSIC

29 Early Baroque Music   234

30 The Birth of Opera: Florence, Mantua, and Venice   240

31 The Concerted Style in Venice and Dresden   251

32 Religious Music in Baroque Rome   262

33 Instrumental Music in Italy   274

34 Instrumental Music in Germany and Austria   288

35 Music in Paris and at the Court of Versailles: Vocal Music   301

36 Music in Paris and at the Court of Versailles:
Instrumental Music   310

Musical Interlude 5   From Ancient to Modern: Aspects of Baroque
Music Theory   319

37 Music in London: Henry Purcell   322

38 Music in London: George Frideric Handel   330

39 Johann Sebastian Bach: Instrumental Music in Weimar
and Cöthen   340

40 Johann Sebastian Bach: Vocal Music in Leipzig   352

DETAILED CONTENTS

Preface   xxv

ANTIQUITY AND THE MIDDLE AGES

1   MUSIC IN ANCIENT GREECE   2

Music in Greek Society   3
  LISTENING CUE Euripides, *Orestes*, Stasimon Chorus (fragment)   4
  LISTENING CUE Seikilos, Skolion (Epitaph), *As long as you live*   5
The Nature of Greek Music   6
Music in Greek Philosophy   7
Greek Music Theory   8
Summary   11
Key Terms   12

2   ANTIQUITY TO THE MIDDLE AGES: MUSIC IN ROME, JERUSALEM, AND THE EARLY CHRISTIAN WORLD   12

Rome   12
Jerusalem and the Rise of Early Christian Music   14
Summary   17
Key Terms   17

3   MUSIC IN THE MONASTERY AND CONVENT   17

The Monastery of St. Gall, Switzerland   18
The Canonical Hours: The Work of the Lord   19
Gregorian Chant in the Monastery   20
Gregorian Chant for Vespers   21
  LISTENING CUE Chants of Vespers   23
    Antiphon, *Tecum principium*   23
    Psalm, *Dixit Dominus*   23
    Hymn, *Jesu, Redemptor omnium*   23
Gregorian Chant for the Mass   23
  LISTENING CUE Chants Beginning the Mass for Christmas Day   27
    Introit, *Puer natus est nobis*   27
    Kyrie   27
    Gloria   27
    Gradual, *Viderunt omnes*   27
    Alleluia, *Alleluia. Dies sanctificatus*   27
Summary   27
Key Terms   28

4 MUSIC THEORY IN THE MONASTERY: JOHN OF ST. GALL AND GUIDO OF AREZZO 28

The Eight Church Modes 29
Chant Notation 30
Musical Staff and Pitch Names 30
Hexachords 31
The Guidonian Hand 33
Summary 34
Key Terms 34

5 LATER MEDIEVAL CHANT: TROPES, SEQUENCES, AND THE LITURGICAL DRAMA OF HILDEGARD OF BINGEN 34

Tropes 35
LISTENING CUE Tuotilo of St. Gall, Introit trope, *Hodie cantandus est nobis* 35
LISTENING CUE Tuotilo of St. Gall, *Kyrie* trope, *Omnipotens genitor* 35
Sequences 36
LISTENING CUE Anonymous, *Dies irae* 37
Music in the Convent: The Chant and Liturgical Drama of Hildegard of Bingen 38
LISTENING CUE Hildegard of Bingen, *O rubor sanguinis* 40
LISTENING CUE Hildegard of Bingen, *Ordo virtutum* (excerpts) 41
Summary 41
Key Terms 41

6 TROUBADOURS AND TROUVÈRES 41

LISTENING CUE Beatriz de Dia, *A chantar m'er* 43
The Court of Eleanor of Aquitaine 43
LISTENING CUE Bernart de Ventadorn, *Can vei la lauzeta* 45
Trouvères 45
LISTENING CUE Richard the Lionheart, *Ja nus hons pris ne dira* 45
Summary 46
Key Terms 46

7 EARLY POLYPHONY 47

Organum in Music Theory Sources 47
Organum in Practical Sources 49
LISTENING CUE Anonymous, *Viderunt Hemanuel* 50
LISTENING CUE Master Albertus of Paris, *Congaudeant Catholici* 51
Summary 51
Key Terms 52

8 MUSIC IN MEDIEVAL PARIS: POLYPHONY AT NOTRE DAME 52

Notre Dame of Paris 53
Leoninus and the *Magnus liber organi* 54
   LISTENING CUE Leoninus, *Viderunt omnes* 56
Perotinus the Great 58
   LISTENING CUE Perotinus the Great, *Viderunt omnes* 60
Summary 61
Key Terms 61

9 MUSIC IN THE CATHEDRAL CLOSE AND UNIVERSITY: CONDUCTUS AND MOTET 61

Conductus 63
   LISTENING CUE Anonymous, *Orientis partibus* 65
   LISTENING CUE Philip the Chancellor, *Dic, Christi veritas* 65
Motet 65
   LISTENING CUE Anonymous motet, *El mois d'avril/O quam sancta/Et gaudebit* 68
   LISTENING CUE Anonymous motet, *On parole de batre/A Paris/Frese nouvele* 69
Summary 69
Key Terms 70

10 IN THE PARISIAN MASTER'S STUDY: MUSIC THEORY OF THE *ARS ANTIQUA* AND *ARS NOVA* 70

Franco of Cologne and the *Art of Measured Song* 71
Jean des Murs and Philippe de Vitry: The *Ars Nova* 72
Summary 74
Key Terms 75

11 MUSIC AT THE COURT OF THE FRENCH KINGS 75

The *Roman de Fauvel* 76
   LISTENING CUE Gervès de Bus, *Roman de Fauvel* 76
   LISTENING CUE Anonymous, *Quare fremuerunt gentes* 77
Philippe de Vitry 77
   LISTENING CUE Philippe de Vitry, *Garrit Gallus/In nova fert/Neuma* 78
Royal Dances 78
   LISTENING CUE Anonymous, *La quinte estampie real* 80
Musical Instruments at Court and in Church 80
   LISTENING CUE Anonymous, Robertsbridge Codex, *Estampie* 81
Summary 81
Key Terms 82

12 FOURTEENTH-CENTURY MUSIC IN REIMS: GUILLAUME DE MACHAUT   82

Machaut, the Black Death, and the Hundred Years' War   83
   LISTENING CUE Guillaume de Machaut, *Hoquetus David*   84
Machaut and the *Formes fixes*   84
   LISTENING CUE Guillaume de Machaut, *Je puis trop bien*   86
   LISTENING CUE Guillaume de Machaut, *Douce dame jolie*   87
Machaut and the Mass of Our Lady   87
   LISTENING CUE Guillaume de Machaut, *Kyrie* of the *Mass of Our Lady*   88
Summary   89
Key Terms   89

13 AVIGNON, SYMBOLIC SCORES, AND THE ARS SUBTILIOR   89

Papal Avignon   89
Baude Cordier and Symbolic Scores   91
   LISTENING CUE Baude Cordier, *Tout par compas suy composés*   92
Philippus de Caserta: The *Ars Subtilior*   93
   LISTENING CUE Philippus de Caserta, *Par les bons Gedeons*   93
Summary   95
Key Terms   95

Musical Interlude 1
From Medieval Manuscript to Modern Performance   95

Part II THE LATE MIDDLE AGES AND EARLY RENAISSANCE

14 MUSIC IN FLORENCE, 1350–1450   104

Trecento Music and the Squarcialupi Codex   105
   LISTENING CUE Jacopo da Bologna, *Non al suo amante*   106
Francesco Landini   107
   • *Women Making Music in Boccaccio's* Decameron   *109*
   LISTENING CUE Francesco Landini, *Or su, gentili spirti*   110
Summary   110
Key Terms   110

15 MUSIC AT THE CATHEDRAL OF FLORENCE   110

   • *Musical Number Symbolism*   *113*
   LISTENING CUE Guillaume Dufay, *Nuper rosarum flores*   114

Summary   114
Key Terms   115

16   MUSIC IN ENGLAND   115

Rondellus and Rota   116
   LISTENING CUE Anonymous, *Sumer is icumen in*   118
English Faburden and Continental Fauxbourdon   118
King Henry V: The Old Hall Manuscript and the Carol   119
   • *Vestiges of English Traditions in the "Country" Music of Today*   121
   LISTENING CUE Anonymous, Agincourt Carol   121
John Dunstaple and the *Contenance Angloise*   121
   LISTENING CUE John Dunstaple, *Quam pulcra es*   123
Summary   123
Key Terms   123

17   MUSIC AT THE COURT OF BURGUNDY   123

Gilles Binchois and the Burgundian Chanson   125
   LISTENING CUE Gilles Binchois, *Dueil angoisseus*   126
Guillaume Dufay: A Lament and a Mass for the Christian Soldier   127
   LISTENING CUE Guillaume Dufay, *Lamentatio sanctae Matris Ecclesiae Constantinopolitanae*   129
   LISTENING CUE Guillaume Dufay, *Kyrie* of the *Missa L'Homme armé*   131
Summary   131
Key Terms   131

18   MUSIC AT THE FRENCH ROYAL COURT   131

Johannes Ockeghem and Musical Canons   132
   LISTENING CUE Johannes Ockeghem, *Prenez sur moi*   133
   LISTENING CUE Johannes Ockeghem, *Kyrie* of the *Missa Prolationum*   134
A Musical Joke for the French King   135
   LISTENING CUE Josquin des Prez, *Guillaume se va chaufer*   136
Philippe Basiron and the Paraphrase Motet   136
   LISTENING CUE Philippe Basiron, *Salve, Regina*   137
Antoine Busnoys and the Imitative Chanson   137
   LISTENING CUE Antoine Busnoys, *Je ne puis vivre ainsy tousjours*   138
   • *Women Poets and Performers*   139
Summary   139
Key Terms   140

19   MUSIC IN THE LOW COUNTRIES   140

Jacob Obrecht and the Multiple Cantus Firmus Mass   140
   LISTENING CUE Jacob Obrecht, *Credo* of the *Missa Sub tuum presidium*   142

Musical Instruments   142
The *Basse Danse*   143
   LISTENING CUE Heinrich Isaac, *La Spagna*   144
Summary   145
Key Terms   145

THE LATE RENAISSANCE

Musical Interlude 2

Musical Humanism and the Renaissance   148

20 POPULAR MUSIC IN FLORENCE, 1475–1540: CARNIVAL SONG AND LAUDA, FROTTOLA, AND EARLY MADRIGAL   150

The Carnival Song and the Lauda   150
   LISTENING CUE Lorenzo de' Medici, *Sian galanti di Valenza*   151
   LISTENING CUE Girolamo Savonarola, *Giesù, sommo conforto*   153
The Frottola   153
   LISTENING CUE Josquin des Prez, *El grillo è bon cantore*   155
The Early Madrigal in Florence   155
   LISTENING CUE Jacques Arcadelt, *Il bianco e dolce cigno*   157
   LISTENING CUE Orazio Vecchi, *Il bianco e dolce cigno*   158
Summary   158
Key Terms   158

21 JOSQUIN DES PREZ AND MUSIC IN FERRARA   158

Josquin des Prez   159
Josquin's Music for Duke Hercules of Ferrara   159
   LISTENING CUE Josquin des Prez, *Sanctus* of the *Missa Hercules dux Ferrarie*   161
   LISTENING CUE Josquin des Prez, *Miserere mei, Deus*   163
Josquin and an Artist's Temperament   163
Summary   164
Key Terms   164

Musical Interlude 3

Music Printing in the Renaissance   165

22 MUSIC IN RENAISSANCE PARIS   168

The Parisian Chanson   168
Claudin de Sermisy   169
   LISTENING CUE Claudin de Sermisy, *Tant que vivray*   170
Instrumental Arrangements   171
   LISTENING CUE Claudin de Sermisy, *Tant que vivray* arranged for lute   171
   LISTENING CUE Claudin de Sermisy, *Tant que vivray* arranged for voice and lute   172
   LISTENING CUE Claudin de Sermisy, *Tant que vivray* arranged for keyboard   173
Dance Music   173
   • *Thoinot Arbeau: The Dancing Priest*   175
   LISTENING CUE Anonymous, Pavane and
      Galliard   176
Summary   177
Key Terms   177

23 RENAISSANCE INSTRUMENTS AND INSTRUMENTAL MUSIC   177

Keyboard Instruments   178
String Instruments   179
Wind Instruments   181
Instrumental Genres   182
   LISTENING CUE Miguel de Fuenllana, Fantasia   184
   LISTENING CUE Claudio Merulo, Canzona 5   185
Summary   185
Key Terms   186

Musical Interlude 4
Music Theory in the Renaissance   186

24 MUSIC IN THREE GERMAN CITIES: THE PROTESTANT-CATHOLIC CONFRONTATION   190

Innsbruck: Music under Emperor Maximilian I   191
   LISTENING CUE Heinrich Isaac, *Innsbruck, ich muss dich lassen*   193
   LISTENING CUE Paul Hofhaimer, *Salve, Regina* for Organ   194
The Reformation: Music in Augsburg   194
   LISTENING CUE Martin Luther, *Ein feste Burg ist unser Gott*, Chorale   197
   LISTENING CUE Johann Walter/Martin Luther, *Ein feste Burg ist unser Gott*, 4-part
      setting   198
Orlande de Lassus and the Court of Munich   198
   LISTENING CUE Orlande de Lassus, *De profundis clamavi*   200
Epilogue: The Psalter in Other Protestant Countries   201
Summary   202
Key Terms   202

25   ROME AND THE MUSIC OF THE COUNTER-REFORMATION   203

Giovanni Pierluigi da Palestrina   204
  LISTENING CUE Giovanni Pierluigi da Palestrina, *Sanctus* of the *Missa Aeterna Christi munera*   206
  LISTENING CUE Giovanni Pierluigi da Palestrina, *Tu es Petrus*   207
  LISTENING CUE Giovanni Pierluigi da Palestrina, *Kyrie* of the *Missa Tu es Petrus*   208
Spanish Music during the Counter-Reformation   209
Summary   209
Key Terms   209

26   MUSIC IN ELIZABETHAN ENGLAND: EARLY VOCAL MUSIC   210

Henry VIII as Musician and Church Reformer   210
  LISTENING CUE King Henry VIII, *Pastyme with Good Companye*   211
  • *The Education of a Renaissance Queen*   212
Thomas Tallis and the English Psalm   212
  LISTENING CUE Thomas Tallis, *Psalm 2*   214
William Byrd and the English Anthem   214
  LISTENING CUE William Byrd, *O Lord, make thy servant, Elizabeth*   216
Summary   216
Key Terms   217

27   MUSIC IN ELIZABETHAN ENGLAND: INSTRUMENTAL MUSIC AND LATER VOCAL MUSIC   217

English Keyboard Music   218
  LISTENING CUE Thomas Morley, *Goe from my window*   219
The English Madrigal   219
  LISTENING CUE Thomas Weelkes, *As Vesta Was from Latmos Hill Descending*   220
The English Lute Ayre   221
  LISTENING CUE John Dowland, *Flow my tears*   222
Summary   222
Key Terms   222

28   THE LATER MADRIGAL IN FERRARA AND MANTUA: GESUALDO AND MONTEVERDI   222

The Madrigal in Ferrara   223
Carlo Gesualdo   225
  LISTENING CUE Carlo Gesualdo, *Moro, lasso*   227

Music in Mantua: Isabella d'Este   227
Claudio Monteverdi   228
   LISTENING CUE   Claudio Monteverdi, *Cruda Amarilli*   230
Summary   230
Key Terms   231

BAROQUE MUSIC

29   EARLY BAROQUE MUSIC   234

Characteristics of Early Baroque Music   236
Summary   239
Key Terms   240

30   THE BIRTH OF OPERA: FLORENCE, MANTUA, AND VENICE   240

Early Opera in Florence   240
   LISTENING CUE   Jacopo Peri, *Euridice*, "Funeste piagge"   243
   LISTENING CUE   Giulio Caccini, *Le nuove musiche, Filli, mirando il cielo*   244
Early Opera in Mantua: Monteverdi's *Orfeo*   244
   LISTENING CUE   Claudio Monteverdi, *Orfeo*, Toccata   244
   LISTENING CUE   Claudio Monteverdi, *Orfeo*   247
     Recitative, "A l'amara novella"   247
     Arioso, "Tu se' morta, mia vita"   247
     Aria, "Possente spirto"   247
Early Opera in Venice   248
   LISTENING CUE   Claudio Monteverdi, *L'incoronazione di Poppea*, Duet, "Pur ti miro"   249
   • *Did Monteverdi Write the Finale? Does It Matter?*   250
Summary   250
Key Terms   251

31   THE CONCERTED STYLE IN VENICE AND DRESDEN   251

Giovanni Gabrieli and the Concerted Motet   254
   LISTENING CUE   Giovanni Gabrieli, *In ecclesiis*   254
Claudio Monteverdi and the Concerted Madrigal   254
   LISTENING CUE   Claudio Monteverdi, *Hor che 'l ciel e la terra*   256
Barbara Strozzi and the Early Baroque Cantata   256
   LISTENING CUE   Barbara Strozzi, *L'Amante Segreto: Voglio morire*   258
The Concerted Style Moves North: Heinrich Schütz in Dresden   258
   LISTENING CUE   Heinrich Schütz, *Symphoniae sacrae; Saul, Saul, was verfolgst du mich?*   261

Summary   261
Key Terms   261

32   RELIGIOUS MUSIC IN BAROQUE ROME   262

The *Cappella Pontificia Sistina* and the *Stile Antico*   263
  • *Mozart Pirates Allegri's* Miserere   265
  LISTENING CUE Gregorio Allegri, *Miserere mei, Deus*   265
St. Peter's Basilica and the Colossal Baroque   265
  LISTENING CUE Unknown, *Kyrie of the Missa Salisburgensis*   267
Organ Music by Girolamo Frescobaldi   267
  LISTENING CUE Girolamo Frescobaldi, *Fiori musicali*, Mass for Sundays   269
    Toccata   269
    Kyrie   269
    Ricercar   269
Sacred Opera and Oratorio: Giacomo Carissimi's *Jephte*   269
  LISTENING CUE Giacomo Carissimi, *Jephte*   271
    "Plorate, colles" (solo)   271
    "Plorate, filii Israel" (chorus)   271
The Chamber Cantata: A Christmas Cantata by Alessandro Scarlatti   272
  LISTENING CUE Alessandro Scarlatti, Cantata *Oh di Betlemme*   273
    Recitative, "Oh di Betlemme"   273
    Aria, "Dal bel seno d'una stella"   273
Summary   273
Key Terms   274

33   INSTRUMENTAL MUSIC IN ITALY   274

The Violin Family   274
Formation of the Baroque Orchestra   275
  • *The Violin Then and Now*   276
Church and Chamber Music   277
Salomone Rossi and the Early Baroque Sonata   277
  LISTENING CUE Salomone Rossi, *Sonata sopra l'aria di Ruggiero*   279
Arcangelo Corelli: Solo Sonata and Trio Sonata   279
  LISTENING CUE Arcangelo Corelli, Opus 4, No. 1   282
    Preludio   282
    Corrente   282
    Adagio   282
    Allemanda   282
Trumpet Music by Giuseppe Torelli: The Beginnings of the Solo Concerto   282
  LISTENING CUE Giuseppe Torelli,
    Trumpet Sinfonia in D Major   284
Antonio Vivaldi: Solo Concerto and Concerto Grosso   284
  LISTENING CUE Antonio Vivaldi, Opus 3, *L'estro armonico*, Concerto Grosso, No. 8,
    1st movement   287
Summary   287
Key Terms   288

34 INSTRUMENTAL MUSIC IN GERMANY AND AUSTRIA 288

Johann Froberger and the Baroque Dance Suite   289
   LISTENING CUE Johann Froberger, Suite No. 6 in C Major   291
      Lamento (Allemande)   291
      Courante   291
      Sarabande   291
      Gigue   291
Biber and Kuhnau: The Programmatic Sonata   291
   LISTENING CUE Heinrich Biber, "Mystery" Sonatas, *The Resurrection*   293
   • *The Doctrine of Affections*   295
Dieterich Buxtehude and the North German Organ Tradition   296
   LISTENING CUE Dieterich Buxtehude, *Wie schön leuchtet der Morgenstern*   298
Johann Pachelbel and the South German Tradition   299
   LISTENING CUE Johann Pachelbel, *Wie schön leuchtet der Morgenstern*   299
   LISTENING CUE Johann Pachelbel, Canon in D Major   300
Summary   300
Key Terms   301

35 MUSIC IN PARIS AND AT THE COURT OF VERSAILLES: VOCAL MUSIC 301

Ballet de cour   302
Jean-Baptiste Lully and *Tragédie lyrique*   303
   • *Lully Kills Himself Conducting*   306
   LISTENING CUE Jean-Baptiste Lully, *Armide*   306
      Overture   306
      "Enfin il est en ma puissance"   306
Religious Music   307
Elizabeth Jacquet de La Guerre and the *Cantate française*   307
   LISTENING CUE Elizabeth Jacquet de La Guerre, *Jephté*   309
      Aria, "Jephté revient"   309
      Recitative, "La Fille de Jephté"   309
Summary   309
Key Terms   310

36 MUSIC IN PARIS AND AT THE COURT OF VERSAILLES: INSTRUMENTAL MUSIC 310

The Gaultiers: French Lute Music   310
   LISTENING CUE Denis Gaultier, *La Rhétorique des dieux, Tombeau de Madamoiselle Gaultier*   313
The Couperins: French Harpsichord Music   313
   • *The Eighteenth-Century French Harpsichord*   317
   LISTENING CUE François Couperin, *Pièces de clavecin . . . premier livre, La Favorite*   317

LISTENING CUE François Couperin, *Pièces de clavecin . . . quatrième livre*,
L'Arlequine   318
Summary   318
Key Terms   319

Musical Interlude 5

**From Ancient to Modern: Aspects of
Baroque Music Theory   319**

37 MUSIC IN LONDON: HENRY PURCELL   322

Henry Purcell and Theater Music   323
   LISTENING CUE Henry Purcell, *Dido and Aeneas*   326
      Recitative, "Thy hand, Belinda"   326
      Aria, "When I am laid in earth"   326
Purcell's Odes and Funeral Music for Queen Mary   326
   • *Art Music Displaced by Folk Music*   327
   LISTENING CUE Henry Purcell, *Come, ye sons of art*   328
      Chorus, "Come, ye sons of art"   328
      Duet, "Sound the trumpet"   328
      Chorus, "Come, ye sons of art"   328
   LISTENING CUE Henry Purcell, Funeral Music for Queen Mary, March and Canzona
      329
Summary   329
Key Terms   330

38 MUSIC IN LONDON: GEORGE FRIDERIC HANDEL   330

Handel and the Dance Suite   331
   LISTENING CUE George Frideric Handel, *Water Music*, Suite No. 1   333
      Minuet and Trio   333
      Hornpipe   333
Handel and Opera   333
   • *The Castrato in Handel's Operas*   334
   LISTENING CUE George Frideric Handel,
      Giulio Cesare, Aria, "V'adoro, pupille"   335
   • *Opera Then and Now*   336
Handel and Oratorio   336
   LISTENING CUE George Frideric Handel, *Messiah*   338
      Aria, "He shall feed his flock"   338
   LISTENING CUE George Frideric Handel, *Messiah*   339
      "Hallelujah" chorus   339

Summary 340
Key Terms 340

39 JOHANN SEBASTIAN BACH: INSTRUMENTAL MUSIC IN WEIMAR AND CÖTHEN 340

Bach in Weimar: The Organ Music 342
- *The Organ in Bach's Day* 343
LISTENING CUE Johann Sebastian Bach, *Orgelbüchlein*, "In dulci jubilo" 345
LISTENING CUE Johann Sebastian Bach, *Orgelbüchlein*, "Durch Adams Fall ist ganz verderbt" 345
Bach in Cöthen: Chamber and Orchestral Music 346
LISTENING CUE Johann Sebastian Bach, The Well-Tempered Clavier, Prelude and Fugue in C Minor 348
- *Pitch and Tuning in Bach's Day* 349
LISTENING CUE Johann Sebastian Bach, Brandenburg Concerto No. 5 in D Major, 1st movement 352
Summary 352
Key Terms 352

40 JOHANN SEBASTIAN BACH: VOCAL MUSIC IN LEIPZIG 352

The Lutheran Chorale Cantata 353
- *Bach's Choir and Orchestra: Where Were the Ladies?* 355
LISTENING CUE Johann Sebastian Bach, Cantata, *Wachet auf, ruft uns die Stimme*, Movement 1 356
  Movements 2, 3, 4 357
  Movements 5, 6, 7 358
- *Bach's Four-Part Chorale Harmonizations and Teaching Music Theory Today* 358
Bach's Later Musical Projects 358
LISTENING CUE Johann Sebastian Bach, B-Minor Mass, *Credo* 361
  "Crucifixus" 361
  "Et resurrexit" 362
Summary 362
Key Terms 363

Notes 364
Bibliography 366
Credits 368
Glossary 370
Index 386

PREFACE

The decision to write a new history of Western music must appear to others, as it occasionally still does to its authors, as an act of madness. Of course, we have taken up this challenge in order to create a book that will best serve our students and our own goals as teachers. But it seems appropriate at the outset to inform prospective readers—and even to remind ourselves—what these goals are and what specific things we think make this text better than other histories of Western music.

THE "PLACE" OF MUSIC

Music is the expressive voice of a culture, and often that voice is clearest in one particular city, country, or region. For this reason, we have centered our discussion of music in the places where it took deepest root. For example, we link much of the presentation of medieval music to the city of Paris; Handel to London; Beethoven to Vienna; Richard Strauss to Berlin; jazz to Harlem. We have not attempted daring or esoteric connections. But by placing music in a culturally resonant setting, we can help our students to see and hear how the sociopolitical life of certain places not only gave rise to musical genres and styles but also broadened and shaped all of Western civilization. To accomplish our overarching goal, we made certain pedagogical decisions based on our many years of teaching music history.

CONTENT AND ORGANIZATION

The most visible difference in the organization of this book is its arrangement of topics into 83 brief chronological chapters. The book includes everything we thought most important to cover, and its many brief chapters promote three main goals. First, the arrangement of chapters makes it easier for instructors to present the material to students in any order that best suits their courses. For example, we are accustomed to teaching the instrumental music of Bach before his vocal music. But instructors more comfortable leading with vocal music can easily do so by assigning Chapter 40 before Chapter 39. Second, as instructors all know, students do not invariably bring to their studies an unquenchable desire to read the assigned text material. We have found that assigning a smaller passage for every class session yields better results than long chapters. Third, short chapters allow time for supplementary or source readings, and thus promote a better-rounded treatment of the subject at hand.

To provide variety for the student while studying the basic materials and musical selections, we engage special topics in **Boxes.** These are always germane to the subject under discussion, and they give the student a momentary diversion on some relevant issue in the history of music. For example, students enjoy the quirky observations on sixteenth-century social dancing made by aging priest Thoinot Arbeau, so we have highlighted his *Orchésographie* in Chapter 22. Similarly, students are generally astonished to find that people were paid to attend opera performances in the nineteenth century and to applaud on cue, so a box in Chapter 62 explains the existence of the *claque*. Nine longer **Musical Interludes** appear between various chapters. These discussions—music printing in the Renaissance, the critical concept of romanticism, and the birth of rock, among others—deal with larger issues that characterize an entire musical and cultural age, and their greater length and placement between chapters reflect their added importance.

A comprehensive **Timeline** of composers interwoven with the important political, social, and artistic events of that era opens each of eight parts of the book. We intend each timeline to provide a visual synopsis of a major historical period and a cultural context for the many musical events that we will discuss in the chapters that follow.

At the root of any study of music history, of course, lies the music itself, and our 267 CD tracks represent the major genres, composers, and works in the history of Western music. The discussion in each chapter moves quickly from a geographical and cultural context to a close study of these works, which are placed in students' hands in the form of excellent recordings and scores. A **Listening Cue** in the text alerts the reader whenever the time is right to leave the text, pick up headphones and the Anthology, and grapple with the primary materials of music.

In our selection of music, we have emphasized the **coverage of women composers** by including works by Hildegard of Bingen, Beatriz de Dia, Barbara Strozzi, Elizabeth Jacquet de La Guerre, Clara Schumann, Alma Mahler, Lili Boulanger, Bessie Smith, Ruth Crawford Seeger, and Joan Tower. We are mindful that many important composers—male as well as female—have of necessity been omitted from our discussion to produce a text of reasonable size. We invite comments about our choices and have appended our e-mail addresses to the end of this preface for this and any other issues readers may wish to discuss with us. In rare instances, where we were unable to include a piece on the CD set, the Listening Cue directs the reader to the book's website or to the Internet.

MATERIAL TAILORED TO YOUR COURSE

Most schools offer music history for music majors in a sequence covering one, two, or three semesters. A few lucky colleagues have four or more semesters to cover this subject. We both teach at schools that devote three semesters to the history survey, and we are well aware of the problems that arise in adapting any one text to sequences of different durations. But the emerging web economy has taught us and our students that we must provide greater choices.

Accordingly, we offer the book, the Anthology, and the thirteen CDs that accompany the text in combinations that match a typical two- or three-semester course—march time or waltz time, as it were. The book is also available, of course, as a single-volume text, in hardcover for durability over the course of a year or more. Students rightly complain if they must buy a book and then are assigned only part of it. Our flexible configuration of print and audio material allows instructors to require students to buy only as much material as they will actually use. The ISBN and order information for these several print and audio options appear on the back cover of the text.

For teaching formats that we have not anticipated but may best fit your unique course syllabus, please write your local Cengage Learning sales representative to craft a print medium customized to your course. For help contacting this person, use the Rep Locator on the Cengage Learning home page: www.cengage.com.

ANCILLARIES

Several remarkable ancillaries accompany the text.

Anthology

Timothy Roden of Ohio Wesleyan University has joined us to create a splendid anthology of Scores. It contains all of the central works discussed in the text with the exception of a few jazz and modern pieces that lack scores. Tim has added informative introductory notes to each selection and supplied new translations for all works with texts in foreign languages. As mentioned earlier, the complete Anthology is available in two or three volumes.

Audio CDs and Web

Virtually every piece that we discuss in the text appears on one of thirteen audio CDs; recordings of a few works can be located on the book's website (academic .cengage.com/music). The recordings are of the highest quality; for example, much of the recorded medieval music comes from the prestigious Harmonia Mundi label. Recordings of hitherto unrecorded pieces have been specially commissioned from professional groups and performers, including The Washington Cornett and Sackbut Ensemble.

Workbook

Timothy Roden has also written a unique student workbook of analytical exercises and probing questions that will help students examine each piece of music in the Anthology and prepare for exams and quizzes. Nothing like it exists now, and by engaging the student, these exercises bring the music to life. The Workbook also includes an essay by Sterling Murray, "Writing a Research Paper on a Musical Subject," as well as a bibliography for students designed to help in the process of writing papers. The bibliography can also be found on the website (academic.cengage.com/music).

Instructor's Resource CD-ROM

An all-inclusive CD ROM contains ExamView computerized testing, as well as an electronic version of the Instructor's Manual/Test Bank. Also found here are PowerPoint presentations that include outlines for lectures, additional illustrations, musical examples in the text, audio clips, and other materials for use in the classroom.

ACKNOWLEDGMENTS AND THANKS

A project this comprehensive and complex is naturally the work of many hands. We are grateful to colleagues who gave generously of their time, ideas, and good will to make this undertaking a success. Some read and critiqued large portions of the text, others answered specific questions, and still others graciously provided materials. We are sincerely grateful to all of the following for their help.

Jonathan Bellman, *University of Northern Colorado*

Jane Bernstein, *Tufts University*

Francisco Lorenzo Candelaria, *University of Texas, Austin*

Tim Carter, *University of North Carolina, Chapel Hill*

Cynthia J. Cyrus, *Blair School of Music, Vanderbilt University*

Jeffrey Dean, *The New Grove Dictionary of Music and Musicians*

Charles Dill, *University of Wisconsin, Madison*

Christine Smith Dorey, *Case Western Reserve University*

Lawrence Earp, *University of Wisconsin, Madison*

Robert Eisenstein, *University of Massachusetts and Mount Holyoke College*

Robert Galloway, *Houghton College*

David Grayson, *University of Minnesota*

James Grymes, *University of North Carolina, Charlotte*

Barbara Haggh-Huglo, *University of Maryland*

James Hepokoski, *Yale University*

Michael Holmes, *University of Maryland*

Derek Katz, *University of California, Santa Barbara*

Terry Klefstad, *Southwestern University*

Walter Kreyszig, *University of Saskatchewan*

James Ladewig, *University of Rhode Island*

Paul Laird, *University of Kansas*

Bruce Langford, *Citrus College*

Charles S. Larkowski, *Wright State University*

Lowell Lindgren, *Massachusetts Institute of Technology*

Dorothea Link, *University of Georgia*

Daniel Lipori, *Central Washington University*

Ralph Lorenz, *Kent State University*

Patrick Macey, *Eastman School of Music*

Thomas J. Mathiesen, *Indiana University*

Charles Edward McGuire, *Oberlin College Conservatory of Music*

Bryce Mecham, *Brigham Young University*

Donald C. Meyer, *Lake Forest College*

Sharon Mirchandani, *Westminster Choir College of Rider University*

Sterling Murray, *West Chester University*

Giulio Ongaro, *University of Southern California*

Leon Plantinga, *Yale University*

Keith Polk, *University of New Hampshire*

Hilary Poriss, *University of Cincinnati*

John Rice, *Rochester, Minnesota*

Anne Robertson, *University of Chicago*

Ellen Rosand, *Yale University*

David Rothenberg, *Colby College*

Ed Rutschman, *Western Washington University*

Christopher J. Smith, *Texas Tech University School of Music*

Tony C. Smith, *Northwestern State University of Louisiana*

Kerala Snyder, *Eastman School of Music*

Pamela Starr, *University of Nebraska*

Marica Tacconi, *Pennsylvania State University*

JoAnn Taricani, *University of Washington*

Susan Thompson, *Yale University*

Jess B. Tyre, *State University of New York at Potsdam*

Zachariah Victor, *Yale University*

Scott Warfield, *University of Central Florida*

Mary A. Wischusen, *Wayne State University*

Gretchen Wheelock, *Eastman School of Music*

Several colleagues who specifically asked to remain anonymous

Closer to home, we wish to thank our respective wives, Sherry Dominick and Charlotte E. Erwin, for reading and evaluating the text, for giving advice on many fronts, and, most of all, for their support and patience. Having ready access to the music libraries at Yale and the University of Southern California has been a special boon, and we are grateful to Kendall Crilly, Richard Boursy, Suzanne Lovejoy, and Eva Heater for help in acquiring materials, and to Karl Schrom and Richard Warren for advice with regard to recordings. Also offering invaluable assistance during the creation of new recordings were Richard Lalli and Paul Berry. At the end of the project we could not have done without the indefatigable labors of graduate students Pietro Moretti and Nathan Link in researching, editing, proofreading, and preparing materials for the instructor's CD; in the course of this project the students became the mentors.

Finally, the authors wish to thank the staff of Cengage Learning that has helped to produce this volume. First of all, the guiding light, from beginning to end, was our publisher and friend, Clark Baxter; in many ways, this book is his. Joining Clark in this enterprise were a number of exceptionally talented people including Trudy Brown, who coordinated with great finesse the production of every part of this massive undertaking. Judy Johnstone merged, with her accustomed skill and forbearance, countless print and electronic chapters, images, and autography into a book that Diane Beasley's design has made exceptionally attractive. Sharon Poore and Sue Gleason helped us develop the manuscript itself. Julie Yardley worked closely with us and with Tim Roden on the ancillaries, especially on the Anthology. Emily Perkins, Clark's remarkable assistant, kept an ocean of paper and electronic material moving in the right direction, and on schedule. Matt Dorsey oversaw the development of the book's website and the Instructor's Resource CD-ROM. Finally, a word of thanks to Diane Wenckebach, who brought boundless energy and commitment to the marketing of this text, and who, with Patrick Rooney, prepared its promotional material.

Craig Wright
(craig.wright@yale.edu)

Bryan Simms
(simms@usc.edu)

Music in Western Civilization

ANTIQUITY AND THE MIDDLE AGES

*T*he period between 750 B.C.E. and about 1400 C.E. brought sweeping changes to the West. Our story of Western music begins during the age of antiquity in ancient Greece, where our democratic institutions, modes of critical thought, and the value we place on athletic contests and on the arts—especially music—find their roots. Greek music theory was later passed in voluminous amounts, sometimes by Roman interpreters, to the Middle Ages and the Renaissance. Monasteries provided centers of learning in the West during the early Middle Ages. They also preserved the great body of Western religious music, namely monophonic Gregorian chant, or

800 B.C.E.	700	600	500	400	300	200	100	0	100 C.E.	200	300

ANTIQUITY (800 B.C.E.–476 C.E.)

● 776 B.C.E. First Olympic Games include songs and hymns

c580–500 B.C.E. Pythagoras explores science of sound

c500–400 B.C.E. Euripides', Sophocles', Aeschylus', Aristophanes' plays include songs

Socrates (469–399 B.C.E.), continuing with Plato (c429–347 B.C.E.) and Aristotle (384–322 B.C.E.), expound ideas on music and education

Arithmetical basis of intervals and durations beginning fourth century B.C.E.

c6 B.C.E.–c30 C.E. **Jesus Christ**   Ambrose

1st century C.E. **Epitaph of Seikilos**

432 B.C.E. The Parthenon

Corbis

Part I

plainsong, intended for use with the Mass and canonical hours. Only after many centuries, around 900 C.E., was a written system of notation devised for Western plainsong. Shortly thereafter, polyphony emerged in England, France, and Spain. By 1300 C.E. Western musicians had not only developed a method for notating pitch but also one for regulating the increasingly complex rhythms of polyphony. On the eve of the Renaissance, in the late 1300s, composers began to turn away from this complexity and employ simpler rhythms and textures and more sonorous harmonies.

400	500	600	700	800	900	1000	1100	1200	1300	1400	1500

MIDDLE AGES (476–1450)

(340?–397) Ambrosian chant

c850–950 Earliest musical notation of plainchant and polyphony

c435 Martianus Capella develops *quadrivium*, including music

1100 John of St. Gall writes *De Musica* on 8 church modes

476 Western Roman Empire ends

King Richard I of England (1157–1199), trouvère

c612 St. Gall founded

Hildegard of Bingen (1098–1179)

Augustine of Hippo (354–430) *De Musica* on music and rhythm

Charlemagne (742–814)

800 C.E. Gallican chant merges with Roman

mid-1100s Beatriz de Dia, trobairitz

1200 Motet emerges in Paris

Boethius (c480–524) *De institutione musica*, compendium of Greek music theory

c1316 *Roman de Fauvel*

c1320 *La quinte estampie real*

Benedict of Nursia (c480–c550) establishes Benedictine order

Machaut, *Messe de Nostre Dame* (1360s)

Tuotilo of St. Gall (c850–915) composes tropes

1380s Philippus de Caserta, *Ars subtilior*

Notker Balbulus (c840–912) composes sequences

1030 Guido of Arezzo establishes musical staff and solfege

Jean des Murs (c1290–c1351), *Ars novae musicae*

Philippe de Vitry (1291–1361), *Ars nova*

Jacques de Liège (c1260–c1330), *Ars antiqua*

Guillaume de Machaut (c1300–1377)

Gargoyle on Notre Dame of Paris, built 1163–1285. Leoninus and Perotinus the Great compose polyphony there.

Corbis

1348–1350 Black Death

1337–1453 Hundred Years' War

Baude Cordier (c1365–1398), circular canon

First clavichord 14th century

Bridgeman Art Library

1378–1417 Great Western Schism

Chapter 1

Music in Ancient Greece

We in the West owe much to the ancient Greeks. Our democratic institutions, modes of critical thought, and the value we place on athletic contests and on the arts—especially music—trace their roots directly back to ancient Greece. In a real way, music in Western civilization began with the music and culture of that country.

Although Greece today is a rather small country, 2,500 years ago it exerted vast influence as the center of the civilized world in the West. Between 750 and 500 B.C.E. Greek colonists spread out around the shores of the eastern Mediterranean Sea (Map 1-1). Later, under the leadership of Pericles (c495–c429 B.C.E.), Greek political power was concentrated in the area around the city-state of Athens. During this period, called the Periclean Age, Athens saw the flowering of democratic principles as well as extraordinary artistic excellence. All male citizens had an equal voice in deciding affairs of state, and all citizens, male or female, enjoyed equal protection under the law. On a hill within Athens, an area called the Acropolis, the Greeks built a temple to the patron goddess of their city, Athena Nike (literally, Bringer of Victory). Here, in the Parthenon (see Part I timeline), architecture and sculpture expressed the qualities of beauty we have come to associate with classical art: symmetry, balance, an absence of excessive detail, and harmony in all things. During the fifth century B.C.E., Western drama had its beginnings in the powerful plays of Aeschylus, Sophocles, and Euripides. So too the philosophers of Athens, beginning with Socrates (469–399 B.C.E.) and continuing with Plato (c429–347 B.C.E.) and

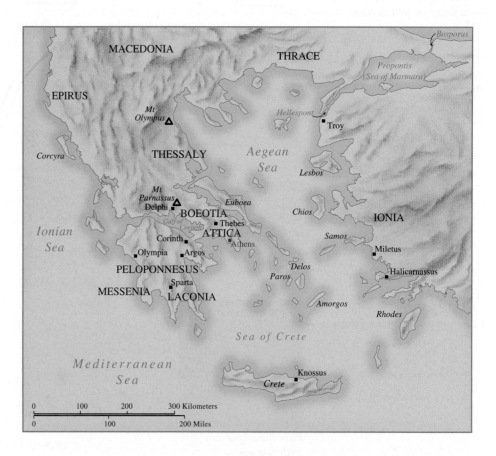

MAP 1-1
Ancient Greece.

Aristotle (384–322 B.C.E.), set the foundation for Western philosophical inquiry, which seeks to know the nature of reality. Thus, the Greeks of Athens established many of the political and intellectual systems, as well as the standards for beauty, that we still cherish today.

Sports and music, too, were basic to Greek life. Early on, festivals involving athletic competitions and music were offered in honor of the chief Greek god, Zeus, who was believed to dwell on Mount Olympus. From there, it was said, he hurled a thunderbolt that landed two hundred miles away, on what is called the plains of Olympia. On that spot in 776 B.C.E., and at four-year intervals thereafter, the best athletes of the world gathered to compete. From these games our modern Olympic Games have descended. The philosopher Socrates taught that music and gymnastics were the two essentials of every good education. His pupil Plato said in *Republic* that these two disciplines must be kept in proper balance, believing that too much music made the body weak and too much sport made the spirit insensitive.

But music was more than a mere counterbalance to athletic activity. All Greek poetry was sung, and most Greek drama was chanted, not spoken, to various metrical patterns. In these contexts, the Greeks refused to separate word from musical sound. Nor could dance be separated from her two sister muses, poetry and music. Greek vases frequently depict musical scenes in which the figures seem to move with the music. Figure 1-1 shows a line of lyre players stepping high as they sing and play. Such illustrations suggest that for the Greeks the sister arts of music, poetry, and dance were inextricably linked.

FIGURE 1-1

Mid-sixth century amphora shows the close association among text, music, and movement. The players of the lyre seem to be executing the "fine high steps" described in a contemporary hymn.

MUSIC IN GREEK SOCIETY

Music set the rhythm of Greek life. There were drinking songs, work songs, love songs, wedding songs, bridal chamber songs, funeral dirges, odes for heroic warriors, and hymns for the gods. Depending on the social context, Greek song might be performed by a chorus or by a solo singer, and it might be accompanied by a musical instrument such as the lyre, kithara (type of lyre), or aulos (wind instrument).

Public Religious Festivals

The ancient Greeks honored their gods by means of public religious festivals recurring every year, every two years, or every four years. The Olympic Games, as mentioned, was one such festival that was held on the plains of Olympia every four years before some 40,000 spectators who had walked to the site. In addition to athletic competitions and horse races, the games involved contests in poetry, dancing, and music. Related to the Olympic Games were the Panhellenic Games and the Pythian Games, both of which emphasized the arts. Prizes were awarded to the best performers on instruments such as the kithara and the aulos. All of these festivities, like our modern Olympic Games, were preceded by an elaborate procession with musical accompaniment during which a unison chorus sang praises to the gods. The stately **paean,** for example, was a hymn that celebrated the deeds of primary gods such as Zeus (the chief god) and Apollo (the god of the sun, of music, and of reason). On the other hand, the passionate **dithyramb** was a wild choral song, mingled with shouts, which did honor to playful Dionysus (the god of wine and fertility). Religious rites and bacchanals—both infused with music—were part of the original Olympics.

Music in the Theater

Public festivals also included Greek dramas. Drama gave poets, actors, and citizens of the chorus an opportunity to create large-scale musical structures on themes important to Greek life. At one annual festival held in Athens in honor of the god Dionysus, five comedies and three tragedies were presented over the course of five days. Prizes were awarded to the best playwright and the best actor. Greek theater usually allowed on stage two or three actors and an all-male chorus, numbering around fifteen. The chorus was far more important in ancient Greek drama than it is in the theater today. It commented on and moralized about the action occurring on stage (just as it would in later Baroque opera). The actors sang some parts and spoke others, while the chorus sang, gestured, and danced with dignity. A player of the aulos accompanied the chorus, in order to enhance the emotional response of the audience. Two papyrus scraps with musical notation for two plays by Euripides (d. 406 B.C.E.) are all that remain of the music of this once-great union of the musical and dramatic arts. Fortunately, one of these is the climactic Stasimon Chorus from Euripides' play *Orestes*. Euripides himself may have composed the music as well as the text. Because the papyrus is fragmentary, what we hear are really phrases from a Greek chorus, rather than the chorus in its entirety. Nonetheless, the fragment is sufficient to give us a sense of the power and the strange beauty of Greek dramatic music.

LISTENING CUE

EURIPIDES	CD 1/1
Orestes (c408 B.C.E.)	Anthology, No. 1
Stasimon Chorus (fragment)	

Private Festivities: The Symposium

In addition to religious and dramatic festivals, Greek music was integral to everyday life. Work songs, love songs, and bawdy tunes appeared spontaneously. Other types of music-making occurred within carefully regulated domestic parties. Of these, the most elaborate was the symposium. The **symposium** was a tightly organized social gathering in which adult male citizens came together for conversation and entertainment—an after-dinner drinking party. Inside a well-to-do residence a special room accommodated seven or eleven couches set end to end along three of the walls. Reclining one or two to a couch, the men communicated, debated, and posed riddles across the open space in the center of the room. A symposiarch (master of ceremonies) laid down the rules for the evening and established the order of events. He decided the number of kraters (large wine bowls) to be drunk and set the proportion of water to wine for each krater (Fig. 1-2). (The ancient Greeks thought drinking undiluted wine barbaric.) A well-balanced mixture of wine and water brought relaxation and conviviality to the group. Everyone conversed. Some recited poetry to musical accompaniment. Professional musicians, dancers, and courtesans (prostitutes for aristocrats) provided entertainment as well as sexual favors. A well-conducted symposium was thought to be a highly civilized event providing liberation from everyday restraints within a carefully regulated environment. As Athenaeus wrote in his *Deipnosophistae* (*The Learned Banquet*):

❀ FIGURE 1-2

A fifth-century B.C.E. wine krater carries this image depicting a symposiast reclining on a couch as he is entertained by female aulete (player of the aulos).

Réunion des Musées Nationaux/Art Resource, NY

> Drink with me, play music with me
> love with me, wear a crown with me,
> be mad with me when I am mad,
> and wise with me when I am wise.[1]

The primary musical entertainment at the symposium was the **skolion,** a song setting a brief lyrical poem. As a wreath of myrtle (symbol of the poetic muse) was
passed around the room, each guest in turn was asked to sing a skolion and to accompany himself on the lyre. Those who refused were thought to be uncultured.
Surviving today is a poem by Seikilos, written in the first century C.E., and long
thought to be one of the few skolia to survive with music (Ex. 1-1). Some scholars
call it an epitaph—a short piece of prose or verse eulogizing someone deceased.
Here, the four lines expound a fatalistic "eat-drink-and-be-merry" philosophy appropriate for a symposium. They inform a complete, albeit short, composition in
which the notation allows for an unambiguous transcription into modern symbols.

EXAMPLE 1-1[†]

1. As long as you live, shine   2. Grieve you not at all
3. Life is of brief duration   4. Time demands its end

🔘 LISTENING CUE

SEIKILOS   CD 1/2
Skolion or Epitaph (first century C.E.)   Anthology, No. 2
As long as you live

The ancient Greek musical notation clearly indicates the pitches and sets the
rhythmic durations. The basic unit of time was a short value called the **chronos**
(here, the eighth note). Two chronoi formed a long value called the **diseme** (quarter note) and three a triple-unit long called the **triseme** (dotted quarter). In the
skolion of Seikilos, the final syllable of each line is emphasized by means of a
triseme. The song spans an octave and is written in what some Greek music theorists called the Phrygian tonos (discussed below)—the equivalent of our white-note
scale on D. At the outset, the melody immediately reaches for the top-most note of
the Greek Phrygian mode and at the end concludes with the bottom-most note.
How are we to judge the impact of such a brief piece? Surely the effectiveness of the
skolion of Seikilos would depend entirely on the degree of enthusiasm and convic-
tion with which a wine-inspired singer might perform it.

[†]Adapted from Thomas J. Mathiesen, *Apollo's Lyre: Greek Music and Music Theory in Antiquity* (Lincoln,
1999), pp. 149–50.

THE NATURE OF GREEK MUSIC

Musical Notation

Most Greek music was not written down but was transmitted orally from performer to performer, generation after generation. Much of the music that was written has been destroyed over time; very little Greek music survives today, no more than fifty pieces. Most are carved in stone monuments or written on papyrus. Moreover, many of these papyrus leaves are mere fragments. Consequently, our understanding of the sound of Greek music is limited. We can talk in general terms about the place of music in Greek society but it is very difficult to recreate its sounds.

The Greeks did, nevertheless, create a system of musical notation. Yet it was very different from our modern-day clefs, round note heads, and letter names for pitches. Instead, the Greeks assigned to each pitch a specific symbol derived from letters and grammatical signs. Several of these symbols can be seen positioned above the modern musical staff at the beginning of Example 1-1. Because the Greeks did not repeat a sign when reaching the octave, as we do, and because they divided the octave into many more than twelve pitches, Greek notation involved a great number of signs, more than sixty in just a three-octave span. To complicate matters further, the Greeks employed one set of symbols for vocal sounds and a second set of symbols for instrumental music, bringing the total number of signs to more than one hundred twenty. Given this complexity, it is no wonder that Greek musical notation was not adopted by later Western European musicians. Our present Western system of musical notation, which makes use of a staff and round notes with letter names, did not begin to evolve until more than a thousand years after the heyday of ancient Greek music (see Chapter 4).

Musical Instruments

Greek music, being closely tied to poetry and drama, was fundamentally vocal music and therefore literary in character. Both Plato and Aristotle stated that instrumental music was inferior to vocal music. Yet the Greeks did have musical instruments: percussion instruments similar to our timpani, and the snare drum, tambourine, and cymbals; wind instruments including a rudimentary flute; and a variety of plucked string instruments such as the psaltery and harp. (Oddly, they had few "stopped" or "fretted" string instruments like the violin or guitar.) Foremost among these Greek instruments were those of the family of the lyre (a plucked string instrument) and the aulos (a reed wind instrument). These were associated, respectively, with the restrained music for Apollo, and with the wilder, more excited sounds in honor of Dionysus.

The **lyre** was a medium-sized instrument usually fitted with seven strings of sheep gut and plucked by a plectrum of metal or bone (see Fig.1-1). The resonator at the bottom was simply a large turtle shell to which the strings were indirectly attached. The lyre rarely played solo melodies, being used most often to accompany a solo singer—usually the player himself—by providing a few stable pitches, perhaps a scale.

The largest of all Greek string instruments was the **kithara,** an especially big lyre. The kithara, too, usually had seven strings, but the resonator at the bottom was a sound-box made of wood rather than tortoise shell. Figure 1-3 shows a performer, head thrown back in song, singing to the sounds of a kithara. The right hand, which has just finished a stroke, strums the strings with a plectrum attached to the bottom of the sound-box with a string. By means of a wristband, the left forearm braces the

FIGURE 1-3

A player of the kithara sings to his own accompaniment.

The Metropolitan Museum of Art

instrument against the body, while the left hand damps the strings. The kithara enjoyed high status in Greek society because it was most often used to accompany paeans offered to Apollo, the god of music. In Greek mythology, Apollo himself played the kithara and vanquished his enemy Marsyas, inventor of the aulos, in a famous musical battle of the gods.

The **aulos,** by contrast, was a wind instrument fitted with a round single reed or with a flat double reed. It consisted of two basic parts, the mouthpiece containing the reed(s) and the body or resonator. The resonator was made of wood or bone and was drilled through with a cylindrical bore and four or five finger holes. In later more advanced instruments, rudimentary key mechanisms were added so that additional finger holes might be set into the instrument and its range thereby extended. Paintings of the period show conclusively that the aulos was played in pairs (see Fig. 1-2); the left hand played one instrument, the right hand another. Together the two might produce ten or more pitches, and perhaps over-blowing would have allowed even more. In such cases, some rudimentary polyphony, playing in parallel fifths for example, was surely possible. While we might be tempted to think of the aulos as creating a sound similar to that of the modern clarinet or oboe, in fact it is really impossible to characterize the timbre of this early Greek woodwind instrument. A few instruments survive, but they can only be studied, not played. Contemporary writers, however, report that the aulos produced a high, clear, penetrating sound.

 ## MUSIC IN GREEK PHILOSOPHY

The Ethical Power of Music

Music was not only a pleasant amusement, improving the quality of life, but it could also affect human behavior, so the Greeks believed. For this reason both Plato (in *Laws*) and Aristotle (in *Politics*) declared music to be the most powerful of all the arts. To change a citizen's behavior, one need merely change the music! Thus, only the most upright sort of music should be taught to the youth of Athens. The Dorian mode (associated with Apollo) was thought appropriate because it was orderly and relaxed in its manner and rhythms, whereas the Phrygian (appropriate for Dionysus) was more frenzied and ecstatic, and more likely to encourage wanton behavior and drunkenness. Thus music had the force of law. In the words of Plato (*Republic*): "Our songs are our laws." Although the Greeks' attempts to regulate behavior by controlling music may seem repressive to us, do we not exhibit some of the same mentality in the "parental advisory" labels that go on some of today's compact discs?

To be sure, the ethical power of music, and the need to regulate it, was a notion deeply embedded in the Greek mythology. The following story recounts how the famous mathematician Pythagoras used music to save one member of his community from the crime of arson.

> Who is unaware that Pythagoras, by means of a spondaic melody, calmed and restored to self-control a youth of the city of Taormina who had become intoxicated by the sound of the Phrygian mode? For one night a prostitute was shut up in the house of the youth's rival, and he in his frenzy was about to set fire to it. Meanwhile Pythagoras, who was observing the motion of the stars, as was his custom, learned that the youth, agitated by the sound of the Phrygian mode and deaf to the many pleas of his friends, refused to desist from his crime. Pythagoras ordered that the mode be changed, and thus reduced the youth's fury to a state of perfect calm.[2]

Music of the Spheres

Notice in the preceding legend that **Pythagoras** (sixth century B.C.E.) was outdoors observing the motion of the stars. This is important, for Pythagoras was an astronomer and mathematician as well as a musician. As we shall see, because the sounds of music can be expressed as numbers, music was viewed as a science as well as an art in pre-modern times. Greek philosophy held that behind the surface appearance of everyday life rested universal truths that could be expressed in motion, in number, and in music. When the stars and planets rotated in balanced proportions, they made heavenly music—**music of the spheres** (see also Chapter 2). The soul on earth was to be in harmony with the heavens, so it too needed to embody a harmonious music. Body and soul resonate with earthly music (instruments and voices) because music consists of vibrations that are sympathetically felt by the body. If a mental or physical illness occurs, then a therapeutic music should be administered. This was the Greek world-view of music, and it persisted in the West until the time of Shakespeare and beyond.

GREEK MUSIC THEORY

Greek philosophers spoke of a wondrous harmony throughout the universe. Music on earth was simply the audible expression of that harmony, and it sounded by means of mathematical ratios. By studying these ratios, we might comprehend truths about the sounds and secrets of the universe. But it remained for the Greek philosopher-musicians to explain how this worked—to demonstrate the arithmetical basis of musical intervals and durations. Thus, beginning with Aristoxenus in the fourth century B.C.E., continuing through Ptolemy, Cleonides, and Aristides Quintilianus in the centuries after Christ, and finally ending with Boethius about 520 C.E., a succession of great minds probed with astonishing rigor the nature of musical intervals, consonance and dissonance, and the scales. At no time in the history of music has the arithmetical basis of music been more thoroughly explored than under the penetrating eyes of the Greek theorists. These men were not interested in analyzing pieces of music. They were scientists seeking to understand the very essence and meaning of music. Aristoxenus, for example, was one of Aristotle's closest associates and a master of his methods of observation and classification; Claudius Ptolemy (flourished 127–148 C.E.) was an astronomer whose celestial observations were considered authoritative for the next fourteen hundred years. For these theorists, music was a science: pure, but not simple.

Intervals and Scales

Our understanding of musical intervals and our scale can be traced back to another myth involving the legendary Pythagoras. One day, when passing a forge, Pythagoras heard a blacksmith simultaneously bang two iron hammers and produce the sound of an octave. Investigating further, Pythagoras observed that the hammer giving the higher sound weighed exactly half that of the hammer producing the lower one. Hammers whose weights were in a 3:2 proportion produced the sound of a fifth, those in a 4:3 proportion produced a fourth. Inherent in a few simple mathematical ratios were the basic consonances of music. Pythagoras then went home, so the story goes, and replicated this experience with strings of different lengths.

   In truth, iron hammers do not produce musical intervals in this fashion, and the pitches of strings depend not only upon their length but also their diameter and the tension placed upon them. But Pythagoras' principle was correct: strings or pipes with lengths having a 2:1 ratio produce an octave, 3:2 a fifth, 4:3 a fourth, and 9:8 a whole tone. Almost magically, the essence of music could be understood in ratios of four integers: 12:9:8:6.

Using these ratios, Greek theorists could construct a scale. They had no clefs or staff, simply the idea of ratios and intervals. With the aid of a device called the **monochord** (a single string stretched over a wooden block and anchored at each end; see Fig. 4-1) they took a string and divided it in parts to produce the intervals of an octave, fifth, fourth, and whole step. By applying these ratios at different points on the monochord, they created a regular succession of pitches—a scale. The building block within the scale was a **tetrachord** (a succession of four pitches) whose intervals begin with a semitone (S) followed by two full tones (T). Within the octave two successive tetrachords sounded above the pitch of the basic string. Today we would call the basic string (the lowest-sounding pitch) low A (the Greeks called it the **proslambanomenos**). The two tetrachords shared a common pitch and are thus conjunct tetrachords. Next, above this octave scale, two more conjunct tetrachords were added. The two tetrachords in the middle of the scale were separated by a whole tone and thus were disjunct. These four tetrachords, along with the proslambanomenos, formed the Greek **Greater Perfect System,** the framework of the Greek two-octave scale. Example 1-2 sets this within our modern great staff.

EXAMPLE 1-2

└→ Proslambanomenos

Notice the similarities of the Greater Perfect System to our own white-key scale. From the Greeks' successive derivation of pitches from basic ratios (2:1, 3:2, 4:3 and 9:8) resulted a scale in which each octave-span contained seven pitches (five whole tones and two semitones), an arrangement that has endured to the present day. Thus from the very beginning of music theory, the scale has only a semitone between what we call E and F, and between B and C; the basic ratios of music required it be so.

Although the Greeks had no grid (staff) to indicate relative pitch height, their Greater Perfect System can be placed on our modern great staff. Moreover, the Greeks had scale patterns, just as we have our major and minor scales. They called each scale a **tonos** (plural, **tonoi**). Some Greek theorists identified as many as thirteen or even fifteen scales. The astronomer-musician Ptolemy, however, reduced the number to seven, one pattern for each of the seven species of diatonic scale within the octave. When placed within a modern representation of the Greater Perfect System, the seven tonoi appear as in Example 1-3.

EXAMPLE 1-3

| Mixolydian | Lydian | Phrygian | Dorian | Hypolydian | Hypophrygian | Hypodorian |

Greek theorists derived the names for these scales from the modes of singing associated with particular ethnic groups living around the Aegean Sea (Phrygia, for example, is in what is now western Turkey). Originally, these names may have reflected not only a scale pattern preferred in a particular region but also a style of singing, vocal quality, and mood that was favored there. Although Ptolemy's system contained seven scales, three were always thought more important: Lydian (corresponding to our diatonic C-C), Phrygian (D-D), and Dorian (E-E).[†]

The skolion of Seikilos mentioned earlier (Anthology, No. 2) would accord perfectly with Ptolemy's Phrygian tonos. Similarly, the Stasimon Chorus from Euripides' *Orestes* (Anthology, No. 1) is notated, according to Ptolemy's system, in the Phrygian tonos (transposed to E), but with chromatic inflections.

To accommodate chromaticism within the Greater Perfect System, the Greeks allowed for three different types of tetrachords, three "genera," as they were called. In all three genera the first and fourth pitches of the tetrachord were fixed (see capital letters below), while the inner two pitches were movable. The basic genus within the Greek system was called the **diatonic genus** (to the Greeks, "diatonic" meant "through the tones"). The diatonic genus reflected the primary tetrachord spanning the intervals S-T-T.

In its unaltered form, the Greater Perfect System is a succession of diatonic tetrachords, one disjunct point in the middle separating two conjunct tetrachords on either side. For chromaticism, however, another tetrachord was employed called the **chromatic genus** ("chroma" in Greek means "color"). A chromatic tetrachord consisted of two semitones and a minor third. It allowed more semitones to be inserted into the greater perfect system. Music demanding more subtle variations of pitch made use of the **enharmonic genus** ("enharmonic" means "in harmony" or "same sounding"). The enharmonic genus required a tetrachord consisting of a major third and two quartertones (pitches sounding nearly the same). Finally, as if the three genera were not enough, the Greeks further subdivided each genus into two "shades." Obviously, Greek melody was far more nuanced than our own, making use of what we call microtones—tones smaller than our semitones.

> tetrachord of the diatonic genus: E, f, g, A
>
> tetrachord of the chromatic genus: E, f, f♯, A
>
> tetrachord of the enharmonic genus: E, e+, f, A

In practice a melody might be written in any one of the Greek tonoi, and the basic diatonic genus might be altered as well; that is, for greater expression, the chromatic or the enharmonic genus might be inserted momentarily. Moreover, entire melodies could be constructed using nothing but the chromatic or the enharmonic genus. Following is the Dorian tonos in each of the three genera.

> Dorian tonos in the diatonic genus: E, F, G, A, B, C, D, E
>
> Dorian tonos in the chromatic genus: E, F, F♯, A, B, C, C♯, E
>
> Dorian tonos in the enharmonic genus: E, E+, F, A, B, B+, C, E

Today in music we have two distinctly different scalar patterns: major and minor. The Greeks, as we have seen, had multiple tonoi, further inflected by the various

---

[†]Later, in the Middle Ages, these names would be associated with different scale patterns.

shades of the diatonic, chromatic, and enharmonic genera. Today we clearly hear the difference between a piece in major and one in minor—recognizing that they have different moods. The ancient Greeks felt even more acutely the effects of their different tonoi and their shades. As Aristotle stated in his *Politics*:

> The musical scales differ essentially one from another, and those who hear them are differently affected by each. Some make men sad and grave, like the so-called Mixolydian. Others weaken the mind, like the relaxed scales. Yet others produce a moderate and settled mood, which appears to be the special effect of the Dorian. The Phrygian inspires enthusiasm![3]

SUMMARY

Music informed life in ancient Greece to a surprising degree. Greek poets, philosophers, and scientists (themselves often musicians) frequently spoke of music. Because much Greek music was unwritten, and because much of what was written has been lost over time, there are only about fifty pieces (many fragmentary) surviving today. But Greek music theory was passed to the Middle Ages and Renaissance in voluminous amounts. Totaling more than a thousand dense pages and written over many centuries, ancient Greek music theory demonstrates a mathematical rigor and complexity that would never again be seen in the music theory of any people, East or West. Yet, not only does Greek music theory exhibit complexity but it also reveals that Greek music was in some ways richer and more subtle than our own. The Greeks enjoyed a greater number of scale patterns, for example, and employed microtones not possible on our modern keyboard.

Aspects of Ancient Greek Music Passed On to the West
1. A system of consonance and dissonance (octaves, fifths, fourths, and their multiples were consonances) that would remain unchanged until the fourteenth century
2. A system recognizing octave duplication and dividing each octave into seven pitches (five whole tones and two semitones)
3. The concept of scale patterns, each with its own name, incorporating different intervallic sequences
4. A system of tuning, called Pythagorean, that involved mathematically exact octaves, fifths, and fourths; it remained the only system of tuning discussed by music theorists until the late fifteenth century
5. Important musical terms such as "tetrachord," "diatonic," "chromatic," "enharmonic"

Aspects of Greek Music Passed to the Middle Ages
But Then Gradually Abandoned
1. Notation: the Greeks had notational symbols for vocal music and a separate set of signs for instrumental music, but their system was cumbersome and was abandoned by the ninth century
2. Microtones
3. A belief in the music of the spheres
4. A belief that music is a quantitative science

What Was Not Passed On by the Ancient Greeks
1. A large musical repertory
2. Analysis of compositions

3. Instruments (only images survive, but few real artifacts)
4. A musical staff or clefs (the Greeks had no grid or staff; they thought only in terms of intervals and scale patterns)
5. A theory of musical rhythm (rhythm in Greek music, as discussed in the theory treatises, did not affect the development of written rhythmic notation in the West)

KEY TERMS

paean	lyre	proslambanomenos
dithyramb	kithara	Greater Perfect System
symposium	aulos	tonos
skolion	Pythagoras	diatonic genus
chronos	music of the spheres	chromatic genus
diseme	monochord	enharmonic genus
triseme	tetrachord	

Antiquity to the Middle Ages: Music in Rome, Jerusalem, and the Early Christian World

 ROME

During the two centuries before the birth of Christ, the growing Roman Empire largely overran and absorbed the civilization of ancient Greece (Map 2-1). Typified by the brilliant general Julius Caesar (100–44 B.C.E.), the Romans personified military might, engineering skill, and administrative efficiency. Roman architecture, which endures today from the British Isles to the Near East, remains one of the wonders of the Western world. Roman dramatists such as Plautus and Terence gave us comic plays that are produced in schools today, just as Latin poems by Ovid and Virgil are still studied in Latin classes for their wit and elegance of style. But, oddly, the Romans left us little that is truly original by way of painting, sculpture, and music. Roman sculptures are often copies of earlier ones by Greek masters, and what little Roman painting survives seems to be equally derivative. With regard to music, once again the Romans borrowed heavily from the Greeks.

To be fair, it is difficult to know precisely what the music of ancient Rome was like, for not a note of it survives. Whereas approximately fifty examples of Greek music are extant from the Hellenic world, from the Romans there are none. This may suggest that Roman music was overwhelmingly oral in its transmission and not a written art. Roman historians comment about music in religious and civic ceremonies—in theatrical productions, during religious processions, and at athletic

MAP 2-1
The Roman Empire, 117 C.E.

FIGURE 2-1
Roman *tuba*, preserved in the Instrument Collection of the Museum of Fine Arts, Boston.

contests. These same writers mention musical instruments, but the instruments they name are mainly those already played by the Greeks. The Romans in their turn adopted the simple wood flute, the lyre, the kithara, and the aulos, which they named the **tibia,** perhaps because of its bone-like appearance. In only one respect did the Romans exhibit what might be called a distinctly Roman musical instrument, and that was the trumpet.

Almost all writers, Greek and Roman, attribute the origin of the trumpet to the Etruscans, distant forebears of the Romans who lived in northern Italy nearly a thousand years before Christ. The Roman name for the trumpet was **tuba.** Images embedded in sculpture and pottery show that the *tuba* was a long, straight instrument with a cylindrical bore and a bell at the end. Writers say that it was made of bronze and iron, and was played with a bone mouthpiece (Fig. 2-1). Like the later straight-pipe trumpet of the Middle Ages, the *tuba* could play the fundamental pitch of its pipe as well as the harmonic series above it, depending on the capabilities of the player. The *tuba* served, among other things, to signal commands during battle, for its sound was said by various writers to be booming, roaring, loud, and clear. Given the military might of the Romans, it is not surprising that their principal contribution to music history was an instrument of war. From it developed the trumpet and, ultimately, beginning in the fourteenth century, the trombone.

As to music theory, here again the Romans owed a heavy debt to the Greeks. As much as 95 percent of what appears in early theoretical writings in Latin was culled from even earlier Greek sources. Among the Roman theorists of note was Augustine of Hippo (354–430 C.E.), who became a Christian theologian and was later canonized as St. Augustine. His *De Musica* (*On Music*) is a six-book study of rhythm in music and poetry. Martianus Capella (flourished c435 C.E.), who, like Augustine, lived in a Roman colony in North Africa, set forth a framework of seven intellectual

❦ FIGURE 2-2

Boethius and Pythagoras. Boethius sets pitches with a monochord while Pythagoras measures them with bells.

disciplines called the **seven liberal arts.** The first three—grammar, logic, and rhetoric—formed the **trivium;** these deal with language, logic, and oratory. The final four—arithmetic, geometry, astronomy, and music—constituted the **quadrivium;** they are scientific disciplines, for each uses number and quantitative reasoning to arrive at the truth. Henceforth, and throughout the Middle Ages, music would be classified among the sciences, not the language arts. Eventually, the "liberal arts" were taken to mean subjects of study that free the mind for critical thinking rather than prepare it for a particular trade or profession. The term is still used in this sense within colleges and universities today.

No Roman music theorist was more important, and certainly none more dependent on Greek models, than Anicius Manlius Severinus Boethius (Fig. 2-2). **Boethius** (c480–524 C.E.) was a descendent of an aristocratic family of Roman senators. His birth came a few short years after barbarian Goths from north of the Alps swept down and seized Rome in 476 C.E., thereby putting an end to the Roman Empire. Eventually, Boethius became a minister in the government of the new Gothic king Theodoric. But in 523 he was accused of treason and imprisoned; he was executed the following year. In his short life Boethius wrote, among other works, a treatise on each of the four disciplines within the quadrivium. His *Fundamentals of Arithmetic* was adopted as the standard text for the study of mathematics throughout the Middle Ages, and his *De institutione musica* (**Fundamentals of Music**) became the required school text for music theory. When universities were formed in twelfth-century Europe, the *Fundamentals of Music* became the established music text for the liberal arts curriculum, and it remained so into the eighteenth century at the universities of Oxford and Cambridge.

Boethius spoke and read Greek fluently. He read great amounts of Greek music theory and translated it into his native Latin tongue. More than any other writer, Boethius served as a conduit through which the great treasury of ancient Greek music theory passed to medieval Europe. Specifically, he reaffirmed three important tenets of Greek music theory. First, he reemphasized that music was a science and that numerical ratios determine the pitches of the scale, melodic intervals, and consonances and dissonances. Second, by drawing from Plato and others, he posited that the entire universe resonated with music. These harmonies, Boethius said, could be divided into three general types: ***musica mundana*** (music of the spheres), ***musica humana*** (music of the human body), and ***musica instrumentalis*** (earthly vocal and instrumental music). Cosmic music (*musica mundana*) was the true music, while earthly music (*musica instrumentalis*) was a poor approximation of these divine and unchanging proportions. Finally, Boethius set forth a distinction between the ***musicus*** and the ***cantor***—the musicologist who studies and understands music as distinguished from the practitioner who performs it. All three of these concepts were held dear by writers on music throughout the Middle Ages. Preserved today in 137 medieval manuscripts, Boethius' *Fundamentals of Music* remained the single most influential work on the discipline of music for more than a thousand years.

✿ JERUSALEM AND THE RISE OF EARLY CHRISTIAN MUSIC

Christ was a Jew, and so were his early followers. Thus it is not surprising that the liturgy of the Christian Church had elements in common with the liturgical rites of the Jewish Temple in Jerusalem. **Liturgy** is the collection of prayers, chants, readings, and ritual acts by which the theology of the church, or any organized religion, is practiced. **Chant,** generally speaking, is the monophonic religious music that is sung in a house of worship. The first liturgical service to grow within the emerging Christian Church in Jerusalem was the commemoration of the Last Supper, a common evening meal shared in small groups around the city. A leader, serving as a priest, partook of the blood of Christ in the form of wine, and the faithful partook of the body in the form of bread. During this religious meal, worshipers prayed, sang psalms, and read passages of scripture, rituals also practiced in the Jewish Temple. But the early Christian Church did not derive its music directly from the Temple of Jerusalem. While the liturgies of the two religions arose from common elements (prayers, scripture-reading, and psalm-singing), the music of Jews and Christians developed along quite different lines. The issue is complicated by the fact that no music, Christian or Jewish, survives in written form from that period. Indeed, no written Jewish music with exact pitch notation survives at all much before 1700 C.E. Jewish music was passed along mainly by oral tradition. So, too, was Christian music for the first eight hundred years of its existence.

The service of the early Christians was very informal, with no fixed order of events. St. Paul suggests as much when he writes to the Corinthians (1 Cor. 14: 26–7): "When ye come together, every one of you hath a psalm, hath a doctrine, hath a tongue, hath a revelation, hath an interpretation." Early Christian liturgical texts, when written down, were primarily compiled in Greek, the universal learned language of the East. Much of the music must have been improvised or performed as the occasion demanded. What can be said with certainty is that, by the fourth century, faithful Christians gathered for services of prayer several times during the day. Singing at these services was led by a **cantor,** a person specially trained to lead the music of the community.

Not all Christians were in the city of Jerusalem, or any other city for that matter. As early as the third century a few particularly devout souls detached themselves from urban centers and went out to live as hermits in the desert, notably throughout Egypt and Syria. Some formed communities of monks and nuns whose chief liturgical activity was the recitation of the entire Book of Psalms. In the rituals of these desert hermits can be found the seeds of monasticism in the European Middle Ages.

The wanderings of hermits in the deserts of Egypt and Syria signified that Christianity was on the move, both west and east. Soon a Christian Church appeared in Alexandria, Egypt, that was called the Coptic Church. It developed its own liturgy and its own music, called Coptic chant. **Coptic chant,** the music of the Christian Church of Egypt, still exists today, passed along for nearly two thousand years entirely by oral tradition. Equally important, the liturgy of Jerusalem spread to the city of Byzantium (later Constantinople, and now Istanbul, Turkey). In 395 C.E. the aging Roman Empire was divided into two parts. Rome served as capital of the West and Byzantium of the East. A patriarch (the counterpart of the Roman pope) ruled over the Byzantine Church. This church, too, developed its own liturgy and a special dialect of chant called **Byzantine chant.** Unlike Coptic chant, Byzantine chant eventually came to be notated, and a body of music theory emerged to explain it. The chants of the Byzantine rite were organized into eight church modes, a practice later to be adopted by the Roman Church. Today's Eastern (Greek) Orthodox Church, as well as the Russian Orthodox Church, are institutions descended from the Byzantine Church.

Because the Apostles Peter and Paul were sent to preach in Italy, the Christian message arrived in Rome not long after the death of Christ. Here too the Church developed its own particular forms of devotion, in part because the persecuted Christians worshiped in secret. The style of liturgical singing in the early churches of Rome, today simply called **Roman chant,** was also passed along for centuries in

Cathedral de Leon, Spain

❀ FIGURE 2-3

An early example of Mozarabic chant coming from the cathedral of Leon, Spain. Although the music is for the feast of St. Aciscius, the pitches cannot be read with precision.

oral, but not written, form. Roman chant was the principal source from which Gregorian chant later would emerge.

In 312 C.E. the Roman Emperor Constantine converted to Christianity and the persecution of Christians in Rome ceased. If Christianity was not declared the official religion of the Empire, at least now it might compete on an equal footing with the older pagan gods. Historians estimate that in 300 C.E. only 10 percent of the populace of the Roman Empire was Christian; by 400 C.E. the number had risen to approximately 50 percent. Soon other independent Christian churches appeared in the West. By the late fourth century, Ambrose (340?–397 C.E.) established a separate church and liturgy in Milan in northern Italy. Here **Ambrosian chant** was sung, named in honor of the church's patron. Ambrose himself wrote a number of hymns that survive today. Surprisingly, the Ambrosian rite did not embrace the liturgical practices of nearby Rome, but drew upon those with origins in Jerusalem and elsewhere in the East.

So, too, pilgrims to the Holy Lands, both male and female, carried back to Spain some of the liturgical practices of Jerusalem. In 711 C.E. the Arab Moslems invaded Spain, but they did not entirely stamp out the old Christian music there, called **Mozarabic chant** (the word "Mozarabic" refers to Christians living under Moslem rule). Mozarabic chant survives today in more than twenty manuscripts dating from the ninth through the fourteenth centuries (Fig. 2-3). Unfortunately, it is nearly impossible to transcribe or perform Mozarabic chant because the notation does not specify clearly the distance between pitches.

Uncertainty also surrounds the Gallican chant sung north of the Alps in the early Middle Ages. **Gallican chant** is the Christian music of early-medieval Gaul, which roughly comprised modern-day France and parts of Switzerland. Gallican chant is believed to have been mostly improvised. When Charlemagne imported Roman chant into Gaul around 800 C.E. (see Chapter 3), the indigenous Gallican chant was almost entirely suppressed. At least fifty chants, however, survive today, having been copied down in later books of Gregorian chant. When compared to chants of other Western liturgies of this time, Gallican chant generally appears longer, more flowery, and more exuberant. A fine example of Gallican chant, one with great sweep and grandeur, is the Offertory of the Mass *Collegerunt pontifices* (*The Pontiffs Gathered*; Ex. 2-1). Gallican chant is important in the history of music because it played a primary role in the formation of Gregorian chant. During the ninth and tenth centuries, chant coming north from Rome mixed with the local Gallican chant to create Gregorian chant, the largest body of religious music ever created.

EXAMPLE 2-1

The pontiffs and pharisees gathered in council and said:

SUMMARY

Compared to the Greeks, the Romans made little contribution to the history of Western music. Roman music theory was essentially an elaboration and clarification of earlier Greek music theory. The *tuba*, a long straight-pipe military trumpet, seems to have been the only musical instrument created by the Romans.

The early Christian church had two centers: Jerusalem in the East, and Rome in the West. All of the music of the early Christian church was unwritten; it was in some measure improvised and largely communicated orally from one musician to the next. After 395 C.E., Byzantium gradually replaced Jerusalem as the center of the Eastern Church. The chant of the Byzantine Church, as well as Coptic chant, Ambrosian chant, and Mozarabic chant, had ties to the liturgical traditions of Jerusalem. Rome developed its own liturgy and music, called simply Roman chant. Gaul, the area north of the Alps, was Christianized by missionaries coming from Rome. Historically, the chant of that region, called Gallican chant, had strong ties to Rome. Later, in the eighth, ninth, and tenth centuries, Roman chant and Gallican chant would form a new dialect of chant called Gregorian chant.

KEY TERMS

tibia	*musica mundana*	Coptic chant
tuba	*musica humana*	Byzantine chant
seven liberal arts	*musica instrumentalis*	Roman chant
trivium	*musicus*	Ambrosian chant
quadrivium	*cantor*	Mozarabic chant
Boethius	liturgy	Gallican chant
Fundamentals of Music	chant	

Music in the Monastery and Convent

When the Roman Empire fell to barbarian invaders around 476 C.E., the centers of civilization—the cities—began to disintegrate. Rome itself, which had a population of more than a million around the time of Caesar, had shrunk by the sixth century to fewer than a hundred thousand souls. Some devout Christians retreated to the countryside, where they set up centers of learning and worship called monasteries. In the Middle Ages a religious man living by himself was referred to by the Latin word **monachus** (a solitary person), and a woman as a **monacha**—today we would call them a monk and a nun. Their dwelling, too, was a solitary place, a monastery. In fact, monks and nuns did not live alone but in separate communities, separated by sex, ranging from a dozen like-minded souls to, sometimes, more than a hundred. Of course, there had been monks in the East shortly after the time of the Apostles, but they were few and far between, isolated hermits scattered about the deserts of Egypt, Palestine, and Syria. Now, during the sixth century, monasteries appeared everywhere on the Italian peninsula (Map 3-1). Soon missionaries went out from

MAP 3-1

Important European monasteries established before 1200.

Italy to establish new communities in Ireland and England, and from there other missionaries brought monasticism back to France, Germany, and Switzerland.

The force behind the monastic movement was Benedict of Nursia (c480–c550 C.E.), a Roman aristocrat who decided to exchange wealth for a life of religious poverty in the mountains south of Rome. About 530 C.E. Benedict compiled what is called the **Rule of St. Benedict,** a code of conduct to regulate daily life in a monastic community. It applied equally to both men and women. Those following the Rule of St. Benedict belonged to the Benedictine Order, and the founder's rule dictated their daily life.

Life in a rural monastery was not easy. Monks or nuns were required to profess vows of chastity, poverty, and obedience (obedience to the abbot or abbess in charge of the monastery or convent). The Benedictines spent most of the day in silence. They worked the land to feed their bodies, and prayed and chanted to save their souls. They were not so much interested in helping others as in personal salvation. Their life's goal was to overcome the sins of this world so as to enjoy eternal bliss in the next. If their vision of the world proved correct, they would rise among the elect on the Day of Judgment and sit everlasting with their Lord.

THE MONASTERY OF ST. GALL, SWITZERLAND

Of all the monasteries in the West, the most important for music is the Benedictine house of St. Gall, Switzerland (see Map 3-1). Certainly there are more early-music manuscripts preserved from St. Gall than from any other monastery. St. Gall was founded around 612 C.E. by an Irishman named Gallus, who arrived in the company of other Irish monastic missionaries to the Continent. In the northern foothills to the Alps, in what is now Switzerland, Gallus erected a simple wooden house of prayer and soon began to gather disciples around him. By 750 C.E. the number of monks at St. Gall had reached 53. About this time, these religious men constructed a **scriptorium** (writing room) for the production of books, some from which to study and others from which to sing. All books were, of course, copied by hand and some were beautifully illuminated with pictures (Fig. 3-1). About 850 C.E. the monks of St. Gall commissioned a drawing for an enlarged version of their monastery. From it we can reconstruct the **cloister,** the area around which the monks lived (Fig. 3-2).

As with other monasteries, St. Gall served as a center of learning. The Bible, of course, was copied and studied, but so were the writings of the great theologians, as well as Roman writers such as Virgil and Horace. Indeed, there were no universities or colleges in Western Europe at this time. We owe our knowledge of church music prior to 1000 C.E., as well as the preservation of the great works of Roman literature, to monasteries such as St. Gall.

❀ FIGURE 3-1

Early twelfth-century St. Gall manuscript showing the monk Luitherus presenting a book of chant to St. Gallus. Above them are early chant neumes, many different Alleluias for the Virgin Mary for use at different Masses.

❁ THE CANONICAL HOURS: THE WORK OF THE LORD

At the heart of monastic life were the canonical hours, so-called because they were prescribed by the Rule of St. Benedict (the Latin word for rule is "canon"). The **canonical hours** (also called the **liturgical offices**) were a set of eight periods of worship occurring throughout the day. During these times the monks or nuns would cease their work and gather in the church for prayer, reading of scripture, and singing. The Rule of St. Benedict refers to these services as the "work of the lord" (**opus dei**) because they required as much or more attention and effort than physical labor. In reality, the exact times for manual work and for the celebration of the canonical hours varied from church to church and season to season. Following is a reconstruction of the daily activities at a typical monastery during the summer months.

Summer Schedule for a Benedictine Monastery

2 a.m.	Office of Matins in the church (about one hour), then back to bed
6 a.m.	Offices of Lauds in the church, followed by breakfast in the refectory
7 a.m.	Office of Prime in the church (about a half-hour)
	Business meeting of the monks in the chapter house
	Work or study
9 a.m.	Office of Terce in the church, followed by High Mass
	Work or study
12 noon	Office of Sext in the church, followed by main meal of the day
	Short nap or silent reading
3 p.m.	Office of Nones in the church (about a half-hour)
	Work or study
5 p.m.	Office of Vespers in the church (about a half-hour)
	Work or study
6 p.m.	Abbot's speech to the monks, followed by supper
	Period of conversation
7 p.m.	Office of Compline in the church (about half-hour)
	To bed (later in summer than winter)

✿ FIGURE 3-2

Reconstruction of the monastery of St. Gall, showing the cloister (2), the cellar for wine and beer (3), the dining hall or refectory (4), and the dormitory (5). Adjacent to the church (1) were the scriptorium, where chant books were created, and the library, where books were stored and consulted.

Thus the canonical hours, along with the High Mass of the day, provided the framework for life in the monastery. Some hours were longer and more important than others. The night office of **Matins,** for example, required much singing, and on high feasts such as Christmas or Easter, might go on for four hours. Other services, such as Prime and Nones, were brief, involving little more than singing a few psalms and a hymn. Of the eight canonical hours, the late-afternoon service of **Vespers** is the most important for the history of music. As we shall see, Vespers involved singing, not only psalms and a hymn but also the Magnificat, a text that would remain a favorite with composers throughout the history of music. The liturgical day ended with the office of Compline, which usually concluded with a chant in honor of the Virgin Mary.

Taken altogether, medieval monastic life was an unceasing cycle of manual labor in the fields and spiritual labor before God in the church. Its unbending monotony challenged even the most devout of souls. Thus it was in the Middle Ages, and thus it is still today, in those few monastic communities around the world that continue to follow the rule of St. Benedict.

✿ GREGORIAN CHANT IN THE MONASTERY

The music sung daily at the eight canonical hours of prayer and at Mass was what we today call **Gregorian chant** (also, **plainsong**). Gregorian chant is a vast body of monophonic religious music setting Latin texts and intended for use in the Roman Catholic Church. Plainsong is entirely monophonic music sung in unison, and almost always without the accompaniment of instruments. It was composed over the course of fifteen hundred years—from the time of the Apostles to that of the Council of Trent (1545–1563), a conclave that brought sweeping reforms to the Church. Although Gregorian chant is named in honor of Pope Gregory the Great (c540–604), ironically, Gregory wrote little if any of this music. Pope Gregory was more a church administrator than a musician, and he merely decreed that certain chants should be sung on certain days of the liturgical year. Gregorian chant remained the official music of the Roman Catholic Church until the Second Vatican Council (1962–1965), when it lost its privileged status. Today plainsong is sung daily in only a few churches and monasteries. Yet because of its extraordinary beauty, Gregorian chant continues to be an object of great interest to historians and musicians alike.

Most Gregorian chant was created during the early years of the **Holy Roman Empire.** In 800 C.E. the Frankish warrior-king **Charlemagne** (742–814 C.E.) marched to Rome and had himself crowned emperor by Pope Leo III, thereby becoming the first Holy Roman Emperor. His aim was to resuscitate the western half of the old Roman Empire but to have it "holy"— under Christianity, not paganism as it had been in Caesar's day. To bring stability and political uniformity to his vast territories, Charlemagne mandated that the chant and liturgical traditions of the Church of Rome be imposed on all his lands, including those north of the Alps. Thus, religious music originating in Italy was carried north by Roman singers and, in the course of time, mixed with the local Gallican traditions. In addition, many new chants were composed in northern monasteries during this period. During the ninth century, plainsong first came to be called Gregorian chant, apparently to suggest that it enjoyed the ancient authority of the papacy.

In sum, the core of what we still call Gregorian chant was created north of the Alps during the ninth and tenth centuries, and it was an amalgam of Italian, French, and German religious music. During the next hundred years, the newly refurbished and enlarged repertory was carried back to Italy, and to Spain and England as well. On any given day, monks in central Italy, for example, would sing the same chants, in more or less the same way, as those in southern England or northern Germany. Although the Holy Roman Empire soon lost its political cohesion, the liturgy and music of the church continued to provide a common cultural thread throughout the entire Middle Ages. Indeed, Gregorian chant provided the West with its first international musical repertory.

 GREGORIAN CHANT FOR VESPERS

Why sing? The purpose of singing in the monastery was for the entire community to offer praises to God in a heartfelt, joyful way. Each monk or nun gave voice to the communal song; they sang as if with one voice in a unison chorus. Above all, chanting in the monastery involved singing the **Psalter,** the book of one hundred fifty psalms found in the Old Testament—that portion of the Bible mainly compiled by Jewish teachers before Christ's ministry on earth. According to the Rule of St. Benedict, all one hundred fifty psalms had to be rendered to God each week, ninety at Matins, thirty at Vespers, and so forth. The act or process of singing the psalms is called **psalmody.** Because Vespers was the canonical hour to have the greatest impact on later Catholic and Protestant church music, the psalmody of Vespers will serve as an example for all eight canonical hours.

When the monks or nuns entered the church for Vespers, they said and sang a small number of preliminary chants and prayers. But the bulk of the service consisted of singing four psalms on Sunday, another four on Monday, another four on Tuesday, and so on. After the psalms came a hymn appropriate for the season and, finally, the Magnificat. The clergy were divided and placed on benches or choir stalls on either side of the church. Everyone was required to sing, no matter how poor the voice. A **cantor** (chief musician) sat with one of the two groups and led the singing. He began the psalm so as to give the pitch to the full monastic community and his side of the aisle completed the first verse—each psalm has many verses. The second psalm verse was sung by the other side of the choir, and so on. Such a method of musical performance, in which a divided choir alternately sings back and forth, is called **antiphonal singing.** Once all the verses of a psalm had been sung antiphonally, a two-verse **doxology** ("Gloria Patri," a standard formula of praise to the Holy Trinity) was added at the end. But there is more to psalmody. The entire psalm and its doxology were surrounded by another chant. That is to say, a short chant specific to the day came before the psalm and was repeated after it. Because that short chant began and concluded the antiphonal singing of the psalm, it came to be called an **antiphon.** The following shows the process of singing just one psalm.

Antiphon (begun by the cantor and completed by all)
    Verse 1: begun by the cantor and completed by his side of the choir
    Verse 2: sung by the opposite side of the choir

> Verse 3: sung by the cantor's side of the choir
> Verse 4: sung by the opposite side of the choir
> etc. through the remaining verses
> Doxology: first verse sung by one side of the choir
> second verse sung by the opposite side of the choir
> Antiphon (sung by all)

Psalms were chanted to very simple repeating patterns, rather than elaborate melodies. These simple recitation formulas are called the **psalm tones.** Each psalm tone begins with an intonation sung by the cantor, continues with a recitation on a single pitch followed by a pause (mediation), and, after more recitation on the reciting tone, concludes with a termination. The mediation helps separate the two units of syntax of each verse, and gives the singers a chance to breathe. Example 3-1 shows the parts of a psalm tone in diagrammatic form.

EXAMPLE 3-1

After the first verse, each successive verse is sung in the same fashion, except that the intonation is not repeated. Because each psalm had as few as a half-dozen verses or as many as twenty, the amount of time needed to sing a psalm varied considerably. The first psalm sung each Sunday at Vespers, Psalm 109 *Dixit Dominus* (*My Lord said unto me*) requires about four minutes. The Rule of St. Benedict stipulates that four psalms should be sung in this fashion, each with its antiphon, at every Vespers service. The antiphon-psalm-antiphon unit was the bedrock of this and every canonical hour.

Following the singing of four psalms at Vespers, all the monks chanted a hymn. In the Middle Ages, as now, a **hymn** was a relatively short chant with a small number of phrases, often four, and a rather narrow vocal range (Ex. 3-2). One melody served for as many as five or six stanzas of text, as is true for the Christmas hymn *Jesu, Redemptor omnium* (*Jesus, Redeemer of All*). Like the psalms, the hymn was sung antiphonally, each side of the choral community taking a stanza in turn.

EXAMPLE 3-2

Je-su, Re - demp - tor_____ om-ni-um, Quem__ lu - cis an-te o - ri - gi - nem, *etc.*

Jesus, redeemer of the world, who was the light before the beginning…

Finally, the office of Vespers concluded with the singing of the **Magnificat,** the culmination of the service. The Magnificat is a **canticle,** a particularly lyrical and memorable passage of scripture usually drawn from the New Testament of the Bible. The Magnificat is the canticle of Mary, and it comes from the Gospel of St. Luke (1: 46–55), in which Mary joyfully responds to the news that she will bear the son of God ("My soul doth magnify [*magnificat*] the Lord"). The Magnificat is sung much like a psalm, except that its recitation pattern is slightly more ornate than that of a psalm tone (Ex. 3-3). The particularly beautiful quality of the text, and its emphasis on Mary, has endeared the Magnificat to church composers, including Monteverdi, Bach, and Mozart.

EXAMPLE 3-3

Mag - ni - fi - cat
Et ex - sul - ta - vit   spi - ri - tus me - us___
Qui - a   re - spe - xit hu - mi - li - tat - em an - cil - lae su - ae___

a - ni - ma me - a Do - mi - num___
in De - o sa - lu - ta - ri me - o___
ec - ce e - nim ex hoc be - a - tam me di - cent o - mnes ge - ne - ra - ti - o - nes___

etc.

My soul magnifies the Lord and my spirit rejoices in God my Savior, for he has regarded the low estate of his handmaiden. For behold, henceforth all generations will call me blessed.

🌿 FIGURE 3-3

Nuns of the Benedictine convent of Regina Laudis, in Bethlehem, Connecticut, singing chant.

The following is a summary of the important parts of the canonical hour of Vespers.

> Brief introductory prayers and petitions:
> Antiphon-Psalm-Doxology-Antiphon
> Antiphon-Psalm-Doxology-Antiphon
> Antiphon-Psalm-Doxology-Antiphon
> Antiphon-Psalm-Doxology-Antiphon
> Hymn
> Antiphon-Magnificat-Doxology-Antiphon

Vespers was, and is, sung each day in the evening at Benedictine monasteries around the world (Fig. 3-3).

Abbey of Regina Laudis Archives

💿 LISTENING CUE

CHANTS OF VESPERS

Antiphon, *Tecum principium*
Psalm, *Dixit Dominus*
Hymn, *Jesu, Redemptor omnium*

CD 1/3–4
Anthology, Nos. 3, 4

✿ GREGORIAN CHANT FOR THE MASS

The central and most important religious service each day in the monastery was the **Mass.** The term comes from the final dismissal of the service: "Go, [the congregation] is dismissed" ("Ite, missa est"). The high point of the Mass is the sacrament of the Eucharist (taking communion). Before, during, and after the ritual of the Eucharist, chants are sung, scripture read, and prayers said. The chants are of two sorts, Proper and Ordinary. The **Proper of the Mass** consists of chants whose texts change each day to suit the religious theme, or to honor a particular saint on just that one day. The **Ordinary of the Mass,** on the other hand, includes chants with unvarying texts, and these can be sung almost every day of the year. All Masses include Ordinary and Proper chants. Later, from the late Middle Ages onward, when a composer such as Dufay, Mozart, or Beethoven sat down to write a polyphonic Mass, he set only the Ordinary chants. Setting just the Ordinary allowed the choir to perform the polyphonic Mass more than on just one day each year. The Mass, of course, was not created all at once by any single church father or theologian. Rather, parts were added to it gradually over a period of roughly eight hundred years, from the time of the Apostles until after the reign of Charlemagne (d. 814 C.E.). The following shows the standard parts of the Mass.

Proper of the Mass	Ordinary of the Mass
Introit (an introductory chant for the entrance of the celebrating clergy)	
	Kyrie (a petition, in Greek, for mercy)
	Gloria (a hymn of praise to the Lord)
(reading of the Epistle)	
Gradual (a reflective chant)	
Alleluia or Tract (a chant of thanksgiving or penance)	
Sequence (a chant commenting on the text of the Alleluia)	
(reading of the Gospel)	
	Credo (a profession of faith)
Offertory (a chant for the offering before the ritual of communion)	
	Sanctus (an acclamation to the Lord)
	Agnus dei (a petition for mercy and eternal peace)
Communion (the chant accompanying communion)	
	Ite, missa est (short dismissal)

Every Mass begins with the singing of an **Introit,** a chant that accompanies the entry of the priests and abbot or bishop into the church and up to the high altar. Notice that singing an Introit is much like singing a psalm. The Introit for Mass on Christmas Day, *Puer natus est nobis* (*A boy is born to us*), begins with an antiphon intoned by the cantor and completed by the full choir (Ex. 3-4). Next comes, not a full psalm but a single verse of a psalm, then the doxology, and finally the antiphon is repeated by the choir in full. Thus, singing an Introit is a kind of abbreviated psalmody: instead of singing many verses of a psalm, the choir chants only one. The psalm verse of the Introit, beginning "Cantate Domino cantium novum" ("Sing to the Lord a new song"), is an example of what is called **syllabic chant**—there is usually only one note for each syllable of text. The antiphon of the Introit provides an example of **neumatic chant**—there are often three, four, or five notes for each syllable of text. The *Kyrie* that follows the Introit in the Mass has many notes per syllable and exemplifies **melismatic chant** (a **melisma** is a lengthy vocal phrase setting a single syllable). Generally speaking, the more important services (Matins, Vespers, and the Mass) have the most melismatic chants.

EXAMPLE 3-4

Pu - er na - tus est___ no - bis, et fi - li - us da - tus est no - bis___
[Antiphon]

cu-jus im-pe - ri - um su-per hu - me - rum___ e - jus___

et ___ vo-ca - bi-tur ___ no-men e - jus, ___ mag - ni con - si - li - i

An - ge - lus. Can - ta - te Do - mi - no can - ti-cum no - vum___
[Psalm verse]

qui - a ___ mi - ra - bi - li - a fe - cit.___ Glo - ri - a Pa - tri.
[Doxology]   etc.

A boy is born to us, and a Son is given to us; whose government is upon His shoulder;
and His name shall be called the Angel of great counsel. Sing ye to the Lord a new song,
because He hath done wonderful things. Glory be to the Father… [A boy is born to us…]

The **Kyrie** of the Mass, an ancient Greek text, is the only portion of the Mass not sung in Latin. Here the congregation petitions the Lord for his mercy and does so in threefold exclamations:

> "Kyrie eleison" ("Lord have mercy upon us") three times
>
> "Christe eleison" ("Christ have mercy upon us") three times
>
> "Kyrie eleison" ("Lord have mercy upon us") three times

The musical structure of the *Kyrie* often mirrors this tripartite arrangement. In the *Kyrie* for the Christmas Mass (Anthology, No. 6), each musical phrase is to be sung three times, as indicated by the symbol "iij."

For both the *Gloria* and *Credo,* the full choir sings from beginning to end, once a soloist has set the pitch. The **Gloria** (Anthology, No. 7) is a hymn of praise going back to early Christian times, while the **Credo** is a profession of faith formulated as the result of the Council of Nicaea in 325. Both are lengthy chants because they set long texts, yet the *Gloria* is more neumatic than the highly syllabic *Credo*. The text of the *Gloria* was sung to any one of approximately fifty melodies during the Middle Ages, while the *Credo* was usually chanted to just one, the widely known melody given below.

EXAMPLE 3-5

Cre - do in u - num De - um, Pa - trem om - ni - po - ten - tem,

fac - tor - em cae - li et ter - rae, vi - si - bil - li - um om - ni - um,___

(Continued on next page)

I believe in one God, the father almighty, maker of heaven and earth, and of all things visible and invisible. And in one Lord Jesus Christ, the only begotten Son of God, begotten of the Father before all worlds…

Placed between the *Gloria* and *Credo* are two chants of unusual length and breadth, the Gradual and the Alleluia. The **Gradual** is so-called because it was originally sung from an elevated position, a step (Latin "gradus") in the choir area of the church. The Gradual consists of two parts: an antiphon and a psalm verse. But because the psalm verse is not sung by the chorus antiphonally, the opening chant is not called an antiphon. Instead, it is called a **respond;** the full chorus prefaces and responds to the psalm verse, which is sung by a soloist. Accordingly, the Gradual exemplifies **responsorial singing** (choral respond, solo verse, choral respond). The Gradual *Viderunt omnes fines terrae* (*All the ends of the earth have seen*; Anthology, No. 8) exhibits the sweeping range of many graduals. All Graduals are melismatic chants. Notice, for example, the fifty-two-note melisma on the syllable "Do" of the word "Dominus" (Ex. 3.6). Here in the verse, standing high for all to see, the soloist is able to "showcase" his virtuosic skills as he literally sings praise to the Lord (which is what "Dominus" means in Latin). Following this elaborate solo, the full chorus is meant to repeat the respond, although not all monastic choirs do so today.

EXAMPLE 3-6

All the ends of the earth have seen the salvation of our God; sing joyfully to God, all the earth.
The Lord hath made known…

The **Alleluia,** of course, is a cry of joy (Hallelujah!). It, too, is a responsorial chant as well as a highly melismatic one. The most distinctive part of the Alleluia is a melisma on the final syllable "a" of "alleluia." It is called the **jubilus** because at this moment the full choir and community celebrates with jubilation the redemptive life of Christ. The verse of the Alleluia is sung by a soloist, as can be seen in *Alleluia. Dies sanctificatus* (*Alleluia. Day Sanctified*; Anthology, No. 9). To this the full chorus again responds with "Alleluia." Thus, the structure of the Alleluia is Alleluia-verse-Alleluia (respond-verse-respond). Finally, both the Gradual and the Alleluia are reflective chants during which there is no "action" in the service. Here all attention is turned to the singing of the sacred text, a fact that likely accounts for the greater length and elaborate, melismatic style.

Although the ritual of communion is theologically the high point of the Mass, the chants attending this rite are less melismatic than the preceding Gradual and Alleluia. The Offertory and Communion chants are now stand-alone antiphons, which, in the course of time, have been stripped of their psalm verses. The *Sanctus* and *Agnus dei* are rather similar in musical style to the *Kyrie*. Indeed, like the *Kyrie*, the *Agnus dei* is a threefold petition to the Lord. To conclude the Mass, the priest sings forth "Go, the congregation is dismissed," to which the community replies "Deo gratias" ("Thanks be to God").

LISTENING CUE

CHANTS BEGINNING THE MASS
FOR CHRISTMAS DAY

Introit, *Puer natus est nobis*
Kyrie, *Omnipotens genitor*
Gloria
Gradual, *Viderunt omnes*
Alleluia, *Alleluia. Dies sanctificatus*

CD 1/5–9
Anthology, Nos. 5–9

SUMMARY

Religious life in the West during early Middle Ages was centered in monasteries and convents. The Rule of St. Benedict regulated life within these communities, including the singing of Gregorian chant, or plainsong. Gregorian chant is a vast body of monophonic religious music consisting of thousands of melodies. The repertory was gradually assembled over the course of many hundreds of years by clerics of several different lands, primarily in Italy, Germany, Switzerland, and France. The music for the Western Latin Church assumed its virtually final shape within the confines of the Holy Roman Empire during and after the reign of Charlemagne (768–814 C.E.). Partly because of this long and diverse history, and partly because plainsong serves many functions within the liturgy, Gregorian chant has many diverse musical styles. Some chants are narrow in range and very syllabic (the psalm tones) and others are melismatic and involve a wide vocal range (the Graduals and Alleluias).

Despite the diversity of musical styles, there are several qualities common to all chants. All Gregorian chant is sung in unison (even if doubled at the octave by choirboys or female voices during those rare occasions when monks and nuns sang together). Chant tends to move stepwise, avoiding large leaps, so that the full community can easily participate in the singing. Chant is written without regular rhythms, and it has no meter (you can't tap your foot to it). Finally, chant does not try to convert the listener by overt musical gestures, as a Beethoven symphony might. On the contrary, when sung correctly, chant seems to float, spirit-like, through the air. Its aim is to create a quiet, nonconfrontational environment in which the faithful soul might experience a transcendental union with the divine. In the medieval world, chant was not to be enjoyed for itself, but to lead to God.

  KEY TERMS

monachus	Psalter	Introit
monacha	psalmody	syllabic chant
Rule of St. Benedict	cantor	neumatic chant
scriptorium	antiphonal singing	melismatic chant
cloister	doxology	melisma
canonical hours (liturgical offices)	antiphon	*Kyrie*
opus dei	psalm tone	*Gloria*
Matins	hymn	*Credo*
Vespers	Magnificat	Gradual
Gregorian chant (plainsong)	canticle	respond
Holy Roman Empire	Mass	responsorial singing
Charlemagne	Proper of the Mass	Alleluia
	Ordinary of the Mass	jubilus

Chapter 4

Music Theory in the Monastery: John of St. Gall and Guido of Arezzo

Almost all educated musicians of the Middle Ages were churchmen or churchwomen, because the monasteries, and later the cathedrals, were the sole centers of learning. These church musicians borrowed greatly from ancient Greek music theory. Among other things, they adopted the Greek system of consonance and dissonance, a diatonic scale with the octave divided into seven pitches (five whole tones and two half-tones), and a musical vocabulary including words such as "chromatic" and "tetrachord." But the ancient Greeks were essentially interested in the science of the sound, not in the performance and analysis of music. Medieval musicians, on the other hand, looked upon music theory less as an arcane science, and more as a tool to aid in the daily singing of the canonical hours and Mass. Medieval monks needed a theory that could explain and facilitate their principal activity in life, singing praises of the Lord, the *opus dei* (the work of the Lord). They also needed a system to capture and preserve the music they sang. Perhaps because Charlemagne wanted the services of the church to be the same everywhere in the Empire, Carolingian clerics created a musical notation that allowed them to write down the plainsong of the church and send it from place to place.

THE EIGHT CHURCH MODES

By the year 900 C.E. the repertory of Gregorian chant had grown to nearly 3,000 melodies. To keep track of all this music, church musicians first began to group chants by function within the liturgy and by category of melodic pattern—that is to say, by "mode." Every melody was placed in one of just eight melodic groups, or modes. To give these groups identity, theorists borrowed ethnic names from the ancient Greeks, names such as Dorian and Phrygian. The scale patterns to which these names were assigned, however, were entirely different from the patterns used by the Greeks. Moreover, initially different medieval theorists proposed different names or numbers for the modes. Around 1100 a monk from St. Gall, called **John of St. Gall** (also known as John Cotton), wrote a treatise entitled *De Musica (On Music)*. In it he set forth the eight church modes in a system with numbers to which were added Greek names, and these have remained in use for chant down to the present day. The modality of a melody—the scale-group in which it belonged—was determined by two factors: the range of the chant and its final note. John identifies the eight **church modes** as in Example 4-1.

EXAMPLE 4-1

Number	Name	Range	Final Pitch	Type
1	Dorian		D	authentic
2	Hypodorian		D	plagal
3	Phrygian		E	authentic
4	Hypophrygian		E	plagal
5	Lydian		F	authentic
6	Hypolydian		F	plagal
7	Mixolydian		G	authentic
8	Hypomixolydian		G	plagal

As can be seen, the eight church modes consist of four pairs: the Dorian, Phrygian, Lydian, and Mixolydian. The first mode within each pair is called the **authentic mode** and the second, the **plagal** (meaning "derived from") **mode**. The plagal modes are all a fourth below their authentic counterpart. (The prefix "hypo" in Greek means below, as in hypodermic needle—a needle that goes beneath the skin.) Yet, although the plagal modes are lower than the corresponding authentic ones, each pair has the same final. In simple terms, we have a regular-sounding Dorian mode and a lower-sounding one, for example. Although the range of each chant was in principle only an octave, in practice a melody might embrace one note on either side of that octave. Finally, it is worth remembering that there was no such thing as absolute pitch in the music of the Middle Ages. A choir director had the freedom to transpose any chant, no matter what its mode, into a range that was comfortable for the singers.

❁ CHANT NOTATION

Musicians of the earliest Western church created chant without a system of written notation. Following certain formulas, cantors composed melodies in their heads to fit a given Latin text and then taught them orally to other clerics. But how might music be sent from place to place, or how might it be preserved for future monks and nuns, if the cantor were not present? The limitations of the oral tradition gradually encouraged the development of a system of written musical notation. In this development, however, the notational signs of the ancient Greeks proved to be useless; they were simply too numerous and complex. Indeed, by the year 900 Western musicians had abandoned Greek notation almost entirely. They were engaged in devising a new way to notate music. What they ultimately created—the staff, note heads, and letter names for the pitches—has remained the basis of Western musical notation down to the present.

During the Carolingian era (768–987), Western Europe was transformed from an almost entirely oral culture to one more grounded in written symbols. At first the musical monks simply wrote signs on parchment to indicate that the voice was to go up or down. (They may have been imitating the grammatical accents and punctuation marks found in Greek and Latin texts at this time.) The signs themselves were generally not higher or lower but, like modern texts' accents in French, for example, they suggested whether the voice should go up or down (acute = up, grave = down, circumflex = up-down). Often several pitches were contained within one sign. Signs for single pitches as well as for groups were called **neumes** (see Ex. 4-2). At the beginning, around 900 C.E., the neumes were just laid out on the parchment above the text, as a way of reminding the singer how a melody ought to be sung (see Fig. 3-1). The neumes suggested whether the music went up or down. But how far up or down?

❁ MUSICAL STAFF AND PITCH NAMES

By 1000 C.E. musicians had begun to answer the question "how far up or down" by setting neumes on horizontal lines placed one on top of the other, signaling the beginning of our modern musical staff. In addition, the lines and spaces between were given letter names, starting with low A. Sometimes the horizontal lines indicating A, F, or C were color-coded to make pitch identification easier. At first there were only two lines, but by the twelfth century the number had grown to four. The neumes themselves were also changed so as to emphasize precise pitches and not the space between; curving lines were replaced by square note heads connected by lines. Sometimes the connecting lines were omitted. Simultaneously, theorists began to speak of a pitch sign not only as a neume (a collection of pitches) but also as a **nota**—a symbol on a line or space representing a single, precise pitch. Soon the notes came to be thought of in terms of the letters marking the lines and spaces (the note A or the note D). Example 4-2 shows the opening chant for the Mass of Christmas Day, the Introit *Puer natus est nobis* (*A boy is born to us*): (a) in early non-heightened neumes—the notes are all pretty much on the same horizontal plane—from St. Gall; (b) in later heightened neumes with a staff using a C clef from late-medieval England; (c) in modern chant neumes from a modern edition of plainchant called the *Liber usualis*; and (d) transcribed into standard modern musical notation.

EXAMPLE 4-2

a.
Puer   natus   est   nobis,   et   filius   datus   est   nobis:

b.
Pu-er   na - tus   est   no - bis, et fi - li   us da - tus est no - bis:

c.
Pu-er   na - tus   est   no - bis, et fi - li   us da - tus est no - bis:

d.
Pu - er na - tus est no - bis, et fi - li - us da - tus est no - bis:

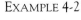

❀ FIGURE 4-1
Guido and his pupil Theodor picking out pitches on a monochord. Miniature from a twelfth-century manuscript.

The leader in the creation of the musical staff and note names was an Italian monk named **Guido of Arezzo** (c991–c1033; Fig. 4-1). In a music theory treatise called the *Micrologus* (*Little Essay*; c1030), Guido set forth all that a practicing church musician needed to know to sing the liturgy: the scale, intervals, church modes, how to transpose, and even a bit about singing simple polyphony. The *Micrologus* became, in today's terms, a bestseller, second only to Boethius' *Fundamentals of Music* as the most popular treatise on music in the Middle Ages. In another writing (a preface to a book of chant) Guido set forth his new system for a musical staff and note names. Guido was proud of his invention; now, he said, it no longer took days to teach novices a new chant orally (by rote memorization); instead, they could look at a chant written in chalk on a slate board or in ink on a piece of parchment and know what pitches to sing. Guido's invention—placing notes on a staff—had made it possible for musicians to sight sing!

❀ HEXACHORDS

But the musical staff and note names were not Guido's only contributions to music history. In the famous *Letter to Brother Michael*, Guido set forth the beginnings of a system that is today known as **solfege**—singing different pitches to the syllables "do, re, mi, fa, sol, la, ti, do." (From the middle syllables "sol" and "fa" comes the Italian "solfeggio," and from it the English "solfege.") Guido derived these syllables from lines of a Latin hymn to St. John the Baptist. Each phrase of the hymn began with a vowel and started on a successively higher degree of the scale (Ex. 4-3).

EXAMPLE 4-3

UT que-ant la - xis **RE**-so-na-re fi-bris **MI** - ra ge-sto - rum **FA**-mu-li tu - o - rum,

SOL - ve pol-lu - ti **LA**-bi - i re - a-tum, San - cte Jo - an-nes.

So that your servants may sing with all their voice the wonders of your deeds,
clean the guilt from our stained lips, O Saint John.

Thus the pitch C also became known as "ut," D as "re," E as "mi," and so forth. But why were solfege syllables needed? Why two names ("C" and "ut," for example) for each note?

Solfege syllables solve a problem inherent in the diatonic scale. In the eight church modes (and in our major and minor scales) some consecutive pitches are only half the distance apart compared to others (a half step as opposed to a whole step). To the vast throng of musically illiterate monks of the Middle Ages, this was a serious problem. If all notes looked equidistant, how did you know when to sing just half a step? By reducing the number of pitches from eight to just six, and by following a constant pattern of TTSTT (T = tone, S = semitone), Guido was able to isolate the semitone. The half step would always fall in the middle, between the syllables "mi" and "fa." Isolating the half step removed uncertainty from the minds of beginning singers as to the whereabouts of whole and half steps in the diatonic scale. All successive intervals were whole steps, except between "mi" and "fa." Guido then laid out these six-note units starting on the notes C, F, and G across the full diatonic scale. Guido's six-note pattern is a hexachord. In the course of time the hexachord placed on C was called the **natural hexachord**, the one set on F the **soft hexachord**, and the one on G the **hard hexachord**. The soft hexachord was so-called because it included a rounded symbol for "b" (whence our flat sign ♭), whereas the hard hexachord derived its name from the fact that it was signaled by a square natural sign ♮ for "b." The following example shows the diatonic scale (with both B♭ and B♮) as it was in Guido's day. Upon it the three hexachords are situated and repeated so as to cover the full range of the scale.

EXAMPLE 4-4

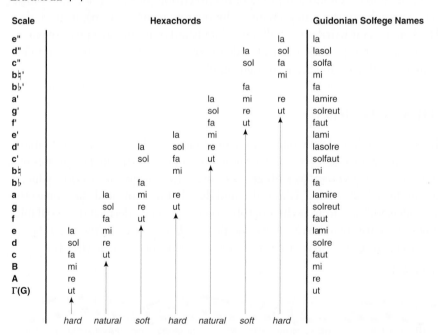

Scale	Hexachords							Guidonian Solfege Names
	hard	natural	soft	hard	natural	soft	hard	
e"							la	la
d"						la	sol	lasol
c"						sol	fa	solfa
b♮'							mi	mi
b♭'						fa		fa
a'					la	mi	re	lamire
g'					sol	re	ut	solreut
f'					fa	ut		faut
e'				la	mi			lami
d'			la	sol	re			lasolre
c'			sol	fa	ut			solfaut
b♮				mi				mi
b♭			fa					fa
a		la	mi	re				lamire
g		sol	re	ut				solreut
f		fa	ut					faut
e	la	mi						lami
d	sol	re						solre
c	fa	ut						faut
B	mi							mi
A	re							re
Γ(G)	ut							ut

The Guidonian system of hexachords remained the standard framework for sight-singing Gregorian chant and later polyphony into the seventeenth century, at which time "ti" (or sometimes "si" or "pha") was added, and the rule of the hexachord gave way to that of the octave. By then singers had gradually learned to deal with two half-steps, and the octave replaced the hexachord as the basic unit of musical measurement.

❀ THE GUIDONIAN HAND

To facilitate sight-singing with hexachords, Guido added a further innovation, the **Guidonian hand** (Fig. 4-2). In truth, it is not certain whether Guido himself devised the musical hand or later theorists simply attributed its innovation to him—the medieval mind loved to ascribe many diverse inventions to a few male authority figures.

In the Middle Ages the human hand, usually the left hand, served as a mini-calculator on which a variety of computations might be performed. By pointing to the lines and joints of the left hand with the index finger of the right, a medieval monk or nun would be able to calculate the day on which Easter would fall the coming year, the sequence of the signs of the Zodiac, the number of days in each of the twelve months, the arrival of the next full moon, the letters of the alphabet (for those who were deaf), and, from the eleventh century onward, the notes of the scale. The left hand was thus the original Palm Pilot computer.

Example 4-5 demonstrates how the syllables of the Guidonian hexachords might be applied to a particular chant, in this case a *Kyrie* (given in full in the Anthology, No. 6). The melody begins in a range best sung in the hard hexachord. In the second phrase, however, it goes lower, and a new hexachord must be chosen, specifically the natural hexachord. On the opening pitch of the second phrase, for example, the singers would "mutate" hexachords, as it was called, the "re" of the hard hexachord giving way to the "la" of the natural.

EXAMPLE 4-5

hard: re re ut re fa mi re ut re   re
natural: la sol fa re mi   mi sol la re   mi sol fa mi fa re re

For musicians, the hand provided not only a mnemonic aid but also a portable musical staff that could be easily carried into rehearsals of the monastic choir. Each of the notes of the Guidonian scale, from low G to high E, was mentally inscribed on the hand. The choirmaster needed only point with the index finger to the spot on the hand, and the choir would know which pitch to sing. Before organs became widespread in church (the fourteenth century) and long before the advent of the piano, the hand provided, if not a keyboard, at least a "hand-board," for teaching music.

Why did the choirmaster need to point to his hand and not simply have the monks sing from books? Because there were no books, or at least very few books. In the Middle Ages a single volume of chant might take a year or more to copy (to say nothing of the lives of many sheep, which were necessary to make parchment, the basic writing material of the Middle Ages). In most monasteries and convents, usually only the cantor personally owned a music book. When music was written in a classroom, then as now, it was most often done with chalk on a small slate board. If the music teacher had a book, a voice, and a hand, that was sufficient to teach religious vocal music following Guido's new system.

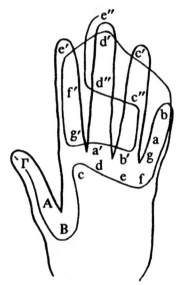

❧ FIGURE 4-2

(a) In this thirteenth-century Italian manuscript, a monk points at the joints of his hand to indicate musical pitches. (b) In modern times, the Guidonian hand may be represented like this.

SUMMARY

Memory and oral learning were enormously important in the ancient world and during the Middle Ages. The musicians of the early church composed plainsong without a system of written notation. Cantors created chants in their heads to fit a given Latin text and taught them orally to other clerics. Only after many centuries, around 900, was a system of notation devised for Western plainsong. Notation allowed for the production of chant books, and with these the repertory could be passed from one church to the next. A staff (horizontal lines) with pitches identified by letter names appeared in rudimentary form around 1000. By 1200 it consisted of four lines of what would later be called the F or bass clef. In order to organize the vast repertory of Gregorian chant, church melodies were grouped in one of the eight modes. To facilitate the learning of chant, a system of hexachords emerged, initiated by Guido of Arezzo. This made it easier for beginning musicians to sing up and down the diatonic scale by isolating the interval of a half-step ("mi" to "fa"). The hexachords were then superimposed on the hand so novices and musicians generally could more easily teach and learn new melodies. Most church music was taught literally "by hand" in the Middle Ages and not by reading from manuscripts. The Guidonian hand remained in use in some areas until the end of the seventeenth century.

KEY TERMS

John of St. Gall	nota	soft hexachord
church modes	Guido of Arezzo	hard hexachord
authentic mode	*Micrologus*	Guidonian hand
plagal mode	solfege	
neume	natural hexachord	

Chapter 5

Later Medieval Chant: Tropes, Sequences, and the Liturgical Drama of Hildegard of Bingen

By 1000 C.E. the liturgy and music of the Western Catholic Church had assumed a form it would retain for the next five hundred years and more. The various canonical hours, as well as the Proper and Ordinary of the Mass, were all firmly in place. Yet musicians continued to feel a need to express themselves. They did so by creating three new genres, or types, of chant: tropes, sequences, and liturgical dramas. Tropes and sequences were not sung every day, but only on about thirty high feasts of the church year. Liturgical dramas (church plays) were even less frequently inserted into the liturgy, usually only on a half-dozen important days around Christmas and Easter. These new chants did not change the basic shape of the services of the church. They simply made the musical portions of these services longer and more splendid.

TROPES

A **trope** is an addition of music or text, or both, to a pre-existing chant. Musicians inserted tropes into the liturgy to elaborate upon the religious theme of an older, pre-existing chant, which remained unchanged. Most tropes were added to chants of the Proper of the Mass, especially the Introit. The new music and text might alternate with the old, or it might come entirely before it, and thereby serve as a musical preface. The trope *Hodie cantandus est nobis* (*Today we sing of a child*; Anthology, No. 10) introduces the Introit for Mass on Christmas morning. It was composed by **Tuotilo of St. Gall** (c850–915 C.E.) around the year 900. Tuotilo was a talented monk who has left us paintings, ivory carvings, and poetry, in addition to a collection of tropes for the high feasts of the church year. Elaborating on the meaning of the Christmas Introit, the trope *Hodie cantandus est nobis* proclaims that the Christ Child was born of a heavenly father and an earthly mother, his coming predicted long ago (Ex. 5-1). Thus tropes more fully explain the theology inherent in the chants to which they are added. As is typical of tropes, the musical style of *Hodie cantandus est nobis* is very similar to that of the Introit it introduces, *Puer natus est nobis* (*A boy is born to us*).

EXAMPLE 5-1

Today we sing of a child…
A boy is born to us, and a Son is given to us…

Sources also attribute to Tuotilo of St. Gall the most famous of all *Kyrie* melodies, *Omnipotens genitor* (Ex. 5-2). Some medieval chant manuscripts include an additional text in Latin for this *Kyrie*—in other words, the *Kyrie* has been troped, or elaborated upon. There is uncertainty, however, as to which came first, the version of the melody with Latin text or the more melismatic version without it. Nevertheless, today scholars refer to the Latin texted version as a *Kyrie* trope—a *Kyrie* with added text.

EXAMPLE 5-2

Almighty father, God, creator of all things, have mercy.
Font of love, source of goodness, everlasting light, have mercy.
May your love save us, good ruler, have mercy.

LISTENING CUE

TUOTILO OF ST. GALL
Introit trope, *Hodie cantandus est nobis* (c900)
Kyrie trope, *Omnipotens genitor* (c900)

CD 1/10–11
Anthology,
Nos. 10, 11

❁ SEQUENCES

The **sequence** began life much like the trope, as an addition of music with text to a pre-existing chant. The sequence did not precede another chant, but followed it, hence the Latin name "sequentia" ("a following thing"). Specifically, the sequence follows the Alleluia of the Mass. From the ninth century onward, sequences were appended to the Alleluia on high feast days as a way of extending through music the joy associated with the word "Hallelujah."

The story of the sequence begins once more at St. Gall with a famous writer of sequences, **Notker Balbulus** (c840–912; Fig. 5-1). (*Balbulus* means "stammerer" in Latin, and Notker actually referred to himself as "the toothless stammerer" [*balbulus et edentulus*]). Despite his physical challenges, Notker was a fine poet and musician, and he compiled a collection of sequences called the *Liber hymnorum*. In the preface to his book, Notker recounts the story of its genesis. About 850 a monk of the monastery of Jumièges north of Paris fled his abbey to escape marauding Vikings. Seeking refuge, he arrived at St. Gall carrying a few notated sequences. Notker thought he could compose better texts, and he set about the task. In the end he compiled a collection of forty sequences. This he showed to his master, Marcellus, who had them copied out individually on parchment rolls (medieval sheet music) so that they could be taught to other monks. From there, Notker's creations spread across the Holy Roman Empire.

The opening work in Notker's book of sequences is *Natus ante saecula* (*Born before the ages*) for high Mass on Christmas Day. As with all sequences, it is an entirely syllabic chant. As Notker himself said: "Each movement of the melody must have its own syllable." It also possesses another distinctive feature of the sequence: **double verse structure.** Each musical phrase is sung twice to accommodate a pair of verses. One side of the choir sings the first verse, the other repeats this music with the second verse. Thus sequences exemplify antiphonal singing. Example 5-3 gives only the first two of six double versicles of Notker's sequence *Natus ante saecula*.

❁ FIGURE 5-1

With inkwells by his right arm, monk and musician Notker Balbulus sharpens his quill and prepares to write.

Jagiellonian Library, Krakow

EXAMPLE 5-3

Na - tus an - te sae - cu - la de - i fi - li - us in - vi - si - bi - lis, in - ter - mi - nus,
Per quem fit ma - chi - na cae - li ac ter - rae, ma - ris et in his de - gen - ti - um.

Per quem di - es et ho - rae la - bant et se i - te - rum re - ci - pro - cant,
Quem an - ge - li in ar - ce po - li vo - ce con - so - na sem - per ca - nunt:

The Son of God, born before time, invisible, and without end.
Through him heaven, earth, and sea and all the things in them were informed.
Through him days and hours pass and repeat their course.
Of him the angels in heaven always sing with harmonious voice.

Today the most famous of all medieval sequences is the **Dies irae** (*Day of Wrath*). It was written during the thirteenth century and serves as the sequence for the

CHAPTER 5 • LATER MEDIEVAL CHANT   37

Requiem Mass (Mass of the Dead) in the Roman Catholic Church. The text speaks of the hellfire that threatens every soul on the Day of Judgment. Over the centuries numerous composers, most notably Mozart, Berlioz, and Verdi, have set the sequence *Dies irae* in spectacular fashion. Consequently, the melody has come to be associated with the macabre and spooky, and has been used in such horror films as *The Shining, Nightmare before Christmas,* and *Sleeping with the Enemy.* As verses one and two of the sequence show, clearly the *Dies irae* is frightening only because of the words—the mostly stepwise melody is very typical of medieval syllabic chant (Ex. 5-4). This demonstrates a point about Gregorian chant: rarely is there an attempt to emphasize or intensify particular words through special musical processes— a text that speaks of descending into Hell is just as likely to go up as down. Chant is a somewhat abstract medium that does not try overtly to "convince" the listener, only to provide an environment for individual contemplation.

EXAMPLE 5-4

Day of wrath, that day
Will dissolve the earth in ashes
As David and the Sibyl bear witness.

What dread there will be
When the Judge shall come
To strictly judge all things.

A trumpet, spreading a wondrous sound
Through the graves of all lands,
Will drive mankind before the throne.

Death and Nature shall be astonished
When all creation rises again
To answer to the Judge.

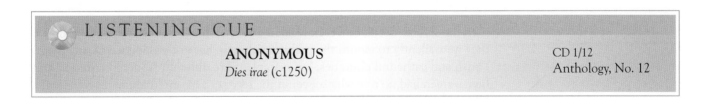

LISTENING CUE

ANONYMOUS
Dies irae (c1250)

CD 1/12
Anthology, No. 12

Tropes and sequences, being somewhat later additions to the music of the church, were not as fixed and unchanging as were the older parts of the Mass and canonical hours. Tropes fell completely out of fashion in the thirteenth century and then virtually disappeared. Sequences, on the other hand, only grew in popularity. Finally, during the Renaissance, these lengthy musical additions came to be viewed with suspicion as fabrications of the superstitious Middle Ages: thus sequences were cast out of the church by the reform-minded Council of Trent (1545–1563). Only five sequences were allowed to remain in the liturgy of the Roman Catholic Church, among them the justly famous *Dies irae* for the Requiem Mass.

✾ MUSIC IN THE CONVENT: THE CHANT AND LITURGICAL DRAMA OF HILDEGARD OF BINGEN

Medieval society was broadly divided into three groups: those who worked (the peasants), those who fought (the nobles), and those who prayed (the clergy). Roughly a quarter of the population was clerical, and nearly one-half of these people were women. Celibate Christian women had banded together in cloistered groups since at least the fourth century. In the sixth century they, too, began to follow the monastic life prescribed in the Rule of St. Benedict. They lived in what was then called a monastery, but today is most often referred to as a **convent** or a **nunnery.** Here, almost entirely removed from all male associations, they worked, prayed, and sang. An abbess governed the convent, and the main female singer, the **cantrix,** directed the choir. Nuns sang the same chants and read the same lessons as the monks, but they could not celebrate the sacrament of the Mass (for that a priest had to be called). Cloistered nuns also received training in singing, according to the rules of music theory of that day. Some musical exercises added to a Psalter from an English convent suggest what this instruction might have been like. The nuns practiced scales and leaps—but all (except at the end) within the confines of a single hexachord (Ex. 5-5).

EXAMPLE 5-5

In the secular world, however, women were encouraged to be seen but not heard; they were silently to mouth the psalms in church, but not pronounce or sing them! Parish and cathedral churches, for example, were different from monasteries, and here women had no role whatsoever in the service. This interdiction derived from a biblical admonition of St. Paul: "A woman must be silent in church."

The life of **Hildegard of Bingen** (1098–1179) demonstrates that sometimes a woman might rise above her traditionally subordinate position within the church to become a figure of renown, even veneration. Hildegard was born on the banks of the Rhine River in 1098. The tenth daughter of a minor nobleman and his wife, her parents gave her over to the church at the age of eight. At fourteen Hildegard chose to profess vows of chastity, poverty, and obedience, and formally join the convent. There she studied the Rule of St. Benedict, the liturgy, and the seven liberal arts, in order to understand the scriptures. When her abbess died in 1136, Hildegard herself was chosen mother superior. Later, she founded a new and larger community of nuns on the slopes of a mountain called Rupertsberg, near the small town of Bingen. It was for this convent that she composed most of her seventy-seven chants and her liturgical drama. Indeed, we have more monophonic chants surviving from the pen of Hildegard of Bingen than from any other single figure during the Middle Ages, male or female. But Hildegard was far more than a musician and church administrator. She was also a botanist, zoologist, pharmacologist, theologian, preacher, and religious visionary. Indeed, she wrote books in each of these and other areas of endeavor—thirteen in all. Toward the end of her life, clergymen, nobles, kings, and even the pope sought her opinion in various matters of church and state.

From an early age, Hildegard possessed unusual spiritual gifts. During moments that we might today identify as severe migraine headaches, she heard voices and saw visions accompanied by great flashes of light: a serpent-like Satan devouring the petals of a scarlet rose, or the blood of Christ streaming in the heavens, for example. These she gathered into a single volume called **Scivias** (**Know You the Ways**), which reads much like the Book of Revelation, the phantasmagorical conclusion of the New Testament. Hildegard's visions also found their way into her musical compositions. More than any other religious poet of the Middle Ages, her musical texts are filled with extraordinarily colorful images. Hildegard's poems are not so much verbal structures as pictures transferred to words. Flowers, serpents, blood, drops of dew, all commingle to almost surreal effect. Toward the end of her life, Hildegard arranged her music in a book called **Symphonia,** of which two manuscript copies are preserved today. Hildegard took no credit for what she created: "The words I speak come from no human mouth. I saw and heard them in visions sent to me . . . I am carried along as a feather on the breath of God."

Hildegard's music consists mainly of hymns, antiphons, and sequences for saints important in her region (Disibod, Rupert, Ursula, and others) as well as for Christ and the Virgin Mary. Typical of Hildegard's life in general, her chants do not conform to the accepted norms of the time. For example, she does not always stay within the confines of the prescribed church modes, her antiphons are not always neumatic but sometimes wildly melismatic, and her sequences do not strictly follow double-verse form. Viewing herself merely as a conduit for the voice of God, Hildegard seems to have had little concern for the norms of Gregorian chant that had been established here on earth.

One thing in the music of Hildegard, however, is consistent with the chant of her day: the structure of the text determines the shape of the music. Hildegard's words form a phrase, and she provides each phrase with its own music. The verbal phrases taken together convey the meaning of the sacred text; the musical phrases cohere into a compelling composition. Take, for example, Hildegard's antiphon for St. Ursula, O rubor sanguinis (O, Redness of Blood; Ex. 5-6). It is written in the Dorian mode, but with a B♭ so as to avoid the tritone F-B. In the Middle Ages, musicians sought to avoid the dissonant tritone, which came to be called the **diabolus in musica** (devil in music). The chant starts on D and ends on D. Every separate phrase of text ends on A (the reciting pitch in the Dorian mode) or D. The text dictates the structure of the music. Normally antiphons are neumatic in style (two, three, or four notes per syllable). But the spirit often moved Hildegard to write melismatic exclamations, such as we see on "O" and the thirty-one-note melisma on "numquam" ("never") as the antiphon gradually wends its way back to the final pitch of the Dorian mode. There is rhapsodic beauty, even ecstasy here, but it unfolds within a clear musical structure.

EXAMPLE 5-6

O   ru - bor san - gui - nis   qui   de

ex - cel -   -   so   il - lo flu - - - xi - sti

etc.

O redness of blood, which flowed down from on high...

LISTENING CUE

HILDEGARD OF BINGEN
O rubor sanguinis (c1150)

CD 1/13
Anthology, No. 13

❀ FIGURE 5-2

A twelfth-century illumination depicting Hildegard of Bingen receiving divine inspiration, perhaps a vision or a chant, directly from the heavens. To the right, her secretary, the monk Volmar, peeks at her in amazement. This illumination was painted twenty-one years after her death.

Otto Miller Verlages, Salzburg

Perhaps the most extraordinary musical creation of Hildegard is her **Ordo virtutum (Play of the Virtues),** a collection of some eighty chants that form a full-length music drama. Specifically, it is a **liturgical drama**—a religious play-with-music intended to be inserted into the liturgy, usually before Mass. Many liturgical dramas were at first simple tropes (additions to the pre-existing liturgy); eventually they grew so elaborate as to stand as separate, independent dramas. Almost all religious plays of the Middle Ages had a scriptural basis, drawing upon some event described in the Bible (the story of Daniel escaping from the lion's den or King Herod slaughtering the innocent children, for example). But Hildegard's *Ordo virtutum* is not drawn from any story in the Bible. Instead, hers is an original work that, according to the prologue, God created and commanded she record. The protagonist in these ninety minutes of musical theater is the human Soul, a woman who represents everywoman. The Soul is torn between the difficult road to spiritual salvation, recommended by the Virtues, and the easy path of worldly fame and fortune urged by the Devil.

The climax of the drama centers on a confrontation between the Soul and the Devil, who encourages the Soul to know and enjoy the pleasures of the human flesh. The Soul sings of her fears and weaknesses. Satan shouts but cannot sing—Hell is a noisy place and its lord is unmusical. The Virtues, on the other hand, sing alluringly of a life removed from the temptations of this world. Needless to say, in this earliest Christian morality play the Virtues ultimately win out. The triumphant final chorus gathers together the Virtues and every Soul. All are urged to witness the suffering and sacrifice of Christ and to follow his example.

Hildegard's *Ordo virtutum* was likely first performed in her convent at Rupertsberg in 1152. The roles of the Soul and the fourteen Virtues were presumably sung by fifteen of the approximately fifty nuns in residence. Abbess Hildegard herself surely played the part of the narrator, while the only male at the convent, her secretary Volmar (Fig. 5-2), likely portrayed the Devil. By excluding all male characters except Satan, Hildegard's *Ordo virtutum* reinforces the first rule of the convent: a woman of virtue is married only to Christ.

LISTENING CUE

HILDEGARD OF BINGEN
Excerpts from *Ordo virtutum* (c1150)

CD 1/14
Anthology, No. 14

SUMMARY

By 1000 C.E. the Mass and canonical hours had assumed their final form. Thereafter, the new chants added to the liturgy usually came in one of three types: trope, sequence, or liturgical drama. Tropes were inserted almost everywhere in the liturgy, though most often they came at the beginning of the Introit of the Mass. Sequences were always inserted after the Alleluia of the Mass as a way of extending this moment of jubilation. Sequences are longer pieces than tropes, usually follow a prescribed form (double verses), and are invariably syllabic. Liturgical dramas are religious plays-with-music inserted into the service, usually before Mass. Tropes and liturgical dramas fell out of fashion later in the Middle Ages. Sequences, however, remained in favor into the Renaissance. Ultimately, all but five were removed from the Catholic liturgy by the reforming authorities of the Council of Trent (1545–1563).

Hildegard of Bingen (1098–1179) was one of the most remarkable figures of the Middle Ages. A polymath who wrote lengthy books on many subjects, she has left us a collection of nearly eighty chants preserved in her *Symphonia* as well as a lengthy liturgical drama entitled *Ordo virtutum*, the earliest morality play to be set entirely to music. Hildegard's texts are extraordinarily vivid, and the music to which she sets them is beautifully effusive.

KEY TERMS

trope
Tuotilo of St. Gall
sequence
Notker Balbulus
double verse structure
Dies irae

Requiem Mass
convent
nunnery
cantrix
Hildegard of Bingen
Scivias (Know You the Ways)

Symphonia
diabolus in musica
Ordo Virtutum (Play of the Virtues)
liturgical drama

Chapter

Troubadours and Trouvères

6

Not all music in the Middle Ages was religious. There were songs for the knights as they rode into battle, songs for the men in the fields and the women around the hearth, and songs and dances for the nobles in their castles. Unfortunately, most of this secular music, and virtually all of it coming from the common folk, is now lost because it was never written down. Only the church music is preserved in any significant amount, because only the men and women of the church were trained in musical notation and educated generally. Even the nobility was more or less illiterate in Latin, the universal language of the Western church. This was the state of affairs in the West until the high Middle Ages of the twelfth and thirteenth centuries.

During the high Middle Ages the court first emerged as a center for the patronage of the arts. Kings, dukes, counts, and princes assumed greater responsibility for defense, commerce, and justice—affairs previously handled largely by the church. To enhance the ruler's prestige and show that he or she was a person of refinement and sensibility, the noble often engaged bands of trumpeters to herald an arrival, instrumentalists to provide dance music for festivals of the court, and singers and poets to create lyric verse. Simultaneously, vernacular tongues began to emerge from the shadow of Latin and become literary languages in their own right. Poetry in French, German, Italian, and Spanish first appears at this time. Some poems were meant to be recited, others sung.

Southern France was the center of this new courtly art. The poet-musicians who flourished there went by the name of **troubadour** (for men) and **trobairitz** (for women). Both terms derived from the verb "trobar," which meant "to find" in their vernacular tongue. Thus the troubadours and trobairitz were finders or inventors of new modes of verbal and vocal expression. Their tongue, the language of southern France, was called **langue d'oc** (also **occitan**). By the early thirteenth century the art of the troubadours had spread to the north. Here the poet-musician was called a **trouvère** (both masculine and feminine) from the word "trouver" (again, "to find"). The language of the north was called **langue d'oïl.** (Both "oc" and "oïl" meant "yes" in medieval French.) A song of the south was called a **canso,** while one of the north was a **chanson.** By gathering many songs into a single volume, the musicians of the north created a **chansonnier** (a book of songs). The scribes of the first chansonniers, whether troubadour or trouvère, simply borrowed the musical notation of the monastery and brought it into the castle. All told, the troubadours created approximately 2,600 courtly poems, about a tenth of which survive today with music. Similarly, the trouvères have left us 2,100 poems, about 1,400 of which have melodies.

The social standing of the troubadours and trobairitz was varied. Many were noblemen or noblewomen—dukes or countesses, for example. Others, however, were the humble servants of such aristocrats. Contrary to popular belief, a troubadour was not a carefree minstrel wandering from town to town. He was a serious verse-technician, usually attached to a single court, who wrote a particular kind of love poetry about **fin'amors** (ideal love). Fin'amors expressed the values of chivalric society as they applied to the art of love, the love of a knight or a poet for his lady. The noble poet-musician placed his beloved woman on a pedestal and swore to honor and obey her, as a vassal would a lord. From this great flowering of troubadour poetry emerged a new view of women in courtly society. The female was now thought to be the more virtuous, purer, yet weaker sex, worthy of both veneration and protection. But the woman, too, had her point of view. Included among the southern repertory are about forty poems by trobairitz, though unfortunately for only one has the music been preserved.

Countess Beatriz de Dia wrote the sole extant song by a trobairitz. She lived in southern France during the middle of the twelfth century. Though married to Count William of Poitiers, she fell in love with a fellow troubadour, Raimbaut of Orange (1146–1173). Her song *A chantar m'er* (*I must sing*) laments her failure in love, despite her self-proclaimed charms. Almost all troubadour and trouvère songs are strophic, and this one has five stanzas. Were we to strip away the text, the melody alone might at first be taken for a chant from the church. Like chant, troubadour and trouvère music is monophonic and has no regular rhythmic pattern or meter. So, too, the song moves predominantly in step-wise motion and has a strong sense of a church mode (in this case, the Dorian mode). Nevertheless, the Countess de Dia's canso exhibits a repetitive formal plan (**ABABCDB**). Such clear-cut repetition schemes are common in the music of the troubadours and trouvères, but virtually unknown in the chant of the church. Often it is the rhyme scheme of the vernacular poem that creates regularity in the music. Throughout the high Middle Ages and into the Renaissance, the secular music of the court will exhibit formal repetitions far more than the sacred music of the church.

LISTENING CUE

BEATRIZ DE DIA
A chantar m'er (c1175)

CD 1/15
Anthology, No. 15

THE COURT OF ELEANOR OF AQUITAINE

More than any other place, the art of the troubadours and trouvères flourished at the court of **Eleanor of Aquitaine** (c1122–1204). Eleanor was arguably the most remarkable woman of the high Middle Ages, and certainly the most powerful. Her grandfather, Duke William IX (1071–1126) of Aquitaine, was the first recorded troubadour—the first to leave us love songs in the vernacular tongue. From her father, Duke William X, Eleanor inherited the duchy of Aquitaine in southwestern France. In 1137 she married Louis of France and, when he succeeded to the French throne that year, Eleanor became queen. But the temperaments of the royal couple were ill-suited: Louis thought Eleanor strong-willed and promiscuous; Eleanor considered Louis a pious wimp. By mutual consent, their marriage was annulled in March 1152. Eight weeks later Eleanor married Henry of Anjou, who in 1154 succeeded to the throne of England as King Henry II. Now Eleanor was queen of England, as well as countess of Anjou, and duchess of Normandy and Aquitaine. The territorial holdings of Eleanor and Henry extended from Scotland through England and down through western France to Spain (see Map 6-1). Because the geographic center of this realm was the French county of Anjou, these holdings came to be called the **Angevin kingdom.** In land and population, the twelfth-century Angevin kingdom was far better endowed than the kingdom of France.

✿ MAP 6-1
The Angevin kingdom (France) in the twelfth century.

Queen Eleanor and King Henry moved frequently, and usually separately, to rule their vast lands. Her preferred abode was the castle of Chinon near Anjou. Here Eleanor drew poets and musicians and encouraged her own children to pursue these arts. At her court was Marie de France, the first writer, male or female, to put the legend of King Arthur into verse.

Foremost among the troubadours at Chinon was **Bernart de Ventadorn** (c1135–c1195). We know something of the life of Bernart owing to the chansonniers that preserve his compositions. In these song books, the works of each composer are grouped separately and prefaced by a small portrait of the artist, as well as a brief biographical sketch called a ***vida.*** Here is the beginning of the "vita" of Bernart de Ventadorn.

> Bernart de Ventadorn was from the Limousin, from the castle of Ventadorn. He was poor by birth, the son of a servant who fired the ovens for baking bread at the castle. But he became handsome and clever and knew well how to sing and make songs, and became courteous and wise. His lord, the Viscount, liked him and did him great honor. The Viscount had a wife, young, noble and joyful; she liked Bernart and his songs, and fell in love with him and he with her; and he made songs and verses for her, about the love he had for her and her worthiness. Their love lasted a long time before anyone noticed. But when the Viscount found out, he separated Bernart from her, and his wife was locked up and guarded. She was made to advise Bernart to leave and go far away. And he left and went to the Duchess of Normandy—Eleanor of Aquitaine—who was young and of great valor, and who understood merit and words of praise. The songs of Bernart pleased her well, and she received him and welcomed him warmly. For a long time he stayed at her court, and he was enamored of her and she of him, and he made many fine songs about her.[1]

Bernart of Ventadorn has left forty-five poems, of which eighteen are supplied with melodies. By far his most popular song is *Can vei la lauzeta* (*When I see the lark*). It was copied and translated into four other languages, including Spanish and German. The "Lark" here refers to Eleanor of Aquitaine. The *vida* of Bernart, again, tells us something about how this song came to be:

> Bernart de Ventadorn called Eleanor of Aquitaine "Lauzeta" because of a knight who loved her and whom she called "Rai" [short for Raimond]. One day the knight came to the duchess and entered her room. Eleanor, seeing him, lifted the front of her skirt and put it over his head, and fell back onto the bed. Bernart de Ventadorn saw all this, because one of the lady's maids had shown him where to hide. On this subject Bernart made the song *Can vei la lauzeta.*[2]

Given these events, no wonder the song *Can vei la lauzeta* is full of bitterness. The idealistic poet Bernart has been deceived. In seven eight-line stanzas he gives vent to his feelings: the joy of love has left his heart because the "lark" has done what is forbidden her—she has broken the rules of *fin'amors*. To the final stanza, Bernart adds an **envoi,** literally a "send-off." Here he calls forth the image of the knight Tristan, the great lover in medieval legend:

Tristans, ges no'm auretz de me,	Tristan, you will hear no more of me,
Qu'en m'en vau, chaitius, no sai on.	For I am going sadly away, I do not know where
De chantar me gic e'm recre,	I am going to stop singing,
E de joi d'amor m'escon.	And I flee from the joy of love.

Indeed, Bernart de Ventadorn did go away. His *vida* says that he withdrew from the secular court of Eleanor of Aquitaine and ended his days in a monastery. Ulti-

FIGURE 6-1

Tomb of Eleanor of Aquitaine and her son Richard the Lionheart at Fontevraud Abbey. At far left is the tomb of Eleanor's husband, Henry II. Notice that Eleanor holds a book, a symbol intended to suggest that she was both learned and a person of authority within the convent.

Bridgeman Art Library

mately, Eleanor of Aquitaine, too, withdrew to a monastery. In her eighties she took up residence among the Benedictine nuns at Fontevraud near Chinon. Her funeral monument remains there today (Fig. 6-1), along with those of her husband, King Henry, and son, Richard.

LISTENING CUE

BERNART DE VENTADORN
Can vei la lauzeta (c1165)

CD 1/16
Anthology, No. 16

TROUVÈRES

Eleanor of Aquitaine had eleven children. Her eldest daughter was Marie of Champagne, herself a patroness of poets. Of Eleanor's five sons her favorite was Richard, who ultimately became King Richard I of England (1157–1199). Richard set to music poetry written in the *langue d'oïl*, for he spoke the language of the north, as did his father, King Henry II of England. Thus Richard was a trouvère—indeed, one of the first. Contemporaries called him **Richard the Lionheart,** for he displayed great courage during the third crusade to the Holy Lands. On his journey home, however, King Richard was ambushed, taken prisoner, and held for ransom. To while away the hours, Richard wrote verse and set it to music. His most famous song is *Ja nus hons pris ne dira (Truly, a captive doesn't speak his mind)*. Obviously written during his period of captivity (1192–1194), it is a beautiful complaint: the lords of the Angevin kingdom have failed to produce the ransom that will set him free. Each of the six stanzas is carried by music in the simplest of musical forms (**AAB**).

LISTENING CUE

RICHARD THE LIONHEART
Ja nus hons pris ne dira (1192–1194)

CD 1/17
Anthology, No. 17

🌺 FIGURE 6-2

A thirteenth-century miniature from the court of King Alfonso the Wise, showing a medieval fiddle (the rebec) on the left and a lute on the right. Both instruments were brought into Spain by the Arabs and then carried northward into the lands of the troubadours and trouvères.

By the beginning of the thirteenth century, imitations of the French love song were being written in Italian, German, Spanish, and even English. In Germany a poet-musician writing love songs in the native tongue was called a **Minnesinger** and the song he created a *Minnesang* ("song of love" in old high German). Spain, however, was geographically closer to southwestern France than any other country, and the mixing of troubadour poetry with the melodic traditions of Arabic Spain produced a distinctive new vocal genre. A medieval Spanish or Portuguese monophonic song is called a *cantiga.* Hundreds of these were created on subjects of love, epic heroism, and everyday life, but few of these secular poems are preserved today with music. One special group of some four hundred songs surviving with music goes by the name **Cantigas de Santa Maria.** About 1270 this anthology was collected, and perhaps some songs composed, by **Alfonso the Wise,** king of Castile, Spain. While the texts of these *cantigas* all honor the Virgin Mary and tell of her miracles, their musical style is more secular than sacred. Many incorporate the **AAB** form often used by both troubadours and trouvères, and some are believed to be pre-existing secular songs just outfitted with sacred words. Most remarkable, however, are the beautiful illuminations contained in the various manuscripts of Alfonso's *cantigas.* These depictions constitute a rich source of information about medieval musical instruments, as can be seen in Figure 6-2. Here, before a backdrop of Arabic geometric patterns, we see clear illustrations of the lute (an instrument of Arabic origin), and a medieval fiddle. Such instruments, which are discussed in further detail in Chapter 11, undoubtedly were used in the performance of Spanish songs at the court of King Alfonso.

SUMMARY

Not all music in the Middle Ages was religious. Secular love music also existed in Western Europe but was not written down until the late twelfth century. The courtly tradition of creating love poems with music was centered in France. The troubadours and trobairitz held forth in southern France during the twelfth century, and they were succeeded in the thirteenth century by the trouvères in northern France. Most troubadour and trouvère songs are syllabic, mainly stepwise melodies setting poems in strophic form. The French tradition of the monophonic courtly chanson inspired the rise of the German *Minnesang* and the Spanish *cantiga*. Equally important, the monophonic canso and chanson of the troubadours and trouvères established the genre of the courtly love song, and from this tradition would emerge the pan-European polyphonic chanson of the late Middle Ages and Renaissance.

KEY TERMS

troubadour	trouvère	chanson
trobairitz	langue d'oïl	chansonnier
langue d'oc, occitan	canso	*fin'amors*

Countess Beatriz de Dia	*vida*	*Minnesang*
Eleanor of Aquitaine	envoi	*cantiga*
Angevin kingdom	Richard the Lionheart	*Cantigas de Santa Maria*
Bernart de Ventadorn	Minnesinger	Alfonso the Wise

Chapter 7

Early Polyphony

Western music has one distinctive characteristic: polyphony. By contrast, Chinese music, Indian music, Korean music, Japanese music—all of these venerable musical traditions—have enormously intricate melodies, ones filled with subtle microtones not present in the melodies of the West. Similarly, sub-Saharan African music employs rhythms so complex as to make those of Westerners look childish by comparison. But for music making with many simultaneously sounding pitches—polyphony—no musical tradition is richer than that of the West. To be sure, Western classical music has cultivated polyphony (expressed in both harmony and counterpoint) to a degree unknown in other musical cultures. One consequence of this can be seen, for example, in the colossal orchestral scores of Gustav Mahler and Richard Strauss. But how, when, and where did this Western obsession with polyphony begin?

Perhaps polyphony began when individuals singing in different vocal ranges noticed their harmoniously different sounds and began to cultivate them; perhaps it began when people singing the same tune in slightly different ways created polyphonic intervals from time to time; perhaps polyphony emerged when a group sang a round and enjoyed the resulting polyphonic sound. Obviously, we do not know where or why polyphony first appeared, but very likely singing polyphonically is as innate to human expression as singing itself.

ORGANUM IN MUSIC THEORY SOURCES

What we do know is that the first documented appearance of polyphonic music comes from a Benedictine abbey in northwestern Germany and dates from the 890s. It is found in a music theory treatise entitled **Musica enchiriadis (Music Handbook)** that describes a type of polyphonic singing called organum. Soon the term **organum (pl., organa)** came to be used generally to connote polyphony. As one theorist explained, polyphony is called organum because voices singing in harmony show "a resemblance to the instrument that is called the organ."[1]

The author of the *Musica enchiriadis*, identified as Abbot Hoger (d. 906) in the earliest sources, does not address his discussion of organum to composers, nor does he intend it for music theorists who wish to analyze music. Instead, Abbot Hoger's sole aim is to teach church singers how to improvise polyphonic music on the spot—to take a given piece of Gregorian chant and make it sound more splendid by adding one or more additional lines around it. This sort of improvised polyphony would be cultivated in Western churches for nearly a thousand years, up to the time of the French Revolution. Thus, the *Musica enchiriadis* and other similar treatises taught musicians, not the rules of composition but a technique for improvising music extempore.

Exactly how did this work? Most organum described in the *Musica enchiriadis* is called **parallel organum** (organum in which all voices move in lockstep, up or down, with the intervals between voices remaining the same). In its most basic form, parallel organum proceeds with only two voice parts. One, called the ***vox principalis*** (principal voice), is a pre-existing chant to be enhanced; the other, called the ***vox organalis*** (organal voice), is a newly created line to be added to the chant. The intervals at which the two voices proceed, not surprisingly, are the primary consonances of the early Middle Ages: the octave, the fifth, and the fourth. The *Musica enchiriadis* allows for parallel organum at either the fourth or the fifth below the plainsong; thus, the *vox organalis* always moves along with the *vox principalis* at the interval of either a fourth or a fifth below. What is more, both voices may be doubled an octave above or below. Thus four-voice parallel organum is also permissible (Ex. 7-1).

EXAMPLE 7-1

May the glory of the Lord, throughout the ages…

Singing in parallel fourths or fifths often results in a dissonant tritone, as when F and B sound together. To avoid the tritone, the author of the *Musica enchiriadis* urges the organal voice to remain stationary at those potentially dangerous moments. In Example 7-2, the organal voice would normally start on D in parallel organum at the fourth, but here starts on G so as not to create an F-B tritone while the principal voice rises through B. Such a moment is called organum with **oblique motion** (one voice repeating or sustaining a pitch while another moves away or toward it).

EXAMPLE 7-2

The humble servants, venerating you with pious melodies.

More than a century passes before we find further discussions of polyphony. They appear in the writings of two music theorists of the eleventh century, Guido of Arezzo and John of St. Gall, both of whom we have previously met. Guido introduced the musical staff with pitch-letter names as well as a system of hexachords and a musical hand that facilitated sight-singing; John was the first to expound a complete system for the eight church modes as we know them today. In his *Micrologus* (c1030) Guido devotes the last of nineteen chapters to polyphony. He does not advocate four-voice organum, only two-voice organum, with the *vox organalis* usually a fourth below. He, too, was concerned about avoiding the offensive tritone. He advocates parallel organum whenever possible, but where a tritone might lurk it should be avoided by means of oblique motion. Guido was the first theorist to be concerned about the cadence, which he called the **occursus**—a running together.

Example 7-3 demonstrates not only oblique motion at a final cadence, but also contrary motion. In brief moments such as these, with the voices moving against one another, we see the earliest signs of what will later be called counterpoint.

EXAMPLE 7-3

Vox principalis

Vox organalis Ve - ni ad do - cen-dum   nos   vi - am pru - den - ti - ae

Come to teach us the path of wisdom.

John of St. Gall devotes only one chapter of his *De Musica* (c1100) to organum, but he has two important things to say: (1) contrary motion and voice crossing in organum are to be encouraged, and (2) the *vox principalis* (the chant) should appear beneath, not above, the *vox organalis*. Hereafter, from the late eleventh through the sixteenth century, the given Gregorian chant is placed toward the bottom of the musical texture as voices are added around it. The old chant serves as a scaffold supporting the newly added voices.

ORGANUM IN PRACTICAL SOURCES

Our best information about early polyphony comes from music theorists who were intent on instructing medieval singers how to improvise organum around a given chant. But contemporary manuscripts survive that contain written polyphony as well. The earliest of these comes from a Benedictine monastery at Winchester, England, and dates from c1000 C.E. The collection is called the **Winchester Troper,** because it contains mainly tropes—a troper is a chant manuscript mainly preserving additions to the liturgy called tropes (see Chapter 5). The Winchester Troper dates some thirty years before the invention of the musical staff, and its pitches are written in unheightened neumes. Moreover, the two-voice polyphony is not notated in one manuscript. Since the singers already knew the chant by memory, only the newly composed voice was notated in the Winchester Troper. Consequently, because the notation does not specify relative pitch and because the two voices are not placed one on top of the other in the same book, it is impossible today to sing the music with any confidence. All we can say is that, from the Winchester Troper, singers could generate a repertory of about 150 two-voice organa—*Kyries* and Alleluias for the Mass, for example. The Winchester Troper was clearly not a prescriptive document for sight-reading, but a memory aid—the singers had all of this organum in their heads and just needed a reminder from time to time.

In contrast to the notational uncertainty of the Winchester Troper, the next significant collection of organum can be read with great clarity. Surviving today from southern France is a repertory of about sixty-five pieces of two-voice organum. It is called **Aquitanian polyphony** because many of the works come from various monasteries in the region of Aquitaine in southwestern France (see Map 6-1). Most are tropes, sequences, and a later musical form called the conductus (see Chapter 9). All pieces date from the twelfth century. Fortunately, with the Aquitanian repertory we can read the pitches with no difficulty. Yet the rhythm still poses a problem; the notation seems not to imply rhythmic durations. We can transcribe the notes as a series of eighth-notes, for example, but the music was most likely performed extempore:

🌼 FIGURE 7-1

Viderunt Hemanuel, a two-voice organum of the twelfth century coming from southern France. Notice the alphabetical pitch indicators to the left of each staff.

one singer (the bottom voice) simply held and waited for the other (top part) to sing the more complex line. Indeed, many Aquitanian pieces exemplify passages of what is called **sustained-tone organum**—the bottom voice holds a note while the faster-moving top voice embellishes it in a florid fashion. In Aquitanian polyphony, sustained-tone organum most often occurs at cadence points at the ends of musical lines.

A fine example of Aquitanian polyphony is the anonymous two-voice *Viderunt Hemanuel* (Fig. 7-1). This is a two-voice trope of the Gradual of the Mass for Christmas, *Viderunt omnes* (see Chapter 3 and Anthology, No. 8), and it would have been sung at a monastery on Christmas morning. The bottom voice begins like the Gradual chant *Viderunt omnes* while the top voice is newly composed. Intervals of thirds and sixths are plentiful in the middle of phrases but more consonant fifths and octaves always sound at the beginnings and ends. At several end points the bottom voice holds while the top voice cascades a full octave down the scale to form a final cadence, a clear instance of sustained-tone organum (see Ex. 7-4). Aquitanian polyphony gives the distinct impression of being music that is rhythmically free, luxuriant, even sensual. There is little that is prescribed in the written score other than the pitches. The ultimate effect of a performance depended greatly upon the tempo, rhythms, and vocal nuances the singers chose to employ.

EXAMPLE 7-4

They saw Emmanuel…
Israel in ruin…

LISTENING CUE

ANONYMOUS   CD 1/18
Viderunt Hemanuel (c1125)   Anthology, No. 18

Related to the repertory of Aquitanian polyphony is a small collection of some twenty pieces preserved today at the cathedral of **Santiago (St. James) de Compostela,** Spain. Next to Rome, the pilgrimage site of greatest importance in medieval Europe was the cathedral of Santiago, for it was believed to house the relics (bones) of the Apostle James. So important was it that a grand street in Paris was (and is still) called Rue St. Jacques, and each year along this road thousands of pilgrims went south on their way out of Paris walking toward Compostela in northwestern Spain. It is estimated that, in all, 500,000 pilgrims took this and various other routes to Compostela annually. Thousands still do so today, sleeping in monasteries and youth hostels along the way.

Surviving today at the church of St. James in Compostela is a manuscript called the **Codex Calixtinus,** written around 1150 and once believed to be the work of Pope Calixtus II. It contains a service for St. James, which includes twenty polyphonic pieces, mostly for Mass and Vespers. Once again, the musical notation does not suggest rhythms, only relative pitches. The singers must fit the two parts together as the spirit and the meter of the text move them. The Codex Calixtinus is an important monument in the history of Western music because it is the first manuscript to ascribe composers' names to particular pieces (Fig. 7-2). Among the composers named in the manuscript is **Master Albertus of Paris.** To him is attributed one of the earliest three-voice compositions in Western music, *Congaudeant Catholici* (*Let the faithful rejoice*), the beginning of which is given below. Master Albertus did, in fact, exist; he was the cantor of the cathedral of Notre Dame of Paris in the mid twelfth century. Thus it is to Paris and the music of the so-called Notre Dame School that we now turn.

FIGURE 7-2
Congaudeant Catholici from the Codex Calixtinus. Two voices are notated in different-colored ink on the bottom staff and one voice only on the top staff.

EXAMPLE 7-5

Let the faithful rejoice…

LISTENING CUE

MASTER ALBERTUS OF PARIS
Congaudeant Catholici (c1150)

CD 1/19
Anthology, No. 19

SUMMARY

The first discussions of polyphony in any musical culture appear in northwestern Europe in the ninth century. Early polyphony was called organum, and our knowledge of it comes from two different types of sources: theory treatises and music manuscripts. The treatises begin by emphasizing parallel organum but increasingly come to recognize the need for oblique and contrary motion to avoid the dissonant tritone. Organum, unlike monophonic chant, was not an everyday affair. Singers wishing to adorn the liturgy in a special way employed it on the highest feast-days of the church year. In all early organum—in England, France, and Spain—the general tendency was to assign polyphony to those chants traditionally sung by soloists, such as the tropes and the difficult responsorial chants. Simple syllabic chants, such as psalms and hymns, continued to be sung chorally in monophonic Gregorian chant.

The largest collections of early written organum are found in the Winchester Troper (c1000 C.E.), which contains about 150 pieces that cannot accurately be deciphered, and a twelfth-century repertory from medieval Aquitaine (southwestern France), which includes about sixty-five compositions, some in sustained-tone, florid style. The Codex Calixtinus, a manuscript preserved at the pilgrimage church of St. James in Compostela, Spain, contains twenty examples of organum dating about 1150. It is the first source to ascribe compositions to particular composers.

KEY TERMS

Musica enchiriadis (*Music Handbook*)
organum (pl., organa)
parallel organum
vox principalis

vox organalis
oblique motion
occursus
Winchester Troper
Aquitanian polyphony

sustained-tone organum
Santiago de Compostela
Codex Calixtinus
Master Albertus of Paris

Chapter

8

Music in Medieval Paris: Polyphony at Notre Dame

Today Paris is breathtaking, arguably the most beautiful, sophisticated, and visually stunning city in the world. But it was not always this way. At the time of the collapse of the Roman Empire (fifth century C.E.), Paris was home to no more than a few thousand souls who huddled on an island (the *Île de la Cité*) in the middle of the Seine River. The early Merovingian kings (ruled c500–751) made Paris their first city; but Holy Roman Emperor Charlemagne, the founder of the Carolingian dynasty, moved his capital to Aachen in western Germany around 790. When Charlemagne died in 814 he left gifts to the twenty-one most important cities in his empire—Rome, Milan, Cologne, even Arles—but nothing to insignificant Paris. Forgotten, Paris declined further. Not until the tenth century, upon the extinction of the Carolingian line and the ascent of a new dynasty of French kings (the Capetians), did the center of government return to Paris. Two centuries later the city experienced a renaissance.

During the twelfth century a new style of architecture emerged in Paris and surrounding territories, one that replaced the older, heavy, Roman-dominated (Romanesque) style. Today we call this new, lighter manner **Gothic architecture,** but contemporaries called it *opus francigenum* ("work in the French style"). Churches in cities near Paris and in Paris itself were built or rebuilt in the new Gothic style. In the main these were urban cathedrals, not rural monasteries. As the new church steeples reached toward the heavens, they signified a rising urban power.

Also in the twelfth century, education moved from the monastery to the cathedral, from the country to the city. In Paris church schools appeared next to the cathedral and eventually spilled over onto the south (left) bank of the Seine River. Here theologians taught the seven liberal arts so that clerical students might read and correctly interpret the scriptures. Spellbinding teachers such as Peter Abelard (1079-1142) attracted thousands of students from across the length and breadth of Europe. In 1215 a university was recognized by the Pope, a *Universitas magistrorum et scholarium* (university of masters and scholars), as it was called. Soon overrun by students, the population of Paris swelled, from 25,000 in the early twelfth century, to 80,000 in the mid-thirteenth, to nearly 200,000, according to a census of 1329. Paris had become the largest and most important city in northern Europe.

NOTRE DAME OF PARIS

At the center of it all, geographically and spiritually, was Notre Dame. Like most cathedrals in France, the one in Paris was dedicated to the Blessed Virgin Mary, Our Lady (*Notre Dame*). Typical of most Gothic cathedrals, the campaign to construct Notre Dame took more than a century. The church we see today was begun about 1163 but was not finished until more than a hundred years later (Fig. 8-1). Today, eight hundred years after the fact, we have become accustomed to the size and beauty of Notre Dame, standing ten stories tall (108 feet). In the Middle Ages, however, visitors to Paris were stunned. Notre Dame towered over the surrounding buildings like a colossus. A vision of the house of the Lord, celestial Jerusalem, had been placed on earth, indeed in the very center of the city.

By far the largest building in any major medieval city was the cathedral. The western end of the church was called the **nave.** This was the public part of the church. People came and went as they pleased. Goods and services were bought and sold, pilgrims slept on the floor, preachers preached, and heralds made public announcements. The nave functioned as town hall and civic auditorium, all contained within the west end of the Lord's temple. But where were the musicians?

Most music was made in the east end of the church, in the area called the **choir,** which included the high altar. In fact, the name for this part of the church was derived from the group of singers (Latin *chorus*) that performed therein. The clergy, as many as a hundred at a time, sat in stalls divided in half—half sat on the north side of the choir aisle and half on the south. Six to eight choirboys occupied benches on the floor. Everyone—the full clerical community—sang the basic Gregorian chant. For solos in the chant and for singing polyphony, however, specialists were needed. At Notre Dame this more professional choir of specially trained singers numbered about a dozen. When these soloists performed polyphony, they stepped down from their choir stalls and gathered around a single

FIGURE 8-1
East end of Notre Dame Cathedral, a fine example of Gothic architecture.

FIGURE 8-2

Hypothetical reconstruction of original choir of Notre Dame of Paris executed by the architectural historian Viollet-le-Duc in the nineteenth century. The medieval roodscreen at the very front was torn down in the eighteenth century during the Enlightenment. Note the choir stalls for the clergy to the left and right of the main aisle.

lectern in the center of the choir (Fig. 8-2). Here they sang the organum made famous throughout Europe by the composers of Notre Dame.

LEONINUS AND THE *MAGNUS LIBER ORGANI*

Among the many students drawn to the University of Paris in the late thirteenth century was an Englishman with a particular interest in music. After his studies in Paris he returned to England and wrote a music theory treatise commenting on contemporary music in Paris. We do not know his name and therefore call him Anonymous IV, because later his treatise was published as the fourth in a series of anonymous writings on music.[†] In the course of a discussion of the principles of musical notation, Anonymous IV inserts the following brief history of polyphonic music at Notre Dame.

> And note that Magister Leoninus, according to what was said, was the best creator of organum (*optimus organista*), who made a great book of organum for both the Mass and canonical hours to adorn the divine service. And this was in use until the time of Perotinus the Great, who abbreviated it and made many better substitute clausulae or sections, because he was the best composer of discant, better than Leoninus . . . . This Magister Perotinus composed the best four-voice works, such as *Viderunt* and *Sederunt*, with an abundance of artful harmonic color; and similarly he composed the most noble three-voice works, such as Alleluia *Posui adiutorium, Nativitas*, etc.

And he made three-voice conducti [see Chapter 9], such as *Salvatoris hodie*, and two-voice conducti, among them *Dum sigillum summi patris*, as well as monophonic conducti, such as *Beata viscera* among many others. The book or books of Magister Perotinus were in use in the choir of the cathedral of Notre Dame in Paris until the time of Magister Robertus de Sabilone and from his time until the present day.[1]

Anonymous IV says three important things: (1) that there was a composer named **Leoninus** who wrote a great book of polyphony called the **Magnus liber organi** to make the Mass and the canonical hours more splendid; (2) that Leoninus was succeeded by Perotinus the Great, who altered the contents of the *Magnus liber organi* and also wrote, among other things, his own three- and four-voice music; and (3) that this Gothic polyphony was sung in the choir of Notre Dame of Paris for as long as a century, until the time that he, Anonymous IV, set pen to parchment about 1280. By happy coincidence, three music manuscripts survive from the thirteenth century that contain almost all of the music Anonymous IV mentions. Let us start with Magister Leoninus and his great book, the *Magnus liber organi*.

Magister Leoninus (Latin for "Little Leo") flourished during the period 1160–1201. He was educated in Paris, earning the degree master of arts (thus "Magister" Leoninus). He was also a priest, poet, and canon (high-ranking official) of the cathedral of Notre Dame. Anonymous IV calls Leoninus "*optimus organista*," meaning the best singer-composer of organum. Indeed, his *Magnus liber organi* contains nearly a hundred pieces of two-voice organum. He composed it, as Anonymous IV attests, so as to make the divine service at Notre Dame more splendid on the high feasts of the church year—on Christmas, Easter, and the feast of the Assumption of

---

[†]The all-female early-music performing group called Anonymous IV derived its name from this medieval theorist.

the Virgin, for example. For the Mass he did not set all of the Ordinary and Proper, but only the two responsorial chants of the Proper, specifically the Gradual and the Alleluia, melismatic chants in which soloists played a leading part. Similarly, for Vespers and Matins, Leoninus set in two-voice polyphony only the lengthy and difficult responsories. All other music at Notre Dame remained monophonic chant. As we review the parts of the Mass, the boldface type shows where Leoninus adorned this morning service:

ORDINARY	PROPER
	Introit
Kyrie	
Gloria	
	Gradual
	Alleluia
Credo	
	Offertory
Sanctus	
Agnus dei	
	Communion

Recall that the Gradual and the Alleluia of the Mass were lengthy, florid chants in which soloists stepped forward to sing a verse within the context of choral respond (see Chapter 3). Leoninus added polyphony only to the solo portions of these two responsorial chants—his organum was difficult music far beyond the skill of the average, musically challenged cleric. Taking the Gradual *Viderunt omnes* for Mass at Christmas as an example, we can see how Leoninus allocated his polyphony to the chant. How many new parts, or voices, did Leoninus create? Only one: the top voice—the lower voice was a pre-existing Gregorian chant then already centuries old.

Soloist

++++++++++

------------- ********************************

Soloists:	Chorus (monophonic chant)
Viderunt omnes fines terrae salutare Dei nostri: jubilate Deo omnis terra.	
RESPOND	

Soloist

+++

-- *********

Soloists	Chorus (chant)
Notum fecit **Dominus** salutare suum ante conspectum gentium revelavit justitiam suam.	
VERSE	[Return to RESPOND]

+++++++ = new upper voice created by Leoninus and sung by soloist in organum

--------- = pre-existing Gradual sung by two or three soloists

******** = pre-existing Gradual sung by full choir in plainchant

To begin the piece (and set the pitch for all), the soloists commenced in organum ("Viderunt omnes"). A single soloist sang the top part while a small group of soloists, probably two or three, sang the chant. Then the full choir, perhaps as many as a hundred voices, concluded the respond in monophonic chant. The soloists then performed the verse in polyphony, again with just one on top. Toward the end, the full choir joined in to render the last word or two in chant. Finally, the respond was repeated. Almost all of the approximately one hundred two-voice organa in Leoninus' *Magnus liber organi* were performed in this way.

Biblioteca Laurenziana, Florence

❀ FIGURE 8-3

A thirteenth-century manuscript preserving Leoninus's organum for Christmas, *Viderunt omnes*. Leoninus' newly created voice is notated on each of the odd-numbered staves, while the slower-moving Gregorian chant appears below it on each of the even-numbered staves.

Leoninus was a composer and singer. He may have served as the soloist who negotiated the difficult upper part. Figure 8-3 shows his two-voice organum for *Viderunt omnes* as it appears in a thirteenth-century manuscript coming from Paris; indeed, one compiled within the shadow of the cathedral. It begins with a large illuminated initial for the letter "V" with scenes from the Christmas season (top to bottom): the adoration of the three kings, the flight into Egypt, and the slaughter of the innocents. Next comes the music, set on the page in pairs of staves. On the top is Leoninus' added voice; supporting it below in long notes is the chant *Viderunt omnes*. Because the bottom voice holds or draws out the notes of the chant, it is called the **tenor** (from the Latin *teneo*, to hold). While the tenor holds the chant, the upper voice undulates and cascades around it with vocal flourishes. From time to time the voices momentarily pause on a consonance, namely the octave, fifth, fourth, or unison. In general, the style of Leoninus' two-voice piece is that of older sustained-tone organum, which now is called **organum purum** (pure organum). *Organum purum* is florid two-voice organum.

Yet Leoninus also created something very new. Look carefully at the bottom of the Figure 8-3. Suddenly, on the syllable "do" (the beginning of "dominus" = Lord), the tenor begins to move more rapidly, almost as quickly as the upper voice. At the same time, notice how the upper voice, which had been moving up and cascading down, is now organized into neat little units of two or three notes. Instead of pure organum we now hear **discant,** a style of music in which both voices move at roughly the same rate and are written in clearly defined rhythms (see Ex. 8-2). Each separate section making use of discant style is called a **clausula** (section, phrase, or "musical clause"). "Dominus" is a clausula. What is radically new here is the introduction of music with a strong rhythmic profile. There is contrast and excitement in the music of Leoninus as it moves from polyphony to monophony and from the older, florid style of pure organum to the newer Gothic style of discant with its clearly articulated rhythms.

To execute the rhythmically precise discant clausulae in *Viderunt omnes* requires that the singer read a new type of musical notation. This is called **modal notation,** and it came into music gradually, beginning around 1150–1170. By the early thirteenth century it had evolved into a system of six **rhythmic modes.** The rhythmic modes were simple patterns of repeating rhythms: one pattern for mode one, another for mode two, and so on. Variants of these patterns could be created by extending or subdividing elements of these six. Music theorists such as Anonymous IV set out the six basic patterns of modal notation as given below. The important point is this: In mensural notation (from which our modern system derives), each sign has a separate and distinct shape and thereby denotes a specific value. In older modal notation, the context determines the rhythm; the performer looks at the context of an entire passage (a group of ligatures) and extrapolates an unvarying rhythm to be applied from beginning to end (Ex. 8-1).

EXAMPLE 8-1

Mode	Combination	Example	Transcription
I	3 2 2 2 2		
II	2 2 2 2 3		
III	1 3 3 3		
IV	3 3 3 1		
V	3 3 3		
VI	4 3 3		

In modal notation, individual square notes are grouped into units of two, three, or perhaps four notes. Each group is called a **ligature** (from the Latin "ligare," to bind). The order of ligatures signals to the singer the rhythmic mode to be applied. For example, a ligature of three notes might be followed by several ligatures of two notes. This indicates that the singer is to sing the pattern for mode 1 throughout the entire passage. If, however, the performer sees a succession of two-note ligatures followed by one of three notes, he sings the passage in rhythmic mode 2. In modal notation there are no durational values inherent in any one symbol or ligature. The performer scans the passage, recognizes the mode to be applied, and then sings it with the implied rhythmic pattern. Look again at Leoninus's *Viderunt omnes* (see Fig. 8-3) at the discant clausula on "dominus." The music is given in modal notation in Example 8-2a and the singer sings as in the modern notation found in Example 8-2b.

EXAMPLE 8-2A   EXAMPLE 8-2B

do   -   -   [minus]   do   -   -   -   -   -   -   -   -   -[minus]

For the history of music, this was a monumental development. Now it was possible to indicate and control rhythm, as well as pitch, with precision. Modal notation was in favor for more than a hundred years, from roughly 1150 to 1280 when, because of the somewhat rigid nature of the patterns, it was gradually replaced by a more flexible system called mensural notation, in which each symbol signifies one, and only one, duration (see Chapter 10).

Rhythm in music is primeval. What was new and exciting for Leoninus and his colleagues at Notre Dame of Paris was the capacity to notate and control it. Never before did any culture have a system to write down complex rhythmic patterns. Not surprisingly, the musicians of Notre Dame decided to play with their new discovery. Composers began to isolate particular sections of the organum, specifically the discant clausulae, and apply different rhythmic and melodic solutions. For the clausula "Dominus," for example, they composed more than a dozen alternatives. These were compositional essays—attempts to explore new rhythmic opportunities. Some were written in mode 2, others in 3, 4, and 5. Some of these creations were later inserted into the pre-existing organum of Leoninus, thereby creating what is called a **substitute clausula,** one clausula written in discant style intended to replace another. Example 8-3 shows the beginnings of just two of the substitute clausulae that might be inserted in *Viderunt omnes* in place of the original clausula "Dominus." In these musical experiments there was an element of adventure and amusement. One clever follower of Leoninus created a substitute for "Do-mi-nus" which he entitled "Nus-mi-do." Appropriately, he made the chant in the tenor go backwards—the first written example of retrograde motion in the history of music!

EXAMPLE 8-3

PEROTINUS THE GREAT

Perotinus the Great (c1160–c1236) took the rhythmic innovations of Leoninus and used them to create polyphonic works of unprecedented length, complexity, and grandeur. Yet we know little of his life. Like Leoninus, he was called by the diminutive (Little Peter), had a degree from the University of Paris, and was associated with Notre Dame. He may have been the Petrus Succentor who served as canon and then choirmaster at the cathedral from 1198–1238. Anonymous IV names seven compositions by him, and he likely wrote hundreds more. His settings of the Graduals *Viderunt omnes* and *Sederunt principes* were sung at Notre Dame in 1198 and 1199, respectively. So little biography for so great a composer!

Perotinus' *Viderunt omnes* and *Sederunt principes* are extraordinary compositions. Each is long, extending more than ten minutes, and each is written for four voices. Few pieces of polyphony before this time had been composed for three or four voices. Leoninus wrote for only two voices, and thus it was not necessary to regulate all aspects of rhythm at all times; the performers could simply look at one another and sense when each was moving to the next harmony. But, when the texture was increased to three or four voices, stricter rhythmic discipline was required to coordinate all parts. Thus Perotinus dispensed with the older, improvisatory style and created a new type of organum. The tenor still holds out the chant in long notes, but all of the upper voices proceed in strict rhythms. Occasionally, when the chant is especially melismatic, Perotinus shifts into discant style, the tenor now moving with the same degree of rhythmic organization as the upper voices.

Most remarkable, the great four-voice organa of Perotinus display a unique modular construction. He creates units of carefully shaped phrases, each two, three, four, or more of what we would call measures in length. These phrases are interchangeable, that is, a unit in the **duplum** (second voice) may appear a few measures later in the **triplum** (third voice), and then shortly thereafter in the **quadruplum** (fourth voice). Modules are also repeated within one and the same voice. Example 8-4 shows the beginning of Perotinus' setting of the old Christmas Gradual *Viderunt omnes*. All four voices begin with a held note on an open fifth chord built on F. Then, while the tenors hold this pitch, the upper voices sing through a succession of phrases each four units (in $\frac{3}{8}$ meter) in length. Rhythmic mode 1 is in play. The duration of sound in one part is carefully coordinated with that in all others. The boxes show the repetitions and interlocking exchanges of the musical modules. Notice also that, at the beginning of each phrase, two and sometimes all three upper voices have a pitch that is dissonant (a major seventh) with the tenor F; by the end of the four-unit phrase, however, all voices have reached a perfect consonance with the tenor on the open-fifth chord with which the piece began.

EXAMPLE 8-4

Notice also in Perotinus' *Viderunt omnes* how the voices are all in a rather narrow range, usually within the octave above the tenor. Thus there is no clear differentiation of sonority by register; each unit looks and sounds like all the others, like so many interlocking stones on a great Gothic wall. Notice as well not only the shifts between organum and discant but also the moments when the tenor presents a new syllable of text. Perotinus calls attention to these important points by creating a crunching dissonance and then moving to a pure, open fifth, an effect especially stunning inside a stone church with sonorous acoustics. Much of the power and strength of his work derives from the tension, and ultimate resolution, of the dissonance-consonance conflict. Finally, note the feeling of rest and repose that descends when, after the excitement of the polyphony of Perotinus, the full clerical community returns with the sounds of the ancient chant. The Lord has revealed his righteousness, and the world is at peace on Christmas day.

LISTENING CUE

PEROTINUS THE GREAT
Viderunt omnes (1198)

CD 1/21
Anthology, No. 21

🌸 FIGURE 8-4
The floor plan of the cathedral of Paris reveals the almost endless repetition of a few basic geometric patterns, just as the great four-voice organum of Perotinus repeats various melodic patterns.

The importance of Perotinus in the history of Western music can hardly be exaggerated; he can fairly be called the first modern composer. Whereas previous performer-creators of liturgical polyphony, including Leoninus, had sought to capture and notate what was at heart a free improvisatory vocal style, Perotinus undertook a radically new approach to musical organization. He replaces the expansive and wide-ranging melismas of earlier composers with shorter, complementary blocks of sound, and these in turn are balanced, shaped, and interposed to produce a brilliantly original musical architecture. Indeed, the analogy to architecture is appropriate here. Consider Figure 8-4, which shows the floor plans of Notre Dame of Paris. Notice how the full design is created by replicating again and again a few simple geometric patterns. Like the musical phrases in *Viderunt omnes*, these units are reciprocal and interchangeable. Finally, like an architect conceiving an entire edifice in the abstract and then drawing a blueprint, Perotinus thinks about the long-term implications of each musical decision. He composes each voice with an immediate eye toward the others, as well as toward what might come later in the piece. The architectonic quality of *Viderunt omnes* suggests that here we are dealing with a composer in the modern sense of the word, an artist who had a plan and who designed *a priori* all parts of his composition. The composer has replaced the improviser.

Notre Dame of Paris has now survived more than eight centuries. Yet never was Notre Dame more important in the history of music than during the period 1160–1260. Leoninus, Perotinus, and their colleagues created a huge musical repertory, more than a thousand pieces. So numerous were their compositions and so influential their style that historians later came to speak of the **Notre Dame School.** There had been other, earlier centers of organum, in monasteries in England and in southern France, as we have seen (Chapter 7). But the polyphonic pieces created in these churches were comparatively few and were unique to them; almost never did an organum from one center reappear in a manuscript produced at another. By the thirteenth century things began to change. The fledgling University of Paris was attracting theology students from across Europe. When these masters and scholars returned to their native lands, they carried with them not only what they had learned of scholastic theology but also the most up-to-date music from Paris. The works of Leoninus and Perotinus came to be heard in Spain, Germany, England, Italy, the Low Countries, and even Poland. Now for the first time it was possible to speak of an international repertory of polyphonic music.

SUMMARY

During the late twelfth century, Paris became the center of music, as well as architecture and theology, for Western Europe. All that was new in music could be seen in the compositions of two leading figures, Leoninus and Perotinus. Leoninus compiled a *Magnus liber organi* containing nearly one hundred two-voice organa, mostly settings of the Gradual and Alleluia to adorn the Mass on high feast days. Perotinus updated this and composed many new pieces for three and four voices. Perhaps the most impressive musical works of the high Middle Ages can be found in the four-voice organa of Perotinus. These are long, complex works that would have required a great deal of "pre-planning," or composition as we think of it today. Large-scale, multi-voice composition had been made possible by a new development: rhythmic control. By means of a system of rhythmic modes, Leoninus and Perotinus developed a way to regulate rhythm through musical notation. The innovative style of the Notre Dame School spread throughout Western Europe, thereby becoming the first international repertory of polyphonic music.

KEY TERMS

Gothic architecture	*organum purum*	substitute clausula
nave	discant	Perotinus
choir	clausula (pl., clausulae)	duplum
Leoninus	modal notation	triplum
Magnus liber organi	rhythmic modes	quadruplum
tenor	ligature	Notre Dame School

Chapter 9

Music in the Cathedral Close and University: Conductus and Motet

Leoninus and Perotinus created organa to adorn the liturgy celebrated in the choir of Notre Dame on high feasts. But they and their later musical colleagues also wrote polyphony that was not so strictly tied to the church. New musical genres such as the conductus and motet were equally at home in the cathedral, outside the church in the adjoining close, and at the university.

Situated next to almost every medieval cathedral was an independent urban enclave called the **close.** The close was a gated community for the men employed in the cathedral: canons, chaplains, vicars, musicians, choirboys, sacristans, and vergers, as well as several hundred assistants and servants, most male but a few female. As a territory free from control of the king, the close at Notre Dame of Paris enjoyed its own weights and measures, police force, and jail. Within its walls sat several dozen houses for the clergy, the cathedral school where music was taught, and the dormitory for the choirboys. Figure 9-1, the earliest surviving map of Paris,

Bridgeman Art Library

✿ FIGURE 9-1

Île de la Cité and close of Notre Dame of Paris as they appear in the earliest map of Paris. The area of the close is to the left of the cathedral.

shows the *Île de la Cité*, the cathedral, and the close ("le cloistre") to the north (left) of the church.

Of all the clerics to reside in the close of Notre Dame, none was more famous, or infamous, than **Peter Abelard.** Abelard, a nobleman turned cleric, set up shop as a professor of logic in the close of Notre Dame in 1114. Soon he obtained lodging in the house of canon Fulbert, and was given charge of the education of Fulbert's niece, the gifted **Héloise.** The relationship led to one of the most passionate and scandalous romances of the Middle Ages, culminating in the birth of a child and the castration of Abelard. Banned from the close, he became a monk, she a nun. Despite the shame and pain, their love affair produced an outpouring of poetry and music from the pen of Abelard, as Héloise reveals in the first of her famous letters to him:

> You had besides, I admit, two special gifts whereby to win at once the heart of any woman—your gifts for composing verse and music, in which we know other philosophers have rarely been successful. This was for you no more than a diversion, a recreation from the labors of your philosophic work, but you left many love-songs and verse which won wide popularity for the charm of their words and tunes and kept your name continually on everyone's lips. The beauty of the melodies ensured that even the unlettered did not forget you.[1]

Although the words and music of a hymn and six laments by Abelard are preserved, none of the love songs that the great philosopher wrote in the close of Notre Dame has survived.

The scandal of Abelard and Héloise, along with related disorders, caused the churchmen of Notre Dame to expel the unruly scholars and masters from the close. In the course of the twelfth century, the schools moved across the Seine and onto the left bank. In 1215 the pope gave formal recognition to the new ***Universitas***—a unified collection of all the schools and colleges under a single administrative head. By then, there were approximately ten thousand students enrolled at the university of Paris, about one-fifth of the total population of the city.

Life in a medieval university was very different from university life today. To begin with, all students were male, usually ranging in age from fourteen to twenty-two. To the extent that women received an education in the Middle Ages, this occurred in the home or in a convent. Students paid their money directly to the master for the instruction they received, and the teacher's income was proportional to the number of students he attracted. Lectures were given in Latin, and on the streets students spoke the international language of all scholars, again Latin (hence the term "**Latin Quarter**" of Paris). There were few textbooks, and what books the student possessed he copied by hand, section by section, from an exemplar rented from a local bookstore. Most learning was done by oral repetition and rote memory. After six years of study, including one term devoted to Boethius' *the Fundamentals of Music*, a student could petition to be examined. If successful, he was admitted to the group of masters licensed to teach the seven liberal arts—he had graduated.

At the head of the University of Paris was the chancellor of the cathedral of Notre Dame. In matters of education he spoke for both the cathedral and the university. During the years 1217–1236 the head of the University of Paris was Philip of Nemours, called **Philip the Chancellor** (c1160–1236). From Philip's pen flowed no fewer than seven hundred sermons for the cathedral and the university. He was also a poet and apparently a composer of some merit. Seventy compositions with religious or moralistic texts by Philip survive today. Most of Philip's creations can be classified among one of two new musical genres that arose during these years: the conductus and the motet.

CONDUCTUS

The term **conductus** derives from the Latin infinitive *ducere*, to lead. From a related word *educere* (to lead forward or elevate) come our words "educate" and "education." As the name suggests, the conductus was sung as the clergy moved from place to place or was engaged in some other type of kinetic activity, such as dance. The prefix "con" may also imply that this music was sung as part of a gathering of clergy, perhaps for a festal or convivial event. Thus conducti[†] appear as processional pieces to convey celebrants from one spot to another within the church, as musical accompaniments to the movements of characters in liturgical drama, and as songs to lead the clergy into and out of the church. They are not part of the formal liturgy (Mass and canonical hours). Conducti are written for one, two, three, and occasionally four voices. Their texts are metrical Latin poems arranged in successive stanzas. Most are serious and moralistic in tone. Many conducti, however, have ties to the Christmas and New Year's season. As such, these seasonal conducti served as the medieval equivalent of today's Christmas carols—joyous pieces, often with a refrain, sung by a group in the church or in the close.

A good example of a lighter conductus can be seen in the anonymous three-voice *Orientis partibus* (Ex. 9-1). Known throughout the musical world today as the *Song of the Ass*, it parodies the solemnities of the Christmas season. To understand its meaning, we must set the context in which this conductus was sung.

For the medieval clergy, most of the fun of Christmas came, not on Christmas day but during the following week, when the services of the church were handed over to the younger clergy to celebrate in place of their superiors. The most raucous revels came on Circumcision (1 January), also known as the **Feast of Fools,** when the youngest of the adult clerics took charge of the church. Standing in the choir and at the high altar, the youths engaged in a blasphemous mockery of the liturgical service. Some dressed as women, others threw bones across the choir aisle, while the "celebrant" lit an old shoe and censed the altar with its smoke. Before all this began, however, the youths processed around the town and then back into the church. Leading the procession was an ass, the humble beast of burden that had carried Mary and her baby to Bethlehem (see Fig. 8-3). Picture in your mind's eye several dozen inebriated teenagers driving a frightened donkey up the aisle of Notre Dame on New Year's Eve. As they proceeded, they sang a conductus, one that imitated the hey-hawing ("Hez, va") of the ass and concluded with a reference to what this beast did most often on the floor.

[†]In the Middle Ages "conductus" appears as both a second- and fourth-declension noun. The plural, thus, can be either "conducti" or "conductus."

EXAMPLE 9-1

From Orient lands	With a leap he out-jumped the stag
Came an ass,	The antelope and deer
Handsome and most strong,	Faster than dromedaries
An excellent beast of burden	From Media
Hey, ho, hey, Sir Ass, hey!	Hey, ho, hey, Sir Ass, hey!

Orientis partibus (c1200) is a short, simple conductus. Yet in many ways it is typical of the genre. The text setting is syllabic, and all parts sing a single text simultaneously. The text itself is metrical and strophic, each of its seven strophes ending with a refrain. It speaks to the asinine moment, but is full of sacred allusions to scripture. Notice the tuneful nature of the tenor. As in other genres of polyphony in the Middle Ages, the tenor came first and the other voices were built upon it. But what is most important in the conductus is that the tenor is not a pre-existing chant, but a newly composed melody. This is the first polyphonic music in which the composer has free rein to create all the voices. The style of the conductus is that of discant—all voices move at about the same rate and create consonances on the strong beats. In Orientis partibus, the first rhythmic mode predominates, synchronized to the troachic meter of the Latin poetry. At the end of each musical phrase the upper voices cadence with the tenor, thereby clarifying the structural division of the work. Orientis partibus is immediately accessible because the tenor sounds strongly tonal to our ears, centered as it is around what we would call a C major triad. Medieval ears, however, would have heard this as a piece in the Lydian mode (with B♭) transposed to C. Perhaps because of the tuneful, tonal quality of the tenor, the medieval Orientis partibus survives today in many books of Christmas carols under the title The Friendly Beast.

LISTENING CUE

ANONYMOUS
Orientis partibus (c1200)

CD 1/22
Anthology, No. 22

Orientis partibus is exceptional for its humor, specifically for its parody of the liturgy of Christmas. Far more typical, however, are the serious moralistic conducti of Philip the Chancellor. His texts range from pious prayers to the Virgin to stinging condemnations of corrupt clergymen, kings, and popes. In his sermons and poems he fought for the rights of the chancellor of the university, fending off the encroaching masters (the faculty) and their ally, the pope. His conductus *Dic, Christi veritas* (*Speak, Christian Truth*) shows how Philip used the musical genre of the conductus as a bully pulpit from which to excoriate his enemies, namely the masters, as well as the pope, who rarely came to his aid in these academic disputes. *Dic, Christi veritas* is a rhetorical composition, one in which text and music work together for maximum effect. The effect is achieved by means of what the music theorists of the day referred to as a **cauda** (pl., **caudae**)—literally a "tail" (whence our word "coda"), a long melisma on a single syllable. A *cauda* might come anywhere—beginning, middle, or end—of a conductus to set off key words. The most distinctive *cauda* in *Dic, Christi veritas* comes at the end of the first stanza where Philip the Chancellor depicts the rantings of the pope with a lengthy melisma on "fulminante" ("fulminating")—a rare moment of word painting in medieval music. *Dic, Christi veritas* may have been sung as the Chancellor processed to the pulpit to deliver a sermon. Yet it could also stand alone outside the church, for this conductus is itself both a sermon and a lecture in music.

LISTENING CUE

PHILIP THE CHANCELLOR
Dic, Christi veritas (c1230)

CD 1/23
Anthology, No. 23

 MOTET

Medieval Paris was also home to another new genre of music that emerged around 1200, the motet. Originally a **motet** (diminutive of the French *mot* meaning "word") was a discant clausula (see Chapter 8) to which sacred words were added. Recall that a discant clausula was simply a self-contained section of organum in discant (note-against-note) style involving just one or two words in the original chant. With the motet, however, things are different. Instead of all voices singing just one word in melismatic fashion, each upper voice declaims its own new poetic text. These new words comment upon the significance of the single Latin word sung by the tenor. Throughout the Middle Ages theologians had taken a passage of scripture and expanded upon it, offering their own views as to the meaning of the holy writ. Now this practice, called "glossing," was applied to music. The upper voice or

University of Montpellier

✿ FIGURE 9-2

The motetus and tenor (bottom system) of the motet *El mois d'avril/O quam sancta/Et gaudebit* as it appears in a manuscript compiled in the area of Paris around 1300. In the upper minature a cleric venerates a statue of the Virgin, while the lower scene depicts events associated with spring.

voices glossed the meaning of the tenor. For example, while the tenor voice sang the word "Lord," a second voice (now called the **motetus**) would speak of Christ's birth and the hope for humankind that the Lord brings, while the third voice (still called the triplum) would relate the Lord's ultimate fate on the cross. Thus the early motet was polytextual, involving at least two Latin texts and sometimes three or four, in cases of three- or four-voice motets. Soon French texts were inserted along with those in Latin. In the course of the thirteenth century the motet gradually replaced organum and conductus as the preferred genre of musical composition. By 1300 more than a thousand motets had been created. One manuscript alone, called the Montpellier Codex (Fig. 9-2), contains 345 motets, some with Latin upper voices, some with French, and some with both languages sung simultaneously.

To understand the historical development of the motet, consider the text of the Alleluia *Alleluia. Non vos reliquam* and Example 9-2a–c. The clausula (and subsequent motets) grew out of the words "Et gaudebit" ("And it will rejoice") of the chant. Example 9-2a shows the beginning of the two-voice discant clausula *Et gaudebit* as it appears in the *Magnus liber organi*. The clausula belonged to organum added to the Alleluia of the Mass for Ascension, that joyful day on which Christ ascended into heaven. The Alleluia text borrows from John (14:18)—*Alleluia. Non vos relinquam orphanos; vado et venio ad vos et gaudebit cor vestrum* (Alleluia. I will not leave you orphans; I come and go among you, and your heart, it will rejoice). Thus the spiritual theme of these motets is Christian rejoicing.

Alleluia - - - .   Non vos relinquam orphanos; vado et venio ad vos **et gaudebit** cor vestrum.
Organum-chant. Organum - **clausula** - organum

EXAMPLE 9-2A

Example 9-2b shows the beginning of the same piece but with text now added to the upper voice, thereby creating a motet. The new text in this motetus voice sings the praises of the Virgin and of the joy of the angels, and it ends with an obvious expansion of the spiritual theme of the tenor (*Et gaudebit*): *Gaude in filio, gaudens ego gaudeo in Domino* (Rejoice in the Son, rejoicing I will rejoice in the Lord).

EXAMPLE 9-2B

Example 9-2c shows the same two-voice motet, but now with a third voice. The text here is in old French and speaks of the beauties of spring. At first glance, this poem seems to have little to do with the spiritual message of the tenor.

EXAMPLE 9-2C

In the month of April, when winter begins to depart and the birds begin again their song,
one morning I was riding through the woods . . .
Oh, how holy, how benign, shines the mother of the Savior . . .
And [my heart] will rejoice.

Let us examine more carefully this anonymous three-voice bilingual motet *El mois d'avril/O quam sancta/Et gaudebit*, written in Paris around 1230. Once again, we see the basic principle of medieval composition at work: a phrase of Gregorian chant provides a scaffold for the entire composition. That is to say, the pitches of a pre-existing chant, placed in the tenor, determine the harmonies created by the upper voices—the motetus and triplum form consonances with the tenor on strong beats and dissonance off the beat. The favored consonances are the unison, fifth, and octave, with the fourth also appearing from time to time. Notice that the three voices are moving at different rates of speed. The French triplum has more text than the Latin motetus and thus must move in shorter note values. In fact, the triplum is in rhythmic mode 6, the motetus in mode 1, and the slow moving tenor in mode 5 (on the medieval rhythmic modes, see Chapter 8). Here the modes are slightly obscured because of extensions and subdivisions of the basic modal patterns. At the beginning, for example, the tenor extends or elongates the mode 5 pattern, changing two dotted quarter-notes into a single dotted half-note. What results in the tenor is an unvarying rhythmic pattern four bars in length.

Most important, the entire tenor melody is repeated, starting in measure thirty-six. The decision to repeat the tenor required the composer to write the piece a second time, providing a new musical response above the same tenor melody and rhythm. The texts of the upper voices respect, indeed emphasize, the sectional division within this motet. Part I (bars 1–35) of the motetus offers praises to the Virgin Mary, extolling her virtues; Part II (bars 36–70) is a supplication to Mary, imploring her to pray to Christ on behalf of the sinners of this world. Similarly, Part I of the triplum tells of a wandering knight who visits a magical garden, whereas Part II describes the wondrous maiden he found there. But how did a knight and a maiden get into this story of Christ's ascension?

To understand the full meaning of the motet *El mois d'avril/O quam sancta/Et gaudebit* we must enter into the mindset of a medieval university student. A literal reading of the story of the handsome knight and the beautiful maiden (*El mois d'avril*) suggests an earthly love. A medieval university cleric, however, would have understood it much differently, applying an allegorical interpretation to the text, just what the theologians taught at the University of Paris. The magical garden is the sacred garden of Gethsemane; the maiden is not any maid but the Virgin Mary; the fine spring day in April is the period around Ascension; and the new love is the love for the newly risen Christ. Mary has given herself to Christ and, in the end, so will every faithful Christian. Motet texts of this type can be read at two levels, the literal and the allegorical. The students and masters of the day delighted in multiple meanings just as they delighted in multiple texts. The polytextual motet of the Middle Ages is as subtle intellectually as it is pleasing musically.

Given the intellectual quality of the medieval motet, for whom was it written? Who was the audience? Music theorists of the period tell us that the motet was created for an educated elite. Johannes de Grocheio, for example, writing in Paris around 1300, says that the motet was intended for the "literati"—a literate class who could properly understand it. In the thirteenth century there was only one literate, elite class: the clerical students and masters who lived at the cathedral and university. Only they could have appreciated, for example, the richness of the Latin poem in the motetus (*O quam sancta*) with its biblical references to Jacob's ladder and the tree of Jesse. In sum, the polytextual motet was created for clerical recreation and edification, to be sung in private moments in private residences. This is religious music, but not necessarily music for the church, and certainly not for the masses.

🄭 LISTENING CUE

ANONYMOUS MOTET
El mois d'avril/O quam sancta/Et gaudebit (c1230)

CD 1/24
Anthology, No. 24c

Music of the Notre Dame School began at the cathedral and gradually spread beyond its confines, to the close, to the university, and then to other countries. As it did so, new genres of music, the conductus and motet, were created. By the second half of the thirteenth century polyphony began to lose its historical connection to the cathedral. Motet tenors were no longer drawn exclusively from the repertory of cathedral chants that had served Leoninus for the *Magnus liber organi*, for example. Instead, tenor tunes came from other chants, from trouvère melodies, from popular songs, from street cries, and from new melodies fashioned for the occasion by the composer.

By the end of the thirteenth century, the subject matter of the motet in Paris ranged from the esoteric to the frivolous. Similarly, no one motet style dominated.

Instead, we find remarkable diversity of borrowed tenors and formal procedures, as the motet runs the gamut from high to low art. A more popular style can be found in the three-voice *On parole de batre/A Paris/Frese nouvele*, a simple piece which extols the simple pleasures of medieval Paris. As both motetus and triplum voices assure us, Paris was renowned for its food, wine, and beautiful women. In keeping with the urban theme, here the tenor is a street cry—the call of a wandering peddler of the sort who could still be heard on the streets of Paris into the 1970s. This medieval street vendor is hawking fresh strawberries and ripe blackberries. The musical structure of his cry is as basic as his merchandise: the same eight-bar phrase is heard four times. We are now very far from the esoteric allegory of cathedral close and university. While it may be going too far to call this the "rap music" of the high Middle Ages, nonetheless this motet shows that, in late thirteenth-century Paris, popular urban polyphony was alive and well.

EXAMPLE 9-3

They talk of threshing and winnowing, of digging and cultivating
In Paris morn and night one can find good bread and good clear [wine]
Fresh strawberries, ripe black berries…

LISTENING CUE

ANONYMOUS MOTET

On parole de batre/A Paris/Frese nouvele (c1280)

CD 1/25
Anthology, No. 25

SUMMARY

The art music of the thirteenth century is marked by the appearance of two new musical genres, the conductus and motet. The conductus was not part of the canonical liturgy but something of an "add-on"—it was most often sung as the clergy moved from place to place. In musical style the conductus might be from one to as many as four voices. The conductus does not make use of a pre-existing Gregorian chant. All voices are newly composed, even the tenor, and all sing the same Latin text. The subject matter of the conductus ranges widely, from holiday carol texts to political sermons. The musical style, however, is consistently discant.

The motet came into being around 1200 and soon became the most favored type of polyphonic music of the thirteenth century. It began life within the service of the church, when clerics added a text to the upper voice of a two-voice clausula within an organum. Soon, however, more voices were added, with texts in French as well as Latin. The upper texts glossed (commented upon) the spiritual theme carried by the pre-existing chant in the tenor. Gradually, the motet moved away from the liturgy inside the cathedral to the close and university, where clerics enjoyed it for both spiritual enlightenment and entertainment. By the end of the thirteenth century, popular refrains, even street cries, had made their way into the motet, occasionally transforming it into a type of urban popular music.

KEY TERMS

close	Latin Quarter	*cauda* (pl., *caudae*)
Peter Abelard	Philip the Chancellor	motet
Héloise	conductus	motetus
Universitas	Feast of Fools	

Chapter 10

In the Parisian Master's Study: Music Theory of the *Ars Antiqua* and *Ars Nova*

In the Middle Ages people did not think of the world as we do today. To begin with, they believed that the sun revolved around the earth, that Jerusalem sat at the exact center of the earth, and that the world was no more than seven thousand years old, extending back only a few years before the Flood. Reality was explained by the Bible, not science, and it was flexible. The time needed to boil an egg was calculated by the length of time necessary to say a *Miserere* (Psalm 50). The New Year might begin on 1 January, 25 March, or Easter, depending on where you lived. Time was regulated by the seasons, by night and day, or perhaps by a sundial if it were not dark or too cloudy. An "hour" of the day was longer in the summer than during the winter (the span of daylight was divided by twelve no matter how long an hour might last). Everywhere the progress of time was marked by the unfolding of the liturgy of the church and announced to the people by the ringing of bells. Needless to say, this was an inexact measurement that depended upon local religious traditions. Evening (Vespers), for example, might be signaled in one town at one time and many, many minutes later in another. What difference did it make?

Around 1300 all this began to change. Within fifty years on either side of this date, mechanical clocks were invented, cannons fired, organs placed in Gothic cathedrals, and nautical charts written—all inventions dependent upon the precise measurement of time, distance, space, or pitch. Clocks and organs were most often placed in the nave of the church, so that all the people could see and hear these astonishing technological innovations. Harmony, whether produced by instrument or by voice, was possible because pitches could be precisely measured and adjusted so as to achieve a harmonious sound. Music theorists since Greek antiquity had measured two pitches against each other, seeing in them a worldly manifestation of divine number. In order for three or four voices to sing separate parts, however, time had to be precisely measured. Music theory throughout the thirteenth century was concerned with the measurement of time. By the end of the century both harmonic intervals and musical time were rationalized within coherent systems of pleasing regularity.

Once again Paris, and specifically the University of Paris, was the epicenter of these important developments—the music theorists of the day were almost all masters at the university. These musicians were perhaps as much "teacher-reporters" as what we would call music theorists. They prepared lectures on music for the students of the various schools and colleges. They delivered these orally, but over the decades their various pronouncements on music were arranged in logical fashion by students or other masters and written down. The masters were concerned with measuring and classifying pitch, but more so with rhythm.

FRANCO OF COLOGNE AND THE ART OF MEASURED SONG

The clearest exposition of the music theory of the thirteenth century is found in Franco of Cologne's *Ars cantus mensurabilis* **(Art of Measured Song)**. **Franco of Cologne,** sometimes called Franco of Paris, was a German who had come to Paris to teach around 1280. His treatise contains the first fully systematic classification of harmonic intervals, one that he frames in terms of consonance and dissonance in the following way:

CONSONANCES

Perfect consonances:	*Intermediate consonances:*	*Imperfect consonances:*
unison and octave	fifth and fourth	major and minor thirds

DISSONANCES

Imperfect dissonances:	*Perfect dissonances:*
minor seventh,	minor sixth, semitone,
major sixth,	tritone, major seventh
whole tone	

From our modern perspective, it is surprising to find the fourth classified here as a consonance (by the fifteenth century it will come to be viewed as a dissonance). Similarly, it is surprising to see that the sixths, which sound "sweet" to us, were dissonant to medieval ears; a minor sixth, for example, was thought to be just as dissonant as a semitone!

Most important, Franco's hierarchy of consonance and dissonance suggests that music was developing much like philosophy and logic at this time. Intellectuals divided material, even musical intervals, into categories, sets, and then subsets. They created a revolutionary approach to "information management" by constructing chains of hierarchical categories and relationships. This mode of thinking is called **scholasticism,** and it rose to prominence at the University of Paris during the thirteenth century. When we prepare an outline with topics and subtopics, headings and subheadings, we engage in a scholastic exercise.

Time, too, could be divided and subdivided into many separate parts. If the newly invented clock allowed the day to be broken into exact hours, minutes, and seconds, so the theorist might divide music into temporal units such as the double long, the long, and the short. The smaller units were interchangeable subsets of the larger. Franco of Cologne organized these into reciprocal relationships and explained temporal duration in music in terms of an overarching system. Franco recognized three basic note shapes: the **long** (◌), the **breve** (♩) and the **semibreve** (♪). Each unit stood in a triple relationship to the unit nearest it so as to honor, Franco said, the Holy Trinity—the fundamental meter of all written music was still triple, as in the days of modal rhythm. This was the theory, although Franco allowed that in practice a long or a breve could be made duple (reduced by a third) by a neighboring note. He also acknowledged the presence of the duplex long, a value equal to two longs. The important point, however, is that from Franco onward each note has a unique shape and a specific duration (Ex. 10-1).

EXAMPLE 10-1

| Duplex Long = 2 Longs | Long = 3 Breves | Breve = 3 Semibreves |

Rests, too, have their own symbols (Ex. 10-2).

EXAMPLE 10-2

| Duplex Long | Long | Breve | Semibreve |

By giving each note value and rest its own distinctive sign, Franco signaled the end of the older, contextual system for indicating rhythmic duration in the Notre Dame era. In brief, modal notation (contextual notation) now gave way to **mensural notation** (symbol-specific notation). Again, Franco's system can fairly be called "scholastic" because, like the famous *Summa theologica* of Parisian master Thomas Aquinas (1225–1274), it is both comprehensive and hierarchical, progressing in categories from largest to smallest values. Time in music was now thought of as a continuum involving division and further subdivision. The next generation of Parisian masters would extend Franco's scholastic system to radical lengths.

❁ JEAN DES MURS AND PHILIPPE DE VITRY: THE *ARS NOVA*

Significantly, both masters Jean des Murs and Philippe de Vitry were Parisian mathematicians as well as music theorists. As we have often seen, the medieval mind might occupy itself equally with the manipulation of numbers, the motion of the stars and planets, or the duration of musical sounds. **Jean des Murs** (c1290–c1351) was an astronomer, mathematician, musician, and convicted murderer (for which crime he was exiled to Cyprus for seven years). **Philippe de Vitry** (1291–1361) was a mathematician, astronomer, poet, diplomat, and bishop, as well as composer. Each compiled an important musical treatise. Jean des Murs called his *Notitia artis musicae* (*Knowledge of the Art of Music*), but it also went under the title *Ars novae musicae* (*Art of New Music*). Philippe de Vitry's work simply went by the name *Ars nova* (*New Art*). That the title *Ars nova* was given to these treatises suggests that Jean and Philippe were keenly aware of the power and originality of their ideas; they knew that they were creating a new art, an *avant garde* that would soon affect polyphony generally. Thus later historians have given the title *Ars nova* to all music of the first half of the fourteenth century. But what is new about the *Ars nova*?

The *Ars nova*—music of the first half of the fourteenth century—is characterized by four innovations: (1) The theorists acknowledge a new short note value, the **minim,** as a subdivision of the semibreve. In the course of the thirteenth century the duration of each note in performance had become longer, and this had necessitated the addition of a new note sign (the minim) to express a shorter value. (2) For the first time in the history of music, musicians divide durations into duple as well as triple units (Ex. 10-3). The long, for example, might consist of either two or three breves, and the breve of two or three semibreves. What we call duple meter is now sanctioned by music theory. This further extends the scale of musical time. Note values now run from the triplex long to the minim (the very shortest conceivable unit of time). Duple or triple divisions were possible at all levels of duration. When duple divisions were in play, a **dot** could be added after the note to turn it temporarily into a triple value; thus the dot, adding 50 percent to the value of the note, enters music history at this time. Taking the division of the notes, duple or triple, from largest to smallest: the division of the long was called the **mode** (*modus*), that of the breve the **time** (*tempus*), and that of the semibreve **prolation** (*prolatio*). (3) By coloring certain notes red, triplets and hemiola could be introduced in what were otherwise duple meters. (4) Meter signatures (time signatures) now appear for the first time in the history of music. To signal to performers what relationships hold sway in a composition (duple or triple), signs are placed at the beginning of the work. Originally there were six signs indicating a duple or triple division for the mode, time, and prolation. Soon, however, those for mode were dropped, leaving these four time signatures. One of these signatures, the C indicating "common time," is still in use today.

EXAMPLE 10-3

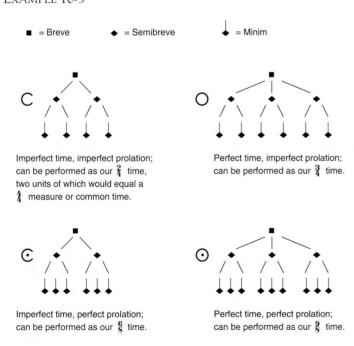

■ = Breve   ◆ = Semibreve   ♩ = Minim

Imperfect time, imperfect prolation; can be performed as our 2/4 time, two units of which would equal a 4/4 measure or common time.

Perfect time, imperfect prolation; can be performed as our 3/4 time.

Imperfect time, perfect prolation; can be performed as our 6/8 time.

Perfect time, perfect prolation; can be performed as our 9/8 time.

The practical result of all this was that the musicians of the *Ars nova* saw before them a brave new world of rhythmic flexibility. A composition need not have the same monorhythmic sound from beginning to end; it need not thump along in repetitive patterns like the discant of Leoninus and Perotinus. Rhythmic textures could change with surprising rapidity. Although the tempo would remain the same, the music might seem to speed up and then suddenly slow down, faster here, slower there, as radically longer or shorter values were introduced. The shortest note in the system (the minim) was eighty-one times faster (shorter) than the longest note (the triplex long). Musicians had gained total control over the second of the two fundamental parameters of music: pitch and time. The composer could create and express on parchment, in the most precise and detailed terms, these two axes, pitch written vertically and time horizontally. The West had its first graph, and it was created in music. The composer, consciously or not, stood at the forefront of science.

But not all musicians were pleased. One in particular, the music theorist **Jacques de Liège** (c1260–c1330), inveighed against the radical innovations of the **Ars nova** with its duple relationships and small note values. He preferred instead the earlier style of Parisian music, with its uniform pace and clear ternary units—the sort of music that we have seen in the motet *El mois d'avril/O quam sancta/Et gaudebit* (see Chapter 9). Jacques dubbed this older repertory the **Ars antiqua.** Battle lines were drawn between the conservative music of the thirteenth century and the radical new music of the fourteenth—between the *Ars antiqua* and the *Ars nova*. Even **Pope John XXII** charged into the fray to defend conservative church music. In his bull *Docta sanctorum patrum* (*Teachings of the Holy Fathers*; 1324) he fumed:

> But certain exponents of a new school, who think only of the laws of measured time, are composing new melodies of their own creation with a new system of notes, and these they prefer to the ancient, traditional music; the melodies of the Church are sung in semibreves and minims and with gracenotes of repercussion. . . . These composers, knowing nothing of the true foundation upon which they must build, are ignorant of the church modes, incapable of distinguishing between them, and cause great confusion. The great number of notes in their compositions conceals from us the plainchant melody, with its simple well-regulated rises and falls that indicate the character of the church mode. These musicians run without pausing. They intoxicate the ear without satisfying it; they dramatize the text with gestures; and, instead of promoting devotion, they prevent it by creating a sensuous and indecent atmosphere. . . . Consequently, we intend to prohibit, cast out, and banish such things from the Church of God.[1]

But the pope's opinion had little sway. The music of the *Ars nova* continued to develop unchecked. Why? Because, as history shows, it is futile to legislate progress or regulate personal preference in the arts. In fact, in this specific instance, the voice of the pope grew fainter and fainter, as the authority of the church generally declined during the fourteenth century. The balance of power in the arts—in poetry and literature as well as music—was shifting away from the church to the courts of secular rulers.

   ## SUMMARY

The single most important development in Western music in the thirteenth century was the movement away from a system of notation based on context (modal notation) to one based on specific signs (mensural notation). By the end of the century, there were four basic note values as expounded by Franco of Cologne: duplex long, long, breve, and semibreve. But these values began to slow down (last longer), so yet a new smaller value, the minim, was introduced around 1300 to carry the faster-moving notes. Musicians continued to be fascinated with the possibilities of measuring and controlling time, and they experimented with rhythm in the main musical genre of the day, the motet. Music theorists Jean des Murs and Philippe de Vitry promoted several rhythmic innovations, including duple meter, triplets, and hemiola, and the use of time signatures. A wide range of durations as well as a greater variety of patterns were now possible. This new style of music (*Ars nova*) was far more complex rhythmically than thirteenth-century music (*Ars antiqua*) with its simple patterns, all in triple meter. By the end of the fourteenth century musicians would take the rhythmic innovations of the *Ars nova* to extraordinary extremes.

KEY TERMS

Art of Measured Song	mensural notation	time
Franco of Cologne	Jean des Murs	prolation
scholasticism	Philippe de Vitry	Jacques de Liège
long	minim	*Ars nova*
breve	dot	*Ars antiqua*
semibreve	mode	Pope John XXII

Chapter

11

Music at the Court of the French Kings

Notre Dame of Paris sits on the east end of an island (*Île de la Cité*) in the Seine River, and has traditionally served as a symbol of religious and spiritual authority in French life. The government and the courts, however, have historically been situated at the west end of the island. In medieval times, secular power rested with the kings who resided there in a fortified palace. By the early fourteenth century, the royal compound included, among other buildings, apartments for the king and his courtiers, a donjon, a meeting hall for parliament, and a two-story chapel, the famous Sainte-Chapelle that still stands today. Yet the largest and most impressive part of the royal palace was the Grande-Salle. Measuring 70 meters in length and 27 meters in width, it was then the largest hall in Western Europe. Here, surrounded by mounted statues of the ancient rulers of France, the king welcomed heads of state and gave royal banquets. All such events were adorned with secular music of various sorts.

The Grande-Salle was built during the reign of King Philip IV (1285–1314) by his chief financial minister Enguerran de Marigny (c1275–1315). Marigny had risen to a position of great power at court, but had accumulated equally powerful enemies along the way; moreover, he was skimming money from the king's treasury. Immediately upon the death of his royal protector in 1314, Marigny was accused of corruption, tried, convicted, and hanged high above Paris on the gallows at Montmartre. So sensational were these events that they gave rise to a long poetic satire called the *Roman de Fauvel*. In one copy of the *Roman de Fauvel* (Fig. 11-1), the story is brought vividly to life through the addition of illustrations and music. With its 135 monophonic and 34 polyphonic compositions, and its pictures, this version of the *Roman de Fauvel* constitutes the most important music manuscript of the first half of the fourteenth century.

FIGURE 11-1

A plate from the *Roman de Fauvel*, showing Fauvel the ass, in the top panel, on his wedding night.

Bridgeman Art Library

THE *ROMAN DE FAUVEL*

The ***Roman de Fauvel*** (*Tale of Fauvel*) is a fable about political power gone awry. In it Enguerran de Marigny and his corrupt henchmen are collectively portrayed as a witless ass, Fauvel. The animal's name is an acronym derived from the first letters of six worldly sins—*Flaterie*(flattery), **A**varice (avarice), *Vilanie* (villainy), *Variété* (fickleness), *Envie* (envy), and *Lascheté* (loose morals) = FAUVEL. Most of the poem was written in 1314 by Gervès de Bus, though the poet Chaillou de Pesstain and the composer Philippe de Vitry made insertions a few years later. All three men were young notaries at the French royal court. Thus they had the "inside scoop" on what was happening behind the back of old King Philip IV. They intended their satirical creation to serve as a warning to the next ruler to root out graft and corruption; if the king would only follow the poet's advice, he could not fail to become an excellent ruler. In Fauvel's world, Lady Fortune has turned everything upside down: lawyers pervert the law; justices are unjust; and pope and king bow down, fawning before Fauvel. (Our expression "to curry favor" is derived from "to curry Fauvel.") Most of the *Roman de Fauvel* is a poetic recitation to be delivered in medieval French by a narrator, perhaps with simple improvised instrumental accompaniment in the background. The following selected lines give a taste of this political morality tale.

De Fauvel que tant voi torcher	I see so many people curry Fauvel
Doucement sans lui escorcher,	Softly without skinning him,
Sui entréz en merencolie,	I've fallen into a melancholy state
Pour ce qu'est beste si polie. . . .	Because he is so well groomed. . . .
Fauvel ne gist mès en l'estable,	Fauvel no longer lives in a stable
Il a meson plus honorable:	He has a more honorable house
Haute mengoere demande	A high manger he requests,
Rastelier bel et assez viande	A handsome haystack and plenty of food.
Il s'est herbergiéz en la sale,	He lodges himself in the great hall
Pour miex demonstrer sa regale. . . .	The better to show that he is royal. . . . .
Fortune, contraire a raison,	Fortune, contrary to reason,
L'a fait seigneur de sa meson;	Has made him lord of her house
En lui essaucer met grant peine,	And taken great pains to raise him
Car ou palais roial le maine;	Because in the Palais Royal she leads him
De lui fere honorer ne cesse. . . .	To have him honored without ceasing. . . .
Vicontes, prevos et baillis;	Viscounts, provosts, and sheriffs
A bien torcher ne sont faillis;	To curry well, not are lacking;
Bourgois de bours et de cités	Bourgeoisie of the towns and cities
Torchent par grans subtiltés,	Curry with such great subtlety,
Et villains de ville champestre	And rustics from the country towns
Sont empres Fauvel pour li pestre.	Gather round Fauvel to ask for favors.

LISTENING CUE

GERVÈS DE BUS
Roman de Fauvel (1314)

CD 1/26
Anthology, No. 26

Music regularly interrupts the poetic narrative of the *Roman de Fauvel*, as singers comment upon the events unfolding before them. In the anonymous two-voice *Quare fremuerunt gentes* (*Why do the people rage*), for example, they ask why the people are discontent. The answer: because never have they seen such corruption and discord. *Quare fremuerunt gentes* is a reworking of a century-old conductus, here refashioned and bedecked with all of the rhythmic finery of the *Ars nova*. Each metrical unit consists of three breves; each breve is divided into two semibreves, and each of these in turn into three minims. Thus the mensuration that governs is perfect mode, imperfect time, and perfect prolation. Note values of widely different duration allow for passages of rapid movement, effected by minims, to be set against clearly articulated points of arrival, signaled by longs. This use of widely divergent rhythmic durations is typical of the exploring spirit of the composers of the *Ars nova*.

EXAMPLE 11-1

Why do the people and nations rage? Because they did not see the monsters with their own eyes…

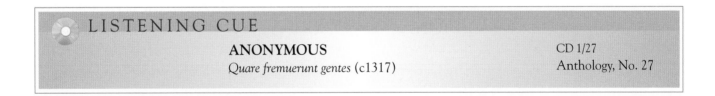

LISTENING CUE

ANONYMOUS

Quare fremuerunt gentes (c1317)

CD 1/27

Anthology, No. 27

PHILIPPE DE VITRY

"The only true poet among the French"—this is how the renowned Italian poet Petrarch characterized **Philippe de Vitry** (1291–1360).[1] We have already seen that Vitry was a notary at the royal court and an influential music theorist (see Chapter 10). He was also a mathematician, astronomer, politician, soldier, and diplomat, and he ended his career as the bishop of the city of Meaux. Typifying the medieval intellectual with diverse interests, Vitry was living proof that we need not wait until the Renaissance to meet "the Renaissance man."

Vitry's involvement in royal politics can be seen in one of his contributions to the illustrated *Roman de Fauvel*. His three-voice motet *Garrit Gallus/In nova fert/Neuma* is an animal allegory. The text speaks of the rooster, chicken, and lamb (the French people), who are devoured by the wicked fox (Enguerran de Marigny) because the blind lion (King Philip IV) does not see the deceit. To this scalding political satire Vitry adds biblical and classical references, creating a dense web of textual allusions. His music is equally complex. The tenor voice employs a new technique called isorhythm.

In **isorhythm** (same rhythm) a rhythmic pattern is repeated again and again in a line, usually in the tenor voice. Here in Vitry's motet a rhythmic pattern of ten measures is stated six times in the tenor. The rhythmic pattern, or unit, is called a **talea** (a segment or slice). There are three statements of the talea, and then the melody of the tenor is sung a second time to another three statements of the talea. In an isorhythmic motet the melodic unit is called the **color**. Thus, in this motet, two statements of the color coincide with six of the talea, as can be seen in the example below.

EXAMPLE 11-2

In Vitry's motet, the upper voices offer their complaint at a blistering pace but the isorhythmic regularity of the tenor holds the work tight. Isorhythm presupposes forethought and careful planning. Every rhythm of the tenor is predetermined. Like fugal procedure in the eighteenth century or twelve-tone technique in the twentieth, isorhythm helped the medieval composer give structure to a lengthy musical composition. Eventually, with the next generation of composers, not only the tenor but also the upper voices will come under strict isorhythmic control.

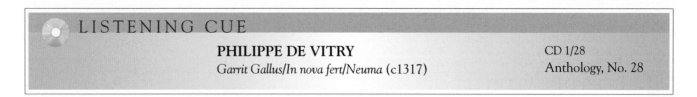

LISTENING CUE

PHILIPPE DE VITRY   CD 1/28
Garrit Gallus/In nova fert/Neuma (c1317)   Anthology, No. 28

ROYAL DANCES

The kings of France welcomed and amused their guests in the Grande-Salle of the royal court. King Charles V, for example, entertained Holy Roman Emperor Charles IV and a group of eight hundred courtiers there in 1378 (Fig. 11-2). In good weather the king and his entourage might repair to the royal garden at the westernmost tip of the island. Here shaded walkways, soft grass benches, colorful flowers, and succulent fruits were to be found. Yet whether in the Grande-Salle or in this royal garden of delights, the most popular musical entertainment was dancing.

Broadly speaking, people in the Middle Ages enjoyed two types of dances, each with a distinctive form. One type was a song and dance called the **carole**. It made use of a musical form called strophe plus refrain, in which a series of stanzas would each end with the same refrain. The singers and dancers grouped in a circle. As they danced around, a soloist sang each successive strophe of text, while everyone else joined in for the refrain (Fig. 11-3). The subject matter of the carole might have to do with Christmas or Easter, spring, the month of May, or love. A second type of dance was called the **estampie** or "stomp" (likely derived from the Old French *estampir*, to stamp or make resound). The estampie, like all medieval dances in Western Europe, was originally a sung dance. That is to say, the dancers of the early estampie sang a text, usually a poem about love, as they danced. During the thirteenth and fourteenth centuries, the text was often dropped, leaving a purely instrumental piece, either monophonic or polyphonic. A French chronicler of the fourteenth century emphasizes the instrumental nature of the estampie, and perhaps the choral quality of the carole: "And as soon as [the minstrels] had stopped the estampies that they beat, those gentlemen and ladies who had amused themselves dancing began, without hesitation, to take hands for carolling."[2]

This and other evidence suggests that the carole was danced and sung by a group holding hands, alternating male and female. The estampie, however, was for couples. We know nothing about the choreography of the estampie, beyond the fact that couples of all ages danced in stately procession.

The most characteristic feature of the estampie is its musical structure. It comprises a succession of couplets, or pairs of musical phrases. Each pair is called a **punctum** (phrase, pl. **puncta**) and, although the puncta of the dance may be of different lengths, all end with the same music, a refrain. Most important, this concluding refrain has both an **open** and a **closed ending.** Thus the form of the estampie can be represented: **AxAyBxByCxCyDxDy** etc. (Ex. 11-3). It is here in the repertory of medieval dance music that first and second endings appear for the first time in the history of music.

We do not know for which French king *La quinte estampie real* (*The Fifth Royal Estampie*) was composed, only that it appears as the fifth in a collection of eight estampies, all called "royal." Typical of the estampie, the melodic range here is narrow, and there are no chromatic inflections. The four puncta appear to be constructed by linking small melodic-rhythmic units. Medieval performers may well have improvised, or elaborated upon, such dance tunes as the occasion demanded. As with all French estampies, this one enjoys a solid modal grounding. Indeed, part of the charm of *La quinte estampie real* is the continuous interplay between the C-grounded first ending and the A-based second. A theorist of the fourteenth century would say that this interchange was between the Lydian mode (with B♭ and transposed to C) and Dorian (with B♭ and transposed to A). Later, in the sixteenth century, theorists would designate these modes as Ionian and Aeolian. Today we would simply call them major and minor.

🌿 FIGURE 11-2

Holy Roman Emperor Charles IV and his nephew French King Charles V at a banquet given in honor of the emperor in 1378.

🌿 FIGURE 11-3

To the accompaniment of shawms and a bagpipe, dancers execute a carole in a garden while holding hands.

EXAMPLE 11-3

LISTENING CUE

ANONYMOUS   CD 1/29
La quinte estampie real (c1320)   Anthology, No. 29

Finally, what is perhaps most striking about medieval dance music is how little of it is preserved. No more than fifty instrumental pieces prior to 1450 have survived. What does that say—that there were few dances and little music? Likely not. Rather it suggests that the dances played by the minstrels of the court belonged to a tradition of improvised music that was passed orally from one generation of musicians to the next without benefit of written notation. Indeed, the first evidence that instrumentalists were required to read written notation does not appear until much later, in the 1470s.

Instrumental music was not a sacred object to be preserved in a splendid manuscript. Much of it survives as an after-thought to music history; it was added at the end or copied in the margins of manuscripts of vocal music. Instrumental music did not require a great deal of pre-compositional planning, but came alive during performance. It was everyday music, which might be written down, but more likely was not. In this sense, medieval instrumental music has more in common with our modern-day jazz than it does with the ancient Mass and motet.

MUSICAL INSTRUMENTS AT COURT AND IN CHURCH

 FIGURE 11-4

Vielle as depicted in an illumination from late thirteenth-century Paris. The medieval vielle had a very flat bridge and was often used for playing chords by employing drones and multiple stops.

Bodleian Library

What instruments played dance music at the French royal court during the thirteenth and fourteenth centuries? Music theory treatises, poems, and paintings reveal that in Paris, as elsewhere throughout Europe, a great variety of instruments were heard. Most likely to accompany an estampie was the **vielle** (Fig. 11-4), a large five-string fiddle capable of playing the entire Guidonian scale. Players of the vielle are mentioned performing alone, in pairs, or occasionally in groups of four, as a contemporary poem recounts: "Then the servants hurried and quickly took away the napery [table linen]. Four minstrels of the vielle played a new estampie before the lady."[3] The harp, psaltery, and gittern (an early cousin of the lute) likewise played at court, though the sounds of these soft-stringed instruments may have been too faint to accompany a party of energetic dancers. Indeed, louder sounds were needed if the dance took place out of doors. Thus such instruments as the pipe and tabor (fife and drum), played by one or two persons, as well as a bagpipe and two shawms, often appear in illustrations of dances (see Fig. 11-3). The **shawm** (an ancestor of the modern oboe) was a double-reed instrument with a loud penetrating tone; by the late fourteenth century it came in two sizes, treble and tenor pitched a fifth below. Trumpets were present but they did not play dance music; rather, they sounded fanfares and heralded pronouncements.

Prior to 1300 the only "keyboard" instrument that existed was the organ, but it was rare and, in truth, used sliders and not keys. Sliders were flat pieces of wood that could be pulled in and out to allow air to pass through the pipes. The invention of the keyboard was a technological innovation of the fourteenth century. Now, instead of sliding boards in and out, keys could be pushed to let air rush through the pipes to make sound. The keyboard was added to both the portative and positive organ, which differed only in size. The **portative organ** was a small movable instrument that sounded at courtly entertainments, though more often to accompany singers than dancers. The organist played with one hand and pumped the bellows with the other (or an assistant might pump the bellows; Fig. 11-5). The **positive organ** was a large stationary instrument that began to appear in large numbers shortly after 1300. Because the positive organ was considered to be one of the technological wonders of the day, it was usually attached high on a wall in the nave of the church for all the populace to see and hear. The organ at this time was called, as it is today, "the king of instruments." It was the only musical instrument officially sanctioned within the church by ecclesiastical authorities, all others being viewed as worldly profanations of sacred space.

Finally, the fourteenth century witnessed the development of the **clavichord** (literally "key-string"), a keyboard instrument that makes sound when a player depresses a key and thereby pushes a small metal tangent in the shape of a "T" upward to strike a string. The clavichord was initially called the **chekker,** likely from the medieval English word for counting board, which had a checkered look. The first mention of the chekker is found at the court of the king of France in 1360, when King John II received one as a gift from the English King Edward III. From the French royal court in this period comes our earliest surviving collection of keyboard music, called the **Robertsbridge Codex.** This manuscript preserves three estampies and arrangements of three motets from the *Roman de Fauvel*, music typically heard at the French royal court during the mid fourteenth century. The music of the second estampie sounds fresh yet untutored, being full of lively rhythms but endless parallel octaves as well.

FIGURE 11-5

A fifteenth-century domestic scene in which a gentleman plays a portative organ, assisted by a lady who pumps the bellows. Today, wind pressure is created in the organ by means of electronically activated pumps.

EXAMPLE 11-4

 LISTENING CUE

ANONYMOUS
Robertsbridge Codex (c1350)
Estampie

Book Companion Website (http://schirmer.wadsworth.com/wright_1e)
Anthology, No. 30

 SUMMARY

Historians have long recognized the fourteenth century as a period of decline in the power of the church and a corresponding increase in the influence of the secular court. During this period no court was more brilliant than that of the French kings.

Bridgeman Art Library

The two principal northern European composers of the fourteenth century, Philippe de Vitry and Guillaume de Machaut (see Chapter 12), both had strong ties to the French monarchy. The most important music manuscript of the first half of the fourteenth century, the *Roman de Fauvel*, is a scathing attack on the power and corruption within the court. It contains several isorhythmic motets of Vitry, a genre of music that reflects the continued desire of composers to give structure to their music by the precise measurement and repetition of units of musical time. The French court was also home to dances, called caroles and estampies, as well as the first surviving pieces for keyboard in the history of music.

KEY TERMS

Roman de Fauvel	estampie	portative organ
Philippe de Vitry	punctum (pl., puncta)	positive organ
isorhythm	open ending	clavichord
talea	closed ending	chekker
color	vielle	Robertsbridge Codex
carole	shawm	

Chapter 12

Fourteenth-Century Music in Reims: Guillaume de Machaut

🌿 FIGURE 12-1

The poet-composer Guillaume de Machaut at work, one of the earliest portraits of a Western artist.

Bibliothèque Nationale, Paris

With its 200,000 inhabitants, Paris was by far the largest city in Western Europe in the mid fourteenth century. But it was not the only French town of musical and artistic importance. Situated a hundred miles to the northeast of the capital, the city of **Reims** could boast a cathedral as large and impressive as Notre Dame of Paris. Here, at Notre Dame of Reims, all kings of France were crowned. Today we think of Reims as the home of great champagne. In the Middle Ages it was known as the city that crowned the French king. Among the 20,000 residents of Reims in the mid fourteenth century was Guillaume de Machaut (c1300–1377; Fig. 12-1), the most renowned poet and musician of the age. Machaut himself sang in two royal coronations, that of King John II in 1350 and Charles V in 1364.

Guillaume de Machaut was born about 1300, educated in the schools of the cathedral of Reims, and apparently obtained the degree master of arts, probably at the University of Paris. Around 1323 he became the secretary of John, duke of Luxembourg and king of Bohemia, in whose service he traveled widely—to Bohemia (Czech Republic), Poland, and perhaps to Lithuania and Russia as well. In 1337 Machaut was appointed a canon at the cathedral of Reims and began to adopt a more settled life. During his mature years he spent most of his time writing lyrical verse and music on commission for members of the French royal family. Kings John II and Charles V were among his principal patrons. In all, Machaut composed 23 motets, 19 lais (monophonic songs using the form of the sequence), 42 ballades, 22 rondeaux, 33 virelais, a hocket, and a four-voice polyphonic Mass, as well as fifteen long narrative stories and a collection of 280 short poems that he chose not to set to music—a sizable body of music and poetry! By 1350 Machaut had begun to gather this enormous literary and musical *oeuvre* into neatly organized manuscripts. Machaut is the first composer in the history of music for whom we possess a "complete works"—almost all of his music survives. He died in Reims in 1377 and was buried in the nave of the cathedral.

MACHAUT, THE BLACK DEATH, AND THE HUNDRED YEARS' WAR

Guillaume de Machaut was the companion and confidant of kings. As a man of the times, he personally experienced some of the horrific events that marked what one historian has called "the calamitous fourteenth century." In 1348 a bubonic plague known as the **Black Death** swept Europe, carried by fleas hosting upon rats. A human victim would develop a high fever and soon buboes would appear (black welts in the armpits and around the groin). Death was as sudden as it was sure. By 1351 fully a third of the population of Western Europe, perhaps 20 million people, had died. Among them was Bonne of Luxembourg, mother of King Charles V of France, for whom Machaut wrote a memorial motet *Trop plus est bele/Biauté paree/Je ne sui mie certeins*. In one of his narrative poems, Machaut reveals that he spent the winter of 1337–1349 shut up in his house in Reims. In this fashion he survived the plague while many of his friends, he tells us, were "mors et en terre mis" (dead and buried).

A decade later another calamity came to the gates of Reims, the **Hundred Years' War** (1337–1453). The English kings wanted to control not merely the western side of modern France (the old Angevin kingdom; Map 6-1) but all of it. And because the English and French royal houses had intermarried, the king of England had a distant hereditary claim to the French throne, should the French king die leaving no male heir. The hostilities that resulted—sporadic bloody battles interrupted by fragile peaces—occurred between 1337 and 1453. They ended only after **Joan of Arc** rallied the French royal forces and led the dauphin (the future king Charles VII) to be crowned at Reims.

Indeed, Reims was central to the Hundred Years' War, for, to be king of France, an aspirant had to be crowned in Reims. To this end, the English King Edward III led a large army across northern France to the walls of the city in the fall of 1359. The nearly 60-year-old poet-composer Guillaume de Machaut put on armor and mounted the ramparts prepared to enter battle. (The famous English poet Geoffrey Chaucer was captured by the French during the same campaign.) After forty days of futile assaults on Reims, the English king raised his siege and marched away. Machaut commemorated these events in three isorhythmic motets. In one, *Christe qui lux es/Veni creator spiritus/Tribulatio proxima*, his triplum speaks of those "Who tear us apart in the wars that have now arisen," while his motetus cries "Our enemies surround us"—a fitting description of the English siege of Reims.

Because the walls of Reims held firm, King Edward III of England never became king of France. The crown remained in the French royal house, passing to Charles V at Notre Dame of Reims on 19 May 1364. Machaut himself participated in the coronation ritual; the canons of Reims traditionally played an important role in the ceremony, leading the new king into the church. Indeed, Machaut seems to have composed a work specifically for the event. It is entitled *Hoquetus David* (the French king was often called David in these years by way of analogy to the biblical king of that name). **Hocket** is both a contrapuntal technique and a musical genre. It occurs when the sounds of two voices are staggered by the careful placement of rests, thereby creating a highly syncopated piece. The term "hocket" derives from the Latin word *hoquetus* (hiccup), and indeed the sound is similar to a musical hiccup. In Machaut's *Hoquetus David*, an isorhythmic tenor is fashioned from the end of *Alleluia. Nativitas*, which speaks of the kings of the Old Testament. Tenor talea and color overlap in a highly complex fashion (see Anthology, No. 31). But although the tenor is crafted with arithmetic precision, the profiles of both talea and color are almost wholly inaudible to the listener. As is often the case in medieval music, a mathematical structure rests unheard beneath the audible surface. What catches our ear is not the isorhythmic tenor, but the snappy hocketing above in the duplum and triplum. Hocketing was a popular technique during the thirteenth and fourteenth centuries, but it disappeared thereafter. Most hockets are without texts. They might be sung by voices alone or performed on instruments. Wind instruments, with their aggressive attacks, are particularly effective at bringing out the syncopations. Example 12-1 offers a small sample of the technique of hocket from *Hoquetus David*.

EXAMPLE 12-1

LISTENING CUE

GUILLAUME DE MACHAUT   CD 2/1
Hoquetus David (c1364)   Anthology, No. 31

MACHAUT AND THE *FORMES FIXES*

The troubadours and trouvères had bequeathed to Western Europe a great treasury of lyrical love poetry set to music (see Chapter 6). Many of these monophonic songs and dances were composed in just a few patterns, or musical forms. By the early fourteenth century, most French secular art songs were written in one of just three forms: ballade, rondeau, and virelai. Because each of these forms was always prescribed, or fixed, in advance (like a *prix fixe* menu), they were called the ***formes fixes*** (fixed forms). The French *formes fixes* are not religious pieces but secular songs and dances setting texts in medieval French. Thus there is no pre-existing Latin tenor, as is true for motets and hockets: in *formes fixes* pieces all voices are newly composed. Guillaume de Machaut did not invent these forms; rather, he popularized them, cultivating these to the exclusion of all other secular musical forms. For Machaut, and continuing for composers a hundred years later, almost all secular music setting a French text was composed in one of these three fixed forms.

A **ballade** is a song setting a poem with from one to three stanzas, or strophes. Each stanza usually contains seven or eight lines of text, and the last line serves as a refrain (a highlighted résumé at the end of the stanza). In addition, lines one and two are sung to the same music as lines three and four, usually with first and second endings for each pair; lines five through seven or eight have new music. Thus the musical form of each stanza of a ballade is **AAB.** The text below is the first strophe of Machaut's three-stanza ballade *Je puis trop bien,* with boldface letters indicating the musical sections and italic type showing the textual refrain.

Machaut's *Je puis trop bien* (*I can well compare*) is an excellent example of a piece composed in **ballade style** (Ex. 12-2). Here a treble voice sings a text to a lyrical melody while a slower moving tenor and contratenor provide a harmonic support. The lower voices may also be sung, or they may be played on musical instruments. Noteworthy here is the new attention given to the upper voice, the melody. It is more tuneful, rhythmically flexible, and melismatic than in previous secular poly-phonic music. Now for the first time the melody voice is called the **cantus,** mean-ing "the song," perhaps because the singer can luxuriate on a single syllable so as to enjoy the sheer beauty of the human voice. The syllables on which these vocalises occur in the cantus are usually not important to the meaning of the poem; in much medieval music, musical line and poetic intent work independently. The tenor pro-vides a foundation, and the contratenor fills out the harmony. In ballade style we see for the first time a true accompanied song. The text of the song recalls the story of the ancient Greek sculptor Pygmalion, who creates a statue so beautiful he falls in love with it. The same story served as the basis of George Bernard Shaw's play *Pygmalion* and the Broadway musical *My Fair Lady.*

Je puis trop bien madame comparer	**A**	I can well compare my lady
A l'ymage que fist Pymalion		To the statue Pygmalion made
D'yvoire fu, tant belle et si sans per	**A**	Of ivory so beautiful and without equal
Que plus l'ama que Medee Jazon.		That he loved it more than Jason did Medea.
Li folz toudis la prioit,	**B**	Mad with love, he cried out,
Mais l'ymage riens ne li respondoit.		But the image did not respond.
Einssi me fait celle qui mon cuer font,		Thus does she treat me, the one who melts my heart,
Qu'ades la pri et riens ne me respont.	(refrain)	*For I pray to her ever, but she does not respond.*

EXAMPLE 12-2

LISTENING CUE

GUILLAUME DE MACHAUT   CD 2/2
Je puis trop bien (c1355)   Anthology, No. 32

The virelai and rondeau are generally more playful than the serious ballade. Indeed, these *formes fixes* originated with the troubadours and trouvères as monophonic dances that involved choral singing. The **rondeau** consists of two musical sections, **a** and **b.** At the outset everyone sang a text refrain to these two sections. Then a soloist sang a new line of text to **a,** to which the chorus responded with part of the refrain set to **a.** Next the soloist sang two new lines to **a** and **b,** followed by a concluding choral refrain. The complete form of a rondeau was thus **ABaAabAB** (the capital letters indicate the refrain). Below is the text of Machaut's three-voice rondeau *Ma fin est mon commencement et mon commencement ma fin* (My end is my beginning and my beginning my end). It is famous in the history of music because the text suggests the mode of performance: the cantus voice goes forward while the tenor sings the same music backward against it; a contratenor, only half as long as the other two voices, sings to its end and then returns to the beginning. Here retrograde motion is ingeniously joined to a clear example of rondeau form. The numbers below represent units of time (modern measures) in Machaut's famous rondeau.

Cantus:	1	5	10	15	20	25	30	35	40
Tenor:	40	35	30	25	20	15	10	5	1
Contratenor:	1	5	10	15	20	15	10	5	1

Ma fin est mon commencement	**A**	*My end is my beginning*
Et mon commencement ma fin.	**B**	*and my beginning my end.*
Et teneüre vraiëment	**a**	This much is clear.
Ma fin est mon commencement	**A**	*My end is my beginning*
Mes tiers chans iij fois seulement	**a**	My third voice sings three times only
Se retrograde et einsi fin.	**b**	in retrograde, and then is done.
Ma fin est mon commencement	**A**	*My end is my beginning*
Et mon commencement ma fin.	**B**	*and my beginning my end.*

The form of the **virelai** can simply be represented as **AbbaA.** There are two musical sections (**a** and **b**) as well as a textual refrain (**A**) sung to music **a.** Unlike the rondeau, the virelai may have more than one stanza. For a three-stanza virelai, such as Machaut's monophonic *Douce dame jolie,* the form that results is **AbbaAbbaAbbaA.** Machaut's *Douce dame jolie* (Fair sweet lady) is a simple poem of unrequited love set to an equally simple, but charming melody.

Douce dame jolie,	(refrain)	**A**	*Fair sweet lady*
Pour Dieu ne pensés mie			*for God's sake never think*
Que neulle ait signourie			*that any woman rules*
Seur moy, fors vous seulement.			*my heart, except you alone.*
Qu'adès sans tricherie, chierie		**b**	I have cherished you long
Vous ay, et humblement			and served you faithfully
Tous les jours de ma vie servie		**b**	All the days of my life
Sans vilein pensement.			without a base thought.

Helas! Et je mendie	**a**	Alas! I must do without
D'esperance et d'aïe,		hope and help, and thus
Dont ma joie est fenie,		my joy has ended,
Se pité ne vous en prent.		unless you pity me.
Douce dame jolie . . . . (refrain)	**A**	*Fair sweet lady . . .*

LISTENING CUE

| **GUILLAUME DE MACHAUT** | CD 2/3 |
| *Douce dame jolie* (before 1350) | Anthology, No. 33 |

Originally, both the virelai and the rondeau were dance pieces in which a soloist sang the verses and a chorus the refrain. In the course of the fourteenth century, however, a new performance practice emerged in which a single voice sang the choral refrain as well as the verses. A lively dance had become more intimate chamber music.

MACHAUT AND THE MASS OF OUR LADY

By far Machaut's most famous work is his *Messe de Nostre Dame* (*Mass of Our Lady*), one of the greatest artistic achievements of the Middle Ages. Composed for four voices during the 1360s, Machaut's Mass is revolutionary on several counts. It is the first complete treatment in polyphony of the Ordinary of the Mass. Prior to this, to create a polyphonic Mass, composers had usually chosen to set the responsorial chants of the Proper of the Mass (see Chapter 8). Because these earlier Mass settings were therefore proper to a specific day in the liturgical calendar, each could, in principle, be performed only once a year. By composing music for the Ordinary of the Mass (chants heard at nearly every Mass) Machaut created a composition that was appropriate for, and thus could be performed on, many days of the year. In addition, Machaut's *Mass of Our Lady* is the first **cyclic Mass,** meaning that all of the movements of the Mass are linked together by a common musical theme (see Anthology, No. 34). A distinctive motive occurs in each of the six movements of the Mass (*Kyrie, Gloria, Credo, Sanctus, Agnus dei,* and *Ite missa est*), and this recurring gesture binds together into a coherent unit what would otherwise be six separate, disconnected movements. Taken in sum, Machaut's Mass movements constitute a work that requires nearly twenty-five minutes to perform, by far the longest polyphonic composition before the fifteenth century.

The sound of Machaut's Mass is brilliant, indeed startling, because of a new approach to choral sonority. In earlier polyphony, two, three, or four voices were written in approximately the same range, within an octave or so of what we call middle C. Now Machaut has expanded the vocal texture to two full octaves. The cantus (triplum) sings in a high range and stays there; the tenor does similarly in a tenor range. Between these Machaut adds a third voice, as well as a fourth one, both called contratenor. The lower contratenor works in conjunction with the tenor and often goes below it, providing a true bass within the four-part harmony. Soon after Machaut's time the contratenor below the tenor would be called the **contratenor**

bassus, whence our term "bass," and the contratenor above the tenor **contratenor altus,** whence our term "alto" voice. Here for the first time we have a clear separation of the vocal parts by range. Something akin to true four-part harmony has been created, and this generates a fuller, richer choral sound.

Machaut's sound is exhilarating for other reasons as well. The listener senses a formal rigidity, perhaps because of the isorhythm and pre-existing chant in the slow-moving tenor; yet hocket and frequent syncopation add an element of daring to the upper two voices (Ex. 12-3a). The contrapuntal fabric bristles with unprepared dissonances. Throughout it all, Machaut poses and resolves conflicting forces, creating a *concors discordia* (harmony through discord) typical of medieval art: sustained chords vie with quick-moving hockets; rich triads yield to hollow open fifths; and biting double leading tones pull to perfect consonances (Ex. 12-3b).[†] The sound that results is one of extraordinary excitement and power.

EXAMPLE 12-3A   EXAMPLE 12-3B

LISTENING CUE

GUILLAUME DE MACHAUT
Kyrie of the Mass of Our Lady (c1360)

CD 2/4
Anthology, No. 34

Guillaume de Machaut composed his Mass to honor the Virgin Mary, and he established an endowment of 300 French *livres* (a huge donation in the fourteenth century) so that it might be performed every Saturday of the year. Upon his death in 1377 prayers for his departed soul were added to the Mass, and both Mass and prayers were celebrated weekly before a statue of the Virgin in the nave of the cathedral of Reims. It was here that the composer had asked to be buried. By endowing such a votive service Machaut was simply conforming to the religious beliefs of the age. He hoped to reduce the length of time his spirit might languish in Purgatory and ensure that it arrived at the gates of St. Peter well recommended by the Virgin.

[†]For a description of the double leading-tone cadence, see Musical Interlude 1.

SUMMARY

During the fourteenth century, musicians continued to exploit the potential of musical rhythm first explored by the composers of the *Ars nova*. Isorhythm remained a structural force in both motet and Mass. French musicians, led by the preeminent figure of Guillaume de Machaut, consolidated their secular polyphonic music into just three fixed forms: ballade, rondeau, and virelai. The ballade was the most serious in tone of the three, while the rondeau and virelai were generally lighter pieces that only gradually gave up their ties to sung dance. Machaut made use of large-scale isorhythmic structure in his motets and in his most important work, the *Mass of Our Lady*. In this four-voice Mass, he places the voices in distinctly different registers, thereby creating a new, expanded sense of tonal sonority. Machaut's *Mass of Our Lady* is the first complete polyphonic setting of the Ordinary of the Mass, and it established a precedent; hereafter, when composers created a polyphonic Mass, they almost always set only the Ordinary of the Mass.

KEY TERMS

Reims	hocket	rondeau
Guillaume de Machaut	*formes fixes*	virelai
Black Death	ballade	cyclic Mass
Hundred Years' War	ballade style	contratenor bassus
Joan of Arc	cantus	contratenor altus

Chapter

Avignon, Symbolic Scores, and the *Ars Subtilior*

 ## PAPAL AVIGNON

In 1335 the renowned Italian poet **Francesco Petrarch** (1304–1374) called the city of Avignon in France "this profane Babylon that knows no shame."[1] Petrarch, an official of the papal court, was writing from Avignon because the popes had moved the papacy there from Rome. As a result, the population of this once-small southern French town (Map 13-1) swelled from 5,000 in 1300 to 120,000 by 1340. People squeezed themselves together within the protective walls of the city, which encircled no more than six square miles (an area about the size of Central Park in New York). They lodged in any available space along narrow tortuous streets, along the ramparts, even in cemeteries. Crime and prostitution were rampant. Soon, however, these urban ills were temporarily relieved by another: in 1348 the Black Death killed 62,000 souls, spreading rapidly among the densely packed citizens. Avignon was a microcosm of all that might go wrong in a medieval city. Thus Petrarch

 MAP 13-1
Avignon.

Bridgeman Art Library

✳ FIGURE 13-1

Avignon, France, Palace of the
Popes. The towers at the palace
were a continuation of families'
towers in Italian city-states where
families had sought refuge during
the furious vendettas of the Middle Ages.

equated it with ancient Babylon, the city of luxury and vice.
Following his example, historians now call the period in which
the papacy resided in Avignon the **Babylonian Captivity**
(1309–1403). But how did it come to pass that the popes had
left Rome? How did it happen that the most progressive music
of the late fourteenth century was written, not in Paris or
Rome, but in the southern French city of Avignon?

Throughout much of the Middle Ages, the papacy was not
in Rome; the Eternal City was the symbolic center of the
Church but often not its physical home. At the height of the
Roman Empire the population of Rome was more than a million; by 1350 it had shrunk to about 20,000. Rome was in
ruins. Warring families as well as crime, both organized and disorganized, made it
dangerous. Not surprisingly, the popes preferred safer, more salubrious cities in Italy
(Florence, Pisa, and Genoa) and in southern France (Lyon, Vienne, and Avignon),
and so they moved from place to place. Indeed, the medieval papal court (the pope
and his retinue of about three hundred officials and servants) moved almost as often
as today's circus.

Thus when Pope Clement V entered Avignon in March 1309 he did not expect
that he and his successors would remain there for nearly a hundred years. But remain they did. In 1378 an Italian pope, Gregory XI, attempted to return the papacy
to Rome, but he died just after arriving there. Under pressure from the Roman mobs,
one group of cardinals elected an Italian as the next pope, while a pro-French group
chose a Frenchman, who immediately returned to Avignon. The **Great Western
Schism** had begun, and it would remain until 1417.

The Avignonese popes were mindful of their prestige and so built a worthy palace
(Fig. 13-1). Contemporaries called it "the most beautiful and most fortified house in
the world." The papal banquet hall was 162 feet in length. The chapel, constructed
between 1345 and 1352 by Pope Clement VI, was the largest palace chapel in the
world (Fig. 13-2). Appropriately called the **Clementine Chapel,** it served as a model
for the one that Pope Sixtus IV would later build at the Vatican, the Sistine Chapel
(see Fig. 25-2). In the Clementine Chapel, the Avignonese popes heard Mass as the
papal chapel sang chant and polyphony. Indeed, during the Babylonian Captivity
the word **cappella** begins to assume two separate and distinctly different meanings:
a building consecrated for religious worship, as well as an organized group of highly
trained musicians who sang at these services.

✳ FIGURE 13-2

Long view of the chapel of Pope
Clement VI within the Palace
of the Popes.

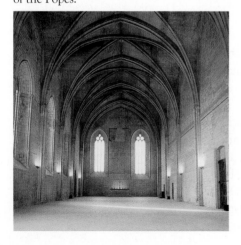

Given its location roughly halfway between Paris and Rome, papal Avignon became a crossroads for arts and ideas. Poets, painters, and musicians sojourned there, or simply passed through. Composer-theorists
Philippe de Vitry and Jean des Murs were both in Avignon during the
1340s. When Vitry was there in 1342 he composed an isorhythmic motet,
Petre Clemens/Lugentium, in honor of the election of Pope Clement VI.
The Great Western Schism (1378–1417) did little to dim the allure of
Avignon. Some composers continued to live there permanently as members of the papal chapel, some were employed in the service of the thirty-
two cardinals who resided with the Avignonese pope, and others simply
visited the city in the retinues of counts, dukes, and kings. At the end of
the fourteenth century, Avignon was the center of the most progressive
music then written in the West.

BAUDE CORDIER AND SYMBOLIC SCORES

Among the musicians passing through Avignon at the end of the fourteenth century was **Baude Cordier.** Cordier's music is marked by unusual rhythmic sophistication, as can be seen in his French rondeau *Tout par compas suy composés* (*All by a compass am I composed*). This is an ingenious piece on several counts. As is immediately apparent (Fig. 13-3), the shape of the music bears out the title of the piece, for it is written in circular notation on lines drawn by a compass. Other scores in this period are shaped like a heart, a harp, and a labyrinth to symbolize, through music, the meaning of the text. Indeed, the late fourteenth century was a fanciful age in which musical shapes, rhythmic symbols, riddle canons, and pseudonyms helped create an almost make-believe world of sound.

The name Cordier literally means "String Man," and it apparently served as the professional nickname of Baude Fresnel (c1365–1398), a harper employed by Duke Philip the Bold of Burgundy. In 1391 and 1395 Cordier traveled with Duke Philip to Avignon. His presence there is confirmed by the text of the rondeau *Tout par*

Bridgeman Art Library

❀ FIGURE 13-3

Baude Cordier's symbolic score *Tout par compas suy composés*. There are four rondeau poems in the four corners. The refrain of that in the upper left (*Tout par compas suy composés*) is also set beneath the music of the outer circle. The outer circle generates a two-voice canon, or round (hence the symbolism). The inner circle is a tenor support for the two-voice canon.

compas suy composés. At each of the four corners of the manuscript (see Fig. 13-3) is a stanza of text; each is encompassed by a circle, and each is fixed in the poetic form of a rondeau. The stanza at the bottom left literally says that Cordier's music was known as far as Rome but, in fact, it refers to Avignon. For in this period the Avignonese popes advanced the doctrine of **Ubi papa, ibi Roma** (Wherever is the pope, there be Rome). The palace of the popes in Avignon was called "Rome" in the official documents of the day.

Maistre Baude Cordier se nomme	**A**	*His name is master Baude Cordier*
C'ilz qui composa ceste rode.	**B**	*Who composed this round.*
Je sui bien scavoir a toute homme,	**a**	I make it known to all,
Maistre Baude Cordier se nomme	**A**	*His name is master Baude Cordier*
De Reims est et jusqu'à Romme	**a**	From Reims, whose music circulates
Sa musique appert et a rode.	**b**	To Rome and is known.
Maistre Baude Cordier se nomme	**A**	*His name is master Baude Cordier*
C'ilz qui composa ceste rode.	**B**	*Who composed this round.*

Line two calls this piece a "rode" (Latin *rota*) or round, and so it is in two senses: it goes around, three times completely; and it is a round, or canon. In Latin the word **canon** literally means "rule." In music the rule is that a second voice must duplicate exactly the pitches and rhythms of the first, as in "Row, row, row your boat," for example. Here, the leading voice begins at about eleven o'clock as we view the music (see Fig. 13-3). After one measure a second voice enters and follows the melody exactly, note for note, thereby creating the canon. Beneath this canonic duet a tenor provides a harmonic foundation. The text set beneath the music instructs the voices to make three full turns around the circle as they sing. The three trips around the circle come in the rondeau form as follows: 1 (**AB**), 2 (**ab**), and 3 (**AB**).

Tout par compas suy composés	**A(1)**	*All with a compass am I composed*
En ceste rode proprement		*Properly, as befits a round*
Pour moy chanter plus seurement.	**B**	*To sing me more surely.*
Regarde com suy disposés	**a**	Look how I am disposed,
Compaing, je te pri chierement.		Companion, I pray you kindly.
Tout par compas suy composés	**A**	*All with a compass am I composed*
En ceste rode proprement.		*Properly, as befits a round.*
Trois temps entiers par toy posés	**a(2)**	Three times you go around me entirely
Chacer me pues joyeusement,		You can chase me joyfully,
S'en chantant as vray sentiment.	**b**	If in singing you're true to me.
Tout par compas suy composés	**A(3)**	*All with a compass am I composed*
En ceste rode proprement		*Properly, as befits a round*
Pour moy chanter plus seurement.	**B**	*To sing me more surely.*

LISTENING CUE

BAUDE CORDIER   CD 2/5
Tout par compas suy composés (c1391)   Anthology, No. 35

Finally, look carefully once again at the original manuscript of Cordier's rondeau (see Fig. 13-3). Notice that there are symbols and numbers situated in both the cantus and tenor parts. These are mensuration signs (time signatures) and indicators of proportions (see below). They control the temporal flow of the music and give this already artful piece great rhythmic complexity.

 PHILIPPUS DE CASERTA: THE *ARS SUBTILIOR*

Just how complex rhythm became at the end of the fourteenth century can be seen in the music of **Philippus de Caserta,** an Italian composer working in Avignon during the reign of Pope Clement VII (1378–1394). In fact, Caserta's two-stanza ballade *Par les bons Gedeons* (*By the Good Gideon*) is written in honor of Pope Clement VII. Here the tenor establishes a solid rhythmic foundation, sounding firmly on the beat in modern $\frac{2}{4}$ time. Against it, the contratenor altus offers a light rhythmic counterpoint, providing syncopations and occasional moments of hocket. Above this framework, Caserta sets a flowing but difficult cantus. This melodic line is challenging to any singer, owing to the variety of rhythmic and metrical patterns that the voice must employ against the other voices: 4 against 1, 3 against 2, and 4 against 3. Long stretches of syncopation create polyrhythms that in turn suggest **polymeter,** two or more meters sounding simultaneously. In measures 23–25, for example, the cantus appears to be in $\frac{3}{4}$ while the lower voices are in $\frac{2}{4}$. Moreover, one and the same meter can be set against itself. In measures 10–16 all voices are in $\frac{2}{4}$, yet the cantus enters an eighth-note after the other two voices, thereby creating a lengthy passage of metrical syncopation (Ex. 13-1). This sort of music has been dubbed the **Ars subtilior** (more subtle art)—a style of music radiating out from Avignon to other parts of southern France and into northern Italy during the late fourteenth century. The *Ars subtilior* is marked by the most subtle, sometimes extreme, rhythmic relationships.

EXAMPLE 13-1

Ge - - de - ons   et   San - son
ser - - vi - tud   au - quel   es - [toit]

LISTENING CUE

PHILIPPUS DE CASERTA

Par les bons Gedeons (c1385)

CD 2/6
Anthology, No. 36

Philippus de Caserta was not only a composer but also a music theorist. In his *Tractatus figurarum* (*Treatise on Note-Shapes*; c1385) he offers one of the earliest discussions of the *sincopa* (syncopation). Syncopation is, in effect, a temporary shift of the downbeat, just as occurs in twentieth-century ragtime and jazz. The rhythmic pattern of one voice can be shifted so that it is out of sync with that of another. Certainly a good deal of the rhythmic subtlety found in Cordier's *Tout par compas suy composés* and Caserta's *Par les bons Gedeons,* as we have seen, is due to syncopation. But not all of it. The most complex passages are those involving **proportions,** time signatures often written as fractions that modified the normal value of notes.

Proportions in early music often produced "irrational" groupings of notes (groupings not involving an exact doubling or tripling of the note value). The characteristic division of the beat in one voice might differ from that in another. For example, in the music of the *Ars subtilior,* three eighth-notes in the cantus might sound against two in the tenor, or four against three, five against two, or nine against four. Proportions create polymeters that may last for only a beat or two, or for several measures. They make it difficult for performers to stay together because the parts are in metrical conflict. Below are two passages from the *Ars subtilior* repertory typifying such moments of difficulty (Exs. 13-2a, 13-2b). They approach the limits of what vocal performers can execute.

EXAMPLE 13-2A   EXAMPLE 13-2B

In the music of the *Ars subtilior,* proportional changes are most often assigned to the cantus voice. To signal to the performer when to apply proportions, musicians introduced a host of new note-shapes. In his *Treatise on Note-Shapes,* Philippus de Caserta set forth several new notational forms (*figurae*). Example 13-3 shows first the standard note shapes of the *Ars nova* and then several new *figurae* of Caserta and his colleagues of the *Ars subtilior.*

EXAMPLE 13-3

Not surprisingly, these odd-looking shapes were never widely adopted. Instead, musicians soon began to indicate proportions by writing arabic numerals, such as $\frac{4}{3}$ or $\frac{5}{2}$, in the score. Nonetheless, these shapes reveal to what extremes musicians were willing to go in search of rhythmic novelty. They also suggest just how far musicians had come. In little more than a century, rhythm in Western music had progressed from the simple triple-meter patterns of the *Ars antiqua* music of Leoninus and Perotinus to the astonishing intricacies of the *Ars subtilior*.

SUMMARY

During the early fourteenth century, musicians of the *Ars nova* began to unleash the full potential of rhythm. They discovered that sounds might have many different durations and relationships, and that these could be used for expressive purposes. By 1350 there were six different note values (ranging from triple long to semiminim), and duple or triple relationships were possible among them all. Musicians pushed these rhythmic discoveries to greater lengths, ultimately creating the intricate rhythms and complex proportions of the *Ars subtilior*. Early on, in 1324, the Avignonese Pope John XXII inveighed against such rhythmic excesses (see Chapter 10). Yet, ironically, Avignon and the region around it soon became the center for rhythmic experimentation in music, as can be seen in the compositions of Baude Cordier and Philippus de Caserta. It was almost as if composers had found a new musical toy (rhythm) and were intent on driving their elders crazy with it. Indeed, at no time in the history of music before the twentieth century did composers go to such rhythmic extremes as during the late fourteenth century. Soon, having reached the practical limits of what is rhythmically performable, the avant-gard (*Ars subtilior*) of Western European music retreated. Composers began to do away with difficult syncopations and to employ simpler rhythms and textures and more sonorous harmonies. In these developments we see harbingers of a musical Renaissance.

KEY TERMS

Francesco Petrarch
Babylonian Captivity
Great Western Schism
Clementine Chapel
cappella

Baude Cordier
Ubi papa, ibi Roma
canon
Philippus de Caserta
polymeter

Ars subtilior
sincopa
proportions

Musical Interlude

From Medieval Manuscript to Modern Performance

When we listen to a piece of medieval music today, we are likely to think it sounds as it did during the Middle Ages. But how do we know? Surely the performers are doing their best to be faithful to the written score, but does that written document provide sufficient information to generate a faithful rendition of something seven hundred years old? In truth, the recordings we hear reflect a great deal of speculation by the modern editors and performers. Musicians today must make many more decisions when they engage the repertory of early music than they do when performing a symphony by Mahler or a ballet by Stravinsky, for example. The reason for this is easy to understand: the medieval manuscript contains only the barest of information. It is a mere sketch for a performance, and the farther back we go in music history, the more this is true.

Complicating things further is the fact that improvisation, and unwritten music generally, played an enormous role in the Middle Ages. Medieval culture was to a great extent an oral culture, not a visual one, as ours is. A teacher at a cathedral school in medieval France would read a prescribed text, and the pupil would memorize it orally and aurally. Only after the student had learned the entire text by ear (or by heart) would he be given a written version of it—the textbook—as a status symbol of his learned accomplishment. In medieval music, some entire repertories—organum and instrumental music, for example—grew out of a tradition, not of *a priori* composition as we know it, but the practice of spontaneous improvisation following various rules and procedures commonly accepted at that time. Today we, too, have entire repertories of music—jazz, much rock, hip-hop, funk, and rap— that involve traditions of spontaneous musical creation that use the ear but are not dependent on written notation.

As the Middle Ages unfolded, the growing complexity of the music caused more and more of it to be committed to a written format. More voices and a greater interdependence among them made it increasingly necessary to have a notated blueprint to keep everyone together. Consider the progress of medieval music: in the seventh century C.E. an important music theorist, Isidore of Seville, wrote: "Unless sounds are remembered by man, they perish, for they cannot be written down."[1] Yet two centuries later, monks and nuns had started to do just that—to capture and write down the melodies of the church (see Ex. 4-2). A basic staff was in place by the beginning of the eleventh century, and in the twelfth century churchmen devised a system to regulate and record rhythmic durations (see Ex. 8-1). By the fourteenth century, the heyday of Vitry, Machaut, and the *Ars subtilior,* a way to capture sounds not only existed but had also become enormously complicated, as we have seen (see Ex. 13-3 and Anthology, Nos. 35 and 36). This transition—from a completely oral music, and the belief that music could not be preserved, to the creation of complicated musical scores—is one of enormous importance and far-reaching implications. The composer gradually began to replace the improvising performer as the determinant force in a musical creation. As the centuries progressed, the composer gained more and more control over the way the music sounded. The dominance of the composer and a heavy dependence on a written score are two distinctive aspects of Western art music that separate it from the art music of other cultures around the world. These two distinctive Western characteristics first appeared during the Middle Ages.

Despite the increasing control of the composer and the growing importance of the written score, a medieval music manuscript is a far cry from our modern orchestral score, which contains various stylistic marks in virtually every measure. The medieval performer had to make decisions regarding a long list of musical elements, which were never notated. Medieval notation specified just pitch and duration, and even these only in a relative way. Following are listed the many elements that medieval performers had to regulate, which are also those that modern performers must confront in order to make early notated manuscripts come to life as sounding music.

PITCH

Pitch was the first element of music to be notated, and this occurred in the late ninth and early tenth centuries. Nevertheless, medieval pitch was only relative (the pitch of a written note was determined in relation to the pitch of other written notes). There was no such thing as absolute pitch. Indeed, an "international" standard for precise pitch was not finalized until the twentieth century. Medieval musicians simply transposed the music, whether plainchant or polyphony, secular or sacred, into a range that comfortably fit the voices and instruments at hand. Pieces 38 and 40 in the Anthology, for example, have been transposed by modern editors to make them easier to sing. Medieval musicians would have done this as well, just by singing and playing higher or lower at sight.

DURATION AND TEMPO

Similarly, medieval musicians developed a system to notate different rhythms in the twelfth century, but only for relative durations (how long this note is compared to that one). This system, however, said nothing about how long the notes should be. Presumably a long should be long and a breve short, but how long or how short? Not before 1496 did a music theorist (Gaffurius, *Practica musicae*) suggest any sort of absolute standard for duration, and even that wasn't very precise: the beat (then the semibreve) should go at the rate of the heartbeat of a person breathing normally. Composers did not begin to specify tempo markings until the seventeenth century, and even then they did so in an inexact way with terms such as *allegro* (fast) and *adagio* (slow). The ability to specify the exact duration of the beat (the tempo in music) came only with the advent of the metronome in the early nineteenth century.

VOLUME AND EXPRESSION

Here again indications for how loud or soft the music should be do not appear written into manuscripts and prints until the early seventeenth century. Expression marks such as "gravely" or "gaily" don't generally appear until the eighteenth. The medieval composer left it entirely to the performers to adjust the volume and shape the phrase to suit the demands of the music at any given moment.

PRONUNCIATION AND TEXT UNDERLAY

Needless to say, English, French, Italian, Spanish, and even Latin are not pronounced today as they were during the Middle Ages. Singers today need to study languages and perhaps work with a **philologist** (a scholar of early languages) to approximate a correct pronunciation of earlier texts. One key to correct pronunciation is the rhyming patterns within medieval poetry. Sometimes, too, the text is missing from a part in a vocal piece, often the alto or tenor. Does this mean that the part is to be played on an instrument, or rather that the scribe assumed the performer would insert the text in the untexted voice? That depends on local scribal practices. For Anthology, No. 38, for example, a literary account says that the upper two parts were sung, but the only surviving manuscript to preserve the piece has no text in the lower of these two voices (the alto). Thus we have supplied the text for the alto part, allocating the syllables according to the example of other texted pieces of this period and region.

ORNAMENTATION

Given the importance of improvisation in the music of the Middle Ages and Renaissance, it is not surprising that medieval musicians added embellishment to the notated music. Should not modern performers do the same? For an idea of the sort of ornamentation that instrumentalists added, compare the beginning of the vocal version of Jacopo da Bologna's *Non al suo amante* (Anthology No. 37) with a slightly later written instrumental version of it, also from Italy (Exs. 1-1a, 1-1b). Again, the instrument on which the ornamented version is to be played is not specified in the manuscript; rather, the choice is left to the performer.

EXAMPLE 1-1A

EXAMPLE 1-1B

ACCIDENTALS (ADDING *MUSICA FICTA*)

Not only did medieval performers have to supply their own ideas about tempo, dynamics, expression, pitch, and many other things but they also sometimes had to insert accidentals into the written score. Sometimes the composer (or scribe) wrote in all the accidentals, sometimes not. It was up to the performer, and now the modern editor, to supply missing accidentals according to various rules of music theory of the period. Notice in the preceding example how a B♭ is provided in the vocal version, but not in the instrumental one. In the latter case flats have been added by the modern editor, as indicated by the fact that they are written above the note, not before it. Two melodic rules require the B♭ here. The first is simple: wherever possible, perfect consonances such as the fourth should be kept perfect (hence the F-B ambitus of the melody requires a B♭). Second and more complex: a melodic line in which the hexachord is exceeded by only the step above "la" in the Guidonian system should always be sung as a half-step (thus here in a melody in the natural hexachord a B♭ is required).

Other rules for adding accidentals emerged from the growing awareness of counterpoint and voice leading during the fourteenth century. Indeed, our term **counter-**

point begins to appear at this time and is derived from the Latin expression *punctus contra punctum* (one note moving against another note). When writing for two or more voices, certain intervals were to be avoided. The augmented octave and the tritone, for example, were proscribed; in fact, the disagreeable tritone eventually came to be known as the ***diabolus in musica*** (the devil in music). Other intervals were highly desirable at certain moments in contrapuntal part writing. The aim was to have the voices get as close as possible to the most common perfect intervals, which at this point in history were the unison, fifth, and octave. At cadences, for example, thirds moving to fifths were to be major thirds, and sixths moving to octaves should be major sixths. To make these thirds and sixths major usually required the insertion of accidentals by the performers. Such accidentals, with the exception of B♭, were not to be found on the limited medieval scale as developed by Guido of Arezzo (see Chapter 4). Because these accidentals were theoretically "off the scale" and had to be imagined, they were called ***musica ficta*** (false music), as opposed to the notes on the medieval scale, which were called *musica recta* (correct music).

Recall that the earlier Guidonian system made use of three hexachords: the natural starting on C, the soft on F with a B♭, and the hard on G with a B♮ (Chapter 4). Thus in Guido's eleventh-century scale, B♭ was the only allowable chromatic note. Now, in the early fourteenth century, musicians began to place hexachords on pitches other than C, F, and G. By starting on other pitches, but keeping the interval pattern of the hexachord intact (1, 1, 1/2, 1, 1), they produced other accidentals such as F♯, C♯, and E♭. By 1375 a fully chromatic keyboard was in place. Nevertheless, because all chromatic notes other than B♭ were new additions to the system, they still were considered false, or *ficta*, notes.

To see how *musica ficta* works, consider the final cadence of the first *Kyrie* of Machaut's *Mass of Our Lady* (Ex. 1-2). The *ficta* C♯ in the bass in the first measure (bar 25) should be added by the performers so as to avoid an augmented octave with the C♯ that Machaut wrote in the alto voice. The *ficta* C♯ in the alto in measure two (bar 26) was also placed in the manuscript by Machaut, yet the *ficta* G♯ in the bass and in the soprano should be added by the performers for two reasons: to avoid a tritone and to make the third expanding to a fifth a major third. Music theorists said that voices should be "less distant from that location which they intend immediately to reach."[2] Accordingly, the G♯ and C♯ change a minor third and minor sixth to a major third and major sixth, and thus make these voices closer to the notes A and D they intend to reach in the final D-A-D chord. They thereby form what is called a **double leading-tone cadence,** here in the Dorian mode. Double leading-tone cadences create the biting, pungent sound characteristic of much fourteenth-century music.

EXAMPLE 1-2

✺ PREPARING A SCORE

Throughout this book the term "score" refers simply to polyphony in written notation. In a strict sense, however, "score" should be applied only to written notation in which the various parts are superimposed on one another. Medieval music was rarely written in score in the strict sense. Instead, to save space and valuable parchment, the parts were simply copied in succession; there was no attempt to align them vertically. By the late Middle Ages, the tradition had evolved whereby the music manuscript was opened and the soprano voice placed on the upper left, alto or tenor on the bottom left, alto or tenor on the upper right, and bass on the bottom right. Such a layout, particularly common for religious music, is called **choirbook format.** Below is a diplomatic facsimile (a reconstruction) of the original notation of the beginning of the *Sanctus* of Machaut's *Mass of Our Lady* set forth in choirbook format and then in a modern transcription (Ex. 1-3). Notice that neither the meter signature nor the bar lines were included in the original. Adding them likely helps the modern performer, but it may also create a more rhythmically "square" performance than Machaut intended. These are the sorts of issues the modern performer must engage when coming to terms with medieval music.

EXAMPLE 1-3

In sum, the relationship between the performer and the written artifact (the musical score) is very different now from what it was in the Middle Ages. Today a pianist can pick up a score of the Chopin études or a violinist can open the Brahms violin sonatas and play the music pretty much as the composer intended—because the composer provided most of the essential information. When dealing with early music, however, the performer needs to know so much more, because the composer provided so much less. Today it is not enough to be simply a performer of early music, you must also be something of a **musicologist** (a scholar of music).

KEY TERMS

philologist	*musica ficta*	choirbook format
counterpoint	double leading-tone	musicologist
diabolus in musica	cadence	

THE LATE MIDDLE AGES AND EARLY RENAISSANCE

*H*istory passes continuously through time. To make sense of it, historians have invented terms such as "Middle Ages" and "Renaissance" to divide this ceaseless continuum into shorter, more manageable units. Yet, needless to say, the arts do not change from one style to another all at once. For example, what we call the "Renaissance" (a period of "rebirth") began at different times at different places. While there are signs of a renaissance in Italy by 1350, there is little evidence of a cultural rebirth in France before 1500, and England did not see much of a reawakening before 1550.

1300	1350	1400	1450

MIDDLE AGES (–1450)	RENAISSANCE (1350–1600)

- **Trecento: Century of the 1300s in which the arts flourished in Italy**
- **c1300 Summer Canon, using rondellus technique and circular canon**

Antoine Busnoys

● 1440

Francesco Petrarch (1304–1374) popularizes the madrigal as a poetic form

Babylonian Captivity (1309–1403)

Jacopo da Bologna (c1310–c1386) gives musical accompaniment to madrigals

Joan of Arc executed 1431

Francesco Landini (c1325–1397), most important composer of the trecento

Hundred Years' War (1337–1453)

◆ **1350 Giovanni Boccaccio's *Decameron***

Christine de Pisan (c1364–c1430) writes the text of Binchois's chanson *Dueil angoisseus*

Filippo Brunelleschi (1377–1446) designs the dome of Florence Cathedral

Great Western Schism (1378–1417)

John Dunstaple (c1390–1453), composer, astronomer,

Guillaume Dufay (c1397–1474), principal

Gilles Binchois (c1400–1460), singer and

Johannes Ockeghem (c1410–1497),

Henry V of England (r. 1413–1422)

Antonio Squarcialupi (1416–

● 1420s Old Hall

King Charles VII

1300s, Oxford University established

Francesco Petrarch (1304–1374), popularizes madrigal as poetic form

Similarly, the styles we associate with the Renaissance appear in the different arts at different times. Art historians would say that the Renaissance began in painting during the 1330s. Literary historians would argue that it commenced with the humanistic efforts of the poet Francesco Petrarch (see timeline) around 1350, while musicologists would suggest that in music many qualities of Renaissance style do not show themselves before the 1420s. In truth, during the early Renaissance (1350–1475), music did not experience a wholesale rebirth, but it did change dramatically. Thirds and sixths became primary consonant intervals, dissonance is more carefully regulated, and voices begin to work together in harmonious imitation. These are just a few of the important stylistic changes that music experienced while her sister arts underwent a reawakening.

1450	1500	1550	1600

(c1435–1492), important composer

Martin Le Franc, French poet, confirms Dunstaple's continental influence

Philippe Basiron (c1449–1491), composer and singer at king's Sainte-Chapelle in Bourges

◆ May 29, 1453, Ottoman Turks defeat the Byzantine Christians and capture Constantinople

Jacob Obrecht (1457/8–1505), master of the multiple cantus firmus Mass

Louis XI of France (r. 1461–1483)

◆ 1477 Charles the Bold, last duke of Burgundy, killed at Battle of Nancy

● c1483 Trumpets and shawms permitted at church services in Bruges

● c1500 Cornett joins the wind band

● 1500 *La Spagna (The Spanish Tune)* is widely popular

1507–1530 Margaret of Austria (1480–1530) serves as official regent of the Low Countries

and mathematician

musician for the pope and the dukes of Burgundy

composer at the court of Burgundy

composer for the French royal court

1480), organist at the cathedral of Florence

Manuscript, large collection of English polyphony

of France (r. 1429–1461)

Chapter 14

Music in Florence, 1350–1450

What city, not merely in Italy, but in all the world, is more securely placed within its circle of walls, more proud in its palazzi, more bedecked with churches, more beautiful in its architecture, more imposing in its gates, richer in piazzas, happier in its wide streets, greater in its people, more glorious in its citizenry and more inexhaustible in wealth.[1]

Thus said humanist Coluccio Salutati of Florence in 1403. Even today, no city in the world has more great art per square foot than Florence. Stunning frescoes, paintings, sculptures, enamels, and fine pieces of jewelry attract millions of tourists annually. What is more, although many treasures remain in Florence today, this local patrimony is only a small fraction of what the city once produced; art museums around the world have their galleries of "early Renaissance art" filled with works drawn primarily from Florence and the surrounding region of Tuscany. Giotto, Donatello, Masaccio, Brunelleschi, Botticelli, Leonardo da Vinci, and Michelangelo are only a few of the painters, sculptors, and architects who graced Florence between 1320 and 1490. What caused this extraordinary artistic florescence? Among the stimulants were social mobility between classes, municipal support for the arts, and competition, both between individual artists and between cities.

Florence was an independent **city-state,** a city that governed itself and the territory immediately around it (Map 14-1). While France and England were ruled by kings during the fourteenth century, there was no such central authority in Italy (nor would there be until the nineteenth century; see Chapter 56). Northern Italian

✿ MAP 14-1
Renaissance Italy.

cities, among them Milan, Pisa, Ferrara, Venice, Siena, and Florence, controlled their own destinies. Most were ruled by despots. Florence, however, was a republic. Its citizens elected the government, established rules of commerce, and hired an army. By 1340, 100,000 people lived within the high city walls, though 40,000 of these would perish during the Black Death of 1348. Florentine society was not rigidly hierarchical, as was generally true elsewhere in the Middle Ages. No sections of the city were reserved for the rich, no ghettoes inhabited solely by the poor. Individuals of talent could move freely among all classes. Thus physicians conversed with architects, and musicians dined with wealthy bankers. A growing pride in civic accomplishment, and a new emphasis on individual achievement marked Florence and the early Renaissance generally.

✸ TRECENTO MUSIC AND THE SQUARCIALUPI CODEX

Florentine pride and respect for individual creativity can clearly be seen in the sumptuous **Squarcialupi Codex,** a music manuscript containing 354 compositions (Fig. 14-1). Its large size, rich colors, and brilliant gold leaf typify the tradition of Florentine excellence in the arts and crafts. Copied about 1415, the Squarcialupi Codex is a retrospective anthology of music important in Florence during the **trecento** (short for *mille trecento,* or the century of the 1300s) in which the arts flourished. It derives its name from one of its first owners, Antonio Squarcialupi (1416–1480), organist at the cathedral of Florence. All the songs included here are settings of Italian texts, for during the trecento this vernacular tongue emerged as a major literary and poetic language. Some pieces are monophonic, some for two voices, and others for three. Together they represent the sum total of the written song repertory of trecento Florence.

Biblioteca Medicea Laurenziana

※ FIGURE 14-1

A page of the Squarcialupi Codex showing the blind organist Francesco Landini playing the organ and the music of his ballata *Musica son.*

The compositions preserved within the Squarcialupi Codex belong to one of three musical genres: the madrigal, the caccia, and the ballata. These are the Italian *formes fixes.* The fourteenth-century **madrigal** was originally a poem in the vernacular tongue (Italian, not Latin) to which music was added for greater emotional effect. The poem, usually about love, consists of two (sometimes three) three-line stanzas followed by a two-line **ritornello** (refrain). It was Petrarch who elevated and popularized the madrigal as a poetic form. By the mid fourteenth century his madrigals were given musical accompaniment by composers working in northern Italy, among them Jacopo da Bologna.

Jacopo da Bologna (c1310–c1386) took Petrarch's madrigal text *Non al suo amante* (*Not to her lover*) and set it in typical madrigal style for two voices. The text consists of two three-line units, each sung to the same music, followed by a ritornello. Thus the musical form of this and all trecento madrigals is **AAB.** Rhythmically, the voices in Jacopo's madrigal are rather square, even mechanical; section **A,** for example, has not a single instance of syncopation, as frequently found in the contemporary songs of Machaut, for example. However, lyricism abounds in the florid upper voice, which begins and ends each line with a melisma. If the Italians are not concerned with rhythmic complexities, they are nevertheless enamored with long, almost sensual, musical lines. Typical of the madrigal, here the ritornello is in a different musical meter from that of the preceding stanzas ($\frac{3}{4}$ instead of $\frac{4}{4}$). Petrarch, as was his custom, concludes this madrigal poem with a vivid image, allowing composer Jacopo da Bologna to underscore it through a change to triple meter. Their madrigal ends with a lovely oxymoron: the lover experiences a shiver of passion in the heat of the noonday sun.

EXAMPLE 14-1

Non al suo amante più Diana piacque	**A**	Not to her lover did Diana ever more please
Quando per tal ventura tutta ignuda		As when, through good fortune,
La vidi in mezzo de le gelide acque.		He saw her naked in the midst of the cool waters.
Ch'a me la pastorell'alpestre e cruda,	**A**	As did please me the cruel shepherdess,
Posta a bagnar un leggiadretto velo,		Washing her white veil, which protects
Ch'a l'aura il vago e biondo capel chiuda.		Her fine blond hair from blowing free.
(ritornello)	**B**	
Tal che mi fece quand'egli arde 'l cielo,		Thus it made me, now when the sky is fiery,
Tutto tremar d'un amoroso gielo.		All tremble with the chill of love.

🎵 LISTENING CUE

JACOPO DA BOLOGNA
Non al suo amante (c1350)
(text by Francesco Petrarch)

CD 2/7
Anthology, No. 37

The caccia and the ballata constitute the two other genres of secular music in trecento Italy. A **caccia** is a piece involving a musical canon in the upper two voices supported by a slower moving tenor. In Italian, *caccia* means "hunt," and many of the texts recreate vivid hunting scenes. For example, an archer may chase a doe through a wooded landscape, accompanied by musical shouts, and perhaps hocket. Often such texts are merely allegories of an amatory pursuit, as the lover pursues the beloved. The canonic quality of the upper voices exemplifies the process of the hunt, one voice chasing after the other at an exact interval of pitch and time.

As the name suggests (from the Italian *ballare*, to dance) the **ballata** was a dance song with a choral refrain. Its musical and poetic form is very similar to the French virelai: **A** (ripresa) **b** (piede) **b** (piede) **a** (volta) **A** (ripresa). The terms *piede* (foot), *volta* (turn) and **ripresa** (refrain) recall the origins of the ballata as a monophonic dance. The Florentine composer Francesco Landini was the first to write two- and three-voice ballatas. During the second half of the trecento, the ballata replaced the madrigal as the most popular Italian musical genre. Landini has left us thirteen madrigals and only one caccia, but 140 ballatas.

✿ FRANCESCO LANDINI

By all standards, Francesco Landini (c1325–1397) was the most important composer of the trecento. As a child he was blinded by smallpox. To compensate, he developed his aural faculties, becoming proficient on a number of string, wind, and keyboard instruments. In time he also became a leading Florentine intellectual, a respected authority on politics, religion, ethics, and even astronomy. Sometime during the 1360s the king of Cyprus crowned Landini poet laureate, thereby acknowledging his excellence in verse as well as music. Thus, in his portrait in the Squarcialupi Codex (see Fig. 14-1) Landini wears the laurel wreath around his cap. In his hands he holds a portative organ, the instrument on which he excelled above all others. From 1365 until his death Landini was organist at the church of San Lorenzo in the center of Florence. It was here that he was buried in 1397, and here that his tombstone can be seen today.

The society that enjoyed Landini's music is described in two important literary works, Giovanni Boccaccio's *Decameron,* which recreates events in Florence in 1348, and Giovanni da Prato's *Il Paradiso,* set in 1389. The *Decameron* is a collection of one hundred short stories, told by ten persons over the course of ten days. Music, and the women who make it, play an important role in these novellas (see Box). Giovanni da Prato's *Il Paradiso* is a similar collection of stories told by a group of Florentine intellectuals who gather in the homes of leading citizens. Francesco Landini is among the guests, and is introduced by da Prato with the following words:

> At that time, wondrous to recount, still flourished Francesco of the Organs, a theorist and practical musician. Blind almost since birth, he showed himself to be of such divine intellect that in all the most abstract aspects of music he understood the most subtle proportions of musical numbers, and realized them with such sweetness on his organ that it seemed unbelievable even when one heard it. Moreover, he discussed with every artist and philosopher not only his music but also all the liberal arts because he was knowlegible [sic] in all of them.[2]

As was the custom, the circle of friends moves to a garden where Landini, like the other guests, is asked to tell a story. When he has finished, two young ladies step forward to sing a ballata he composed:

> And soon with the approval of all, and especially the musician Francesco himself, two young ladies began to sing a ballata to the accompaniment of Biagio di Sernello, with such grace and angelic voices that not a single man or woman was unmoved; and soon the birds, up among the cypresses, came near and imitated the singing with even greater sweetness. The words of the ballata are these: *Or su, gentili spiriti* [sic].[3]

This eyewitness description shows that the upper two parts of Landini's ballata were sung by young women, while a gentleman sang the tenor or played that line on an instrument. Other accounts demonstrate that instruments such as the vielle and lute might accompany, or even replace, one or more voices. The poem that

Landini set is likely his own, and its high quality suggests that he well merited the title "poet laureate" bestowed upon him by the king of Cypress.

EXAMPLE 14-2

(ripresa) Or su, gentili spirti, ad amar pronti,	A	Come now, gentle spirits, ready to love,
Volete voi vedere 'l Paradiso?		Do you want to see Paradise?
Mirate d'esta petra 'l vago viso.		Admire the beautiful face of this [precious] stone.
(piede) Nelle sue luce sancte ard' e sfavilla	b	Victorious love burns and glows
Amor victorioso, che divampa		In her holy eyes, which inflames he who
Per dolcezza di gloria chi la mira.		Gazes upon her through the sweetness of glory.
(piede) Ma l'alma mia, fedelissima ancilla	b	But my soul, most faithful helpmate,
Piatà non trova in questa chiara lampa		Finds no pity in this clear light,
E null'altro che lei ama o disira.		Nor does it love or desire anything else than her.
(volta) O sacra iddea, al tuo servo un po' spira	a	O holy image, to your servant show some
Mercé; mercé sol chiamo, già conquiso:		Mercy; already conquered, mercy I alone ask:
Dé, fallo pria che morte m'abbia anciso.		Come, do this before death kills me.
(ripresa) Or su, gentili spirti. . . .	A	Come now, gentle spirits. . . .

Landini's *Or su, gentili spirti* demonstrates several stylistic features of late-trecento music. The principal vocal line is still the cantus, but now this part is more fluid, rhythmically less rigid, than in earlier trecento music. Evidently, Landini was much influenced by the French *Ars nova*. Syncopations occur frequently and sometimes run across the bar line. Primitive-sounding parallel fifths are still present. Yet parallel thirds and sixths appear in greater abundance, lending to the music a sweeter sound typical of the emerging Renaissance. At cadences, the sixth in the outer voices expands to an octave. Landini liked to ornament these cadences by adding a lower neighbor-tone to the upper part as it moves up to the octave. So prevalent is this cadential gesture in his music that it has come to be called the **Landini cadence.** The final cadence of *Or su, gentili spirti* has both syncopation in the cantus

Women Making Music in Boccaccio's *Decameron*

Giovanni Boccaccio was inspired to write his *Decameron* by the horrific events of 1348, when "into the distinguished Florence, more noble than any Italian city, came a deadly pestilence."[4] Like all Florentines, Boccaccio suffered greatly from the Black Death, but he survived, thanks to the assistance of several woman friends. To repay their kindness, he determined to create a set of stories that would center around women. Thus was born *Decameron*, a work of fiction in which a group of wealthy young Florentines briefly escape to the Tuscan hills. Their life of idyllic beauty in the countryside contrasts sharply with the city below that is festering with the plague. *Decameron* means "ten days," and Boccaccio's book is a collection of one hundred stories, told over ten days by ten persons, each day's activities concluding with a ballata that is both sung and danced. Seven of the ten characters are women. They sing ballatas, play musical instruments, and lead the dancing (Fig. 14-2). Indeed, to judge from the *Decameron* and other contemporary writings, women predominated in the performance of secular songs and dances throughout the trecento.

But women were not taught to be composers, partly because they were not given instruction in musical notation. A lady could learn by rote to sing and play an instrument such as the vielle, psaltery, or harp, or to dance. But in the Middle Ages musical notation was written in arcane symbols and explained in a language that remained the preserve of the church. All medieval music theory treatises were written in Latin, which women generally did not study. Nor were women allowed to enroll in the university—neither in church-controlled universities such as that in Paris nor in municipally supported ones such as in Florence. Conse-

quently, they were deprived, among other things, of the study of ethics and moral philosophy. Boccaccio says that his *Decameron* intends to correct this inequity. A moral can be drawn from each of his one hundred tales, as well as from the texts of his ten ballatas that conclude each day, and, from these, women can learn the ways of the world. In this fashion, Boccaccio says, "I will make up in part the wrong done [to women] by Fortune."[5]

Bibliothèque Nationale, Paris

FIGURE 14-2

Queen Pampinea in the garden in an illustrated copy of *Decameron*. The women dance; the men watch.

and a Landini cadence. As you can see, the first line of Landini's text invites the participants to enjoy love and thereby experience Paradise, the general theme of Giovanni da Prato's *Il Paradiso*.

EXAMPLE 14-3

LISTENING CUE

FRANCESCO LANDINI
Or su, gentili spirti (c1389)

CD 2/8
Anthology, No. 38

SUMMARY

The polyphonic music created in Florence and other northern Italian cities during the trecento consists mainly of secular songs, a total of more than six hundred madrigals, caccias, and ballatas. The majority of these are preserved in a single manuscript, the Squarcialupi Codex, a compendium assembled in Florence about 1415. Almost all songs set texts written in Italian, which emerges in this period as an important literary and poetic language. Trecento music has rhythms that are more regular than the French music of this period. At the same time, it often luxuriates in long melismas for the soprano or uppermost voice at the end of lines of text. By the end of the century, however, some French influences—specifically greater syncopation, and first and second endings—can be seen in the ballata. The repertory culminates in the three-voice ballatas of Francesco Landini, which combine Italian lyricism with French rhythmic subtlety. Simultaneous thirds and sixths (6/3 chords) become more frequent in Landini's music, especially at cadences. These create a sonority that will become basic to the music of the emerging Renaissance: parallel 6/3 chords. In addition, the overwhelmingly secular nature of the repertory suggests that the focus of composers is turning away from religious music to music for purely human pleasure, recreation, and delight. In this more secular, less sacred world can be seen the beginnings of musical humanism—music not offered solely to God, but made by humans to be enjoyed by humans.

KEY TERMS

city-state	ritornello	Landini cadence
Squarcialupi Codex	caccia	Giovanni Boccaccio
trecento	ballata	*Decameron*
madrigal	ripresa	

Chapter

15

Music at the Cathedral of Florence

Like the Colosseum in Rome, the cathedral of Florence (Fig. 15-1) serves as a cultural icon for all of Italy. When the gigantic dome was finished in 1436, the authorities in Florence called upon a Frenchman, not a native Italian, to create new music for the ceremony of dedication. They did so in part because Italy had no strong tradition of large-scale polyphonic church music. Italian sacred music during the Middle

Ages and early Renaissance was overwhelmingly monophonic Gregorian chant, the age-old music of the Western Church. By the early fifteenth century a few polyphonic Masses and motets began to appear in Italian music manuscripts. But most of these were the work of French and English composers, not native Italians. Just as Gothic architecture was brought down to Italy from France in this period, so too musicians and musical genres, such as the isorhythmic motet, were imported from the north.

Among the northern musicians who came to Italy in this period was Guillaume Dufay (c1397–1474), a native of the region of Cambrai in northern France. (His name should be pronounced with three syllables "Du-fa-y" for in his day it rhymed with the French word "me-lo-die.") During the 1420s and 1430s Dufay served a number of patrons, working his way up to become the pope's **magister cappellae** (leader of the chapel). During the summer of 1434, Pope Eugenius IV and his court were chased from Rome by unruly mobs and took up residence in Florence. Thus it was convenient for the citizens of Florence to call upon their pope and his principal musician, Dufay, to celebrate the completion of the cathedral of Florence in 1436.

The dome of the cathedral of Florence is one of the architectural wonders of the Western world. The citizens of fifteenth-century Florence planned to construct a church with an enormous dome that would loom large as testimony to the glory and power of their republic. But no dome this size had been constructed since Roman times. The challenge was to build a colossal structure that would go upward and then progressively inward, but not collapse, and do so without supports. (At Notre Dame of Paris, and all other Gothic churches, the high vaults were built above a wooden scaffold that supported them from beneath; then, when the mortar of the vaults had dried, the scaffold was removed.) But no trees were large enough to go across the expanse planned for the dome of Florence (140 feet across), and steel beams did not exist. To solve this engineering problem, the Florentine architect **Filippo Brunelleschi** (1377–1446) went to Rome to study the ancient Pantheon. Using the secrets of classical architecture, he then built for the Florentines a dome with a double shell, the inner shell lightening the load of the outer one. Further, he contained the outward thrust of the bricks by tying them together with bands of stones linked together by iron rings.

On the morning of 25 March 1436, the pope and the citizens of Florence gathered to celebrate Brunelleschi's accomplishment. To make the ceremony more splendid, Guillaume Dufay composed a motet, *Nuper rosarum flores* (*Recently roses*). Because this was a solemn state occasion, Dufay chose to make it an isorhythmic motet, creating one of the last pieces in this medieval genre; throughout history composers have made use of old-fashioned, conservative musical styles for ceremonial and state occasions.

Dufay built his motet upon the opening phrase of a chant, *Terribilis est locus iste* (*This is a redoubtable place*), the Introit of the Mass for the dedication of a church. This melody resounds with double force because two tenors sing the notes of the chant, tenor I a fifth lower than tenor II. Both melody and rhythm in the tenors are stated four times, once in each of the four sections of the motet. Each of these sections begins with a duet in the upper two voices and to these the two tenor parts are

CORBIS

✿ FIGURE 15-1

The cathedral of Florence with its giant dome designed by Filippo Brunelleschi was dedicated in 1436.

soon joined. In medieval notation each section is twenty-eight longs in length (twenty-eight double whole-notes, i.e., twenty-eight bars in modern notation). Mensuration signs (medieval time signatures) control the length of each section. In Section I the long lasts for six semibreves (six half-notes in modern notation), in Section II for four, in Section III for two, and in Section IV for three. Thus the four sections unfold with a durational ratio of 6:4:2:3.

I	II	III	IV
Duet then	Duet then	Duet then	Duet then
four voices	four voices	four voices	four voices
28 × 6 half-notes	28 × 4 half-notes	28 × 2 half-notes	28 × 3 half-notes

But there are more numbers at work in Dufay's motet. Each section consists of fourteen bars of two-voice and fourteen bars of four-voice music. The two tenors each sing the same fourteen notes of the chant in each of the four sections. The motet text, which speaks of the dedication of the church, consists of four stanzas each of seven lines and each line has seven syllables. The numbers 1, 2, 4, 7, 14, and 28 inform the entire motet. Thus, *Nuper rosarum flores* is no less architectonic (constructed by a master builder) than the architecture of the cathedral.

In fact, *Nuper rosarum flores* mirrors the proportions of the cathedral. The cathedral of Florence was built according to a measurement called the *braccio* (a length of about 22 inches, or an arm's length, from the Italian word for "arm"). The nave of the church is 72 *braccia* wide (outside wall to outside wall), 72 *braccia* long, and 72 *braccia* high. Brunelleschi's dome, moreover, is 72 *braccia* in diameter and 2 × 72 (144) *braccia* high. The numbers basic to Dufay's motet, 6, 4, 2, 3, when multiplied, also equal 144. Dufay's motet is the only piece by a major composer in the history of music to attempt to replicate the proportions of a building through sound.[1]

We estimate that some 20,000 citizens of Florence crowded into their new cathedral on the day of its consecration. Did they hear the intended unity of music and architecture as they listened to Dufay's motet under Brunelleschi's magnificent dome? Did they sense any of the other musical symbolism inherent in this music (see Box)? Perhaps not. The steady stream of small note values and the unequal distribution of the text obscure the changing proportions among the four sections. Meaning in early music often lurks unseen or unheard beneath the surface, accessible only to an intellectual few. What apparently struck the people of Florence was the grand sonorities of the music. Here is what one eye-witness said of the music that day:

> All the places of the Temple resounded with the sounds of harmonious symphonies [of voices] as well as the concords of diverse instruments, so that it seemed not without reason that the angels and the sounds and singing of divine paradise had been sent from heaven to us on earth to insinuate in our ears a certain incredible divine sweetness.[2]

This "incredible divine sweetness" may refer to the new sonorities of Dufay's motet. *Nuper rosarum flores* has none of the dissonant parallel seconds and sevenths of fourteenth-century music. Gone, too, are all antiquated parallel fifths and octaves. (Here in the early fifteenth century music theorists decree for the first time that perfect intervals should not come one after the other in direct succession.) Moreover, intervals are now carefully regulated so that dissonance does not occur on a strong beat, but rather off the beat in some sort of passing fashion. Any dissonance that does fall on the beat is carefully prepared and resolved. In this motet of the late Middle Ages and early Renaissance we see the rules of counterpoint and good part-writing beginning to take shape.

Musical Number Symbolism

Meaning in music of the Middle Ages and Renaissance was conveyed as much through **number symbolism** as it was through overt explanation. Numbers came to possess rich theological associations. Christ was represented by 8 and, by extension, 888; Satan by 666, according to the Book of Revelation; the Virgin Mary by 7, because of her seven sorrows, seven joys, seven acts of mercy, seven virginal companions, and seven years of exile in Egypt; the temple by 4 and 7 because of its four cornerstones and seven pillars of wisdom; the Trinity by 3; and so forth. Silent, unseen numbers informed all of God's creations, including Dufay's motet.

Dufay chose the structural proportions 6:4:2:3 to mirror not only the cathedral of Florence but also the ancient temple of Solomon in Jerusalem, the prototype and spiritual authority of all churches throughout Christendom. The Bible (I Kings: 6) tells us that Solomon's temple measured 60 cubits in length (divided into 40 and 20 cubits for the nave and sanctuary, respectively) by 20 cubits in width and 30 cubits in height. It was begun in the fourth year of Solomon's reign and took seven years to complete. The service of dedication occurred in the seventh month of the seventh year and required twice seven days.

In *Nuper rosarum flores*, Dufay has wedded the symbolic numbers of the biblical temple to those of the Virgin, to whom the cathedral of Florence was dedicated. He thereby created a perfect union, one centering around 28, the number inherent in the four sections of his motet. Since ancient times, 28 was recognized as a perfect number ($1 \times 28 = 2 \times 14 = 4 \times 7$; $1 + 2 + 4 + 7 + 14 = 28$).

We may not hear any of this number symbolism, but that is how the intellectuals of the Middle Ages and Renaissance understood the world, how they perceived the theological concepts of the universal church and the Virgin. The numbers were embedded in the music and that was all that mattered. Early music often conveys meaning through abstractions rather than overt, mimetic expression. Yet some twentieth-century composers also engaged in number symbolism. For a discussion of the "Golden Section" in the music of Béla Bartók, see the Box in Chapter 71.

Finally, Dufay graces his motet with abundant thirds and sixths (Ex. 15-1). Parallel sixths, for example, often form the structural backbone of the piece. In addition, the composer frequently places the third of a chord in the soprano voice to give it prominence. In the final chord of the piece he ends on a third, as if to say "I like this new sound," but then moves away to a more traditional ending with an open-fifth chord. Not for another seventy years would composers actually finish with the sweeter-sounding third. Last of all, notice such important phrases as "the temple, majestic in its engineering" and "this same most enormous temple." Here Dufay requires the alto part to divide, thereby momentarily creating a richly sonorous five-voice texture. This is truly a grand motet for what was and remains the largest dome in the pre-modern world.

EXAMPLE 15-1

Section I: 28 × 6 half-notes

(Two voices) Nuper rosarum flores	Recently roses given by the pope
Ex dono pontificis	Have not ceased to adorn,
Hieme licet horrida,	Cruel winter having past,
Tibi, virgo celica,	The Temple,
Pie et sancte deditum	Majestic in its engineering,
(Four voices) Grandis templum machinae	Dedicated to the Virgin
Condecorarunt perpetim.	In piety and holiness.
Hodie vicarius	Today the vicar
Jesu Christi et Petri	Of Jesus Christ and successor
Successor Eugenius	Of Peter, Eugenius,
Hoc idem amplissimum	This same most enormous Temple
Sacris templum manibus	With sacred hands
Sanctisque liquoribus	And holy oils

Section II: 28 × 4 half-notes

(Two voices) Consecrare dignatus est.	Has deigned to consecrate.
Igitur, alma parens	Therefore, sweet parent
Nati tui et filia	And daughter of your son,
Virgo decus virginum,	God, virgin of virgins,
(Four voices) Tuus te Florentiae	To you your devoted
Devotus orat populus	Populace of Florence petitions
Ut qui mente et corpore	So that whoever begs for something,
Mundo quicquam exorarit,	With pure spirit and body,

Section III: 28 × 2 half-notes

(Two voices) Oratio-	May, by
(Four voices) ne tua	your prayer
Cruciatus et meritis	And the merits,
Tui secundum carnem	Owing to his carnal torment,

Section IV: 28 × 3 half-notes

(Two voices) Nati domini sui	Of your son, their lord,
(Four voices) Grata beneficia	Be worthy to receive
Veniamque reatum	Gracious benefits and
Accipere mereatur.	Forgiveness of sins.
(Four voices) Amen.	Amen.

LISTENING CUE

GUILLAUME DUFAY
Nuper rosarum flores (1436)

CD 2/9
Anthology, No. 39

SUMMARY

The early fifteenth century is a period of gradual transition between the Middle Ages and the Renaissance that is revealed in painting, architecture, and music. The architect Filippo Brunelleschi, for example, went to Rome to study structural designs from classical antiquity, and he used these to create a renaissance in architecture, specifically at the cathedral of Florence. But only half of the cathedral of

Florence is Renaissance in style. The nave of the church was constructed during the fourteenth century in the older Gothic-style architecture. Thus art historians say that the west half of the church (the nave) is medieval and the east half (the choir covered by the dome) is Renaissance in style. So too Dufay's motet *Nuper rosarum flores* has qualities of the old and the new. It is medieval in the sense that the composer builds upon the older framework of isorhythmic structure and uses medieval number symbolism. The motet is of the Renaissance, however, in that Dufay embraces the sweeter sounds of thirds and sixths, avoids parallel fifths and octaves, and carefully controls all dissonances. Significantly, the final cadential phrase "Amen" (mm. 169–170) is added on to, and lies beyond, the medieval isorhythmic structure. This powerful final moment of choral homophony points most clearly toward the newer, more richly sonorous harmonies of the Renaissance.

KEY TERMS

magister cappellae	Filippo Brunelleschi	number symbolism

Music in England

Before the fifteenth century, England had no single great musical figure, like Guillaume de Machaut in France or Francesco Landini in Italy. Nor were there any English cities with a population of more than 10,000 except London (Map 16-1), which in 1300 counted 75,000 souls, about a third of the number in Paris at this time. England was fundamentally a rural society. About ninety percent of its six million inhabitants were engaged in one way or another in agriculture. They worked the lands of the lords or those of the church. Monasteries exerted an especially strong presence in this rural environment. Thus English music written during the thirteenth and fourteenth centuries consists mostly of compositions for monastic communities. Almost all pieces are anonymous—religious music written by nameless monks who lived and died in the service of the church.

From the moment Frenchman William the Conqueror seized England in 1066 until the early fifteenth century, the kings of England spoke French at their court. French culture dominated English high society in other ways as well. French-born and French-educated clerics held the major offices of church and state. English students flocked to the University of Paris. When Oxford University was established in the 1300s, its founders modeled the new institution on the older French one. So too in music, things French informed English institutions. Organum from Paris was heard at the English royal chapel; and the French conductus provided a model for composition in the English monasteries.

At the same time, however, a few distinctly English musical practices coexisted with imported French styles. From time immemorial the English

MAP 16-1
England during the early Renaissance.

had a love of unaccompanied polyphonic singing; the Winchester Troper, dating from around 1000, preserves some of the West's earliest organum (see Chapter 7). And England enjoyed its own special dialect of Gregorian chant, called **Sarum chant** from the old Latin name of the cathedral town of Salisbury; the melodies and texts of this English repertory were different from the more "standard" chant sung on the Continent.

RONDELLUS AND ROTA

One distinctly English musical practice is a technique called **rondellus.** In rondellus, two or three voices engage in voice exchange or, more correctly, phrase exchange. Each voice starts with its own phrase and then they switch. After each part has sung all phrases, the voices begin new phrases and then switch again, as the following scheme demonstrates:

Voice 1	a	b	c	d	e	f
Voice 2	b	c	a	e	f	d
Voice 3	c	a	b	f	d	e

Rondellus technique was part of a long unwritten tradition of choral singing. Welsh people in the western part of England are known to have sung rondellus in the twelfth century when, according to one observer, "you could hear as many songs (phrases) as you could see heads, yet they all accord in one consonant polyphonic song."[1] A rondellus might stand as an independent song, or the technique might be worked into a motet or conductus. Finally, the simple process that generates a rondellus (singing in a round) may imply that at least some of this English music was improvised on the spot. The English love of singing glees and catches (canons or rounds) continued well into the nineteenth century.

The most famous of all medieval English compositions makes use of rondellus technique as well as canon. It is entitled *Sumer is icumen in* (*Summer is coming in*), or simply the **Summer Canon,** and was written about 1300 (Fig. 16-1). Here, the bottom two voices engage in a brief rondellus, continually exchanging a short, two-bar phrase. The English called a bottom voice that continually repeats a **pes.** Thus in the Summer Canon the pes is a rondellus. Above the pes unfolds a four-voice canon in which each new voice enters at a distance of two measures in modern notation. Once the first voice reaches the end, it and its followers are instructed to return to the beginning to start again in a potentially never-ending cycle. The English called this type of canon that endlessly circles back to the beginning a **rota** (Latin for wheel, from which the English word "round"). The Summer Canon, or rota, is not only the first canon but also the first circular canon in the history of music. In addition, it is also the first surviving composition for six voices. Like most simple canons, this one works because the strong beat of each metrical unit (downbeat of each measure) creates, or implies, one and the same chord, in this case what we today call an F major triad, here transposed to D to make it easier to sing.

The original manuscript of the Summer Canon (Fig. 16-1) shows two texts written below the music (Ex. 16-1). The upper one is in Middle English (*Sumer is icumen in*) and the lower is in Latin (*Perspice Christicola*). The English text tells of the exuberant sights and sounds of a rural spring:

FIGURE 16-1

The Summer Canon, with its two-voice pes at the bottom.

the singing cuckoo, the bleating lamb, the lowing cow, and the farting goat, among
them. The Latin text speaks of the death and resurrection of Christ on Easter Sunday (see below). While these themes might at first seem unrelated, both joyfully
celebrate the eternal process of rebirth and regeneration that occurs each spring.
All the while, the singers sing of this ceaseless re-creation as they continually repeat their endless round. The anonymous Summer Canon is a delight to sing (try it
with a few friends), and it also demonstrates several qualities of early English music:
a folksy tune, a predilection for canon, a preference for many voices, and a love of
consonant, often triadic, sonorities.

EXAMPLE 16-1

Middle English	Modern English
Sumer is icumen in,	Summer is coming in
Lhude sing cuccu!	Loudly sing, cuckoo!
Groweth sed and bloweth med	Seeds sprout and the meadow blooms,
And springeth the wde nu.	And new wood growth appears.
Sing cuccu!	Sing cuckoo!
Awe bleteth after lomb,	Ewe bleats after lamb,
Lhouth after calve cu.	Cow lows after calf,
Bulluc sterteth, bucke verteth,	Bullock leaps, he-goat farts,
Murie sing cucu!	Merrily sing cuckoo!
Wel singes thu cuccu.	Well sing you cuckoo.
Ne swik thu naver nu!	Don't ever stop!

Latin	Modern English
Perspice Christicola,	Observe, worshipers of Christ
que dignatio!	what gracious condescension!
Celicus agricola	How the heavenly husbandman
pro vitis vicio,	for the sin of the vine [in Eden]
filio	not sparing his son

non parcens exposuit	exposed him
mortis exicio.	to the pains of death.
Qui captivos semivivos	Those half-dead captives
a supplicio	sentenced [to Purgatory]
vite donat	he restores to life
et secum coronat	and crowns them next to him
in celi solio.	on the heavenly throne.

Pes: Sing cuccu!

 LISTENING CUE

ANONYMOUS
Sumer is icumen in (c1300)

Book Companion Website (http://schirmer.wadsworth.com/wright_1e)
Anthology, No. 40

 ENGLISH FABURDEN AND CONTINENTAL FAUXBOURDON

The English passion for choral singing and consonant sound can be heard in a style of music called faburden. **Faburden** arose when singers improvised around a given chant: one voice sang above the plainsong at the interval of a fourth, and another sang below it at a third; at cadences the bottom voice would drop down to form an octave with the top one (Ex. 16-2). The sound that resulted was a succession of parallel 6/3 chords punctuated by occasional 8/5 chords at the beginnings and ends of phrases. Singers declaimed the sacred text simultaneously in the free rhythm of plainsong. Below is the process of faburden as singers of the fourteenth and fifteenth century might have improvised it around a *Kyrie* (Anthology, No. 6).

EXAMPLE 16-2

Because faburden was an improvisatory technique, almost no written examples of it survive—we know it was popular because music theorists tell us so. The importance of faburden is that English composers incorporated this unwritten improvisatory style into their more formal written works. Indeed, much of the English music that survives from the early fifteenth century is overrun with parallel 6/3 chords. This same technique is sometimes more generally referred to as **English discant**—adding two improvised voices upon a chant so as to increase its sonority. What results is a euphonious stream of consonant chords.

Most late-medieval English polyphony, whether strict faburden or the more general English discant, was composed for three voices, each of which had a different name. The lowest part was called, of course, the tenor. The middle voice was often called the "meane" (middle, as in "mean average") and the highest part the **treble** (perhaps from "triple" because this was the third voice). The term "meane" was of no lasting importance, but not so the term "treble." From this word comes our general musical term "treble," meaning top part. In the course of time, English-speaking musicians also came to refer to the highest clef in music, the G clef, as the "treble clef."

Three-voice faburden originated in England and was carried into France in the fifteenth century by the followers of the English kings. Soon Continental composers developed a related style called fauxbourdon. In **fauxbourdon** singers of sacred music improvised at pitches a fourth and a sixth below a given plainsong. Thus in faburden the chant is in the middle voice, but in fauxbourdon it is on top. Both styles, however, produce parallel 6/3 chords. Many written-out examples of this improvisatory process survive in fifteenth-century French, Italian, and German manuscripts. Sometimes the composer would lightly ornament the chant (marked by "x" in Ex. 16-3) on the top as well as the bottom part, so as to break the monotony of the parallel 6/3 chords. Rather than writing out the middle voice, however, he then simply inserted the word *fauxbourdon* in the score, thereby telling the middle part to sing a fourth below the chant. In the fauxbourdon applied by Guillaume Dufay to the following popular Christmas hymn, we are midway between improvisation and composition.

EXAMPLE 16-3

You whose suffering...

Both English faburden and Continental fauxbourdon suggest that, in addition to the composed music preserved in written form, late medieval musicians engaged in a great deal of improvised singing. What little we can glimpse today of these improvisatory practices is likely only the tip of an iceberg that went deep into the ancient tradition of English choral song.

KING HENRY V: THE OLD HALL MANUSCRIPT AND THE CAROL

Of all the late-medieval kings of England, **Henry V** (r. 1413–1422) was the most dashing and successful. He has been immortalized by Shakespeare (*Henry V*), whose kingly creation, in turn, has been portrayed in several twentieth-century films. Henry conquered northern France, and would have taken all of it had he not died

British Library

❧ FIGURE 16-2

A polyphonic *Gloria* ascribed to King Henry in the Old Hall Manuscript.

suddenly in 1422. Though Henry was a valiant soldier, he also possessed a taste for literature, poetry, and music. He supported two important chapels, one that traveled with him around England and to the Continent and one that was resident at Windsor Castle, the traditional home of the English kings and queens just west of London. Among the musicians employed by the royal family was Leonel Power (c1380–1445), a composer important in the history of the unified Mass cycle (see Chapter 17). In addition, King Henry V himself seems to have been something of a composer.

Surviving today are a polyphonic *Gloria* and *Sanctus* ascribed to "Roy Henry," presumed to be Henry V. Both are preserved in an important music manuscript compiled during the 1420s. It is called the Old Hall Manuscript (now in the British Library, but formerly at the College of St. Edmund in Old Hall, England). The **Old Hall Manuscript** contains 147 compositions, mostly Mass movements and motets, many by composers serving the royal household (Fig. 16-2). Several motets in honor of the warrior St. George may link the book to the chapel of St. George on the grounds of Windsor Castle. Not only is the Old Hall Manuscript the largest collection of English polyphony from the late fourteenth and early fifteenth centuries, it also contains music of the most advanced English style, a style that would soon come to influence music in France and Italy. England at this moment in history was no longer an isolated island, but a potent force in both music and politics.

In 1415 King Henry V of England invaded northern France, landing at Harfleur near the mouth of the Seine River. His army was small, fewer than 10,000, and it relied on an infantry of fast moving archers and pike-men. The French army was nearly four times as large, but depended upon the mainstay of the older medieval military: knights in heavy armor. When the two forces clashed on a muddy field near Agincourt on 25 October, the agile English made numerical inferiority work to their advantage and cut the lumbering French to shreds. With the French defenses weakened, Henry V gradually moved south. In 1419 he captured Paris and was declared regent of France.

Henry V's stunning victory at the **Battle of Agincourt** was soon celebrated in song, in a genre of music called the carol. The English **carol** was a strophic song for one to three voices, all of which were newly composed. It began with a refrain, called the **burden,** which was also repeated after each stanza. What results is a common musical form called **strophe plus refrain.** Usually the strophe, or stanza, was sung by a soloist while all the singers joined in with the burden, or refrain. The text was in Latin or English (or a combination of the two) and usually dealt with Christmas, Easter, the Virgin Mary, or the saints. More than 120 polyphonic carols survive from fifteenth-century England. Some were inserted into the liturgy, at the end of Mass or an office, and others served as popular spiritual recreation at home. Our modern Christmas carol—often a strophic song with refrain graced with a few words of Latin—traces its ancestry to the English carol of the fifteenth century.

Not all carols were for Christmas, however. Some were political and nationalistic. Witness the anonymous **Agincourt Carol,** which celebrates the victory of Henry V over the French (Ex. 16-4). It begins with a two-voice refrain (or burden), to be sung by all. Thereafter comes a verse performed by soloists, and finally an expanded version of the refrain, now for a chorus of three voices. The harmonic framework consists of 5/3, 6/3, and 8/5 chords, but here the essential note-against-note sonorities are animated through melodic ornamentation. In the exciting Agincourt Carol, the English exhibit pride in their monarch as well as their traditional love of choral singing and full, harmonious sounds.

Vestiges of English Traditions in the "Country" Music of Today

The musical form strophe plus refrain appears in the music of many western European countries by the late Middle Ages, but it is perhaps most deeply rooted in English music, especially in the carol. Over the course of the centuries, strophe plus refrain would continue to provide formal structure for much of the popular and folk music of the British Isles.

During the seventeenth and eighteenth centuries, English, Scottish, and Irish settlers brought their folk music to America, and to the Appalachian region in particular. Much of the "folk" and "country" music we hear today still relies on the late-medieval form of strophe plus refrain. In addi-

tion, American "country" music often perpetuates the ancient English love of euphonious singing. The next time you hear a medley of "country" tunes, especially hymns and gospel music, notice that many of them have a melody accompanied quietly by one or two other singers who move in identical rhythms in thirds, sixths, and fifths (singing in harmony) against the lead voice. This practice, too, has its origins in the ancient discant-like improvised folk singing of the British Isles. Both strophe-plus-refrain form and tight vocal harmony can be heard on many of the tracks of the Grammy Award–winning soundtrack for the film *O Brother, Where Art Thou?*

Burden I (two voices):	Deo gratias, Anglia, redde pro Victoria!
	(England, give thanks to God for the victory!)
Stanza I:	Our king went forth to Normandy
	With grace and might of chivalry;
	There God for him wrought marv'lously
	Wherefore England may call and cry. Deo gratias.
Burden II (three voices):	Deo gratias, Anglia, redde pro Victoria!

EXAMPLE 16-4

England, give thanks to God for the victory.

 LISTENING CUE

ANONYMOUS
Agincourt Carol (c1420)

CD 2/10
Anthology, No. 41

JOHN DUNSTAPLE AND THE *CONTENANCE ANGLOISE*

Among the English musicians who traveled to France in the wake of the invasion of King Henry V was John Dunstaple (c1390–1453). He may have sung in the chapel of King Henry and been at Agincourt, for the royal chapel accompanied the

English army. Dunstaple was not only a composer but also an astronomer and mathematician, and he thus stood squarely in the medieval tradition that associated music and the sciences. He left us approximately sixty compositions, mostly polyphonic Mass movements and motets. One isorhythmic motet (*Veni creator spiritus/Veni sancte spiritus*) is of special note because it is **pan-isorhythmic**; isorhythm is applied to all voices, not merely the tenor.

Most of Dunstaple's compositions are preserved in manuscripts coming, not from England, but from the Continent. Indeed, Dunstaple's Continental influence is confirmed by a French poet, Martin Le Franc, writing around 1440. Le Franc reports that the leading French composers, Dufay and Binchois, followed Dunstaple and adopted the **contenance angloise** (English manner). But what is the "English manner" that the French found so appealing?

A hint may be found in Dunstaple's motet *Quam pulcra es* (*How beautiful thou art*). The music makes use of **pan-consonance**; almost every note is a member of a triad or a triadic inversion and not a dissonance. Likely this dissonance-free environment is one stylistic feature of the *contenance angloise* that Dufay and Binchois adopted from Dunstaple. Notice also that Dunstaple gives the text an almost entirely syllabic setting in which the voices clearly declaim the text. Words such as "Veni" ("Oh come") are highlighted through music for rhetorical effect. Here we see some of the earliest signs of a growing affinity between word and sound, one that will become more pronounced as the Renaissance gains force.

Dunstaple drew the text of *Quam pulcra es* from the **Song of Songs** (also called the Song of King Solomon), a particularly lyrical book in the Old Testament of the Bible. Throughout the ages Jewish rabbis and Christian exegetes have interpreted these surprisingly sensuous texts as allegories; the beautiful woman of *Quam pulcra es* can be seen as the nation of Israel, the entire Christian community, or the Blessed Virgin Mary. Often in English churches motets drawing from the Song of Songs were sung in front of a statue of the Virgin at the end of the liturgical day. Here the sensual poetry and pure, dissonance-free music of the *contenance angloise* were intended to inspire an almost mystical spiritual union with the Virgin.

EXAMPLE 16-5

Quam pulcra es et quam decora,	How beautiful thou art, and fair,
Carissima in deliciis.	My beloved, in thy delights.
Statura tua assimilata est palme	Thy stature is like a palm tree,
Ubera tua botris	Thy breasts like unto round grapes.
Caput tuum ut Carmelus	Thy head is like Mount Carmel and
Collum tuum sicut turris eburnea.	Thy neck like a tower of ivory.
Veni, dilecte mi	Oh come, my beloved;
Egrediamur in agrum et videamus	Let us go into the fields and see

Si flores fructus parturierunt	If the blossoms have borne fruit,
Si floruerunt mala punica	If the pomegranates have flowered
Ibi dabo tibi ubera mea.	There I will give to you my breasts.
Alleluia.	Alleluia.

LISTENING CUE

JOHN DUNSTAPLE
Quam pulcra es (c1420)

CD 2/11
Anthology, No. 42

SUMMARY

At no time before the arrival of the Beatles in the 1960s was English music more influential than during the fifteenth century. Fifteenth-century English music represented a culmination of centuries of indigenous choral practices. These include a fondness for two seemingly opposite styles: a preference for contrapuntal techniques such as rondellus and rota yet a love for strongly homophonic textures such as those produced by faburden and exhibited in the carol. Faburden helped establish the chord we call the "triad" as a building block of music and transform the interval of a sixth from a dissonance to a consonance in the eyes and ears of Continental musicians. Some of these practices were not limited to England—parallel 6/3 chords can be found in the Italian music of Landini, for example—but they were heard with greater frequency in England. Perhaps most important for the future of Renaissance music, Dunstaple and his colleagues were the first to begin to tie text to tone, to underscore the meaning of the word through an appropriate musical gesture. Finally, faint echoes of medieval English musical practices can still be heard today, in that institution we call the Christmas carol and in authentic Appalachian "folk music."

KEY TERMS

Sarum chant	treble	strophe plus refrain
rondellus	fauxbourdon	Agincourt Carol
Summer Canon	Henry V	pan-isorhythmic
pes	Old Hall Manuscript	*contenance angloise*
rota	Battle of Agincourt	pan-consonance
faburden	carol	Song of Songs
English discant	burden	

Chapter 17

Music at the Court of Burgundy

Today Western Europe looks very different than it did more than five hundred years ago (Map 17-1). In the fifteenth century there was no Spain, Italy, Germany, Belgium, or the Netherlands as we know them. What we now call Spain, for example,

MAP 17-1

Western Europe in the fifteenth century.

MAP 17-2

Burgundian lands in 1477.

was three smaller kingdoms (Navarre, Castile, and Aragon), and Italy consisted of a patchwork of territories and independent city-states. Much of central Europe, including modern Germany, was embraced by the Holy Roman Empire; but this empire, as every student of history knows, was neither holy, nor Roman, nor an empire—it was a loose confederation of some two hundred principalities, all to varying degrees under the control of an elected German prince. Scotland was largely independent of England, yet the king of England still held territories in France. France, only two-thirds the size of its modern self, had been weakened politically and economically by the Hundred Years' War. Into this vacuum of power marched the dukes of Burgundy. They were cousins, increasingly distant and hostile, of the kings of France. By the mid-fifteenth century they had made Burgundy an independent state and the most powerful military force in Europe.

We think of Burgundy as an agricultural region in eastern France that produces great wine. But in the fifteenth century it was much more. By 1477 the dukes of Burgundy had inherited, purchased, and conquered large portions of present-day northern France and the Low Countries (Belgium, Luxemburg, and the Netherlands; Map 17-2). Thus it is preferable to speak more broadly of the **Burgundian lands,** rather than simply the duchy of Burgundy. The court of Burgundy and the Burgundian lands are important at this moment in music history for two reasons. First, the court was an important center for the patronage of the arts, and music in particular. At its height in the mid fifteenth century it comprised more than four hundred attendants, including cooks, heralds, poets, painters, minstrels, trumpeters, and a chapel of about twenty singers. Second, within the Burgundian lands were born nearly all of the great polyphonic composers who flourished in the West between 1425 and 1550.

Figure 17-1 shows the two most famous musicians of the court of Burgundy. To the left is Guillaume Dufay (c1397–1474), and to the right, Gilles Binchois (c1400–1460). These two, along with the Englishman John Dunstaple, were the most important composers in Europe in the decades before 1450. We have met Dufay before in Florence as a member of the papal chapel (see Chapter 15). In this portrait Dufay stands next to an organ, the quintessential instrument of the church, perhaps to suggest that he was primarily a church musician. Binchois holds a harp, the instrument of the educated courtier, perhaps to suggest that he associated more with a worldly court.

FIGURE 17-1

Guillaume Dufay and Gilles Binchois as depicted in a manuscript copied c1440.

GILLES BINCHOIS AND THE BURGUNDIAN CHANSON

For nearly thirty years, from roughly 1430 until his death in 1460, Gilles Binchois was a singer and composer in the chapel of Duke Philip the Good (r. 1419–1467). As an ordained priest and chapel singer, he wrote religious music—Masses and motets, and simpler liturgical forms such as hymns. Yet, as a composer of sacred music, Binchois broke no new ground. He composed no large-scale cantus firmus Masses, for example, of the sort that Dufay would make famous (see below). Binchois was a musical jeweler—he created small gems and he did so in the genre of the French chanson.

Chanson is simply the French word for song, be it monophonic or polyphonic. The troubadours and trouvères had written monophonic chansons. Machaut had composed more than sixty polyphonic ones. Now, during the fifteenth century, the French polyphonic chanson became the dominant genre of secular music. More than four hundred of them survive, not merely in manuscripts from France, but also from Spain, England, Italy, and Germany—such was the dominance of the French language and culture in this period. When performers sang and played a chanson, they did so from an oblong sheet of paper or parchment called a **rotulus** (Latin for "roll"); this was the sheet music of the late Middle Ages and early Renaissance (see Fig. 18-2). Chansons were also sometimes copied together in a single volume called a **chansonnier,** a collected anthology of chansons (Fig. 17-2). A chansonnier might contain as few as twenty to as many as two hundred songs by many different composers. Gilles Binchois composed nearly sixty chansons, each written in one of the three French *formes fixes* (ballade, rondeau, or virelai). As is true of most pop songs today, those of Binchois are about affairs of the heart, even though he was a priest. Indeed, most composers of secular art music in this period were clerics in holy orders, because the church still had a monopoly on formal education as well as on the secrets of musical notation.

Gilles Binchois's chanson *Dueil angoisseus (Anguished mourning)* is about love lost. It is a setting of a ballade by the Burgundian poet **Christine de Pisan** (c1364–c1430), who had lost her husband at an early age and here laments his passing; thus, this poem affords us the chance to hear about love from the woman's perspective (see Box, Chapter 18). Pisan's ballade has three stanzas, though we will concern ourselves only with the first. As typical of ballade settings, Binchois assigns the eight lines of text to the musical structure **AAB.**

FIGURE 17-2

Opening of the Cordiforme Chansonnier. As its name "heart-shaped" suggests, both the form and the content deal with affairs of the heart (love songs).

Dueil angoisseus, rage demesuree,	**A**	Anguished mourning, immeasurable rage
Grief, desespoir plein de forsennement,		Grief, despair full of madness
Languor sans fin et vie maleuree,	**A**	Languor without end, a life accursed,
Plaine de plour, d'angoisee et de tourment.		Full of lamentation, anguish, and torment.
Coeur doloreux qui vit obscurement,	**B**	A dolorous heart which lives in darkness,
Tenebreux corps sur le point de partir,		A shadowy corpse on the point of death,
Ay sans cesser continuellement,		These have I without cessation,
Et si ne puis ne garir ne morir. (refrain)		*And so can neither recover nor die.*

Knowing that the text is a lament by a woman who has lost her one true love, the modern listener will be struck by the almost cheerful tone of the music—but cheerful to our ears only. Early music had its own notions of beauty. Musicians had not yet developed the convention that grief and pain were to be expressed musically by the minor mode and painful dissonances, for example. On the contrary, here the Lydian mode with an added B♭ (our major mode) rules most of the piece. An intensely personal text is matched by an intensely beautiful melody. Indeed, Binchois surpassed composers of his generation in his lilting, seemingly effortless melodies that move gracefully through a succession of short, well-directed phrases. Gone are the rhythmic complexities of the *Ars subtilior* and the rigid structure of isorhythm. Here, all is simplicity and grace. Yet each line has a role to play: the cantus carries the melody, the slower-moving tenor provides a support below, and the contratenor moves alternately above and below the tenor, filling out the texture. All three parts can be sung, or just the cantus alone, with the lower two parts played on instruments such as the vielle and lute (Ex. 17-1).

EXAMPLE 17-1

Anguished mourning, immeasurable rage,
Languor without end, a life accursed,

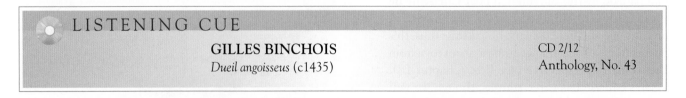

LISTENING CUE

GILLES BINCHOIS
Dueil angoisseus (c1435)

CD 2/12
Anthology, No. 43

Notice the final cadence of Binchois's *Dueil angoisseus* (Ex.17-2b). Whereas in the fourteenth and early-fifteenth centuries the basic three-voice cadence involves a double leading tone with a third pulling to a fifth and a sixth expanding to an octave

(Ex. 17-2a), now in the mid fifteenth century the contratenor has been placed below the tenor so as to achieve a wider, richer sonority. In that lower position the only note that is consonant with the interval of a sixth above (and which will not create forbidden parallel octaves or fifths) is a fourth below the ultimate final note of the cadence (here C below the final F). When only three voices are present, the contratenor often jumps an octave to fill in the texture of the final chord, producing what is called a **Burgundian cadence** (octave-leap cadence), as seen in Example 17-2b. In the newer four-voice writing used later by both Binchois and Dufay, however, the presence of both bass and alto contratenors makes it unnecessary for the bass to jump an octave. Still, the only consonant note to which it can move in the final octave-fifth chord is the final or "tonic" (Ex. 17-2c). Thus what we today call a "dominant-tonic" (V-I) cadence arose in the mid-fifteenth century partly as a desire for greater sonority and partly as a result of a part-writing constriction.

EXAMPLES 17-2A, 17-2B, AND 17-2C

✿ GUILLAUME DUFAY: A LAMENT AND A MASS FOR THE CHRISTIAN SOLDIER

Although Guillaume Dufay was never officially a member of the musical chapel of the dukes of Burgundy, nevertheless he was a frequent visitor to their court. In 1439 he is referred to as a "familiar" of Duke Philip the Good. When Dufay died in 1474 he left six books of music to Duke Charles the Bold (r. 1467–1477), a bequest that signals an unusually close relationship between prince and composer. Dufay was born in the area around Cambrai, France, about the year 1397. Although he was the illegitimate son of a single woman and a priest, he rose to become a trusted friend of the major rulers of the day. In addition to being a "familiar" of the dukes of Burgundy, Dufay served at various times as master of the chapel of Pope Eugenius IV (see Chapter 15), as private counselor to the duke of Savoy, as a canon of the cathedral of Cambrai, and as a confidant of the Medici rulers in Florence. The Medici referred to Dufay as "the chief ornament of our age"; Dufay's intellect and artistic talent brought him into contact with the major players on the political stage of mid fifteenth-century Europe.

On 29 May 1453 the Christian world suffered a grievous loss when the Ottoman Turks defeated the Byzantine Christians and captured their capital, Constantinople (today Istanbul, Turkey). Now the Turkish Muslims not only controlled the Near East but they also began to push farther into the Balkans and to threaten Italy by sea. The pope in Rome called upon the rulers of the West to mount a holy war against these so-called infidels. But among the Christian princes only Duke Philip the Good of Burgundy responded enthusiastically.

In February 1454, Duke Philip summoned his knights and courtiers to the town of Lille in northern France. His aim was to rally support for the crusade, and to this end he staged the **Feast of the Pheasant,** where the guests ate pheasant, then an exotic bird imported from the Muslim East. Though heavy with ethnic symbolism, the Feast of the Pheasant proved to be one of the great parties of the fifteenth century. The banquet hall was organized around three large tables. On one was a mock church "in which was a sounding bell and four singers who sang and played on organs when their turn came." Another table supported a huge pastry so formed that it could house "twenty-eight living persons playing on divers instruments." At a third table "three children and a tenor sang a very sweet chanson, and when they had finished a shepherd played on a bagpipe in a most novel fashion." Later, two gentlemen came forward, hidden within the costume of a stag.

> Then entered a wondrously great and beautiful stag. Mounted upon the stag was a young lad, about twelve years old. The boy held the two horns of the stag with his hands. As he entered the hall be began the upper part of a chanson in a very high, clear voice; and the stag sang the tenor, without there being any other person except the boy and the artifice of said stag. The song that they sang was named *Je ne vis onc-ques la pareille* [ascribed to Binchois in one chansonnier and to Dufay in another].[1]

Finally, an elephant was led into the hall and upon its back was a little castle in which was a man disguised as a woman to represent the figure of the Holy Mother Church. In falsetto voice he sang a lament bemoaning the fall of Constantinople and appealing for aid from Duke Philip and his knights.

Guillaume Dufay composed four polyphonic laments on the fall of Constantinople, though only one survives; it is entitled *Lamentatio sanctae Matris Ecclesiae Constantinopolitanae* (*Lament for the Holy Mother Church of Constantinople*; 1454). This four-voice lament is a cross between a motet and a chanson. Such a hybrid is called a **motet-chanson,** a genre in which a vernacular text in an upper voice is sung simultaneously with a Latin chant in the tenor. Here in the cantus, the Virgin Mary melodiously pleads in French for aid ("O merciful fountain of all hope") for the Holy Mother Church, while the tenor chants a passage in Latin from the Lamentations of Jeremiah (1: 2) of the Old Testament: "All her friends have deserted her, among all her lovers she hath none to comfort her." Just as the Jews were endangered during the first Babylonian Captivity (597 B.C.E.), now it is the Latin Church of the West that is threatened.

EXAMPLE 17-3

I come to lament at your sovereign court…
All her friends have deserted her…

LISTENING CUE

GUILLAUME DUFAY

Lamentatio sanctae Matris Ecclesiae
Constantinopolitanae (1454)

CD 2/13
Anthology, No. 44

In the end, the dukes of Burgundy did little to help the church. No Burgundian crusade set forth, no sword was raised in battle, no Turk slain. Yet the militant spirit of the moment did have a musical resonance. Surviving today in music manuscripts of the late fifteenth century and beyond are more than thirty-five polyphonic Masses built on a favorite melody, the **L'Homme armé tune** (*Armed Man* tune; Ex. 17-4). No other melody has been borrowed as often for religious purposes. Significantly, many of these Armed Man Masses were written by Burgundian composers. While the text of the Armed Man tune is a call to arms, the music forms an unexpectedly bouncy triple-meter melody in **ABA** form.

EXAMPLE 17-4

The armed man, the armed man, should be feared.   A
Everywhere the cry has gone out,
Everyone should arm himself   B
With a breastplate of iron.
The armed man, the armed man, should be feared.   A

Clearly, this jaunty tune is a secular song, not a sacred Gregorian chant. But how was it possible to use a popular tune in a sacred Mass or motet for the church? In the late Middle Ages and early Renaissance, profane songs could be given sacred meaning. For example, the distraught woman described in Binchois's song *Comme femme desconfortée* (*Like a woman disconsolate*) becomes the tearful Virgin Mary at the cross when the melody is used in a motet for the church during Holy Week—the tune still has meaning even though the original words are now removed. Likewise, when placed in a Mass, the soldier of the Armed Man tune becomes the Christian soldier—be he a crusader about to fight the Turk, or every Christian soul who daily wages war with the devil in this world of sin and temptation. In a larger theological sense, the Armed Man, the ultimate warrior, is Christ himself who, according to scripture, defeated the forces of evil by his act of sacrifice on the cross. When he arose in a fifteenth-century Mass, the Armed Man was Christ and all those good Christians who marched with him.

Sometime during the late 1450s, Guillaume Dufay took the *L'Homme armé* tune and made it serve as a tenor scaffold in a new setting of the Ordinary of the Mass. In so doing he created what is called a **cantus firmus Mass**—a cyclic Mass in which the five movements of the Ordinary are unified by means of a single **cantus firmus** (a Latin adjective meaning "firm" or "well-established"). Thus a cantus firmus is a well-established, previously existing melody, be it a sacred chant or a secular song. By employing one and the same cantus firmus in all five movements of the Ordinary of the Mass, a composer could effect unity. Invariably, the composer placed the cantus firmus in long notes in the tenor voice. The five movements of the Mass, each of which has a different text, were thus tied together by a common melody and a common theological theme—in this case the ideal of the Christian soldier fighting a war against the forces of evil. In Dufay's *Missa L'Homme armé,* the Armed Man cantus firmus appears in the tenor once in the *Kyrie,* twice in the *Gloria,* three times in the *Credo,* twice in the *Sanctus,* and three times in the *Agnus dei.* Significantly, in the final two statements in the *Agnus dei,* Dufay makes the Armed Man tune move backward and then forward to the end. Dufay was just one of many composers of the period who used retrograde motion to symbolize Christian faith in the round-trip journey of the Lord: Christ (the Lamb of God, or "Agnus dei") journeyed to earth, descended into Hell to defeat the forces of Satan, and then returned to Heaven. Thus, cantus firmus technique brought not only musical unity to the five sections of the Ordinary of the Mass but also theological unity, sometimes by symbolic means. Example 17-5 shows the beginning of Dufay's *Kyrie* with the *L'Homme armé* tune serving as a cantus firmus in the tenor.

EXAMPLE 17-5

LISTENING CUE

GUILLAUME DUFAY
Kyrie of the *Missa L'Homme armé* (c1460)

CD 2/14–15
Anthology, No. 45a-b

SUMMARY

Music at the court of Burgundy was dominated by two composers, Gilles Binchois and Guillaume Dufay, and it emphasized two musical genres, the chanson and the cantus firmus Mass. Continuing to compose in the secular *formes fixes* established by Machaut during the fourteenth century, Gilles Binchois composed about sixty ballades, rondeaux, and virelais, all relatively short pieces but many with exceptionally beautiful melodies. Although likely invented by English composers such as John Dunstaple and Leonel Power, the cantus firmus Mass reached maturity in the hands of Dufay around 1460, becoming a five-movement work full of contrapuntal artifice yet united by a single religious theme. The symbol-laden cantus firmus was placed in long notes in the tenor. So dominant did the cantus firmus Mass become that it quickly replaced the isorhythmic motet as the large-scale musical structure in which a composer might demonstrate profound technical mastery. In fact, after 1450 no more isorhythmic motets were composed. Finally, in the music of the court of Burgundy and elsewhere in this period, we begin to see a cadence that we now call dominant-tonic (V-I)—the first hints of functional harmony as we know it.

KEY TERMS

Burgundian lands	Christine de Pisan	*L'Homme armé* tune
chanson	Burgundian cadence	cantus firmus Mass
rotulus	Feast of the Pheasant	cantus firmus
chansonnier	motet-chanson	

Music at the French Royal Court

Who has not heard of **Joan of Arc** (c1412–1431), the miraculous Maid of Orléans who rescued France from the English? Joan's heroics occurred in the last stages of the Hundred Years' War. In 1415 the English army, under King Henry V (1387–1422), had won a stunning victory at the Battle of Agincourt (see Chapter 16). From there the English invaders had gone on to capture large portions of northern France. Henry's son, King Henry VI (1421–1471), was eventually crowned king of France at Notre Dame of Paris. The French claimant to the throne, the future Charles VII, was pushed out of Paris and took up residence 200 miles south in the Loire Valley. Owing to the heroism of Joan of Arc, Charles was led to Reims and crowned king there on 16 July 1429. Thus there were two kings of France, one

French, one English. Gradually, Charles gained allies among the nobility and repelled the English. In 1436 the French retook Paris, and by 1450 most of northern France had been returned to the French crown.

The lands of the French kings may have been restored, but not their confidence. King Charles VII (r. 1429–1461) and his successor Louis XI (r. 1461–1483), still fearful of Paris, continued to reside in the beautiful Loire Valley as they expanded their royal authority. Just as the French royal court enjoyed a resurgence at this time, so too did the royal chapel. By 1451 King Charles had engaged fourteen singers to celebrate the Mass and Vespers daily in plainchant and polyphony. Only one of these musicians was a composer of renown, but that one, Johannes Ockeghem (c1410–1497), enjoyed unusual longevity and influence.

JOHANNES OCKEGHEM AND MUSICAL CANONS

Johannes Ockeghem, too, was born in Burgundian lands, in the hamlet of St. Ghislain south of Brussels. By 1451 he had moved further south and joined the French royal chapel. There he remained as a singer for nearly fifty years, working his way up, from chaplain to first chaplain (1454), to master of the chapel (1465), and finally "to counselor and master of the chapel of the king" (1477). Perhaps because of his central position at the French royal court, Ockeghem seems to have influenced the development of many major composers of the day. Dufay was his friend and confidant, and many composers whom we shall meet (Josquin, Basiron, Busnoys, and Tinctoris) studied directly or indirectly with this much-loved figure. A visitor to the French court in 1470 said the following about Ockeghem:

FIGURE 18-1
The French royal chapel with Johannes Ockeghem (presumably) at far right, wearing glasses.

> I am sure that you would not dislike this man, so pleasing is the beauty of his person, so noteworthy the sobriety of his speech and of his morals, and his graciousness. He alone of all the singers is free from vice and abounding in all virtues.[1]

Figure 18-1 is a later illustration of the French royal chapel. The elderly gentleman to the far right is likely Ockeghem, since we know that he served the chapel until a ripe old age, wore spectacles, and, in addition, sang bass.

Surviving today from the pen of Johannes Ockeghem are twenty-five chansons, six motets, and fifteen Masses—not a large *oeuvre* for a man who lived so long and was held in such high esteem by his musical colleagues. Yet in each of these three genres Ockeghem demonstrated exceptional technical skill, a fact that may account for his great fame in his own time. His twenty-five chansons are important because as a group they show the first systematic attempt to structure compositions by using **imitation** (one voice duplicates the notes and rhythms of another for a brief span of time). Other composers, extending back into the fourteenth century, had used imitation from time to time, but the generation of Ockeghem and his pupils Philippe Basiron and Antoine Busnoys (see below) was the first to employ it consistently as a structural tool. From the mid-fifteenth century onward, imitation would come to dominate the texture of written polyphonic music to the point that the entire Renaissance might well be called "the age of imitative counterpoint." We will see shortly an imitative chanson by Ockeghem's pupil Antoine Busnoys. For the moment let us concentrate on an extreme application of imitation, imitative technique as found in Ockeghem's three-voice *Prenez sur moi* (*Take from me*; Ex. 18-1).

Usually when we speak of imitation we refer to only a short span of exact imitation, a measure or so. When, however, the imitation is exact from the beginning to the end of a piece, a stricter form of counterpoint, canon, is at work. We have met musical canons before. They first appear with the famous English Summer Canon of about 1300 (see Chapter 16) and continue with the French *chace* and the Italian *caccia* of the fourteenth century. But in these earlier canons only the upper voices are canonic. The lower voice stands apart from the canon, supporting it with various notes from below. Now, with the generation of Ockeghem and his pupils, fully canonic writing takes hold.

Ockeghem's three-voice *Prenez sur moi* was one of his most popular chansons. It is something of a musical game, or at least a musical pun. The text is ostensibly a love song in the form of a rondeau, and the first voice begins "Take from me your example of love." And take from the leader the subsequent voices do; the second and third voices enter in turn and duplicate exactly the pitches and rhythms of the first, thereby producing a three-voice canon. Note that the voices do not enter at simple intervals of unison, fifth, or octave, but rather at successively higher fourths. Although the complete song is a three-voice canonic rondeau with lyrics, it can be performed with equal effect simply as a three-voice instrumental piece.

EXAMPLE 18-1

Take from me your example of love…

LISTENING CUE

JOHANNES OCKEGHEM
Prenez sur moi (c1460)

CD 2/16
Anthology, No. 46

As this canon and other works indicate, Johannes Ockeghem was a master of musical artifice, posing and solving difficult technical problems in music. In fact, Ockeghem is said to have written a canonic piece for no fewer than thirty-six voices, the sacred motet *Deo gratias*. Among Ockeghem's Masses, two are famous for their erudite construction. The *Missa Cuiusvis toni* (*Mass on Whichever Mode*) is composed so that it can be performed in any one of the eight church modes. Ockeghem notates the Mass only once, but requires the performers to read the music in any one of four different clef combinations, thereby covering the four pairs of authentic and plagal modes. Clearly, this was a test to see how well singers were able to read different clefs.

The epitome of Ockeghem's ingenious constructions, however, is found in his *Missa Prolationum* (*Mass of the Prolations*). Indeed, it has been called the most extraordinary contrapuntal achievement of the fifteenth century. Here the four voices simultaneously sing two two-voice mensuration canons. A **mensuration canon** is one in which two voices perform the same music at different rates of speed; they start at the same time, but one moves through the notes faster—and progressively away from the other in time. In early music, one and the same note shape could have different values depending on the mensuration sign (meter signature) specified by the composer; for example, a long note in a perfect time (triple meter) would be held for three beats but in imperfect time (duple meter) for only two beats. Thus the voice in duple meter sang through the notes more quickly and moved progressively ahead. In the *Kyrie* of Ockeghem's Mass, for example, cantus and altus begin in unison and sing a canon in extended $\frac{2}{4}$ and $\frac{3}{4}$ time, respectively; the tenor and the bass are likewise in unison and sing a second canon in $\frac{6}{8}$ and $\frac{9}{8}$. In the original manuscript only the higher voice is notated for each pair; it was up to the performers to extract from this notation the two missing canonic voices. In Example 18-2 the music is realized in modern edition for all four voices. A mensuration canon is extremely difficult to construct and Ockeghem has two working together simultaneously. Even the great contrapuntalist J.S. Bach never fashioned musical canons this complex or technically difficult.

EXAMPLE 18-2

LISTENING CUE

JOHANNES OCKEGHEM
Kyrie of the Missa Prolationum (c1475)

CD 2/17
Anthology, No. 47

Obviously Ockeghem intended his *Missa Prolationum* to be a brain teaser for performers, and he was not alone in playing these erudite musical games. A spirit of playful artifice is a hallmark of this generation of musicians. Ockeghem's pupil Antoine Busnoys is credited with having written a set of six Masses on the *L'Homme armé* tune (see Chapter 17). In these, the melody is made to go forward, backward (retrograde), upside-down (inversion), and upside-down and backward (retrograde inversion). To effect these permutations, the composer gives instructions to the performers by means of riddle canons (enigmatic rules) written in the language of ancient Greek music theory. In all of music history, no generation of composers was more intent on posing and then solving such esoteric musical puzzles. In fact, there is little in the twelve-tone music of the twentieth century (see Chapter 69) that had not already been worked out during the fifteenth century by Ockeghem, Busnoys, and their ingenious colleagues.

 ## A MUSICAL JOKE FOR THE FRENCH KING

The ingenuity of composers in this period was sometimes put to use just for fun. French King Louis XI (1461–1483) clearly loved music, and he paid the master of his chapel, Johannes Ockeghem, handsomely. Toward the end of his reign he hired the young Josquin des Prez (see Chapter 21) and commissioned him to set in polyphony psalm texts with special meaning for him. And when Louis was ill, having suffered a stroke, he asked for his instrumentalists to play quietly beneath his window. But, despite his passion for music, Louis seems to have had little talent. A sixteenth-century music theorist, Heinrich Glarean, tells the story of how the king asked a singer of the court, apparently Josquin, to write a piece in which he, too, could participate.

> Some relate such [humorous] stories about Josquin des Prez, and it is of such a kind which we are now going to tell. Louis [XI], the French king, is said to have had a very inadequate voice. He had formerly been pleased by some song and asked the chief of his singers if there was anyone who would compose a song in several voices in which he could also sing some part. The singer, wondering at the demand of the King, whom he knew to be entirely ignorant of music, hesitated a while and finally decided what he would answer. "My King," he said, "I shall compose a song in which your Majesty will also be given a place in the singing." The following day, after the King had had breakfast and was to be refreshed with songs, according to royal custom, the singer produced this song, composed in four voices. . . .
>
> He had composed the song so that two boys would sing very lightly and delicately the *cantus*, taken from a single theme, evidently so that the exceedingly thin voice of the King would not be drowned out. He had given the King the next voice, notated on one continual tone in the range of the alto, a range which would be suitable to the royal voice. . . . And so that the King would not waver in pitch, the composer, who was going to sing the bass, arranged this bass voice so that at regular intervals he would support the King at the octave, on the alternate tone of the *tempus*. But the octave is like the unison, through which octave the voice of the King was helped exceedingly. The King laughed merrily at the trick and gladly dismissed the composer with a present.[2]

Fortunately, this musical joke survives today in a manuscript copied in France about 1510. It is called "The French Song of Louis XI, King of France" and carries a simple, rustic text *Guillaume se va chaufer* (*William is going to warm himself*). As you can see, the king was, in fact, apparently tone deaf, for he sang only a single long pitch on D. Against him, the two choirboys produced a short, continually repeating canon, while the bass supported the king with octaves and fifths below. Surely this is the only piece in the history of music written for a royal monotone. But even in this short, humorous piece, the composers of the royal court were able to work in a clever canon.

EXAMPLE 18-3

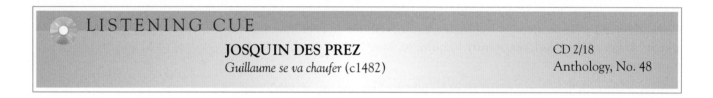

William is going to warm himself.

LISTENING CUE

JOSQUIN DES PREZ
Guillaume se va chaufer (c1482)

CD 2/18
Anthology, No. 48

✿ PHILIPPE BASIRON AND THE PARAPHRASE MOTET

Philippe Basiron (c1449–1491) was a singer at the king's Sainte-Chapelle in the central French town of Bourges. Although not a major figure in the history of music, his compositions were nonetheless known in Spain, Italy, and Bohemia (Czech Republic) as well as France. Basiron's significance rests in the fact that he was an early practitioner of paraphrase technique, though in truth he borrowed this from earlier English composers and from his apparent mentor at the French court, Johannes Ockeghem. In **paraphrase technique** a composer takes a pre-existing plainsong (Gregorian chant) and embellishes it somewhat, imparting to it a rhythmic profile; the elaborated chant then serves as the basic melodic material for a polyphonic composition. Unlike cantus firmus technique, in which the borrowed melody is usually placed in long notes in the tenor, with paraphrase technique the ornamented chant can appear in any and all voices, though most often it is heard in the cantus. The paraphrased chant might appear in a motet, thereby creating a **paraphrase motet.** Similarly, paraphrase technique might be applied to all five movements of a polyphonic Mass. A Mass in which the movements are united by a single paraphrased chant is called a **paraphrase Mass.** Josquin des Prez's famous *Missa Pange lingua* is such a Mass, one in which a continually ornamented hymn tune, Thomas

Aquinas's hymn *Pange lingua*, permeates all voices and binds all five movements into a unified whole.

Basiron's *Salve, Regina* (sometimes attributed to Ockeghem himself) takes the famous Marian antiphon of that name as its point of departure. The beautiful *Salve, Regina* (*Hail queen*) melody was one of the most popular chants of the Middle Ages and Renaissance; in many locales it was sung daily at the end of the canonical hours before retiring for the night. A comparison of the chant with Basiron's polyphonic setting shows how he added rhythmic energy, even syncopation, to the chant, while keeping its melodic contour essentially intact. Here the paraphrased chant appears almost exclusively in the cantus, the lower three voices providing counterpoint and structural support. Later in the fifteenth century, composers will be more inclined to allow the paraphrased melody to migrate to all voices in the polyphonic complex. The virtue of Basiron's setting, however, is that no matter how rich the supporting harmonies below, the borrowed melody is always clearly audible on top.

EXAMPLE 18-4

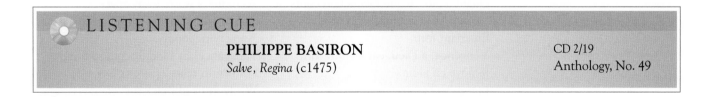

LISTENING CUE

PHILIPPE BASIRON
Salve, Regina (c1475)

CD 2/19
Anthology, No. 49

ANTOINE BUSNOYS AND THE IMITATIVE CHANSON

The fact that such a fine composer as Antoine Busnoys is little known today simply underscores the fact that in the late fifteenth century there were many great composers; Busnoys was only one star in a bright firmament. Antoine Busnoys (c1435–1492) was apparently born in the hamlet of Busnes in the Burgundian lands of northern France. By 1461 he had journeyed south and was employed as a singer in the town of Tours, the abode of the king of France and his chapel master Johannes Ockeghem. Indeed, for the coronation of King Louis XI in 1461, Busnoys composed a motet-chanson *Resjois toi terre de France/Rex pacificus*. Shortly before 1467, Busnoys left the orbit of the French king and became a singer at the court of the king's arch-rival, Duke Charles of Burgundy.

Like his mentor Ockeghem, Busnoys delighted in musical cryptograms. In one motet, *Anthoni usque limina*, he wrote the instructions for performance in Latin and Greek around a picture of a bell; this musical puzzle has never been satisfactorily solved. In four chansons Busnoys makes use of literary codes to allude to a special lady. For example, *Je ne puis vivre ainsy tousjours* (*I cannot live like this forever*) contains an **acrostic** (a poem in which the first letters of each line form a word or phrase). Here the first letters of each line produce the name Jaqueljne d'Aqvevjle" (Jacqueline de Hacqueville). The lady secretly signaled here may have been a devotee or lover of Busnoys, or she may have been the author of the text (see Box). Regardless, *Je ne puis vivre ainsy tousjours* is a charming virelai (**AbbaA**) of one stanza, with the music of section **a** in triple meter and that of **b** in duple. Typical of the newer-style chanson of the Ockeghem-Busnoys generation, the texture is infused with imitation, which in turn creates an equality of rhythmic and melodic activity among the voices. A hallmark of Busnoys's personal style can be seen at the very beginning of the chanson, when each voice rises quickly up the scale to the distance of a tenth, thereby clarifying the mode of the piece; Busnoys would say that it is in the Lydian mode (with a B♭) transposed to C; we would call it simply C major.

Je ne puis vivre ainsy tousjours	**A**	*I cannot live like this forever*
Au mains que j'aye en mes dolours		*Unless I have in my distress*
Quelque confort,		*Some comfort,*
Une seule heure ou mains ou fort;		*A single hour, more or less*
Et tous les jours		*And every day*
Léaument serviray Amours		*Loyally I will serve Love*
Jusqu'a la mort.		*Until death.*
Noble femme de nom et d'armes	**b**	*Noble woman of name and arms*
Escript vous ay ce dittier-cy,		*I have written you this ditty*
Des jeulx pleurant à chaudes larmes	**b**	*With crying eyes full of warm tears*
Affin qu'aiez de moi mercy.		*That you may have mercy on me.*
Quant a moy, je me meurs bon cours	**a**	*As to me, I waste away apace*
Vellant les nuyt, faisant cent tours,		*Awake at nights, tossing a hundred times,*
En criant fort:		*And crying loudly:*
Vengence! a Dieu, car a grant tort		*Vengeance! by God, because wrongly*
Je noye en plours		*I drown in tears*
Lorsqu'au besoing me fault secours,		*While in need I lack succor*
Et Pitié dort.		*And Pity sleeps.*
Je ne puis vivre ainsy tousjours	**A**	*I cannot live like this forever . . . .*

LISTENING CUE

ANTOINE BUSNOYS
Je ne puis vivre ainsy tousjours (c1460)

CD 2/20
Anthology, No. 50

Women Poets and Performers

While it may seem that early music was an all-male activity, often it was not. The text of Binchois's chanson *Dueil angoisseus* (see Chapter 17) was written by Christine de Pisan (c1364–c1430) and that of Busnoys's *Je ne puis vivre ainsy tousjours* possibly by Jacqueline de Hacqueville. Pisan was a single mother and a feminist before her time, compiling a lengthy chronicle of the deeds of illustrious women throughout Western history. Jacqueline de Hacqueville was apparently a lady-in-waiting at the French royal court. One of the pastimes of such women was the composition of poetry. The ladies serving at the court of King Charles VII of France were criticized for "staying up too late writing rondeaux and ballades." However, when women wrote love poetry they sometimes employed the female voice and sometimes they adopted the male perspective (referring to the lover as "he" and the beloved as "she"). In addition, although women were proscribed from singing in church, except in convents, they were encouraged to do so at court. The majority of illustrations of secular music-making in the fifteenth century prominently shows women as performers. They appear as singers, presumably of the cantus part, or as instrumentalists (usually playing string instruments), or as both. Clearly, women participated formally and informally in secular music-making, but they were "off the books" because they occupied the somewhat ill-defined position of "ladies-in-waiting." All the official musical positions at court—those of chaplain, minstrel, trumpeter, and organist—still went to men.

FIGURE 18-2

A garden of love wherein two gentlemen and two ladies perform a chanson. Both ladies are singing from a rotulus (sheet music).

SUMMARY

Like their contemporaries at the court of Burgundy, composers in the orbit of the French king in the Loire Valley—Ockeghem, Josquin, Basiron, and Busnoys, among them—composed chansons, Masses, and motets. They were concerned with developing new localized formal devices, such as imitation, as well as large-scale structural procedures, such as cantus firmus and paraphrase techniques. By applying imitation to all the voices within a composition, stratification between voices was reduced; by its very nature imitation makes all vocal parts, if not exactly equal, at least rather similar in their melodic content and rhythmic activity. The royal composers also began to popularize the paraphrase motet and the paraphrase Mass. In these a single pre-existing chant was taken, lightly ornamented, and then spun through the various voice parts, appearing most prominently in the cantus. Johannes Ockeghem and his pupils also explored more esoteric textual and musical procedures such as acrostics, mensuration canons, and modal transpositions, as well as inversion and retrograde motion. Rarely in the history of music have composers been more interested in learned contrapuntal processes.

KEY TERMS

Joan of Arc   paraphrase technique   paraphrase Mass
imitation   paraphrase motet   acrostic
mensuration canon

Chapter 19

Music in the Low Countries

During the fifteenth century, the region that we now call the Low Countries fell mostly within the Burgundian lands (see Chapter 17). In fact, the dukes of Burgundy derived most of their wealth from these northern territories, the countries of modern-day Belgium, the Netherlands, and Luxemburg. Towns such as Ghent, Bruges, Brussels, and Antwerp enjoyed bustling trade by boat with England and by land with Italy. These cities, not those in France or Germany, formed the commercial center of northern Europe. The dominant language was what is now called Dutch (also called Flemish). In these Dutch- or Flemish-speaking cities new churches sprang up and fine musical choirs appeared. Commerce fostered support for religious institutions, and these, in turn, supported education. Many churches began to sponsor a **choir school**—a school that took in boys at about the age of six, gave them an education with a strong emphasis on music and especially singing, and prepared them for a lifetime of service within the church. These schools and the intense musical education they provided may account for a remarkable historical fact: most of the major composers of learned polyphony in western Europe during the period 1425 to 1550 were born in the Burgundian Low Countries. These musicians are sometimes called Burgundian composers, sometimes Franco-Flemish composers, or sometimes just the Netherlanders. In addition to Binchois, Dufay, Ockeghem, and Busnoys, they include, among others, Jacob Obrecht, Josquin des Prez, Heinrich Isaac, Cipriano de Rore, Adrian Willaert, and Orlande de Lassus. Some of these musicians served the court of Burgundy, some the court of the king of France, and others migrated south to gain fame and fortune at courts in Italy. But many musicians avoided the vicissitudes of court life. They stayed at home in the Low Countries, earning a stable living as church singers or city instrumentalists. One musician who did so was Jacob Obrecht.

✿ JACOB OBRECHT AND THE MULTIPLE CANTUS FIRMUS MASS

Jacob Obrecht was born in 1457 or 1458 in Ghent, the son of a trumpeter who served his city for more than thirty years. Young Jacob may have been trained as a trumpeter, learning to play fanfares and to improvise on well-known tunes. Yet, for most of his adult career, Obrecht was a choir director in churches in and around the Low Countries: in Bergen op Zoom, Cambrai, Bruges, and Antwerp. He composed many of his nearly three dozen Masses, for example, for the urban church of St. Donatian in Bruges. Not until 1504 did Obrecht yield to the temptation to accept a more lucrative position at a secular court, specifically as *magister cappellae* for Duke

Hercules d'Este in Ferrara, Italy. It was an unwise decision; Obrecht died in Ferrara shortly after his arrival, the victim of a sporadic outburst of bubonic plague.

Perhaps as no other composer in the history of music, Jacob Obrecht was a master at combining several melodies, either simultaneously or successively. When several secular tunes are brought together, the process creates a genre of music called a **quodlibet** (Latin for "whatever you like"). Obrecht wrote many of these popular medleys, several in his native language of Dutch. (The practice of writing quodlibets for the amusement of an urban public, which begins here in the late fifteenth century, continued to the time of Bach and beyond.) In a more serious vein, Obrecht often combined several cantus firmi in a single motet or Mass. In his Mass for St. Martin, for example, he incorporates no fewer than nine chants taken from the liturgy of St. Martin; as the singers sing these in succession they allude to the major events in the life of the saint, thereby creating a sort of musical *curriculum vitae*. When two or more cantus firmi sound simultaneously or successively in a Mass a **multiple cantus firmus Mass** results. In all, Obrecht composed approximately thirty chansons, thirty-four motets, and thirty-five Masses. About a dozen of his sacred works, both motets and Masses, make use of multiple cantus firmi.

Obrecht's most impressive multiple cantus firmus Mass is his *Missa Sub tuum presidium* (*Mass Under Your Protection*), a Mass in honor of the Virgin Mary. As the following chart shows, Obrecht at first borrows only a single sacred cantus firmus, then two, three, and four as more and more voices are added in succeeding movements of the Mass. The climactic *Agnus dei* calls for seven voices, four to sing various cantus firmi simultaneously and three to sing free counterpoint against them. (Perhaps it is not mere coincidence that the Mass concludes with seven voices, for seven was the symbolic number for Mary.) The principal cantus firmus of the Mass, the antiphon *Sub tuum presidium*, was sung in many churches before a favorite painting of the Virgin Mary; for faithful Catholics, the Virgin served as the great protector of humankind. Other chants allude to other attributes of Mary and Christ. In the *Credo*, for example, the composer sets two cantus firmi in the highest two voices, *Sub tuum presidium* and another borrowed petition to the Virgin, *Audi nos* (*Hear us*). Beneath these the lower three voices weave a dense web of counterpoint. Just as the Virgin protects the people beneath her, so the chants sound down from on high. Yet of such beauty is Obrecht's *Missa Sub tuum presidium* that one barely notices that the composer has built a musical scaffold of extraordinary complexity. If you think this is easy, take three or four folk songs or pop tunes and adjust the rhythms so that all three or four will sound simultaneously and make good harmony—and then write free counterpoint against these in three other voices!

Structure of Jacob Obrecht's *Missa Sub tuum presidium*

	Kyrie	*Gloria*	*Credo*	*Sanctus*	*Agnus dei*
Cantus 1	S	S	S	S	S
Cantus 2	—	—	CF	CF	CF
Alto 1	—	—	—	—	CF
Alto 2	O	O	O	O	O
Tenor 1	—	—	—	CF	CF
Tenor 2	O	O	O	O	O
Bass	—	O	O	O	O

S   Cantus firmus taken from antiphon *Sub tuum presidium*
CF Other sacred cantus firmi
O   Free counterpoint setting text of Ordinary of the Mass
— Voice is silent

LISTENING CUE

JACOB OBRECHT
Credo of the *Missa Sub tuum presidium* (c1500)

CD 2/21

Anthology, No. 51

 MUSICAL INSTRUMENTS

Not all music in the cities of the Low Countries was vocal in nature. Towns throughout northern Europe employed instrumentalists, mostly wind players, to signal the approach of an invading army, salute a visiting nobleman, or herald an important announcement. Wind bands for these communal events performed in the market square, from the city gates, from the belfry of the highest church, and from the balcony of the town hall. Our tradition of literally broadcasting sacred tunes from church belfries began in this era in the Low Countries and Germany. As a result, toward the end of the fifteenth century the separation of secular and sacred repertories by place of performance began to break down. In Bruges in 1483, for example, trumpets and shawms were permitted to play at services in the church nave, sometimes adding secular tunes to the otherwise-sacred repertory. Conversely, sacred chants and motets were taken out into the streets and performed as part of religious processions, thereby linking music to civic spectacle. Motets of Obrecht, for example, are known to have been performed outdoors by wind bands in cities from Bruges to Venice.

Civic and courtly instrumental music at this time centered around dancing and the early-Renaissance equivalent of chamber music. Trumpets and shawms were needed here for dancing, but so too were lutes, vielles, recorders, and even the harpsichord for quieter music. The first detailed description of a **harpsichord** comes from the Low Countries about 1440. Dating more than two hundred and fifty years before the advent of the piano, this instrument was designed by Henri Arnaut de Zwolle (c1400–1466), master of medicine, astronomy, and astrology to Duke Philip the Good of Burgundy. As can be seen in Figure 19-1, Zwolle describes four key-jack mechanisms, and his nearly-three-octave keyboard (B to a") is fully chromatic. Like the portable organ, the early harpsichord could easily be carried from place to place and was meant to be played when set upon a table top. On it a single performer could easily play an arrangement of a dance piece or a popular song.

Throughout the fifteenth century, instruments were classified according to one of two types: *haut* (loud) or *bas* (soft). The **hauts instruments** included trumpets, shawms, bagpipes, drums, and tambourine. The straight-pipe military trumpet (*trompette de guerre*) and the folded trumpet with slide (*trompette des menestrels*) were made of brass, or sometimes silver. The slide trumpet, also known as the **sackbut** (from the French *sacque-boute* meaning roughly "push-pull"), was the precursor of our modern trombone. The shawm, ancestor of the modern oboe, was a brilliant-sounding double-reed instrument that played in one of two ranges, treble and tenor (pitched

 FIGURE 19-1

Henri Arnaut de Zwolle's plans for his harpsichord, c1440.

❋ FIGURE 19-2

An ensemble of *hauts instruments* (two shawms and a sackbut) accompanying a *basse danse* as represented in a miniature executed for the duke of Burgundy, 1468–1470.

a fifth below). The typical wind band consisted of a sackbut along with two or three shawms and perhaps an accompanying drum (Fig.19-2). Later, by around 1500, the wind band was sometimes joined by a **cornett,** a wooden, lip-vibrated wind instrument with finger-holes and a cup-shaped mouthpiece that produced a soft trumpet sound, but with a somewhat wooden or hollow tone. The cornett sounded in the range of the soprano voice.

Unlike the *hauts instruments,* the **bas instruments** constituted no set group. These soft instruments (recorder, vielle, lute, harp, psaltery, portative organ, and harpsichord) might appear individually or in any one of a number of possible combinations. These were best used as chamber instruments, their quickly diminishing sounds being less well suited for the noisy dance hall and the outdoor pageant. Women frequently played string instruments, but rarely wind instruments, with the exception of the flute. Usually only one instrument played a given musical line; there was no doubling or tripling of parts. Finally, most of the instrumentalists of the period may not have been able to read musical notation. Certainly much of this instrumental repertory was improvised, and performers most likely learned by aural memory, not by reading music.

❋ THE *BASSE DANSE*

When Duke Charles the Bold of Burgundy died at the battle of Nancy in 1477, he left no male heir. The Burgundian lands in the Low Countries passed to Charles's daughter, Mary of Burgundy. More for protection than love, Mary immediately married Maximilian I of the house of Hapsburg, who was soon to be Holy Roman Emperor (r. 1493–1519). The children of Maximilian and Mary in turn married the offspring of Ferdinand and Isabella of Spain (patrons of Christopher Columbus), and thus the Low Countries came under Spanish rule. During this gradual transition from Burgundian to Hapsburg-Spanish control, the old court of Burgundy was

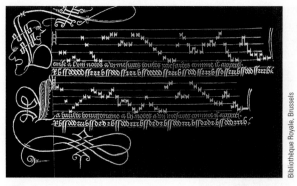

Bibliothèque Royale, Brussels

❧ FIGURE 19-3

A *basse danse* book from the court of Margaret of Austria. The parchment has been dyed black, and the writing is executed in gold and silver ink.

directed by **Margaret of Austria** (1480–1530), daughter of Mary and Maximilian. Ruling from the town of Mechlin, Margaret served as official regent of the Low Countries from 1507 to 1530.

Like her father and grandfather before her, Margaret of Austria was a great patron of music. She was skilled as a singer and keyboard player, and she wrote poetry, some of which was set to music by court composers. But Margaret was also a victim of bad luck, for she was thrice married and thrice widowed. A shroud of mourning thus descended upon her Burgundian-Hapsburg court, and even joyful activities such as dancing assumed a moribund tone. Witness the famous *basse danse* book of Margaret of Austria: its parchment has been dyed black (Fig. 19-3).

The **basse danse** was the principal aristocratic dance of court and city during the early Renaissance. As its name "low dance" suggests, the *basse danse* was a slow, stately dance in which the dancers' feet glided close to the ground (see Fig. 19-2). Proceeding in a line of couples, the participants executed any one of four choreographic gestures (see Ex. 19-1): a single step (s), a double step (d), a step backward (r), or a shake (b), all preceded by a reverential bow by the gentleman (R). Margaret of Austria's *basse danse* book (see Fig. 19-3) preserves fifty-eight dance tunes, each with its own name. The titles often allude to the musician who created the tune, or the region in which the melody originated. Music was provided by a standard wind band. The sackbut played the tune in slow notes of equal value. During each note the dancers executed one of the four steps of the choreography. As the tune progressed, shawms and perhaps a cornett wove a polyphonic accompaniment above, much like a jazz quartet of today in which a piano and saxophone improvise above the fundamental bass notes provided by the double bass or guitar.

One of the most popular dance tunes around the year 1500 was *La Spagna* (*The Spanish Tune*; Ex. 19-1). It survives in more than two hundred polyphonic arrangements, ranging from settings for solo lute to Mass movements for multiple voices. In fact, the setting by Heinrich Isaac was also made to serve as a movement in a Mass by that composer. Written arrangements such as *La Spagna* capture in notation, after the fact, what was at first an improvisatory dance tradition. Later, in the early sixteenth century, the *basse danse* would be followed by a faster dance called the *tordion*. But although the *basse danse* was slow and stately, the music for it, as demonstrated by this version of *La Spagna*, could be very lively indeed!

EXAMPLE 19-1

LISTENING CUE

HEINRICH ISAAC
La Spagna (c1500)

CD 2/22
Anthology, No. 52

SUMMARY

Composers in the Low Countries during the late fifteenth century continued to write large-scale compositions, specifically the sacred motet in Latin and the five-movement Latin Mass. To bring unity to these large-scale works, composers used cantus firmus, paraphrase, or multiple cantus firmus technique, thereby creating, for example, a cantus firmus Mass, a paraphrase Mass, or a multiple cantus firmus Mass. Jacob Obrecht was the master of the multiple cantus firmus Mass. In these, several borrowed melodies would appear both successively and simultaneously.

Instruments proliferated and instrument makers flourished in cities of the Low Countries during the late fifteenth century. *Bas instruments* provided most of the softer, quieter instrumental music for court and private home. The louder *hauts instruments*, on the other hand, were especially well suited for playing dance music, the principal dance of the era being the stately *basse danse*. Instrumentalists also began to play polyphonic motets both inside and outside the church. They simply sounded the notes and omitted the text. Here, for the first time in the history of music, instruments other than the organ—specifically the shawm, cornett, and sackbut—began to be associated with music of the church.

KEY TERMS

choir school	harpsichord	*bas instruments*
quodlibet	*hauts instruments*	Margaret of Austria
multiple cantus firmus Mass	sackbut	*basse danse*
	cornett	

THE LATE RENAISSANCE

*S*trictly speaking, the word *renaissance* means "rebirth," but it also connotes "recovery" and "rediscovery." Nineteenth-century historians invented the term to describe the great flowering of intellectual and artistic activity that occurred first in Italy and then elsewhere in Europe during the years 1350–1600. In the early part of this period, roughly 1350–1475, music underwent profound changes. Such stylistic changes continued and even accelerated during the late Renaissance (1475–1600). Yet, what specifically was "reborn," or at least new, about the music of the late Renaissance? First, the Renaissance unleashed the expressive, indeed rhetorical, power of music as the result of the

1350	1400	1450	1500

EARLY RENAISSANCE (1350–1475)   **LATE**

Johannes Gutenberg (c1400–1468), inventor of printing with movable type

Emperor Maximilian I (1459–1519)

Lorenzo the Magnificent (b. 1449), Medici prince

Girolamo Savonarola (1452–1498), perhaps the most famous, or infamous, writer of laude

Josquin des Prez (c1450–1521), Renaissance

Ottaviano Petrucci (1466–1539),

● 1470 Buxheim Organ Book,

Hercules d'Este (r. 1471–1505),

Michelangelo

Claudin de Sermisy

Pierre Attaingnant

Sistine Chapel,
constructed 1477–1481

CORBIS

Bridgeman Art Library

Martin Luther
(1483–1546)

humanists' concern with literature. Music increasingly came to intensify the meaning of the text. Second, there was with the Renaissance a growing sense that music might be not only for religious solace and salvation but also for personal enrichment and entertainment. Third, a new technology (music printing) made possible the widespread dissemination of written music to a much broader segment of society and generally increased musical literacy. Fourth, the Renaissance witnessed a gradual shift in the perception of music as a discipline among the sciences to one among the fine arts. Finally, attending this new view of music as a fine art was an increased awareness of the composer as an individual— indeed an artist—worthy of special honors and financial rewards.

Part III

| 1500 | 1550 | 1600 | 1650 |

RENAISSANCE (1475–1600)

● 1524 Johann Walter (1496–1570) publishes *Geistliche Gesangbüchlein*

● 1530 Madrigal arises in Italy

● 1567 Giovanni Pierluigi da Palestrina (1525–1594) composes *Mass for Pope Marcellus*

of Austria

who wrote texts of carnival songs

Queen Elizabeth I (r. 1558–1603) of England

1545–1563 Council of Trent

Carlo Gesualdo (1561–1613) publishes 7 books of madrigals and 3 volumes of motets

composer

John Dowland (1563–1626), greatest composer of English lute ayres

Venetian printer first to publish polyphonic music

containing 256 compositions for organ

William Shakespeare (1564–1616)

patron of musicians

Claudio Monteverdi (1567–1643), important composer of late madrigals and early operas

Queen Mary (r. 1553–1558)

(1475–1564)

(c1490–1562), composer of Parisian chansons

1589 *Orchésographie*, a treatise on dance, is published by Thoinot Arbeau (Jehan Tabourot)

(c1495–c1552), official printer of music for the French crown

Jacques Arcadelt (c1505–1568), early proponent of madrigal

Thomas Tallis (c1505–1585) composes for Catholic, Anglican, and Puritan faiths

King Henry VIII (r. 1509–1547) of England, musician, composer, and church reformer

King Francis I (r. 1515–1547) of France, brings Italian Renaissance to France

Orlande de Lassus (1532–1594) composes in all genres of his day

William Byrd (1543–1623), preeminent composer under Queen Elizabeth

◆ **1555 Peace of Augsburg**

Thomas Morley (1557–1602), important composer and theorist in London

El Greco (1541–1614), "Christ Clasping the Cross" (1600–1605)

Musical Interlude 2

Musical Humanism and the Renaissance

Although the historians who coined the term "renaissance" greatly exaggerated the difference between the old "dark" Middle Ages and the newly "revivified" Renaissance, they had a point. Observers of the day were aware that something new was in the air. As the important music theorist **Johannes Tinctoris** (c1435–1511) said in his *Art of Counterpoint* (1477): "There is no composition written over forty years ago which is thought by the learned as worthy of performance." What mattered to Tinctoris was all that was new. To be sure, the Renaissance brought with it a new way of looking at things. During the period 1475–1600, music generally would come to be governed by strict rules of counterpoint. Perhaps more important, musicians came to believe that in vocal music a composition should reflect the meaning of its text in the fullest and most vivid manner. This new attitude about text and tone, and about music generally, was derived largely from the study of the arts and letters of ancient Greece and Rome, a discipline called *studia humanitatis*.

Humanism was the study of ancient texts and monuments with the aim of extracting a model for thinking and acting in the emerging society of the Renaissance. It began in the fourteenth century with Francesco Petrarch's (see the introduction to Part II) exploration of the literature of ancient Rome. Now in the late fifteenth century scholars intensified their interest in the poetry, philosophy, and arts of classical Greece and Rome and tried to make the principles found therein work for the present day. By learning from the past, humanists expected to create a society full of truth and beauty populated by morally upright citizens.

Implicit in humanism is the notion that human beings have the capacity to shape their world. If the Middle Ages had placed great emphasis on God and relegated man to a minor, faceless role in a great divine pageant, the Renaissance placed its faith in human achievement and individual creativity. The fact that Michelangelo sculpted his David (1501–1504) as a huge figure fully nude—something never done in medieval religious art—suggests a new artistic imperative (Fig. 1). Humans must give free rein to their creative instincts and fashion a world, not so much in the image of God as in the image of man. These were lofty aspirations, but how specifically did they affect the composition and performance of music in this period?

For musicians the study of the musical artifacts of antiquity was less direct than it was for other disciplines. The reason was simple: as far as they knew, no music survived from ancient Greece and Rome. Instead, the musical humanists studied the writings in music theory of classical Greece and the attitudes about music held by the ancient philosophers such as Plato and Aristotle (see Chapter 1). Greek music theory greatly influenced Renaissance theory and brought about changes both in theory and practice, as we shall soon see. Musicians of the Renaissance eagerly embraced the ancient belief that music could affect the emotions. Plato had told stories of how music had calmed the agitated spirit and made the warrior brave. Accordingly, Renaissance musicians tried to create a more affective, more emotionally expressive music. Because the poet and the musician were one and the same in Greek society, Renaissance musicians came to insist upon a closer union between text and tone. During the sixteenth century, composers developed a vocabulary of

❧ FIGURE 1

Michelangelo's giant statue *David* (1501–1504) expresses the heroic nobility of man in near-perfect form. Like Leonardo da Vinci, Michelangelo made a careful study of human anatomy.

Bridgeman Art Library

expressive musical gestures that mimicked, or sounded out in onomatopoeic fashion, the meaning of the text.

In practical terms the lessons of antiquity influenced music-making in the Renaissance in the following ways. Composers set to music the ancient verse of Virgil and Horace, among others, and did so in simple four-voice settings in which the rhythms of the music matched those of the ancient poetry. Influenced by Greek music theory, the Renaissance theorist Heinrich Glarean expanded the number of modes to twelve, and composers such as Cipriano de Rore and Nicola Vicentino wrote highly chromatic pieces that tried to re-institute the microtonal inflections of the ancient Greek genera. Everywhere composers strove to make their works convey the syntax and sense of the poetry as clearly as possible. Finally, the study of antiquity caused Renaissance musicians to adopt new attitudes with regard to music-making and musical instruments.

A single example may be enough to show how antique attitudes about music influenced Renaissance thinking about musical instruments and performance. Writers throughout the Renaissance consistently declare that the most noble instruments are the strings such as the viol, but not the organ of the church or the brilliant-sounding trumpet. Why? Because Plato and Aristotle considered the strings more noble than the winds. These philosophers were influenced by Greek mythology, which spoke of **Apollo,** god of the sun and of music, who sat atop Mount Olympus playing a string instrument. Here he was attended by nine goddesses called the **muses,** who presided over the arts and sciences and from whom we ultimately derive our word "music." Apollo and the muses shunned woodwind instruments because to play them required a forced blowing that deformed the face. Accordingly, Renaissance painters such as Raphael depicted Apollo expressing the divine powers of music by means of a string instrument (Fig. 2). Similarly, Renaissance writers, such as Baldassare Castiglione in his influential *The Book of the Courtier* (1528), encouraged the socially ambitious to learn to play string instruments but to avoid the deforming winds. Woodwinds and brasses were fine for the servant class of professional musicians, but not for the upwardly mobile concerned with their appearance. Thus the mythical status of Apollo, and the humanists' response to it, was just one way classical antiquity shaped musical thought during the Renaissance. Humanistic values touched performers and composers in equal measure.

 FIGURE 2

Apollo among the Muses, painted by Raphael for the papal apartments in 1509–1511. "Music," in the form of the god Apollo, plays a *lira da braccio,* surrounded by personifications of other fine arts, including song, dance, poetry, and drama.

 © Scala/Art Resource

KEY TERMS

Johannes Tinctoris
humanism
Apollo
muses
The Book of the Courtier

Chapter 20

Popular Music in Florence, 1475–1540: Carnival Song and Lauda, Frottola, and Early Madrigal

Historians dub the fifteenth century in Italy the **quattrocento** (Italian for what we call "the 1400s"). It was a period of enormous creativity in the visual arts, especially in cities such as Florence, Venice, Ferrara, and Mantua. Among the native painters and sculptors working in Florence during the 1400s were Donatello, Botticelli, Leonardo da Vinci, and Michelangelo. Earlier, during the trecento (1300s), Florence had been the center of a rich musical life, the place of creation of several hundred secular compositions (see Chapter 14). Given this activity in the visual arts and the rich musical tradition of Florence, we might expect to see a comparable level of Florentine musical productivity during the quattrocento. Strangely, however, during the fifteenth century the Florentines, and Italians generally, seem not to have encouraged native Italian musicians to develop skills as learned contrapuntists. When "high art" music was needed, especially for their churches, wealthy Italian patrons were inclined to hire singers and composers from northern Europe. Thus, northern luminaries such as Guillaume Dufay and Josquin des Prez were lured to Italy to serve the pope and other secular princes. These Franco-Flemish composers created the bulk of the learned art music—Masses, motets, and chansons—written in Italy during the fifteenth century.

Native Italians, and the Florentines in particular, cultivated a somewhat different kind of music. They preferred music in a more popular style and music improvised on the spot—music without canons and contrapuntal complexity. Unfortunately, not much of this Italian music survives in written form. Popular music generally tends not to be set down in complicated musical notation, and improvised music, by definition, is not written at all. Thus, much of what we know of Italian music-making during the quattrocento comes from literary accounts rather than from surviving music manuscripts. Beginning around 1500, however, some of this exuberant musical life was being committed to ink and paper, and published by printers in Venice and Rome. In these publications we can see a vibrant musical culture and discern distinctly Italian musical genres: specifically, the carnival song, the lauda, the frottola, and, soon, the madrigal (a new genre appearing under an old name). Indeed, by the end of the sixteenth century the madrigal would be the most distinctive of all Italian musical genres.

THE CARNIVAL SONG AND THE LAUDA

For most of the Middle Ages, Florence had been a republic administered by an oligarchy of leading families.[1] During the 1400s, however, one clan in particular became dominant: the wealthy Medici family. Most important among the Medici leaders was **Lorenzo de' Medici (the Magnificent),** who controlled the city from 1469 until his death in 1492. Like other Italian rulers at this time, Lorenzo brought northern composers to his city, in this case to sing at the famous cathedral of Florence (Fig. 15-1) as well as in the Medici palace. The most famous of these Franco-Flemish imports was Heinrich Isaac, whom we shall meet later (see Chapter 24). Lorenzo himself was a fine poet, and he encouraged Isaac and others to set his words to music. The genre of music Lorenzo seems to have enjoyed most is the carnival song.

Carnival season comes immediately before Lent. To understand the fun and frivolity of the Italian carnival, think of *Mardi gras* in New Orleans or *carnaval* in Rio with masked revelers, music, and dance, all fueled by appropriate drink. In Renaissance Florence the leading revelers were called *mascherati* (masqueraders), men and boys in costume (frequently, in "drag"). They would go about the city singing songs appropriate for the moment. Sometimes they would stop in a city square or beneath the window of an important lady, and her lover would pay them to sing. Figure 20-1 shows five Florentine *mascherati* so performing. To their left stands Lorenzo de' Medici, purse prominent. Lorenzo wrote poems that he then had set to music to serve as a **carnival song** (*canto carnascialesco*). Most carnival songs are short, homophonic pieces in three vocal parts. Texts usually deal with everyday life on the streets of Florence and are sometimes sexually explicit. One of the best known of the carnival songs was the *Canto de' profumieri* (*Song of the Perfume Sellers*). Here simple, declamatory music accommodates a refrain and seven strophes of text. The refrain introduces the *mascherati*, who in this case claim to be a group of gentlemen merchants of the Spanish town of Valencia. The first two stanzas extol their wares, including soothing oils that bring relief to women in the heat of love, a clear *double entendre*. The text of this carnival song was by Lorenzo the Magnificent. The music was likely improvised by singers in the streets; only later, when it had become part of the oral tradition of Florence, was the musical version written down.

Biblioteca Riccardiana, Florence

🌿 FIGURE 20-1
Lorenzo de' Medici and carnival singers.

EXAMPLE 20-1

We are the gallants of Valencia, who in passing are smitten…

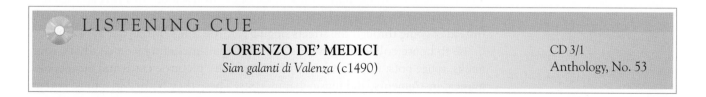

LISTENING CUE

LORENZO DE' MEDICI
Sian galanti di Valenza (c1490)

CD 3/1
Anthology, No. 53

Florence was and remains a city of extremes—of wealth and poverty, tradition and novelty, passion and piety. The secular carnival song had its sacred counterpart in the lauda. A **lauda** (Italian for "a song of praise"; pl., **laude**) was a simple, popular sacred song written, not in church Latin but in the local dialect of Italian. From its beginning in the thirteenth century, the lauda had been sung by members of a

confraternity, a society of laymen devoted to one or another aspect of Christian faith, such as the Virgin Mary or the Holy Cross. Florence had no fewer than twelve such confraternities, and performing laude was an essential part of their fraternal life. Hundreds of their lauda texts survive, but few melodies. The reason for this is simple: most laude were sung to pre-existing melodies, and many different texts could be sung to the same tune. A prescription at the top of a text would instruct the brothers to sing the lauda "just as to the Song of the Fisherwoman" or "just as to the Song of the Perfume Sellers." The newly fashioned piece was called a **contrafactum** (pl., **contrafacta**)—something fabricated from something else, in this case a religious piece from a very secular one. (In a similar manner the reform-minded Lutherans would soon make contrafacta by retexting popular songs with religious texts, thereby creating Lutheran chorales.) Lorenzo the Magnificent also wrote lauda texts, and his lauda *O maligno, e duro core* (*O, malignant, evil heart*) was to be sung to the *Song of the Perfume Sellers*. As comparisons of just the refrains show, the number of syllables per line (eight) and the rhyme scheme (**abba**) of the lauda was the same as that of the carnival song; thus one tune easily works for both texts.

Lauda	Rhyme scheme	Carnival song
O maligno e duro core,	a	Sian galanti di Valenza,
Fonte d'ogni mal concetto,	b	Qui per passo capitati,
Che non scoppi a mezzo il petto,	b	D'amor già presi e legati
Che non t'apri di dolore.	a	Delle donne di Fiorenza.
(O, evil, bitter heart,		(We are the gallants of Valencia
Source of all malicious thought,		Who in passing are smitten,
Who bursts from the breast not even a little,		Taken and tied by the love
And opens not for sadness.)		Of the ladies of Florence.)

Perhaps the most famous, or infamous, writer of laude was **Girolamo Savonarola** (1452–1498). Savonarola was a Dominican friar, a member of a monastic order that still exists today. Born and raised in Ferrara, Italy, Savonarola came to Florence in 1482. By 1490 he had advanced to become the principal religious orator of the city. Preaching to thousands in the nave of the gigantic cathedral (see Fig. 15-1), the friar railed against the laxity of the clergy, including the pope, as well as against the idleness of the aristocracy. Part populist, part rabble-rouser, and part religious fanatic, Savonarola's critical attacks earned him a following among many reform-minded citizens of Florence.

By 1497 the devout Savonarola had become the most powerful figure in the city and, needless to say, he didn't think much of carnival season. In 1497, and again in 1498, Savonarola instigated a practice now known as the **bonfire of the vanities.** Instead of going through the streets singing carnival songs, his supporters went from house to house collecting "useless" worldly items including women's hats, wigs, masks, rouge pots, mirrors, chessboards, perfumes, pictures, cards and dice, books, musical instruments, and music manuscripts. These they burned in a huge bonfire in the Piazza della Signoria (the central square of Florence; Fig. 20-2). Such bonfires were a powerful symbol of the friar's fanaticism and his belief that the Florentines must lead simple, virtuous lives if they themselves hoped to avoid the eternal bonfire of Hell. Savonarola was, to say the least, anti-humanist.

But Savonarola was not entirely anti-music. He himself was the author of twelve lauda texts, and each of these was supplied with music by means of a contrafactum; a carnival song provided music for a lauda. Savonarola's numerous followers went through the streets of Florence lamenting the sinful world as they sang his laude. Savonarola's most popular lauda text, *Giesù, sommo conforto* (*Jesus, highest solace*), survives with an anonymous popular tune serving as a cantus. Against this, a tenor provides a harmonic support while an alto adds simple counterpoint, mostly in parallel thirds often above the cantus. Originally, the duet between the cantus and altus might have been improvised, and it is easy to imagine that this entire setting faithfully records what was essentially an oral, improvisatory practice. Such an approach did not create a musical masterpiece, but it was sufficient to convey Savonarola's spiritual message: every good Florentine should be willing to join Christ on the cross and burn with "holy fire," as the text of this lauda says.

Ultimately, such a fiery fate befell Savonarola himself. Followers of the pope and the Medici family united and took him prisoner. As punishment for having rendered "false prophecies," Savonarola was tied to an elevated crucifix in the Piazza della Signoria and burned to death on 23 May 1498 (Fig. 20-2).

❀ FIGURE 20-2

Savonarola instituted the "bonfire of the vanities" to rid the city of objects of personal adornment and enjoyment. Eventually, the citizens of Florence rid themselves of Savonarola by subjecting him to the same fate. This anonymous painting shows the burning of Savonarola and two of his followers.

EXAMPLE 20-2

Jesus, highest solace...

🔘 LISTENING CUE

GIROLAMO SAVONAROLA
Giesù, sommo conforto (c1495)

CD 3/2
Anthology, No. 54

❀ THE FROTTOLA

In addition to the carnival song and lauda, another genre of Italian popular music arose during the quattrocento, the frottola. The term **frottola** (pl., **frottole**; believed to derive from the Latin "frocta," a collection of random thoughts) was used as a catch-all word to describe a polyphonic setting of a wide variety of strophic Italian poetry. Although the frottola flourished between the years 1470 and 1530, its roots lie in a tradition of improvisatory, solo singing that arose in Italy during the 1400s. A singer would recite poetry while accompanying himself on a string instrument. This practice was especially popular among Italian aristocrats. Lorenzo de' Medici was fond of improvisatory singing and accompanied himself on a Renaissance fiddle called the **lira da braccio**, a bowed five-string instrument tuned in fifths and played on the shoulder (Fig. 20-3). Improvisation of this sort should be seen as

National Music Museum

🌺 FIGURE 20-3

Lira da braccio of 1563. The *lira da braccio* was similar in design and function to the medieval vielle (see Fig. 11-4 and Fig. 2 on p. 149). It had five strings and two drone strings off the fingerboard.

a humanistic effort to recover the simplicity associated with the music of classical antiquity. With a *lira* in hand, the Renaissance musician appeared as ancient Orpheus reborn. In his influential *The Book of the Courtier* (1528), Baldassare Castiglione argues that the ability to sight-read polyphonic music is important. But even more desirable is the capacity to perform self-accompanied solo song:

> In my opinion, the most beautiful music is in singing well and in reading at sight and in fine style, but even more in singing to the accompaniment of the *lira*, because nearly all the sweetness is in the solo and we note and follow the fine style and the melody with greater attention in that our ears are not occupied with more than a single voice, and every little fault is the more clearly noticed—which does not happen when a group is singing, because the one sustains the other. But especially it is poetic recitation with the *lira* that seems to me most delightful, as this gives the words a wonderful charm and effectiveness.[2]

The frottola began life in this fashion, as poetry sung to an improvised string accompaniment; the performer would sing successive strophes of the text while bowing an accompaniment. It first took deep root in the northern Italian city of Mantua, where two Italians, Marchetto Cara (c1465–1525) and Bartolomeo Tromboncino (born 1470–died after 1535), perfected the genre. Some Franco-Flemish musicians working in Italy also turned to the frottola from time to time. Josquin des Prez wrote at least three, the best known of which is *El grillo* (*The Cricket*).

As Josquin's work shows, by 1490 the frottola could be fully sung, as well as performed by a solo voice with accompanying instrument(s). Here four singing parts are all assigned the same lively rhythms, a procedure that creates a highly homophonic texture. Curiously, just as rock guitarists in the 1950s and 1960s accompanied tunes almost exclusively in root-position chords, so here Josquin makes use of nothing but root-position triads in his harmony. This again suggests the ancestry of the frottola, that originally it was a poem sung to the accompaniment of simple chords bowed on a *lira da braccio* or strummed on a lute. The text of *El grillo* is typical of the lighter, sometimes comic, quality of the frottola. On one level, the subject of the poem, the cricket, can be taken to represent a singer who sings for love rather than for money. On the other hand, a *double entendre* may lurk here; the cricket's "long cry" and his singing "when the weather is hotter" may suggest a coarser interpretation. Either way, the music and the text are a long way from the lofty expression of the courtly Burgundian chanson. *El grillo* has the same zest for life and lighter musical style as the Florentine carnival song.

EXAMPLE 20-3

The cricket, the cricket is a good singer...

El grillo è bon cantore	The cricket is a good singer
Che tiene longo verso.	Who has a long cry.
Dale beve grillo canta.	The cricket sings of drinking.
El grillo è bon cantore.	The cricket is a good singer.
Ma non fa come gli altri ucelli,	But he is not, like other birds,
Come li han cantata un poco,	When they have sung a little,
Van' de fatto in altro loco,	Go off elsewhere,
Sempre el grillo sta pur saldo.	The cricket stays still.
Quando là maggior el caldo	When the weather is hotter
Alhor canta sol per amore.	Then he sings for love.
El grillo è bon cantore	The cricket is a good singer
Che tiene longo verso.	Who has a long cry.
Dale beve grillo canta.	The cricket sings of drinking.
El grillo è bon cantore.	The cricket is a good singer.

LISTENING CUE

JOSQUIN DES PREZ   CD 3/3
El grillo è bon cantore (c1500)   Anthology, No. 55

THE EARLY MADRIGAL IN FLORENCE

The **madrigal,** like the frottola, was a catch-all term used to describe settings of Italian verse. Earlier (see Chapter 14) we met the Italian trecento madrigal, a strophic secular piece for two or three voices in **AAB** form. The sixteenth-century madrigal, however, is musically unlike its earlier namesake. The sixteenth-century madrigal is invariably **through composed** (new music for every line of text), rather than strophic. Moreover, it employs a variety of textures and compositional techniques—simple homophonic declamation, imitative counterpoint, and extended melismatic passages among them. Thus, the madrigal is capable of a much wider range of expression than the usually uniform, strophic frottola. So too the madrigal displays a more serious tone, for the poetic texts are of a higher quality. The lofty aspiration of the madrigalists can be seen in the fact they often took their texts from the finest poets in the Italian language, their favorite being the great Francesco Petrarch (see introduction to Part II).

Given the importance of the madrigal to Italian musical culture during the Renaissance, it is ironic that most of the composers first associated with the genre were French or Flemish. Chief among them was Jacques Arcadelt (c1505–1568), a Frenchman who was active in Florence during the 1530s and spent much of his later career in the service of the pope in Rome. While in Florence, Arcadelt became one of the chief proponents of the madrigal. His first essays into the genre were published in 1538 or 1539 under the title *Primo libro di madrigali d'Archadelt* (*The First Book of Madrigals by Arcadelt*). The collection was so popular it was reprinted more than fifty times, and it secured Arcadelt's reputation as the preeminent composer of the early madrigal.

Opening Arcadelt's *Primo libro di madrigali* is his enduring *Il bianco e dolce cigno* (*The gentle white swan*). Typical of the madrigal, it sets a single stanza of poetry written in seven- or eleven-syllable lines. The subject is love and death. Legend has it that the swan sings a last song before dying—hence the term "swan song," meaning one's last act. The death of a beautiful white swan is not a happy image, yet here this conceit is sharply contrasted to the death of the speaker who dies with "joy and desire." Once again we have a *double entendre*, for in Renaissance poetry "death" was a metaphor for sexual release. Poetic antitheses and extremes of emotion such as these lie at the heart of madrigal poetry. They afford the composer the opportunity for equally diverse and extreme musical expression, but how does this play out in the music?

Il bianco e dolce cigno begins with soft, tranquil music worthy of the noble swan. The initial image of the swan quickly gives way to the "weeping" ("piangendo") of the narrator, which is underscored by an almost painfully surprising chord built on the flat seventh degree of the scale. Perhaps for rhetorical effect, this striking musical moment is immediately repeated. Similarly, a few bars later (mm. 21–23) the painful joy of a blessed "death" is highlighted by a flood of suspensions (dissonances releasing to consonances). Finally, the notion that a thousand such deaths would be desirable is conveyed through music by a passage of pervasive imitation, the phrase "di mille morti il dì" ("a thousand deaths a day") being sung by the voices seemingly a thousand times. Obviously, in the madrigal, as in no other musical genre of the Renaissance, there is a tight bond between text and music.

EXAMPLE 20-4

The gentle white swan dies singing, and I, weeping, approach the end of my life.

Il bianco e dolce cigno	The gentle white swan
Cantando more, e io	dies singing, and I,
Piangendo giung'al fin del viver mio,	weeping, approach the end of my life.
Stran'e diversa sorte,	Strange and diverse fates,
Ch'ei more sconsolato,	that he dies disconsolate,
E io **moro beato,**	and I die happy.

Morte che nel morire	Death, that in the [act of] dying
M'empie di gioia ela e di desire.	fills me wholly with joy and desire.
Se nel morir, altro dolor non sento,	If in dying I feel no other pain,
Di mille mort'il dì, sarei contento.	I would be content to die a thousand deaths a day.

LISTENING CUE

JACQUES ARCADELT
Il bianco e dolce cigno (c1538)

CD 3/4
Anthology, No. 56

The use of striking chord shifts, musical repetition, controlled dissonance, and abrupt textural changes to highlight the meaning of the text is called **text painting** in music; the music overtly sounds out the meaning of the text, almost word by word. Text painting (also called **word painting**) became all the rage with madrigal composers, in Italy and later in England. Even today such musical clichés as sighs and dissonances for "harsh" words are called **madrigalisms.**

Just how far composers of the Italian madrigal might go along the path of overt text expression can be seen in a five-voice setting of the same text, *Il bianco e dolce cigno,* by Orazio Vecchi (1550–1605). Vecchi's remake is an homage to, and perhaps even a parody of, Arcadelt's famous setting (Ex. 20-5). Both works are in the same mode (what would then be called the Ionian mode transposed to F), and Vecchi quotes the opening five bars of the earlier work (mm. 1–9). However, the entrance of the upper two voices in bars 6 and 7, which feature a playful melisma on "canTANdo," signals an entirely different tone and expressive intent. The remainder of the work is saturated with abrupt changes in texture and with word painting. Here Vecchi seems to want to make this piece do everything a madrigal "should" do and then some. Vecchi so exaggerates the moments of word painting that the madrigal becomes comic, as if poking fun at itself. As highly social music for both male and female singers, the madrigal intended to please performers and listeners alike. If it was funny as well as fun, so much the better.

EXAMPLE 20-5

The gentle white swan dies singing...

LISTENING CUE

ORAZIO VECCHI
Il bianco e dolce cigno (1589)

CD 3/5
Anthology, No. 57

SUMMARY

During the fifteenth century, composers from northern Europe thoroughly dominated the creation of learned polyphonic music in Italy (Masses, motets, and chansons). But there was much native music-making as well. Quattrocento Italian music tended to be lighter in style and more popular in expression. Because Italian music was often improvised on the spot, little of it was written down. Music with the Italians, and the Florentines in particular, involved perpetuating popular traditions in which complicated counterpoint had no place. The carnival song and the lauda were part of this vigorous, more spontaneous, Italian approach to music. The frottola, too, began life as an improvised genre, albeit inside the court rather than on the streets of the city. Yet in musical style it likewise manifests aspects of native Italian popular music: abundant root-position chords, snappy rhythms, and light, sometimes frivolous, texts. The madrigal, which arose in Italy about 1530, had a more serious tone and was part of a general movement in the Renaissance to elevate vernacular poetry to a higher status. The madrigal originated in Florence and then spread to other Italian cities, and eventually the Low Countries and England. The extent of its dominance in sixteenth-century musical life can be measured in the fact that many thousands were published. Above all, the madrigal is marked by an exceptionally close relationship between music and word.

KEY TERMS

quattrocento
Lorenzo de' Medici
(the Magnificent)
carnival song
lauda (pl. laude)
confraternity

contrafactum
(pl., contrafacta)
Girolamo Savonarola
bonfire of the vanities
frottola (pl., frottole)
lira da braccio

madrigal
through composed
text painting (word
painting)
madrigalism

Chapter

21

Josquin des Prez and Music in Ferrara

Political power in Renaissance Italy was concentrated in three separate areas: the kingdom of Naples in the south; the papal lands, with Rome at its heart, in the center of the peninsula; and the city-states in the north (see Map 14-1). Florence, Milan, and Venice were the most important northern city-states. But other smaller cities claimed attention, and one of the most important of these was **Ferrara.** Owing to a central location and a succession of strong rulers, Ferrara became a center of musical activity. Ferrara, unlike Venice and Florence, was not a republic. In the late fifteenth century it was ruled by a succession of despots, all members of the d'Este family. The d'Este were a rough, sometimes brutal, bunch but they did know a good composer when they heard one. The important musicians who at one time or another associated with the d'Este family included major composers such as Josquin des Prez, Adrian Willaert, Cipriano de Rore, and Carlo Gesualdo. By the end of the sixteenth century, the population of Ferrara had grown to about 60,000, and the court of Ferrara employed as many as forty full-time musicians, both singers and instrumentalists.

✼ JOSQUIN DES PREZ

Although the Renaissance produced many fine composers, Josquin des Prez (c1450–1521) is surely among the very best (Fig. 21-1). His fame was so great that at a time when composers from previous generations quickly became forgotten, his music continued to be published some fifty years after his death. Today ardent admirers place Josquin des Prez alongside Bach, Mozart, and Beethoven in the Pantheon of great composers. Josquin (as he was known by his contemporaries) wrote in all the musical genres of his day: approximately twenty Masses, seventy motets, seventy secular songs (chansons and frottole), as well as a few instrumental pieces carry his name. Martin Luther favored Josquin's music above that of all other composers: "Josquin is master of the notes, which must express what he desires; other composers can do only what the notes dictate."[1] The Florentine humanist Cosimo Bartoli compared Josquin to the great Michelangelo (1475–1564), who decorated the ceiling of the Sistine Chapel where Josquin was once a singer:

🌿 FIGURE 21-1
The only surviving likeness of Josquin des Prez.

> Josquin may be said to have been a prodigy of nature, as our Michelangelo Buonarroti has been in architecture, painting, and sculpture; for, as there has not thus far been anyone who in his compositions approaches Josquin, so Michelangelo among all those who have been active in these arts, is still alone and without a peer; both Josquin and Michelangelo have opened the eyes of all those who delight in these arts or are to delight in them in the future.[2]

Yet despite his greatness, the details of Josquin's life are still somewhat sketchy. His full name was Josquin Lebloitte dit (called) des Prez and he was born in northern France—we are not sure where—around 1450. In his youth, Josquin seems to have been a choirboy in the northern French town of St. Quentin, then a singer at the court of René d'Anjou in Provence in southern France, and later an employee of King Louis XI of France in Paris and Tours (see Chapter 18). By 1484 Josquin had migrated to Italy, and here he moved rather often between the courts at Milan, Mantua, Ferrara, and the papal curia in Rome. The records of the papacy show that Josquin sang in the Sistine Chapel between 1489 and 1495, and his name, which he carved on the wall of the singers' gallery, can still be seen there today (artistic license, or graffiti?). Eventually, Josquin left Rome and entered the service of Duke Hercules of Ferrara.

✼ JOSQUIN'S MUSIC FOR DUKE HERCULES OF FERRARA

At the end of the fifteenth century, Ferrara was ruled by Hercules d'Este (r. 1471–1505). Hercules was a professional soldier whose army was often hired to fight for other, larger Italian city-states such as Florence and Milan. Thus, the most famous

© Alinari/Art Resource, NY

❀ FIGURE 21-2

A portrait of Josquin's patron in
Ferrara, Duke Hercules d'Este
in full military armor.

portrait of Hercules shows him in full battle armor (Fig. 21-2).
Yet Hercules was also a devoutly religious man, attending Mass
daily, going on religious pilgrimages, and washing the feet of
the poor during Holy Week. Throughout his life Hercules
modeled his conduct after his namesake Hercules, the hero of
classical Greek mythology. Images of the ancient Hercules appeared everywhere at the court of Duke Hercules—painted on
walls, woven into tapestries, stamped on coins, and sculpted as
statues for the ducal garden. Why all this Herculean imagery?
During the Renaissance the hero Hercules became something
of a role model for Christian rulers because he had fought and
defeated the forces of evil in Greek antiquity. Hercules, both
modern duke and ancient hero, was a warrior who ultimately
chose a life of piety. As a sign of his piety, and of his love of
music, Duke Hercules supported a chapel that in 1503–1504
counted thirty-one singers and three organists, the largest in
western Europe at that time. Chief among them was Josquin
des Prez.

The esteem in which Josquin was held can be judged from
letters of 1502, when Duke Hercules was in need of a new director for his court chapel. The duke had recruiters searching
for the best composer of the day, and had narrowed the choice down to two musicians: Josquin des Prez and the renowned Heinrich Isaac, court composer for the
Holy Roman Emperor. One recruiter urged the duke to hire Josquin, whose presence, it was suggested, would make the Ferrarese chapel the equal of that of a king:

> My Lord, I believe that there is neither lord nor king who will now have a better
> chapel than yours if Your Lordship sends for Josquin . . . and by having Josquin in our
> chapel I want to place a crown upon this chapel of ours.[3]

Yet another agent felt Josquin, although the better composer, was too temperamental an artist:

> To me [Isaac] seems well suited to serve Your Lordship, more so than Josquin, because
> he is more good-natured and companionable, and will compose new works more often.
> It is true that Josquin composes better, but he composes when he wants to and not
> when one wants him to, and he is asking 200 ducats in salary while Isaac will come for
> 120—but Your Lordship will decide.[4]

To his credit, Duke Hercules chose the moody, more expensive Josquin, who became ducal chapel master in 1503.

Josquin's *Missa Hercules Dux Ferrarie*

Josquin des Prez composed a four-voice Mass in honor of Hercules, and he did so in
a novel fashion, knowing that the duke liked to see his name everywhere. Josquin
took the Latin title "Hercules dux Ferrarie" and extracted the vowels (e, u, e, u, e,
a, i, e). These he equated with the Guidonian solfege syllables to produce the
pitches "re," "ut," "re," "ut," "re," "fa," "mi," and "re," and he made these serve as
the cantus firmus of the Mass (Ex. 21-1). A cantus firmus extracted from the vowels
of a name is called a *soggetto cavato dalle vocali* ("subject cut out from the vowels").
It can simply be called a **soggetto cavato** ("a cut-out subject"—you can make one of
your own name). Josquin's *Missa Hercules dux Ferrarie* is one of the first compositions to use this procedure. Like the Guidonian hexachord itself (see Chapter 4),

the *soggetto cavato* could, in principle, appear in its natural form set on C, in the soft form set on F (with B♭), or in the hard form set on G (with B♮).

EXAMPLE 21-1

In fact, Josquin uses the *soggetto* only in its natural and hard positions. He strings the two together to form a twenty-four-note cantus firmus (Ex. 21-2). In the course of the Mass this twenty-four-note unit appears twelve times, perhaps as a symbolic reference to the twelve labors of the ancient hero Hercules.

EXAMPLE 21-2

Josquin's *Missa Hercules dux Ferrarie* begins with a statement of the cantus firmus in the soprano, so as to introduce the *soggetto* and make it clearly audible. Thereafter, the cantus firmus is assigned to the tenor, which does nothing other than sing the vowels of *Hercules dux Ferrarie* for the duration of the Mass; Josquin wanted to make sure we knew for whom this Mass was written! It seems likely that the ducal tenors sang the syllables of the duke's name rather than the text of the Ordinary. In fact, Hercules himself may have sung the motto with his tenors, since he is known to have "sung solfege on books of Masses for his amusement." The *Sanctus* may be taken as typical of Josquin's Mass as a whole (Ex. 21-3). At the conclusion of this movement the motto appears without interruption and in short note values, which creates the sense of driving excitedly toward the end.

EXAMPLE 21-3

LISTENING CUE

JOSQUIN DES PREZ

Sanctus of the *Missa Hercules dux Ferrarie* (c1503?)

CD 3/6

Anthology, No. 58

In the *soggetto cavato* Josquin had found a simple new way to unify all five parts of the Ordinary of the Mass and at the same time honor a generous employer. The *Missa Hercules dux Ferrarie* was first printed in 1505, the year of the duke's death, and the act of publication was seen as a tribute by a great composer to a famous patron. Although Josquin was the first to create a musical *soggetto cavato*, the process continued for centuries. Bach, Schumann, Berg, and Shostakovich were among the later composers who in similar ways fashioned themes, and sent coded messages, by means of musical letters.

Josquin's Motet *Miserere Mei, Deus*

In his day, Josquin des Prez was renowned above all else as a composer of motets. The unique quality of Josquin's motets rests in the relationship between music and text. Josquin is among the first composers to assess the meaning of the words of each section of a sacred text and craft music that captures the emotional content of those words. This is an important development in the history of music. It signals the end of the abstract, emotionally noncommittal music-text relationship of the Middle Ages, and the beginning of a new kind of expressive music designed to reflect and enhance the meaning of the words. Such text-specific music was inherent in the early madrigal of the 1530s, as noted in Chapter 20. It first appeared, however, around 1500 in the motets of Josquin des Prez.

One of Josquin's most powerful motets is his *Miserere mei, Deus* (*Have mercy upon me, O Lord*). It was inspired by, and modeled upon, a sermon by Girolamo Savonarola (1452–1498).[5] As we have seen (see Chapter 20), Savonarola, a native of Ferrara, was a religious fanatic who had gained control of Florence late in 1494. He urged spiritual reform and ordered that objects of idle pleasure, including musical instruments and music manuscripts, be burned in the central square of Florence. Ultimately, Savonarola was arrested, tried for heresy, and himself burned on a cross in the central square. While awaiting his execution, Savonarola penned a sermon in which he assumes the voice of a penitent soul who has sinned against God. The words of the sermon are periodically interrupted by a refrain, the opening line of Psalm 50, *Miserere mei, Deus*.

Psalm 50 is one of the seven so-called **Penitential Psalms,** seven psalms among the one hundred fifty of the Psalter that are especially remorseful in tone and sung in the rites of the Catholic Church surrounding death and burial. Savonarola's sermon quickly came to the attention of Duke Hercules of Ferrara, himself something of a religious fanatic. Hercules commanded his chapel master Josquin des Prez to create a musical counterpart to Savonarola's meditation on impending death.

In constructing his great work, Josquin drew inspiration from the psalm tone (see Ex. 3-1) to which *Miserere mei, Deus* is traditionally sung at the burial service. At the heart of the psalm tone is a **recitation** (reciting) **tone,** a constantly repeating pitch followed by a mediation. Here the mediation is an upper neighbor tone. Such an up-down motion, particularly by a half-step, has been traditionally associated with sighing or lamenting. This mournful reciting tone provides a structural grid for the motet, appearing as a cantus firmus in the tenor (Ex. 21-4).

EXAMPLE 21-4

Josquin's *Miserere mei, Deus* begins with second tenor, bass, soprano, and alto presenting the reciting tone in turn and then continuing with imitative counterpoint. The tenor soon enters with the reciting tone in long notes starting on the pitch e'. At the end of the first verse it returns with words "Miserere mei, Deus" on the reciting tone, but now a pitch lower, starting on d'. Here all voices join in with the cry "Have mercy upon me, O Lord," as if all humanity were petitioning for forgiveness. In this fashion the motet proceeds: duets and trios present the verses of the psalm and each verse ends with the choral refrain "Miserere mei, Deus" led by the tenor, each time beginning on a pitch a step lower. Josquin divides the twenty verses of Psalm 50 into three parts, consisting of eight, seven, and five verses per part. The reciting tone "Miserere mei, Deus" falls by step (starts a step lower each time) in part one, rises by step in part two, and falls again in part three. One might hear this as a repentant sinner falling to his knees, rising, and then falling once again before the Lord. Every time the tenor enters with its phrase, all other voices join his mournful cry.

How does Josquin paint, through music, the deeply sorrowful tone of the text? First of all, he makes plentiful use of the sorrowful quality of the reciting tone with its rise and fall. Moreover, he sometimes isolates a single word, setting it off on either side by rests, so as to highlight the meaning of that word, as he does in verse one on the petition "dele" ("remove [my sin]"). Also, Josquin uses "word painting" from time to time to emphasize the meaning of the text. For example, at the beginning of verse two all the voices sing together with a full choral sound on the word "amplius" ("more fully"). Finally, the entire psalm is oriented around the Phrygian mode, a scale that has historically possessed a strangely mournful quality, likely owing to the half-step relationship between scale degrees one and two. Exploiting these text expressive techniques within a masterful treatment of counterpoint leads to a work of extraordinary beauty and power. Josquin's *Miserere mei, Deus* is one of the greatest choral works ever written. In it we clearly hear how one composer achieved a primary goal of Renaissance humanists and musicians: to endow music with the persuasive power of rhetoric.

LISTENING CUE

JOSQUIN DES PREZ
Miserere mei, Deus (1503)

CD 3/7
Anthology, No. 59

A few months after Josquin composed this motet, the bubonic plague returned to Ferrara. The composer fled the city and left Italy for good, returning to the small town of Condé, his family's home, on the border of modern-day France and Belgium. There he died, a much-respected musician, in 1521. But the legend of Josquin only continued to grow.

✿ JOSQUIN AND AN ARTIST'S TEMPERAMENT

Upon the death of Josquin at least a half-dozen composers penned musical tributes to his memory. Publishers issued more and more of his chansons, Masses, and motets, making Josquin the most published composer of his age. Indeed, in Germany printers began issuing motets falsely under Josquin's name in order to capitalize on his reputation. This led one important figure, thought to be Martin Luther, to remark wryly: "Now that Josquin is dead, he is putting out more work than when he was still alive." Josquin is the first composer in the history of music for whom we have contemporary anecdotes, stories that reveal something of the personality and working habits of a truly exceptional composer. The Swiss music theorist Heinrich Glarean says, for example, that Josquin worked laboriously on his compositions, revising them and holding them back for many years before releasing them to the public. Another Swiss humanist, Johannes Manlius, reports that each time Josquin composed a new work he would give it to the choir to try out. As they sang, he would walk around, listening to the harmony. When he heard something he disliked, he would say "Be quiet, I will change that." To a singer who was so bold as to add notes to what the master had written, Josquin angrily responded: "You ass, why did you add those embellishments? If I had wanted them, I would have written them myself. If you want to correct musical works that have been composed in a natural or plain style, then write your own, but don't change my works."[6] Like other composers of the Renaissance, including Dufay and Obrecht (see Chapters 15, 17, and 19), Josquin would sometimes insert his own name, and information about himself, into the text of a motet. And let us not forget that Josquin was said to compose only when he wished and demanded a salary twice that of his principal competitor (Heinrich Isaac). In sum, Josquin comes across as one of a new breed, the artist of the Renaissance: moody, egotistical, demanding of himself and others, and supremely confident in the rightness of his own human creations.

 ## SUMMARY

Ferrara, Florence, and Venice were among the northern Italian city-states that encouraged the arts, and especially music, during the Renaissance. Ferrara in particular had a rich musical history, extending from the composer Josquin des Prez at the beginning of the sixteenth century to Carlo Gesualdo at the end. Josquin des Prez is one of the greatest composers in the history of music. In his nearly twenty Masses he used many erudite procedures (canon, retrograde motion, and *soggetto cavato*, for example) yet surrounds them with such beautiful sounds that these technical devices are barely noticeable—ingenious craftsmanship embedded within sublime sound. In his seventy-odd motets, Josquin reveals himself a master of text expression, one of the earliest composers to create musical gestures that intensify the meaning of individual words and phrases of the text. Numerous documents and anecdotes from Josquin's own day show that his contemporaries accorded him and his music a degree of respect like that of no other composer.

 ## KEY TERMS

Ferrara	Penitential Psalms
soggetto cavato	recitation tone

Musical Interlude

Music Printing in the Renaissance

Before the year 1450 all books in the West were written by hand; that is why they are called "manuscripts" (a combination of the Latin "manus" and "scriptus"). During the 1450s, however, a German craftsman working in the city of Mainz perfected a new method to produce books. His name was **Johannes Gutenberg** (c1400–c1468). Gutenberg invented printing with **movable type,** and it works in the following way. Hundreds of small pieces of metal type are cut, each containing a letter of the alphabet; these are arranged to form words in a series of lines that in turn create a page; after completion of the appropriate number of pages, the type is locked into an iron frame, called a "forme," and then is ready to be placed in the press. The type is then covered with ink and a sheet of paper pressed against it. When all the sheets for that forme are printed, the pieces of type can now be disassembled and reused to produce other formes. Finally, when all the sheets of a book are printed, they are arranged in order, and sent to a bookbinder to be stitched together.

Figure 1 shows a Renaissance printing press at work, as a sheet is pressed down tightly onto a metal forme full of movable, and reusable, type. Printing significantly reduced the amount of time needed to produce a book, and therefore its cost. A book was no longer something owned only by the nobility and high-ranking clergy, but could be had by lawyers, doctors, and tradesmen as well. Printing with movable type remained the standard method for generating books and newspapers until the advent of the computer-compositor in the late twentieth century.

Johannes Gutenberg printed mainly religious works, including the famed "Gutenberg Bible." The first examples of printed music also involved the sacred, specifically monophonic Gregorian chant. Printing polyphonic music, however, was a more difficult task because of the complexity of the different rhythmic values. It would not be until 1501—some fifty years later—that printing polyphonic music with movable type was successfully achieved.

The Germans had invented book printing in the West, and they soon carried the idea to Italy, specifically to Venice, where it became a huge commercial success. In fact, Venice became the center of publishing not only for Italy but also for all of Europe. Here technology went hand in hand with learning, for publishing and debating ancient Greek and Roman texts became, of course, the principal activity of Renaissance humanists. During the sixteenth century about 35,000 different titles were published in Venice, each with a press run of about 1,000, resulting in the publication of approximately 35 million books!

In 1501 the first book of polyphonic music from movable type was printed in Venice by **Ottaviano Petrucci** (1466–1539). He called it the ***Odhecaton,*** a Greek term meaning one hundred songs ("od" is Greek for "song," as in "melody" and "prosody"). Most of the songs in this collection were not by

🌿 FIGURE 1

A French printing shop about the year 1530. On the right, proofreaders check the text for errors.

Italians but were works of the great northern masters of counterpoint such as Ock-eghem, Busnoys, Obrecht, and Josquin. During the next two decades Petrucci went on to publish additional collections of songs, as well as Masses, motets, and frottole. Yet no matter what he printed, Petrucci executed everything with great care and clarity.

Petrucci's music prints are uniformly elegant because he used a complicated process called **multiple-impression printing**. First, he printed the lines of the staff horizontally across the page. Then he carefully pressed down the sheet a second time on a new metal plate and printed the notes onto the staff. Finally, he pressed the page down yet a third time to add text, title, composer's name, and any written instructions. Multiple-impression printing was time consuming, making the price fairly high and the number of buyers comparatively low. Indeed, Petrucci's press runs were modest; usually he printed no more than 500 copies of any one collection of songs or Masses.

An economical way of printing music was not realized in Italy or Germany, but in France, specifically in Paris during the late 1520s. Here **Pierre Attaingnant** (c1494–c1552), a printer and book seller living in the university quarter of the Left Bank, popularized a method called single-impression printing. In **single-impression printing** both the note and a small vertical section of the staff are fashioned onto a small piece of movable, reusable type. Dozens of such small pieces are needed to represent every possible pitch and rhythmic value, including multiples of them necessary to create many lines of music at once. A typesetter would set down staff, music, and text all in one forme, and press the sheet of paper only once, thereby substantially reducing production time and cost. The finished product had slight disjunctions where the individual pieces of type fit together. Compare the smooth look of a Petrucci print with the more utilitarian result of Attaingnant, where the breaks in the staff appear as small, jagged lines (Figs. 2 and 3). Attaingnant's method was not elegant, but it got the job done. With the single-impression method, music printing

🌿 FIGURE 2

The soprano part of a Mass by Pierre de la Rue in Petrucci's print of 1503.

became a commercially viable enterprise, and it quickly spread throughout Europe to become the usual mode of production of music books during the Renaissance. Single-impression printing remained the norm for printing music until the late seventeenth century, when the process of musical engraving gradually came to replace it.

Most early prints of music, whether from the press of Petrucci in Venice or Attaingnant in Paris, were issued not in score but in what are called part books. A **part book** is a volume that contains the music of one voice part and only one voice part. Even the new printed books were expensive. If you were a soprano, did you really need the alto's music? If you sang bass, why pay for what the tenor would sing? (Some well-to-do collectors, of course, bought sets with all the parts.) Because it was easier and cheaper for the printer to lay out the voice parts in separate books, the part book helped further reduce the cost of printing, and this stimulated a mass market for music. The part book format remained the main vehicle for disseminating vocal music until the middle of the seventeenth century, when printing music in score became more common.

Much as printing affected intellectual life in general during the Renaissance, so printing music affected musical life. Printed part books contributed to the growth of musical literacy, not so much at court or in church, but at home. "How to" manuals encouraged ordinary men and women to learn to read musical notation, to sing, and to play an instrument. Here, for the first time in music history, we see the appearance of the musical amateur. Moderately priced musical anthologies provided the music the amateur needed.

Finally, the fact that printing music required skilled craftsmen to cut the fonts of type, pressmen to manufacture the books, and shops in which to sell them, suggests that printing music was very much an urban phenomenon dependent on technology and commerce. Large cities such as Venice, Rome, and Paris became centers of the music publishing business, and the fledgling industry grew along with the ever-increasing urban populations. During the Renaissance a printer such as Petrucci or Attaingnant acquired the press and the fonts of type, gathered the musical compositions and arranged them into a pleasing collection, printed the books, and sold them in the same shop where he printed them. Music lovers came to the shop, acquired the music, and took it home to perform. This model of the urban music store, where printed music could be bought for performance in the home, remained in place until a mere fifty years ago. It was gradually replaced by the record store and then the CD store, where it was possible to buy music that others had performed and to listen to their performances at home. Now even the music shop has become obsolete. Most music today is performed by others—by professionals—and is downloaded from the Internet.

FIGURE 3

The soprano part of a Mass by Jean Mouton in Attaingnant's print *Viginti missarum musicalium* of 1532. Note the wavy lines created by the many small pieces of movable type.

Boston Athenaeum

KEY TERMS

Johannes Gutenberg	multiple-impression printing	single-impression printing
movable type		
Ottaviano Petrucci	Pierre Attaingnant	part book
Odhecaton		

Chapter 22

Music in Renaissance Paris

During the late Middle Ages (1150–1350), Paris was at the center of all that was new in polyphonic art music. The composers of organum, motets, and conductus, as well as the later isorhythmic motets, were, at least at first, nearly all Parisians. They wrote Europe's most "cutting edge" music. But the Black Death of 1349–1350 and the Hundred Years' War (1337–1453) brought calamity to late medieval Paris, and not until the Renaissance did the capital of France finally recover.

When Paris did regain its former glory it did so under the aegis of an especially powerful, yet artistically sensitive, king: **Francis I** (ruled 1515–1547) (Fig. 22-1). Almost single-handedly, he brought the Italian Renaissance north to France. To adorn the royal court, Francis hired some of the greatest Italian artists of the day (Leonardo da Vinci and Benvenuto Cellini among them). He encouraged the study of classical literature in both Latin and ancient Greek by founding a college in Paris that still exists today (the *Collège de France*). The number of students living in the university section of Paris—the Latin Quarter on the Left Bank—grew to nearly 16,000. For religious music, King Francis supported a large chapel of the best singers and composers he could find; for secular entertainment he employed lutenists, string players, chamber singers, trumpeters, and shawmists, among others. His singers were mostly French, but many of his instrumentalists were imported from Italy. Yet perhaps the greatest contribution Francis made to the growth of art music in Renaissance Paris was his support for the fledgling music industry of Paris, specifically his sponsorship of the new industry of music publishing. For Francis, art, industry, and technology progressed hand in hand.

As we have seen (Musical Interlude 3), the commercial music business as we know it first began in Paris with **Pierre Attaingnant** (c1494–c1552), a book printer and seller with a shop on the Left Bank. In 1528 King Francis gave Attaingnant a copyright on the music he published and a patent on the technology that made it possible. In 1537 the king named Attaingnant the official printer of music for the crown. Attaingnant had received, in effect, a monopoly to print music, at least in and around Paris. It must have been a lucrative business, because Attaingnant produced music book after music book, more than 170 different titles in all.

✳ FIGURE 22-1

King Francis I as painted by Jean Clouet about 1525.

Bridgeman Art Library

✳ THE PARISIAN CHANSON

What kind of music did Attaingnant print? He issued books for all kinds of music-making, from large, luxurious choir books of polyphonic Masses for professional church choirs, to cheaper, small-size books containing collections of motets, lute music, keyboard music, and dances for instrumental ensembles. But, above all, Attaingnant printed anthologies of polyphonic chansons, a total of more than a hundred of them. Each book contained about thirty songs, and for each he ran off about 500 to 1,000 copies. Most chansons were for four voices, a few for three. Like the Italian printers before him, Attaingnant published these songs (as well as his motets) not in score, but in part books. A singer need not purchase an entire set, only the music for his or her vocal part (Fig. 22-2).

In all, Pierre Attaingnant printed more than two thousand separate secular chansons. Many of these songs are of a type referred to as the **Parisian chanson.** Before 1500 the poetry of the French chanson was essentially a courtly affair that spoke of ideal love in a somewhat abstract way. For nearly two centuries it followed the rigid rules and rhyme schemes of the *formes fixes*. The musical setting, too, was abstract, meaning that there was little attempt to write music to convey the sense of particular words, or to capture the natural rhythm of the text. Often the text could be set almost anywhere beneath the music with no specific tying of the words to particular notes. In the newer Parisian chanson, however, the rhythm of the text begins to animate the rhythm of the music. Now, almost every note has its own syllable, and the duration of that note is often determined by the length or stress of the syllable. Similarly, the subject matter of the lyrics is far more "down to earth" in tone. These chansons sometimes speak of love, but love of a less ideal, more physical sort—of lusty lovers or libidinous priests and their all-too-willing companions, for example. Some songs depict drinking scenes, others, particularly those of Clément Janequin (c1485–c1560), are medleys of battle sounds or the street cries of Parisian vendors. Many texts are funny, some obscene.

The musical style of the Parisian chanson is almost entirely syllabic, because the stresses of the words largely determine the duration of the notes. All four voices often declaim the text together, thereby creating a generally chordal texture. Homophonic declamation now takes precedence over linear counterpoint. Pitches are frequently repeated in snappy recitation called **patter-song**—the rapid delivery of text on repeated notes. The form of the song flows naturally from the particular structure of the text. Indeed, every song seems to have its own form. By 1530 the stiff, medieval *formes fixes* had been driven from the scene, replaced by a multitude of formal types; the old courtly chanson gave way to a more flexible, urban (and urbane) popular song.

FIGURE 22-2

Tapestry from Bourges, France, depicting four singers performing a chanson from part books. As the scene suggests, this was music for all literate musicians to enjoy, female as well as male.

 ## CLAUDIN DE SERMISY

The master of the new Parisian chanson was Claudin de Sermisy (c1490–1562). Claudin (as he was known in his day) was primarily a church musician. Between 1508 and 1562 he served as a singer and then master of the royal chapel for three successive French monarchs. Though an ordained priest, Claudin's fame now rests, not on his religious music, but on his 169 surviving secular songs. Like Paul McCartney in the twentieth century, Claudin was one of the greatest melody writers of his day.

It is no surprise, therefore, that Claudin's chansons dominate Pierre Attaingnant's inaugural publication, the *Chansons nouvelles* of 1528, and that the second song in that set was his *Tant que vivray* (*As Long as I Live*). The seductive melody and infectious rhythm suggest why *Tant que vivray* went on to become one of the hit tunes of the sixteenth century, the object of many reprints, not just in Paris but in places like England, Italy, the Netherlands, and Spain. Here the structure of the text determines the structure of the music, each line beginning with a new idea and ending in a clear cadence (Ex. 22-1). Notice, again, how the rhythm of the text determines the rhythm of the music. Except for the short melisma in the cantus and tenor in bar 10, the piece is entirely syllabic—each syllable generates one note, but no more. At the very beginning, the poetic unit is that of a dactyl (long-short-short-long), and for that Claudin creates a corresponding rhythm: "Tant que vivray" (♩♩♩♩). Toward the end, the dactyls come faster as short, four-syllable lines pile one on top of the other in patter-song style, and likewise the musical rhythms reflect the increased verbal speed: "Son alliance, c'est ma fiance" (♩♪♪♩♩). Yet while the music reflects the rhythm of the text, it does not overtly sound out its meaning, as is true of many Italian madrigals. *Tant que vivray*, like most Parisian chansons, is strophic, and multiple stanzas cannot accommodate text painting.

EXAMPLE 22-1

As long as I live in the prime of life,…
Her allegiance, that is my faith, her heart is mine, and mine is hers.

LISTENING CUE

CLAUDIN DE SERMISY
Tant que vivray (c1528)

CD 3/8
Anthology, No. 60a

INSTRUMENTAL ARRANGEMENTS

The popularity of Claudin's *Tant que vivray* can be judged by the fact that it was not only reprinted many times as a vocal piece but also arranged for a variety of instruments: solo keyboard, lute, lute and voice, and even for three lutes; of course, it could also be played as a four-part instrumental piece simply by eliminating the text. No sooner did Pierre Attaingnant publish the song as a four-voice vocal piece in 1528 than the very next year he printed an arrangement of it for solo voice with lute accompaniment as well as another for lute alone. The version for solo lute is called a lute **intabulation,** in part because it is written in lute **tablature.** (Lute tablature is explained in Chapter 23 in connection with Ex. 23-2.) An intabulation implies that a preexisting polyphonic vocal piece has been arranged for a single instrument.

The lute intabulation of Claudin's *Tant que vivray* takes into account the technical and sonorous limitations of that instrument. First of all, the alto part has been removed, a standard practice when reducing a four-part song to a more manageable number of lines on a solo instrument (Ex. 22-2). But, more important, because no lute can sustain for long the delicate sound of the plucked strings, embellishment is added. To fill in sonic voids—the long notes in the original song—figural ornamentation is inserted, mainly in and around the melody line.

EXAMPLE 22-2

 LISTENING CUE

CLAUDIN DE SERMISY
Tant que vivray arranged for lute (1529)

Book Companion Website (http://schirmer.wadsworth.com/wright_1e)
Anthology, No. 60b

In Attaingnant's arrangement for voice and lute, on the other hand, the voice now carries the melody. Consequently, the lute is free to restore the original alto line and need not supply as much sound-filling ornamentation (Ex. 22-3). Needless to say, what Attaingnant and his arranger have given us by way of lute accompaniment is only one possibility. A talented instrumentalist would have improvised many alternative accompaniments as the singer sang subsequent strophes of the song. Instrumental music at this time was only gradually moving from a mainly aural and improvisatory tradition to one of written musical notation or, in this case, written musical tablature.

EXAMPLE 22-3

Tant que vi - vray en aa - ge flo - ris - sant

etc.

LISTENING CUE

CLAUDIN DE SERMISY

Tant que vivray arranged for voice and lute (1529)

CD 3/9

Anthology, No. 60c

In 1531 the always enterprising Pierre Attaingnant issued Claudin's *Tant que vivray* in yet another arrangement, this time for keyboard. A translation of the title of that print reads: *Twenty-one chansons reduced to tablature for organ, harpsichord, clavichord, and similar musical instruments.* Clearly, the publisher wanted to sell as many volumes as possible by making it known that this music could be played on any sort of keyboard instrument. A quick glance at the keyboard version of Claudin's *Tant que vivray* shows that Attaingnant's arrangement makes use of all of the old-fashioned, stereotypical organ embellishments of the fifteenth century and grafts them onto the chanson (Ex. 22-4). These older keyboard figures include the quick turn around the initial note of the piece, simple scales, and seemingly aimless "noodling" (see bar 8). Occasionally, the keyboard ornamentation results in out-dated parallel fifths (entry to bar 8) and parallel octaves (bar 21, see Anthology, No. 60d). In truth, this keyboard transcription, burdened with antiquated features, possesses none of the charm or airy grace of the lute arrangement or the vocal origi-nal. In general, one can safely say that the keyboard music of the early sixteenth century only rarely attains the generally high level of musical excellence found in the secular and sacred vocal music of that period.

EXAMPLE 22-4

etc.

LISTENING CUE

CLAUDIN DE SERMISY
Tant que vivray arranged for keyboard (1531)

Book Companion Website (http://schirmer.wadsworth.com/wright_1e)
Anthology, No. 60d

Finally, a group of instruments might perform Claudin's popular *Tant que vivray* simply by playing, rather than singing, the vocal lines. In sixteenth-century Paris a family of viols (see Chapter 23) or of recorders, or of a flute for the melody with recorders below, would have been common. Attaingnant mentions what he calls the "German flute" (our transverse flute; Fig. 22-3) as well as the recorder. All instrumentalists, with the possible exception of the bass part, were expected to improvise around the written chanson lines. Indeed, today's performers of early music do this as a matter of course when recreating the sounds of the Renaissance. When improvising in the style of the Renaissance, modern instrumentalists employ, among other things, the ornamental patterns set forth in Attaingnant's own lute and keyboard transcriptions.

DANCE MUSIC

Parisian chansons had direct, pleasing rhythms, and often these songs, when played by an instrumental ensemble, served well as dance music. Claudin's *Tant que vivray*, for example, was transformed, later in the century, into a duple-meter Italian dance known as the *passamezzo*. Popular chansons, however, were not the only kind of music used for dancing. Beginning in 1529 Attaingnant issued a series of volumes containing pieces specifically created to be dance music. Most of the collections were filled with dance pieces for an instrumental consort—for a quartet of viols or of recorders, for example. Attaingnant's first publication for instrumental consort, *Six Gaillardes et six Pavanes avec Treze chansons musicales a quatre parties* (*Six Galliards and Six Pavanes with Thirteen Songs in Four*

FIGURE 22-3

A lutenist playing from a rotulus (sheet music) and a player of a transverse flute, performing from a printed part book, execute a Parisian chanson about 1540. Notre Dame of Paris can be seen in the background.

Parts; 1530), contains just what the title says: a dozen dances along with thirteen songs that could be sung or played as dance music. That the dances are entirely pavanes or galliards suggests the importance of these two dance types. By the mid sixteenth century the pavane and galliard had supplanted the *basse danse* and the *tordion* (see Chapter 19) as the most favored pair of what might fairly be called the "couples" type of ballroom dances.

The pavane gradually replaced the fifteenth-century *basse danse* as the primary slow dance of the court. Like the earlier *basse danse*, the **pavane** is a slow, gliding dance performed by couples holding hands, but it is in duple rather than triple meter. The stately quality of the pavane is indicated by the fact that it also served— and still serves today in some regions of France—as wedding music while entering the chapel, as well as processional music for ecclesiastics entering and exiting the church. The pavane is perhaps the simplest of all Renaissance dances. It consists of only four steps, as described in the introduction to Anthology, No. 61. The music, too, was rigorously organized into phrases of four bars in our modern notation, which could be extended to eight- or twelve-bar units.

The anonymous third pavane from Attaingnant's *Second Livre de danceries* (*Second Book of Dances*; 1547) is comprised of such four-bar phrases (Ex. 22-5). Each beat and each step of the dance occupies a half note (semibreve) in a measure of cut time. Finally, each four-, eight- or twelve-bar section is repeated, and the entire piece could be repeated as many times as necessary, according to the will and stamina of the dancers.

EXAMPLE 22-5

Thoinot Arbeau: The Dancing Priest

Most of what we know about dance in sixteenth-century France comes from an unexpected source, an elderly canon and priest of Langres, in the eastern part of France. His name was Jehan Tabourot (1520–1595) but he chose to write about dance under the *nom de plume* of an anagram of that name: **Thoinot Arbeau.** In 1589 Arbeau published a lengthy treatise on dance called ***Orchésographie,*** the name of which is derived from the fact that in the theater of ancient Greece the chorus sang and danced in what was called "the orchestra." It may seem strange that a man of the cloth would write about dance, but male clerics frequently danced in the pre-modern church, just as spiritual men such as shamans and dervishes have in other cultures throughout the ages.

Arbeau writes his dance treatise in the form of a master-pupil dialogue. His pupil is a young law student who, like Beethoven some two hundred years later, wished to improve his social graces by taking dancing lessons. Arbeau patiently describes the popular dances of the day, laboriously detailing the steps for each. He tells us what is in fashion and what is not. From him we glean unexpected information about the performance practices of the day: that a harpsichord playing octaves regularly in its low range could simulate and replace a drum beat; that a tambourine might also give the beat; that a solo violin might accompany a dance; or that, if instruments were not at hand, singers could sing a tune for the dancers. Arbeau specifically recommends

the dance music "of the recently deceased Pierre Attaingnant" and gives his address in Paris, should the reader wish to buy dance music from his shop.

Arbeau provides an amusing insight into the social mores of the day. The pupil is encouraged to improve himself because "by learning fencing, dancing, and tennis you may be an agreeable companion to ladies and gentlemen alike." Ladies should do likewise because "they lead sedentary lives, intent upon their knitting, embroidery, and needlework, and are subject to a variety of ill-humours, which have need to be dispelled by some temperate exercise." After dancing, the gentlemen are permitted to kiss their mistresses "to ascertain if they are shapely or emit an unpleasant odor as of bad meat." Finally, Arbeau, who was sixty-nine when he wrote his treatise, suggests how to deport oneself on the dance floor:

When you dance in company never look down at your feet to see whether you are performing the steps correctly. Keep your head and body erect and appear self-possessed. Spit and blow your nose sparingly, or if needs must, turn your head away and use a fair white handkerchief. Converse affably in a low, modest voice, your hands at your sides, neither hanging limp nor moving nervously. Be suitably and neatly dressed, your hose well secured and your shoes clean; and remember this advice not only when you are dancing the galliard but in performing all other kinds of dance as well.[1]

FIGURE 22-4

A couple executing a "révérence" as depicted in Thoinot Arbeau's *Orchésographie* (1589), as reproduced in the English edition of Mary Steward Evans, p. 80.

The pavane was usually followed by the **galliard,** a fast leaping dance in triple meter. The basic unit of this dance and its music involves six beats and six steps in $^6_4$ time. The galliard proceeds at a much faster tempo than the pavane, and the beat is now carried by the quarter note (minim), as can be seen in the third galliard from Attaingnant's *Second Livre de danceries* (Ex. 22-6). Most important, the steps of the galliard are much different from those of the pavane. The galliard involves a succession of fast steps with periodic leaps (*sauts*) into the air. Each step takes place within the space of a single quarter note. The principal leap (*saut majeur*) occurs on beat five of the six-beat phrase, and this accounts for the frequent use of rhythmic hemiola, with stress suddenly coming on beats three and five of the six-beat phrase. Thus if the stately pavane was a slow dance for the old, the leaping galliard was a show dance for the young. An athletic couple would enter the dance floor together but then dance separately as one or the other took the lead. Queen Elizabeth I of England was famous as a dancer of the galliard and a related dance called the volta, in which the woman was tossed so high that she "will feel her brain reeling and her head full of dizzy whirlings" (see Fig. 27-1).[2] With leaps by solo dancers, the galliard and similar dances must have approached what we today call ballet.

EXAMPLE 22-6

LISTENING CUE

ANONYMOUS
Pavane and Galliard (1547)

CD 3/10 and
Book Companion Website (http://schirmer.wadsworth.com/wright_1e)
Anthology, Nos. 61a, 61b

Ultimately, in the course of the sixteenth century, other dances were added to, or replaced, the pavane and galliard. The allemande, for example, made its first appearance in an Attaingnant print in 1557, and Arbeau discusses the courante and gavotte in his treatise of 1589. The practice of stringing together several dances, each with its own tempo, meter, and mood, intensified in France and Italy after 1550, and eventually led to the Baroque instrumental suite, which culminated around 1720 in those of Bach and Handel.

SUMMARY

Paris regained its position as an important cultural and artistic center in the first half of the sixteenth century. King Francis I (r. 1515–1547) encouraged the growth of scholarship and the cultivation of music as well as the medium by which to disseminate both, namely printing. Between 1528 and 1557 the firm of Pierre Attaingnant published virtually all of the music that survives today from Paris in the first half of the sixteenth century, to wit, Masses, motets, instrumental dances, and, especially, popular songs. During this period, composers in and around Paris developed a new style of polyphonic song called the "Parisian chanson." Here the subject matter is topical and speaks of everyday life in a realistic way. The poetic text determines the overall structure of the music, and the rhythm of the poem usually sets the rhythm of the music as well. Pierre Attaingnant also published instrumental arrangements of songs, as well as ten collections of dances for lute, keyboard, or instrumental consort. These include the older *basse danse* as well as the newer pavane and galliard. The pavane is a slow, stately dance in duple meter constructed of four-bar phrases, while the galliard, made up of six-beat units, is a faster dance in triple meter involving quick steps and athletic leaps. Combining several dances of different moods and styles ultimately led to the Baroque dance suite.

KEY TERMS

Francis I	intabulation	Thoinot Arbeau
Pierre Attaingnant	tablature	*Orchésographie*
Parisian chanson	pavane	galliard
patter-song		

Chapter

23

Renaissance Instruments and Instrumental Music

The greatest glories of Renaissance music, without doubt, are to be found in its vocal pieces, specifically in the Masses, motets, madrigals, and chansons of composers such as Josquin, Lassus, Palestrina, and Byrd, for example. Measured purely in terms of musical sales, vocal music was more in demand in the Renaissance than instrumental music. Around 1550 music publishers produced about fifteen prints of vocal music for every one of instrumental. But there is an explanation for this seeming imbalance: before 1500 almost all instrumental music was performed by aural memory and not from written scores, and after 1500 much of it continued to be performed in this way. Also, lute intabulations and keyboard scores were generally more expensive to print than vocal part books. Nevertheless, the sixteenth century was an important moment in the history of instrumental music. The printing press enabled instrumental music to circulate farther afield than before. Finally, new instruments appeared, including the guitar, viol, and violin, and new instrumental genres were created, such as the prelude, ricercar, and fantasia.

✿ KEYBOARD INSTRUMENTS

Organ

The organ was first widely introduced into churches only during the late Middle Ages, specifically in the fourteenth century. Most organs were "show pieces" embodying the newest technology in metallurgy and scientific measurement. For that reason organs were usually put in the people's part of the church at the back (west end), where they could be seen and heard by all. By the sixteenth century, many churches in Europe had two organs, a large one at the back and a smaller one in the area of the church called the choir (east end). This second instrument could more easily accompany singers near the altar. The largest of the church organs had two keyboards for the hands and a pedal keyboard as well. Smaller portative organs possessing a single keyboard were also present in the dwellings of monks and canons (high-ranking churchmen) in monasteries and cathedrals, as well as in residences of the aristocracy and well-to-do (see Fig. 11-5). On these domestic organs, performers played keyboard arrangements of both sacred vocal music and popular songs. The monks enjoyed a good tune as much as their secular brethren.

In fact, one of the largest sources of Renaissance organ music was once owned by a monastery. It is called the **Buxheim Organ Book,** Buxheim being the site of a monastery that still exists today near Munich in southern Germany. The manuscript (Fig. 23-1) was written about 1470 and contains 256 compositions for organ, almost all of them anonymous arrangements of sacred and secular vocal music. Notice that the Buxheim Organ Book is written in **keyboard tablature,** a combination of note symbols (for the fast-moving upper part) and pitch-letter names (for the lower parts). In principle, tablature in music directs the performer's fingers to a specific spot on an instrument, in this case a key called A or F, for example. Tablature of this sort continued fashionable for three centuries, and was sometimes used by J.S. Bach when he composed for the organ.

Notice also in Figure 23-1 that for the first time we see what appear to be bar lines, or measure lines, in the music. The lines are not always consistently placed, but they generally mark off units (measures) of equal duration. Bar lines are found in keyboard and lute tablatures much earlier than they appear in vocal music, perhaps because composers thought it necessary to show vertical alignment in music where the notes are superimposed in score format. To hear an organ from the Renaissance, go to CD 3/13.

Clavichord, Harpsichord, and Virginal

The **clavichord** is a medieval instrument (see Chapter 11) that produces sound when a tiny metal tangent in the shape of a "T" is pushed into the string from beneath. The tangent does not so much pluck as caress the string by vibrating against it from below. Consequently, the sound of the clavichord is very quiet, the softest of any musical instrument. Yet in one important way it is the most expressive of the keyboard instruments; because the tangent remains in contact with the string, the performer can push slightly up or down on the key and create a vibrato, as on the violin.

✿ FIGURE 23-1

An anonymous setting of the chant *Salve, Regina,* written in keyboard tablature and preserved in the Buxheim Organ Book. Notice the presence of measure or bar lines.

Bayerische Staatsbibliothek, Munich

The **harpsichord** first appeared in the Low Countries around 1440 (see Chapter 19). It creates sound when a key is depressed, and this in turn pushes a lever upward. Attached to the lever is a plectrum or pick (then made of crow's quill, today made of plastic) that plucks the tight wire string. A **virginal** is a smaller harpsichord with the strings running at right angles to the keys. (For more on the virginal, see the discussion of the Fitzwilliam Virginal Book, Chapter 27.) In the Renaissance these keyboard instruments did not have legs or a stand, but were simply set upon a table (Fig. 23-2). The harpsichord was best known in Italy, the virginal in northern Europe, and the clavichord everywhere.

Although the organ, clavichord, harpsichord, and virginal differ greatly in size and sound, they all shared the same musical repertory during the Renaissance. Publishers encouraged this "one size fits all" approach to keyboard music because they sold more copies of the printed score. A uniform method also applied to fingering for all keyboard instruments. This approach to fingering differed greatly from what we do today on the organ, harpsichord, and piano. Renaissance performers had essentially a "thumbless" approach to the instrument. Even when running up and down the scale, they would avoid using the thumb and would continually cross 2 over 3 or vice versa, as can be seen in Example 23-1. To see how this looked in practice, turn to Figure 27-2, which shows a young woman playing a virginal using this 2-3 technique. To hear a clavichord, go to CD 7/8; to hear a harpsichord, go to CD 3/22.

🌿 FIGURE 23-2

Emperor Maximilian I in his music room, from Hans Burgkmair the Elder's woodcut entitled *Maximilian I Surrounded by His Court Musicians and Instruments* (c1514). On the table we see a keyboard instrument, most likely a clavichord. Above it is a viol, and next to it on the lower left, a crumhorn. Many other instruments, including organ, harp, drums, lute, sackbut, shawm, recorder, and transverse flute, are also visible.

EXAMPLE 23-1

🌸 **STRING INSTRUMENTS**

During the Renaissance the medieval psaltery, harp, and vielle gradually disappeared, supplanted by members of the viol and violin families, while the medieval lute only grew in popularity.

Lute

The **lute** is a pear-shaped instrument with six sets of strings called courses, then usually made of animal gut, now of wire. The most distinctive feature of the lute is the peg box that turns back at a right angle to the fingerboard (Fig. 23-3). Wrapped around the fingerboard at measured intervals are thin strips of leather that create frets, as on a modern guitar. These make it possible to mark and play the half-steps of the scale with ease. The performer stops the string at a fret to produce the desired pitch.

During the sixteenth century, the lute became the most popular of all musical instruments. Although the lute has many strings, and thus takes a long time to tune, it enjoys one distinct advantage—you can walk around with it. The French publisher Pierre Attaingnant issued more than ten times as many lute collections as he did those for keyboard. Similarly, in England surviving lute pieces outnumber keyboard works about 4 to 1, there being roughly sixteen hundred lute pieces but only about four hundred for keyboard.

Lute music, like keyboard music in the Renaissance, was written in a special type of notation called tablature. **Lute tablature** directs the fingers to stop strings at specific frets so as to produce sounds. Example 23-2 provides a diplomatic facsimile of a page of French lute tablature as printed in Paris by Pierre Attaingnant in 1529, along with modern transcription (above). A staff of six spaces serves to represent the six courses, or strings, of the lute. The top space visually indicates the highest sounding string. The lute, then as now, is usually tuned G, c, f, a, d', g', and thus the highest space represents the open string g' above our middle c'. All open strings are indicated by the letter "a", all first frets by "b", and so forth. The duration of each pitch is set by a simple system of vertical stems with each additional flag on a stem indicating a duration half as long as that of the next higher value. Exact duration matters less on the lute than on other instruments, because the sounds die away so quickly. The essential features of Renaissance lute tablature are still in use in guitar notation today. To hear the sound of the lute, go to CD 3/9.

Bridgeman Art Library

✿ FIGURE 23-3
Young ladies performing a chanson by Claudin de Sermisy. The singer in the back reads from a rotulus (sheet music) accompanied by a small lute and transverse flute. The flutist plays from a soprano part book, and two other part books are stacked before her.

EXAMPLE 23-2

New String Instruments from Spain: *Vihuela* (Spanish Guitar) and the Viol

The lute entered western Europe via Spain, having been brought there by the Arabs in the early Middle Ages. During the late fifteenth century, two new fretted string instruments related to the lute emerged in Spain and then, like the lute, spread around the West. These were the *vihuela* (Spanish guitar) and the viol.

The **vihuela** is a plucked string instrument with a waisted body, and a long pole-neck that serves as a fingerboard (Fig. 23-4). Our modern classical guitar is a direct descendant of the *vihuela*. Because the *vihuela* was plucked, it was often called the *vihuela de mano* (hand guitar). Related to it was a similar Spanish instrument called the *vihuela de arco* (bowed guitar) that was better known in its day as the viol.

Contrary to general opinion, the viol was not a medieval instrument, but one that developed in Spain around 1475. The **viol** (see Fig. 24-2) had six strings and was fretted and tuned like the lute and *vihuela*, but it was bowed and not plucked. It came in three sizes—treble, tenor, and bass—and was played with the instrument resting on the lap and legs. Thus the viol is often called by the Italian name **viola da gamba** (leg viol). Having entered Italy from Spain, the viol quickly spread to all of northern Europe, including England. Throughout the Renaissance it served as the principal bowed string instrument for high art music. Only in the Baroque period did the viols yield in prominence to the members of a different string family, that of the violin. To hear the sound of a viol, go to CD 3/10.

Violin

The violin is only slightly younger than the viol. Violins first appear in northern Italy around 1520 in towns such as Cremona, Brescia, Mantua, and Ferrara. Indeed, Cremona became the center of violin building, made famous by generations of the Amati family, who standardized its shape and size. Unlike the viol, which is played off the chest or the legs, the violin is held off the shoulder. From its inception, the violin was smaller than the viol, and this may account for the diminutive name *violino* (little viol), from which the final "o" was eventually dropped, giving us in English "violin." Naturally, its small size caused the violin to produce higher pitches, and its tone generally was brighter and more penetrating. The early violin had only three, or sometimes four, strings and did not make use of frets. It was tuned in fifths (g, d', a' or g, d', a', e") instead of fourths, as was generally true of the viols. Because of its brighter, more penetrating sound, the violin was preferred for dance music. In the course of time, larger, lower-sounding instruments of the violin family were developed, namely the viola and the violoncello. The modern double bass, however, is not a relative of the violin family, but is a descendent of the viol, being tuned not in fifths but fourths.

Throughout the sixteenth century, the viol, not the violin, was considered the aristocrat of string instruments. Members of the violin family were thought more low class, appropriate for professional and semi-professional musicians to play for dancing in taverns or cavorting through the streets. Because of their "wilder" associations, the Roman Catholic Church sometimes ordered violins destroyed. Not until the seventeenth century, during the Baroque period, would the violin become the dominant bowed string instrument, the *sine qua non* for the early orchestra.

✤ WIND INSTRUMENTS

Recorders and flutes

Recorders were usually called *fleuste* (French), *flauto* (Italian), or *flöte* (German) during the Renaissance. What we today call the flute (the transverse flute) was known as the **German flute**, *fleuste d'Allemande* (Fig. 23-3). Recorders and flutes were made of wood, or occasionally of ivory. Recorders came in many sizes, from smaller than soprano down to the great-bass. Each had a range of about an octave and a sixth, and each sounded an octave higher than written. When a group of recorders, or viols, or any instruments of the same family played together they produced a **consort**—an

❁ FIGURE 23-4

A representation of Orpheo (Orpheus) playing a *vihuela* (Spanish guitar) from the *Libro de musica de vihuela* of Luis Milán (1535/1536).

Bridgeman Art Library

ensemble of instruments all of one family. When instruments of different types played together, as was the case in the loud wind band, what resulted was called a **broken consort** (or mixed ensemble). Generally speaking, Renaissance instrumentalists did not double musical lines; a five-part piece was played by five instruments, and a three-part piece by a trio, for example.

The Renaissance Wind Bands: Trumpet, Sackbut, Shawm, Crumhorn, and Cornett

During the early Renaissance two bands of wind instruments emerged from the group originally called the *hauts instruments* (see Chapter 19). One was an ensemble of trumpets, which sometimes combined with kettledrums (early timpani). This group was ceremonial, its music essentially restricted to fanfares. During the sixteenth century, though, some trumpeters developed the ability to play very high, in the so-called **clarino register.** Later, in the Baroque period, the clarino register was exploited by such composers as Torelli, Handel, and Bach (see Chapter 33).

A second ensemble, more important musically, also developed at this time: the loud wind band. By about 1500 it usually included two or three shawms and one or two sackbuts, and thus was a broken consort. As we have seen (Chapter 19), the sackbut was the predecessor of the modern trombone and the shawm of the oboe. In fact, already in 1589 Thoinot Arbeau (see Chapter 22) refers to the shawm as the "**hautboys**" (oboe). In the course of the Renaissance, the loud wind band expanded to as many as eight players and new instrumental colors were added, mainly the sound of the crumhorn and cornett. The **crumhorn** (curved horn) is a capped double-reed wooden instrument with a curving shape (see Fig. 23-2). It has a range of a tenth and produces a buzzing sound similar to the noise of a kazoo. The **cornett** is also a wooden instrument with fingerholes, but is played with a mouthpiece and sounds in the soprano range. Its tone is something like that of a soft trumpet but with a more hollow, "wooden" sound, and it blends particularly well with the sackbut.

During the late Renaissance the loud wind band went by various names, among them *alta cappella* (loud choir) in Italy and *Stadtpfeifer* (town pipers) in German-speaking lands. Figure 23-5 shows a group of town pipers playing during a religious progression in Antwerp. Clearly visible are (right to left) sackbut, tenor shawm, alto shawm, cornett, tenor shawm, and an early bassoon. Most important, from the early sixteenth century onward, many wind bands accompanied church choirs in the performance of sacred music during religious services. Wind instruments, particularly cornett and sackbut, came to enjoy a special association with sacred music during the Renaissance, and they would continue to do so through the time of Mozart. To hear the instruments of a Renaissance wind band, go to CD 2/22 or CD 3/11.

❧ FIGURE 23-5

Detail from painting by Denis van Alsloot of a religious procession in Antwerp showing, from right to left, sackbut, tenor shawm, alto shawm, cornett, tenor shawm, and early bassoon.

© Museo del Prado, Madrid

✿ INSTRUMENTAL GENRES

The Renaissance witnessed the creation of several new musical genres that sprang forth because of the quickening interest in instrumental music. Many of these genres would remain in vogue for centuries hereafter.

Arrangements, Intabulations, and Variations

Chansons, madrigals, motets, and Masses—the four principal genres of Renaissance vocal music—were often arranged for keyboard, lute, or guitar. We have seen how one arranger refashioned Claudin de Sermisy's chanson *Tant que vivray* for lute and for keyboard, for example (see Chapter 22). Such arrangements were called intabulations simply because they were written in lute or keyboard, or even guitar, tablature. When adapting a vocal work for instrument, the arranger invariably made use of the ornamental style of instrumental writing favored at the time (see Ex. 22-4). Ornaments had the practical advantage of sustaining sounds that would quickly decay on softer instruments.

In addition to instrumental arrangements, composers wrote variations on preexisting melodies, be they the ancient chants of the church or the hit tunes of the day. Such variations were not transcriptions or arrangements of preexisting works, but entirely new compositions. By the end of the sixteenth century, many composers were also writing variations on popular bass lines and harmonic patterns. For an example of a set of variations on a popular tune, see Thomas Morley's setting of *Goe from my window* (Chapter 27).

Dances

Dance music, of course, had been popular during the Middle Ages (see Chapter 11)—indeed, since time immemorial. During the early Renaissance, dances came to be grouped in pairs. A slow duple dance was followed by a fast triple one: the *basse danse* by the *tordion* (see Chapter 19), for example, and the pavane by the galliard (see Chapter 22). Toward the end of sixteenth century the allemande would come to precede the pavane and galliard. Thus the nucleus of the Baroque dance suite, later exploited by Corelli, Handel, and Bach (see Chapter 34), was already in place by the end of the Renaissance.

Prelude

As the name suggests, a **prelude** is a preliminary piece, one that comes immediately before and introduces the main musical event. An organ prelude might precede a Magnificat at Vespers, for example, or a lute prelude might introduce a lute intabulation of a chanson. The prelude had its roots in earlier improvisatory practices. It often opens with chordal strumming and follows with freely running scales or moments of light imitation. But the prelude had a function, perhaps several. While playing, the performer might make sure that the strings of the instrument were in tune. At the same time, the player could establish the mode of the piece to follow and even prefigure some of its themes. Finally, a prelude could stop conversation in its tracks and call attention to the fact that serious music was about to begin.

Ricercar

Originally the ricercar was closely related to the prelude. Indeed, the Italian word *ricercare* (to seek out) suggests much the same function as the prelude: in a short preliminary piece the performer searches for the mode and the themes of the larger piece to follow. By the mid sixteenth century, however, the ricercar had changed noticeably. Composers in Italy, influenced by the sacred vocal music of the day, now wrote fully independent pieces that contained a number of imitative sections, each with its own imitative theme. A **ricercar** can be defined as an instrumental piece, usually for lute or keyboard, similar in style to the imitative motet of the sixteenth century. During the next several centuries, composers such as Frescobaldi, Pachelbel, and Bach would continue to breathe new life into a musical genre that had originated during the Renaissance. To hear a slightly later ricercar, go to CD 4/15.

Fantasia

The word fantasia suggests a kind of music in which the composer might give free rein to the imagination. Indeed, in its early stages during the first decades of the sixteenth century, the fantasia was a freeform, seemingly spontaneous creation. By mid-century, however, the fantasia, like the ricercar, had evolved into a predominantly imitative, motet-like piece. Thus a definition of the Renaissance **fantasia** must reflect its changing style: an instrumental piece that at first allowed the composer to indulge flights of chordal or scalar fancy, but that gradually evolved into work displaying imitative counterpoint from beginning to end. Ironically, as the fantasias of Bach and Mozart demonstrate, the fantasia later shed its imitative skin and reverted back to its earlier, freer, more whimsical form.

Consider the fantasia for Spanish guitar (*vihuela*) by Miguel de Fuenllana (c1510–c1585) published in Seville, Spain, in 1554. With its predominantly imitative texture, it typifies the contrapuntal fantasia of the mid sixteenth century. Fuenllana works out four different imitative themes in succession. The first theme unfolds in four-voice imitation in the ranges of soprano, then alto, tenor, and finally bass; yet immediately the soprano and alto lines vanish. This is typical of the fantasia, and particularly of those for lute and guitar in which the sound dies quickly—the imitative voices seem to enter and disappear at will.

 LISTENING CUE

MIGUEL DE FUENLLANA
Fantasia (1554)

Book Companion Website (http://schirmer.wadsworth.com/wright_1e)
Anthology, No. 62

Canzona

Originally, "canzona" was simply an Italian word designating a French chanson, more specifically the Parisian chanson of the mid sixteenth century. By the end of the century, however, a **canzona** denoted a freely composed instrumental piece, usually for organ or instrumental ensemble, which imitated the lively rhythms and lightly imitative style of the Parisian chanson. Canzonas seem to have been particularly favored by the wind bands of northern Italy, especially in Venice. The canzona composed by the Venetian organist Claudio Merulo (1533–1604) exemplifies the genre (Ex. 23-3). Although no specific instruments are called for in the score, this canzona contains the kind of music that cornetts, shawms, and sackbuts can execute well. The performers must sharply attack repeated pitches, but rarely do they play scales where speed and intonation may be an issue. Notice the repeating notes at the beginning. This is an opening rhythmic figure found in almost all canzonas: long, short, short. Notice also how the composer pairs the imitative entries so that an echo often results, a particularly exciting effect in a resonant church. In this

late-Renaissance canzona by Merulo, as in most, pulsating sound is all that is needed
to animate the music.

EXAMPLE 23-3

 LISTENING CUE

CLAUDIO MERULO   CD 3/11
Canzona 5 (c1600)   Anthology, No. 63

SUMMARY

By the sixteenth century many, but by no means all, of the instruments with which
we are familiar today had already come into existence. Some of these, namely the
sackbut (our modern trombone) have changed very little since the Renaissance.
Others, such as the organ, guitar, violin, recorder, flute, shawm (modern oboe), bass
shawm (bassoon), and trumpet were in place but would continue to undergo a
process of evolution well into the nineteenth century. Other instruments existed in
rudimentary form but were not used for art music—notably the hunting horn (the
later French horn). Still others, among them the piano and clarinet, would not
emerge until the eighteenth century. Yet, not all Renaissance instruments remained
popular. The viol, cornett, and crumhorn fell victim to changing musical tastes. By
the mid eighteenth century they had become something like musical dinosaurs,
nearly extinct.

During the Renaissance several new genres appeared that remained exclusively
associated with instrumental music. Of these, only the instrumental transcription
did not continue to thrive during the Baroque era. The other genres—variations,
the newly emerging dance suite, the prelude, ricercar, fantasia, and canzona—were
intensely cultivated during the Baroque era and far beyond. Today when we practice and perform a canzona by Gabrieli, a dance suite by Handel, a prelude by Bach,
or a fantasia by Mozart, Schubert, or Schumann, we perpetuate venerable musical
genres that originated during the Renaissance.

KEY TERMS

Buxheim Organ Book	viol	crumhorn
keyboard tablature	*viola da gamba*	cornett
clavichord	*violino*	prelude
harpsichord	German flute	ricercar
virginal	consort	fantasia
lute	broken consort	canzona
lute tablature	clarino register	
vihuela	hautboys	

Musical Interlude

Music Theory in the Renaissance

Medieval music theory had been concerned with practical issues: singing the notes of the scale, identifying the consonant and dissonant intervals, and explaining the complicated notation used to signify rhythmic durations in music. Renaissance music theory is practical as well. It too was concerned with how the composer should write music and how the performer should sing or play it. But Renaissance theorists also inquired into the meaning of music. Why do we have music? What is unique about it? Why does it move us the way it does? In posing these questions, the theorists explored the aesthetics and emotive power of music, just as had the ancient Greeks. They also tried to reconstruct the particulars of ancient Greek music theory.

THE REBIRTH OF ANCIENT GREEK MUSIC THEORY

Beginning shortly before 1500, musicians began to embrace the writings on music of the ancient Greek theorists. In this they demonstrated the same humanistic desires as their fellow scholars in the other arts and sciences. Many Greek texts on music were now translated into Latin for the first time. Some musical humanists learned enough Greek to study the ancient texts in the original language. Greek terminology was again adopted by the theorists. During the late Middle Ages, for example, the modes had usually been identified simply by numbers (mode 1, mode 2, and so on); now the ancient Greek ethnic names—Dorian, Phrygian, and the like—were again commonly invoked. The complicated issue of tuning, whether that of Pythagoras or others, again came to the fore (see below). Finally, the ancient Greek genera—diatonic, chromatic, and enharmonic—were revisited. One theorist in particular, **Nicola Vicentino** (1511–c1576), championed the reinstitution of the chromatic and the enharmonic genera as a way to re-impose the power of ancient Greek music (on the genera, see Chapter 1). To this end he composed madrigals with microtonal inflections that sought to capture the shadings of the enharmonic genus in particular. He also constructed a strange new keyboard instrument called the arcicembalo. The **arcicembalo** was a harpsichord that had two keyboards, each with three rows of keys (Ex. 4-1). The two keyboards supplied thirty-six keys within each octave, an ample number to accommodate the microtonal inflections of the Greek genera. Surely a nightmare to tune, the arcicembalo did not catch on. Yet it suggests the lengths to which Renaissance musicians might go to capture the specifics, as well as the general spirit, of ancient Greek music.

EXAMPLE 4-1

✸ NEW RULES FOR HARMONY AND COUNTERPOINT

Where did we get the rules for harmony and counterpoint that we study today? Most originated with the composers and theorists of the Renaissance. During the Middle Ages, theorists were occupied in large measure with identifying the consonances and dissonances. As a rule, they prescribed that consonances fall on strong beats but they allowed great freedom as to how dissonance might come between consonances. Renaissance theorists, beginning with **Johannes Tinctoris** (c1435–1511), set up precise rules as to where, in what way, and for how long dissonance might last. Below is an example of three-voice counterpoint from Tinctoris's *The Art of Counterpoint* (1477). It shows how passing tones, neighboring tones, suspensions, and even a chain of suspensions should be created (Ex. 4-2). The beat is called the **tactus.** As a general rule, dissonance should come between one tactus and the next. If it comes on the tactus (beat), it should be prepared by the same pitch and sound for one tactus at most. All dissonance should be approached and left by stepwise motion, although a leap away from dissonance is occasionally tolerated.

The octave, unison, and fifth remain the primary musical consonants. Yet from the fifteenth century onward, theorists legislate that perfect consonances should not come in succession—no parallel fifths or octaves. Why? Because such sounds lack variety and diminish the integrity of the individual voices. Thirds and sixths are now considered imperfect consonances. The fourth, however, which had been a consonance during the Middle Ages, is increasingly treated as a dissonance and handled with care. Often it appears in what we today call a "4-3" suspension. Indeed, it is at this time that the concept of a suspension, called a **syncope** by Renaissance musicians, is first described by music theorists. Example 4-2 has a 9-8 and then a 4-3 suspension properly prepared and resolved in the upper voice.

EXAMPLE 4-2

Tinctoris was the first to set out strict rules of counterpoint. Later, these would be refined by other theorists such as Pietro Aaron (c1480–c1554) and Gioseffo Zarlino (1517–1590). Zarlino recognized two forms of what later would be called the triad (major and minor); he posited that the major was particularly appropriate for heroic sounds, and the minor for sad, plaintive music. The rules for chords and counterpoint further came to be codified in musical practice, particularly in the contrapuntally conservative compositions of Giovanni Pierluigi da Palestrina (1525/26–1594). By the end of the sixteenth century the pristine compositional style of Palestrina had become the model for good counterpoint. Implicit everywhere in Palestrina's music is the notion that contrary motion is to be preferred to similar motion among the outer voices, and that large leaps should be followed by a stepwise movement in the opposite direction—cardinal rules of counterpoint that we still follow today. Indeed, Palestrina's contrapuntal precepts, distilled into a teaching manual by Johann Fux in 1725, were studied and taught by Bach, Haydn, Mozart, and Beethoven, among others, into the nineteenth century and beyond.

NEW MODES

During the Middle Ages, tonal structure was controlled and determined by the eight church modes (see Chapter 4), and this continued to hold true into the 1550s. But, as early as the 1470s, Renaissance theorists showed an interest in analyzing particular pieces so as to identify the modal structure of a work. Theorists now provided the names of pieces by well-known composers such as Dufay and Josquin and asked the reader to consider the modal structure of these works.

Modality in Renaissance music, the theorists tell us, should be judged by the progress of the tenor line. The final note and the range of the tenor are important considerations, but so are the position of melodic fourths and fifths within the tenor line as well as the pitches of the internal cadences. By analyzing music according to these criteria, a musician can determine the mode of a Renaissance composition.

Here, for the first time in the history of music, theorists seem to be as much interested in musical analysis—understanding and assigning value to works of art—as they are in giving prescriptive rules to composers and performers.

Equally important, Renaissance theorists expanded the number of modes, or what we would call scales. In 1547 a Swiss musical humanist named **Heinrich Glarean** (1488–1563) published his *Dodecachordon* (*Twelve-String Instrument*). It acknowledged the presence of two new modes, both running up and down the white keys, one beginning on A and the other beginning on C (Ex. 4-3). By supplying each of these two new modes with a plagal partner, Glarean raised the number of modes from eight to twelve. Reaching back to Greek music theory for names, he called the first of these the **Aeolian** mode and the second the **Ionian.** Their plagals he called Hypoaeolian and Hypoionian.

EXAMPLE 4-3

Number	Name	Range	Final Pitch	Type
9	Aeolian		A	Authentic
10	Hypoaeolian		A	Plagal
11	Ionian		C	Authentic
12	Hypoionian		C	Plagal

Glarean thought he had rediscovered the ancient Greeks' system of modes—no matter that his modes were rather different from the scales the Greeks associated with these names. The important fact is that the major (Ionian) and minor (Aeolian) modes were now officially recognized. In the course of the next two centuries, these two new modes would gradually come to be used to the exclusion of all others, foreshadowing the dominance of the major and minor scales today.

✿ NEW TUNINGS AND TEMPERAMENTS

A fully chromatic keyboard with twelve half-step pitches within each octave was recognized in western Europe by the end of the fourteenth century. However, the distance between these half-steps was by no means equal. Renaissance theorists fought over what type of tuning a musician should use. Those favoring the oldest Greek method argued for what is called **Pythagorean tuning,** a process in which the octaves, fifths, and fourths are tuned in perfect 2:1, 3:2, and 4:3 ratios. While this produced fine-sounding fifths and fourths, the half-steps were not equal. Some Renaissance theorists favored a system called **just tuning,** in which the major and minor thirds were also tuned according to strict ratios (5:4 and 6:5). Just intonation reflected the growing importance of thirds and sixths in Renaissance music. But just intonation resulted not only in unequal half-steps, but unequal whole steps as well. The distance from C to D was much greater than that from D to E, for example.

Some basic triads, those around C, were beautifully tuned in perfect intervals, but those far away from C were badly out of tune. To remedy these defects, practicing musicians began to shave just a bit off the perfect fifths. The result was a **temperament**—the tuning of intervals in something slightly more or less than strict mathematical ratios.

By the early sixteenth century, however, some musicians were advocating a division of the octave into twelve equal half-steps, each with the ratio of approximately 18:17. This was called **equal temperament.** The composer Adrian Willaert (c1490–1562) wrote a motet that progressed entirely around the circle of fifths without sounding out of tune; this was possible only with equal temperament. But equal temperament did not immediately carry the day. Most harpsichords and organs continued to be tuned in Pythagorian or just tuning, or some variant thereof, well into the eighteenth century. (On the adoption of equal temperament in the eighteenth century, see Chapter 39.)

Finally, during the Renaissance there was no such thing as standardized pitch—an A in one locale might be as much as a whole step lower or higher than that pitch in another place. A set of three recorders pitched in f-c-f ' made in one town might be slightly sharper or flatter than those of a similar set made by another craftsman in a neighboring city, but the players could adjust in several ways. There were rules and standards in the Renaissance, but that did not stop the process of music-making.

KEY TERMS

Nicola Vicentino
arcicembalo
Johannes Tinctoris
tactus

syncope
Heinrich Glarean
Aeolian
Ionian

Pythagorean tuning
just tuning
temperament
equal temperament

Chapter 24

Music in Three German Cities: The Protestant-Catholic Confrontation

Throughout its history, the country we now call Germany has assumed many territorial forms. During the late Middle Ages and Renaissance, German-speaking lands belonged only to a loose confederation of two hundred principalities and city-states called the **Holy Roman Empire** (Map 24-1). These lands and cities owed allegiance to the Holy Roman Emperor. There was no fixed capital of the Empire, nor in fact were there any German-speaking cities of any significant size before the sixteenth century. Perhaps for this reason, polyphonic music was not as rigorously cultivated in Germany as it was in the Low Countries, France, England, or Italy. As we have seen, the creation of polyphonic music was mainly either a courtly or an urban phenomenon. While Germany had its own dialects of Gregorian chant, what poly-

MAP 24-1
The Holy Roman Empire, c1500.

phonic art music there was in medieval Germany was often derived from the genres and styles of music coming from France.

In the later fifteenth century, however, German commerce, technology, and culture generally began to flourish. The printing industry, for example, first saw the light of day in the 1450s in the German town of Mainz. Eventually, as the quickening pace of commerce encouraged the growth of German cities, music printing began to appear in such centers as Leipzig, Nuremberg, Augsburg, and Munich.

Some of these German printers issued both religious music and religious pamphlets. They were soldiers engaged in the war of words fought between the reform-minded Protestants and the tradition-based Roman Catholics. The Protestant Reformation, as we shall see, occurred first in German-speaking lands, before spreading to Switzerland, France, the Low Countries, and England. Generally speaking, the southern (Alpine and Italian) parts of the Empire remained Catholic, while those cities and principalities to the north tended to go over to the Protestant side. Thus Alpine Innsbruck stayed in the Catholic fold, the more-northern Augsburg became Protestant, while Munich was geographically and spiritually somewhere between the two.

INNSBRUCK: MUSIC UNDER EMPEROR MAXIMILIAN I

Surrounded by snow-capped mountains, the beautiful Alpine city of Innsbruck, Austria, owes its importance to its location. Since Roman times it has sat on the main route between Germany and Italy, where that road goes across a bridge (German, "Brücke") traversing the fast-moving river Inn. In the fifteenth century, Innsbruck and the surrounding lands, called the Tyrol, were under the control of the Hapsburg family, whose greatest figure was **Emperor Maximilian I** (1459–1519). In 1477 Maximilian married Mary of Burgundy, thereby uniting the old Burgundian territories in the Low Countries to the Hapsburg lands in Germany and Austria. Eventually, Maximilian left the government of the Low Countries to his daughter Margaret (see Chapter 19), while he ruled the German and Austrian parts of the Empire from Innsbruck, Augsburg, or Vienna. Among these, Innsbruck was the preferred residence: as Maximilian said, "Innsbruck and the Tyrol are the center of the German Empire." It was here that he built a mausoleum to honor his accomplishments, and it was here that he brought his chapel.

At the center of religious and musical life at the Hapsburg court was the **Hofkapelle** (German for "court chapel"), a group of approximately twelve singers responsible for the religious music of the court. In 1496 Maximilian added a jewel to the crown of imperial singers when he hired the illustrious composer Heinrich Isaac (c1450–1517). Though born in the Low Countries, Isaac had spent many years in Florence as the principal musical ornament at the court of the ruling Medici family. But in 1494 the Medici were expelled from Florence, leaving Isaac temporarily unemployed. Two years later Maximilian recruited him for his chapel. For the next twenty years Isaac moved with the imperial court from Innsbruck, to Vienna, to Augsburg, to Constance, and elsewhere throughout the German-speaking part of the Empire. Ultimately, old and sick, Isaac was given leave to return to Florence, where he died in 1518.

Although reform-minded German Protestants began their verbal attack on the power and privileges of Rome during the early sixteenth century, Emperor Maximilian steadfastly remained a Catholic. Thus the religious music that Heinrich Isaac composed for the imperial court was polyphony for the traditional Catholic liturgy. Maximilian was fond of large-scale projects, and sometime during the early 1500s he encouraged Isaac to set polyphonically all of the Proper chants of the Catholic Mass for the major feasts of the church year. Ultimately, nearly three hundred fifty motet-like compositions appeared in Isaac's collection. It is called the **Choralis Constantinus** because it sets in polyphony chants from the German diocese of Constance. The *Choralis Constantinus* was the first systematic attempt to provide polyphony for the entire church year since the twelfth-century *Magnus liber organi* of Leoninus (see Chapter 8).

Heinrich Isaac wrote not only serious Catholic church music for the imperial Hofkapelle but also more light-hearted secular music. When in Innsbruck, the versatile Isaac set in polyphony popular strophic songs in the local vernacular tongue, in this case German. A popular or art song in German is simply called a **Lied** (pl., **Lieder**). Isaac wrote thirty-four polyphonic Lieder, almost all during his years of service to Maximilian. In these he took a simple preexisting popular tune and reworked it in one of two ways. The first way was the more traditional German approach, that of the Tenorlied. In a **Tenorlied** the preexisting tune is placed in the tenor and two or three other voices enhance it with lightly imitative polyphony. Thus the Tenorlied continues the tradition of the tenor cantus firmus. Isaac's second approach to setting a German Lied was to place the tune in the cantus and support it with chords below. In this second type of setting, with the melody on top and all voices beginning and ending phrases at the same time, we see an early manifestation of the four-part chorale style later used so effectively by J. S. Bach (see Chapter 40).

Examples 24-1a and 24-1b show the beginnings of two different settings by Heinrich Isaac of the same popular tune. The first is in the style of the Tenorlied, with the tune in the tenor; here, the alto closely imitates the tenor. The second, and later, setting by Isaac provides a more homophonic harmonization, with the melody now in the cantus.

EXAMPLE 24-1A

EXAMPLE 24-1B

Innsbruck, I must now leave you, I'm going on my way…

The popular tune that Isaac employed, one still well known by every citizen in Innsbruck today, is a love song, addressed not to a man or woman, but to a city. As the title and text show, in *Innsbruck, ich muss dich lassen* (*Innsbruck, I must now leave you*), a musician laments his departure from this beloved place, a sentiment Isaac must have felt as he moved all too often with Emperor Maximilian from one imperial German city to another. Soon Protestant Germans would alter the text to make the music serve as a religious piece, creating *O Welt, ich muss dich lassen* (*O World, I must now leave you*).

LISTENING CUE

HEINRICH ISAAC
Innsbruck, ich muss dich lassen (c1510)

CD 3/12
Anthology, Nos. 64a
and 64b

Among the musicians at Innsbruck in these years was the organist Paul Hofhaimer (1459–1537), who first arrived there in 1478. For more than thirty years Hofhaimer served the family of Emperor Maximilian I, first in Innsbruck and later in Augsburg. When Maximilian died in 1519, Hofhaimer assumed the post of organist at the cathedral of Salzburg, a position that Mozart would occupy some two hundred sixty years later.

Contemporaries agreed that Hofhaimer had no equal as an organist. They marveled at his powers of invention as he improvised at the keyboard. Unfortunately, only a small portion of Hofhaimer's improvisatory art comes down to us in notated form. His *Salve, Regina*, one of two surviving sacred pieces for organ, is built on the old Gregorian antiphon in honor of the Virgin Mary. As in much organ music of the Renaissance, Hofhaimer's setting makes use of **alternatim technique**—the verses of the chant are assigned to alternating performing forces. Here, the first verse is given to the organ, the second to a choir to sing in monophonic chant, the third back to the organ, and so on. A glance at the score of *Salve, Regina* (Ex. 24-2) will show that Hofhaimer makes use of cantus firmus technique here as well. He has the ancient chant *Salve, Regina* (see Ex. 18-4) sound forth in long notes in the range of the tenor voice. Above this cantus firmus the right hand plays an array of ornamental patterns; from the very beginning, keyboard music has always demanded more of the right hand than the left. The right-hand figuration is technically demanding, yet sometimes mechanical and repetitious. We must remember, however, that the organ at this time had no centuries-old tradition behind it, as was true for vocal music. Even in the fifteenth century, church organs were something of a novelty. Much of the allure of the organ came, not from the beauty of the part-writing, but from the unusual brilliance and power of the instrument itself—from sound rather than idea.

EXAMPLE 24-2

LISTENING CUE

PAUL HOFHAIMER
Salve, Regina for Organ (c1510?)

CD 3/13
Anthology, No. 65

✳ THE REFORMATION: MUSIC IN AUGSBURG

One of the cities that Heinrich Isaac, Paul Hofhaimer, and their patron Emperor Maximilian I often visited was Augsburg, Germany. Because Augsburg was a republic (free city) beholden to no prince and situated near the geographical center of the Empire, it was an ideal site for meetings of the imperial Diet. The **Diet** (or **Reichstag**) was a legislative assembly that met almost annually to voice opinions on the finances of the Empire and on affairs of state. So often did Emperor Maximilian convene the Diet in Augsburg, and his court reside there for extended periods, that the citizens jokingly came to call him "Burghermeister" (mayor) of the city. Figure 24-1 shows the imperial Hofkapelle in Augsburg about 1518 with a Mass in progress. To the center right, Maximilian kneels in prayer; in the lower right, the singers of the Hofkapelle group before a large music manuscript; and to the left, seated at the organ, is imperial court organist Paul Hofhaimer.

In the early sixteenth century, Augsburg was a thriving commercial center of more than 25,000 inhabitants, the most progressive city in southern Germany. Foremost among the citizens was Jacob Fugger, appropriately nicknamed "the Rich" (1459–1525). Fugger and his descendants were money lenders, the first family north of the Alps to institute the now-popular practice of "private banking" for rulers such as Emperor Maximilian. They were also patrons of intellectuals and artists, and they collected music manuscripts and printed part books, many of which survive today. In 1514 Jacob Fugger lent a large sum of money to Pope Leo X to rebuild St. Peter's Basilica in Rome. To repay him, Leo sold indulgences to true-believing Catholics; this led Protestant reformers to protest the "commercialization of the Gospel." But, as fate would have it, the staunchly Catholic Fuggers came to be linked to the radical reformer Martin Luther; in 1512 they chose as the site of their private chapel in Augsburg the small monastic church of St. Anne, a church that Luther would soon come to call home.

On 31 October 1517, **Martin Luther** (1483–1546) nailed his **Ninety-Five Theses** (objections to current church practices) to the door of the castle church in Wittenberg, Germany. This defiant act was an important moment in the **Reformation**—the religious revolution that began as a movement to reform Catholicism and ended with the establishment of Protestantism. Soon Luther's theses were widely circulated, and he was called to Augsburg, to the church of St. Anne, to defend himself against the charge of heresy brought by the pope. In brief, Luther and other Protestant theologians wished to bring an end to the following church practices:

- The selling of indulgences—a forgiveness of sin sold by the church with the promise that the buyer, and members of his family, might thereby spend less time in Purgatory after death
- The selling of church services (such as last rites and funeral services)
- The selling of church offices to the highest bidder
- The excessive veneration of saints, which was seen as idolatry
- The growth of religious holidays, especially saints' days, on which commercial activity could not take place
- The use of writings other than the Bible (medieval legends of the saints, for example) as sources of religious truth
- The insistence that leaders of the church remain celibate (unmarried)
- The existence of monks and nuns and thus monasteries and convents

Augsburg, with a tradition of independent thinking, was particularly sympathetic to Luther's views. On Christmas Day 1524, the church of St. Anne celebrated the Mass according to the reformed version of Martin Luther. Two years later, in 1526, Luther published this as his *Deudsche Messe* (German Mass). It encouraged the use of the German language rather than Latin and allowed a larger role for the congregation in the service. Luther was concerned that each person understand and

FIGURE 24-1
Emperor Maximilian I hears Mass in his chapel at Augsburg around 1518.

participate in the service in his own language. Unlike the Catholic Church, which tried to effect a uniform Mass from one church to the next, Luther allowed Protestant churches a great deal of local freedom as to how the service might unfold. Rural communities tended to say the Mass in German, while more "learned" city churches retained much Latin. In the university town of Leipzig, for example, reformed churches continued to sing portions of the service in Latin beyond the time of Bach. Nevertheless, the Lutheran service everywhere differed from the Catholic in several important ways:

- The Mass and the canonical hours were reduced to just the Mass and an evening service.
- The vernacular language was allowed to replace Latin within the service.
- The congregation, and not just the trained choir, was expected to sing during the service.
- The Gloria of the Mass was omitted.
- Simple hymns replaced several parts of the Proper of the Mass.
- Sermons were regularly preached at both Mass and the evening service.

Martin Luther had a fine voice, played flute and lute, could compose pleasing melodies, and could harmonize a tune in four parts. He had come to love the splendor and richness of Gregorian chant from his years of service as a Catholic priest, and he especially enjoyed the polyphony of Josquin des Prez (see Chapter 21). Thus Luther was not disposed to remove music from the service of the reformed church, only to simplify it, making it more accessible to the people. To that end, he and his followers began to assemble a body of church music that centered around the chorale.

A **chorale** is a monophonic spiritual melody or religious folksong, what many Christian denominations today would simply call a "hymn." Chorale melodies are usually simple and their text strophic. To fashion a collection of tunes appropriate for the new Protestant churches, the reformers pressed into service many old Gregorian chants, changing their texts from Latin to German. In this way the Easter chant *Victimae Paschali laudes* (*Hail the Paschal Victim*) became the chorale tune *Christ lag in Todesbanden* (*Christ Lay in Death's Dark Prison*), for example. Popular tunes became chorales, too, by switching the text from profane to sacred. ("Why should the Devil have all the good tunes?" was asked at the time.) Thus, the charming melody *Innsbruck, ich muss dich lassen* became the sacred tune *O Welt, ich muss dich lassen*, as we have seen. Such a transformation—secular piece to sacred, or sacred to secular—is called a **contrafactum (pl., contrafacta).** Perhaps the most famous example of a German contrafactum is the conversion of the love song *Mein Gmütt ist mir verwirret* (*I'm all shook up*) into the chorale *O Haupt voll Blut und Wunden* (*O Sacred Head Now Wounded*), which later became the central chorale of J.S. Bach's *St. Matthew Passion* (1727). Others chorales were newly composed. Luther himself created about twenty new chorale tunes, setting them to simple German texts that explained the Scriptures.

Of the chorales composed by Martin Luther, the most famous is *Ein feste Burg ist unser Gott* (*A Mighty Fortress Is Our God*). As with many of his chorales, Luther shaped the music into an **AAB** form. The melody has a simple rhythm, is predominantly step-wise without difficult leaps, has short clear-cut phrases and a strongly implied tonal center—all qualities designed to make the tune easy to learn and remember. The text, again by Luther himself, is simply his German adaptation of Psalm 46, *God is our refuge*.

EXAMPLE 24-3

Ein feste Burg ist unser Gott, ein gu-te Wehr und Waf-fen.
Er hilft uns frei aus al-ler Not, die uns jetzt hat be-trof-fen.

Der al-te bö-se Feind, mit Ernst er's jetzt meint, gross Macht un viel

List sein grau-sam Rüst-ung ist, auf Erd' ist nicht seins Glei-chen.

Ein feste Burg ist unser Gott	**A**	A mighty fortress is our God
Ein gute Wehr und Waffen.		A bulwark never failing.
Er hilft uns frei aus aller Not	**A**	Our helper he amid the flood
Die uns jetzt hat betroffen.		Our mortal ills prevailing.
Der alte böse Feind	**B**	For still our ancient foe
Mit Ernst er's jetzt meint,		Does seek to work us woe,
Gross Macht und viel List		His craft and power are great
Sein grausam Rüstung ist,		And armed with cruel hate,
Auf Erd' ist nicht seins Gleichen.		On earth is not his equal.

LISTENING CUE

MARTIN LUTHER
Ein feste Burg ist unser Gott (1529)

CD 3/14
Anthology, No. 66a

To spread the new music among his followers, Luther encouraged the publication of his chorales as broadside sheets (sheet music) and in printed hymnals. He also urged a colleague, **Johann Walter** (1496–1570), to set the chorales in polyphony, so as to create a repertory for trained church choirs. In 1524 Walter published his ***Geistliche Gesangbüchlein*** *(Little Book of Spiritual Songs)*. This collection of settings of thirty-eight Protestant hymns and five Latin motets became the first monument of Protestant church music. Walter's *Gesangbüchlein* provided a core repertory for Lutheran church choirs, and over the course of the century it appeared in many different editions. Its purpose, however, was as much pedagogical as it was theological. The preface by Luther himself explains:

> And therefore [these songs] were arranged in four parts [some in fact are written in three voices and others in five] to give the young—who should at any rate be trained in music and other fine arts—something so that they will put aside love ballads and dirty songs, and learn wholesome things in their place, thus combining the good with the pleasing, as is proper for the young.[1]

Accordingly, these chorale settings were taught in Lutheran schools as part of a student's education in the arts. Once the chorale setting had been learned by heart in school, it might be sung in the service of God in the church.

In a later edition of the *Geistliche Gesangbüchlein*, Johann Walter published a four-voice setting of Luther's *Ein feste Burg ist unser Gott*. The chorale tune is placed in the tenor, following the tradition of the Tenorlied. Above and below it, the other three voices provide a chordal support and lightly animated counterpoint. For modern ears it is difficult to hear the chorale because the tenor is covered by the surrounding voices. Yet sixteenth-century listeners, long familiar with tenor cantus firmus technique, would have had no difficulty perceiving the chorale and its intended message: God alone is a refuge for devout Protestants.

LISTENING CUE

MARTIN LUTHER   CD 3/15
Ein feste Burg ist unser Gott (1529)   Anthology, No. 66b
Arranged by Johann Walter

Augsburg continued to be a hotbed of religious conflict as most, but by no means all, of its citizens converted to Lutheranism. At the Diet of Augsburg in 1530, supporters of Luther presented to the new emperor, Charles V, what has come to be called **The Augsburg Confession,** the definitive doctrinal statement of the Lutheran faith. (Exactly three centuries later Felix Mendelssohn would commemorate this event in his *Reformation* Symphony and quote Luther's famous hymn *Ein feste Burg ist unser Gott*.) In 1555 supporters of Luther and Catholic Emperor Charles V agreed to the **Peace of Augsburg.** This treaty marked a milestone in the history of Western political processes, for it was the first attempt to grant Protestants and Catholics alike a measure of religious freedom within the same city.

ORLANDE DE LASSUS AND THE COURT OF MUNICH

If Innsbruck remained steadfastly Catholic and Augsburg became a stronghold of Lutheranism, the city of Munich, Germany, found itself somewhere in the middle, both in terms of religion and geography (see Map 24-1). Though situated just north of the Alps, sixteenth-century Munich, the capital of the duchy of Bavaria, still felt the pressure of Protestant reform. In the 1560s the leader of the Munich court chapel, Ludwig Daser, was a Protestant; its foremost composer, Orlande de Lassus (1532–1594), was a Catholic; and the leader of the court, Duke Albrecht V, vacillated between the two religions, ultimately siding with the Catholics.

Like the art of the great German painter Albrecht Dürer, the music of Orlande de Lassus found favor with Protestants as well as Catholics. Orlande de Lassus (known to Italians as Orlando di Lasso) was by far the most famous composer of his day. His music was published in all of the important printing centers of Europe, including Venice, Rome, Nuremberg, Antwerp, Paris, and London, as well as Munich. An international figure, he wrote more than two thousand works in all genres of his day: sixty Masses, more than one thousand motets, and countless Italian madrigals, French chansons, and German Lieder. Yet Lasso was above all a great master of the motet. When it came to writing religious music, the more diversified nature of the motet text suited his expressive genius.

Orlande de Lassus was not born in Germany, but in the Low Countries near the small town of Mons, south of Brussels. As a youth, Lassus was a choirboy at the church of St. Nicolas in Mons, and tradition has it that he was kidnapped three times owing to the beauty of his voice. He spent his early adulthood as a singer in Italy, and his first publication, a collection of madrigals and chansons, appeared when he was only twenty-three. In 1558 Lassus was recruited to be a tenor in the chapel of Duke Albrecht of Bavaria in Munich; here he stayed for the remainder of his life, working his way up to master of the chapel and personal confidant of the duke. Figure 24-2 shows the chapel of Albrecht, along with the instrumentalists of the court, as if they were all about to provide chamber music for a ducal banquet. In fact, this banquet hall, especially built by Albrecht for such ceremonial occasions, was often a place for music-making, for what the Germans call *Tafelmusik* (chamber music, both vocal and instrumental, for the dinner table).

Duke Albrecht was not only a lover of music but also of the visual arts. During the 1550s he constructed next to his residence in Munich an art gallery (the first art gallery north of the Alps) to house the treasures from classical antiquity that he had purchased in Rome—an appreciation of ancient art symbolic of the Renaissance. The rooms above the art gallery were configured to serve as a library, and here the duke put the splendid books he purchased or commissioned. The most lavish of the ducal books is a two-volume set of Penitential Psalms newly composed by Lassus—lavish because each page of Lassus's music is surrounded by color paintings of the biblical scenes and themes expressed by the psalms (Fig. 24-3). So artistically splendid was this pair of books that Duke Albrecht kept them in the new library, rather than with the music books in the chapel. This was sacred music in the service of the visual arts, but what music it was!

Many aspects of Lassus's musical style are immediately audible in his Penitential Psalms: the richness in harmonic color, quick changes in texture, rapid shifts in the number of voices, and forceful yet clear text declamation. Lassus's music is more compact, more harmonically conceived, and more economical in utterance than that of his contemporaries. His aim was not to weave together long strands of imitative counterpoint, but rather to convey the intensity of a bold text through an equally bold musical gesture, as he does superbly in his Penitential Psalms. Lassus's expressive, text-oriented style can be heard nowhere better than in his settings of the Penitential Psalms.

The **Psalter** (150 psalms of the Old Testament) is one of the great treasures of both the Christian and Jewish faiths. Early in the history of the Christian church, seven psalms were given special attention. They are called the **Penitential Psalms** because their texts express a sense of sin and because they petition God for mercy in an especially personal, heartfelt way. In the liturgy of the Catholic Church, the Penitential Psalms were traditionally sung on Ash Wednesday, during Holy Week, and as part of the Office of the Dead. (For Josquin's setting of the Penitential Psalm *Miserere mei, Deus*, see Chapter 21). Protestants, however, found these biblical texts provided a means for a direct appeal to the Lord; an individual might plead for mercy in the

Bayerische Staatsbibliothek, Munich

FIGURE 24-2

An illumination, painted by Hans Mielich (c1560), that appears at the front of a luxurious manuscript containing the Penitential Psalms of Orlande de Lassus. Lassus is seated at the harpsichord. Behind and around him are the instrumentalists of the court and, behind them, the chapel singers.

Bayerische Staatsbibliothek, Munich

�$$ FIGURE 24-3

The soprano and bass parts
of Orlande de Lassus's motet
De profundis.

quiet and solitude of the home, without the liturgical ritual of the established church. Lassus was the first composer to set all of the Penitential Psalms in polyphony. In so doing, he created one of the great monuments of Renaissance choral music.

The sixth of the seven Penitential Psalms (Psalm 129) begins: *De profundis clamavi ad te Domine: Domine, exaudi vocem meam* (*From the depths I cried to you, O Lord: Lord hear my voice*). The illustrations accompanying Lassus's music (see Fig. 24-3) depict those heroes who throughout sacred history have been imprisoned and have implored the Lord for deliverance, among them Joseph in the dungeon of the Pharaoh, Daniel in the den of the lions, and Jonah in the belly of the whale—all Old Testament precursors of Christ. At the outset, Lassus's music too poignantly expresses deep despair as the basses fall down to great F and climb back up an octave only to plummet again—an excellent example of text painting in music. Clearly, Lasso was greatly affected by his early exposure to the Italian madrigal. Furthermore, because the Penitential Psalms, like all other psalms, comprise a succession of short verses, the music for them is made up of short sections, each one setting one verse of text. Accordingly, in *De profundis clamavi*, Lassus continually changes the number of voices and moves boldly from one harmony to another as he proceeds from one verse to the next (Ex. 24-4). In this way the distinction between verses is clear and the text emphatically expressed.

EXAMPLE 24-4

From the depths I cried to you, O Lord:

LISTENING CUE

ORLANDE DE LASSUS
De profundis clamavi (c1560)

CD 3/16
Anthology, No. 67

For the first twenty years of their existence, Lassus' seven Penitential Psalms were kept in Duke Albrecht V's library above his art gallery; this was his private music. Members of the court called it **musica reservata,** text-sensitive music reserved for a small circle of connoisseurs. Only after the death of the duke in 1579 did the Penitential Psalms receive their first public performance. Lassus and the singers of the ducal chapel sang them in a darkened gymnasium of a Jesuit college in Munich during Holy Week 1580.

✿ EPILOGUE: THE PSALTER IN OTHER PROTESTANT COUNTRIES

The Book of Psalms was important to Catholics like Lassus, but even more so to Protestants in Germany and elsewhere. Some extreme reformers such as Ulrich Zwingli (1484–1531) in Switzerland banned all music from the church. Others, however, allowed music in the sanctuary, but limited it exclusively to singing the Psalter. One such reformer was John Calvin (1509–1564), a Frenchman exiled to the Swiss town of Geneva. Calvin believed that polyphonic Masses and motets sung by a trained choir distracted the faithful from the Word of God. For him the only true church music was the Psalter sung monophonically in unison by the congregation. To this end, Calvin published what is called **The Geneva Psalter** (1539; revised 1551) containing a translation of all one hundred and fifty psalms into metrical and rhyming French. Many of the psalms were supplied with simple melodies, most created by the Geneva musician Louis Bourgeois (c1510–c1560). Among them was the pleasing tune for Protestant Psalm 134: *Or sus, serviteurs du Seigneur* (*Ye servants of the Lord of might*; Ex. 24-5).

EXAMPLE 24-5

Ye servants of the Lord of might,
Who in his house do watch by night,
Attending there, your selves address,
The Lord our God to praise and bless.

Two decades later the Psalter was translated into poetic English. It too was published, not in England but in Geneva, Switzerland, where English reformers had temporarily taken refuge during the reign of Catholic Queen Mary I (1553–1558). In this collection the melody of Louis Bourgeois was also made to serve Psalm 100, which subsequently became known in the English-speaking world as "Old Hundreth" (*All people that on earth do dwell*; Ex. 24-6).

EXAMPLE 24-6

The principals behind the English Psalter were Thomas Sternhold and John Hopkins and their collection, the **Sternhold and Hopkins Psalter,** enjoyed enormous popularity, appearing in nearly five hundred editions in the course of the next hundred years; in these, a small number of melodies did service for the many "Englished" psalm texts. When the Pilgrims (English reformist refugees) landed on the shores of America in 1620, they carried with them the Sternhold and Hopkins Psalter. Even today, psalm settings from this book as well as the Geneva Psalter appear in Protestant hymnals. Thus has the Book of Psalms inspired music for worship for Jews, Catholics, and Protestants over the span of more than three thousand years.

 SUMMARY

German-speaking lands had a long tradition of monophonic Gregorian chant. Yet composed polyphonic art music did not become deeply rooted there until the Renaissance. With the growth of German cities, and especially with the advent of music printing, polyphonic music in the German tongue began to flourish. The German song (Lied) was set in polyphony by a number of composers, most notably Heinrich Isaac. Composers placed the tune in the tenor, thereby producing a Tenorlied. Having more in common with the French chanson than the Italian madrigal, the strophic Tenorlied rarely indulged in word painting or bold chromatic harmonies. It was unadorned, pleasing music designed to appeal to the general public.

So too was the music of the early Protestant church. Martin Luther and his followers reduced the complexity of the Catholic service, introduced German into the Mass, and allowed for congregational singing of a new type of religious song called the chorale. Like hymns today, the strophic German chorale was intentionally simple and tuneful so that all could sing it. Lutheran musicians, especially Johann Walter, set chorale tunes in a four-voice, lightly imitative style, usually with the chorale in the tenor. Later the chorale migrated to the soprano, which is where it appears in the four-part chorale harmonizations of J.S. Bach.

Southern-most Germany and Austria remained Roman Catholic during the Renaissance. Composers working in these lands continued to write in the traditional genres of religious music—the Mass and motet, both still using the Latin language. The most prominent of these was Orlande de Lassus at the court of Munich. Having been influenced at an early age by the Italian madrigal, Lassus made use of text painting and harmonic coloring in his sacred music for the Catholic service. Lassus's style generally is more vivid, direct, and rhetorical than the somewhat ethereal, abstract style then coming forth from Counter-Reformation Rome.

 KEY TERMS

Holy Roman Empire	Tenorlied	Reformation
Emperor Maximilian I	*alternatim* technique	chorale
Hofkapelle	Diet (Reichstag)	contrafactum
Choralis Constantinus	Martin Luther	(pl., contrafacta)
Lied (pl., Lieder)	Ninety-Five Theses	Johann Walter

Geistliche Gesangbüchlein   *Tafelmusik*   The Geneva Psalter

The Augsburg   Psalter   Sternhold and Hopkins

    Confession   Penitential Psalms   Psalter

Peace of Augsburg   *musica reservata*

Chapter

25

Rome and the Music of the Counter-Reformation

Rome was the greatest city on earth at the height of the Empire, during the reigns of Julius Caesar and his successors. It fell into disarray and often chaos in the Middle Ages, only to regain much of its former splendor in the fifteenth and early sixteenth centuries. Indeed, Rome epitomized the rebirth expressed by the term "Renaissance." Just how bad had things become in the Eternal City? By the fourteenth century the population of Rome, which once numbered more than a million, had shrunk to about 20,000; the great monuments of the Empire lay in ruin, covered by debris and vines; the papacy was no longer in Rome, having moved to Avignon (see Chapter 13); and, at night, wolves roamed the streets, looking for the latest victims of plague or malaria.

✿ FIGURE 25-1

A joust in progress inside the gardens of the papal apartments at the Vatican. The Sistine Chapel is at the top. Workers constructing the new St. Peter's Basilica can be seen in the background at the upper right.

Things began to improve, however, when Pope Martin V returned the papacy to Rome in 1420. Clergymen now journeyed to the city to receive the benefits and privileges that only a pope could bestow. Pope Nicholas V declared 1450 a jubilee year, and thousands of spiritual pilgrims flocked to Rome, bringing not only their questing souls but also the money of the tourist. Gradually, streets were refurbished, monuments were restored, and fallen statues resurrected. New construction began in the area of the Vatican on the western edge of the city. Pope Sixtus IV built the Sistine Chapel between 1477 and 1481, and popes Julius II, Leo X, and Paul III began to erect a new St. Peter's Basilica, which would take a century to complete. By the sixteenth century the papacy had regained administrative and financial control over religious practices in much of western Europe. From Rome went orders as to how the universal church should be administered; to Rome came the money contributed by the faithful.

In the early sixteenth century, after nearly a century of improving fortunes, the papacy ran headlong into an implacable foe: Martin Luther. Luther and his fellow reformers sought to bring an end to the persistent corruption within the Roman Catholic Church: the sale of indulgences, graft in appointing church officers, and personal excess by the popes. The very worldly nature of the papacy can be seen in Figure 25-1, which shows a joust going on near the papal apartments as the new St. Peter's rises in the background; the pope was a warlord as well as a spiritual leader. By the time the Protestant Reformation had run its course, most of Germany, Switzerland, the Low

Countries, and all of England, as well as parts of France, Austria, Bohemia, Poland, and Hungary, had gone over to the Protestant cause. The established Roman Catholic Church was shaken to its very foundation.

In response to this religious challenge, the Church of Rome began to clean its own house. The cleansing applied not only to matters of spirituality and church administration but also to art, liturgy, and music. Nudity in religious paintings, musical instruments within the church, secular tunes in the midst of polyphonic Masses, and married church singers were now deemed inappropriate to a truly pious environment.

The movement that fostered this reform within the established Roman Church is called the **Counter-Reformation.** Its spirit was institutionalized in the **Council of Trent** (1545–1563), a congress of bishops and cardinals held at the small town of Trento in the Italian Alps. Although the assembled prelates debated many aspects of reform within the Church of Rome, the liturgy and its music occupied much of their time. In essence, they put the contrapuntal style of sacred music on trial. They considered banning all polyphony from the church. What bothered the Catholic reformers most about the church music of the day was the incessant entry of voices in musical imitation, which created an overlapping of lines that obscured the text; in other words, excessively dense counterpoint was burying the sacred word of the Lord. As one well-placed bishop said derisively:

> In our times they [composers] have put all their industry and effort into the writing of imitative passages, so that while one voice says "Sanctus," another says "Sabaoth," still another says "Gloria tua," with howling, bellowing, and stammering, so that they more nearly resemble cats in January than flowers in May.[1]

This states what sacred polyphony should not be. But how should good music for the church sound? In September 1562 deputies of the Council declared the following:

> All things should indeed be so ordered that the Masses, whether they be celebrated with or without singing, may reach tranquilly into the ears and hearts of those who hear them, when everything is executed clearly and at the right speed. In the cases of those Masses which are celebrated with singing and with organ, let nothing profane be intermingled, but only hymns and divine praises. The whole plan of singing in musical modes should be constituted not to give empty pleasure to the ear, but in such a way that the words be clearly understood by all, and thus the hearts of the listeners be drawn to desire of heavenly harmonies, in the contemplation of the joys of the blessed.[2]

✿ GIOVANNI PIERLUIGI DA PALESTRINA

Clarity of the text—the word of the Lord—was of primary importance to the church fathers at the time of the Counter-Reformation. Immediately, composers such as Giovanni Pierluigi da Palestrina (1525/26–1594) set about to produce polyphonic Masses that demonstrated that sacred polyphony for four, five, or six voices could be written in a clear, dignified manner. Among these works was Palestrina's **Mass for Pope Marcellus** (1567), a Mass which later generations came to view as the model of the clear, serene style of the Counter-Reformation. For his role in maintaining a place for composed polyphony within the established Church, Palestrina, rightly or wrongly, came to be called "the savior of church music."

Palestrina was born in the small hill town of that name outside Rome. He spent almost his entire professional life as a singer and composer at various churches in and around the Vatican: St. Peter's Basilica, St. John Lateran, St. Mary Major, and the **Sistine Chapel** (the pope's private chapel within his apartments; Fig. 25-2). Al-

FIGURE 25-2
Interior of the Sistine Chapel.
The high altar and Michelangelo's
Last Judgment are at the far end;
the balcony for the singers is at
the lower right, just on the other
side of the choir screen.

though Paul IV, one of the more zealous of the reforming popes, dismissed him from
the Sistine Chapel in 1555 because he was a married layman not conforming to the
rule of celibacy, Palestrina returned to papal employment at St. Peter's in 1571,
holding the title *maestro di cappella* (master of the chapel) and ultimately *maestro
compositore* (master composer). In the course of his lengthy career as a church musician, Palestrina composed more than 700 sacred works, including 104 polyphonic
Masses. All of this music was conceived for voices alone. It was the custom in most
Roman churches at this time to sing polyphony without the accompaniment of musical instruments. The Sistine Chapel in particular had never made use of instruments, even the organ. The expression *"a cappella Sistina"* (in the style of the Sistine
Chapel) eventually would be reduced simply to *a cappella*—singing without instrumental accompaniment. Palestrina's music is invariably performed *a cappella*.

The *Sanctus* of Palestrina's *Missa Aeterna Christi munera* (*Mass: Eternal Gifts of
Christ*) epitomizes the musical spirit of the Counter-Reformation that then radiated
from Rome. Palestrina's *Sanctus* unfolds slowly and deliberately with long notes gradually giving way to shorter, faster-moving ones, but without catchy rhythms or a
strong beat. The sober mood is created in part by the careful use of imitative counterpoint. Each phrase of text is assigned its own motive, which appears, in turn, in each
voice. A motive used in this fashion is called a **point of imitation.** Palestrina's *Sanctus* has four points of imitation (mm. 1, 13, 23, and 30). The first enters in the order
soprano, alto, tenor, bass, and the music works to a cadence. While the soprano and
bass conclude the cadence, the alto and tenor begin the second point of imitation.
Soon this section cadences in the soprano and alto as the bass and tenor enter with
the third point. Palestrina was a master at sewing a cadence to the beginning of a
new point of imitation (Ex. 25-1). The listener experiences not only a sense of satis-
faction on arrival at the cadence but also a feeling of ongoing progress as the new
point pushes forward. Notice the individual musical lines. Each voice moves primarily in step-wise motion. The largest leap is an octave, which occurs only in

ascending motion. Diminished and augmented intervals are prohibited. Dissonance occurs off the beat or, if on the beat, is carefully controlled. This conservative style of writing continued an old tradition, going back to Ockeghem and Josquin, that would soon come to be called the *prima pratica* (first practice)—a traditional style for church music that is in contrast to the freer writing found in some madrigals of the late sixteenth century. In this conservative style, the Church of Rome found the musical embodiment of the restrained spirit of the Counter-Reformation.

EXAMPLE 25-1

Lord God of Sabaoth, the heavens are full of your glory...

LISTENING CUE

GIOVANNI PIERLUIGI DA PALESTRINA   CD 3/17
Sanctus of the Missa Aeterna Christi munera (1590)   Anthology, No. 68

 FIGURE 25-3

The high altar of St. Peter's Basilica and, above it, the Latin inscription beginning *Tu es Petrus* and ending *regni caelorum*. Palestrina set this text on several occasions.

Scala/Art Resource

The **Vatican,** the compound in which the pope resides today, derives its name from the old Roman name of the hill (*mons Vaticanus*) on which it sits. The site was chosen to be the seat of the Church of Rome because in 324 C.E. Emperor Constantine, the first Christian emperor, had built a church there, where the earliest Christians venerated the bones of St. Peter, Christ's apostle to Rome. Today on this site we see the largest church in the world, the gigantic **St. Peter's Basilica.** Designed in part by Michelangelo, it is a Renaissance replacement for Constantine's Roman church. Thus, St. Peter has been the object of devotion in the area of what we call the Vatican for nearly two millennia.

The source of the Apostle Peter's special status within the Roman Church is found in the Bible where, in the Gospel according to St. Matthew (16:18–19), Christ says to Peter: "Tu es Petrus et super hanc petram aedificabo ecclesiam meam" ("You are Peter and upon this rock I will build my church"). This decree that Peter be the foundation of the church is inscribed in giant letters in the dome of St. Peter's Basilica (Fig. 25-3). The scene of Christ presenting the keys of the church to Peter also appears in a fresco painted on a wall of the Sistine Chapel. Similarly, the theme of this transfer of power from Christ to Peter resounds in much music by Palestrina.

Palestrina worked at various times in both St. Peter's Basilica and in the Sistine Chapel. Not surprisingly, he composed three motets setting the text *Tu es Petrus* (*You are Peter*), one each for five, six, and seven voices. The six-voice motet makes use of points of imitation, but it also employs a less strict musical process called **rhythmic imitation** (Ex. 25-2). Here each voice in turn sings the same rhythmic motive, but to melodic motives that differ slightly in pitch.

EXAMPLE 25-2

[I will build] my church…

Rhythmic imitation creates roughly the same effect as strict imitation, but it does not require the same contrapuntal rigor. Generally speaking, in the late sixteenth century, the more voices for which a composer writes, the greater the likelihood he will use rhythmic imitation rather than strict imitation.

Palestrina composed motets not only for six voices but also for eight, divided into two choirs of four parts each. In Palestrina's *Tu es Petrus* the six voices are often divided into two groups of three, a harbinger of the double chorus style that became popular for sacred music in both Rome and Venice at the end of the sixteenth century. Throughout this motet, one group of voices will respond to the music of another, often in a chordal declamatory style. The musical lines are not long and undulating, but short and energetic. Important phrases of text are repeated again and again for special emphasis. The motet *Tu es Petrus* demonstrates that Palestrina relied not only upon imitation but also upon straightforward chordal declamation to project the meaning of a sacred text. To make the word of the Lord clearly audible to all was a spiritual imperative for composers of the Counter-Reformation.

LISTENING CUE

GIOVANNI PIERLUIGI DA PALESTRINA
Motet *Tu es Petrus* (1573)

CD 3/18
Anthology, No. 69

Sometime about 1585 Palestrina composed a six-voice *Missa Tu es Petrus* in which he borrowed musical material from his six-voice motet *Tu es Petrus*. For example, the beginning *Kyrie* of the Mass draws from the opening of the motet, specifically the music of "Tu es Petrus" (Ex. 25-3); and, in the *Christe*, Palestrina takes from the music of "aedificabo Ecclesiam meam." Earlier composers had also borrowed previously existing material, specifically when making use of cantus firmus technique or of paraphrase technique. Here, however, a different process is involved, one called parody technique. In **parody technique** a composer borrows, not merely a pre-existing melody from another work, but an entire polyphonic complex. That is to say, in parody technique one or more short passages involving several simultaneously-sounding voices are taken over by another composer. The new composer then goes on to elaborate upon and add to the borrowed material, thereby creating an entirely new composition.

EXAMPLE 25-3A   EXAMPLE 25-3B

Today "to parody" usually means "to make fun of," but that is not the case with the term "parody technique." Rather, the second composer pays homage to the first by suggesting that the earlier model is worthy of emulation. For that reason, parody technique is sometimes called **emulation technique.** One composer emulates another by borrowing portions of a musical mentor's polyphonic work. In the case of *Tu es Petrus*, however, Palestrina is simply emulating himself.

LISTENING CUE

GIOVANNI PIERLUIGI DA PALESTRINA   CD 3/19
Kyrie of the *Missa Tu es Petrus* (c1585)   Anthology, No. 70

Finally, toward the end of sixteenth century, it was not uncommon for the soprano part in the choirs of the Sistine Chapel and St. Peter's Basilica to be sung by one or more castrati. The **castrato** was a type of high-voice male singer created by castrating boys who showed promising voices before they reached puberty. Castrati sang in church choirs and, later, in opera houses in Italy and elsewhere until the early twentieth century (see also Chapter 38). They first entered the Sistine Chapel in 1562, and many of the earliest ones came from Spain, which at the time had close musical ties with Rome.

SPANISH MUSIC DURING THE COUNTER-REFORMATION

Rome was the epicenter of the Counter-Reformation, but other cities in Italy also adopted the clear, conservative style of church music. So too did other countries, most notably Spain. Throughout the sixteenth century there were close political and artistic ties between Spain and Italy. And, because there had been a history of Spanish popes during the early sixteenth century, the Sistine Chapel in particular welcomed Spanish singers. Cristóbal de Morales (c1500–1553), Francisco Guerrero (1528–1599), and Tomás Luis de Victoria (1548–1611) were three important Spanish composers who came to Rome to learn the style of the musical Counter-Reformation. Victoria may have studied with Palestrina himself during the 1560s. To the uninitiated, his style of composition is virtually indistinguishable from that of Palestrina. Indeed, Victoria is the Spanish Counter-Reformation composer *par excellence*. His dark, austere, somewhat mysterious sound provides a musical equivalent to the paintings of El Greco (1541–1614; see timeline for Part III). Like El Greco, who painted almost no secular subjects, Victoria wrote no secular music. Both Victoria and Palestrina composed serenely beautiful sacred vocal music appropriate for the solemn mood of the Counter-Reformation Church.

 SUMMARY

The Counter-Reformation was born of a desire to rid the Church of Rome of administrative abuses—and secular influences generally. In specifically musical terms, it proscribed the use of popular tunes in Masses and motets, and it encouraged the clearest possible exposition of the sacred text. Simple contrapuntal imitation and straightforward chordal declamation were the preferred means of expression. Above all, the musical style of the Counter-Reformation was conservative in its harmony and counterpoint. Indeed, the "rules" of good voice-leading and part-writing for music came to be extracted from the music of Palestrina, Victoria, and their contemporaries. Later, during the Baroque period, these practices would be codified into method books of counterpoint that were studied by great composers such as Bach and Mozart. The conservative style of church writing, first called the *prima pratica* and later the *stile antico* (old or traditional style), provides the foundation for the study of modal and species counterpoint in universities even today. Thus, for the first time in music history, a historical style became the basis of a pedagogical theory.

 KEY TERMS

Counter-Reformation	point of imitation	parody technique
Council of Trent	*prima pratica*	(emulation
Mass for Pope Marcellus	Vatican	technique)
Sistine Chapel	St. Peter's Basilica	castrato
a cappella	rhythmic imitation	

Chapter 26

Music in Elizabethan England: Early Vocal Music

Prior to 1560 the winds of the Renaissance were slow in reaching the British Isles. England had experienced little of the humanistic study of classical authors that flourished in Renaissance Italy. The architecture of the period was a particularly English brand of flamboyant gothic and small-window manor house, rather than the broad, grand, symmetrical style of the Italian Renaissance. English composers in general concentrated on liturgical texts for use in the services of the Catholic Church. Their secular vocal pieces showed little of the close cooperation between music and word that was then evident in the Italian madrigal. When the Renaissance finally came to England—in the plays of Shakespeare, the poetry of Edmund Spenser, the architecture of Inigo Jones, and the music of William Byrd and John Dowland, for example—it arrived late, but stayed longer, well into the seventeenth century. Shakespeare, for example, lived from 1564 until 1616. For much of the Bard's life, England was ruled by a wise and temperate monarch, Elizabeth I, who encouraged the arts and letters generally and loved music in particular. To understand how this extraordinary woman became the sole ruler of England, we return to the early sixteenth century and the tumultuous reign of Henry VIII.

✿ HENRY VIII AS MUSICIAN AND CHURCH REFORMER

During most of the first half of the sixteenth century, England was governed by a single dominant figure, King **Henry VIII** (r. 1509–1547). Henry did nothing in moderation. At his court he employed no fewer than fifty-eight musicians, many of whom were skilled instrumentalists brought over from the Continent. He owned fifty-six keyboard instruments, twenty "horns" of various sorts, nineteen bowed string instruments, thirty-one plucked strings, and no fewer than 220 wind instruments of various kinds. Moreover, Henry himself was a musician. He sang and played the recorder, flute, lute, and even cornett, and he danced with enthusiasm. What is more, Henry was a composer of some thirty-five secular pieces. Among the best of these—and certainly the best-known in Henry's day—is his *Pastyme with Good Companye* (Ex. 26-1). Its robust, vigorous sound reflects the assertive personality of the king.

EXAMPLE 26-1

Pastyme with Good Companye is a fine example of an English **partsong**—a strophic song with English text intended to be sung by three or four voices in a predominantly homophonic musical style. With its lively, dance-like rhythms and chordal texture, the English partsong has much in common with the Parisian chanson of the 1530s (see Chapter 22). In fact, Henry seems to have purloined the melody for this piece from a chanson (*De mon triste et desplaisir*) by the Parisian composer Jean Richafort.

LISTENING CUE

KING HENRY VIII

Pastyme with Good Companye (c1520)

CD 3/20

Anthology, No. 71

Henry VIII was a larger-than-life figure with an immense appetite: he devoured food; he devoured women; and, ultimately, he devoured the Roman Catholic Church. In 1528 Henry, in dire need of a male heir, asked Pope Clement VII to annul his nineteen-year marriage to Catherine of Aragon (daughter of Ferdinand and Isabella of Spain). When the pope refused, Henry proceeded to divorce Catherine and marry Anne Boleyn, the second of his six wives. Soon the pope retaliated, excommunicating Henry and, in effect, all English citizens. Henry responded by establishing a new Church of England with himself, the king, as its Supreme Head. He adopted some of the beliefs of the Protestants on the Continent. For example, Henry came to view all monasteries and convents as leeches on society and closed them. Some churchmen in England, influenced particularly by the Calvinists in Switzerland and France, went even further than Henry wished to go toward religious reform; they insisted upon a complete break with the liturgy of the Church of Rome and argued for a new, far simpler, religious service. Consequently, by 1547, the last year of Henry's reign, there were three branches of formalized religion in England, comprising the Church of Rome as well as two Protestant offshoots—the Church of England (later called the Anglican Church, and related to the Episcopal Church in America), and the more progressive, reform-minded group of Protestantism called the Puritans. After Henry's death, church composers working in England wrote for one, or all, of these three religious persuasions.

This was the religious situation in England when on 17 November 1558, Princess Elizabeth Tudor, daughter of Henry and Anne Boleyn, ascended the throne of England. As Queen **Elizabeth I** she ruled for forty-five years, until her death in 1603. She was called "the Virgin Queen" because she never married. There were eager suitors enough, but for political reasons Elizabeth chose to remain single, fashioning an image of herself as a wise and learned monarch devoted to the interests of her subjects. Alone among her sex, she held the unique position of a woman who exercised power successfully in a deeply patriarchal world.

Religion, and the music that accompanied it, occupied much of Elizabeth's attention during her long reign. Political survival dictated that the queen steer a middle course between the reactionary conservatives of the Catholic faith and radical reformers among the Puritans. In her own chapel, Elizabeth followed the newly truncated service adopted by the Anglican Church—instead of Mass and eight canonical hours observed by Catholics, she attended an Anglican service. The Anglican service consisted of **Morning Prayer** (a compression of Matins and Lauds), Mass, and **Evensong** (a similar compression of Vespers and Compline). Sometimes her large chapel of thirty-two men and twelve boys sang in Latin using the same

The Education of a Renaissance Queen

Elizabeth Tudor was exceptionally well prepared to be ruler of England. Her father Henry VIII, recognizing that she was an unusually bright child, provided tutors in almost every conceivable subject (Fig. 26-1). She studied architecture, mathematics, the fundamentals of astronomy, and geography. But special emphasis was placed on foreign languages. By her adolescence she could speak and write French, Italian, and Latin almost as well as she could English, and she had also acquired some Greek. For practice, she read Cicero and Livy in Latin and the New Testament in Greek. Later, when queen, Elizabeth was known to give, on the spur of the moment, a lengthy harangue to Parliament in fluent Latin. As monarch, she found time to read history three hours a day. She was, in short, a natural scholar. For amusement Elizabeth would ride horseback, play chess, dance, and make music, all skills she learned at an early age. As one of her tutors said of Elizabeth when she was eighteen:

> Her mind has no womanly weakness and her perseverance is equal to that of a man and her memory long keeps what it quickly picks up. She talks French and Italian as well as she does English and has often talked to me readily and well in Latin, moderately in Greek. When she writes in Greek and Latin, nothing is more beautiful than her handwriting. She delights as much in music as she is skilful in it.[1]

Indeed, Elizabeth's skills in music and dance, as we will see, were considerable.

❀ FIGURE 26-1

A portrait of Princess Elizabeth Tudor at the age of thirteen, attributed to William Scrots. She holds a book, and another rests on a lectern, both prominently displayed to symbolize Elizabeth's extraordinary capacity for learning.

CORBIS

---

style of elaborate counterpoint preferred by the Catholics on the Continent. At other times the royal chapel sang simple polyphonic psalm settings of the sort favored by reformed congregations of Calvinists and Puritans. If nothing else, composers in the service of Elizabeth needed to be versatile.

❀ THOMAS TALLIS AND THE ENGLISH PSALM

Thomas Tallis (c1505–1585) was one such versatile composer; he wrote music for all three faiths—Catholic, Anglican, and Puritan. Tallis has left us a stunning set of Lamentations suitable for the Catholic Church during Holy Week, as well as many anthems (see below) in English and motets in Latin, including one for forty voices (*Spem in alium*)—all appropriate for the Church of England. Yet today Tallis is known equally well for simple psalm settings of the sort favored by the Puritans.

As we have seen, the English Puritans were greatly influenced by the Calvinist religion on the Continent, which endorsed no music in the service except simple psalms sung in the vernacular tongue. English reformers soon translated the Psalter into English and supplied it with simple tunes. The most popular of these was the Sternhold and Hopkins Psalter (see the end of Chapter 24), but it was not the only such book. In 1567 Matthew Parker, a clergyman close to Queen Elizabeth, produced another translation and asked royal composer Tallis to provide the music. Parker's volume, *The Whole Psalter Translated into English Metre*, took the Latin prose of the Book of Psalms and turned it into English poetry. Tallis provided music for eight of the translated psalms, one for each of the old church modes (Ex. 26-2). But, because many of the psalms had a common meter, Tallis's eight musical settings were able to accommodate most of the one hundred fifty psalms in Parker's book; one setting served many psalms. Below is Parker's metrical translation of Psalm 2 as set by Tallis, preceded by the Latin previously used in England, and followed by the later English as it appeared in the early-seventeenth-century King James version of the Bible.

Ps. 2: Latin of Vulgate Bible
Quare fremuerunt gentes,
et populi meditati sunt inania?
Astiterunt reges terrae,
et principes convenerunt in unum,
adversus Dominum,
et adversus Christum ejus.

Ps. 2: Parker's translation, set by Tallis
Why fum'th in sight the Gentiles spite,
in fury raging stout?
Why tak'th in hand the people fond,
vain things to bring about?
The kings arise, the Lords devise,
in counsels met thereto,
against the Lord with false accord,
against his Christ they go.

Ps. 2: King James Version
Why do the heathen rage
and the people imagine a vain thing?
The kings of the earth set themselves
and the rulers take counsel together,
against the Lord, and against his
Anointed.

EXAMPLE 26-2

Why fum'th in sight the Gen-tiles spite, in fu-ry rag-ing stout?

Appropriate for the simple musical needs of the English reformed church, Tallis's *Why fum'th in sight* is a straightforward, chordal setting of Psalm 2 for four voices. Like the reformers of the German Lutheran Church, who often borrowed from the chant of the Church of Rome when fashioning a chorale tune, Tallis here adopted a melody from the medieval Catholic liturgy. His tune is nothing other than a reworking of the old Gregorian psalm tone for the Phrygian mode (mode 3). In

Parker's book, Tallis describes the Phrygian mode as one that "doth rage and roughly brayth." And, like German musicians who often placed the tune in the tenor voice when setting a chorale, Tallis puts his melody in the tenor. Finally, just as the German chorale tune migrated over the centuries from the tenor to the soprano, Tallis's melody eventually moved to the highest voice. Today an arrangement of Tallis's psalm setting, with the melody in the soprano, can be found in the hymnal of both the Anglican (Episcopal) and Lutheran church. The tune continues to be well known to lovers of later orchestral music, for in 1910 the English composer Ralph Vaughan Williams made it the basis of his hauntingly beautiful *Fantasy on a Theme of Thomas Tallis* (see Chapter 61).

LISTENING CUE

THOMAS TALLIS
Psalm 2 (1567)

Book Companion Website (http://schirmer.wadsworth.com/wright_1e)
Anthology, No. 72

 ## WILLIAM BYRD AND THE ENGLISH ANTHEM

When Tallis died in 1585, his place as the preeminent composer of the Elizabethan age devolved to his pupil William Byrd (1543–1623). Byrd faithfully served Elizabeth for forty-five years, and she in turn rewarded and protected him. Protection was needed, for Byrd was a Catholic in an increasingly anti-Catholic country. He, like all Romanists, was forced to practice his faith in secret at small, clandestine gatherings in private homes and chapels. The music that Byrd wrote for these underground Catholic services includes three polyphonic Masses, for three, four, and five voices, respectively. He also composed many motets setting Latin texts. Several of these recount the fall of Jerusalem, because, for Byrd and other English Catholics, the decline of the homeland Catholic Church was tantamount to the fall of Jerusalem in biblical times.

Despite his personal faith, duty required that Byrd write motets for the Anglican Church. These works, reflecting the reformed service, used English instead of Latin texts, and were called anthems. Thus an **anthem** is a sacred vocal composition, much like a motet but sung in English, in honor of the Lord or invoking the Lord to preserve and protect the English king or queen. Most anthems were composed for Morning Prayer or Evensong, some in honor of the monarch. Later, Henry Purcell and George Frideric Handel would write anthems for church and crown. One of Handel's *Coronation Anthems*, "Zadok the Priest," has been performed at the coronation of every English king and queen since its creation in 1727.

Byrd's anthem *O Lord, make thy servant, Elizabeth* was written for Elizabeth I, sometime around 1570. Byrd has simply reshaped a few lines from the beginning of Psalm 21 to make them apposite for his royal patron, turning "the King" into "our Queen."

Psalm 21, verses 1, 2, and 4:
The King shall joy in thy strength,
    O Lord.
Thou hast given him his heart's desire,
and hast not withholden the request
    of his lips.

Byrd's text in honor of Elizabeth:
O Lord, make thy servant, Elizabeth
    our Queen to rejoice in thy strength;
Give her her heart's desire,
and deny not the request
    of her lips.

He asked life of thee, and thou gavest in him,
even length of days for ever and ever.

But prevent her with thine everlasting blessing,
and give her a long life, ev'n for ever and ever.
Amen.

Appropriate for the royal subject matter, Byrd adorns this text with a large-scale, five-voice setting. In musical style, this Anglican anthem is similar, in the most general way, to the learned, imitative polyphony created by Catholic composers on the Continent at this time, among them Lassus and Palestrina. There are moments of choral declamation for emphasis, such as the opening entreaty "O Lord," that remind us of Lassus. But throughout most of the anthem Byrd spins out points of imitation, first on the words "Give her her heart's desire" and then on "And give her a long life," a contrapuntal technique reminiscent of Palestrina. But there are also moments here that sound distinctly English. Look carefully at measures 14, 15, and 42, where a crunching dissonance occurs. In each case a B♭ in the soprano sounds against a B♮ in the alto. Both conflicting notes are correct, however, and indeed are required by the rules of proper voice leading—the line with the flat is moving down, that with the natural is moving up, ultimately to serve as a leading tone at the cadence (Ex. 26-3).

EXAMPLE 26-3

Such moments of harmonic (but not melodic) conflict were heard on the Continent at this time, but were especially relished by English composers throughout the sixteenth and seventeenth centuries. The sound is called the **English cross (false) relation**—the simultaneous or adjacent appearance in different voices of two conflicting notes with the same letter name. The intensity, even shock, of such conflicting moments adds expressive power to the music.

Finally, Byrd's anthem for Queen Elizabeth ends with a quiet "Amen," and this too is a peculiarity of the English music at the time. German Lutheran chorales never end with "Amen" because these texts are not derived from the psalms. In the medieval Catholic liturgy, psalms end with a lengthy doxology concluding with "Amen." English Protestants shortened the doxology to simply the last word "Amen" (the old Hebrew "and so be it"). English composers in turn gave this short, emphatic conclusion special attention, developing what we call the **Amen cadence.** They usually set the word "Amen" as a **plagal cadence,** a term drawn from the Greek word *plagalis*, meaning "derived from" or "not direct." Today we describe the plagal cadence as a IV-I chordal movement with the bass in root position falling down by the interval of the fourth. In Byrd's anthem, the main body of the piece ends with a V-I authentic cadence; the appended "Amen," however, ends with a IV-I plagal, or Amen, cadence (Ex. 26-4).

EXAMPLE 26-4

LISTENING CUE

WILLIAM BYRD
O Lord, make thy servant, Elizabeth (c1570)

CD 3/21
Anthology, No. 73

SUMMARY

The Renaissance came late to England but lasted longer, well into the seventeenth century. During the Middle Ages, English polyphonic music was cultivated widely in monasteries and cathedrals around the country. During the Renaissance, however, the composition and performance of written art music was centered around the person of the king or queen, first Henry VIII and then his daughter Elizabeth I. Most of the English Renaissance occurred during the reign of Elizabeth, and without this remarkable monarch there likely would have been no golden age of English music. Elizabeth was a practical ruler who tolerated Puritan, Anglican, and Catholic music alike. Her chapel singers, Thomas Tallis and William Byrd, were both versatile composers able to create simple psalm settings, or more elaborate English anthems and Latin motets as the occasion demanded.

KEY TERMS

Henry VIII	Morning Prayer	English cross (false) relation
partsong	Evensong	Amen cadence
Elizabeth I	anthem	plagal cadence

Music in Elizabethan England: Instrumental Music and Later Vocal Music

27

Early in her reign, in 1575, Queen Elizabeth had favored her two chapel composers Thomas Tallis and William Byrd with a special privilege: a monopoly on the printing of music in England. This was a way to augment a musician's salary without draining a queen's purse. Armed with their new commercial authority, Tallis and Byrd immediately issued a collection of religious music called *Cantiones sacrae* (1575). In the preface they thanked their benefactor with seemingly fulsome praise: "Her Royal Majesty, the glory of our age, is accustomed always to have Music among her pleasures. Not content simply to hear the venerable works of others, she herself sings and plays excellently." Flattery this was not.

Like her father, King Henry VIII, Queen Elizabeth I was enamored of music. She too apparently tried her hand at composition, for in 1598 she related to the French ambassador that as a girl she had "composed measures [dance steps] and music and played them herself and danced them." And she kept on dancing, almost to her end (Fig. 27-1). In 1599 the Spanish ambassador reported that the 66-year-old "head of the Church of England and Ireland was to be seen in her old age dancing three or four galliards."[1] As to her performing skills, Elizabeth sang and played the lute and harpsichord. Her music making seems to have transpired, not so much in public, but more in the solitude of her privy chamber, as the following report of the Scottish ambassador suggests:

> That same day after dinner [I was taken] up to a quiet gallery that I might hear some music, where I might hear the Queen play upon the virginals. After I had hearkened a while, I took by the tapestry that hung before the door of the

🌿 FIGURE 27-1

A painting believed to show Queen Elizabeth dancing the volta with the Duke of Leicester.

Photo credit to come

✻ FIGURE 27-2

The title page of *Parthenia* (1612), a collection of keyboard music by Byrd, Gibbons, and Bull, showing a young performer seated at a virginal. Notice the prominent use of "2-3 fingering" with the thumb little engaged.

chamber, and seeing her back was toward the door, I entered within the chamber, and stood a pretty space hearing her play excellently well. But she left off immediately, so soon as she turned her about and saw me. She appeared to be surprised to see me, and came forward, seeming to strike me with her hand; alleging she used not to play before men, but when she was solitary, to shun melancholy.[2]

Indeed, more than one visitor to the English court reports that the queen played on an instrument with strings "of pure gold and silver." That instrument was called a virginal.

✿ ENGLISH KEYBOARD MUSIC

A **virginal** (often "virginals") is a diminutive harpsichord possessing a single keyboard with the strings placed at right angles to the keys (Fig. 27-2). The instrument was small enough to rest easily on a table. Because of its modest size, sound, and cost, it was the ideal beginning instrument for young girls—hence the term "virginal." Indeed, it is clear from paintings and drawings of the period that women played the virginal far more often than men, who tended to prefer the lute.

A young woman can be seen seated at a virginal on the cover of *Parthenia* (1612), the first collection of keyboard music printed in England and one of the earliest English examples of musical engraving, a new method for printing music (see Fig. 27-2). Behind this title page are twenty-one keyboard works by William Byrd, Orlando Gibbons (1583–1625), and John Bull (1562–1628), all three employed at one time or another as singers or organists at the royal chapel. A much larger collection of keyboard music is preserved today in a manuscript at the Fitzwilliam Museum in Cambridge, England. Copied during the early seventeenth century, this giant anthology is now called the **Fitzwilliam Virginal Book** (c1615). In previous centuries it was known, incorrectly, as Queen Elizabeth's Virginal Book, because so much of the music emanated from her royal court.

Among the 297 compositions in the Fitzwilliam Virginal Book are many keyboard fantasias, settings of dances such as the pavane and galliard, descriptive pieces including William Byrd's *The Bells*, and even intabulations of a few Italian madrigals and French chansons. But almost all the compositions in this collection, in one way or another, employ **variation technique,** a procedure in which successive statements of a theme are changed or presented in altered surroundings.

Typical of these is a set of variations composed by Thomas Morley (1557–1602) on the popular song *Goe from my window.*[3] Morley's setting of *Goe from my window* gives seven variations of the tune. As with most variations on top hits in Elizabethan England, the tune itself is not given prominently at the beginning. By contrast, later composers—Bach, Beethoven, Haydn, and Mozart, among others—always give the listener the tune clearly before they begin to vary it. But, in the Renaissance, when aural traditions were more strongly ingrained, composers thought it unnecessary to provide the unadorned melody. Everyone knew the tune, so they just started with the first variation. Because we do not know the tune, the melody of *Goe from my window* is given in Example 27-1.

EXAMPLE 27-1

Goe from my win-dow my love, Goe from my win-dow my dear, The wind and the rain will drive you back a-gain, you can-not be all de-spair.

In truth, Morley focuses his attention more on the harmonic pattern supporting *Goe from my window* than on the tune itself. The challenge he sets himself is to create seven equally compelling versions of the same harmonic plan. At the same time, Morley seems intent upon improving the performer's technique in one way or another. Variation four, for example, emphasizes the need to play parallel sixths cleanly, while six and seven develop the ability to play scales rapidly and evenly, first in the right hand and then the left. Yet there is more here than mere mechanical figures: Morley's variation one has rich chords and fine part-writing, while his variation two begins with a masterful demonstration on how to create a chain of suspensions. Moreover, variation five contains a remarkable driving, leaping bass that seems to prefigure those of Handel and Bach more than a century later (Ex. 27-2). This is keyboard music of a very high quality. Could Queen Elizabeth ever have played up to tempo music with such complexity and technical difficulty? Judging from what contemporaries said of her musical skills, likely yes.

EXAMPLE 27-2

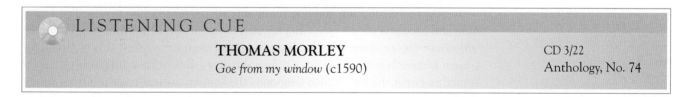

LISTENING CUE

THOMAS MORLEY

Goe from my window (c1590)

CD 3/22

Anthology, No. 74

THE ENGLISH MADRIGAL

As the years went by, Elizabeth found it difficult to keep up the image of the youthful virgin queen. Servants applied wigs, teeth whiteners, perfumes, and powders to this end. Courtiers, too, were expected to do their part to perpetuate the myth of the ageless queen. Playwrights like Ben Jonson curried favor by means of plays and masques (elaborate court entertainments that praise the ruler through music and dance). Composers were left to flatter the queen through the verse of their madrigals.

In 1601 Thomas Morley fashioned a remarkable volume of royal adulation when he engaged twenty-three colleagues to join him in creating a collection of madrigals to honor Queen Elizabeth. The resulting set of twenty-five pieces (Morley provided two) was published under the title **The Triumphes of Oriana**—Oriana and Gloriana being two names the Elizabethans had adopted for their beloved queen. To promote her patriotic cult, Morley demanded that each contributor end his madrigal with the acclamation "Thus sang the nymphs and shepherds of Diana / Long live fair Oriana."

That Morley might call upon so many English madrigalists suggests the great popularity of the madrigal in England. Indeed, England was the only country outside Italy to develop a native variety of the madrigal. Madrigals performed outside Italy were usually Italian pieces sung in Italian, not in the native tongue. At first English composers too were strongly influenced by the Italian madrigal, but gradually they transformed the genre into something distinctly English. Simultaneously, the English adopted and adapted a lighter form of sixteenth-century Italian vocal music called the balletto, transforming it into the English ballett with dance-like rhythms and a "fa, la, la" refrain. In 1588 this vogue for Italian music was first made manifest in England in print with **Musica transalpina** (*Music across the Alps*). Although the thirty-three madrigals contained herein were mainly by Italian composers, the Italian texts were replaced by English translations. Two years later, a second publication of this sort appeared under the title *Italian Madrigals Englished*. Soon English composers, many employed at the royal court, began to issue madrigal collections of their own, including Morley's *The Triumphes of Oriana*.

Typical among the madrigals in *The Triumphes of Oriana* is the six-voice *As Vesta Was from Latmos Hill Descending* by Thomas Weelkes (1576–1623), a gentleman of the royal chapel. The text, likely created by Weelkes himself, is a rather confused mixture of images from classical mythology: the Roman goddess Vesta, descending the Greek mountain of Latmos, spies Oriana (Elizabeth) ascending the hill; the nymphs and shepherds attending the goddess Diana desert her to sing the praises of Oriana. This is doggerel with a meaning: Elizabeth is in the ascent. As Vesta descends from her temple of vestal virgins, Oriana takes her place; even the attendants of Diana, goddess of the hunt and chastity, pay homage to this virgin queen. The descriptive text provides many opportunities for madrigalisms (word painting). The music descends, ascends, runs, mingles imitatively, and offers "mirthful tunes" to Elizabeth as the text commands. In many ways *As Vesta Was from Latmos Hill Descending* is typical of the English madrigal. English composers rarely engage in the extremes of emotionalism and chromatic intensity, as the Italian madrigalists Gesualdo and Monteverdi do (see Chapter 28), for example. English madrigals can be serious, but more often they are light, fun, and even funny. Yes, this madrigal for Queen Elizabeth is an example of political flattery. But, with word painting that is sometimes over the top, it also lampoons the Italian musical tradition from which the English madrigal sprang.

LISTENING CUE

THOMAS WEELKES   CD 3/23
As Vesta Was from Latmos Hill Descending (1601)   Anthology, No. 75

The Triumphes of Oriana was just one of more than forty books of madrigals published in London between 1588 and 1627, each volume usually containing some twenty pieces or more. The composers who fashioned this great outpouring of English secular music—among them Byrd, Morley, Weelkes, Wilbye, and Gibbons—have been dubbed the **English Madrigal School,** and their collective creations constitute one of the glories of the English Renaissance.

🌼 THE ENGLISH LUTE AYRE

The popularity of the English madrigal coincided with the end of the Elizabethan Renaissance. Equal-voice counterpoint had long typified music of the Renaissance, but it was not the wave of the future. The future of music, both in England and on the Continent, was to be found in the expressive solo song. The solo art song first flourished in England just before and after 1600, toward the end of Queen Elizabeth's reign, and it appeared in two forms. In one, called the **consort song,** the voice is accompanied by a group of independent instruments, usually a consort of viols. In the other, called the **lute ayre,** the soloist is accompanied by a lute and possibly a bass instrument such as the *viola da gamba*. Both consort song and lute ayre are strophic—the same music serves each of two, three, or four stanzas. It was the job of the solo singer to employ the expressive nuances of the voice to make each stanza sound distinctive. The madrigal, by contrast, was rarely strophic; each word or phrase needed its own very special music. Madrigals were no longer published in England, or elsewhere, after the early decades of the seventeenth century; but the lute ayre, and the solo song generally, flourished in England and on the Continent throughout much of what is called the Baroque era in music.

The principal proponent of the lute ayre in England was John Dowland (1563–1626). Indeed, Dowland (pronounced "Doe-land") is now recognized as the finest English composer of lute songs as well as of music for solo lute. Unlike most of the great Elizabethan composers, Dowland did not enjoy a position at court, at least not at first. Instead, he traveled widely and worked on the Continent in France, Germany, Italy, and even Denmark. Queen Elizabeth heard Dowland's music on many occasions, and in 1596 she sent a messenger to Germany to wish him "health & soon return." Yet Dowland was known to be a difficult person, and not until 1612, well after Elizabeth's death, was he appointed royal lutenist. Between 1597 and 1612, Dowland published four collections of lute ayres. His *Second Booke of Songs or Ayres* (1600) contains *Flow my tears*, a song so powerful that it created something of a sensation. Countless arrangements for keyboard, lute, and instrumental consort survive in more than a hundred manuscripts of the period. The melody became, in effect, Dowland's "signature tune," for he began to sign himself "John Dowland de Lacrimae" (*Lacrimae* being the Latin for "tears"). Dowland published *Flow my tears* with an optional part for *viola da gamba*, which might double the lowest notes of the lute and thereby add weight to the powerful bass he had created. The plaintive melody with strong bass support can most clearly be heard at the words "And tears, and sighs, and groans" (mm. 11–12) where an ascending sequence begins low in the bass and rises spectacularly out of the depths of despair (Ex. 27-3). No wonder this exceptional song became all the rage during the Elizabethan age.

EXAMPLE 27-3

LISTENING CUE

JOHN DOWLAND
Flow my tears (1600)

CD 3/24
Anthology, No. 76

Some of Dowland's most expressive lute ayres have qualities of the solo monody emerging in Italy during the Baroque era (see Chapter 29). He writes an intense solo vocal line and creates a texture with a strong polarity between melody and bass. What Dowland does not compose is a vocal line with elaborate, virtuosic embellishments. Despite some forward-looking elements, *Flow my tears* belongs to the tradition of the unadorned Renaissance air, not the vocally demanding Baroque aria we will soon meet.

 SUMMARY

Queen Elizabeth's court witnessed the creation of the first repertory of keyboard music of high artistic quality and high technical difficulty. Royal composers Byrd, Gibbons, and Morley, among others, wrote lengthy keyboard works, almost all of which use variation technique in one way or another. They intended these to be played on the dominant keyboard instrument of the day, a small harpsichord called the virginal.

Secular vocal music also flowered with Elizabeth's encouragement, the principal genres being the madrigal and the lute ayre. Although at first derived from the style of the Italian madrigal, English madrigals can be lighter, less serious in tone, and less chromatic in design than their Italian counterparts. The lute ayre remained a principal vehicle for solo singing throughout the seventeenth century. The most intense of John Dowland's lute ayres exhibit an expressive solo voice as well as a strong polarity between vocal melody and bass support. These features are also apparent in the solo monody emerging in Italy around the turn of the seventeenth century.

 KEY TERMS

virginal	variation technique	English Madrigal School
Fitzwilliam Virginal Book	*The Triumphes of Oriana*	consort song
	Musica transalpina	lute ayre

The Later Madrigal in Ferrara and Mantua: Gesualdo and Monteverdi

Sixteenth-century Italy witnessed a resurgence of written art music by native composers. If Italian courts in fifteenth-century Italy had been dominated by northern Franco-Flemish composers such as Dufay and Josquin, now at the end of the sixteenth century the Italian scene was ruled by native composers. The advent of the frottola and especially the madrigal gave new energy to musical settings of poetry in the Italian language. The madrigal in particular only continued to grow in popularity. More than a thousand individual collections, each containing about twenty madrigals, were printed between 1530 and 1620. Some Italian madrigals were even printed with Italian texts outside of Italy, specifically in German-speaking lands, England, Denmark, and the Low Countries. Thus the madrigal became the first genre of Italian music to be exported around Europe, as opera and the concerto would be during the seventeenth century. The popularity of the madrigal signaled that Italy was becoming the center of the Western musical world, a position it would continue to enjoy through the eighteenth century.

The birthplace of the madrigal was Florence, but soon popular enthusiasm carried it to Venice, Rome, Ferrara, and Mantua (see Map 14-1). Ferrara and Mantua were city-states but, unlike Florence, not republics. Instead, they were ruled by hereditary, autocratic families, namely the d'Este family in Ferrara and the Gonzaga clan in Mantua. To their court in Ferrara the d'Estes attracted musicians such as Josquin, Cipriano de Rore, and the nobleman-composer Carlo Gesualdo, while the Gonzagas patronized the frottolist Marchetto Cara and, later, the great Claudio Monteverdi.

 ## THE MADRIGAL IN FERRARA

The court of Ferrara had been a beacon for northern composers since the mid fifteenth century (see Chapter 21). Guillaume Dufay provided music for the Ferrarese rulers as early as the 1430s. Josquin des Prez became a singer there in 1503 and was followed by another northerner, Jacob Obrecht, who died of the plague in Ferrara in 1505. In 1515 Obrecht's countryman, Adrian Willaert, moved south to enter the service of the d'Este duke, where he remained until 1527. Willaert was a prolific composer who, as we have seen, experimented with a radically new approach to tuning called "equal temperament" (see Musical Interlude 4). Two of Willaert's pupils, Cipriano de Rore, a northerner, and Nicola Vicentino, an Italian, likewise shared their mentor's enthusiasm for experimental music. We have previously met Vicentino's chromatic keyboard instrument called the arcicembalo, a harpsichord with thirty-six keys (pitches) within each octave (see Musical Interlude 4). Cipriano de Rore's interest in experimental chromatic music can be seen in his *Calami sonum ferentes* published in 1555 (Ex. 28-1). Melodic chromaticism is immediately evident here, as each line rises up the scale in half-steps. But even more novel is the harmony. Chords are built not only on the seven notes within the mode but also on tones that are foreign to it. At the outset, the chromatically rising bass (mm. 8–10) creates chords built on E, F, F♯, G, and A in immediate succession. The results are startling to the ear.

EXAMPLE 28-1

Those who set forth the sweet sounds of the flute with Sicilian rhythm...

During the second half of the sixteenth century, Ferrara maintained its reputation as the center of the musical avant-garde, in both composition and performance. The most forward-looking aspect of musical performance at Ferrara was the **concerto delle donne** (ensemble of ladies). During the 1570s the duke and duchess of Ferrara encouraged performances by a trio of singers, all of whom were women of the minor nobility. Then, in 1580, in an obvious attempt to elevate the standards of musical performance, the duke dismissed the original three singers. In their place he hired three, and sometimes four, women of middle-class background, all with exceptionally fine voices. To maintain propriety, the members of the *concerto delle donne* were classified as ladies in waiting to the duchess, not among the ranks of paid musicians; professional women musicians were still viewed with mistrust at this time, being thought little better than street entertainers. In fact, however, the *concerto delle donne* comprised vocalists of the highest quality and constituted the first professional ensemble of women employed by a court. The excellence of their singing impressed visitors coming to Ferrara, and soon similar all-female vocal groups could also be heard in Rome, Florence, and Mantua.

At Ferrara the *concerto delle donne* performed for the duke and duchess each afternoon, singing usually for two hours. (Playing cards and board games, reading poetry, and listening to live music were the ways in which the aristocracy amused itself in the days before TVs and DVDs.) Each of the ladies of the *concerto delle donne* also played a string instrument—the harp, lute, viol, or harpsichord—that might provide an accompaniment to their singing. They were supported by a single bass singer and sometimes joined by a tenor. Yet, as the following eyewitness accounts suggest, often the ladies had need of neither the bass nor the tenor voice:

> **8 September 1582:** Wednesday after having dined, the duke passed a good deal of time listening to those ladies sing from ordinary music books. Even in that kind of singing the ladies were beautiful to hear, because they sing the low parts an octave higher.

> **29 July 1584:** And then [the duke] favored me [an emissary from Florence] by allowing me to hear for two hours without break his *concerto delle donne*, which is truly extraordinary. Those ladies sing excellently, both when singing by memory and when singing at sight from part books they are secure. The duke favored me continually by showing me written out all the pieces that they sing by memory, with all the virtuosic passages that they do.[1]

As these reports suggest, the *concerto delle donne* did not perform for the full court, but only for the ducal family and a very few important guests. In fact, these concerts went by a special name, **musica secreta** (secret music). At other courts this chamber music was sometimes called *musica reservata* (reserved or private music; see Chapter 24). But, whether termed *musica secreta* or *musica reservata*, this was progressive chamber music reserved for a small, elite audience.

The exclusive nature of *musica secreta,* and the intense emphasis on the text, led to a style of composition that was more virtuosic and dramatic. For example, when singing madrigals in these private chamber concerts, the ladies often performed florid vocal passages either written by the composer or improvised on the spot. So, too, textures became more extreme through the contrast of highs against lows and very long notes against very short ones. Moreover, madrigals appear for single solo voice with instrumental accompaniment. Finally, this elitist chamber music tended to encourage chromatic writing, sometimes of the most intense sort. The result? The equal-voice imitative polyphony commonly found in the madrigal and motet of the earlier sixteenth century began to give way to a more fragmented, dramatic style. The earlier conservative style of composition was called the *prima pratica,* while the newer, text-driven, dramatic style went by the name *seconda pratica*, for reasons we will soon see.

A good example of the new, dramatic madrigal is *O docezze amarissime d'amore* (*O sweet bitterness of love*) by Luzzasco Luzzaschi (c1545–1607), a composer resident in Ferrara from the 1560s onward. Measures 10–14 exhibit widely varying rhythms, difficult vocal passages, and a moderate degree of chromaticism (Ex. 28-2). Yet the music is animated by the sort of text painting we have come to expect in the madrigal: the word "gioisco" ("I enjoy") inspires rapturous melismas, while later the command "fuggite" ("flee") generates flighty imitation. With its three demanding parts for soprano (and optional keyboard accompaniment), this madrigal was a vocal showcase for the ladies of Ferrara.

EXAMPLE 28-2

Why is grief with me if I take pleasure in it...

✿ CARLO GESUALDO

Carlo Gesualdo (1561–1613) is perhaps the most notorious figure in the history of music. He was an aristocrat, prince of the small territory of Venosa east of Naples and dutiful husband of the Marchesa of Pescara, Maria d'Avalos. But on the night of 16 October 1590 Gesualdo discovered his wife and her lover in what was then referred to as "flagrant violation and flagrant sin" and stabbed them both to death. Gesualdo was not punished by any civil court; death was thought an appropriate reward for adulterous women in Renaissance Italy. Instead of going to prison or the gallows, Gesualdo simply repaired to his country villa until the scandal blew over. Here, in semi-isolation, he was able to cultivate all the more intensely his passion for music.

Exactly when and how Gesualdo learned music is not entirely clear, but music became his obsession. During his isolation, Gesualdo composed at least two books of madrigals. By the time of his own death in 1613 he had published seven such books, as well as three volumes of motets and other religious works in Latin. In 1594 Gesualdo was able to rehabilitate his reputation by marrying Leonora d'Este, niece of Duke Alfonso d'Este of Ferrara, and for most of the years 1594–1596 he resided there. Letters to and from Ferrara at this time show that Gesualdo was a somewhat compulsive figure whose craving for music was so strong he could not endure even a single evening without it, as a Ferrarese court official suggests:

15 February 1594: [Gesualdo] discourses on hunting and music and declares himself an authority on both of them. Of hunting he did not enlarge very much since he did not find much reaction from me, but about music he spoke at such length that I have not heard so much in a whole year. He makes open profession of it and shows his works in score to everybody in order to induce them to marvel at his art. He has with him two sets of music books in five parts, all his own works, but he says that he has only four people [in his entourage] who can sing, for which reason he will be forced to take the fifth part himself . . . This evening after supper he sent for a harpsichord . . . so that he could play on it himself along with the guitar, of which he has a very high regard. But we could not find a harpsichord for which reason, so as not to pass an evening without music, he played the lute for an hour and a half.[2]

During his three years in Ferrara, Gesualdo published his first four books of madrigals. Books three and four in particular show the influence of the progressive musical style of Ferrara and of the singing of the *concerto delle donne*. Books five and six, not published until 1611 and 1613, demand even greater aural skills and vocal bravura. Typical of these pieces is the remarkable five-voice madrigal *Moro, lasso* (*I die, miserable*).

Let us first consider its text. As is customary with the madrigal, the poem is a single stanza with lines of seven or eleven syllables. It is also rather short and aphoristic; that is to say, it is packed with intense words and vivid images. Finally, it makes use of oxymoron—two words that mean the opposite. At the beginning of *Moro, lasso* death confronts life: the lover wishes to die because the beloved will not let him live. Gesualdo preferred short, vivid texts full of such antitheses. A brief text allowed him to work through each word very slowly and express it through music as intensely as possible. He gives each word or phrase its distinct meaning by switching textures (from slow chordal-declamatory passages to rapid imitative ones, for example), as well as by means of sudden strong dissonances, and, most important, bold chromatic shifts. These lightning-quick changes of musical style capture the opposite meanings contained in an oxymoron. The opening chords shock because of their chromatic relationship (chords built on C♯, C, and B come in immediate succession). They lend a feeling of uncertainty and strangeness to the music. *Moro, lasso* is intense, chromatic, passionate, often beautiful, and, like Gesualdo himself, sometimes bizarre.

EXAMPLE 28-3

I die, miserable in my despair, and the one who can give me life…

Moro, lasso, al mio duolo	I die, miserable in my despair
E chi mi può dar vita	And the one who can give me life
Ahi, che m'ancide e non vuol darmi aita!	Ouch, that one kills me and gives no aid!
O dolorosa sorte,	Oh, dolorous fate,
Chi dar vita mi può, ahi, mi dà morte.	The one who can give me life, alas, gives only death.

LISTENING CUE

CARLO GESUALDO
Moro, lasso (published 1613)

CD 3/25
Anthology, No. 77

Needless to say, the late madrigals of Gesualdo are not for the timid amateur singer. Rather, the rapid ascents, wide ranges, and difficult leaps suggest a repertory intended for highly skilled professional performers. The chromatic sections in particular challenge the fearless singer to find and cling to the right pitch in the midst of an unsettled sea of harmonic change. When performed without the support of instruments, the madrigals of Gesualdo can be among the most difficult works in the entire repertory of *a cappella* vocal music. Indeed, not before the advent of "atonal" music in the twentieth century do we find chromatic vocal lines as challenging as these. It is not surprising, then, that the modern Russian composer Igor Stravinsky became fascinated with Gesualdo's music, "recomposing" three of Gesualdo's madrigals to create his tribute *Monumentum pro Gesualdo di Venosa* (1960).

MUSIC IN MANTUA: ISABELLA D'ESTE

Like Ferrara, Mantua was a Renaissance city-state of between fifty and sixty thousand citizens ruled by an aristocratic, music-loving family, in this case the Gonzagas. A link between the two cities was forged in 1490 when **Isabella d'Este** (1474–1539; Fig. 28-1), daughter of the Duke of Ferrara, married Francesco Gonzaga, son of the Marquis of Mantua. Isabella moved to Mantua and took with her many of the musical traditions of the Ferrarese court. As a youth she had studied Latin and could recite passages from the poets of Roman antiquity—part of the humanistic curriculum of the Renaissance. Because her husband was a military general often far from home, Isabella frequently ran the affairs of state for Mantua and its subordinate lands. But when business was done, Isabella turned to the arts for recreation and spiritual solace. She was not, however, content merely to listen to the musicians, professional and amateur, of her court. She, too, joined in the music-making. Isabella had a fine soprano voice and made sure her voice teacher at Mantua was a soprano as well. (Because only males served as singing teachers at this time, she found a man who sang in the soprano range in falsetto voice.) Isabella also acquired a singing method book, which contained a program of study and exercises. By the 1490s she had learned to play the harpsichord, clavichord, *lira da braccio*, lute, viol, and *vihuela de mano* (Spanish guitar). All of these instruments she kept in a specially constructed music room at court.

Besides music, Isabella was a connoisseur of the visual arts. She collected ancient Greek and Roman sculpture and commissioned paintings from the most prominent artists of the day, including Andrea Mantegna, Titian, and Leonardo da Vinci (see

FIGURE 28-1

Isabella d'Este was a great patron of both musicians and artists. Here she is seen in a portrait commissioned from Leonardo da Vinci.

Tiroler Landesmuseum Ferdinandeum, Innsbruck

FIGURE 28-2
Portrait of Claudio Monteverdi by Bernardo Strozzi (1581–1644). Strozzi also painted the singer and composer Barbara Strozzi (see Chapter 31).

Fig. 28-1). Similarly, Isabella both wrote and collected poetry and commissioned composers, principally the frottolist Marchetto Cara (c1465–1525), to set this verse to music. Cara's frottola *Forsi che sì, forsi che no* (*Perhaps yes, perhaps no*), which sets the motto of the Gonzaga family, is a typical fruit of Isabella's patronage. Given Isabella's commitment to the arts, it is not surprising that Mantua became a principal center for musical composition during the sixteenth century.

✸ CLAUDIO MONTEVERDI

The cultivation of music continued at Mantua well into the seventeenth century, as can be seen in the career of Claudio Monteverdi (1567–1643; Fig. 28-2). Monteverdi arrived in Mantua in 1591 to be a string player in the ducal orchestra. By 1601 he had worked his way up the musical ladder to become *maestro della musica* at court. In this capacity, Monteverdi provided myriad musical services for the Gonzaga family. He composed, he played, he taught composition and singing, he conducted, and eventually he mounted operas and ballets. Although Monteverdi wrote an important Mass and Vespers service for the church, he was best known in his day as a composer of secular music, including nine books of madrigals and several important early operas. As the years went by, Monteverdi found his duties at Mantua excessively heavy and his pay exceedingly light. Consequently, in 1613 he moved on to Venice to become *maestro di cappella* of the basilica of St. Mark, where he extended his distinguished career into the 1640s.

As a composer of madrigals in Mantua, Monteverdi became embroiled in what is known as the **Artusi-Monteverdi controversy.** Giovanni Maria Artusi (c1540–1613) was a churchman and conservative music theorist. While visiting Ferrara in 1598 he heard several newly composed madrigals, among them *Cruda Amarilli* (*Cruel Amarillis*) by Monteverdi, and was horrified by the "errors" in counterpoint and harmony that he found. In 1600 Artusi published *Delle imperfettioni della moderna musica* (*On the Imperfections of Modern Music*) in which he goes almost measure by measure through Monteverdi's *Cruda Amarilli* pointing out its "mistakes." These "errors" have come about, according to Artusi, because composers such as Monteverdi have given free rein to the ear and not followed reason, that is, the traditional rules of harmony and counterpoint. Even so, he believes, such passages are offensive to the ear.

> They are harsh to the ear, and offend rather than delight it. They bring confusion and imperfection to the good rules of harmony left by those who have established the principles of the science of music. Instead of enriching, augmenting, and ennobling harmony by various means, as so many noble spirits have done, they have created a situation in which the beautiful and purified style is indistinguishable from the barbaric.[3]

Monteverdi responded to Artusi in the preface to his Fifth Book of Madrigals (1605; Fig. 28-3) and more fully (using his brother to speak for him) in the preface to his *Scherzi musicali* (1607). Here, the composer defends his progressive musical style in firm and forceful tones. In a famous phrase he declares that "harmony (music) must be the servant of the words" and not the other way around. He calls his new text-driven approach to musical composition the ***seconda pratica,*** and dis-

🌿 FIGURE 28-3

The preface to the fifth book of madrigals by Claudio Monteverdi, in which the composer defends his text-driven approach to the madrigal, referring to it, as can clearly be seen, in capital letters as *SECONDA PRATICA*. Notice also that he places *Cruda Amarilli* as the first madrigal in the collection, something of an "in your face" response to the music theorist Artusi.

tinguishes it from the older, more conservative *prima pratica*, in which composers often followed the rules of counterpoint regardless of the text (see Chapter 25). The emotional content of the text was of such importance that it justified, indeed required, violations of the standard rules for part-writing in the sixteenth century. But what rules did Monteverdi violate?

The gist of the Artusi-Monteverdi controversy concerns what are called unprepared dissonances—dissonant seconds, fourths, diminished fifths (tritones), and sevenths sounding against the lowest pitch without proper preparation. Taking the offending passages in *Cruda Amarilli* in turn, as did Artusi: in bar 13 the soprano jumps in with a second against the bass (Ex. 28-4a); in bar 19 the quinto (fifth part) rises to a seventh against the bass; in bar 21 the bass itself enters to form a diminished fifth against the tenor; in bar 36 the alto leaps down to create a seventh against the bass, and then the tenor and soprano do the same (Ex. 28-4b).

EXAMPLE 28-4A   EXAMPLE 28-4B

According to Artusi's strict interpretation, each of these spots violates conventional rules of harmony for preparing and resolving dissonance. Monteverdi, on the other hand, believes that each "violation" is justified by the text at that moment. The words "ouch" (m. 13), "bitterly" (mm. 19 and 21), "wasp" (mm. 36–38), and "fierce" (m. 41) require such dissonances—dissonances made all the more stinging, bitter, and fierce precisely because they are not prepared. Are these unprepared dissonances offensive to the ear, as Artusi believes, or do they intensify the meaning of the text, as Monteverdi contends? You be the judge.

LISTENING CUE

CLAUDIO MONTEVERDI
Cruda Amarilli (1598; published 1605)

CD 3/26
Anthology, No. 78

In truth, Monteverdi's unprepared "barbarities" may not be as shocking as Artusi alleges. Monteverdi saw himself, not as a radical innovator but as part of a long continuum of composers. In his reply to Artusi, Monteverdi applied the label *seconda pratica* to the madrigals of text-expressive composers extending back over the last fifty years. Modern historians, however, have seized upon the term as a way to focus attention on the debate between the old and new musical practices around 1600—to contrast the law-abiding music of Palestrina (*prima pratica*) against the illicit, text-driven music of Monteverdi (*seconda pratica*). Ultimately, Monteverdi's vision proved correct, for it is from the *seconda pratica* that the new music of the Baroque emerged.

 ## SUMMARY

Music in late sixteenth-century Italy was marked by an intensification of interest in the textually explicit madrigal. One of the hallmarks of the Renaissance, as opposed to the earlier Middle Ages, was the creation of text-reflective music that forged a close bond between text and tone. Renaissance composers developed a system of onomatopoeic gestures to express text through music. Explained in the simplest terms, the word "ouch" would require a dissonance, and "peace" a soothing major triad, for example. Composers made use of these gestures to varying degrees, and by the end of the century a separation of compositional styles had developed. On the one hand, a conservative contrapuntal idiom was evident, especially in religious music. Called the *prima pratica*, it included the Masses and motets of Ockeghem and Josquin, and eventually those of Palestrina as well. Proceeding with a carefully regulated control of harmony and counterpoint, the *prima pratica* too showed a concern for clear text declamation but did not engage in detailed text painting. At the same time, a second, more progressive musical style developed in northern Italian city-states such as Ferrara and Mantua. Typified by the madrigals of Gesualdo and Monteverdi, this *seconda pratica* delighted in extremes of textures, difficult vocal writing, bold chromatic progressions, and, occasionally, unprepared dissonance—all with the aim of supercharging an already vivid text. Ultimately, this progressive second practice proved to be the path to the future.

Finally, the private concerts of chamber music that emerged at the end of the sixteenth century in Ferrara, Mantua, Florence, and Rome reshaped the relationship between performers and audience. Since its beginnings in Florence and Rome, the sixteenth-century madrigal had been sung largely for the pleasure of the singers themselves—the singers and audience being one and the same. This was social music, in which amateurs eagerly sang music that was not too difficult to read. Toward the end of the century, however, the progressive madrigal became so vocally demanding that professional singers were needed. This resulted in a separation between highly skilled, solo performers and a non-participating, generally aristocratic audience, a division that set the stage for early Baroque opera.

KEY TERMS

concerto delle donne	Isabella d'Este	*seconda pratica*
musica secreta	Artusi-Monteverdi controversy	

BAROQUE MUSIC

$\mathscr{M}$usic historians use the term "baroque" to describe the music, musical theater, and dance during the years 1600–1750. The composition of most art music in the Baroque period was sponsored by aristocratic courts—or by wealthy princes of the church. While France, Germany, England, and Spain were developing distinctive musical languages at this time, Italy had become the arbiter of musical tastes and practices for much of Europe. Italian musicians began to occupy positions at northern courts, and naturally they brought with them the genres that they had created in Italy during the seventeenth century: opera, oratorio, cantata, sonata, sinfonia, and concerto.

| 1500 | 1550 | 1600 | 1650 |

RENAISSANCE (–1600)

BAROQUE (1600–1750)

Giovanni Gabrieli (c1554–1612), first composer fully to exploit sonic opportunities of St. Mark's

Galileo Galilei (1564–1642)

● 1570s Florentine camerata, group of prominent Florentines, gathers

Salomone Rossi (c1570–c1630), violinist

Girolamo Frescobaldi (1583–1643), foremost organist in Rome and most influential organ composer in Europe during the first half of the 17th century

René Descartes (1596–1650), French philosopher

Denis Gaultier (1597?–1672) dominates lute

● 1598 Jacopo Peri creates first true opera, *Dafne*

● Early 1600s Baroque music first appears;

● 1600 Jacopo Peri writes *Euridice*, first

● 1600 Artusi-Monteverdi controversy, war of

● 1602 Giulio Caccini composes *Le nuove*

Giacomo Carissimi (1605–1674), remembered

● 1607 Claudio Monteverdi composes

● 1613 Claudo Monteverdi becomes

Johann Froberger (1616–1667),

Thirty Years' War (1618–1648)

Barbara Strozzi (1619–1677),

● 1621 Heinrich Schütz

Pope Urban VIII (1623–1644)

Louis XIV with Plans for Versailles

CORBIS

Palace of Versailles

CORBIS

George Frideric Handel (1685–1759)

Staats-und Universitätsbibliothek Hamburg

Perhaps the single most important innovation for music during the Baroque era was the advent of opera, and of the dramatic style in general. The madrigal of the late Renaissance had sown the seeds of intense expression that would bear fruit in the form of seventeenth-century opera—and soon oratorio and cantata as well. By the end of the century, the system of dramatic expression that had been developed for dramatic vocal music was extended to instrumental music. Instruments, too, could sound out meaning without the benefit of text, and did so in new genres such as the sonata and the concerto. Thus, to chronicle the development of Baroque music is to see the growth, and ultimate dominance, of dramatic styles in sacred music as well as secular, and in instrumental music as well as vocal.

1650	1700	1750	1800

● 1653 Louis XIV appoints Giovanni Battista Lulli (1632–1687) *Compositeur de la musique instrumentale*

Johann Pachelbel (1653–1706), prolific composer writing hundreds of pieces, vocal and instrumental

● 1722 Rameau publishes *Treatise on Harmony*

to discuss literature, science, and arts

Arcangelo Corelli (1653–1717), violinist-composer of enormous influence in development of Baroque instrumental music

François Couperin (1668–1733), called "the Great," arguably the greatest of French Baroque instrumental composers

Georg Philipp Telemann (1681–1767), important composer and friend of Bach

1668 Dieterich Buxtehude (c1637–1707), greatest north German organ composer, becomes organist at church of St. Mary in Lübeck

playing in Parisian salons at mid-century

Frederick the Great of Prussia (1712–1786), musical enthusiast and skilled flautist

● 1669 Louis XIV establishes *Académie royale de musique* and starts to build Palace of Versailles

composers acknowledge new importance of bass and give it the name basso continuo

completely preserved opera

words over what was more important: music or text

musiche (*The New Music*) and writes opera *Euridice*

today for 14 surviving oratorios

early opera *Orfeo*

maestro di cappella at St. Mark's in Venice

German musician who establishes dance suite as primary genre of string keyboard music

1670 Heinrich Biber (1644–1704), violin virtuoso, enters employment at court of archbishop of Salzburg

daughter of Giulio Strozzi, publishes 8 volumes of vocal music

Johann Sebastian Bach (1685–1750)

The Collection of William H. Scheide, Princeton, NJ

appointed Kapellmeister at German court of Dresden

Antonio Vivaldi (1678–1741), violinist and composer important in development of concerto

Jean-Philippe Rameau (1683–1764), composer and theorist

Giuseppe Torelli (1658–1709), violinist, writes trumpet concertos for St. Petronio's basilica in Bologna

Chapter 29

Early Baroque Music

Music historians agree, with unusual unanimity, that Baroque music first appeared in the early seventeenth century in northern Italy, in cities such as Florence, Mantua, and Venice. Around 1600 the choral polyphony of the Renaissance gradually gave way to a new exuberant style of solo singing that musicians of the day called "the new music." Later, this new music was given a new name: Baroque.

Baroque is the term used generally to describe the art, architecture, and music of the period 1600–1750. It derives from the Portuguese word *barroco*, meaning a pearl of irregular shape then used in jewelry and fine decoration. Critics applied the term "Baroque" to indicate a rough, bold sound in music and excessive ornamentation in the visual arts. To the philosopher Jean-Jacques Rousseau (1712–1778), "A baroque music is that in which the harmony is confused, charged with modulations and dissonances, the melody is harsh and little natural, the intonation difficult, and the movement constrained." Thus originally the term "Baroque" had a pejorative meaning. It signified the extravagant, the excessive, even the bizarre. Only during the twentieth century, with a newfound appreciation of the painting of Peter Paul Rubens (1577–1640) and the music of Antonio Vivaldi (1678–1741) and J.S. Bach (1685–1750), among others, has the term "Baroque" come to assume a positive meaning in Western cultural history. Today we admire Baroque art for its drama, opulence, intense expression, and grandeur.

The period of Baroque art roughly corresponds with what political historians call the **Age of Absolutism.** The theory of absolutism held that a king enjoyed absolute power by reason of divine right. Rulers were said to govern with absolute authority so that citizens might live in a well-ordered society. The pope in Rome, the Holy Roman Emperor, the kings of France and Spain, and, to a lesser extent, the king of England were the most powerful absolute monarchs of the seventeenth century. Much Baroque art, architecture, and music came into being to reflect and extend their absolute power. In almost every way, the church and the aristocratic court remained the principal patrons of the arts, in Italy and elsewhere.

Most striking about many monuments of Baroque art, such as St. Peter's Square in Rome or the palace of Versailles outside of Paris, is their vast scale. The buildings and grounds are massive. St. Peter's Square, designed by Gian Lorenzo Bernini (1598–1680), is so enormous that it seems to swallow people, cars, and buses (Fig. 29-1). The palace of Versailles, built by French King Louis XIV (1638–1715), is not merely a building but was once an entire city under a single roof, designed to be home to several thousand court functionaries (see Part IV timeline).

The music composed for such vast expanses could also be grandiose. No longer was every part played by a single instrument, as had been the case generally during the Renaissance. By the end of the seventeenth century many parts were doubled so as to increase the volume of sound. The orchestra playing for the opera

🌿 FIGURE 29-1
St. Peter's Square, Rome, designed by Bernini in the mid seventeenth century. St. Peter's Basilica, the largest church in the world, is in the center; the smaller Sistine Chapel is to the right.

Archiv fur Kunst Und Geschichte, Berlin

and ballet at the court of King Louis XIV at Versailles sometimes numbered more than eighty instrumentalists, although such an ensemble was exceptional. In Rome and elsewhere composers wrote choral works for twenty-four, forty-eight, and even fifty-three separate vocal parts. These vocal works were generally intended for the great Baroque churches in Italy and Austria, and this style of music for multiple choruses with instrumental accompaniment has come to be called the grand, or colossal, Baroque.

Yet the art and architecture of the Baroque era is marked by strong contrasts. Buildings of enormous scale, for example, are usually adorned by much ornamental detail. Artists filled the long lines and vast spaces of the palaces and churches with abundant decoration. Monumental space created a vacuum, and into this rushed the artist with intense, dramatic energy. In creating his *Throne of St. Peter* for the interior of that basilica in Rome, the sculptor Gian Lorenzo Bernini filled the expanse with twisting forms that energize the otherwise static architecture (Fig. 29-2). Similarly, a Roman ceiling painting entitled *Glorification of Pope Urban VIII* by Pietro da Cortona (1596–1669) epitomizes the size and exuberance of the Baroque art (Fig. 29-3). The architectural space is filled with figures that writhe and clouds that swirl. The painting is monumental yet packed with countless energetic details.

This same approach to artistic expression is found in the music of the Baroque era. Composers too created large-scale compositions and filled them with energetic figures. In both vocal and instrumental music, strong chordal blocks support highly ornamental melodic lines. The florid melodies add energy and

✿ FIGURE 29-2

Bernini's *The Throne of St. Peter* within St. Peter's basilica. This is not the high altar of St. Peter's, merely a rear chapel, which suggests the enormous size of the basilica. Bernini responded to the architectural scale by filling the chapel with exuberant decoration.

✿ FIGURE 29-3

Pietro da Cortona, *Glorification of Pope Urban VIII*. This ceiling fresco, executed in Rome in 1633–1639 for the family of the pope, is both energetic and monumental.

excitement to what would otherwise be a purely static harmonic background. Notice in the following excerpt from Giulio Caccini's aria *Ardi, cor mio* (*Burn, O my heart*) of 1602 how the energetic vocal line is supported by a solid bedrock of simple chords (Ex. 29-1).

EXAMPLE 29-1

CHARACTERISTICS OF EARLY BAROQUE MUSIC

Toward the end of the sixteenth century the madrigal was the most progressive genre of music in Europe. The more forward-looking of the madrigal composers—Gesualdo and Monteverdi among them—wrote experimental works that broke many of the established rules of counterpoint. They valued the text and its meaning above purely musical procedures. In 1600 Monteverdi was attacked in print by a conservative music theorist named Giovanni Maria Artusi and he responded in kind, thereby creating what has come to be called the **Artusi-Monteverdi controversy** (see also Chapter 28)—a war of words over what was more important, music or text. Monteverdi called his new text-driven approach the *seconda pratica* (second practice). This he distinguished from the more traditional *prima pratica*, the conservative, mainly church style that dutifully followed the traditional rules of linear counterpoint. Later, musicians would refer to the conservative church style as the *stile antico* (old or traditional style) and the newer *seconda pratica* as the *stile moderno* (modern style). Composers continued to write in both *antico* and *moderno* styles throughout the seventeenth century.

Monteverdi and his progressive colleagues believed that music had the power to move the soul, as had ancient Greek music. Their faith that the language of music could express many and varied emotions led to an aesthetic theory called the Doctrine of Affections. The **Doctrine of Affections** held that different musical moods could and should be used to influence the emotions, or affections, of the listeners. A musical setting should reinforce the intended "affection" of the text. As early as 1602 the composer Giulio Caccini, in his *Le nuove musiche* (*The New Music*), referred to "moving the affections of the soul." Later music theorists would advocate a unity of affections, holding that each piece of music should project only a single affection, be it anger, hate, sorrow, joy, or love (see Chapter 34). Indeed, Baroque music generally does not change quickly from one mood to another, as might a polyphonic madrigal in the Renaissance or a symphony from the later Classical period. The Baroque artist—whether painter, sculptor, or musician—created emotional units that were clearly defined, distinctly separate, and long-lasting.

Vocal Expression and Virtuosity

During the Renaissance, vocal music was mostly ensemble music—works for groups of vocalists, even if there were only one singer on a part. In the early Baroque, however, emphasis shifted from vocal ensemble to accompanied solo song. Vocal groups might be a useful way to convey the abstract religious thoughts of the multitudes but, to communicate raw human emotions, direct appeal by an individual soloist was now thought more effective. Solo madrigals, solo arias, and solo recitatives were all designated by a single word: **monody** (from Greek terms meaning "to sing alone"). The vogue of monody was simply a continuation of the attempts of poets, scholars, and musicians to emulate the music of ancient Greece by making the words intelligible and enhancing their effect. In Chapter 30 we shall discuss several types of monody (see Anthology, Nos.79–81). For the moment it is enough to say that emphasis on the solo voice quickly led to a more flamboyant style of singing (see Ex. 29-1). Soon the vocal virtuoso would emerge, the star of the court theater and the operatic stage.

Harmonic Conception and the Basso Continuo

During the Renaissance the prevailing texture for music, vocal as well as instrumental, involved imitative counterpoint. In a Renaissance Mass, motet, or madrigal, for example, several equal parts spin out a web of polyphony, one line imitating another in turn. Early Baroque music has a fundamentally different orientation. Instead of having three, four, or five contrapuntal lines, composers now emphasized just the top and bottom parts, using the other voices to add chordal enrichment in the middle. If much of Renaissance music was created polyphonically and horizontally, working line by line, that of the early Baroque period is more homophonically conceived, its chords springing up vertically from the bass.

🌿 FIGURE 29-4

A Lady with Theorbo (c1670) by John Michael Wright. The bass strings are at the top of the instrument and off the fingerboard. Each bass string plays just one note of a low, diatonic scale. The theorbo was often used to play the basso continuo in the seventeenth century.

In the early 1600s, composers acknowledged the new importance of the bass, and they gave it a new name: **basso continuo** in Italian (commonly called "thorough bass" in England). The basso continuo was a bass line that provided a never-ending foundation, or "continuous bass," for the melody above. Early in the Baroque, the basso continuo might be played by a single solo instrument such as the lute or the **theorbo**—a large lute-like instrument with a full octave of additional bass strings descending in a diatonic pattern such as F-E-D-C-B'-A' (Fig. 29-4). Gradually, a low melody instrument such as the *viola da gamba*, cello, or bassoon came to reinforce the bass line. Thus the basso continuo often consisted of an ensemble of two instruments; while one performer played the written bass line, another played a harmony above the bass on a chord-producing instrument—organ, harpsichord, lute, theorbo, or even guitar, for example. (For a clear example of the sound of the basso continuo, turn to the Anthology, No. 85.) The chord-playing instrument linked the melody on top to the bass below by improvising on the spot in a flexible, expressive way. But how did the player know what chords to improvise?

The harmonies of the basso continuo were usually indicated by a notation called **figured bass**—a numerical shorthand placed with the bass line that tells the player which unwritten notes to fill in above the written bass note. Figured bass is similar in intent to the numerical code found in "fake books" used by modern jazz pianists that indicate which chords to play beneath the written melody. Today, music theory courses in conservatories and universities around the world still teach, and test, the capacity to realize (play chords above) a figured bass at sight (Ex. 29-2).

EXAMPLE 29-2

A musician who has mastered the ability to realize a figured bass has a solid understanding of chordal harmony. Indeed, in the early Baroque, chordal harmony was becoming increasingly important. More and more, composers were conceiving music as a series of chordal units, or chord progressions. In addition, they came to write these chord progressions within just the major and minor keys.

Major and Minor Tonalities

In the course of the seventeenth century, two scale patterns, major (the Ionian mode) and minor (the Aeolian mode), came to be employed to the virtual exclusion of all of the other church modes of the Renaissance and before. The old Dorian and Phrygian modes, for example, became less and less important. (For more on the increasing importance of major and minor tonalities, see Musical Interlude 5 following Chapter 36.) Of course, privileging just the major and minor modes meant that melodies were written mostly in just these two scales. But it affected harmony as well. Modal polyphony of the Renaissance had emphasized triads that were often only a second or a third apart; the new tonal polyphony of the Baroque, on the other hand, tended increasingly to construct chords upon notes of the scale that were a fourth or a fifth apart. Viewed from the perspective of harmony alone, the seventeenth century can be seen as a period in which modal harmony gradually gave way to tonal harmony. The difference between the two approaches can be seen by comparing two progressions centering on the home pitch E (Exs. 29-3a, 29-3b), the first by Renaissance composer Thomas Tallis and the second by Baroque composer Arcangelo Corelli.

EXAMPLE 29-3A   EXAMPLE 29-3B

Modal harmony (Tallis, 1567)   Tonal harmony (Corelli, c1690)

As harmonies were reduced to just the major and minor modes, the listener could more easily focus on the distinct properties of each. Composers could play the dark minor mode off against the bright major, or vice versa, to create the emotional effects and shadings of color so important in Baroque music in particular and Baroque art generally.

Instrumental Color and Musical Dynamics

The Baroque era is a crossroads in the progressive development of musical instruments. Some instruments of the Renaissance, such as the lute, theorbo, cornett, recorder, and *viola da gamba*, were peaking in popularity and would disappear with the Baroque era. Others, particularly the members of the violin family, including the violoncello (or cello), were relatively new and would grow in popularity during the Baroque period. In the early 1600s, however, all of these instruments were available and were called for by composers at various times. A variegated ensemble in which a theorbo, *viola da gamba*, cornett, sackbut, violin, recorder, transverse flute, bassoon, cello, and harpsichord played together was not uncommon. The early Baroque orchestra was not yet dominated by members of the violin family; instead it was remarkable for its diverse, colorful sounds.

Similarly, diversity of sound came to include the volume of sound. Certainly there were louds and softs in the music of the Middle Ages and Renaissance. Yet not until around 1600 did composers specify levels of volume in their music. At first they did so in a very simple way: they merely wrote *piano* or *forte* in the score. Generally, in Baroque instrumental music, dynamics do not change gradually within a section of a piece. Rather, a single dynamic range, whether loud or soft, holds fast until abruptly replaced by another. Setting loud against soft, winds against strings, soloist against chorus, major against minor—all these helped create the brilliant colors and strong contrasts that mark Baroque music.

Idiomatic Writing for Instruments and Voice

Finally, Baroque music welcomes for the first time truly idiomatic writing for both instruments and voice. In the Renaissance, melody was more or less all of one type. It was a direct, uncomplicated line that could be performed by either a voice or an instrument. Indeed, Renaissance publishers exploited the generic quality of melody, eagerly advertising their newest print as "suitable for both voices and instruments." Beginning about 1600, however, instrumental style began to diverge from vocal. Composers recognized that the violin, for example, can play a scale faster than the human voice can sing one. Thus they began to write idiomatic (well suited) music for particular instruments—rapid scales for the violin or repeating notes of a triad for brass instruments, for example. Vocal music, too, began to go its own way. Composers wrote vocal lines with starkly different levels of rhythmic activity and with trills and other ornaments that highlighted the acrobatic ability of the voice. Nowhere could this distinctly idiomatic vocal style be more clearly heard than in the newly emerging opera.

    SUMMARY

In Western cultural history the term "Baroque" identifies an artistic style that flourished during the years 1600–1750. Baroque art, architecture, and music are characterized by vivid colors, strong contrasts, and grand designs. Around 1600 the choral polyphony that had dominated the Renaissance gave way to an exuberant style of solo singing. If Renaissance music was mostly conceived contrapuntally and horizontally, line by line, that of the early Baroque period is organized more homophonically and vertically, chord by chord. Attention came to be focused almost entirely on an expressive melody supported by a strong bass. Tonality increasingly came to be limited to just the major and minor modes. Throughout the Baroque era, idiomatic writing created two distinctly different styles, one for instruments and another for voices.

KEY TERMS

Baroque	*seconda pratica*	theorbo
Age of Absolutism	Doctrine of Affections	figured bass
Artusi-Monteverdi controversy	monody	
	basso continuo	

Chapter

30

The Birth of Opera: Florence, Mantua, and Venice

Today opera is an enormously popular medium. While symphony orchestras struggle to stay in business, opera companies flourish, and demand for the best singers pushes ticket prices to the roof. Yet, oddly, opera emerged rather late in the history of Western art music, around 1600. By way of comparison, both China and Japan had had a flourishing tradition of opera since at least 1300. True, something approaching sung drama had existed in the West in the liturgical drama of the medieval church. But liturgical drama flowered only briefly around 1200 and then died, leaving no successor. The opera that we listen to today, and for which there are passionate devotees around the world, emerged in northern Italy about the year 1600.

Opera literally means "work." Musically speaking, the term was first employed in the Italian phrase *opera drammatica in musica* (a dramatic work, or play, set to music). In opera the lines of the actors and actresses are not merely spoken, but sung. At first this sounds like a very odd thing to do; human beings do not sing out their day-to-day conversations ("Please pass the peas as soon as possible," for example). But the fundamental premise of opera is that sung music can heighten the emotional intensity of a dramatic text. The text that conveys the story of the opera is called the **libretto,** and it is written in poetic verse. By combining music, poetry, drama, scenic design, and dance, opera can be the most powerful of all forms of art. Some consider it the supreme expression of the human spirit.

❀ EARLY OPERA IN FLORENCE

Opera in the West first appeared at the court of the Medici princes in Florence, Italy, at the turn of the seventeenth century. In quick succession came *Dafne* (1598) by Jacopo Peri, *Euridice* (1600) again by Peri, and *Euridice* (1602) by Giulio Caccini. All three early operas set a libretto by the Florentine court poet Ottavio Rinuccini (1562–1621). The stories of Dafne and Apollo and of Euridice and Orpheus are based on ancient Greek myths. In fact, most early operas set a libretto drawn from mythology because the creators of opera were trying to recapture the spirit of ancient drama while carrying the listener to a magical world far from reality. The first operas of Peri and Caccini did not emerge out of thin air, however. Rather, they were the result of nearly twenty-five years of discussion and experimentation about the nature of ancient Greek music.

As early as the 1570s, a group of prominent Florentines had gathered in the home of Count Giovanni Bardi (1534–1612) to discuss the literature, science, and arts of the day. Later, one of Bardi's protégés dubbed this society the **Florentine camerata** ("club" or "circle"). Bardi was a soldier by profession, but an antiquarian by passion. Fellow camerata members included the translator and textual scholar Girolamo Mei (1519–1594) and the musician-scientist Vincenzo Galilei (c1528–1591). Galilei is important to history and music on several counts: he was the father of the famous astronomer Galileo Galilei (1564–1642); he was one of the earliest to advocate equal temperament as the most practical way of dealing with tuning in music; and he was one of the first to argue for a new style of solo singing, as stated in his *Dialogo della musica antica, et della moderna* (*Dialogue on Ancient and Modern Music*, 1581). Bardi, Mei, Galilei, and their colleagues shared a common purpose, to create a modern music that approximated the vocal declamation of ancient Greek tragedy. Though they lacked the actual music from ancient Greece, they knew that Greek drama had been sung, or at least declaimed in a musical manner. What the camerata advocated was a new type of vocal delivery called *stile rappresentativo*. **Stile rappresentativo** (dramatic style or theater style) was vocal expression somewhere between song and declaimed speech. The singer emphatically declaimed the text so that the pitches and rhythms of the voice matched exactly the rhythms, accents, and sentiments of the text. What began as an antiquarian study of Greek musical practices became a model for contemporary composition.

In 1589 the leaders of the camerata presented their new experimental style of singing to an aristocratic audience drawn to Florence for the wedding of the grand duke of Tuscany, Ferdinando de' Medici. The principal wedding entertainment was a play. Between each of the acts of the play, however, Bardi and his associates inserted a sung diversion, called an intermedio, a sung play within a play. Figure 30-1 shows Jacopo Peri (1561–1633) portraying the role of the mythological singer Arion in the fifth intermedio of 1589. Typical of such late Renaissance court entertainments, each intermedio was fully sung, yet each was an isolated dramatic scene; they did not form a unified sung drama.

Nine years later Jacopo Peri created the first true opera, *Dafne* (1598), a unified multi-scene drama entirely sung. Unfortunately, only fragments of *Dafne* have survived. The first completely preserved opera dates from two years later: Peri's setting of the story of Orpheus and Euridice, simply called *Euridice* (1600). The story of Orpheus and Euridice is important in the history of opera because numerous composers would set it to dramatic music over the next three centuries.

The **Orpheus legend** tells the tale of Orpheus (Orfeo in Italian), the son of Apollo, the Greek god of the sun and of music. (As mentioned, our word "music" comes from the muses who attend Apollo.) Orpheus, himself a demi-god, falls in love with the beautiful human Euridice. No sooner are they married than she is fatally bitten by a snake and carried off to Hades (the realm of the dead). Orpheus vows to descend into the Underworld and restore his beloved to earthly life. This he nearly accomplishes by exploiting his divine powers of musical persuasion, for Orpheus can make the trees sway, calm savage beasts, and even overcome the furies of Hades with the beauty of his expressive song.

FIGURE 30-1

Composer-singer Jacopo Peri portraying the mythological poet-singer Arion in Florence in 1589.

In his preface to the published score of *Euridice*, Jacopo Peri explained his approach to setting a text "in the manner of the ancient Greeks and Romans":

> I recognized that in our [Italian] language certain words are uttered in such a way that they allow a harmony to be built on them, and that in the course of speech, one passes through many other words that are not stressed, until one eventually returns to another word capable of sustaining a new consonant harmony. Having in mind those affects and stresses that we use to create lamenting, rejoicing, and similar emotions, I set the bass moving at the same pace as human speech, now faster, now slower, according to the affections, and held it firm through dissonances and consonances until, running through the various notes, the voice of the singer arrived at a syllable stressed in ordinary speech that then allows a new harmony.[1]

Exactly the sort of music Peri describes can be heard at the climax of *Euridice*, when Orfeo, having descended into Hades to rescue Euridice, confronts the horrors of that region. In a vocal solo entitled "Funeste piagge" ("Deadly shores") the composer drives rapidly through lines of text, often with quickly repeating pitches. At strategic moments, however, usually at the ends of lines where rhyming words appear, he underscores the text through long notes. The bass moves more rapidly or slowly as the text requires. Along the way dissonance is treated freely—not prepared or resolved according to the traditional rules of counterpoint. The excerpt from "Funeste piagge" in Example 30-1 exemplifies both monody (the term used generally to describe accompanied solo song at the turn of the seventeenth century) as well as the more specific *stile rappresentativo* (the dramatic or theatrical style). The chords above the basso continuo have been realized by a modern editor following the indications of Peri's figured bass.

EXAMPLE 30-1

While with sad accents I lament with you my lost love; and you, oh, pitying my anguish...

LISTENING CUE

JACOPO PERI
Euridice (1600)
"Funeste piagge"

CD 4/1
Anthology, No. 79

Jacopo Peri had a rival on the operatic stage in Florence: the composer, singer, and singing teacher Giulio Caccini (1551–1618). No sooner had Peri performed his *Euridice* (October 1600) than Caccini rushed into print with his own setting of the same libretto (January 1601). Caccini was intent on making sure his *Euridice* was seen to be as timely and as novel as Peri's. In the preface to his *Euridice*, Caccini was quick to point out that he too had set to music the fable of *Euridice* in the *stile rappresentivo* and he too had supported the recited parts with a basso continuo. He also announced that he would soon explain a new method for singing ornaments that he had invented.

The next year, Caccini made good on his promise by publishing **Le nuove musiche** (*The New Music*, 1602). Ironically, not all of *Le nuove musiche* was new music. It is, in fact, an anthology of solo madrigals and strophic solo songs gathered over time. Several of the madrigals, Caccini claims in his preface, had been greeted with "warm applause" when heard by the Florentine camerata as early as 1590. What is truly new about *Le nuove musiche* is Caccini's description of the vocal techniques that grace his monodies. Caccini was the first to describe early Baroque vocal ornaments and the first composer to write them directly in the score. The preface to *Le nuove musiche*, therefore, provides invaluable information on performance practices for modern performers seeking to re-create the true spirit of early Baroque vocal music. His instructions apply equally well to chamber singing and to early Baroque opera, because at that time both used the same techniques of singing.

Caccini has much to say about vocal execution, and his comments guide those singers who re-create Baroque opera today: Singers should inflect longer notes by means of slight crescendos and diminuendos, moments that he calls exclamations (*esclamazioni*); at that time musicians had no symbols to indicate crescendo and diminuendo. (Yet Caccini urges caution with the crescendo because the pitch may go sharp as the voice gets louder.) Singers are encouraged to fill in larger melodic intervals with running scales (*passaggi*). Singers may also vary the written rhythms to add lightness to the music. Most important, singers are urged to insert idiomatic vocal ornaments at cadences for emphasis, but to do so in moderation. To explain the principal two cadential ornaments, Caccini includes the following example (Ex. 30-2). His *trillo* is a repeating percussive effect placed on a single pitch, whereas his *gruppo* is the counterpart of our modern neighbor-note trill.

EXAMPLE 30-2

The monodies that follow the preface of *Le nuove musiche* exemplify Caccini's thoughts on vocal execution. The madrigal *Filli, mirando il cielo* (*Phyllis, admiring the heavens*), for example, is filled with well-placed vowels that offer opportunity for brief crescendos and diminuendos, and it ends with an elaborate *trillo* and *gruppo*. Indeed, the last line "What torment I shall have when my face turns sallow and my hair silver" is set three times with increasingly elaborate ornamentation. The principles of ornamentation set forth here apply not only to solo madrigals such as this but to all Florentine monodies including, as mentioned, those of early opera.

LISTENING CUE

GIULIO CACCINI   CD 4/2
Le nuove musiche (1602)   Anthology, No. 80
Filli, mirando il cielo

 EARLY OPERA IN MANTUA: MONTEVERDI'S *ORFEO*

"There is no lover of music who does not keep Orfeo's songs before him at all times."[2] This contemporary remark attests to the popularity of the newborn opera generally and to the legend of Orpheus in particular. Soon another important composer, Claudio Monteverdi, took up the legend of Orpheus and Euridice. Monteverdi, as we have seen (see Chapter 28), was a composer who wrote madrigals in the manner of the *seconda pratica,* the progressive style that flourished around 1600. During the early 1600s, Monteverdi was director of music at the northern Italian court of Mantua. He apparently got the idea of writing an opera on the Orpheus legend when he heard Peri's *Euridice* in Florence in the fall of 1600. By 1607 Monteverdi was ready to stage his own version of the tale, one built on a new libretto by Alessandro Striggio (1573–1630). Monteverdi's *Orfeo* is Mantua's answer to Florentine operas based on the same subject.

Monteverdi intended his Mantuan *Orfeo* to be a chamber opera heard by a small and elite audience. At the first performance on 24 February 1607 about two hundred aristocrats crowded into a standing-room-only chamber measuring just 30 × 40 feet. (The room, on the ground floor of the ducal palace in Mantua, survives today, but serves as a gift shop!) Monteverdi divides his *Orfeo* into five short acts that together last no more than ninety minutes.

Orfeo opens with a brief fanfare entitled "toccata." A **toccata** (literally a "touched thing") is an instrumental piece, for keyboard or other instruments, requiring the performer to touch the instrument with great technical dexterity. In other words, it is an instrumental showpiece. Here the full orchestra puts on the show. Monteverdi requires a remarkable variety of instruments that feature many distinctly different sounds, as is typical of early Baroque ensembles: strings including violins and viols, recorders, trumpets, trombones, cornetts, harpsichord, theorbo, harp, organ, and reed organ. At no time, however, do all the instruments sound together. In the opening toccata, for example, the trumpets lead the way, racing up and down the scale in brilliant fashion. In his printed score Monteverdi instructs that the toccata be sounded three times: presumably first to get the attention of the audience, then to announce the arrival of the patron, the duke of Mantua, and finally to signal that the action is about to begin.

LISTENING CUE

CLAUDIO MONTEVERDI   CD 4/3
Orfeo (1607)   Anthology, No. 81a
Toccata

Compared to earlier settings of the Orpheus legend, Monteverdi's *Orfeo* is a richer, more opulent score. The luxuriant sound is created partly by the large number and variety of instruments, and partly by the diverse kinds of music Monteverdi creates; his opera has a mix of choral songs, choral dances, instrumental dances, instrumental interludes, and, most important, solo singing of various kinds. The accompanied solo singing, the monody, is stylistically the most progressive music, and he saves it for the dramatic high points of the opera.

The first such moment of high drama comes midway through Act II, when Orfeo learns that his new bride Euridice has been killed by a snake and carried off to the Underworld. Two shepherds relate how the hero took the news. They do so in a style of monody that will soon be called *stile recitativo* ("recited style"). **Recitative** is musically heightened speech. When it is accompanied only by basso continuo, it is usually called **simple recitative** (*recitativo semplice* in Italian). Recitative in opera usually tells the audience what has happened. Because recitative attempts to mirror the natural stresses of oral delivery, it is often made up of rapidly repeating notes followed by one or two longer notes at the end of phrases, after which the reciter might pause to catch a breath. Thus the Second Shepherd relates the bitter news (Ex. 30-3).

EXAMPLE 30-3

At the bitter news the unfortunate one was turned to stone…

Orfeo now reacts to this thunderbolt. He tells us how he feels by using a more flexible, expressive style of monody that will soon be called "arioso." **Arioso style** is a manner of singing halfway between a recitative and a full-blown aria. It involves fewer repeating pitches and is more rhythmically elastic than a purely declamatory recitative, but is not as song-like and expansive as an aria. In Orfeo's arioso-style "Tu se' morta, mia vita" ("You are dead, my life"), Monteverdi uses expressive vocal intervals, changing rhythms of speech, and bitter harmonies to intensify the hero's grief (Ex. 30-4).

EXAMPLE 30-4

You are dead, my life, and I breathe,…

At the peak of his misery and rage, Orfeo vows to go where no human has ever tread: he will descend into Hades and rescue his bride. Here he confronts Caronte (Charon), the guardian of the Underworld. Now Orfeo must use all of his vocal skills to pacify the frightful guard (Fig. 30-2). His song, the central number in the opera, is the aria "Possente spirto" ("Powerful spirit"). An **aria,** Italian for "song" or "ayre," is more florid, more expansive, and more melodious than a recitative or arioso. It tends to have less rapid-fire delivery and more melismas (one vowel luxuriously spread out over many notes), as can be seen in Example 30-5. Occasionally, an aria is set for two or three singers, in which case the terms "duet" or "trio" are appropriate. Finally, an aria invariably sets a short poem made up of several stanzas. In fact, a closed strophic poem created by the librettist became a cue to the composer to create a lyrical aria. The text of "Possente spirto" has three strophes each with three eleven-syllable lines rhyming **aba.** Here is the first of these stanzas.

Possente spirto e formidabil nume,	**a**	Powerful spirit and formidable god
Senza cui far passaggio à l'altra riva	**b**	without whom no bodiless soul,
Alma da corpo sciolta in van presume.	**a**	onto the shore of Hades has trod.

EXAMPLE 30-5

The following two stanzas make use of the same melody and bass, somewhat varied each time. What results is a **strophic variation aria,** an aria in which the same melodic and harmonic plan appears, with slight variation, in each successive strophe. Composers of the early seventeenth century seized upon strophic variation form as a way of giving variety to the otherwise utterly repetitive strophic form.

Finally, an aria in a Baroque opera, unlike a recitative, is often accompanied by more than just the basso continuo, and, the later we go in the seventeenth century, the more this is true. Early in the Baroque, however, treble instruments accompanying the aria melody were rather rare, and Monteverdi was one of the first to experiment with this procedure. In his "Possente spirto" Orfeo's appeal to Caronte is accompanied at various times by organ, theorbo, violins, cornetts, and harps. With its expansive solo singing and rich accompaniment, the aria provides the musical high points of this and almost every opera.

Monteverdi's aria "Possente spirto" with the vocal part in both an ornamented and an unornamented version. Why two versions? Perhaps Monteverdi needed to show the less experienced singer how to ornament this melody, leaving it to the more advanced singer to add ornaments to the simple, unadorned version at will. Notice that the printer is still making use of single-impression printing, a technique developed in Paris nearly a hundred years earlier (see Chapter 22). This accounts for the "wavy" lines on the staves.

LISTENING CUE

CLAUDIO MONTEVERDI
Orfeo (1607)
Recitative, "A l'amara novella"
Arioso, "Tu se' morta, mia vita"
Aria, "Possente spirto"

CD 4/4–6
Anthology,
No. 81b-d

In truth, the terms just used to describe the expressive monody heard in Monteverdi's *Orfeo* were not coined in connection with this opera. The word "aria" was frequently employed to describe solo songs in strophic form in the late Renaissance, whereas the terms "recitative" and "arioso" did not become commonplace until the 1630s. Nevertheless, Monteverdi's use of different styles of monody is an important innovation. *Orfeo* is the first opera to differentiate styles of singing clearly so as to underscore different sorts of dramatic events. He shows that declamatory recitative can be used to deliver impersonal narration, whereas the more expansive aria is best saved for intense personal expression and rhetorical persuasion. As we shall see, the stylistic distinction between recitative and aria, and their different dramatic functions, will become even more pronounced in later Baroque opera.

EARLY OPERA IN VENICE

In 1613 Claudio Monteverdi quit his job as director of music in Mantua and moved to Venice. He had composed two path-breaking operas for the Mantuan court, *Orfeo* (1607) and *Arianna* (1608), but had received neither appreciation nor remuneration. "I have never in my life suffered greater humiliation of the spirit than when I had to go and beg the treasurer for what was mine," he said. Disgusted with Mantua, Monteverdi accepted the much coveted position of *maestro di cappella* (director of music) at St. Mark's Basilica in Venice (see Fig. 31-1), the most prestigious musical post in Italy. Naturally, his new job at this famous church required that he compose much religious music, and this he did for the next thirty years. In 1640, however, Monteverdi returned to the operatic stage, lured there by the sudden appearance of, not one but two, new opera houses in Venice.

When the citizens of Venice first embraced opera in 1637, they did so very differently than elsewhere in Italy. In Florence, Mantua, and Rome, opera was sponsored by aristocratic courts as a way to enhance the prestige of the prince. In Venice, on the other hand, opera became the enterprise of wealthy merchant families who saw it as a way to make money. To be commercially successful, however, an opera had to play night after night in a large theater. Thus the patrician families of Venice created theaters especially for opera. The audience was not a select group of two hundred aristocratic guests, but a fee-paying crowd of as many as 1,500 drawn from a cross section of society: merchants, soldiers, clerics, students, and the like. Soon several opera houses were competing head-to-head, much like Broadway theaters today. Between 1637 and 1678 Venetian audiences saw more than one hundred fifty operas in nine different theaters. To make the business of opera efficient (and to abide by the religious customs of the city), opera in Venice was confined to the carnival season (roughly from after Christmas to the beginning of Lent), when the population of Venice swelled to nearly 150,000. The leveling of social classes, in the streets and in the opera house, was facilitated by the fact that during carnival everyone wore masks. Opera was no longer the private preserve of an elite group. It had become a public spectacle.

The very public nature of opera in Venice soon led to changes. Star singers became more important as opera lovers became enamored with the special qualities of one or another of the leading voices of the day. Competition between opera houses in Venice inflated the salary of the singers, who soon were earning twice as much as the best composers. More and more, composer and librettist were forced to tailor the music to suit a leading singer's vocal range, capacity for ornamentation, and dramatic skills. In addition, stage machinery and elaborate sets created an air of the spectacular (Fig. 30-3). Angels flew across the sky and naval vessels did battle on the high seas of the stage. With its emphasis on glitzy sets and lavish costumes, Venetian opera had all the trappings of a modern-day mega musical.

By 1640 Claudio Monteverdi had reached the age of seventy-two and become the grand old man of Venetian music. Yet, that year, having apparently finished no new operas in more than three decades, he returned to the stage, first with *Il ritorno* d'Ulisse in patria (*The Return of Ulysses*), followed by *Le nozze d'Enea* (*The Marriage of Aeneas*, 1641) and *L'incoronazione di Poppea* (*The Coronation of Poppea*, 1642). *Poppea*, as this last opera is known, would be the final composition of Monteverdi's long and distinguished career.

Many believe *Poppea* to be the greatest opera of the seventeenth century. Certainly, it is a very different sort of opera from those that preceded it. The subject matter is not drawn from Greek mythology but Roman history. It celebrates, not the virtues of the ruling class, but their vices. The somewhat sensational plot goes as follows: The Roman emperor Nero lusts for the beautiful Poppea, a lady of the court; to achieve his desires, he sentences to death his wise but prudish counselor Seneca, banishes his own wife Ottavia, and places the ambitious Poppea triumphantly on the throne of all Rome.

⚜ FIGURE 30-3

Ships sail on the high seas as gods descend from the heavens in Giacomo Torelli's stage set for the opera *Bellerofonte* (Venice, 1642).

In many ways, the realistic dramaturgy of Monteverdi's opera resembles that of his older contemporary, William Shakespeare. Sovereigns share the stage with servants; high tragedy alternates with low comedy; and wise advice goes unheeded by passionate young lovers. But unlike the works of Shakespeare, where ill deeds are condemned if not punished, here vice triumphs over virtue. Poppea is crowned empress and revels in her triumph in a final love duet with Nero. In this duet "Pur ti miro" ("I adore you") the guilty lovers are left on stage to sing a seemingly endless chain of voluptuous dissonance-to-consonance progressions. This ravishing conclusion encapsulates the passionate, sensuous nature of their love and the entire opera as well. Above all, it demonstrates just how far opera had progressed since Monteverdi left Mantua. The orchestral writing is luxuriant and the musical numbers are distinctively different so as to highlight the special qualities of the principal characters. Most important, a clear stylistic distinction exists between recitative and aria—the one syllabic and declamatory, the other florid, even rhapsodic.

LISTENING CUE

CLAUDIO MONTEVERDI? (see Box)
L'incoronazione di Poppea (1642)
Duet, "Pur ti miro"

CD 4/7
Anthology, No. 82

Venetian opera did not end with the death of Claudio Monteverdi in 1643 but lived on in the hands of his pupil Francesco Cavalli (1602–1676) and follower Antonio Cesti (1623–1669). Cavalli composed thirty-three operas, the best known of which was the often-performed *Giasone* (1649), which deals the myth of Jason and the Argonauts. Of the twelve or so operas attributed to Cesti, certainly the most

Did Monteverdi Write the Finale? Does It Matter?

Today, when a composer finishes an opera the creative process usually ends and the score becomes the blueprint for the performance. That was true for the earliest court operas from Florence and Mantua as well. But beginning with public opera in seventeenth-century Venice, composers, librettists, and impresarios (producers) started to tinker with the score, making additions and cuts, right up to the premier and even after. Requirements of the particular theater, the cast, and the tastes of the audience had to be met. As with new Broadway shows today, a mid-century Venetian opera was not so much a finite work of art as a continuing work in progress.

There is reason to believe that the final duet, "Pur ti miro" ("I adore you"), may have been added later to Monteverdi's *Poppea,* and perhaps was not composed by Monteverdi at all. The text of the duet does not appear in the separately published libretto and it can be argued that the musical style differs slightly from Monteverdi's norm. Could the duet have been the work of Monteverdi's pupil Francesco Cavalli, whose hand can be seen elsewhere altering Monteverdi's score, or perhaps that of an admirer, Benedetto Ferrari, who wrote the text of the duet (and possibly the music)? Conversely, did Monteverdi himself write "Pur ti miro" to Ferrari's text and append it to his own score in order to make the finale of *Poppea* even more glamorous?

This issue of authenticity of "Pur ti miro" leads us to ask: Does it matter who creates a work of art? Would the *Mona Lisa* be any less beautiful were it painted, not by Leonardo da Vinci, but by someone else named Leonardo? Authorship should not matter, of course, unless we are more concerned with the life of the composer than the created work, more concerned with biography than art. Whether by Monteverdi or someone in his circle, "Pur ti miro" is an exquisite aria (duet), one perfectly exemplifying mid-century Venetian opera.

spectacular was *Il pomo d'oro* (*The Golden Apple*); in 1668 it received a lavish production with twenty-four different stage sets at the court of the Holy Roman Emperor in Vienna. Generally speaking, the operas of Cavalli and Cesti contain fewer choruses and instrumental interludes and more arias for the star singers. In addition, they distinguished more clearly between the recitative and the aria. Arias became not only more numerous but longer. These trends—more emphasis on solo singing in opera, more and longer arias, and more vocal display—would accelerate during the second half of the seventeenth century. Singers were wresting control of opera away from the composer.

SUMMARY

Nowhere was the new Baroque style more clearly evident than in a new genre of music that emerged around 1600: opera. Fully sung dramatic works were at first dominated by a style of monody called *stile rappresentativo.* Gradually, a distinction emerged between the declamatory recitative used for narration, and the more florid, melodious aria intended for personal expression. Florence, Italy, was the home of early opera, but the genre soon spread to Mantua, Rome, Naples, and Venice, and then north of the Alps. What began as a small-scale courtly experiment in Florence within fifty years had become a large-scale public spectacle. The opening of public theaters for opera in Venice in the 1630s accelerated the growing tendency to turn the operatic spotlight entirely upon the aria and the star singers. By 1650 the framework for Baroque opera was fully in place involving: (1) a multi-act, fully sung drama setting either a mythological or historical subject, and (2) a clear distinction between recitative and aria. Already by mid-century the balance of power within the opera theater was beginning to shift, with less importance placed on the composer and more on the star singers.

KEY TERMS

opera	Orpheus legend	simple recitative
libretto	*Le nuove musiche*	arioso style
Florentine camerata	toccata	aria
stile rappresentativo	recitative	strophic variation aria

The Concerted Style in Venice and Dresden

Venetia, Venetia, chi non ti vede non ti pretia! This sixteenth-century proverb can roughly be translated as: To appreciate Venice, you have to see it! The proverb is still true today. Venice remains a fantasyland of maze-like walkways and exotic buildings, all perched precariously above the waters of a lagoon. Venice was formerly a republic directed by a Doge (duke or chief magistrate) and an oligarchy of leading families. By 1630 the city had a population of 102,000 and was already a mecca for tourists and spies. Visitors came in search of the exotic, the foreign (the city enjoyed a thriving trade with the Near East), and the forbidden (prostitution and gambling flourished). They also came for the music. From the late 1630s onward, opera held sway at several opera houses during carnival season (see Chapter 30). By mid-century, 144 organs could be found in 121 different churches. Religious music in churches, civic music in processions of the Doge, and, later, public concerts at orphanages for females could be heard year-round.

The focus of civic and spiritual life in Venice, then and now, was the **basilica of St. Mark,** where the bones of the Evangelist Mark were believed to be buried. Because St. Mark's served as the chapel of the Doge, the political leader, it functioned as the goal of processions on occasions of state as well as religious festivals. St. Mark's has an architectural plan unique among the major churches of the West. It is built in the form of an equal-sided Greek cross, likely because in its early history Venice had strong ties to the Byzantine Empire in the East.

Beginning in the mid sixteenth century, Venetian musicians exploited the unusual architectural plan of St. Mark's by composing **cori spezzati**—literally "broken choirs," music for two, three, or four choirs placed in different parts of a building. At first these separate ensembles at St. Mark's were situated in the two choir lofts to the left and right of the main aisle (Fig. 31-1). Later, on days of special ceremonial importance, they were also stationed in other elevated galleries that adjoined the central dome. By positioning musicians in groups at points around the central axis of the church, the authorities of St. Mark's created something akin to multiphonic

❋ FIGURE 31-1

A view of singers in a gallery
at St. Mark's Basilica drawn by
Canaletto in the eighteenth
century. A matching gallery for
musicians was at the opposite side
of the church.

Bridgeman Art Library

surround sound for special, festive motets. Into these musicians' galleries crowded
not only singers, but instrumentalists as well.

Seventeenth-century Venice was at the forefront of technology. The city was the
European center for printing generally, and for music printing in particular, as well
as for shipbuilding, glass production, and the fabrication of musical instruments.
Recorders, shawms, cornetts, sackbuts, viols and violins, harpsichords, and clavichords were all produced in Venice for use there or for export to other cities in Italy
and north of the Alps. The tradition of polychoral religious music at St. Mark's
joined happily with the civic interest in musical instruments to foster a new style of
music, the concerted style.

Stile concertato is Italian for "concerted style." It is a term broadly used to identify Baroque music marked by grand scale and strong contrast, either between voices
and instruments, between separate instrumental ensembles, between separate choral
groups, or even between soloist and choir. Our term "concerto" derives from the
same word and has the same connotation, "to act together," perhaps within the
spirit of friendly competition. The first publication that employed the word "concerto" was printed in Venice in 1587: *Concerti . . . continenti musica di chiesa* (*Concertos . . . containing church music*). The church music contained herein was the

creation of two organists and composers at St. Mark's, Andrea Gabrieli (1533–1585) and his nephew Giovanni. A clear example of the concerted style can be seen in Example 31-1, the beginning of a polychoral *Gloria* by Giovanni Gabrieli. Here simple chordal units create an echo-like effect. Generally speaking, the composers at St. Mark's and other large Baroque churches avoided complex counterpoint and quick harmonic changes in favor of short units of homophonic declamation in which the text is clearly audible. Textual clarity is particularly important in a large, stone building such as St. Mark's which, then and now, has "muddy" acoustics.

EXAMPLE 31-1

And peace on earth…

GIOVANNI GABRIELI AND THE CONCERTED MOTET

Giovanni Gabrieli (c1554–1612) was among the first composers fully to exploit the sonic opportunities afforded by the architecture of St. Mark's. Gabrieli had studied with Lassus in Munich and knew well the tradition of the expressive Latin motet. Yet, as a native of Venice, he was intimately familiar with the Doge's windband of cornetts and trombones, as well as the newly emerging violin. In his *Sacrae symphoniae* (*Sacred Symphonies*, 1597), Gabrieli became the first composer in the history of music to indicate dynamic levels in a musical score. Specifically, his *Sonata pian e forte* requires the instruments to play soft and loud at various times; one four-voice choir of cornett and trombones alternates with another of violin and trombones in short bursts of louds and softs. Gabrieli was also one of the first composers to use the term "sonata" (for more on the sonata, see Chapter 33). One sonata by Gabrieli, published posthumously in 1615, is scored for twenty-two separate instrumental parts (mostly violins, cornetts, and trombones), plus basso continuo. For the early seventeenth century, this was a large-scale orchestra.

Giovanni Gabrieli was also the first composer to write idiomatically for particular instruments and specify the instruments in the score. In his motet *In ecclesiis* (*In the Churches*), which appeared in the second volume of *Sacred Symphonies* (1615), he explicitly stipulates the makeup of three separate ensembles: choir 1, an instrumental sextet requiring violin, three cornetts, and two trombones; choir 2, a group of four solo voices (soprano, alto, tenor, and bass); and choir 3, a four-voice chorus covering the same parts. To this is added a basso continuo played by the organ and perhaps a bassoon. Because the concertato style is evident everywhere in the motet *In ecclesiis*, we call it a **concerted motet.** Gabrieli assigned the soloists (choir 2) difficult parts, often with long melismas. To the chorus (choir 3) he gives a completely different kind of music: merely a chordal refrain on the word "Alleluia," a sign of collective rejoicing. The instruments (choir 1) have their own timbre, one distinct from the voices. Sometimes they play entirely by themselves, while at others they merely double the vocal parts; sometimes the instruments insert their own lines independent of the voices. When this occurs, a highly complex texture results with fourteen independent musical strands. *In ecclesiis* is a concerted motet full of luxuriant sounds designed to make more splendid one of the grand occasions of state that culminated beneath the domes of St. Mark's.

LISTENING CUE

GIOVANNI GABRIELI   CD 4/8
In ecclesiis (c1612)   Anthology, No. 83

CLAUDIO MONTEVERDI AND THE CONCERTED MADRIGAL

We have met Monteverdi twice before, first as a creator of a new-style madrigal at the end of the Renaissance (see Chapter 28), and then as the main progenitor of a new musical genre, opera (see Chapter 30). To this might be added the fact that in 1610 he composed a spectacular *Vespers* that brought the new dramatic style into the church. Herein lies the important point: Claudio Monteverdi, more than any other composer, set the standard for early Baroque music. First in Mantua and then in Venice, he led the avant-garde toward the creation of new musical genres and styles.

Monteverdi moved to Venice in 1613 to succeed Giovanni Gabrieli as the principal composer of the basilica of St. Mark. His new job required him to compose religious works and to oversee the performance of music generally in the church. After three years his superiors were pleased with Monteverdi's work. They extended his contract for ten years into the future at an annual salary of 400 ducats (he earned another 200 from freelance work fulfilling commissions from other Venetian churches). The extension was offered, so the contract stipulated, in order to assure that Monteverdi "live and die in the service [of this church]." And this is precisely what happened. Monteverdi served as *maestro di cappella* at St. Mark's until his death in 1643 at the age of seventy-six.

Sadly, most of the music Claudio Monteverdi composed for St. Mark's has been lost. It existed only in manuscript copies. By contrast, Monteverdi's secular music, intended for the large domestic market, was published and thus survives mostly intact. In all, Monteverdi wrote nine books of madrigals; the first five date from his years in Mantua, and the last four from his time in Venice. In the earlier madrigals, five voices sing continually with a uniform texture from beginning to end (see *Cruda Amarilli*, Chapter 28). In the later Venetian madrigals, however, instruments appear, and textures and timbres are strongly contrasting; all are characteristics of the **concerted madrigal.**

The concerted madrigal appears most prominently in Monteverdi's eighth book (1638). He entitled the collection *Madrigali guerrieri, et amorosi* (*Madrigals of War and Love*). Indeed, most of the pieces are about love and battles of the heart. In his preface Monteverdi says:

> I have come to realize that the principal passions or affections of our mind are three: anger, moderation, and humility; so the best philosophers declare. The very nature of our voice suggests this by having a high, low, and middle range. The art of music also points clearly to these three emotions in its terms "agitated," "soft," and "moderate" [*concitato, molle,* and *temperato*]. In all the works of earlier composers I have found examples of the "soft" and the "moderate," but never of the "agitated," a type of music nevertheless described by Plato in the third book of his *Republic* in these words: "Create a harmony that would fittingly imitate the words and accents of a brave man who is engaged in warfare."[1]

In other words, Monteverdi intends to create a new style of music, **stile concitato** (the agitated style), one particularly suited to warlike music. In truth, there had been martial music earlier during the Renaissance, but Monteverdi's agitated warlike music is more direct and insistent. To create it, he tells us, he simply took whole notes and divided them into machine gun–like short notes—sixteenth notes all firing on the same pitch.

The madrigal *Hor che 'l ciel e la terra* (*Now that the heavens and earth*) from the eighth book shows clearly how Monteverdi incorporates *stile concitato* to create bellicose sounds. It is scored for six voices, two violins, and basso continuo. The text is by the venerable Francesco Petrarch (see Chapters 13 and 14), a favorite poet of madrigal composers. It speaks of a quiet night, when the heavens, the earth, and the sea are calm; yet the lover battles the pains of unrequited love. He is both lover and warrior, supple yet violent. At the words "War is my state, full of rage and pain" (Ex. 31-2), Monteverdi unleashes a barrage of notes in *stile concitato*, continually repeating the word "guerra" (war).

EXAMPLE 31-2

War, war, war is my state...

Monteverdi's *Hor che 'l ciel e la terra* is both old and new. By 1638 the madrigal as a genre was then a hundred years old and at the end of its history. Monteverdi's attempt to capture a particular emotion (agitation) following the dictates of Plato is the last gasp of the Renaissance humanists who sought to re-create the affective powers of ancient Greek music. On the other hand, there is much here in the modern Baroque style. In this Baroque concerted madrigal, a basso continuo supports the voices, and here there are two violins as well. Not only do the violins accompany the voices, they also play independently from time to time. Most important, there is strong textural contrast as is typical of the concerted madrigal. All six voices begin and end in chordal harmony. Along the way we hear a duo alternate with interjections from the full chorus, as well as a four-voice chorus set in opposition to a six-voice one. Most striking is the moment when the two violins take charge in *stile concitato* on the word "guerra" ("war"). In this late madrigal by Monteverdi, the coolly uniform texture of the Renaissance gives way to the opulent sonic variety of the Baroque.

LISTENING CUE

CLAUDIO MONTEVERDI
Hor che 'l ciel e la terra (1638)

CD 4/9
Anthology, No. 84

✤ BARBARA STROZZI AND THE EARLY BAROQUE CANTATA

The life of Barbara Strozzi (1619-1677) shows yet another aspect of the colorful world of seventeenth-century Venice: the cultured literary salon where chamber music flourished. Barbara Strozzi (Fig. 31-2) was the illegitimate daughter of Giulio Strozzi, a merchant, diplomat and noted poet who provided texts for Monteverdi, among others. Barbara studied music with opera composer Francesco Cavalli (see Chapter 30) and began to compose herself. In 1637 her father Giulio founded a literary society called the Accademia degli Unisoni (Academy of the Like-Minded) to showcase his daughter's musical skills. Intellectual academies for males only (as was the custom at this time) were popular in Italy because they offered a place to debate the social, moral, and artistic issues of the day. The minutes of the Academy of the Like-Minded show that Barbara sang at their meetings as well as suggested topics that the members of the club might debate. In all, she published eight volumes of vocal music, mostly solo madrigals, arias, and cantatas with basso continuo.

Whereas opera was the dominant form of theatrical music of the Baroque era, the cantata became the primary genre of vocal chamber music. The word **cantata** literally means "something sung," as opposed to the sonata, "something sounded" or played on an instrument. Because it was usually performed before a select group of listeners in a private residence, this genre is called the **chamber cantata** (see also Chapter 32). In the seventeenth century the Italian cantata was usually a piece of accompanied solo vocal music that most often dealt with a secular topic: tales of unrequited love, stories from ancient history and mythology, or discussions of the pressing moral issues of the day. (Later, Bach and his fellow German composers would transform the cantata into a religious work for the church; see Chapter 40.) The cantata grew out of, and ultimately replaced, the monodic madrigal of the early seventeenth century. A solo madrigal will typically last three to four minutes, but a cantata by Barbara Strozzi or one of her contemporaries usually runs eight to twelve minutes or even more. The greater length of the cantata is caused by its sectional design, one in which singing in aria, recitative, and arioso style can come in any order. A single work could thus encompass more moods, or points of view. Aria, recitative, and arioso style yield to one another almost imperceptibly. In fact, a flexible mixture of the three styles typifies the cantata of 1620 to 1680. To hold the various sections together—to bring unity to the cantata—composers of the mid seventeenth century often employed a repeating bass line, or *basso ostinato*.

In Italian "*ostinato*" is the word for someone or something obstinate, stubborn, or even pigheaded. Thus a **basso ostinato** is a bass line that insistently repeats, note for note. Seventeenth-century musicians favored short patterns that had fanciful-sounding names such as *passamezzo antico*, *folia*, *passacaglia*, and *ciaconna*. Above these popular bass lines composers wrote vocal and instrumental variations (much like composers do today above the blues pattern). The beloved English ballad *Greensleeves* is built above a repeating *passamezzo antico*, and from the pen of Corelli we have a well-known violin piece above a repeating *folia* bass.

FIGURE 31-2

A portrait of Barbara Strozzi painted in the 1630s by Bernardo Strozzi, perhaps a relative.

EXAMPLE 31-3

Passamezzo antico   Folia

Passacaglia (minor)   Passacaglia (major)   Chaconne

The *ciaconna* (called *chaconne* in French) and *passacaglia,* both of Spanish origin, originally were separate and distinct bass melodies. But during the seventeenth century the distinction between them began to blur. The two terms came to be used indiscriminately to indicate almost any repeating bass pattern of short duration.

Just how a *basso ostinato* might provide a unifying structure within a lengthy cantata can be seen in Barbara Strozzi's *L'Amante Segreto: Voglio morire (The Secret Lover: I wish to die)* from her collection *Cantate, ariette e duetti* of 1651. Here a four-note descending *passacaglia* bass regulates the flow of most of the piece. Such descending tetrachordal figures, almost always in triple meter, are common in the Baroque period. Most often they are associated with pain, tears, and lamentation. Accordingly, such a tetrachordal *ostinato* is called a **lament bass.** (We will encounter it again in Dido's Lament by Purcell and in the "Crucifixus" of the B-Minor Mass by Bach.) Here the "Secret Lover" cannot reveal his feelings to his beloved, and wishes to die. An aria-like vocal line spins out the lover's despair above the repeating bass in the basso continuo (Ex. 31-4a). Yet periodically, the aria and supporting *ostinato* stop and a passage of declamatory recitative appears so as to move the "plot" along (Ex 31-4b). This is typical of the early Baroque cantata by Strozzi and her contemporaries: triple-meter arias alternate with duple-meter recitatives. Thus in a cantata, *stile concertato* is effected not so much by alternating units of contrasting timbres, but rather by changing to distinctly different vocal styles. What Barbara Strozzi has created is a variegated showpiece for soprano voice.

EXAMPLE 31-4A

I wish to die…

EXAMPLE 31-4B

As if she wished to say "Reveal, reveal your pain,"…

🎧 LISTENING CUE

BARBARA STROZZI   CD 4/10
L'Amante Segreto: Voglio morire (1651)   Anthology, No. 85

✺ THE CONCERTED STYLE MOVES NORTH: HEINRICH SCHÜTZ IN DRESDEN

Venice is only 225 miles from Munich, Germany, about the same distance it is from Rome. Indeed, as the northern-most large Italian city, Venice had frequent commerce—musical and otherwise—with the German and Austrian cities to the north.

Most important among these were Munich, Dresden, and Vienna. Monteverdi dedicated his eighth book of madrigals to the Holy Roman Emperor in Vienna, as did Barbara Strozzi her *Cantate* of 1651. Musicians from Italy went north to study, and vice versa. Both Andrea and Giovanni Gabrieli had gone to Munich to sit at the feet of Lassus in the 1560s and 1570s. Yet in the next generation, the most promising German composer, Heinrich Schütz, came to Venice to study, first with Gabrieli and again later with Monteverdi. When he returned to the court of Dresden, Germany, in 1629, Schütz carried with him seven cornetts of various sizes and numerous collections of Italian music. Paintings, too, flowed north from Italy. Today one of the finest holdings of Italian art of the Renaissance and Baroque is in the former court collection in Dresden, including the famous portrait of Barbara Strozzi (see Fig. 31-2). Similarly, the equally renowned portrait of Monteverdi (see Fig. 28-2) found a home in Innsbruck, Austria. Paintings, instruments, music, musicians, and musical styles—the concerted style in particular—moved from Italy to German-speaking lands during the first half of the seventeenth century.

Heinrich Schütz (1585–1672) was among the first of a long line of seventeenth- and eighteenth-century composers who made their way to Italy to learn the Italian style (Handel and Mozart would follow). Schütz, who came from the area of central Germany not far from Dresden, had shown musical talent as a youth. Consequently, a patron sent him to study with the renowned master Gabrieli in Venice. As Schütz later recounted:

> Since at that time a very famous if elderly musician and composer [Giovanni Gabrieli] was still alive in Italy, I was not to miss the opportunity of hearing him and gaining some knowledge from him. And the aforementioned Princely Highness ordered that a yearly stipend of 200 thalers be presented to me for the journey. Then (being a young man, and eager to see the world besides) I quite willingly accepted the recommendation with submissive gratitude, whereupon I set out for Venice in the year 1609, against my parents' wishes [they intended a career in law for young Schütz].[2]

After two years of tuition with Gabrieli, Schütz published the fruits of his study (a book of madrigals in Italian) and then returned to Germany.

In 1615 Schütz joined the chapel of the Elector[†] of Saxony in Dresden, then the largest musical institution in the largest city in Germany. By 1621 he had been appointed **Kapellmeister**—chief of music at court, the German equivalent of *maestro di cappella* (chapel master) in Italy. The job required that he supervise the selection and performance of the singers and instrumentalists, and oversee the education and musical preparation of the choirboys. Schütz also began to publish sacred music for the court, but his professional activities were severely hindered by the wars of religion that swirled around Saxony, specifically the Thirty Years' War.

The **Thirty Years' War** (1618–1648) was one of the great conflicts in the history of early-modern Europe. It consisted of a series of declared and undeclared wars fought essentially between the Protestants and the Catholics over political control—and religious dominance—in central Europe. On one side were the Protestants, led by the northern German princes and the king of Sweden. Arrayed against them were the Catholic forces of southern Germany and Austria, led by the Holy Roman Emperor. Hostility quickly grew into a "world war," or at least "pan-European war," as France and Denmark joined the Protestants and Spain aided the Catholic Emperor. Saxony, with Dresden as its capital, was politically and geographically caught in the

---

[†]In German history, an elector was one of nine powerful princes with the right to vote in the election to choose the Holy Roman Emperor.

middle. Musical institutions at Dresden and elsewhere in Germany were devastated. Schütz himself began to write for smaller musical forces, fearing there were no German ensembles left capable of performing fully concerted scores for voices and instruments. Even as Kapellmeister, his own salary often went unpaid.

Schütz's publications reflect these troubled times. Two early collections of polychoral motets, *Psalmen Davids* (1619) and *Symphoniae sacrae* Part I (1629), are large-scale works. But his *Kleine geistliche Konzerte* (*Little Sacred Concertos*; 1639 and 1641), written during the middle of the Thirty Years' War, suggests that only reduced forces were now available. Around the end of the war, however, Schütz was hopeful enough to publish large-scale works, specifically his *Symphoniae sacrae* Parts II and III (1647 and 1650). Schütz composed vocal music almost exclusively, most of it setting German texts. His religious music is most often not in the Latin of the Roman Catholic Church but in the German of the Protestant Church—Dresden and its court adhered to the Lutheran doctrine. Schütz was also the first composer to write an opera in German, specifically his *Dafne* (now lost) of 1627. In 1629 Schütz undertook a second trip to Venice, this time to study with Monteverdi, the master of the opulent Venetian style in general and early opera in particular. There, to quote his own words, Schütz learned "fresh devices" used by the newest Venetian composers "to tickle the ears of today."

Schütz's knowledge of the dramatic conventions of opera and the Venetian concerted motet can be seen in his *Saul, Saul, was verfolgst du mich?* (*Saul, Saul, Why doest thou persecute me?*). Published in 1650 as part of the *Symphoniae sacrae* Part III, Schütz's motet sets five short lines from the New Testament book of Acts (26:14–18). Here the Bible recounts how Christian-persecutor Paul, addressed by the Hebrew name Saul, was confronted on his way to Damascus, Syria; a blast of divine light knocks him dumb. The voice of Jesus asks:

> Saul, Saul, why doest thou persecute me? It is hard for thee to kick against the pricks . . . [go preach to] the Gentiles, unto whom now I send thee, to open their eyes, and to turn them from darkness to light, and from the power of Satan unto God.

Saul converts to Christianity, adopts the Christian name Paul, and goes on to write the New Testament epistles (letters) attributed to him. Painters of the early Baroque, among them Caravaggio (Fig. 31-3), were fond of depicting this scene with strong contrasts of light and dark to emphasize this dramatic moment of divine illumination.

Dramatic contrast also lies at the heart of Schütz's motet. A choir of six soloists is set against two four-voice choruses. Two violins and a basso continuo of organ and double bass are the only instruments specified, though others such as cornetts and trombones could double the two choruses if they were available. Throughout the score, the texture switches quickly among passages in *cori spezzati*, monody, and six-voice concerted madrigal style. Equally important, Schütz employs dynamic markings of *forte*, *piano*, *mezzopiano*, and *pianissimo*. As we have seen, his teacher in Venice, Giovanni Gabrieli, was the first to

❧ FIGURE 31-3

Caravaggio, *Conversion of Saint Paul*, 1601. Caravaggio's depiction of Saul's transformation on the road to Damascus uses stark contrast between light and dark to suggest a ray of divine revelation coming from above. This sort of dramatic juxtaposition is typical of both Baroque art and music.

Bridgeman Art Library

include dynamic markings in a musical score. At the very end of *Saul*, Schütz removes the double choruses and asks the soloists to conclude by singing in succession *forte*, *mezzopiano*, and finally *pianissimo*. Clearly, his intent was to end the motet with a *diminuendo*, even though in 1650 there was no musical term or sign for this effect. Thus not only by alternating vocal and instrumental forces but also by the use of different dynamic levels does Schütz masterfully re-create the dramatic conversion of Saul/Paul on the road to Damascus.

LISTENING CUE

HEINRICH SCHÜTZ

Symphoniae sacrae (1650)
Saul, Saul, was verfolgst du mich?

CD 4/11
Anthology, No. 86

SUMMARY

In the early Baroque a new musical style developed, *stile concertato*. The concerted style employed distinctly separate units of voices and instruments to create vivid contrasts. Composers applied the concerted style to several different genres of music, most notably to the motet and madrigal. The solo chamber cantata also developed at this time, but here the concerted style was less pronounced because no chorus was involved. St. Mark's Basilica was the epicenter of musical life in Venice. The polychoral concerted motets of Gabrieli and Monteverdi exploited the particular acoustics of the church. The concerted madrigal and cantata, however, were intended for homes of the well-to-do and the literary academies that enlivened Venetian life.

By 1650 the musical tide had fully turned around. During the Renaissance, northern composers such as Dufay and Josquin brought the newest styles of learned art music to Italy; during the Baroque, however, Italian musicians became the leaders, and they carried the Italian style northward across the Alps. Thus the progressive Venetian concerted style of Gabrieli and Monteverdi made its way to Germany, specifically to the important court centers in Dresden and Vienna. The culmination of the concerted style north of the Alps can be found in the dramatic polychoral works of Heinrich Schütz, Kapellmeister to the Elector at Dresden.

KEY TERMS

basilica of St. Mark	*stile concitato*	*passacaglia*
cori spezzati	cantata	lament bass
stile concertato	chamber cantata	Kapellmeister
concerted motet	*basso ostinato*	Thirty Years' War
concerted madrigal	*ciaconna* (*chaconne*)	

Chapter

32

Religious Music in Baroque Rome

Rome is a city of churches. It is also the home of the largest single organized church in the world, the Roman Catholic Church, which numbers approximately 700 million adherents. So important is the Catholic Church to Rome that it occupies its own nation-state, the Vatican, in the middle of the city. Here resides the pope as well as the numerous cardinals and other officials who direct the affairs of the Church. Within the Vatican are the Sistine Chapel, an interior sanctuary serving the pope, as well as the larger and more public St. Peter's Basilica. St. Peter's, by far the largest church in the world, provides a gathering place for thousands of the faithful during moments of extraordinary religious display. As is true for most of the largest churches in Rome, St. Peter's was completed during the Baroque era. By 1650 the city already possessed no fewer than 250 churches—basilicas such as St. Peter's, parish churches, chapels, and oratories, as well as numerous monasteries and convents.

Naturally, this concentration of religious institutions led to an emphasis on religious art and music. As nowhere else, art and music in Baroque Rome was overwhelmingly sacred, and the men who sponsored it were predominantly high-ranking church officials, specifically the pope and his attending cardinals. In truth, the papacy was very much a family affair. During the first half of the seventeenth century, for example, cultural life in Rome was dominated by Pope Urban VIII (1623–1644) and his three nephews. Urban appointed two of these nephews cardinals—hence the term "nepotism," from the Italian "*nipote*" for "nephew." This unique situation—family sponsorship of almost all high culture in the name of the Church—led to styles of sacred music particular to Rome as well as to one new musical genre, the sacred oratorio.

Art and music in seventeenth-century Rome expressed the spirit of the **Counter-Reformation,** the Church's aggressive response to the Protestant Reformation (for the Counter-Reformation in the Renaissance, see Chapter 25). The Catholic reformers purified the sanctuary by banning secular tunes and painting over nudity in religious art, and they limited corruption by curtailing the sale of indulgences (payment of money for remission of sin). Yet the Counter-Reformation Church also clung to the traditional Catholic practices: the centralization of power in Rome, celibacy for the clergy, a limited role for women, the veneration of images, and the continued support of monasteries and convents. The newly strict Church also strengthened the Inquisition (a Church court with the power of imprisonment) and imposed censorship by means of the Index of Prohibited Books. To foster the teachings of the Church, the popes promoted the work of a relatively new religious order, the **Jesuits.** Jesuit priests established colleges to impart a sense of a true Catholic life by means of education. Today, the Jesuit rule is still the principal sponsor of Catholic universities in the United States and around the world.

By the 1620s the Catholic Church had achieved something of a victory. Territory north of the Alps was no longer being lost to the Protestants, and some regions had even been reclaimed for the Church of Rome. A mood of triumph and celebration came over the Eternal City. Colleges and large churches sprang up everywhere. Into a few large churches on the high feast days went groups of musicians, sometimes as many as a hundred and fifty of them. Taking the largest view, music in Baroque Rome can be seen as belonging to one of three distinctly different types:

(1) a conservative style of vocal polyphony called *stile antico* (the old or traditional style) sung by the papal chapel; (2) a newer style of concerted music intended for a few vast churches and called "the colossal Baroque"; and (3) a highly progressive style in which the innovations of opera (aria and recitative) were manifest in sacred operas, oratorios, and cantatas.

THE *CAPPELLA PONTIFICIA SISTINA* AND THE *STILE ANTICO*

During the seventeenth century, the pope's (pontiff's) private vocal ensemble came to be called the ***cappella pontificia sistina*** (papal Sistine Chapel). As the last name suggests, the home of this group was the Sistine Chapel, which had been constructed during the late fifteenth century (see Chapter 25). In 1625 there were thirty-four singers on the chapel's roster, and thus in principle about eight singers for each vocal part. All singers were male clerics, with the soprano and alto parts allocated about equally to both castrati and falsettists. Yet, despite these impressive numbers, rarely did the entire group perform at once. The long hours needed each day to sing through the lengthy cycle of the Mass and offices required that the singers perform in shifts, usually with no more than one on a particular vocal part.

The *cappella pontificia sistina* employed a distinctive mode of performance and a unique musical repertory. All music was vocal music sung *a cappella* (no instruments, not even the organ, participated). The core of the chapel's music was a conservative repertory centering on the compositions of Palestrina and others engaged at the Sistine Chapel during the Renaissance and early Baroque. This conservative style, at first called the *prima pratica*, emphasized imitative counterpoint and followed strict rules of sixteenth-century part writing. More recent composers of the chapel—among them Tomás Luis de Victoria (1548–1611), Felice Anerio (c1560–1614), Stefano Landi (1587–1639), and Gregorio Allegri (1582–1652)—perpetuated this traditional style well into the seventeenth century. Because the *prima practica* increasingly looked backward rather than forward, the conservative music emanating from the papal chapel came to be dubbed the ***stile antico*** (old or traditional style).

By far the most famous example of *stile antico* music written for the papal chapel is the *Miserere*, composed by Gregorio Allegri in 1638. In truth, were it not for his *Miserere*, Allegri would be virtually unknown today. But this one piece, a setting of Psalm 50 (*Miserere mei, Deus; Have mercy upon me, O Lord*), captivated the imagination of listeners for two hundred and fifty years, including the likes of Goethe, Mozart, Mendelssohn, Ralph Waldo Emerson, and Samuel F. B. Morse (the inventor of Morse Code). Allegri's *Miserere* owed its appeal to the unusual atmosphere in which it was performed in the Sistine Chapel. The Penitential Psalm *Miserere* was the musical high point of each of the three most solemn days of Holy Week: Maundy Thursday, Good Friday, and Holy Saturday. The morning offices of these three days were (and are still) called the **Tenebrae service** (Latin for "darkness"), because the service was sung in almost total darkness. To represent the blackness of the world in which the light of Christ had been extinguished, the candles around the chapel were blown out one by one, leaving the pope and his cardinals prostrate on the floor as the voices of the *cappella pontificia* resounded from on high. The effect of the *a cappella* singing of the castrati and falsettists, as reported by countless visitors, was an eerie, ghostly sound like no other.

Despite its fame, Allegri's composition is a rather simple piece that represents a type of music called **falsobordone.** *Falsobordone* originated in Spain and Italy around 1480. Like its earlier cousin *fauxbourdon* (see Chapter 16), *falsobordone* was at first an improvisatory technique used by church singers. In early *falsobordone,* three voices chanted along with the psalm tone to produce four-voice, root-position chords (Ex. 32-1), an easy way of making simple chant sound more splendid. By the seventeenth century, however, both the psalm tone and improvisation had been largely abandoned, resulting in a newly composed piece for four or even five voices, as can be seen in the opening of Allegri's *Miserere* (Ex. 32-2). The voices chanted in simple psalm-tone style employing root-position chords with slightly ornamented cadences.

EXAMPLE 32-1

The Lord said to my Lord, "Sit on my right [hand]."

EXAMPLE 32-2

Have mercy upon me, O Lord, according to thy great [mercy].

Ironically, the thing that made Allegri's *Miserere* famous was not included in his score: vocal ornamentation. To Allegri's simple *falsobordone* foundation, soloists added unwritten, but carefully calculated counterpoint. As the generations went by, the nature of the ornamentation changed, as did, in fact, Allegri's written score. Nevertheless, visitors to the Sistine Chapel—from musicians such as Mozart, Mendelssohn, and Liszt to writers like Goethe, Shelly, and Dickens—came to marvel at Allegri's *stile antico* music and the eerie beauty of the Tenebrae service.

Mozart Pirates Allegri's *Miserere*

The *cappella pontificia sistina* was a closed men's club. It was a private all-male singing group, controlled by the pope, which elected its own members and selected its own musical repertory. In general, the papal chapel sang only Gregorian chant approved by the pope or polyphony composed by its own members, past or present. After 1638 Allegri's *Miserere* became a popular favorite with the faithful throngs who crowded into the back of the Sistine Chapel to witness the Tenebrae service annually just before Easter. But Allegri's motet was never published or even copied outside the chapel itself. Successive popes banned its reproduction on pain of excommunication. By the eighteenth century, however, pirated editions had begun to leak out. One of those who secretly copied the *Miserere* was the 14-year-old Wolfgang Amadeus Mozart.

How much music can you retain on first hearing: three seconds, seven seconds, ten seconds? It all depends on the capacity of your musical ear and your ability to process and retain musical patterns—on your innate musical talent. Needless to say, Mozart possessed extraordinary talent and he was able to write down by memory the essentials of all of Allegri's *Miserere* during just one performance. Mozart and his father, Leopold, were in Rome in April 1770 and, like many tourists, went to the Sistine Chapel to observe the famous Tenebrae service culminating with Allegri's *Miserere*. But let Mozart's father tell the story:

> You have often heard of the famous *Miserere* in Rome, which is so greatly prized that the performers in the

chapel are forbidden on pain of excommunication to take away a single part of it, to copy it or to give it to anyone. But we have it already! Wolfgang has written it down and we would have sent it to Salzburg in this letter, if it were not necessary for us to be there to perform it. But the manner of performance [the ornamentation] contributes more to its effect than the composition itself. So we shall bring it home with us. Moreover, because it is one of the secrets of Rome, we do no wish to let it fall into other hands, lest we incur, directly or indirectly, the punishment of the Church.[1]

Mozart's sister adds that Wolfgang returned to the Sistine Chapel two days later, hiding his pirated copy in his hat, and made a few corrections to his score.

In truth, remarkable as Mozart's accomplishment was, it may not be quite as astonishing as it first appears. Although Allegri's setting of Psalm 50 can take eight to twelve minutes to perform, depending upon the tempo, it consists of fewer than thirty bars of original music: a five-part *falsobordone* section alternates with a four-voice *falsobordone* section, and between each of these come verses of monophonic chant (see Anthology, No. 87). The amount of original polyphonic music to be copied, in either five or four parts, runs about one minute and thirty seconds. In addition, because the *falsobordone* sections repeat in successive verses, Mozart had a chance to hear each polyphonic section five times. How much of the improvised ornamentation he tried to capture is anyone's guess.

LISTENING CUE

GREGORIO ALLEGRI
Miserere mei, Deus (1638)

CD 4/12
Anthology, No. 87

ST. PETER'S BASILICA
AND THE COLOSSAL BAROQUE

A **basilica** is a special, grand church that happens not to be a cathedral (not the seat of a bishop). St. Peter's Basilica is special, of course, because on this site, directly below the high altar, are believed to be the bones of Peter, the Apostle, to whom Christ gave the authority to build the Church. Emperor Constantine had constructed a sanctuary on this site around 324 C.E., and a new, more magnificent building was begun in the sixteenth century. The central dome of the new St. Peter's, designed by Michelangelo, was completed in 1586; the nave and the great façade went up during the early decades of the seventeenth century. At the height of activity in 1611, more than eight hundred men worked at the site, sometimes at night by torchlight. Pope Urban VIII consecrated the structure in 1626, exactly one hundred years after the first cornerstone had been set. This was a triumphant moment for the Church. St. Peter's symbolized a newfound optimism of the clergy and people of Rome. The Counter-Reformation had purified the Church, and now its splendor could be revealed for all the world to see. St. Peter's was simply the largest visible symbol of this triumphant moment in Roman Church history.

Given its great size and acoustical resonance, it is in no way surprising that the music heard in St. Peter's was very different from that at the smaller Sistine Chapel. Indeed, the vast scale of the basilica invited composers to exploit size to achieve sonic magnificence. Accordingly, the musicians of St. Peter's, who formed an ensemble separate and independent from the singers of the Sistine Chapel, turned to large-scale compositions in the concerted style. Composers at St. Peter's—Paolo Agostini (c1583–1629), Virgilio Mazzocchi (1597–1646), and Orazio Benevoli (1605–1672), for example—wrote Masses and motets for as many as twelve choirs of voices and instruments. We have come to call this idiom of large-scale multiple-choir music for voices and instruments the **colossal Baroque.** Colossal Baroque church style usually involves four or more choirs, both answering each other and sometimes singing together in impressive tutti passages. Echoing units of choral sound provide the fundamental building blocks, and from these one or more solo voices occasionally emerge. This is concerted music, but concerted music on the largest possible dimension. For example, in 1639 musicians from St. Peter's and other choirs around Rome performed a work by Virgilio Mazzocchi, in honor of the patron saint. A contemporary reported that the piece was executed by "twelve or sixteen choirs"—apparently there were so many that it was impossible to count them all with confidence. Moreover, "an echo choir was placed at the top of the

❀ FIGURE 32-1

Interior of the dome of St. Peter's Basilica. This grand church, the largest in Christendom, was dedicated in 1626.

dome [and] in the space of that vast temple it was wonderfully effective." Obviously, Mazzocchi wished to achieve a heavenly effect by having at least one choir echo down from the top of Michelangelo's gigantic dome (Fig. 32-1). For this performance musicians stood on the floor, in the galleries above the floor, and on high in the cupola (dome). Instruments, specifically violins, cornetts, and trumpets, are reported in the dome as early as 1637. On these days honoring the patron saint, St. Peter, the church itself served as a giant resonator for both voices and instruments.

Unfortunately, little of the music in the style of the colossal Baroque survives. These were large pieces designed for specific events and usable within only a few specific churches. None of the large scores was ever published, and only a few manuscript copies are preserved. To get a sense of the sound of the colossal Baroque, therefore, we must turn to a Mass composed for the Catholic cathedral of Salzburg, Austria, where the colossal style had spread. This anonymous Mass, called simply the *Missa Salisburgensis* (*Salzburg Mass*), was first attributed to the Roman composer Orazio Benevoli of St. Peter's, and more recently to the German Heinrich Biber. Most likely, the Mass was composed in 1682 to celebrate the eleven-hundredth anniversary of the founding of the diocese of Salzburg. Despite its likely Austrian origin, however, the *Missa Salisburgensis* arises from the spirit of the Roman colossal Baroque, because during the seventeenth century both the Roman musical style and musicians trained in Rome held sway at this Austrian church. A glance at the gigantic score (Anthology, No. 88) will show that the composer wrote for seven separate musical ensembles and a total of fifty-three independent parts. The choirs were placed around the church, with two trumpet groups somewhat removed from the singers.

To avoid creating a sonic muddle with so many different parts, the composer of the *Missa Salisburgensis* employed only a few basic chords and changed them only very slowly. Because large Baroque churches generally had a long **reverberation time** (the time it took the sound to die out), composers of the colossal Baroque style in particular avoided quick harmonic changes. Otherwise, the simultaneous reverberation of two different chords would yield a dissonance. Of necessity, then, the harmony of the *Missa Salisburgensis* is conservative and the counterpoint very basic. The sound, however, is simply magnificent.

LISTENING CUE

UNKNOWN
Kyrie of the Missa Salisburgensis (1682?)

CD 4/13
Anthology, No. 88

ORGAN MUSIC BY GIROLAMO FRESCOBALDI

Except at the Sistine Chapel, instruments usually accompanied choral singing in the larger Baroque churches. The primary church instrument was the organ, which sounded both by itself and with the singers, providing a basso continuo and helping to keep the voices on pitch. Owing to the city's intense religious activity, Rome had more church organs than any European city; at least two hundred organs had been installed by 1640, and individual organists owned numerous portative organs that they transported from church to church as needed.

The foremost organist in Rome during the first half of the seventeenth century was Girolamo Frescobaldi (1583–1643; Fig. 32-2). By the end of his life Frescobaldi was universally recognized as the greatest organ composer, not just in Italy but in all of Europe. Frescobaldi was born in Ferrara, but by as early as 1601 had moved to Rome. Here he remained, with few absences, for more than forty years. Like many organists today, Frescobaldi was employed at more than one church, and he combined an active career as a teacher with his work as a composer and performer. He also received income for being "musician in residence" to a succession of wealthy clerical patrons, notably Cardinal Francesco Barberini, nephew of Pope Urban VIII. Yet Frescobaldi's principal post, from 1608 until his death in 1643, was organist at St. Peter's Basilica.

As organist at St. Peter's, Frescobaldi performed at the massive displays of concerted polychoral music that marked the feasts honoring St. Peter. He also participated in the more usual music-making at the basilica, playing organ at Sunday and feast-day Masses. For these services, Frescobaldi would have regularly improvised music, such as toccatas, ricercars, and canzonas, to introduce or

FIGURE 32-2

An engraving showing the likeness of Girolamo Frescobaldi. The inscription reads, "Girolamo Frescobaldi of Ferrara, organist of the basilica of St. Peter in the Vatican, thirty-six years of age."

Bridgeman Art Library

replace the choral singing during Mass. The organist might also alternate with the choir, playing a solo in place of the choral chant or polyphony. When the organ played alternate verses of the *Kyrie* or *Gloria*, for example, the result (see Chapter 24) was a performance using **alternatim technique.**

In 1635 Frescobaldi published a collection of Mass music to serve St. Peter's and other churches, his **Fiori musicali** (*Musical Flowers*). It includes organ music for Mass for most of the Sundays and feast days of the church year. Each Mass begins with an organ prelude, and is followed by an *alternatim* setting of the *Kyrie*. Then come other organ solos, in which the instrument replaces the choir in the Proper of the Mass. A Mass in which an organ alternates with, or entirely replaces, the choir is simply called an **organ Mass.** The heyday of the organ Mass was the seventeenth century, and Frescobaldi was its principal exponent.

For an example of an organ Mass from Frescobaldi's *Fiori musicali,* let us turn to the opening piece, the *Toccata avanti la Messa* (*Toccata before the Mass*). A **toccata,** as we have seen (see Chapter 30), is an instrumental work designed to show off the creative spirit of the composer as well as the technical skill of the performer. Although the term sometimes applies to pieces for other instruments, "toccata" most often signifies a freeform keyboard piece in which a "touching" of the keyboard is needed to demonstrate digital dexterity. The opening toccata of this particular organ Mass is shorter than most, being compressed into just thirteen measures (Ex. 32-3). Frescobaldi extended his keyboard figuration into the middle and lower ranges of the instrument, a far different practice from Renaissance keyboard music, in which the figuration is confined mostly to the highest register. Notice the two G sharps in this toccata (mm. 4 and 5) that pull toward the note (A) a fifth away from the home pitch (D); this is clear evidence of a growing awareness of what we today call functional tonality and secondary dominant chords.

EXAMPLE 32-3

A *Kyrie* using *alternatim* technique comes next, and here the organ plays the first verse and the choir chants the next, continuing thus through all nine verses of the *Kyrie.* Each independent organ section in an *alternatim* organ Mass is called an **organ verset,** a short piece that replaces a liturgical item otherwise sung by the choir. The organ versets in this *Kyrie* make use of *cantus firmus* technique; here (Ex. 32-4) the ancient *Kyrie* chant sounds in long notes, not in the tenor, but in the highest line.

EXAMPLE 32-4

Whereas the organ versets of the *Kyrie* employ an old technique from the Renaissance, the following organ ricercar is radically new. In this organ Mass, the ricercar replaces the Offertory usually sung by the choir. A **ricercar,** as we have seen (see Chapter 23), is an instrumental piece, usually for lute or keyboard, that is similar in style to the sixteenth-century imitative motet. Frescobaldi's newer ricercar, however, is very different from its sixteenth-century forebear. To begin with, it is monothematic. The composer has fashioned a single distinct subject and a countersubject (an important counterpoint to the subject; see Ex. 32-5, bar 3). Moreover, when the second voice imitates the subject at the interval of a fifth above, it changes the subject so as to keep the music in the home tonality, thus producing a **tonal answer** (Ex. 32-5, bar 3). Finally, the second section of the ricercar presents a new countersubject, which appears both in a normal and an inverted form. In every measure of this ricercar either the subject or a countersubject can be heard—a remarkably dense web of counterpoint. Developing a contrapuntal piece from a single subject and its countersubjects points directly toward the German fugue of the eighteenth century. In fact, J. S. Bach knew Frescobaldi's *Fiori musicali* well, for he obtained a manuscript copy as early as 1714 and kept it with him to the end of his life.

EXAMPLE 32-5

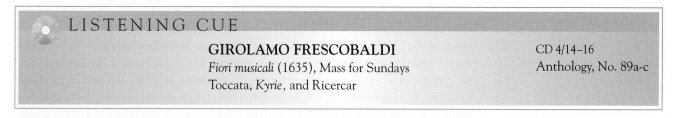

LISTENING CUE

GIROLAMO FRESCOBALDI
Fiori musicali (1635), Mass for Sundays
Toccata, *Kyrie*, and Ricercar

CD 4/14–16
Anthology, No. 89a-c

SACRED OPERA AND ORATORIO: GIACOMO CARISSIMI'S *JEPHTE*

Rome was predominantly a city of religious music, but not exclusively. During the early seventeenth century, opera spread from its home in Florence to Mantua, Venice, Naples, and Rome. Traditional secular operas using plots drawn from classical mythology, such as Stefano Landi's *La morte d'Orfeo* (*The Death of Orpheus*, 1619), saw the light of day in Rome. Even comic opera had a hearing, as evidenced by *Chi soffre speri* (*Who suffers may hope*, 1637), an opera by Virgilio Mazzocchi and Marco Marazzoli based on a story by Boccaccio.

But opera in Rome was not like opera in other cities. First of all, Rome produced a far higher percentage of sacred, or Christian, operas. As early as 1600, Emilio de' Cavalieri's sacred music drama *Rappresentatione di Anima, et di Corpo* (*Representation of Soul and Body*) was performed in a Roman church. In 1631 Stefano Landi set to music a libretto treating the life of St. Alexis (*Il Sant'Alessio*); in subsequent years it was performed spectacularly at the palace of Cardinal Francesco Barberini in a huge hall seating three thousand spectators. Typical of Christian opera, the libretto for *Il Sant'Alessio* was written by a priest, Giulio Rospigliosi (1600–1669), who went on to become Pope Clement IX (1667–1669). In a way unique to Rome, most opera, secular or sacred, was sponsored by clergymen—usually not by the pope himself, but by his cardinals in their lavish palaces. Also peculiar to Rome was the absence of female singers; women were not allowed to appear on stage in Rome or in papally controlled lands (though they could do so in "extraterritorial" foreign embassies!). Thus, Roman opera usually made use of castrati and boys for the highest parts. Finally, religious scruples here as elsewhere dictated that opera, as with spoken drama, be heard during the festive season of carnival, but not during the solemn time of Lent.

To satisfy the Roman desire for dramatic music during Lent, patrons and musicians developed a new musical genre: **oratorio.** Conforming to the solemn tone of Lent, oratorio put away lavish sets, costumes, and choreography. The dramatic text, either in Italian or Latin, usually elaborated upon a story found in the Old Testament, one recounting a tale of sacrifice and self-denial concordant with the spirit of Lent. Oratorio differs from opera because the singers are not in costume and do not fully act out their dramatic roles. A narrator simply reports what happens. Nevertheless, the fundamental musical processes of opera—recitative, aria, and chorus—also animate oratorio. Choruses (even if sung by only one on a part) loom larger in oratorio than in opera, for the chorus often carries a moral message delivered by the people to the people.

As the Italian term "oratorio" suggests, an oratorio was performed in an **oratory,** a prayer hall set aside just for praying, preaching, and devotional singing. Each oratory in Rome was supported by a **confraternity,** a fraternal order emphasizing religious devotion and charity. The most prestigious Roman confraternity was that of the Most Holy Crucifix, a brotherhood of educated noblemen. Every Friday during Lent its members gathered in their oratory in the center of Rome to hear one or more oratorios, works often composed by Giacomo Carissimi.

Giacomo Carissimi (1605–1674) served for more than forty years as director of music at the German College in Rome, an important Jesuit institution of higher learning. In addition to Masses and motets, Carissimi also wrote about a hundred and fifty secular cantatas. He is remembered today, however, mainly for his fourteen surviving oratorios. Most are based on stories from the Old Testament recounting deeds of heroic characters such as David killing Goliath or Jonah escaping from the belly of the whale. Rather than simply quote verbatim from scripture, the text of an oratorio embroiders upon the story; a more elaborate text allowed for a more vivid musical setting.

Just how Carissimi might bring a biblical story to life can best be judged in his oratorio *Jephte* (c1648), which embellishes upon events in the Old Testament book of Judges 11. There are three principal characters, the *Historicus* (narrator), Jephte, and his nameless daughter, as well as a chorus representing the people of Israel. Jephte is the leader of the Israelites, about to do battle against the Ammonites. He promises

God that if victory be granted, he will sacrifice upon his return the first living creature to greet him. This welcomer proves to be his own daughter. Dutifully, the daughter retreats to the mountains to lament her fate and bravely commends her soul to God. Her willingness to sacrifice was meant to inspire every good Christian during Lent.

In mid seventeenth-century oratorio, just as in early opera, the distinction between vocal styles is not always clearly drawn. Generally speaking, simple recitative is used to report events, and arioso style (more expressive recitative) appears for moments of greater intensity, while the aria projects poetic texts of special beauty or feeling. This is true of the climax of *Jephte*, where the daughter's lamentation ("Plorate, colles") is in four sections, each beginning syllabically like a recitative, but ending with a long melisma, as might an aria. Also typical of an aria, the text is often repeated for rhetorical emphasis. At first the daughter repeats her own words, then voices from the chorus provide a mountain echo. The daughter's lamentation is followed by a choral treatment of the same subject ("Plorate, filii Israel"), one of the most beautiful choruses ever written. At the beginning the basses descend in a repeating tetrachord, or lament bass, the musical symbol of despair and suffering. Toward the end, however, they rise by step while the upper voices fall down in a chain of mournful suspensions (Ex. 32-6). Such beauty is timeless, and nearly a century later Handel "borrowed" Carissimi's music and made it serve in his own oratorio *Samson* (1743); the Latin words "Plorate, filii Israel" ("Weep, children of Israel") were simply changed to the English "Hear, Jacob's God."

EXAMPLE 32-6

★ = suspension

🔘 LISTENING CUE

GIACOMO CARISSIMI
Jephte (c1648)
"Plorate, colles" (solo)
"Plorate, filii Israel" (chorus)

CD 4/17–18
Anthology, No. 90a-b

✿ THE CHAMBER CANTATA: A CHRISTMAS CANTATA BY ALESSANDRO SCARLATTI

Late seventeenth-century Rome saw the culmination of the chamber cantata, a genre that had originated in northern Italy and is exemplified in the works of Barbara Strozzi (see Chapter 31). As the name suggests, a **chamber cantata** was performed for a select audience in a private residence. By the end of the century it consisted of a succession of movements for solo voice and accompaniment that alternated between rapid declamation (recitative) and florid song (aria). Most cantatas were in Italian and spoke of love, though some revisited events in Roman history and a few embraced sacred subjects. Compared to an opera or an oratorio, a chamber cantata usually required only a single voice, was accompanied only by basso continuo and a few strings at most, and incorporated only a small number of recitatives and arias. Thus, while an opera or oratorio might extend well beyond an hour, the briefer chamber cantata usually lasted no more than fifteen minutes. Owing to its brevity and concentration, it was customary for a cantata to be repeated several times to allow the audience to savor the poetry and the music. At the end of the seventeenth century no composer in Rome was more celebrated as a creator of chamber cantatas than Alessandro Scarlatti.

Alessandro Scarlatti (1660–1725) belonged to a large family of musicians and was himself the father of the famous keyboard composer Domenico Scarlatti (see Chapter 43). It is not entirely certain with whom Scarlatti studied, but by 1680 he had been appointed composer-in-residence to exiled Queen Christina of Sweden, an important Roman patroness. After her death in 1689, Scarlatti eventually assumed a similar role at the court of Cardinal Pietro Ottoboni, great-nephew of Pope Alexander VIII. With their support, Scarlatti progressed to become the leading composer of opera in Rome, and later in Naples.

Patrons such as Queen Christina and Cardinal Ottoboni sponsored not only operas and oratorios but also chamber cantatas. Cardinal Ottoboni had responsibility for arranging to have Christmas cantatas performed annually on Christmas Eve in the papal apartments at the Vatican. Here, between the celebration of Christmas Vespers and the midnight Mass, the pope and perhaps twenty-five guests enjoyed spiritual refreshment in the form of a Christmas cantata and then moved on to an abundant meal.

We do not know precisely when, where, or for whom Alessandro Scarlatti composed his beautiful Christmas cantata *Oh di Betlemme* (*O Bethlehem*), but surely it was written around 1700 for one of the patrician houses in Rome. In the surviving manuscripts the cantata is identified simply as a *Cantata pastorale. . . . per la Natale* ("Pastoral cantata . . . for the Nativity"). In this work, as in many of his more than six hundred cantatas, Scarlatti developed a new structure for the aria.

In the 1690s Alessandro Scarlatti established the ***da capo*** **aria,** a formal arrangement that would come to enjoy enormous popularity. The text of the aria, usually consisting of just a single stanza, was assigned to two contrasting musical sections, and at the end of the second the first would return exactly, thus producing **ABA** form. The reprise of **A,** of course, was not written out, but simply signaled by the inscription "*da capo*" (take it from the top or, literally, "from the head").

Scarlatti's *Oh di Betlemme* makes exclusive use of the *da capo* aria—all three arias are molded in that form. The cantata begins with a brief instrumental introduction followed by a recitative, "Oh di Betlemme" ("O Bethlehem"), in which the singer contrasts the humble former status of Bethlehem, site of the nativity, with its present glory. The aria that follows, "Dal bel seno d'una stella" ("From a fair bosom of a star"), sets only four lines of text; the first two evoke the image of the sun (and Son), while the third and fourth refer to the Virgin Mary. To form the *da capo* structure, Scarlatti simply allocates his music to the text in pairs of lines, as shown below. He then emphasizes the distinction between **A** and **B** in two ways: he shifts tonalities from D major to B minor (the relative minor), and he assigns an instrumental ritornello to section **A,** but not **B.** As the term suggests, an instrumental **ritornello** (refrain) is a distinctive musical phrase that comes at the beginning of the aria and returns frequently thereafter. Here, in the charming aria "Dal bel seno d'una stella," the instrumental ritornello, played by a solo violin, establishes a dialogue with the voice. Thus, in *Oh di Betlemme*, Alessandro Scarlatti shows clearly why he is important to the history of the Italian cantata and to vocal music generally: he established the form and style of the chamber cantata, which would remain the norm for this genre in the first half of the eighteenth century; and he crafted a particular musical form, the *da capo* aria, that would continue to be favored by composers of operas, oratorios, and cantatas to the very end of the Baroque era.

Dal bel seno d'una stella	**A**	From a fair bosom of a star
Spunta a noi l'eterno sole.		Rises for us an eternal sun.
Da una pura verginella	**B**	From a pure maiden
Nacque già l'eterna prole.		is born an eternal son.
Dal bel seno d'una stella	**A**	From a fair bosom of a star
Spunta a noi l'eterno sole.		Rises for us an eternal sun.

LISTENING CUE

ALESSANDRO SCARLATTI
Cantata Oh di Betlemme (c1700?)
Recitative, "Oh di Betlemme"
Aria, "Dal bel seno d'una stella"

CD 4/19–20
Anthology, No. 91a-b

SUMMARY

More than any European city, Rome was and is dominated by the Roman Catholic Church, and this simple fact accounts for the preeminence of religious music there. During the seventeenth century, at the end of the Counter-Reformation, the fortunes of the Church reached a high point, as symbolized by the completion of St. Peter's Basilica, consecrated in 1626. Generally, the size and function of the church determined the nature of the music to be performed. Three musical styles predominated: (1) a dignified, conservative style of vocal polyphony called *stile antico* (old or traditional style) sung by the papal chapel in the Sistine Chapel; (2) a harmonically conservative style of concerted polychoral music called the colossal Baroque that was intended for a few vast spaces such as St. Peter's Basilica; and (3) a highly progressive style in which the innovations of opera (aria and recitative) were manifest in sacred operas, oratorios, and cantatas, many of which were performed in private residences of aristocratic churchmen. Organ music, most notably that of Girolamo Frescobaldi, also grew in importance at this time as a way of providing sonic variety for what otherwise was a religious service of exclusively vocal music.

Opera was known in early seventeenth-century Rome, but Roman opera usually emphasized moral and especially Christian themes. The religious orientation of

Rome also contributed to the creation of oratorio, a new musical genre. Although oratorio made use of the same conventions as opera (recitative, aria, and chorus), its message was spiritual and its plot usually drawn from dramatic events of the Old Testament, as is the case of the oratorios of Giacomo Carissimi. The chamber cantata, too, involved neither costumes nor histrionics. A lone singer sang a succession of recitatives and arias, accompanied by a basso continuo and a few strings at most. Alessandro Scarlatti solidified the general form and style of the Italian cantata, as well as popularized *da capo* form, a structure that would become the norm for the late Baroque aria in cantata, oratorio, and opera alike.

 KEY TERMS

Counter-Reformation	reverberation time	tonal answer
Jesuits	*alternatim* technique	oratorio
cappella pontificia sistina	*Fiori musicali*	oratory
stile antico	organ Mass	confraternity
Tenebrae service	toccata	chamber cantata
falsobordone	organ verset	*da capo* aria
colossal Baroque	ricercar	ritornello

Chapter 33

Instrumental Music in Italy

Instrumental music came into its own in the Baroque era. During the sixteenth century (late Renaissance) composers had written much instrumental music, and a variety of colorful instruments played it (see Chapter 23). Yet, not until the seventeenth century (early Baroque) did composers write for instruments in a truly idiomatic way, in a way that matched particular musical figures with the strengths of each separate instrument. Not until then was instrumental music printed in abundance. Indeed, during the seventeenth century, publishers began to issue as much instrumental music as vocal music, and by the eighteenth century, publishers' catalogues show a preponderance of instrumental music for sale. New instruments, new styles of playing, and new genres of pieces, including the sonata and concerto, all sprang forth during the seventeenth century.

The place of origin of these innovations was northern Italy (Map 33-1). Northern Italy saw the rise of the violin—the Baroque instrument *par excellence*. The first great violinmakers were all northern Italians and so, too, were most of the composers who satisfied the rapidly growing demand for music for this instrument. From northern Italy the violin and its music spread to the rest of Italy, and eventually to the rest of Europe as well.

MAP 33-1

Northern Italy in the seventeenth century.

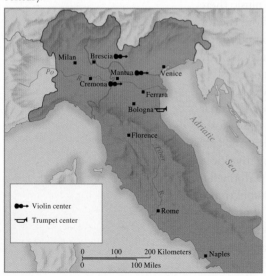

THE VIOLIN FAMILY

As we have seen (see Chapter 23), the violin originated in the sixteenth century as a "low-class" instrument used for playing dance music in inns and taverns. Appearing first in such northern Italian towns as Cremona and Brescia, the violin quickly spread to larger northern cities like Mantua and Venice, and eventually south to Rome and Naples. **Cremona** is crucial to the development of the violin. Claudio Monteverdi, the first great composer to write consistently for the violin, was a native of the city. Here, too, were born and lived many of the great violin-makers, including Antonio, Girolamo and Nicolò Amati, and Pietro and Giuseppe Guarneri, as well as **Antonio Stradivari** (c1644–1737). Today instruments by these exceptional Cremonese artisans are so highly prized that they fetch millions of dollars at auction houses in London and New York.

All members of the violin family have four strings and are tuned in fifths, the violin g-d'-a'-e". Violas and cellos are simply larger-sized violins. The cello developed from an early bass violin called the *violone* (large bass violin) tuned B♭', F, c, g. After 1650 a somewhat smaller instrument, tuned C, G, d, a, became popular, so the diminutive expression "cello" was appended to *violone* creating "violoncello," or "small large bass violin," which we now abbreviate as "cello."

The double bass emerged only at the end of the seventeenth century. Its ancestor was not the violin, but the viol, and it retains to the present day two viol-like characteristics: it is tuned in fourths (rather than fifths, as with the violin, viola, and cello); and it is often played with an "underhand" viol bowing, not "overhand" as used for violin, viola, and cello. Then, as now, the double bass sounded an octave below written pitch, and usually doubled the cello an octave lower. By the end of the seventeenth century, the violin, viola, cello, and often the more distantly related double bass, had come to form the nucleus of the Baroque orchestra.

FORMATION OF THE BAROQUE ORCHESTRA

The symphony orchestra as we know it today had its origins in Italy during the seventeenth century. At its beginning, the early Baroque orchestra was something of a "mixed bag" of instruments. The ensemble accompanying Monteverdi's *Orfeo* (1607), for example, consisted of violins and viols, recorders, trumpets, cornetts, sackbuts (trombones), harpsichord, theorbo, harps, organ with metal pipes, and organ with reed pipes. It was an ensemble of soloists; players did not normally double on the same instrumental part. The sound was diverse and colorful, but not especially powerful.

After the mid seventeenth century, however, several instruments important in the Renaissance—viol, cornett, sackbut (trombone), shawm, and theorbo—began to lose favor.[†] In their place stepped forward the instruments of the violin family to form a core ensemble, and to this group other instruments were gradually added. As the seventeenth century progressed, composers came to specify oboes, bassoons, flutes, trumpets, and, last, horns along with the strings. A single harpsichord (or organ in church) gradually replaced the theorbo and other plucked string instruments as the provider of a chordal support in the basso continuo. By the end of the century more than one player—two, three or even four—might sometimes execute one and the same string part. Yet, even with some parts doubled, what resulted was

---

[†]The large *viola da gamba* remained popular into the eighteenth century as a bass instrument in ensembles and as a solo instrument. The shawm evolved into the modern oboe. The sackbut, generally called the trombone during the Baroque era and thereafter, continued to be heard in church music and provide special effects in the opera theater. It was not added to the symphony orchestra, however, until the time of Beethoven.

The Violin Then and Now

What makes a great violin? They all look remarkably similar, with a common shape and common features, characteristics that were established in the sixteenth century. But the type and place of origin of the wood chosen for the front (usually spruce) and the back (usually maple), the way the wood is cured and then carved, the way the pieces are assembled, the type of final varnish applied—these are just a few of the features that separate a superb instrument from a mediocre one. Antonio Stradivari was among the greatest of the Cremonese violinmakers. Some six hundred fifty Stradivari instruments survive today: violins, violas, cellos, and even guitars. Today professional virtuosos such as Joshua Bell or Midori are willing to pay millions of dollars for the magnificent sound of a Stradivari.

In truth, the Stradivari violin sold today in New York or London is not precisely the one Stradivari made; all Stradivari violins have been rebuilt and significantly modified over the centuries. The size and general shape of the Baroque and modern instruments are the same, but the Baroque violin had a shorter fingerboard, and thus could not play pitches as high as can the modern instrument (Fig. 33-1). The bridge was lower, in part because there was less tension placed on the strings. Strings were made of animal gut (often cat intestine) sometimes spun around with a thin thread of brass or silver wire for added resonance. The Baroque violin bow had a narrower band of horsehair and was under less tension than its modern counterpart. Finally, there was no chin rest in the seventeenth century, and the violin was often played off the shoulder rather than under the chin (Fig. 33-2). With gut strings and less tension on both instrument and bow, the Baroque violin had a light, clean sound, not nearly as loud and rich as that produced by the modern violin. The Baroque violin was prized because it could play rapidly and could clearly articulate the lively rhythmic patterns of the new Baroque style.

(a)   (b)

National Music Museum

❦ FIGURE 33-1
Baroque violin (a) compared to modern one (b), side view.

Elvehjem Museum of Art

❦ FIGURE 33-2
Young Man Playing a Violin, attributed to Pietro Paolini, c1620. Note that the instrument is played off the shoulder rather than under the chin.

a modest-size orchestra with no more than twenty-five players. By way of example: eighteen instrumentalists were on the payroll at the basilica of St. Mark in Venice in 1643; twelve were employed at the basilica of St. Petronio in Bologna about 1680. By contrast, King Louis XIV (r. 1643–1715) sometimes augmented his core of twenty-four string players to more than eighty for performances of court ballet and opera at Versailles, and Cardinal Ottoboni once employed an orchestra of a hundred to play for a sacred opera in Rome. These large orchestras, however, were very much the exception rather than the rule.

In sum, during the seventeenth century the instrumental ensemble gradually coalesced around the instruments of the violin family (violin, viola, and cello) with a low string instrument such as the double bass sometimes added. After mid-century, oboes and bassoons might also double the strings, and a trumpet sound forth for extra brilliance. Beneath them all was the basso continuo held together by a harpsichord or, in church, by an organ.

CHURCH AND CHAMBER MUSIC

Today we distinguish between orchestral music (music with more than one on a part played before a large audience) and chamber music (music with just one on a part played before a small audience). In the Baroque era, the line separating orchestral and chamber music was not as clearly drawn. Most instrumental ensemble music, regardless of the place of performance and size of the audience, was played by just one performer on each part. Similarly, the same sonata or sinfonia might be performed in a church accommodating several thousand or a salon seating only a handful of listeners.

In an age in which there were no public concert halls and few public opera houses, church and chamber were the only two venues for ensemble music. Indeed, in the second half of the seventeenth century, composers gradually began to identify music as **da chiesa** (of the church) and as **da camera** (of the chamber). Thus were born the *sonata da chiesa* and the *sonata da camera*. The chamber sonata was usually made up of a series of dance-like movements, each of which had the name and character of a particular dance such as allemande, courante, and gigue. The church sonata included fewer pieces with dance rhythms, and the titles of the movements were simply tempo markings such as *grave, adagio, allegro,* or *presto;* it was thought inappropriate to have the movements of a piece destined for the church associated with secular dances.

SALOMONE ROSSI AND THE EARLY BAROQUE SONATA

A **sonata** (something to be sounded) is a piece for a single instrument or small instrumental ensemble. The term was first used in Venice around 1600 to indicate a composition intended specifically to be played or sounded, as opposed to one that was to be sung (a cantata). At first a sonata might be written for four, five, or as many as twenty-two, instrumental parts. It consisted of a single movement, which often had distinct sections with different tempos and moods. Thus around 1600 there was little difference between an early-Baroque sonata and a late-Renaissance canzona. In the course of the seventeenth century, however, the sonata took on its own distinctive features and the canzona gradually disappeared. In brief, the sonata experienced a gradual reduction of the number of parts, leaving just the solo sonata and trio sonata (see below); simultaneously, it expanded from a single movement, with separate sections, to multiple movements. Two important figures in this development were Salomone Rossi and Arcangelo Corelli.

To learn that violinist Salomone Rossi (c1570–c1630) was a native of Mantua is not surprising; northern Italian cities such as Cremona, Brescia, and Mantua were among the first to embrace the newly popular violin. More remarkable is the fact that Rossi was a Jew who flourished within the Christian court of Duke Vincenzo Gonzaga at Mantua. Duke Vincenzo showed the esteem in which he held Rossi by exempting him from wearing the identifying yellow star, a requirement of most other Jews in Italy at this time. Not only did Rossi compose instrumental music for the Mantuan court, he also created *Hashirim asher lish'lomo* (*The Songs of Solomon*, 1622), the first print to set Hebrew texts to music. The intent of this collection of thirty-three polyphonic settings of Hebrew psalms and hymns was to provide music for the synagogues thriving within the strictly defined Jewish zones (ghettos) in northern Italian cities such as Ferrara, Mantua, and Venice. Nevertheless, it is not for his vocal music for the synagogue, but rather for his contribution to the instrumental sonata, particularly the trio sonata, that Rossi is today considered most influential.

Salomone Rossi published four collections of instrumental ensemble music in the early decades of the seventeenth century. In these he moves away from the instrumental canzona of the late Renaissance (see Chapter 23) with its four-voice imitative texture. Instead, Rossi prefers a top-bottom texture with a duet for two violins on top and a basso continuo below. He clearly was influenced by the lyrical vocal monody and duets that he heard in the operas and concerted motets of his colleague at Mantua, Claudio Monteverdi. Indeed, a flamboyant vocal style for one or two high instruments dominates Rossi's sonatas. Yet Rossi goes beyond this vocally inspired manner, adding dashing turns, quick repeated notes, and rapid runs to exploit the idiomatic capabilities of the violin; such figures can be played faster and cleaner on the violin than they can be sung. Supporting the acrobatic upper parts is a rock-solid basso continuo that clearly sets out the direction of the harmonies.

Typical of Rossi's early Baroque sonatas is his *Sonata sopra l'aria di Ruggiero* (*Sonata on the song Ruggiero*). *Ruggiero* was a popular tune of the late Renaissance that continued to fascinate learned composers well into the seventeenth century. It possessed not only a melody but also a distinctive bass pattern. In fact, it was one of several bass patterns of the early seventeenth century that often served as a *basso ostinato*, a bass line repeating over and over, above which the composer built a set of variations (see Ex. 31-3). Rossi's *Sonata sopra l'aria di Ruggiero* consists of eight variations upon the *Ruggiero* bass (Ex. 33-1), the last of which is repeated at a faster tempo. Most of Rossi's variations involve a rapid interplay between the two upper violins. At times, the growing competition between them leads to virtuosic display. However, at strategic points (the beginning, and beginnings of variations four and seven), Rossi inserts passages of longer note values that have the effect of creating a much slower tempo. This alternation of slow/fast/slow/fast became a hallmark of the sonata. Here the alternation occurs within a single substantive movement. By the late seventeenth century the sections with differing tempos and moods would be separated and made to stand as independent movements, some of substantial duration, others very brief. Rossi and contemporaries such as Dario Castello and Biagio Marini intuited that the future of the sonata would rest in a multi-movement format.

EXAMPLE 33-1

> ### LISTENING CUE
>
> **SALOMONE ROSSI**
> *Sonata sopra l'aria di Ruggiero* (1623)
>
> CD 4/21
> Anthology, No. 92

ARCANGELO CORELLI:
SOLO SONATA AND TRIO SONATA

From the northern centers of Cremona and Mantua, the violin, and music for it, spread south to the rest of Italy. One important conduit was the composer Maurizio Cazzati (1616–1678), who carried the northern idioms from Mantua to Bologna. Bologna, on the main road south to Rome, soon became a center for the composition and performance of instrumental music. Opportunity for employment at the gigantic basilica of St. Petronio provided a special lure. Among the violinists attracted there was Arcangelo Corelli (1653–1713). Corelli learned his craft in Bologna, but by about the age of twenty had moved farther south to Rome. In Rome he became the darling of the aristocratic salon, admired for the rigor and precision of his playing.

Rome in the late seventeenth century was a city of about 150,000 people, and many contradictions. The Holy City had more than two hundred temples of worship, yet houses were crowded together, sanitary conditions appalling, and crime rampant. Virtually everyone of any means carried a sword, pistol, or dagger. Nonetheless, art and music flourished under the sponsorship of patrons with strong religious convictions. Corelli's first patron was Christina, exiled queen of Sweden, who in 1654 had renounced the Protestant religion and her throne, and moved to Rome to embrace Catholicism. To her Corelli dedicated his first publication, Opus 1 (1681), a set of twelve trio sonatas. Another important patron was young Pietro Ottoboni (1667–1740), who had been elevated to the rank of cardinal by his uncle, Pope Alexander VIII (more nepotism, as discussed in Chapter 32). Ottoboni collected paintings and musical instruments, and maintained an orchestra in his splendid Palazzo della Cancelleria in the center of Rome. In 1690 he engaged Corelli to serve as its *maestro di concerto* (concert master).

Corelli was the first composer in the history of music to make his reputation exclusively as an instrumental composer. He did not compose a great deal, but almost all of what he wrote was instrumental, not vocal, music. Corelli published four sets of trio sonatas, two *sonate da chiesa* (Opus 1 and Opus 3) and two *sonate da camera* (Opus 2 and Opus 4); a set of twelve solo sonatas for violin (Opus 5); and a collection of twelve ensemble concertos (Opus 6). Both of the latter publications contain examples of *da chiesa* as well as *da camera* format. Corelli was also the first composer to achieve international fame primarily from musical publications, because whatever was printed first in Italy under his name was quickly pirated by printers in Amsterdam and London. His solo sonatas in particular became enormously popular; forty-two editions of Opus 5 appeared before 1800, including arrangements for other instruments such as recorder. Appearing in Corelli's violin sonatas are modern bowing practices and frequent use of **multiple stops,** playing two or more notes simultaneously as chords. Corelli set the standard for composers throughout Europe at the turn of the eighteenth century, and his style was often imitated.

To be sure, the sonata was at the heart of Corelli's creative activity, and in his hands this genre became standardized both with regard to instrumentation and form. Earlier sonatas had been written for ensembles of various sizes, from one to as many as twenty-two instrumental players. With Corelli, however, the norm took two types: the solo sonata and the trio sonata. These two instrumental combinations became standard for composers until the end of the Baroque era around 1750. The **solo sonata** comprised a line for a single melody instrument (usually a violin) and basso continuo, while the **trio sonata** had two treble instruments (usually two violins) and continuo. (Because the basso continuo often required two instruments—one playing chords and the other the bass line—the solo sonata actually involved three players, and the trio sonata four.)

Form, too, now coalesced into a stereotypical pattern. Sonatas, whether solo or trio, usually consisted of a succession of four movements alternating slow/fast/slow/fast. All movements were in the same key (or relative major or minor). Sonatas intended for church (*da chiesa*) had movements simply labeled with a tempo marking such as *allegro* or *adagio*; sonatas for the private chamber (*da camera*) usually had not only a tempo indicator but also a title of a dance such as allemande or gigue. These were not real dances, but stylized pieces intending to conjure up in the mind of the listener a sonic image of the dance in question.

Corelli also standardized form within movements through a new emphasis on tonality. He developed a strategy of dividing the music of a movement into two balanced sections and repeating each. The first begins in the tonic key and ends on a dominant chord; the second begins on that dominant and works its way back to the tonic. In this process Corelli helped create what is now known as **binary form,** a structure consisting of two complementary parts, the first moving to a closely related key and the second beginning in that new key but soon returning the music to the tonic. In other words, it uses tonality to clarify form. Binary form became the standard form for single movements in sonatas and dance suites throughout the Baroque era.

In Corelli's music, tonality not only regulates the larger formal plan but also directs the smaller, more localized, harmonic event. Corelli's harmonies sound modern to our ears because they are often composed of triads, the roots of which are a fifth apart. Corelli also modulates, using melodic sequence, around the circle of fifths. One chord moves to the next in a purposeful, well-directed fashion, in a chord progression. The feeling of chords pulling one to another is often created by the use of chromatic inflection. The dominant chord has a leading tone that pulls to the tonic and a secondary chord often has a chromatic inflection (usually a sharp) that leads by half-step to the dominant pitch (see Ex. 33-3). What we hear in Corelli is a strong sense of functional tonality as we know it—the kind of harmonic movement still studied in music theory classes today.

In 1694 Corelli published his Opus 4, a set of *sonate da camera* dedicated to his art-loving patron, Cardinal Ottoboni. All twelve sonatas are trio sonatas scored for two violins and basso continuo (here, cello and harpsichord). In addition, all twelve sonatas proceed in a sequence of movements with alternating tempos: slow/fast/slow/fast. Sonata No. 1 in C Major opens with a slow *Preludio* (*Prelude*), which gives the players a chance to warm up while it sets the general mood of the sonata. Movement two is entitled *Corrente* (from the Italian *correre*, "to run") and proceeds in a fast triple meter. The fourth and final movement is also brisk and carries the title *Allemanda* (literally, "the German dance"). In the *Allemanda* the bass moves consistently in eighth notes, often up or down the scale (Ex. 33-2). A bass moving in a steady pace in this fashion is called a **walking bass.** Here, however, the fast tempo transforms it into something akin to a running or sprinting bass.

EXAMPLE 33-2

Between the fast *Corrente* and the brisk concluding *Allemanda*, Corelli places a slow *Adagio* in A minor, the relative minor key. Notice how, toward the end, a steadily rising bass line moves by half-step chromatic inflection to the tonic (Ex. 33-3). Combining the steady motion of a walking bass with chromatic inflections that pull to neighboring chords, or to those a fifth away, is just one way in which Corelli lends to his music a newfound sense of tonal direction.

EXAMPLE 33-3

In sum, Corelli is important in the history of music for developing modern violin techniques such as multiple stops, for standardizing the Baroque sonata as either a solo sonata or trio sonata, for popularizing binary form, for impressing a four-movement format on the whole, and for creating a purposeful harmonic language, one that other composers throughout Europe would soon eagerly adopt. Today, Corelli remains the only instrumental composer to be buried in Rome's famous Pantheon, a hall of fame for Italy's most illustrious artists and statesmen.

TRUMPET MUSIC BY GIUSEPPE TORELLI: THE BEGINNINGS OF THE SOLO CONCERTO

The violin and members of the violin family were not the only instruments to thrive in seventeenth-century Italy. The harpsichord, which had been around since the fifteenth century, became the workhorse of the Baroque ensemble, holding together the basso continuo. And melody instruments, such as the oboe, flute, and trumpet, saw a body of solo music created especially for them. For the trumpet in particular, the period of the seventeenth and early eighteenth centuries was a glorious moment. The trumpet, of course, had existed in Europe since Roman antiquity (see Chapter 2). But it flourished during the seventeenth century, perhaps because of the growing interest in brilliant instrumental sounds during the Baroque era. Trumpet makers in London, England, and Nuremberg, Germany, produced large numbers of quality instruments; and composers such as Henry Purcell in London and Giuseppe Torelli in Bologna created pieces that exploited its brilliant upper register as well as the advanced playing techniques of virtuoso performers.

During the seventeenth century the most important center for trumpet music was Bologna, Italy. The city had a long history of interest in civic music played by municipal trumpeters, one that extended back into the Middle Ages. Increasingly, trumpet music, and music generally in Bologna, was concentrated in the gigantic basilica of St. Petronio, a church far larger than either the Sistine Chapel in Rome or the basilica of St. Mark in Venice. Music at St. Petronio's entered a golden era with the appointment of Maurizio Cazzati as *maestro di cappella* in 1657. Cazzati, inspired by the skill of several trumpeters in Bologna, published the first sonatas for solo trumpet in 1665. By the early eighteenth century, the music library at St. Petronio's comprised hundreds of instrumental works by Cazzati and other composers, including some eighty-three pieces for trumpet. Foremost among the composers of trumpet music in this collection was Giuseppe Torelli. Indeed, judging from the number of pieces surviving under his name in Bologna and elsewhere (approximately forty-five), Torelli was the preeminent composer of trumpet music of the entire Baroque era.

Giuseppe Torelli (1658–1709) was born in Verona, near Venice, but moved to Bologna and a position at St. Petronio's in 1684. He remained in Bologna, except for a brief sojourn in Berlin and Vienna around 1700, for the remainder of his life. Ironically, Torelli was himself a violinist, not a trumpeter. He published two early sets of trio sonatas for strings (1686) as well as two somewhat-later sets of string concertos (1692 and 1698). The concertos of 1692 are important because they are among the first to specify that the orchestral string parts are to be multiplied—as many as three or four players are to reinforce each orchestra line. Yet, following in the footsteps of Cazzati, Torelli also chose to write for the virtuoso trumpeters of Bologna, who filled St. Petronio's with brilliant sound on the high feast days of the church year.

Between 1684 and his death in 1709, Torelli wrote nearly four dozen trumpet pieces for St. Petronio's. Most were performed as a prelude to the Mass or as a substitute for the Mass Offertory on the feast of St. Petronio (4 October), the patron saint of Bologna. Some of these pieces Torelli called sonatas, others sinfonias, and still others concertos. Some he wrote in the slow/fast/slow/fast movement format typi-cal of a sonata, and others in the fast/slow/fast arrangement that was coming to be common for the sinfonia. By 1700 the term **sinfonia** was used to designate a three-movement instrumental overture, one that might preface an opera or a Mass. In truth, Torelli employed the terms "sonata," "sinfonia," and "concerto" without distinction; there is no difference in form or musical process from one genre to the next. Indeed, this indiscriminate use of the terms is a hallmark of Italian instrumen-tal music around 1700.

Consequently, Torelli's Sinfonia in D Major for trumpet should be heard as a three-movement sinfonia, but one possessing early signs of the solo concerto (on the concerto, see below under Antonio Vivaldi). It opens with an orchestral pre-sentation of a theme that will return repeatedly in the first movement (Ex. 33-4). When the trumpet enters, it emphasizes a rising fourth motive (Ex. 33-5), and it alone plays lengthy trills. Thus a distinction is made between the music assigned the soloist and that given the orchestra. Moreover, the trumpet's rising fourth mo-tive is clearly drawn from the opening theme played by the orchestra. These two procedures—differentiating the music of the soloist from that of the orchestra, and having the soloist expand upon material derived from a recurring orchestral theme (ritornello)—are hallmarks of the emerging Baroque concerto. They will become especially prominent in the mature concertos of Antonio Vivaldi.

EXAMPLE 33-4

EXAMPLE 33-5

By contrast, the trumpet is entirely silent during the slow second movement. Here, Torelli writes a short, simple succession of chords and ends with a half-cadence that leads directly into the finale. Above most of these chords Torelli has placed a small dash, the sign for *spiccato*. **Spiccato** (Italian for "sharp") requires the performers to play in a detached fashion, but not quite as short as *staccato*. Compared to nor-mal playing, *spiccato* produces less resonance but greater clarity, a desirable feature in a large, resonant church such as St. Petronio's, where the reverberation time is an astonishing twelve seconds.

Finally, there is a distinction here as to what the violin can play and what the trumpet cannot. In measures 20–24, the violin leads a modulation that touches on chords moving around the circle of fifths: B-E-A-D. This is effected by means of chromatic notes, some of which, such as g#', c#", and d#", are not easily available on

✿ FIGURE 33-3

Two trumpets by Johann Wilhelm Hass, Nuremberg, c1690–1700. Trumpets like these were frequently purchased by Italian trumpeters.

a trumpet pitched in D. Thus this modulatory passage is assigned to the strings but not the trumpet. The Baroque trumpet could play *in* keys such as tonic and dominant, but it could not easily move *through* different keys.

Recall that the trumpet during the seventeenth century is a natural instrument without keys or valves (Fig. 33-3). The notes it can produce are those of the harmonic series. Most trumpets around 1700 were pitched with a fundamental that sounded low D, and therefore most compositions for them in the Baroque are in the key of D major. Example 33-6 shows the notes of the harmonic series, and thus the pitches available to a natural trumpet pitched in D. Notice that the notes g#', c#'', and d#'', among others, are not present in this series. In addition, some of the harmonics (7, 11, 13, and 14) are not in tune and only approximate the black notes written in the example. A skilled performer, however, could blow more or less hard to produce a sharp or flat inflection (B♮ or C for harmonic 7, for example). As the trumpet entered the highest harmonics, a fully chromatic scale resulted. Only in this highest register could the trumpet play conjunct melodies and not merely jump around in fourths and fifths. Playing in this high register, called the **clarino register,** was a special technique of Baroque trumpeters. By 1760, however, this brilliant upper-register playing had became something of a lost art. The trumpet parts written by Baroque composers Torelli, Purcell, and Bach are much more difficult than those composed by Classical masters Haydn, Mozart, and Beethoven.

EXAMPLE 33-6

◉ LISTENING CUE

GIUSEPPE TORELLI   CD 5/1–3
Trumpet Sinfonia in D Major (c1700)   Anthology, No. 94

✿ ANTONIO VIVALDI: SOLO CONCERTO AND CONCERTO GROSSO

The seventeenth century witnessed the advent of several new musical genres, among them opera, oratorio, cantata, sonata, and concerto. In the early seventeenth century, the term "concerto" appeared in many contexts and meant many things. Generally, it connoted a composition that involved opulent, contrasting sound created by diverse musical forces, whether instrumental or vocal. In this sense it was closely related to the early Baroque term *concertato*, music marked by strong contrasts (see Chapter 31). Only during the last two decades of the seventeenth century did the word **concerto** come to denote a purely instrumental piece for ensemble in which one or more soloists both complemented and competed with an orchestra.

The most prolific composer of Baroque concertos was Antonio Vivaldi. In fact, Vivaldi has left us nearly five hundred concertos. Roughly three hundred fifty of

these are for one solo instrument or another, and thus they belong to the category
solo concerto. Of the solo concertos most (some two hundred thirty) are for violin,
but some are for bassoon, cello, oboe, flute, recorder, and even mandolin. Vivaldi
himself was a virtuoso violinist. He was one of the first to showcase his skill as a
soloist at the end of a movement of a concerto. In 1715 a visitor from Germany to
Venice heard the master play such an improvised conclusion.

> Towards the end Vivaldi played a solo accompaniment—splendid—to which he ap-
> pended a cadenza which really frightened me, for such playing has never been nor can
> be: he brought his fingers up to only a straw's distance from the bridge, leaving no
> room for the bow—and that on all four strings with imitations and incredible speed.
> With this he astounded everyone, but I cannot say that it pleased me, for it was not so
> pleasant to listen to as it was skillfully executed.[1]

Thus the instrumental **cadenza**—a technically demanding, rhapsodic, improvisatory
passage near the end of a movement—entered the concerto in the early eighteenth
century in the music of Vivaldi and other contemporary Italian composers.

Antonio Vivaldi (1678–1741) was a native of Venice and became an important
figure in that city's long and distinguished musical history (see Chapter 31). His father was a barber and part-time violinist on the payroll of the basilica of St. Mark,
the principal church of the city. The young Vivaldi's proximity to St. Mark's naturally brought him into contact with the clergy. Although a violin virtuoso at an
early age, he entered Holy Orders and gained the priesthood in 1703. Yet Vivaldi's
life was by no means confined to the realm of the spirit. He concertized on the violin
throughout Europe; he wrote and produced nearly fifty operas, which brought him
a great deal of money; and for fifteen years he lived with an Italian opera soprano.
The worldly pursuits of *il prete rosso* (the red-haired priest) eventually provoked the
wrath of the Church of Rome, and in 1737 Vivaldi was forbidden to practice his
musical artistry in certain papally controlled lands. This ban seems to have affected
his income as well as his creativity. He died poor and obscure in 1741 in Vienna,
where he had moved in a futile effort to resuscitate his career.

Despite his frequent travels, Vivaldi's career was centered in Venice.
From 1703 until 1740 he served variously as a violinist, music teacher, and
composer-in-residence at the *Ospedale della Pietà* (Hospice of Mercy). The
Hospice of Mercy was a combination orphanage, convent, and music conservatory providing for the care and education of young women. It was one
of four such charitable institutions in Venice that accepted abandoned,
mostly illegitimate, girls, who, as several reports state, "otherwise would
have been thrown in the canals." All girls received religious training and
some instruction in domestic crafts (cooking, embroidery, lace-making,
and the like). The more musically talented were given lessons on instruments and required to practice as much as four hours a day. Each Sunday
afternoon the all-female orchestra offered public performances for tourists
and well-to-do Venetians alike. The girls appeared in the chapel of the orphanage standing on high in a special gallery, a musicians' loft, and played
to the outside world through a grill (Fig. 33-4). The report of a French
diplomat in 1739 is typical of the impression they made.

> These girls are brought up at the expense of the state and trained solely to excel
> in music. Moreover, they sing like angels and play the violin, the flute, the
> organ, the oboe, the cello, and the bassoon; in short, there is no instrument,
> however unwieldy, that can frighten them. They are cloistered like nuns. It is
> they alone who perform, and about forty girls take part in each concert. I vow

�“ **FIGURE 33-4**
Women musicians perform
behind a grill at an eighteenth-
century Venetian orphanage.

Photo Costa

to you that there is nothing so diverting as the sight of a young and pretty nun in a white habit, with a bunch of pomegranate blossoms over her ear, conducting the orchestra and beating time with all the grace and precision imaginable.[2]

Vivaldi composed many of his concertos specifically for his female pupils at the Hospice of Mercy in order that they might develop and demonstrate their musical skills. Some of these concertos he published, but most he left in manuscript copies at the time of his death. Among the works Vivaldi published are a set of twelve concerti grossi, comprising Opus 3, entitled *L'estro armonico* (*Harmonic Whim*, 1711) and a group of twelve solo concertos, comprising Opus 8, called *Il cimento dell'armonia e dell'inventione* (*The Contest between Harmony and Invention*, 1725). The first four concertos of this latter set are the famous **The Four Seasons.** In these, Vivaldi writes some of the earliest program music, for the composer inserts a poem about each season into the first violinist's part and then fashions music to match the poetic images (singing birds, a gathering storm, a babbling brook, and so on). Today Vivaldi's *The Four Seasons* concertos are perhaps the most popular of all Baroque compositions—standard background music in restaurants and coffee houses, as well as films and TV commercials.

Less popular today, but more influential in Vivaldi's day, are the concertos contained in the *L'estro armonico*. This collection, which greatly influenced the leading composers of the day, has been called "the single most important collection of instrumental music to appear during the whole of the eighteenth century."[3] Most of the twelve concertos are of the concerto grosso type. In a **concerto grosso** a larger body of performers, namely the full orchestra, contrasts with a smaller group of soloists. The larger ensemble is sometimes called the concerto grosso ("large concerto"), but more commonly identified as the **ripieno** (Italian for "full"). The smaller group of two, three, or four soloists is called the **concertino** ("little concerto"). In the Baroque era these soloists were not expensive stars brought from afar, but the regular first-chair players of the orchestra. When they were not serving as soloists, these leaders simply melted back into the ripieno to play the orchestral parts.

As with the solo concerto, the Baroque concerto grosso is in three movements, fast/slow/fast. The serious first movement is usually composed in a carefully worked-out structure called **ritornello form.** The Italian word **ritornello,** as we have seen (see Chapter 32), simply means "return" or "refrain." Vivaldi employs ritornello form in both his solo concerto and concerto grosso. A piece in ritornello form begins with a distinct main theme, the ritornello, which returns again and again, invariably played by the *ripieno*. Between statements of the ritornello, the *concertino* (or soloist in a solo concerto) comes forward to expand and elaborate upon musical ideas contained or suggested within the ritornello. The *concertino* also provokes modulations to more distant keys. In general, the *ripieno* provides tonal stability, while it is up to the *concertino* to push the piece farther afield tonally. The tension between these two different sound masses and between the tonal zones of the two groups is what gives the concerto grosso its exciting, dynamic quality.

A classic example of a concerto grosso is the eighth within Vivaldi's *L'estro armonico* (Opus 3, No. 8, in A Minor). No less a person than the young J.S. Bach transcribed it for organ so as to study and absorb Vivaldi's style. The opening movement is in ritornello form. Here the ritornello is comprised of four distinct parts. Part 1 (Ex. 33-7a) begins with three strong chords followed by a descending scale played in unison by the strings (unison string writing is a favorite device of Vivaldi). Part 2 (Ex. 33-7b) presents a repeated figure that soon gives way to a descending melodic sequence (frequent use of melodic sequence is another hallmark of

Vivaldi's style). Part 3 (Ex. 33-7c) is marked by a gesture idiomatic to the violin (rocking back and forth with slurred down bows); while Part 4 (Ex. 33-7d) inserts a striking chord (B♭ chord in A minor) as the violins saw away. All four sections are energized by small repeating rhythmic cells, thereby creating the motor-like rhythms that typically propel Vivaldi's music forward. Now the *concertino* (here two violins and cello) takes over from the *ripieno,* and it interjects an insistent, repeated figure borrowed from Part 1 of the ritornello. Thereafter the movement unfolds as a succession of increasingly ornate elaborations of bits of the ritornello played by the *concertino* and returns of one or more sections of the ritornello performed by the *ripieno* (see below). The *concertino* sounds daring and adventuresome; the *ripieno* solid and secure. The interplay between the two goes to the very heart of the concerto, a spirited give-and-take between opposing musical forces.

EXAMPLES 33-7 A–D

Example 33-7a

Example 33-7b

Example 33-7c

Example 33-7d

Formal diagram of Vivaldi, Opus 3, No. 8, 1st movement

Ritornello part:	1–4	4	2	1	3	1	2+4	4
R (*ripieno*) or c (*concertino*):	R	c	R	c	R	c	R	c	R	c	R	c	R	c	R
Key:	a		a	C		d		a		a		a		a

LISTENING CUE

ANTONIO VIVALDI

Opus 3, *L'estro armonico* (1711)
Concerto Grosso, No. 8, First movement

CD 5/4
Anthology, No. 95

SUMMARY

During the seventeenth century, instrumental music became just as important as vocal music, judging from the amount of music published. For the first time in the history of music, composers began to write idiomatically for instruments. By mid-century the sonata had become the dominant genre of instrumental music, though by the end of the century another new genre, the concerto, began to compete for pride of place. At first the sonata was a single-movement composition with sections having different tempos and moods. Similarly, the early sonata might involve as many as twenty-two individual parts. The sonatas of Salomone Rossi, while still embodying a single movement, reduce the instruments to just two high parts and a basso continuo. Arcangelo Corelli standardized the Baroque sonata as either a solo sonata or a trio sonata, and as either *da chiesa* or *da camera*. He impressed a four-movement format on each sonata and binary form on each movement within each sonata. Corelli also created a purposeful harmonic language by using chromatic inflections, secondary dominant chords, and abundant melodic sequences. Giuseppe Torelli wrote trumpet sonatas, sinfonias, and concertos in which can be seen the beginnings of the solo concerto: a separation of material assigned to soloist and opposing orchestra. Antonio Vivaldi popularized both the solo concerto, as exemplified by *The Four Seasons*, and the concerto grosso. In both genres Vivaldi often employs ritornello form to set up a dialogue involving theme and key between the full orchestra (*ripieno*) and a single soloist, or a group of soloists (*concertino*).

KEY TERMS

Cremona	binary form	*The Four Seasons*
Antonio Stradivari	walking bass	concerto grosso
da chiesa	sinfonia	*ripieno*
da camera	*spiccato*	*concertino*
sonata	clarino register	ritornello form
multiple stops	concerto	*ritornello*
solo sonata	solo concerto	
trio sonata	cadenza	

Chapter 34

Instrumental Music in Germany and Austria

Italy was the fountainhead of Western art music during the seventeenth century. Almost all of the new musical genres of the Baroque era—opera, concerted motet, oratorio, cantata, sonata, sinfonia, and concerto—originated there. So dominant was Italy during this period that the terminology the Italians developed for music soon spread to other countries, and it remains fundamentally the one we use today. Terms for dynamics (such as *piano, forte, fortissimo*), for tempo (*allegro, adagio,* and *moderato*), for processes (*ostinato, obbligato, staccato,* and *spiccato*), and even for instruments (violin, viola, cello) were popularized in Italy during the seventeenth century. But other nations had their own distinctive musical styles and practices. In German-speaking lands (mainly modern Germany and Austria; Map 34-1), intensely contrapuntal pieces and those built upon a sacred melody (either Catholic or Protestant) were especially favored. As we have seen, German musicians journeyed to Italy to study the latest Italian musical styles and, similarly, Italian musicians were much prized at German and Austrian courts. With such comings and goings on the Continent, musical styles (Italian, German, French, and Spanish) inevitably became intertwined, and we are sometimes at pains to know exactly which musical characteristics originated where. Some German-speaking composers restricted themselves

MAP 34-1
Northern Europe in the seventeenth century.

to a distinctly Germanic style. Others were proficient at adopting or adapting several national idioms. One such cosmopolitan master was Johann Froberger.

JOHANN FROBERGER AND THE BAROQUE DANCE SUITE

Who was Johann Froberger (1616–1667) and why should we care? Froberger was a German musician who worked mainly in Austria, spent years studying in Italy, and traveled extensively as a virtuoso performer in France and England. He is important to the history of music because he established the dance suite as an important genre of music for string keyboard instruments (harpsichord and clavichord). Handel and Bach later composed keyboard suites building on Froberger's model; young Bach in particular copied keyboard pieces by Froberger to learn his craft, and held him in high esteem throughout his life. Dance suites for keyboard and instrumental ensembles proliferated during the Baroque era and then disappeared after 1750, only to enjoy a renaissance during the twentieth century in the hands of Debussy, Strauss, Respighi, Schoenberg, Stravinsky, and others.

Johann Froberger was born in Stuttgart, Germany, the son of a court musician. In 1634 he moved to the Austrian capital of Vienna and three years later was appointed organist to the imperial court. That same year, Froberger received a stipend from the emperor, which allowed him to study for several years in Rome with the renowned keyboardist and composer Girolamo Frescobaldi (see Chapter 32). Froberger was again given leave from the imperial court in 1651–1652, when he visited London and Paris, meeting and absorbing the musical styles of the leading Parisian composers in particular. He returned to imperial service in Vienna in 1653, but was released in 1657 when a new emperor came to the throne. He ended his days as artist-in-residence for the aristocratic family that his father had once served in Stuttgart.

Froberger composed almost exclusively keyboard music. Those compositions belonging to the Italian tradition (canzonas, toccatas, and ricercars, for example) he intended mainly for organ, while those showing French influence (mostly the dance suites) were designed for harpsichord or clavichord. In Paris, Froberger had come under the sway of the French school of lutenists centering around Denis Gaultier (see Chapter 36), and he transferred their style to the harpsichord. The French, of course, had enjoyed a long history of composed dance music, and by the seventeenth century their earlier dance pair of pavane and galliard (see Chapter 22) had been greatly expanded. Sometimes as many as a dozen dances were organized by key into a group, and it was left to the performer to pick and choose a set to create the desired mood. Our English word "suite" simply means a succession of pieces coming in an order pleasing to performer and audience. The audience listened but did not dance. These were stylized dances in which the composer aimed to capture in music the spirit of the dance in question. As one musician of the day commented, they are written "for the refreshment of the ear alone."[1]

Johann Froberger crystallized the dance suite by creating some thirty suites that usually had the same four dances: allemande, courante, sarabande, and gigue.[2] Subsequent composers such as Handel and Bach would add one or more other dances, but these four dances henceforth remained the backbone of the suite. A **dance suite** can therefore be defined as an ordered set of dances (often on the sequence of allemande, courante, sarabande, and gigue) for solo instrument or ensemble, all written in the same key and intended to be performed in a single sitting.

Below are listed the main traits of these four core dances as well as those of other dances sometimes inserted into the suite as fashion or fancy demanded:

- **Allemande.** The name suggests the place of origin of this dance ("allemande" is French for "German"); a stately dance in $\frac{4}{4}$ meter at a moderate tempo with an upbeat and gracefully interweaving lines that create an improvisatory-like style
- **Courante.** A lively dance ("courante" is French for "running") characterized by intentional metrical ambiguity created by means of hemiola—measures of two beats with triple subdivision $\frac{6}{4}$ interplay with those of three beats with duple subdivision $\frac{3}{2}$
- **Sarabande.** A slow, stately dance in $\frac{3}{4}$ with a strong accent on the second beat
- **Gigue.** A fast dance in $\frac{6}{8}$ or $\frac{12}{8}$ with a constant eighth-note pulse that produces a galloping sound; the gigue is sometimes lightly imitative and often used to conclude a suite
- **Minuet.** An elegant dance of French origin in triple meter and performed at a moderate tempo; the only Baroque dance to remain popular in the Classical period
- **Bourrée.** A fast dance in $\frac{4}{4}$ (or in cut time) with a quarter-note upbeat that usually follows a slower dance in $\frac{3}{4}$ such as the sarabande
- **Gavotte.** Another dance of French origin marked by a moderate tempo, duple meter, and four-bar phrases
- **Hornpipe.** An energetic dance of English origin, derived from the country jig, in either $\frac{3}{2}$ or $\frac{2}{4}$

Froberger's Suite No. 6 in C Major is typical of his thirty keyboard suites. It also demonstrates a unique peculiarity of his music: Froberger had a penchant for composing a highly expressive lament as a response to personal or national tragedy. When he witnessed a well-known French lutenist take a fatal tumble down a flight of stairs, he composed a lament in honor of the fallen musician; and when he had been robbed by pirates on his way from Paris to London in 1652 he composed a "plaint" (musical complaint). Sometimes Froberger's laments were independent, free-standing pieces, as is true for the one he composed on the death of Emperor Ferdinand III in 1657. In other instances, Froberger placed the descriptive piece at the opening of a suite, where it serves as an allemande. In Suite No. 6 in C Major, the allemande is entitled *Lamento sopra la dolorosa perdita della Real Maestà di Ferdi-*

❦ FIGURE 34-1
Autograph keyboard score from
the end of the opening *Lamento*
(*Allemande*) of Johann Froberger's
Suite No. 6 in C Major. These
final two staves conclude with
a three-octave C-major scale
ascending to heaven. (Turn
sideways to better see the faces
of the angels.)

Österreichische Nationalbibliothek

nando IV Rè de Romani (*Lament on the occasion of the sad loss of his Royal Majesty Ferdinando IV, King of the Romans*). The son and heir of Froberger's employer, Ferdinand IV, died unexpectedly in 1654. Froberger's lament is full of painful dissonance
and ends with a run up the C major scale, a graphic depiction of the hoped-for ascent of the young man's soul. Indeed, Froberger's autograph manuscript, preserved
today in Vienna (Fig. 34-1), shows the soul-bearing scale being welcomed by the
light of three heavenly angels. The remaining dances of the suite are all in the same
mood, key, and form as the opening *Lamento* (*Allemande*).

 LISTENING CUE

JOHANN FROBERGER
Suite No. 6 in C Major (1654)
Lamento (*Allemande*), *Courante*, *Sarabande*, *Gigue*

CD 5/5–8
Anthology, No. 96a-d

❀ BIBER AND KUHNAU:
THE PROGRAMMATIC SONATA

Johann Froberger wrote mainly suites for solo keyboard, while Heinrich Biber, a
contemporary virtuoso violinist, composed mainly sonatas for violin and basso continuo. In the late seventeenth century, the suite and the sonata had much in common. Both were multi-movement instrumental works with the movements generally
in one key, and both were comprised of a succession of dances (the suite always, the
sonata often). Moreover, both suite and sonata began to display programmatic influence. In **program music** some external influence or non-musical event affects the
general spirit and the specific details of an instrumental composition. We have just
seen how the expected upward spiritual journey of King Ferdinand IV received
musical depiction at the end of the opening movement of Froberger's Suite No. 6.

�*/* FIGURE 34-2

Twice-crossed strings on the violin suggests the theme of Christ's resurrection. This arrangement is one possible way to effect the *scordatura* required for Biber's sonata for the resurrection.

🌟 FIGURE 34-3

The image of the resurrection accompanying Biber's sonata of that name. In the autograph manuscript of Biber's "Mystery" Sonatas, each sonata is prefaced by an engraving that suggests the spiritual meaning of the music to follow. The rather dramatic ascent of Christ from the sepulcher may explain the agitated music with which this sonata opens.

So too in Heinrich Biber's "Mystery" Sonatas, things outside of music shape (provide a program for) a lengthy musical creation.

Heinrich Biber (1644–1704) was a Bohemian-born virtuoso violinist. In 1670 he entered employment at the court of the archbishop of Salzburg in northern Austria (where Mozart and his father would serve some hundred years later), and in 1684 he became Kapellmeister (a coveted position neither Mozart attained). Salzburg was a German-speaking city, but, like most of those in Austria and southern Germany, it sat squarely within the spiritual realm of the Roman Catholic Church. Thus Italian music, and especially Roman-style church music, was very much in favor here. Biber wrote *a cappella* Masses in *stile antico* as well as more flamboyant, large-scale *stile concertato* Masses. He is probably the author of the colossal, fifty-three part *Missa Salisburgensis* (*Mass of Salzburg;* c1682), once ascribed to the Roman master Orazio Benevoli (see Chapter 32).

Despite his skill as a composer of sacred music, Biber is best known today for his instrumental pieces, specifically his programmatic "Mystery" Sonatas composed for Salzburg about 1674. The **"Mystery" Sonatas,** also known as the **"Rosary" Sonatas,** are a set of fifteen sonatas for solo violin and continuo that project through music the sacred devotion of the rosary (votive prayers coming in fifteen groups). During the recitation of each of these groups, the faithful Catholic meditates upon one of fifteen events associated with the life of Christ or the Virgin Mary, keeping count of the prayers by means of rosary beads. Thus the program for the fifteen "Mystery" Sonatas follows a sequence of fifteen miraculous, or mysterious, events in the lives of Christ and Mary: the annunciation, visitation, nativity, crucifixion, resurrection, and ascension, for example. The violinist projects each mystery by means of a solo sonata with one to four movements.

Yet there is another "mystery" in the "Mystery" Sonatas, and that has to do with the tuning of the violin. Biber instructs that the violinist must tune the instrument a different way for each of the fifteen sonatas. The first sonata requires the standard violin tuning with the strings in fifths (g-d'-a'-e"). Subsequent sonatas instruct that the strings must be set at an interval of a third or a fourth, or even an octave, apart. Tuning a string instrument to something other than standard tuning is called ***scordatura*** (from an Italian word literally meaning "mistuning"). The purpose of *scordatura* is to make certain passages easier to play, to produce special effects, and to make the instrument sound more brilliant by emphasizing the resonance of particular strings. Biber's "Mystery" Sonatas provide the most extensive use of *scordatura* in the entire repertory of Western music.

Exactly how *scordatura* works, and how it helps project the meaning of Biber's "Mystery" Sonatas, can be seen in Sonata No. 11, *The Resurrection.* Here the violinist must tune the strings to g-g'-d'-d". This may be accomplished one of two ways: (1) by simply switching the two inner strings and tuning them in octaves with the adjacent outer string; or (2) by tuning them g-d'-g'-d" but twice crossing the inner two strings thereby producing g-g'-d'-d" (Fig. 34-2). This crossing of the instrument adds a visible sign of the resurrection (see the cross on Christ's standard in Fig. 34-3).

No violinist could have learned to play these *scordature* in the "Mystery" Sonatas without great labor. To simplify things, Biber writes out his music as if the violinist has the standard tuning in mind (g-d'-a'-e"). This creates an apparently nonsensical collection of notes on the page (top line in Ex. 34-1), but, owing to the *scordatura,* the written notes are mysteriously transformed into pitches that will sound harmonious with those of the basso continuo (second line in Ex. 34-1).

EXAMPLE 34-1

A *scordatura* emphasizing G's and D's, as in Sonata No. 11, naturally works well in the key of G, for here the G-string and D-string are open strings (not stopped), and the tonic and dominant chords sound especially resonant. Sonata No. 11, in fact, is written almost entirely in G major. Notice also that Biber is fond of writing multiple stops to create his virtuosic violin style. This adds to the resonant sound, but it also gives the impression of two, or sometimes three, independent lines working together; polyphony, even when projected on a melodic instrument like the violin, is very much a hallmark of German Baroque music.

Finally, consider the core of this sonata—the stately second movement. Here Biber has constructed a lengthy chaconne upon a popular Latin hymn *Surrexit Christus hodie* (*Christ has risen today*). The hymn first appears in the basso continuo as a chaconne bass, and upon it Biber then constructs a set of variations for the violin. By means of this hymn the "program" of the sonata is communicated to the faithful. Lest the listener miss the point, the movement concludes with the violin playing the hymn in octave double-stops and the continuo an additional octave below (Ex. 34-2)—an emphatic affirmation of the mystery of Christ's resurrection.

EXAMPLE 34-2

mm. 161-167

LISTENING CUE

HEINRICH BIBER
"Mystery" Sonatas (c1674)
The Resurrection, Movements 1–2

CD 5/9–10
Anthology, No. 97a-b

Heinrich Biber, working at the Catholic court of the archbishop of Salzburg, Austria, was not the only composer to embrace the programmatic sonata. To the north, in the Protestant town of Leipzig, Germany, Johann Kuhnau (1660–1722) did the same. Kuhnau was the cantor of the St. Thomas Church, the immediate predecessor of the great Bach in that position in Leipzig. Kuhnau wrote sacred vocal music for the St. Thomas Church (almost all of it unpublished), and two collections of sonatas and two sets of suites for keyboard (all four published). Today Kuhnau's reputation rests almost exclusively on his last published work for keyboard, a set of six sonatas entitled *Musicalische Vorstellung einiger biblischer Historien* (*Musical Representation of a few Biblical Histories*; 1700). Each sonata in the set attempts to illustrate a particular event from the Old Testament: the combat between David and Goliath, Saul cured by David through music, and Jacob's death and burial, for example. To guide the listener, Kuhnau adds a synopsis of each story in phrases of Italian. Thus the first sonata is entitled *Il combattimento trà David e Goliath* (*The Battle between David and Goliath*) and opens with the phrase "Le bravate di Goliath." The dramatic events within the story are depicted musically by a series of self-contained movements, each having a sound distinctly appropriate to the narrative. Example 34-3 suggests the way in which Kuhnau's explicitly pictorial music works.

EXAMPLE 34-3A

The bravado of Goliath [pompous, dotted rhythms]

EXAMPLE 34-3B

The quavering of the Israelites in the face of the giant and their prayer made to God. [trembling chords that fall down and to which is soon added the chorale tune *Out of the Deep I Cry to Thee*]

EXAMPLE 34-3C

The courage of David and his eagerness to prevail over the pride of his terrifying enemy through his confidence found with the help of God. [David steadfastly remains in the key of C major]

The Doctrine of Affections

In the winter of 1645–1646 the French philosopher René Descartes (1596–1650) published an essay entitled *Les Passions de l'âme* (*Passions of the Soul*), in which he sought to classify and explain the full spectrum of human emotions. With each description of an emotion came a physiological diagnosis, as here in the case of sadness:

> *The definition of Sadness.* Sadness is a disagreeable languor in which consists the discomfort and unrest which the soul receives from evil. . . .
>
> *The movement of the blood and spirits in Sadness.* In sadness, the openings of the heart are much contracted by the small nerve which surrounds them, and the blood of the veins is in nowise agitated, which brings it to pass that very little of it goes toward the heart and yet the passages by which the juice of the food flows from the stomach and the intestines towards the liver remain open, which causes the appetite not to diminish at all, excepting when hatred, which is often united to sadness, closes them.[3]

Obviously, Descartes's understanding of the workings of the mind and body was somewhat different from our own. But his views greatly influenced intellectuals generally and music theorists in particular, both French and German. One such theorist was Johann Mattheson (1681–1764) of Hamburg, Germany, who codified a theory of *Affektenlehre*, or what came to be called the Doctrine of Affections. The **Doctrine of Affections** embodies the Baroque belief that emotions are objective phenomena that can be represented by analogous tones and rhythms. As Mattheson explains in his *Der vollkommene Capellmeister* (*The Complete Music Director*; 1739):

> Those who are learned in the natural sciences [i.e. Descartes] know how our emotions function physically, as it were. It would be advantageous to the composer to have a little knowledge of this subject. Since, for example, joy is an *expansion* of our vital spirits, it follows sensibly and naturally that this affect is best expressed by large and expanded intervals. Sadness, on the other hand, is a *contraction* of those same subtle parts of our bodies. It is, therefore, easy to see that the narrowest intervals are the most suitable. Love is a *diffusion* of the spirits. Thus, to express this passion in composing, it is best to use intervals of that nature. Hope is an *elevation* of the spirit; despair, on the other hand, a *casting down* of the same. These are subjects that can well be represented by sound, especially when other circumstances (tempo in particular) contribute their share. In such a manner one can form a concrete picture of all the emotions and try to compose accordingly.[4]

Of course, composers had long been writing music that gave expression to the emotions, in the text painting of the Renaissance madrigal and in the laments and revenge arias of Baroque opera and cantata, for example. Eighteenth-century musician Mattheson is simply providing a theory, or doctrine, for this phenomenon of the "affects" of music well after the fact. This posterior description demonstrates a maxim in music history: theory follows practice. The important point, however, is that when overt musical depiction entered the seventeenth-century sonata, it proved that music without text (instrumental music) could sway the emotions just as much as music with text. Instrumental music had taken on the same emotive power as vocal music.

EXAMPLE 34-3D

And so it goes. This music is overtly descriptive, indeed onomatopoeic, because it sounds out its own meaning. One French composer even went so far as to set in musical tones the gruesome stages of a Baroque kidney-stone operation (without anesthesia)! To our modern ears, program music of this sort is almost comical, like melodramatic silent film scores or even cartoon music. But around 1700 the insertion of such intensely emotional music into the sonata had a profound result. The programmatic sonatas of Biber and Kuhnau deepened the emotional content of the genre, making the sonata far richer and more satisfying than a series of merely pleasing dance pieces. Instrumental music was appropriating the sort of expressive, and sometimes extravagant, gestures that had been the exclusive preserve of vocal music. Gravity and intensity of expression were the legacy the sonata composers of the Baroque bequeathed to those of succeeding generations, specifically to C.P.E. Bach, Haydn, and Mozart.

DIETERICH BUXTEHUDE AND THE NORTH GERMAN ORGAN TRADITION

The pipe organ is known as the king of instruments, in part because in medieval times it was the only instrument sanctioned within the walls of the church. In truth, organs in churches did not become widespread until the fourteenth century, but thereafter most large institutions in the West had at least one, and often two, instruments to support religious music-making. Building an organ requires precise woodworking skills and a knowledge of metallurgy, physics, and acoustics—all attributes German artisans have traditionally possessed. During the years 1650–1750, north Germany produced some of the most remarkable organs ever fabricated. By the early eighteenth century, large organs with three or four manuals (keyboards) and thousands of pipes had been installed in north German port cities such as Hamburg and Lübeck.

At this time, the commercial cities around the Baltic and North Seas (see Map 34-1) formed a distinct region with regard to politics, culture, and music. Here emerged a particular style of organ composition and performance, one beginning with Jan Sweelinck (1562–1621) in Amsterdam and extending to Jan Reincken (1643?–1722) in Hamburg and to Dieterich Buxtehude (c1637–1707) in Lübeck. The practices of the north German organists greatly influenced J. S. Bach, who heard and played for Reincken and studied with Buxtehude.

Dieterich Buxtehude was the greatest of the north German organ composers. He was born in Denmark, but by 1668 had become organist at the church of St. Mary in Lübeck, Germany, where he remained until his death. (Both Bach and Handel apparently had the opportunity to succeed Buxtehude in this post, but both declined because local custom required the new incumbent to marry his predecessor's daughter!) At the time of Buxtehude's arrival, Lübeck was an important shipping center of nearly 30,000 people, a free city loosely linked to the Holy Roman Empire. At Lübeck's center stood its largest church, St. Mary's, which was Lutheran, like all churches in the city; by 1670 the city fathers had expelled most Catholics, Calvinists, and Jews. St. Mary's had two organs, one near the high altar at the east end of the church for votive services and funerals, and the other a gigantic all-purpose instrument at the west end. A guidebook to the church of 1697 says the following about the organs and music at St. Mary's:

> On the west side, between the two pillars under the towers, one can see the large and magnificent organ, which, like the small organ, is now presided over by the world-famous organist and composer Dieterich Buxtehude. Of particular note is the great Abend-Music, consisting of pleasant vocal and instrumental music, presented yearly on five Sundays between St. Martin's and Christmas, following the Sunday vesper sermon, from 4 to 5 o'clock, by the aforementioned organist as director, in an artistic and praiseworthy manner. This happens nowhere else.[5]

The **Abendmusik** proudly advertised in the guidebook was an hour-long concert of sacred music with arias and recitatives—something akin to a sacred opera or oratorio. A single religious theme unfolded in music over the course of five late-afternoon performances on the Sundays immediately before and during Advent (prior to Christmas). Large crowds flocked to the *Abendmusik* at St. Mary's Church. A report from an early eighteenth-century observer suggests, however, that the populace may have been attracted by things other than great music and the opportunity for spiritual enlightenment.

> The composer [Buxtehude] has never failed also to give an artistic and beautiful setting. However, . . . it is also a great inconvenience that the *Abendmusiken* are held at such an unfriendly and bleak time of the year, namely in the middle of the winter, so that after one has already spent three hours in the cold [for Vespers and the Vespers sermon] one must freeze for a fourth hour as well [for the *Abendmusik*]. The atrocious noise of the mischievous young people and the unruly running and romping about behind the choir take away all the enjoyment that the music might have given, to say nothing of the sins and wickedness that takes place under cover of darkness and poor light.[6]

Such a report reminds us of the limited opportunities for fun and recreation during the long, bleak winters of northern Europe before electricity and central heating. Communal religion, enhanced by voices, instruments, and the organ, was then the chief form of public entertainment. So popular did the *Abendmusik* become at St. Mary's that a special police guard was hired to help maintain order. Among those auditors attracted to these Sunday concerts at St. Mary's was young J.S. Bach, who in 1705 walked some 280 miles to hear them (see also Chapter 39) and who later modeled his own six-part Christmas Oratorio on Lübeck's *Abendmusik*.

Sadly, most of the music Buxtehude composed for the *Abendmusik* has been lost, though the many cantatas surviving under his name are sufficient to give us a sense of his sacred music. Similarly, although Buxtehude composed hundreds of organ pieces (toccatas, preludes, fugues, and chorale settings), fewer than eighty works have escaped the ravages of time. To get an idea of the type of organ piece he wrote in Lübeck, we turn to Buxtehude's *Wie schön leuchtet der Morgenstern* (*How Brightly Shines the Morning Star*), built on a chorale of that name. Recall that a chorale is a monophonic spiritual melody or religious folksong of the Lutheran church—what many Christian denominations today would simply call a hymn (see Chapter 24). The chorale *Wie schön leuchtet der Morgenstern* was one of two melodies composed, or at least adapted, by Lutheran pastor Philipp Nicolai in 1599 (the other is discussed in Chapter 40). Here the shining light of the Lord is equated with the bright star leading to the Christ child, and so this chorale was often heard at Advent and during the *Abendmusik* in Lübeck. The entire chorale is given as Example 34-4.

EXAMPLE 34-4

Wie schön leuch-tet der Mor-gen-stern, voll Gnad' und Wahr-heit von dem Herrn, die sü-sse Wur-zel Jes - se;
Du Sohn Da-vids aus Ja-kobs Stamm, mein Kö-nig und mein Bräu-ti-gam, hast mir mein Herz be - ses-sen.

Lieb - lich, freund - lich, schön und herr-lich, gross und ehr-lich, reich von Ga - ben, hoch und sehr präch-tig er - ha - ben.

How brightly shines the Morning Star, With mercy beaming from afar; The host of heav'n rejoices;
O Righteous Branch, O Jesse's Rod! Thou Son of Man and Son of God! We, too, will lift our voices;
Jesus, Jesus! Holy, holy, yet most lowly, Draw thou near to us; Great Emmanuel, come and hear us.

North German organists made a specialty of projecting the Lutheran chorale on their large and colorful instruments. Buxtehude's forty-seven chorale settings constitute the main part of his organ music. Building on the chorale *Wie schön leuchtet der Morgenstern,* Buxtehude creates a **chorale fantasia,** a lengthy composition for organ that takes a chorale tune as a point of departure but increasingly gives free rein to the composer's imagination. In this case, the chorale is first placed in long notes in the bass with two-voice counterpoint set against it (Ex. 34-5a). Then the tune appears a second time, in the treble with the counterpoint coming below. Because the organ can create very different sorts of sonic colors and assign them to separate musical lines on separate keyboards, the chorale tune can be made to stand out distinctively no matter where in the texture it appears. For that reason, chorale settings are more effective on organ than on harpsichord or clavichord. But, as Buxtehude's piece progresses, his creative fancy more and more obscures the tune. Example 34-5b demonstrates how the composer transforms the opening of the chorale into an energetic fugue subject. Example 34-5c shows how he turns the descending scale at the end of the tune into a concluding theme in first three- and then four-voice counterpoint. This is an impressive composition! Remarkably, north German organists such as Buxtehude were expected to improvise such chorale fantasias on the spot as part of every audition. Without this skill, they could not get a job.

EXAMPLE 34-5A

EXAMPLE 34-5B

EXAMPLE 34-5C

 LISTENING CUE

DIETERICH BUXTEHUDE
Wie schön leuchtet der Morgenstern (c1690)

CD 5/11
Anthology, No. 98

JOHANN PACHELBEL AND THE SOUTH GERMAN TRADITION

Who has not heard Pachelbel's Canon? Although he is popularly known today only through this one composition, Johann Pachelbel (1653–1706) was a prolific composer who wrote hundreds of pieces, vocal as well as instrumental. Pachelbel was born in Nuremberg, in southern Germany, studied in the Catholic church tradition in Vienna, worked in the central German Lutheran town of Eisenach (where he befriended the Bach family), and ended his days at the Lutheran church of St. Sebaldus back in Nuremberg (see Map 34–1). Pachelbel himself was keenly aware that he had been trained in the south German and Austrian tradition, not that of the north. What exactly differentiated the north and south German styles?

To contrast the two, compare the beginning of Buxtehude's setting of *Wie schön leuchtet der Morgenstern* (see Ex. 34-5) with that of Pachelbel (Ex. 34-6). First, however, keep in mind that Buxtehude's is a chorale fantasia (with the tune in G), while Pachelbel's is a chorale prelude (with the tune in F), and that north and south German composers wrote both types of pieces. A **chorale prelude** is a work for organ that sets a Lutheran chorale tune, surrounding it with counterpoint and florid embellishment. It is called a "prelude" because the organist played it immediately before the congregation sang the chorale in the Sunday service. (For more on the German chorale prelude, see Chapter 39.) Different from the lengthy chorale fantasia, the chorale prelude sounds the tune just once, enough to remind the faithful of the melody they are about to sing. A typical chorale fantasia takes six or seven minutes to perform, while the average chorale prelude lasts only half that time. So, what is the stylistic difference between the two German traditions? The southern style is a bit more tuneful. Pachelbel's counterpoint flows gently along, whereas Buxtehude's denser counterpoint is marked by a high degree of virtuosic and improvisatory-like gestures. In Pachelbel's chorale prelude, melody and counterpoint are joined in equal measure. It is primarily this greater fondness of lyricism that sets apart the south German tradition from the more rigid north German one.

EXAMPLE 34-6

LISTENING CUE

JOHANN PACHELBEL

Wie schön leuchtet der Morgenstern (c1690)

CD 5/12

Anthology, No. 99

This same mixture of counterpoint and pleasing melody marks Pachelbel's most famous work, his Canon in D Major (c1690). The Canon is part of a brief instrumental suite consisting of just a canon and a concluding gigue. The canonic process unfolds in three violin parts, one imitating another at the temporal interval of two measures. Below the canon, a basso continuo sets forth a relentless two-bar *basso ostinato*, which appears twenty-eight times. As the *ostinato* churns away beneath, the canon above gathers rhythmic energy and ascends to ever-higher peaks (Ex. 34-7). Though a musical commonplace for us today, Pachelbel's Canon amply demonstrates that in this south German music rigorous counterpoint (a three-voice canon) can generate soaring lyricism.

EXAMPLE 34-7

 LISTENING CUE

JOHANN PACHELBEL
Canon in D Major (c1690)

Book Companion Website (http://schirmer.wadsworth.com/wright_1e)
Anthology, No. 100

SUMMARY

Composers in Germany and Austria were important in the development of seventeenth-century instrumental music. Johann Froberger established the dance suite as the primary genre of music for string keyboard instruments (harpsichord and clavichord). Through programmatic works such as his "Mystery" Sonatas for violin, Heinrich Biber added greater gravity and breadth of expression to the sonata. Here we see an early demonstration that purely instrumental pieces could project the same sort of deep emotional expression as did the texted vocal music of the Baroque period.

Historically, the Germans and the French have excelled in organ-making, the German skill in crafting precision instruments of all sorts proving a special advantage in this regard. The organ's multiple keyboards and separate groups of pipes not only encouraged the creation of multiple musical lines but also made it possible to project a religious melody (chorale tune or chant) with distinct clarity. The north German organ tradition, exemplified by the chorale fantasia of Dieterich Buxtehude, is thus marked by intense counterpoint, the use of a chorale tune, as well as plenty of virtuosic display showing vestiges of improvisation. The south German tradition, evident in the chorale prelude of Johann Pachelbel, tempered the Nordic rigor with increased lyricism. The great German organ composer of the next generation, J.S. Bach, would fashion a synthesis of these northern and southern styles.

KEY TERMS

dance suite	bourrée	*scordatura*
allemande	gavotte	Doctrine of Affections
courante	hornpipe	*Abendmusik*
sarabande	program music	chorale fantasia
gigue	"Mystery" Sonatas	chorale prelude
minuet	("Rosary" Sonatas)	

Chapter

Music in Paris and at the Court of Versailles: Vocal Music

Today the French are a proud and sometimes prickly lot, though in fairness they have an extraordinary amount about which to be proud and prickly. Their nationalism, belief in the superiority of their culture, and suspicion of foreign influence is not something unique to modern times. In fact, it is built upon ancient cultural icons extending back to the *Marseillaise* of the Revolution, to Joan of Arc, and to the great Gothic cathedrals—all French creations. But no French man or woman was ever grander, prouder, or more regal than King Louis XIV (Fig. 35-1), the Sun King (*Roi soleil*), source of light for all the French people, or so he said.

Louis XIV personified the absolute monarch. Indeed, his exceptionally long and authoritarian reign (1643–1715) inspired the political theory of **absolutism**—that ultimate power in the state rested in the hands of a king who claimed to rule by divine right. Whatever Louis wanted, Louis got. Wherever Louis was, there was the French government. As he himself famously said: "I *am* the State!" ("L'État, c'est moi!"). Louis strengthened and expanded the nation, pushing its borders to their modern limits and making France the leading power in Europe. He set the standard for monarchs across Europe, to the point that the second half of the seventeenth century and early years of the eighteenth have come to be seen as the "Age of Louis XIV" or the "Age of Absolutism."

As an example of the *grandeur* to which Louis aspired, consider **Versailles** (see Part IV timeline). In 1669 the Sun King determined to build a new home for himself and consolidate his power some twelve miles southwest of Paris. Over the course of twenty years, forests were cleared, rivers diverted, lakes created, and a colossal palace—actually, a complete city—was constructed by a workforce approaching 36,000. When finished, Versailles stood as a monumental symbol of the French absolutist

FIGURE 35-1

King Louis XIV as painted by Hyacinthe Rigaud about 1700. The portrait captures the king's sense of majesty and authority.

Bridgeman Art Library

state. It was also home to thousands of governmental officials, courtiers, and artists. Here ballets and operas were staged, orchestral dance suites performed, and Masses and motets sung in the royal chapel. Toward the end of his reign, Louis XIV employed between 150 and 200 musicians at any given time. Louis controlled and centralized the creation of art music, much as he did governmental administration.

Consequently, musical talent was not scattered around the cities of France. It was concentrated at the king's court, whether at Versailles or the several much-smaller royal residences in Paris, such as the Louvre, the Tuileries, and the Palais Royal. Moreover, the royal musicians usually were not Italians, as was the case at many other European courts at this time, but were mostly French men and women.

The extent of French bias against foreign influence can be seen in the people's reaction to Italian opera. Italian opera was gradually conquering most of late-seventeenth-century Europe. Cardinal Mazarin, an Italian-born prelate who directed the French government during Louis XIV's minority, tried to establish an Italian opera company in Paris by bringing Italian opera there several times between 1645 and 1662. But French listeners did not warm to fully sung drama offered in a foreign language (Italian) in which the highest vocal parts were often sung by castrated males (castrati). "We almost died of boredom," said a lady of the court.[1] Instead, the French preferred their own special genre of theatrical music called *ballet de cour*, one that emphasized not vocal virtuosity, but dance, choral singing, and spectacle.

✦ BALLET DE COUR

If the English historically have been obsessed with choral church music and the Italians with opera, the French have been enamored with dance. Indeed, the roots of modern ballet are to be found in a distinctive French genre of theatrical display called *ballet de cour*. A **ballet de cour** (court ballet) was a type of ballet danced at the French royal court from the late sixteenth to the late seventeenth century in which members of the court appeared alongside professional dancers. Sets of dances and choruses, simple airs (called *airs de cour*), instrumental interludes, pantomime, and lavish scenery all combined to project a loosely assembled dramatic theme. Much of the *ballet de cour* was taken up with eye-popping "production numbers" involving large groups of similarly costumed singers and dancers. Invariably, the ballet opened with a prologue in which allegorical figures sang the praises of the king and the wisdom of his rule. And similarly it concluded with a *grand ballet*, a final grand dance in which the *grands seigneurs* (great lords) of the court, and often the king himself, danced. In all, Louis XIV appeared in some eighty roles in forty major ballets. Through such carefully choreographed exercises, Louis could affirm aspects of an elitist culture then important to the French monarchy: rank, formality, protocol, discipline, and a sense of style.

As for the music of the *ballet de cour*: some of it was choral music sung during dances, and some of it was a special type of French solo song called the **air de cour**— a simple, strophic song for single voice or a small group of soloists. In addition to this vocal music, the *ballet de cour* included purely instrumental music involving sets of dances popular at that time (see Chapter 34): galliards, minuets, bourées, courantes, sarabandes, and the like. These were played by the French court orchestra, which was built around a core of string instruments called the **Vingt-quatre violons du roi**: twenty-four instruments of the violin family (six violins, twelve violas, and six *basse de violons* [oversize cellos]). In the tradition of seventeenth-century French orchestral music, the *Vingt-quatre violons* played five-part music consisting of treble and bass as well as three middle parts played by the twelve violas divided into groups of four. To these could be added harpsichords, trumpets, drums, and the *Douze grands hautbois* (twelve great oboes) of the royal wind band. On occasion, the orchestra for the *ballet de cour* grew to eighty instrumentalists, a size appropriate for the lavish spectacles of the Sun King.

The image of Louis as Sun King first appeared publicly in a *ballet de cour* presented on 3 February 1653 in which the fifteen-year-old king danced the role of the Rising Sun (Fig. 35-2). Louis equated himself with the Greek god of the sun, Apollo, who watched over the arts and sciences generally, and music in particular. Appearing alongside the king that evening was a young Italian-born choreographer and musician named Jean-Baptiste Lully. Lully himself would soon create some twenty-six *ballets de cour*, more than any other composer. The association of King Louis and composer Lully, and the meteoric rise of Lully, date from that moment.

 FIGURE 35-2

Louis XIV as the Sun in the *Ballet de la Nuit*, 1653.

JEAN-BAPTISTE LULLY AND *TRAGÉDIE LYRIQUE*

Giovanni Battista Lulli (1632–1687) was born in Florence and recruited as a youth to serve as an Italian teacher and dancing master to a cousin of the French king. After he caught the attention of Louis XIV in 1653, the king appointed him *Compositeur de la musique instrumentale* (1653). Other titles followed, including *Maître de la musique de la famille royale* (Master of Music for the Royal Family) in 1662. That same year, Lulli became a naturalized French citizen under the name of Jean-Baptiste Lully. With the king's unflinching support, the enterprising and often ruthless Lully gradually gained exclusive authority over public vocal music. Lully's hegemony reached the point that almost no piece of polyphonic art music could be performed before the French aristocracy without his permission. Lully himself had become an absolutist. He might well have said: "La Musique, c'est moi!"

One of the musical institutions over which Lully gained exclusive control was the *Académie royale de musique*. King Louis XIV established this company (under a slightly different name) in 1669 as a way to encourage the growth of French opera, just as he had founded similar academies to foster painting (1648), dance (1661), literature (1663), the sciences (1669), and architecture (1671). The **Académie royale de musique** was, in effect, an opera company directly licensed and indirectly financed by the king. It performed in the center of Paris at the Palais Royal and was, in everything but title, the Paris Opéra. France now had a national opera company, but it had no French operas to perform. During the 1670s, Lully set about to remedy this deficiency, and in so doing created a new and unique genre of theatrical music, French *tragédie lyrique*.

French theater reached its zenith during the second half of the seventeenth century, in the comedies of Molière (1622–1673) and in the classical tragedies of Pierre Corneille (1606–1684) and Jean Racine (1639–1699). For musical theater, the court enjoyed its own special brand of ballet (*ballet de cour*), as we have seen. Now Lully brought a new kind of entertainment to the stage: French opera, first called *tragédie en musique*, then **tragédie lyrique.** To create this distinctly French style of opera, Lully fused classical French tragedy with traditional French ballet (*ballet de cour*). This new genre, French opera, embraced ballet. Accordingly, the action of the opera might be interrupted at any moment by a **divertissement,** a lavishly choreographed diversionary interlude with occasional singing. Thus *tragédie lyrique* was not a solo singer's opera, like Italian opera, but a dancing actor's opera. Indeed, the principal singers were called *acteurs* and *actrices* in keeping with the tradition of French classical theatre. Lully's librettist, Philippe Quinault (1635–1688), drew his subjects from ancient Greek and Roman mythology and from tales of medieval chivalry. But no matter what the plot, the aim was always the same: to praise the king and reaffirm the values of the prevailing aristocratic culture.

Perhaps no *tragédie lyrique* better represents this genre than Lully's five-act *Armide* (1686), the last of his thirteen French operas. King Louis XIV, inspired by an earlier Italian poem, suggested this tale of medieval chivalry and magic-induced love to Lully. The stage is set near Jerusalem during the First Crusade (1095–1099). The sorceress Armide reluctantly falls in love with the most heroic of all the crusaders, Renaud, and then captures his affection by means of a magic spell. Ultimately, Renaud (a shill for King Louis XIV) comes to his senses and rejects Armide, choosing Duty over the illusion of Love.

Armide opens with a **French overture**, a distinctive type of instrumental prelude created by Lully. (Our English word "overture" comes from the French "ouverture," an opening.) A French overture begins with a slow section in duple meter marked by stately dotted rhythms (suggesting the pomp and grandeur of the court), followed by a fast triple-meter section in imitative counterpoint, and finally a return to the slow, stately style of the opening. Because most later composers like Handel and Bach dropped the slow third section, the French overture came to be known as a two-section piece: slow and dotted, then fast and fugal. Thereafter, throughout the remainder of the Baroque period, a French overture could be used to introduce an opera, ballet, oratorio, or instrumental dance suite.

Following the French overture and a prologue obliquely praising the king, the action begins. In Lully's day, *Armide* was known as "the lady's opera" because sorceress Armide dominates the stage. To love or to kill the hero Renaud, that is her dilemma. Armide's inner conflict is most clearly evident at the end of Act II in a scene beginning "Enfin il est en ma puissance" ("Finally, he is in my power"). Here she intends to stab the sleeping Renaud, but love holds her back. Armide expresses her uncertainty in a new type of singing developed by Lully called **récitatif ordinaire** (ordinary recitative). Ironically, this sort of recitative is anything but ordinary. Although still accompanied only by continuo, it is noteworthy for its length, vocal range, and generally dramatic quality. Here we see clearly the difference between Italian recitative of the period and recitative in Lully's *tragédie lyrique*. While the Italian recitative involves rapid declamation within a rather narrow range (see Anthology, No. 91a), French *récitatif ordinaire* is far more elastic. There are rapid passages that recall Italian simple recitative, but also expansive moments that sound much like a florid aria. Notice also the frequent changes of meter. Poet Quinault has fashioned verse with lines of irregular length. Composer Lully sets them within measures of changing length so that the ends of the lines (always stressed in French) come on downbeats (Ex. 35-1). Lully had carefully studied French declamation, as projected on the Parisian stage by actors in the plays of Corneille and Racine. In this example of *récitatif ordinaire*, Lully captures the drama of the moment not only by assigning Armide erratic melodic leaps that suggest confusion but also by inserting unexpected rests that imply hesitation—to kill or not to kill Renaud.

EXAMPLE 35-1

Finally, he is in my power, this superb conqueror. The charm of sleep brings him within my vengeful spell…

For the first performance of *Armide* in 1686, the role of Armide was sung by soprano Marie Le Rochois (1658–1728), who gained something of a cult following because of the way she played this scene. As one fan observed:

> Dagger in hand, ready to pierce the breast of Renaud, Fury animated her features. [Yet] Love took hold of her heart. The one and the other agitated her in turn, pity and tenderness succeeded at the end, and Love was left the victor. What true and beautiful poses! What different movements and expressions in her eyes and on her face during this soliloquy of twenty-nine lines ["Enfin il est en ma puissance"]. . . One can say that it is the greatest piece in all our opera and the most difficult to perform well.[2]

Of course, Armide yields to her heart. To reflect this decision, Lully changes the music from *récitatif ordinaire* to a resolute, yet dance-like air in the style of an *air de cour* (Ex. 35-2). In Lully's French opera, dancers are never far from the center of the action. Moving to the strains of this charming air, magical zephyrs now transport Armide and Renaud to a place where they may enjoy the pleasures of love (Fig. 35-3). Ultimately, Renaud abandons Armide to heed the call of duty. The enraged Armide sets fire to her palace and escapes high across the stage in a flying chariot, bringing the opera to a spectacular end.

🌿 FIGURE 35-3
Armide uses her seductive powers to capture the heart of Renaud in a painting by François Boucher, created about 1733.

Lully Kills Himself Conducting

Jean-Baptiste Lully died shortly after the creation of *Armide*, and he did so in a very odd way. On 8 January 1687 Lully went to a Parisian church to conduct a religious work, his *Te Deum*, in a performance involving more than a hundred musicians. To keep them together, he used a large pointed baton to signal the beat, and in so doing he stabbed himself in the foot. The foot became infected and, little more than two months later, Lully died from gangrene. (Ironically, the performance of the *Te Deum* was organized to give thanks for the recent recovery of King Louis XIV from illness.)

While waving a large stick or staff through the air may seem a strange way to set a beat, this was a common practice when conducting religious music in the seventeenth century. With smaller, single choirs of the Renaissance, it was entirely possible to follow visually the motion of the hand of a leader, and many paintings of the period show a choir director manually giving the beat in the air. With the advent of multiple choirs and polychoral music in the Baroque, however, distances between singers increased and coordination of voices became more of a challenge. A large staff, visible at a great distance, was needed. (Even today experienced performers know that, when multiple groups are separated by distance, or perhaps even placed offstage, it is essential not to listen to the sound, which arrives late, but rather to watch the conductor's beat.) At French churches in the seventeenth century, conductors were urged to strike the beat ("Frappez la mesure"). A Frenchman in Rome in 1638 reports that he saw ten choirs held together by a principal conductor who struck the beat (*battoit la principale mesure*) while ten assistant conductors, one with each of the ten choirs, duplicated his motions. This Baroque practice—musicians watching a staff at a great distance—is still used today in marching bands, where performers follow the beat given by a drum major.

EXAMPLE 35-2

Come, come, support my desires, demons, transform yourselves into favorable winds.

🎵 LISTENING CUE

JEAN-BAPTISTE LULLY
Armide (1686)
Overture
"Enfin il est en ma puissance"

CD 5/13–14
Anthology, No. 101a–b

To sum up: French *tragédie lyrique*, created by Jean-Baptiste Lully, was a new genre of opera that fused elements of *ballet de cour* and traditional French tragic theater. Differing markedly from Italian opera, it possessed the following characteristics:

- **Structure**: requires five acts, following the model of traditional French and English tragedy, rather than the three acts of Italian opera
- **Libretto:** draws on mythological or chivalric topics to create a thinly disguised allegory praising the king and reaffirming the elitist values of the court and the aristocracy generally

- **Overture:** begins with a French overture, not an Italian overture (a sinfonia)
- **Singing:** done mainly in *récitatif ordinaire*; involves little of the virtuosic vocal display then coming into Italian opera
- **Voices:** uses female sopranos, never castrati
- **Chorus:** plays a major role in large-scale choral-dance scenes
- **Dance:** is as important as singing to the overall impact of the work; choreographed *divertissements* regularly interrupt the flow of the drama
- **Spectacle and special effects:** brought about by lavish costumes and elaborate stage machinery, all designed to please the audience and satisfy the ego of the king

❋ RELIGIOUS MUSIC

The fact that Jean-Baptiste Lully was mortally wounded when conducting a lengthy motet (his own *Te Deum*) proves, if nothing else, that not all music at the French court was opera and ballet. As King Louis XIV entered old age, he assumed an increasingly pious life, and his court took on a more devout decor. Not just Lully but other, younger composers were now encouraged to provide sacred music for the king and his relatives. Among these composers were Marc-Antoine Charpentier (1643–1704), who wrote eleven Masses and some 207 motets of various sorts, and Michel-Richard de Lalande (1657–1726), who specialized in writing *grands motets* for the court, some seventy-seven in all. Such works might be heard in religious services at the chapel of Versailles, at many of the Jesuit churches and colleges around Paris, or at the king's Sainte-Chapelle on the Île de la Cité, where Charpentier served as music director from 1698 until his death. When monopolistic Lully departed the scene, Italian-style church music had a chance to gain a foothold. Charpentier studied with Giacomo Carissimi for three years in Rome (see Chapter 32), and he introduced Italian oratorio into France. The sacred cantata, also bearing a strongly Italian imprint, likewise came to France at this time, owing in part to the work of Elizabeth Jacquet de La Guerre (1665–1729).

❋ ELIZABETH JACQUET DE LA GUERRE AND THE *CANTATE FRANÇAISE*

King Louis XIV was not averse to hiring talented female artists. There were professional female dancers in his *ballet de cour*, leading *actrices* in the French opera, and even female sopranos in the royal chapel—this at a time when women did not generally appear as solo singers in churches throughout Europe. About 1670 King Louis heard a five-year-old prodigy named Elizabeth Jacquet sing and play harpsichord, and he granted her a place at court as a performing musician under the care of his principal mistress, Madame de Montespan (Louis's piety came later). A journal of the day commented on her ability to compose and to transpose a piece to any key upon demand. At the age of nineteen, Jacquet left Versailles to marry the organist Marin de La Guerre and thereafter assumed the name Elizabeth Jacquet de La Guerre (Fig. 35-4). She established herself in Paris, giving lessons and concerts, and continuing to compose. Jacquet de La Guerre's output was not large, but what she produced was of high quality, notably her suites for solo harpsichord and her violin sonatas. She also wrote an opera, a *tragédie lyrique* entitled *Céphale et Procris* (1694), the first composed in France by a woman. Her twelve cantatas in French on subjects drawn from the Old Testament are testimony to the growing popularity of the cantata in France in the early years of the eighteenth century.

❀ FIGURE 35-4

Posthumous medallion honoring Elizabeth Jacquet de La Guerre, created in 1732. The reverse of the portrait shows her seated at a harpsichord with the motto "I competed for the prize against the great musicians," implying that she was the equal of her male competitors.

"One talks only of cantatas, only cantatas are advertised at the street corners," said an observer of contemporary Parisian life.[3] Here is evidence that early eighteenth-century France witnessed a flowering of the cantata, both secular and sacred. The cantata, like its instrumental counterpart the sonata, was a product of Italy that by 1700 had made its way over the Alps. By 1730, some 1,200 cantatas had appeared in print in France. Needless to say, the **cantate française,** as it was called, set a French, not an Italian, text. But, in other ways, it was identical to the late seventeenth-century Italian cantata (see Anthology No. 91a–b). A soloist told a story in simple recitative and then, intermittently, the same singer reflected upon these events in ensemble-accompanied arias or in arias with basso continuo only. Succumbing to the Italian rage for the *da capo* aria developed by Alessandro Scarlatti, most of the arias were in **ABA** form. Librettists drew upon either classical mythology (for the secular cantata) or scripture (for the sacred cantata). These were dramas in miniature, for a single character, occasionally two. Thus a *cantate française* can be defined as a piece of chamber music projecting a short mythological or scriptural drama; the story, sung in French, unfolds in a succession of recitatives and arias for solo voice (or duet) accompanied by basso continuo and, occasionally, a small orchestra.

Elizabeth Jacquet de La Guerre published three books of *cantates françaises*, in 1708, 1711, and 1715, respectively. Both of the first two are entitled *Cantates françaises sur des sujets tirez de l'Ecriture* (*French cantatas drawn from subjects from Scripture*). Both portray events in the lives of heroes and heroines of the Old Testament, and both were dedicated to the grandest of all contemporary patrons, King Louis XIV. Like all sacred cantatas, they were intended to provide music for private spiritual reflection, be it in a grand salon or a modest home.

Perhaps it is not surprising that Jacquet de La Guerre, a woman working in the mostly male profession of music, had a special fondness for heroic female characters in biblical history and therefore named cantatas after them: the daughter of Jephte, Judith, Esther, Rachel, and Suzanna, to be specific. We have met the dutiful daughter of Jephte before in Giacomo Carissimi's oratorio of that name (see Chapter 32). Jacquet de La Guerre goes over the same thematic ground as Carissimi but uses neither multiple characters nor a chorus to comment on the action; hers is a cantata, not an oratorio. Her libretto is not in Italian but French, a French that has a certain restrained quality owing to its third-person narrative. Jacquet de La Guerre adopts for all her arias the Italian-born *da capo* aria form (**ABA**). Moreover, she creates luxuriant Italian-style vocal lines with lengthy melismas in the arias (Ex. 35-3) and supports the rapidly shifting emotions of the recitative with rich, Italianate harmonic changes (Ex. 35-4). In sum, Jacquet de La Guerre effects an impressive synthesis of Italian "passion" and French "cool." French musicians of the time referred to this union as "*les goûts réunis*" (the two styles united).

EXAMPLE 35-3

Jephté returns full of glory…

EXAMPLE 35-4

The daughter of Jephté, full of joy, exits from the palace and hastens before him; you will see her all too soon, unfortunate father, alas!

 LISTENING CUE

ELIZABETH JACQUET DE LA GUERRE
Jephté (1711)
Aria, "Jephté revient"
Recitative, "La Fille de Jepthé"

CD 5/15–16
Anthology, No. 102a-b

 SUMMARY

French musical institutions flourished, both in Paris and at the royal palace of Versailles, during the long and absolute rule of King Louis XIV (1643–1715). French *ballet de cour* was a unique blend of ballet and choral singing, interspersed with airs and instrumental interludes, all of which was intended to glorify the monarchy. Beginning in 1673, Jean-Baptiste Lully created a new genre of musical theater called *tragédie lyrique*, French national opera with a distinctly Gallic flavor. Noticeably different from the then-dominant Italian opera, French *tragédie lyrique,* typified by Lully's *Armide* (1686), begins with a French overture and is marked by a style of vocal music in which the singer carefully declaims a French text in a flexible and expansive style of recitative called *récitatif ordinaire.* The heroic-tragic drama is regularly interrupted by *divertissements* involving ballet, solo and choral singing, and

court. Queen Anne (wife of Louis XIII) took up the instrument and so too did Cardinal Richelieu, leader of the French government during the regency of this young king. "It would be difficult to imagine anything more ridiculous than to see him [Richelieu] take his lessons from [lutenist] Gaultier." Though a lute-playing cardinal seemed absurd to this contemporary observer, Richelieu's lessons suggest how pervasive the lute had become in seventeenth-century French aristocratic circles. For the French courtier, playing lute and dancing were two necessary social graces.

The teacher of Cardinal Richelieu, Ennemond Gaultier (1575–1651), was one of a half-dozen musicians working at this time in and around Paris named Gaultier (or Gautier). Equally famous was his younger cousin Denis Gaultier (1597?–1672). The older, and then the younger, Gaultier dominated lute playing in Parisian salons at mid-century. Both seem to have composed only for lute and both seem to have written mainly dance pieces belonging to suites for lute.

The dance suite in France grew out of the practice of pairing dances such as the pavane and galliard during the Renaissance (see Chapter 22). The vogue of the *ballet de cour* (see Chapter 35) made dancing fashionable and brought new dances to prominence, including the allemande, courante, sarabande, and gigue (see Chapter 34). By 1630 these had spread to the repertory for lute and were grouped together in loosely organized suites according to key and/or tuning.

Throughout the Renaissance the standard tuning for the lute involved mainly fourths (G-c-f-a-d'-g'), much like today's guitar tuning (E-A-d-g-b-e'). During the seventeenth century, however, other tunings emerged. Perhaps more important, strings were added to the bass to generate the pitches F, E, E♭, D, and perhaps C'—this so that the lute could participate more effectively as a basso continuo instrument. At mid-century a suite of dances was often preceded by an indication of the tuning appropriate for the group of pieces to follow.

Denis Gaultier's *La Rhétorique des dieux* (*The Rhetoric of the Gods*; c1652) is a sumptuous culmination of the long history of French music for the lute (Fig. 36-1). *La Rhétorique des dieux* is not a widely disseminated print of lute music, but a unique manuscript put together by a group of music-loving admirers of Denis Gaultier. Here are found twelve suites by Gaultier (some incomplete) arranged in pairs of modes—Dorian and Hypodorian, Phrygian and Hypophrygian, and so on—covering all twelve of the late Renaissance church modes. Most of the pieces are dances, but some have emblematic titles and descriptions suggesting to the listener the meaning of the music. For example, one piece is entitled *Apollo the Orator* and is followed by the following lines: "Apollo [god of music] having assumed the human form of Gaultier, displays here all the powers of his eloquence, and by force of his [musical] persuasion makes his listeners pay the keenest attention." Gaultier is the musical "orator" through whom the gods communicate to those on earth.

Commencing the third suite of *La Rhétorique des dieux* is an allemande with the title *Tombeau de Madamoiselle Gaultier* (correctly translated *Lament for Gaultier's Wife*). Here Gaultier speaks to his wife, but only after he is dead! A **tombeau** (French for "tomb") is an instrumental piece commemorating someone's death. Gaultier wanted to commemorate his own demise and leave his wife a brief musical monument of himself; she did, in fact, outlive the composer. The Gaultiers (Ennemond and Denis) were the first to write *tombeaux*, though the tradition continued in France well into the twentieth century. For

✿ F I G U R E   3 6 - 1
The title page of *La Rhétorique des dieux* (c1652), in which one god holds the title of the work interlined with lute tablature and another plays a lute containing as many as ten strings and/or courses (pairs of strings).

this *tombeau* in honor of himself, Denis selected the Phrygian mode, an apposite choice considering the long association of the Phrygian mode and lamentation (see, for example, Josquin's *Miserere*, Chapter 21). But there is more, for Gaultier begins and ends in F♯ minor. In the Baroque era F♯ minor was a highly remote and indeed unusual key, which would have sounded out of tune and thus painful.[1] The full impact of the Phrygian mode, however, may have been lessened by the addition of chromatic inflections and leading tones which have the effect of transforming the Phrygian mode into the more modern melodic minor scale, here transposed to F♯. In fact, the music throughout *La Rhétorique des dieux* conforms more to the newly emerging major-minor tonality than it does to the older sound of the twelve church modes.

A glance at the score of Denis Gaultier's *Tombeau* reveals a musical texture typical of lute music of the period, one called *style brisé*. **Style brisé** (literally "broken style") is a modern term for a type of discontinuous texture in which chords are broken apart and the notes enter one by one. Voices seem to dart in and out. Such a texture is inherent in lute music because the sounds of the lute are delicate and quickly evaporate. Consider the opening of the *Tombeau* (Ex. 36-1). Sometimes there seem to be four voices in the texture, sometimes only two or just one, as on the downbeat of bar four. We hear a bit of plucking here, a bit there—as appropriate to the lute. Yet, in this fragmented environment, a compelling melody is not easily established. In bars 15–17, for example, melody seems to be sacrificed to the pleasures of chordal strumming (Ex. 36-2). Such a style is well suited to the lighter sound and generally lighter musical repertory of the lute, though musicians soon came to adopt it as well for the harpsichord. J.S. Bach's famous opening prelude to the first book of The Well-Tempered Clavier (Ex. 36-3) adopts *style brisé* but transforms it into particularly German rigid arpeggio patterns.

EXAMPLE 36-1

EXAMPLE 36-2

EXAMPLE 36-3

LISTENING CUE

DENIS GAULTIER
La Rhétorique des dieux (c1652)
Tombeau de Madamoiselle Gaultier

CD 5/17
Anthology, No. 103

Adding more and more strings to its lower range made the already-difficult lute even more challenging to play. Larger lutes had as many as twenty-one strings to tune, a time-consuming process. "I have had the pleasure of hearing many a lute tuned, but few played," remarked an exasperated listener of the day. In the second half of the seventeenth century the easily strummed guitar and the colorful, powerful harpsichord replaced the lute as the chamber instrument of choice in France.

 ## THE COUPERINS: FRENCH HARPSICHORD MUSIC

After the Bach family, the Couperin clan forms the most illustrious of all musical dynasties. During the reign of Louis XIV and beyond there were at least a dozen Couperins, both male and female, who made a living as organists, string players, harpsichordists, and composers in Paris. Of these, the most distinguished were Louis Couperin (1626–1661) and his nephew François (1668–1733) called Le Grand ("the Great"). The professional seat of the Couperin family was the parish church of St. Gervais, still standing on the Right Bank of Paris near the Seine River. For nearly 175 years, one Couperin or another served as organist at this splendid Baroque church. In addition, the more talented among them, including Louis and François, were instrumentalists at the royal court.

Louis Couperin is remembered today for one important achievement: he popularized the unmeasured prelude. An **unmeasured prelude** (*prélude non mesuré*) is an opening piece without indications for rhythmic duration or metrical organization. In other words, it has no bar lines and is rhythmically free. The ancestor of the unmeasured prelude for harpsichord was the unmeasured lute prelude. Here a performer moved his fingers freely over the strings to warm up and check the tuning. By the mid seventeenth century, harpsichord composers had adopted the genre as an effective way to open their keyboard suites.

Louis Couperin's unmeasured Prelude in A Minor is the best known of the fourteen that survive under his name. Inspiration for it likely came from the German composer Johann Froberger, for a manuscript preserving this Prelude in A Minor calls it "Prélude à l'imitation de Monsieur Froberger." Froberger, it will be recalled, visited Paris in 1651–1652 and helped standardize the harpsichord suite (see Chapter 34). The opening of the first section of Couperin's prelude (Ex. 35-5), in fact, seems to be an "unmeasuring" of the opening of Froberger's Toccata No. 1 in A Minor (compare Exs. 36-4 and 36-5). Here the unmeasured prelude loosens the already loose toccata.

EXAMPLE 36-4

EXAMPLE 36-5

Publishers eventually tired of dealing with the bizarre-looking notation of the unmeasured prelude. Composers, however, continued to embrace the newfound freedom of the genre in various ways throughout the eighteenth century. J.S. Bach's well-known *Chromatic Fantasy* was conceived in this freer spirit, and his son C.P.E. Bach wrote unbarred fantasias (see Chapter 43). A French composer summed up the main virtue of the unmeasured prelude when he said "because it is unmeasured, one plays it as one wishes."[2]

It was with good reason François Couperin (1668–1733) was called Le Grand ("the Great"). He surely was the greatest of the Couperins and, arguably, of all French Baroque instrumental composers. J.S. Bach copied Couperin's harpsichord music into the keyboard tutorial he prepared for his wife (the Anna Magdalena Bach Book); Johannes Brahms was one of the co-editors of the first complete edition of Couperin's harpsichord music; and both Debussy and Ravel composed pieces in his honor, the latter writing a belated *Tombeau de Couperin* (see Chapter 67).

François Couperin was born and died in Paris and, like his forebears and descendants, served as organist at the church of St. Gervais. But he also was a leading musician at the court of Louis XIV during the declining days of the Sun King, serving as *organiste du roi* and then as the king's personal harpsichordist. Couperin composed most of his sacred music—including the exquisitely beautiful *Leçons de ténèbre* for Holy Week—for the king's chapel at Versailles. Likewise, Couperin wrote most of his chamber music for the court, including his *Concerts royaux* (*Royal Concerts*, 1722) and *Les Goûts réunis* (*The Tastes United*, 1724), an exercise in melding Italian and French musical idioms. Couperin further showed his love of the Italian style in a trio sonata entitled *Apothéose de Corelli* (1724), yet he quickly followed this with one complimentary to the French style called *Apothéose de Lully* (1725).

In his day François Couperin was considered second to none as a teacher of the harpsichord, and among his pupils were the children and grandchildren of the king. In 1716 Couperin published the fruit of his years of teaching: *L'Art de toucher le clavecin* (*The Art of Playing the Harpsichord*). The **clavecin** (French for harpsichord) was then the favorite chamber keyboard instrument, and some French *clavecins* of the period were large and ornate (see Box, p. 317). **The Art of Playing the Harpsichord** is a pedagogical manual in which Couperin leads the *clavecin* student through a discussion of fingering, ornamentation, and other aspects of performance. His comments on fingering show him to be of the old school, in which the third finger crosses over the second or fourth running down or up the scale (the thumb still does not pass under). But most important is Couperin's discussion of ornamentation.

Ornamentation is an indispensable part of almost all Baroque music. Generally speaking, Baroque ornamentation falls into two broad types: that in which an entire line of music is embellished (as in Italian vocal music, for example); and that in which individual notes are decorated (as in French lute and harpsichord music, for example). No musical repertory was more heavily ornamented than French harpsichord music. The ornaments, what the French call **agréments,** are not written out in full in the keyboard score. Rather, they are indicated by a variety of symbols, and it is up to the performer to insert these *agréments* into the music. Couperin's manual tells the performer how to do it. Below are just a few of the *agréments* Couperin presents.

EXAMPLE 36-6

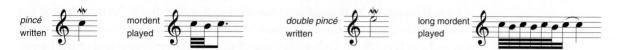

The length of the mordent can be adjusted to the fit the length of the note to which it is applied: the longer the note, the longer the mordent. Most important, the mordent starts on the note, not above it.

EXAMPLE 36-7

Contrary to the mordent, the trill starts above the note. It, too, is to be adjusted to the length of the note it ornaments.

EXAMPLE 36-8

The *port de voix* is a lower, and the *coulé* an upper, appoggiatura. The first note, written as a smaller grace note, is a dissonant note against the bass and must assume at least half of the duration of the larger written note that follows. Finally, all of these ornaments start on the beat, never before it.

In addition to these *agréments,* Couperin discusses performance techniques that are part of the unwritten tradition in French Baroque music. Foremost among these are **notes inégales** in which a succession of equal notes moving rapidly up or down the scale are played somewhat unequally, such as "long-short, long-short." Related to this is the practice of **overdotting,** in which a dotted note is made longer than written, while its complementary short note(s) is made shorter. The performance of *notes inégales* and overdotting appears to have involved more art than science, and was likely much less mathematically exact than the following examples suggest. Couperin does not explain either technique in precise detail, but he makes clear that in French Baroque music, what you see on the page is not always what you play.

> We [French] write [music] differently from the way we play it, which causes foreigners to play our music less well than we play theirs. On the other hand, the Italians write their music in the true note values in which they intended them [to be played]. For example, we dot groups of eighth-notes moving by step [*notes inégales*] despite the fact that we write them as equal notes.[3]

EXAMPLE 36-9

Deciding how to interpret the *agréments* and whether to utilize the practices of *notes inégales* and overdotting are just some of the decisions that a performer must make when engaging Couperin's harpsichord music. Below is one possible realization of two sections of a Prelude by Couperin (Exs. 36-10a and 36-10b). Couperin's original, with his ornamental symbols, appears in the lower system. *Agréments, notes inégales,* and overdotting have been applied in the upper one. This realization suggests just how highly nuanced French Baroque harpsichord music can be, and offers a good example of French rococo style. **Rococo** is a term used to describe the decorative arts and the music of mid eighteenth-century France, with all their lightness, grace, and highly ornate surfaces (Fig. 36-3). Perhaps because of the airy yet brilliant sound of the harpsichord, Couperin's rococo style is very idiomatic to this keyboard instrument.

EXAMPLE 36-10A

EXAMPLE 36-10B

The graceful lines of Couperin's art can best be found in the four collections of harpsichord music he published during his lifetime, each entitled *Pièces de clavecin* (1713, 1717, 1722, and 1730). Containing a total of two hundred twenty pieces, these four books constitute the bulk of the harpsichord music that Couperin wrote and that made him famous in his day. Each book is comprised of a handful of suites (called *ordres*), made up mostly of dance pieces. Like the suite, an **"ordre"** is a group of pieces loosely associated by feeling and key. Couperin's *ordres*, however, differ from the usual suite in that they are filled not only with the standard keyboard dances but also with numerous character pieces—pieces that try to capture the personality of an individual, a place, or an aspect of nature or society.

Take *La Favorite* (piece for the Favorite One) from Couperin's third *ordre* (*Pièces de clavecin,* Book I, 1713). The Favorite One may have been the Dauphin, the much

The Eighteenth-Century French Harpsichord

The harpsichord, as we have seen (Chapter 23), first appeared in the Low Countries around 1440 and soon spread south to neighboring France. By the mid eighteenth century, Paris had replaced Antwerp as the European center of harpsichord fabrication and restoration. Among the notable makers of Parisian harpsichords were Jean and Claude Jacquet, earlier relatives of composer Elizabeth Jacquet de La Guerre (see Chapter 35). The Jacquets were succeeded by four generations of the Blanchet family, who started building harpsichords in Paris in 1689 and continued until the Revolution (1789).

While the basic mechanism of the harpsichord remained unchanged—depressing a key caused a plectrum of quill or leather to pluck a metal string—the instrument became increasingly large and complex during the seventeenth and eighteenth centuries. Parisian harpsichord makers were among the first to standardize a two-manual instrument. A second (upper) keyboard was particularly useful in executing pieces involving cross-handed playing (left hand moving over or on top of the right), a technique often required in the music of both Louis and François Couperin. In addition, the bottom keyboard was equipped with two sets of strings: a larger one (called 8',

though the length of the longest string was actually less than eight feet) and a smaller one (called 4', and sounding an octave higher). The upper keyboard had its own set of 8' strings. Moreover, the two keyboards could be made to play together by means of a "coupler." Thus the large French harpsichord of the eighteenth century might play with one of five string sets or combinations and produce as many sound colors: 8' alone (bottom or top); two 8' together (top and bottom manuals coupled); 8' and 4' together (bottom); 8', 8' and 4' together (bottom and top coupled); or 4' alone (bottom). Finally, the keyboard of the instrument was gradually enlarged from four octaves (C to c'") to five (F' to f'"). Some of François Couperin's earliest *ordres* require such a five-octave instrument.

Figure 36-2 shows a five-octave, two-manual harpsichord made by François Blanchet the Elder in Paris about 1740. It typifies the kind of *clavecin* on which Couperin would have played. The notes of his *La Favorite*, for example, would fit easily within its five-octave compass. Moreover, a performer could clearly elucidate the rondeau structure of *La Favorite* by playing the refrain with the keyboards coupled together, while executing the contrasting "couplets" on a single manual that produced a softer sound.

🌸 FIGURE 36-2
A two-manual harpsichord built by François Blanchet the Elder in Paris c1740.

loved eldest son of Louis XIV, who died of the measles in 1712. A sense of loss is conveyed by the bass line of the main theme, which is a chromatic descending tetrachord, a traditional sign of lamentation throughout the Baroque era (see Chapter 31). The piece, as stated by Couperin himself, is a chaconne in the form of a rondeau—"chaconne" because the tetrachord returns repeatedly and thus forms a chaconne bass, yet "rondeau" because the chaconne bass disappears from time to time to allow other musical ideas to come forward. A **rondeau** in the Baroque era is therefore a composition based on the alternation of a main theme (refrain) with subsidiary sections called *couplets* (couplets) to allow musical diversity. Here the refrain and the various couplets create the pattern **ABACADAEAFA**. Couperin's magnificent chaconne-rondeau, four minutes in length, shows that French harpsichord music of the period is not just marked by abundant surface decoration but, if need be, it can project monumental gravity as well.

💿 LISTENING CUE

FRANÇOIS COUPERIN
Pièces de clavecin . . . premier livre (1713)
La Favorite

CD 5/18
Anthology, No. 104

❀ FIGURE 36-3

"The Harlequin Family" by J. J. Kändler, c1740, a superb example of rococo decoration. Here the passage of time is surrounded by an elegant embellishment and the figures of Harlequin (right) and Columbine (left). Harlequin's smile is somewhat grotesque; the mask of Columbine is that of a bird.

A dancing bear, a beehive, the pleasures of St. Germain-en-Laye, and a famous opera soprano—these are a few of the people, places, and things François Couperin brings to life in the character pieces found within his twenty-seven *ordres*. He also pokes fun at the king's mistresses, the secret societies of the idle rich, and the pretensions of the musicians' union in Paris. One of Couperin's most arresting miniature portraits is his *L'Arlequine* from the twenty-third *ordre* (*Pièces de clavecin*, Book IV, 1730).

Harlequin is a clown from the tradition of Italian *Commedia dell'arte* (improvised slapstick comedy). A troupe of *Commedia dell'arte* players, with clowns Harlequin, Columbine, and Pierrot, was in residence in Paris in the early decades of the eighteenth century. All three clowns wore masks to be funny, certainly, but also to hide a buffoon's pain and humiliation. In a world in which the aristocracy had little to do—the absolute king ran the government absolutely—courtiers tried to while away the hours by creating a make-believe world. This they did with clowns and masks. Harlequin was both comical and grotesque, his smile frightening (Fig. 36-3). Perhaps that is why Couperin has marked his *L'Arlequine* to be performed "*grotesquement*." The piece starts cheerfully enough. But it ends with a swing around the circle of fifths that includes three successive major seventh chords—a shockingly dissonant sound to eighteenth-century ears and a very modern one to ours. Surely, Couperin inserts this unusual harmonic moment to emphasize the grotesque nature of Harlequin's persona. In character pieces such as *L'Arlequine*, Couperin shows himself to be not only a composer of superb music but also a sharp critic of the courtly society, one full of pretension and masquerade.

LISTENING CUE

FRANÇOIS COUPERIN
Pièces de clavecin . . . quatrième livre (1730)
L'Arlequine

CD 5/19
Anthology, No. 105

SUMMARY

Large volumes, both printed and in manuscript, of high-quality lute music were created in mid seventeenth-century France by Ennemond and Denis Gaultier. The Gaultiers wrote mainly dance pieces, grouped in loosely organized suites, which were often marked by *style brisé*, a broken texture in which the notes of chords are played one after the other and the musical lines dart in and out. *Style brisé* was well suited to the evanescent sound of the lute, yet it was soon brought into the repertory of the harpsichord as well.

French harpsichord music of the late seventeenth and eighteenth centuries is one of the glories of that country's musical patrimony. Members of the Couperin family, Louis and François, set the standard. Louis popularized the unmeasured prelude, a genre that allowed the performer great interpretive freedom. His more important nephew, François Couperin, developed the *ordre*—a suite-like collection of dances and character pieces as well. For his *Pièces de clavecin* Couperin composed two hundred twenty harpsichord works arranged into twenty-seven *ordres* and published in four separate books (1713, 1717, 1722, and 1730). His *Art of Playing the Harpsichord* is a teaching manual that sets out in detail the master's recommended manner of fingering and ornamenting these pieces. Couperin's harpsichord works are always elegant and carefully crafted, sometimes monumental, and sometimes filled with musical irony that serves as social commentary on the aristocratic society of eighteenth-century France.

KEY TERMS

tombeau	*The Art of Playing the Harpsichord*	*rococo*
style brisé	*agréments*	*ordre*
unmeasured prelude	*notes inégales*	rondeau
clavecin	overdotting	*couplet*

Musical Interlude

From Ancient to Modern: Aspects of Baroque Music Theory

During the seventeenth century, scientists and philosophers revolutionized some of the most fundamental concepts of Western intellectual thought. In this century, Johannes Kepler (1571–1630) formulated the laws of planetary motion; Galileo Galilei (1564–1642), the son of a musician, posited a heliocentric universe; René Descartes (1596–1650) argued for a mathematically based understanding of the material word; and Isaac Newton (1642–1727) discovered the laws of gravity and optics. So significant was this scientific and philosophical revolution that historians call this the **Age of Reason** and mark the seventeenth century as the beginning of the "modern era" in Western history.

In music, too, old modes of thinking about musical structure were replaced by new paradigms during the seventeenth and early eighteenth centuries. This revolution can be seen as a transition from the ancient to the modern world, for most of the theoretical models put forth by Baroque musicians—musical systems and the terms to describe them—are still used by students and professional musicians when they discuss music today. As in most moments in the history of music, Baroque theorists were simply attempting to formulate a rational explanation for the new music they heard. Much of the theory they posited, however, remains with us today.

MODALITY YIELDS TO TONALITY

The modal scales grew out of the eight tones used for singing the psalms in the medieval church, though their names (Dorian, Phrygian, and the like) had been borrowed from the ancient Greeks. Initially there were eight church modes, but these were expanded to twelve during the late Renaissance. Similarly, the modes were first used as a way of defining and directing monophonic chant, though by the Renaissance they provided a framework and direction for polyphonic compositions, both vocal and instrumental. Pieces composed modally seem, to modern ears, to "float" in harmonic space, shifting side to side and cadencing on unexpected pitches. A piece need not even end with the final or fundamental pitch of the mode sounding in the bass.

During the seventeenth century, however, composers increasingly limited their compositions to just two modes: Ionian on C and Aeolian on A. French music theorists were the first to call these two patterns **major** (*majeure*) and **minor** (*mineur*), because the former scale began with a larger third than the latter. They also recognized that the two patterns might be transposed to other pitches so long as accidentals were included to keep the major or minor scale pattern intact. Around 1650, Denis Gaultier wrote a minor-key piece transposed to F♯, for example (see Anthology, No. 103). By 1725 almost all art music was written in either a major or minor key. Even the esteemed George Frideric Handel noticed that the older church modes had become totally obsolete, as he wrote to a friend around 1725:

> As concerns the Greek modes [church modes], I find that you have said everything that there is to say. Their knowledge is doubtless necessary to those who want to practice and perform ancient music [the music of the sixteenth and seventeenth centuries], which formerly was composed according to such modes; however, since now we have been freed from the narrow bounds of ancient music, I cannot perceive what use the Greek modes [church modes] have in today's music.[1]

When defining a central pitch within a melody, theorists began to replace the old Latin term "*finalis*" with words such as "tone" and "key" (in English), "*tonique*" (French), and "*tuono*" (Italian). That central tone was the first note of a seven-note scale (repeating at the octave). Even this concept of a seven-note unit was revolutionary from a pedagogical perspective, for the old way of teaching music involved the ancient system of Guidonian hexachords organized around six-note units (see Chapter 4). During the seventeenth century the natural, soft, and hard hexachords were challenged by a single seven-note pattern (the term for the seventh pitch was "pha," "si," or "ti," among others). A century later, "do" replaced "ut" as the opening syllable, to complete our present system of "do, re, mi, fa, so, la, ti, do."

✺ CHORD INVERSION, FUNCTIONAL HARMONY, AND THE CIRCLE OF FIFTHS: A CLOSED MUSICAL UNIVERSE

During the Baroque era, musical space, like the physical universe observed by Kepler, Galileo, and Newton, became organized in a systematic way that was radically new. Many musical thinkers were involved in this process of reformulating the sonic world of music. But the most innovative and comprehensive thinker about musical harmony was **Jean Philippe Rameau** (1683–1764). Rameau was a composer as well as a theorist. Indeed, his nearly thirty works for the French musical stage and numerous *Pièces de clavecin* rank him as the most important composer in France of the generation after François Couperin. Because Rameau was a composer, he felt himself well positioned to conceptualize and explain to his fellow musicians the new tonal music of the eighteenth century:

> I could not help thinking that it would be desirable (as someone said to me one day while I was praising the perfection of our modern music) for the knowledge of musi-

cians of this century to equal the beauties of their compositions. It is not enough to feel the effects of a science or an art. Rather, one must fashion a theory in order to render them intelligible.[2]

The foundation of Rameau's theory is set forth in his lengthy **Treatise on Harmony** (*Traité de l'harmonie*), which he published in 1722. Just as Newton had approached the physical sciences through mathematics (*Mathematical Principles of Natural Philosophy*, 1687), so Rameau embraced sounding number, the physical division of string, and later the overtone series, as a way to determine what he called the fundamental bass (root) of a collection of pitches in a chord. In a group of pitches involving two consecutive thirds, such as E, G, C, E, G, C, for example, the fundamental pitch, no matter what actually sounded in the bass, was always C (the bottom note of the only perfect fifth in the aggregate). What Rameau codified was the revolutionary principal of **chord inversion** (Ex. 5-1). To this he added other corollaries, in his *Treatise on Harmony* and later works: that the primary chords in music are the triad and seventh chord; that the basic movement within a succession of chords proceeds through fundamental bass notes a fifth apart; that the fundamental tone (tonic) exerts an almost gravitational force that pulls chords to it; that cadences are perfect or imperfect to the degree that they yield to this force of the pulling fifths. Explicit or strongly implied in Rameau's theory were concepts such as the triad, seventh chord, perfect and imperfect cadences, tonic, dominant, subdominant, and mediant pitches, functional harmonic progressions, and chord inversions—all terms and concepts commonly used by later music theorists.

EXAMPLE 5-1

As the eighteenth century progressed, Rameau and other theorists gradually came to adopt an equal tempering of the scale, and this facilitated the completion of a uniform theory of harmony based on the **circle of fifths.** In his *Treatise on Harmony*, Rameau had emphasized the importance of the interval of the fifth as the primary catalyst for moving the fundamental bass through a harmonic progression. In 1711, and then again in 1728, the German composer and theorist Johann David Heinichen (1683–1729) published a "Musical Circle," showing how a composer might proceed around the tonal globe moving by fifths (with relative minor keys interspersed; Fig. 1). Such a movement by fifths, however, might occur only if the scale were "well tempered" or, even better, tuned to equal temperament in which there is exact enharmonic equivalence (F♯ equals G♭, for example). A closed musical circle such as Heinichen's shows the desire of early eighteenth-century composers to play chords and chord progressions in all possible keys.

🐚 FIGURE 1

Johann David Heinichen's "Musicalischer Circul" from his *Der General-Bass in der Composition* (1728) demonstrates visually the process of moving around the circle of fifths.

Yale University

SUMMARY

The seventeenth and early eighteenth century witnessed a radical reformation of the way in which the pitch content of music was organized and explained. Teachers of music began to replace the hexachord with the octave as the standard unit of measure, and composers gradually reduced the twelve church modes to just two tonalities (major and minor). At the same time, composers also began to transpose these two tonalities to all twelve pitches of the chromatic scale. This created a self-contained tonal universe regulated by movements of a fifth. Within each key, chords a distance a fifth apart pulled toward one another. By means of modulation, a tonal center could be moved to another center a fifth away and then to another, also a fifth away, and so on, allowing a journey that passed through all twelve chromatic keys of the scale and miraculously arrived back at the beginning (because twelve superimposed fifths result in a unison in equal temperament). This early eighteenth-century organization of tonal space into twenty-four keys (twelve major and twelve minor) revolving around a circle of fifths was as revolutionary for music as was Newton's theory of gravity or Kepler's theory of planetary motion for astrophysics. Indeed, Rameau, influenced by the work of Newton, spoke of a gravitational pull moving the subdominant and dominant to the tonic. And, like most of Newton's laws, this remarkable eighteenth-century construct—a closed network of twenty-four keys forming a unified harmonic system—has endured down to the present day.

KEY TERMS

Age of Reason	Jean Philippe Rameau	chord inversion
major	*Treatise on Harmony*	circle of fifths
minor		

Chapter 37

Music in London: Henry Purcell

The seventeenth century was a tumultuous time in English politics. In 1649 the English Parliament seized the king (Charles I) and had him beheaded. Civil war raged between the forces favoring a monarchy and those supporting a more democratic form of government. The royalists regained power in 1660, only to have Parliament depose another king (James II) in 1688, this time by forcing him into exile. Now Parliament invited new rulers, William and Mary, to mount the throne as king and queen. The power of the king and the court was greatly curtailed, while that of Parliament, with its House of Lords and House of Commons, grew proportionally. Individual liberties and democratic self-government expanded (although women were not allowed to vote until 1928!). By the end of the seventeenth century, England had established the first broadly representative government in the West since ancient Greece.

The partial transfer of power from court to commoner that marked the seventeenth century eventually affected music in the Baroque period. Serious opera, for example, rarely flourished in England, in part because it was expensive to produce and received little support from the weakened court. Oratorio, on the other hand, did thrive, because it was less costly to mount and thus appealed to the practical English Puritans. So, too, public concerts and public theaters prospered, because they brought in revenue from daily ticket sales and attracted the increasingly affluent middle class. By 1700 the center of social and artistic life had shifted from the court to public houses (pubs) and public theaters.

London, of course, was the capital and center of art and music for all of England. Its population now numbered nearly 500,000, making it by far the largest city in Europe. Musical life in London was concentrated in three areas. West of the city center was the area of Westminster, where Parliament met. Here, too, stood an old Benedictine monastery called **Westminster Abbey,** providing a venue for ceremonies of state, all with appropriate musical pomp. To the east of Westminster Abbey was Whitehall, where the king and his court resided and entertained, and where the royal chapel sang. Closer to the center of London, then as now, was the theater district. Plays with music, and the occasional opera, were performed here in theaters such as Dorset Garden and Drury Lane, which still exists today.

❀ HENRY PURCELL AND THEATER MUSIC

Henry Purcell (1659–1695) was a child of this changing political and musical environment. Purcell's father was a singer in the royal chapel, and the young Henry too began his career as a chorister in this choir. Here he received instruction in singing, notation, theory, composition, and playing keyboard instruments. After his voice broke in 1673, Purcell became keeper of the royal instruments, then organist at Westminster Abbey and the royal chapel, and finally "composer-in-ordinary" to the court. Toward the end of his life, as the political power and musical interest of the king and queen declined, Purcell increasingly turned his attention to theater music outside the court, where there was more money to be made.

The history of opera in England is somewhat different from that of opera on the European Continent. The Italians and Germans had cultivated opera since the early decades of the seventeenth century. But the English, particularly the Puritans, were skeptical about all-sung opera. Non-stop singing in a theater seemed unnatural to the practical English, especially when it happened in a foreign language. Moreover, the English enjoyed a rich history of purely spoken drama, best exemplified by the plays of Shakespeare. Instead of opera, the English preferred spoken plays (with incidental songs), masques, and semi-operas. The **masque** was an elaborate courtly entertainment using music, dance, and drama to portray an allegorical story that shed a favorable light on the royal family; thus, in many ways, the masque was similar to French *ballet de cour* (see Chapter 35). The **semi-opera** was a spoken play in which the more exotic, amorous, or even supernatural moments in the story were sung or danced. Only rarely was there fully sung opera, such as the excellent *Venus and Adonis* (1685) by John Blow, Purcell's teacher.

Henry Purcell likely acquired his love of the theater at a young age. Since the Middle Ages the roles of women in theatrical productions in Europe had invariably been performed by boys dressed as women; not until 1660 did a woman appear on the public stage in England. For theatrical productions at the English court, the choirboys of the royal chapel often served as female impersonators, and the young Purcell may have got his start in such a role. Regardless of what brought him there, Purcell's compositions for the stage are considerable. They run the gamut of musical theater genres, from simple songs inserted into plays, to incidental music, to semi-opera and fully sung opera. The best known of these today is his only fully sung opera, *Dido and Aeneas*.

Dido and Aeneas (1689)

Purcell's *Dido and Aeneas* apparently received its first performance in 1689 at a school for young women in the London suburb of Chelsea. The school was run by Josias Priest, a friend of Purcell, who was also a choreographer and man of the London theater. The girls presented one major stage production annually, something akin to the senior class play of today, and Priest seems to have provided a role for each and every pupil. They sang in the numerous choruses or danced in the equally frequent dance numbers. All nine solo parts save one (the role of Aeneas) were written for female voices, with the more important solo roles featuring professional singers imported from nearby London.

Appropriately for a school curriculum steeped in classical Latin, the libretto of *Dido and Aeneas* is drawn from Virgil's *Aeneid*. Surely the girls had studied this epic poem in Latin class, and even memorized parts of it. Surely too they knew the story of the soldier-of-fortune Aeneas who seduces proud Dido, queen of Carthage, but then deserts her to fulfill his destiny—sailing on to found the city of Rome. The tale concludes as the abandoned Dido sings an exceptionally beautiful lament, and then runs herself through with a sword (Fig. 37-1). All that remains is for a final chorus to lament her fate.

Dido and Aeneas is an opera in miniature, a chamber opera lasting little more than an hour. Within the three brief acts the music glides quickly between recitative, arioso, and full-blown aria. The climax of the opera comes in the final scene, which culminates in Dido's death. It begins with a brief recitative, "Thy hand, Belinda." Normally recitative is a business-like process that moves the dialogue along through direct, simple declamation. But this one is special. In the stepwise scale that descends an octave, touching almost every chromatic note along the way, we can feel the resignation of the abandoned Dido as she sinks into the arms of her servant Belinda. Here, too, we glimpse one of Purcell's greatest skills: the magical way he sets the English language. He understood where the accents fell in the text of his libretto and gave these stressed syllables greater length and metrical weight in the music; here, the accented syllables generally come on beats one and three, as can be seen in the opening lines "Thy hand, Belinda! Darkness shades me."

❦ FIGURE 37-1

A detail from the painting *The Death of Dido* by Guercino (1599–1666). The servant Belinda bends over the dying Dido, who has fallen on her sword, atop what will become her funeral pyre.

EXAMPLE 37-1

The aria that follows, known as Dido's lament, is one of the most famous pieces in operatic literature. It is constructed of two beautifully shaped musical phrases that carry the following two lines of text:

> When I am laid in earth, may my wrongs create
>   no trouble in thy breast.
> Remember me, but ah! forget my fate.

Each of the two lines is repeated, as are many individual words and pairs. Such repetition of text is typical of an aria, but not a recitative. It is one means by which the composer depicts emotion. The heroine can vocalize, but cannot clearly articulate her feelings in complete sentences. The listener cares less about proper grammar and more that the text and music are emotionally charged. No fewer than six times does Dido plead with Belinda, and with us, to remember her. And, indeed, we do remember, for Dido's plaintive lament is one of the most moving arias in all of opera.

Purcell constructed the lament "When I am laid in earth" on a *basso ostinato*. As we have seen (see Chapter 31), the term *basso ostinato* is an extension of the Italian word *ostinato*, meaning "obstinate," "stubborn," or "pig-headed." In this case, it refers to the fact that the bass line repeats over and over. English composers of Purcell's day called the *basso ostinato* the **ground bass,** because the repetitive bass provided a solid foundation on which an entire composition could be built, or grounded. The repeating pattern might be only a few notes, or several measures, in length.

The ground bass Purcell composed for Dido's lament is five measures long and is heard eleven times. Note that the first half of the musical pattern consists of a chromatic descent that passes through a tetrachord (G, F♯, F, E, E♭, D); the second half moves the harmony from dominant back to tonic. As we have seen (Chapter 31), composers of the Baroque period often used a descending tetrachordal bass as a musical symbol to suggest grief, lamentation, and impending death. Thus, when the basso continuo alone played the descending tetrachord at the beginning of this aria, the audience would have understood the tragic character of the music even before the singer uttered a word. Eight statements of the ground bass then support the repeating phrases of the voice. At the end of Dido's final line, the singer breaks off, as if unable to articulate her sorrow further. But the strings press on, carrying Dido's inconsolable grief across two final statements of the ground bass.

EXAMPLE 37-2

LISTENING CUE

HENRY PURCELL   CD 5/20–21
Dido and Aeneas (1689)   Anthology, No. 106a-b
Recitative, "Thy hand, Belinda"
Aria, "When I am laid in earth"

PURCELL'S ODES AND FUNERAL MUSIC FOR QUEEN MARY

William and Mary (for whom the College of William and Mary is named) were crowned king and queen of England in Westminster Abbey on 11 April 1689. Purcell marched in the procession, composed some of the coronation music, and played organ during the sacral ceremonies. Indeed, Purcell was a busy man that day. It seems that his organ loft gave a good view of the king and queen below, and Purcell made the enormous sum of five hundred pounds selling admission. But the treasurer of the abbey asked for the money back when he learned of the composer's unsanctioned activity. Purcell was not punished further because, as the authorities of the abbey noted, he was "in truth the most excellent musician of his time."

As the years went by, neither William nor Mary proved to be a generous patron of music. Parliament drew their purse strings tight. Moreover, William was a Calvinist (generally called a Puritan in England), and this rather austere branch of Protestantism had little love of music in or out of church. For only one event annually, the queen's birthday, was Purcell required to compose a work for the court.

Art Music Displaced by Folk Music

The music of Henry Purcell belongs to the repertory of what we now call "classical music." Although in its day this kind of brilliant orchestral music and virtuosic singing was appreciated by most of the populace, it was still very much "high art." Yet, even high-born royalty sometimes longed for more commonplace music, if we can trust a story told about Purcell and Queen Mary.

> Having in mind one afternoon to be entertained with music [Queen Mary] sent Mr. Gostling [a singer in the royal chapel] to Henry Purcell and Mrs. Arabella Hunt [see Fig. 37-2], who had a very fine voice, and an admirable hand on the lute, with a request to attend her; [and] they obeyed her commands. Mr. Gostling and Mrs. Hunt sang several compositions of Purcell, who accompanied them on the harpsichord; at length the queen beginning to grow tired, asked Mrs. Hunt if she could not sing the old Scots ballad *Cold and Raw*. Mrs. Hunt answered yes, and sang it to her lute. Purcell was all the while sitting at the harpsichord unemployed, and not a little nettled [annoyed] at the queen's preference of a vulgar ballad to his music.[1]

This anecdote reminds us that a rich tradition of largely unwritten popular music, much of it what we now call Anglo-Irish folk music, coexisted with written art music in England at this time. The Scottish folksong *Cold and Raw*, which apparently originated in the 1500s, was passed along orally for centuries and eventually written down. Several versions of it are currently audible via the internet, some played by electronic synthesizers! To hear one or more of these, simply search under the song title *Cold and Raw*. If the queen found it a pleasant diversion from high art music, you may too.

FIGURE 37-2

Mrs. Arabella Hunt, a much admired soprano in her day, and performing partner of Henry Purcell.

When writing for the royal court, whether for the birthday, wedding, or welcoming of a ruler, English composers traditionally employed a genre of music called the ode. The **ode** is a multi-movement composition, usually lasting about twenty minutes, containing an instrumental introduction, choruses, duets, and solo arias. The ode has no recitative, however, because there is no drama or action to narrate. Instead, the successive movements offer lyrical hymns of praise to a member of the royal family. In a few cases, odes were also written in honor of St. Cecilia, the patron saint of music.

Henry Purcell composed twenty odes for the English royal family and four in praise of St. Cecilia. Six of the royal odes mark the birthday of Queen Mary (30 April), one for each of the six years Mary ruled. The best of these is the last, *Come, ye sons of art* (1694). The text was newly created by Nahum Tate, who had also fashioned the libretto for Purcell's *Dido and Aeneas*. In successive movements it invites "ye sons of art" (musicians) to celebrate Mary's "triumphant day." First the trumpet, then the "hautboy" (oboe), viol, lute, harp, flute, and finally Nature herself are asked to bring forth their special sounds of praise for the queen. The trumpet is represented by two altos who step forward to sing the duet "Sound the trumpet." On either side of the duet Purcell places the title chorus "Come, ye sons of art" to serve as a spirited choral refrain. In Purcell's day, as was the tradition in the Middle Ages and Renaissance, the alto voice was sung by a male in head voice, or falsetto. Today this high, falsetto alto part is performed by a singer called a **countertenor.** Here two countertenors sing music that is appropriately full of major-key fanfare motifs of the sort usually played by trumpets.

But there is irony in the duet "Sound the trumpet." No trumpets actually sound. Instead, as the countertenors sing in trumpet style, the two trumpeters of the orchestra sit silent. Purcell intended this to be an "in joke," for in his day the two royal trumpeters were named John and William Shore, which surely brought a smile at the words "you make the list'ning shores rebound." More-modern musicians, however, have put the trumpet back in Purcell's vocal duet; the music has been arranged for soprano and trumpet and recorded by, among others, trumpeter Wynton Marsalis.

EXAMPLE 37-3

LISTENING CUE

HENRY PURCELL

Come, ye sons of art (1694)
Chorus, "Come, ye sons of art"
Duet, "Sound the trumpet"
Chorus, "Come, ye sons of art"

CD 5/22–23
Anthology, No. 107a-b

Despite Purcell's best wishes, Queen Mary did not live long. An epidemic of smallpox swept London in the fall of 1694, and on 21 December the queen fell ill.

Doctors prescribed various draughts and potions, subjected her to bleeding, and applied red-hot irons to blister her temples. Not withstanding (or perhaps because of) these treatments, she died a week later. The solemn task of composing the music for her funeral fell to Purcell. Like most of her subjects, Purcell seems to have been sincerely fond of his patron and queen. Indeed, her burial occasioned the same sort of outpouring of national grief as did the funeral of Princess Diana in 1997, which was also held in Westminster Abbey, where Purcell's music fittingly was heard once again. For Mary's service the composer fashioned some of the most beautiful burial music ever written. At the center of the service stood an English choral anthem, the famous *Thou knowest Lord, the secrets of our Hearts.* Preceding and concluding the anthem was a march and a canzona. The march is worthy of special attention, for it is the earliest instrumental funeral march to survive.

Purcell's funeral march is noteworthy also for the instruments that played it: four flat trumpets. The **flat trumpet** was a slide trumpet (like the early trombone), but one for which the sliding tube extended backward over the player's left shoulder, rather than extending forward from the right. Actually, little is known about the flat trumpet and no original survives today. Apparently, the name derives from the fact that the slide made it easier for the trumpet to play in minor keys, which employ a "flat" third scale degree. Surely the capacity to play in minor as well as major accounts for the appearance of the flat trumpet in the funeral music for Queen Mary; the traditional non-slide natural trumpet playing in the usual brilliant keys of C, D, or E♭ major would have been out of place at this somber event. Purcell's march is nothing more than five homophonic chord progressions, each three bars in length. Why then did it bring "tears from all," as an eyewitness reported? Likely because of the rich harmonies, the slow and stately tempo, and the mournful tones of the flat trumpets. The more sprightly canzona sounds less like a funeral dirge than a dance, owing to the rapidly moving notes and lightly imitative texture. Its dance-like character is occasioned by an age-old tradition that holds that burials should end with hopeful, lively music, because the dead are said to dance with the angels in heaven in the life beyond. On our accompanying CD recording, modern reproductions of flat trumpets can be heard.

 LISTENING CUE

HENRY PURCELL
Funeral Music for Queen Mary (1695)
March and Canzona

CD 5/24–25
Anthology, No. 108a-b

Less than a year after the death of Queen Mary, Purcell himself died, possibly of tuberculosis. He was barely thirty-six and at the height of his powers. Once again, Purcell's funeral music sounded forth, this time for his own obsequies in Westminster Abbey. He was buried at the foot of the organ, where his memorial plaque can still be read today.

 SUMMARY

Like Mozart and Schubert, Henry Purcell composed a remarkable amount of music during his tragically short life. A fully sung opera, *Dido and Aeneas*, numerous semi-operas, and incidental interludes and songs for plays constitute the bulk of his music for the theater. For the English royal family he composed church anthems, twenty birthday odes, and music for Queen Mary's funeral. Whether writing for theater or court, Purcell's scores show his special gifts for melody, infectious dance rhythms, impeccable handling of the English language, and an unfailing freshness of sound. Like his successor, Handel, much of Purcell's finest writing is to be found in his choruses.

KEY TERMS

Westminster Abbey	ground bass	countertenor
masque	ode	flat trumpet
semi-opera		

Chapter 38

Music in London: George Frideric Handel

George Frideric Handel was German-born but spent most of his life in London, becoming in his time a beloved English institution. Handel and his music were arguably the single most important force for cultural unity in England during the entire eighteenth century, even following the composer's death in 1759.

Handel was born in Halle, Germany, in 1685, the same year as J.S. Bach. His father, a surgeon-barber (the two professions were often joined in Handel's day), wanted the son to be a lawyer. But the young Handel's love and obvious talent for music soon led to a change in plans and a rigorous musical education as organist, harpsichordist, and composer. At eighteen Handel moved to the populous north German city of Hamburg, where he played second violin and then harpsichord in the opera orchestra. There he began to study German opera, which was then heavily influenced by the musical style and theatrical conventions of Italian opera. His principal mentor was Reinhard Keiser (1674–1739), the foremost composer of opera in the German language. In 1706 Handel set off for Italy to learn the Italian traditions firsthand, and there he remained for four years, listening to and composing cantatas and operas in Italian. This Italian experience, one not shared by his contemporary, Bach, gave to Handel's subsequent vocal music an accent thoroughly Italianate. Back in Germany in 1710, Handel accepted a position at the court of the elector of Hanover at an annual salary of 1,000 thaler. The terms of his employment allowed for ample travel, so the composer soon set off for England.

As a friend of Handel said in 1713: "In these times, whoever wishes to be eminent in music goes to England. In France and Italy there is something to learn, but in London there is something to earn."[1] Indeed, the already-famous Handel arrived in England with the aim of making money by bringing Italian opera to London. As we have seen, London, with its population of 500,000, was the largest city in Europe. But opera in England had had a checkered history, owing, among other things, to the English aversion to all-sung drama (see Chapter 37). Yet public demand for real opera sung by top-flight Italian virtuosi was starting to grow, and in 1711 Handel satisfied it with *Rinaldo,* the first fully sung Italian opera designed specifically for London and the first to use an all-Italian cast. Conveniently forgetting his obligations in Germany, Handel remained in London, writing Italian opera and using his music to ingratiate himself with the ruling monarch, Queen Anne. But Anne died in the summer of 1714. As fate would have it, Handel's employer in Germany, the elector of Hanover, acceded to the English throne as King George I. Thus were patron and errant musician reunited. Now the most famous composer in England was a German, and so was the king.

Given his connections to the royals, Handel naturally was the first composer called upon when need arose for festive music to entertain the court or to mark its progress. Thus Handel wrote odes and anthems and, ultimately, the *Coronation Service* for the royal family. Among the purely instrumental works Handel composed for the court are his *Water Music* (1717) and *Music for the Royal Fireworks* (1749). For the general public he published sets of concerti grossi, solo concertos for organ and orchestra, and numerous keyboard suites. All the while, Handel worked tirelessly to make Italian opera a staple of English musical life. Encountering increasing financial problems with opera, however, the composer eventually turned his attention to oratorio. Through oratorio, Handel won the hearts and minds of the court and the well-to-do (mostly high-church Anglicans) as well as the common people of England (mostly Puritans). By the time of his death in 1759, Handel had become a cultural monument to which most people could relate with enthusiasm, albeit a few with cynicism (Fig. 38-1). Embracing his ceremonial music for the English monarchy as well as his ever-popular oratorios, the English developed a special bond with Handel's music and responded to it as one people.

🐚 FIGURE 38-1

Handel did not do things in moderation—he composed 42 operas and at least 22 full-length oratorios. He consumed food and drink with the same enthusiasm as he soaked up national musical styles. This caricature by Joseph Goupy, done in 1754, pokes fun at the composer for his gluttony (food and wine cask) and his penchant for loud music (trumpet, horn, and drum by his left foot).

HANDEL AND THE DANCE SUITE

The versatile Handel composed in virtually every genre of music known in Western Europe during the early eighteenth century. Aside from *Messiah,* today his most popular composition is his dance suite *Water Music.* Recall that a **dance suite** is a collection of dances all in a single key for one instrument or another, be it a solo instrument or a full orchestra (see Chapter 34); moreover, in the Baroque era the dances of a suite were almost invariably in binary form, **AB.** The suite may begin with a prelude or a French overture, and then continue with a succession of dances, usually ranging in number from four to seven. Of course, listeners did not actually dance to these pieces; they were stylized abstractions. But it was the job of the composer to bring each one to life, making it recognizable to the audience by incorporating the salient elements of rhythm and style from each particular dance.

Bach wrote dance suites for orchestra, for harpsichord, and for solo cello. Handel composed suites for orchestra, specifically *Water Music* and *Music for the Royal Fireworks.* He also published eight suites for harpsichord in 1720 and nine more in 1733. (Handel's famous *The Harmonious Blacksmith,* a title bestowed in the nineteenth century, appears in the fifth suite of the first collection.) Both collections for harpsichord are entitled *Suite de Pièces*, reminding us that our English word "suite" comes directly from the French word of the same spelling, meaning "succession" of pieces.

Water Music (1717)

The English royal family, historically, has had a problem with its image. To win favor with the public, the monarchy has traditionally given outdoor concerts, as Queen Elizabeth II did by inviting pop musicians to perform at Buckingham Palace in 2002. Handel's *Water Music* was created for an earlier bit of royal image-building. In 1717 King George I, a direct ancestor of the present queen, was an unpopular monarch. He refused to speak a word of English, preferring his native German. He fought with his son, the Prince of Wales, and banned him from court. London thought King George dimwitted, "an honest blockhead," as one contemporary put it.

To improve his standing in the eyes of his subjects, the king's ministers planned a program of public entertainments, including an evening of music that all the people of London could hear and enjoy. Thus on 17 July 1717, the king and his court traveled by boat up the Thames River. Indeed, so numerous were the boats that it seemed "the whole River in a manner was cover'd." Next to the king's boat was a barge carrying about fifty musicians. As an eyewitness reports, they included "trumpets, horns, hautboys [oboes], bassoons, German flutes [transverse flutes], French flutes [recorders], violins and basses." The account continues: "The music had been composed specially by the famous Handel, a native of Halle [Germany], and His Majesty's principal Court Composer. His Majesty approved of it so greatly that he caused it to be repeated three times in all, although each performance lasted an hour—namely twice before and once after supper."[2] The king and his party did not return to London and the royal residence at St. James until nearly four-thirty in the morning.

To create an hour of music Handel wrote three successive dance suites: one in F major featuring the horn, one in D major highlighting the trumpet, and one in G major and minor centering on the flute. Yet because Handel's complete autograph score of *Water Music* has been lost, and because the surviving contemporary manuscript copies and the early prints do not agree, modern editions differ in the number of movements, titles, and keys. A commonly accepted sequence for the entire work follows.

Suite No. 1 in F Major	Suite No. 2 in D Major	Suite No. 3 in G Major and Minor
1. Overture	10. (Overture)	15. (Sarabande)
2. Adagio e staccato	11. Alla hornpipe	16. Raguadon
3. (Allegro)-Andante-(Allegro)	12. Minuet	17. Minuet
4. (Minuet)	13. Lentement	18. (Andante)
5. Air	14. Bourrée	19. (Country Dance I/II)
6. Minuet (and trio)		
7. Bourrée		
8. Hornpipe		
9. (Allegro)		

The sound of Handel's *Water Music* is both distinctive and historic. It is one of the first English scores to include parts for horn. Although horns had been welcomed into orchestras in Germany, France, and Italy well before 1700, the instrument was introduced into English ensembles only after this date. Oddly, although the home of the horn was Germany and Bohemia (Czech Republic), the English came to call the instrument the **French horn,** having become acquainted with it during visits to the French court of King Louis XIV. Only in the English language is it so named (it is known simply as "the horn" in other countries). The early eighteenth-century French horn was a natural instrument (with no valves) and had a smaller bell, and thus a smaller sound, than the modern horn. Composers frequently assigned a characteristic musical figure called **horn fifths** to the French horn and trumpet, in which the instruments slide back and forth through sixths, fifths, and thirds, sometimes ornamenting along the way as can be seen in Example 38-1 from the Minuet of Suite No. 1. Needless to say, both the French horn and trumpet are featured in *Water Music* because the sound of these brass instruments carries well across outdoor expanses.

EXAMPLE 38-1

LISTENING CUE

GEORGE FRIDERIC HANDEL
Water Music, Suite No. 1 (1717)
Minuet and Trio
Hornpipe

CD 5/26–27
Anthology, No. 109a-b

Water Music proved to be immensely popular; it was played in pubs and in public gardens in London and throughout the British Isles. The work was arranged for small ensemble, for flute and harpsichord, and for solo harpsichord. In short, it conquered England. Today, Handel's *Water Music*, Bach's Brandenburg Concertos, and Vivaldi's *The Four Seasons* constitute the most popular instrumental music of the first half of the eighteenth century.

HANDEL AND OPERA

Handel enjoyed great success when he became one of the first to bring all-sung Italian opera to London during the years 1711–1717, and this inspired a bolder venture. In 1719 he became the musical force behind a remarkable capitalistic enterprise: the formation of a publicly-held stock company for the production of Italian opera. The principal investor was the king, and thus Handel's opera company was called the **Royal Academy of Music.** Handel wrote most of his best operas for the Academy, yet it went bankrupt in 1728 and again in 1734. To understand how this could happen, we must understand something of the economics of Baroque opera, specifically *opera seria.*

Handel composed some forty-two operas, most of which fall into the category of *opera seria.* **Opera seria** (literally, serious opera, as opposed to comic opera) was fully sung Italian opera of the most elaborate and expensive sort. The plots of *opera*

The Castrato in Handel's Operas

Today pop singers make fortunes, and each star has his or her fanatics. Opera singers have cult followings too, and they earn the most money among "serious" musicians. Over the years, tenor Luciano Pavarotti has commanded a hundred thousand dollars for each appearance at Madison Square Garden or Foxwoods Casino, and soprano Renée Fleming (see Fig. 48-2) appears regularly on the David Letterman Show.

Yet the cult of the singer is not new. In the late Baroque era, star singers were the most adored, and by far the best paid, of musicians. Among the men, the most prized was the virtuoso castrato. The castrato, as we have seen, was a male singer who had been castrated, usually between the age of eight and ten; his body would grow but his larynx and vocal cords would remain small, like those of a woman—all this in hopes that he could be trained to sing beautifully in the soprano or alto range. Audiences on the Continent were greatly enamored with the sound of the castrato, for it combined the high range of a female voice with the power of the male frame. Some could hold a note for a full minute and had a range of an incredible three octaves. The popularity of the castrato was enhanced by the fact that on the Baroque stage, high standing was represented by singers, whether male or female, of high vocal range; the roles of Julius Caesar and Alexander the Great, for example, were sung by castrati, and basses and tenors were usually given only minor parts. Castrati gradually disappeared from the operatic stage during the second half of the eighteenth century, but they continued to sing in Italian churches throughout the nineteenth. The last castrato, papal singer Alessandro Moreschi, died in 1921.

Among the most famous castrati of Handel's day was Francesco Bernardi, called **Senesino** (c1690–1759) because he came from Siena, Italy (Fig. 38-2). Senesino was engaged to sing at the Dresden opera in 1717, where he received a carriage—the eighteenth-century equivalent of a limousine—and an annual salary of 7,000 thalers (Bach's base salary about that time was 400 thalers). Senesino's temper tantrums got him fired from the opera at Dresden, and he moved on to London. In the course of the next two decades he sang heroic roles in some twenty operas by Handel, including that of Caesar in *Giulio Cesare*. Opinion of the English public was divided about Senesino, and castrati in general. One observer noted that "Senesino is daily voted the greatest man that ever lived," while another referred to him as a "squeaking Italian." Today the role of Caesar is sung in one of three ways: by a male in chest voice with the part transposed down an octave, by a male singing in falsetto voice (a countertenor), or by a low female voice called **contralto** (a low alto).

🌸 **FIGURE 38-2**

A caricature of the principal singers in a scene from an opera by Handel showing the castrato Senesino (left) and soprano Cuzzoni (center).

seria are usually derived from historical events or mythology, and involve larger-than-life figures—kings, queens, gods, and goddesses. There is little drama on stage. The action is often not seen by the audience, but reported by third parties, generally in the form of recitatives. The leading characters do not act so much as react. One after the other, they step forward to sing a self-contained aria, each expressing one of several stock emotions—hope, anger, hate, frenzy, despair, and vengeance, among others. Above all, *opera seria* is a singers' opera. In Handel's day it provided a platform for those singers who possessed the vocal equipment to quiet a restless, often noisy crowd by the power, range, and beauty of their singing. For this to occur, highly trained virtuosi—the best in the world—were needed. But virtuoso singers, then as now, are expensive. The great sopranos and castrati were each paid £1,500 per season, far more than Handel himself. It was Handel's job to recruit these virtu-osi (all Italian) from opera houses around Europe. English money was used to buy the best vocal talent Italy had to offer.

Giulio Cesare (Julius Caesar, 1724)

The greatest Italian voices of the day sang the leads in *Giulio Cesare*, an unusually successful *opera seria* that Handel composed in 1724 for his Royal Academy in Lon-don. The libretto recounts an episode in Caesar's life in which he pursues and then defeats his rival Pompey, in Egypt. Cleopatra, who rules Egypt jointly with her brother Ptolemy, conspires to seduce the newly arrived Caesar and gain his help in eliminating her despised brother. All this Cleopatra accomplishes, aided by a gener-ous supply of confidants, servants, disguises, and theatrical tricks. By the end of this nearly three-hour opera, she becomes queen to a Roman emperor.

In the 1724 production of *Giulio Cesare*, the famous castrato Senesino (see Box and Fig. 38-2) sang the soprano part of Caesar, while the equally famous female so-prano Francesca Cuzzoni sang the role of Cleopatra. In the aria "V'adoro, pupille" ("I Adore You, O Eyes") from Act II of *Giulio Cesare*, Cleopatra must exert all her charms to win the heart of Caesar, and her music, accordingly, must enchant and captivate. To create seductive sounds, Handel not only constructed an exquisite melody but also called for unusual orchestral instruments—the *viola da gamba*, the theorbo (a large, lute-like instrument), and the harp for heavenly accompaniment. As is true for most arias in *opera seria*, "V'adoro, pupille" is a *da capo* aria (**ABA**; see Chapter 32), though here the return to **A** is interrupted by a bit of recitative deliv-ered by the now-enraptured Caesar. Conventions of the *da capo* aria required the singer portraying Cleopatra to ornament the reprise of **A** to add variety as well as to show off her voice. Example 38-2 gives the beginning of **A** as Handel wrote it (top) and suggests how a singer might have ornamented it (bottom).

EXAMPLE 38-2

```
LISTENING CUE

        GEORGE FRIDERIC HANDEL              CD 5/28
           Giulio Cesare (1724)              Anthology, No. 110
         Aria, "V'adoro, pupille"
```

With beauty such as this, how could Handel's opera company have gone bankrupt? The exorbitant cost of the principal singers has already been mentioned, but there were other factors contributing to the demise of fully sung opera. Among these was the rise of ballad opera (see Chapter 41), a genre of musical theater alternating spoken

Opera Then and Now

In some ways eighteenth century opera was similar to opera today. Handel's company was funded by a combination of subscriptions and daily ticket sales. Operas were given in a public theater to a paying audience during a season that ran from November into June. Singers were expensive and temperamental. Handel constantly fought with his leading castrato, Senesino; he threatened to throw the diva Cuzzoni out a window when she refused to sing an aria he had written; and Cuzzoni and another prima donna, Bordoni (see Chapter 41), once engaged in a hair-pulling fight onstage. Much was spent on costumes and scenery, but comparatively little on the orchestra. Opera's main drawing cards, then as now, were social glamour and star singers.

There were important differences as well. Most operas performed by Handel's Royal Academy of Music were new works, often composed by Handel himself. Today, opera companies mostly perform "revivals" of previously composed operas—by Handel, Mozart, Verdi, or Wagner, for example.

Moreover, in Handel's day the composer was expected to tailor the music to the voices of the singers in a particular production. If an aria was too high or too low, too difficult or not showy enough, Handel would quickly take up the pen to change it. Today's composers, needless to say, are less accommodating.

Finally, what went on in the opera house was much different. The opening overture was played to call the audience to its seats, not when the audience was seated and quiet. The curtain stayed up between the acts, because other performers stepped on stage to play or dance during intermission. Handel is known to have performed his organ concertos between the acts of his oratorios, and Vivaldi played violin concertos between the acts of his operas. How much of this the audience took in is anyone's guess. Clearly, walking and talking during the performance were more tolerated then; to make a mundane comparison, Handel's opera audience probably behaved like the crowd at a baseball game today.

dialogue with traditional ballads. The popularity of ballad opera, the eighteenth-century counterpart of today's Broadway musical, lured people away from Handel's more high-brow art. Finally, in 1733 a second *opera seria* company, called the "Opera of the Nobility," began operation in London in direct competition with Handel's Academy. Eventually both companies failed, and Handel increasingly turned his attention to oratorio.

HANDEL AND ORATORIO

Oratorio, like opera, was born in seventeenth-century Italy. The very name "oratorio" suggests that it originated in an oratory, a large chapel for prayer. As we have seen (see Chapter 32), an oratorio was a large-scale, multi-movement composition setting a sacred text. Oratorio was not part of the regular worship services of the church, but provided extra-liturgical enlightenment and, especially, enjoyment for the faithful. Indeed, by the time of Handel, the oratorio had become in most ways little more than an unstaged opera with a religious subject. Handel originally intended his oratorios to be spiritual substitutes for opera during the six-week Lenten season before Easter, when secular entertainments such as opera were usually not permitted.

To be sure, oratorio and opera in eighteenth-century London had much in common. Oratorio, like opera, was performed in a public theater before a paying audience. Both usually begin with an overture, are divided into three acts, and consist mostly of recitatives and arias. Finally, both oratorio and opera tell a dramatic story by using individual characters and a chorus.

But there are important differences between oratorio and opera. First of all, oratorio, unlike *opera seria,* is not sung in Italian but in the language of the local people.

In the case of Handel's oratorios, they were sung in English. Moreover, oratorio does not involve staging, costumes, or acting; instead, the audience must picture in its mind's eye the drama that is described on stage. Similarly, oratorio does not require expensive operatic voices and the vocal writing generally is less extravagant than in opera. Finally, oratorio, unlike opera, does not draw upon historical events or tales from classical mythology, but on religious subjects, usually those recorded in scripture. The religious nature of oratorio requires moralizing, and this is done best by the collective forces of a chorus; thus, in oratorio, the chorus is generally far more important than in opera.

Given these qualities, it is easy to see why oratorio appealed to Handel. He could do away with the irascible and expensive castrati and prima donnas. He no longer had to pay for elaborate sets and costumes. He could draw on the English love of choral music, a tradition that extended well back into the Middle Ages (see Chapter 16). In addition, social forces were favoring oratorio. The aristocracy and its wealth, the support network for opera from its inception, was weakening in England. Increasing in importance was a new, untapped market of middle-class consumers—the faithful of the Puritan, Methodist, and growing evangelical sects in England, who viewed the pleasures of foreign opera with distrust, even contempt. Similarly, the subject matter of English oratorio—biblical stories of oppressed peoples who threw off the shackles of domination—was not lost on this rising middle class, who saw themselves overburdened by a corrupt government. The enterprising Handel was quick to see that oratorio was a cost-effective way to use music to bring religious enlightenment to his countrymen, remain politically correct, and still make a handsome profit.

Messiah (1741)

Between 1732 and 1751, when he stopped composing because of blindness, Handel wrote twenty-two oratorios. The majority of these depict heroic figures from the Old Testament, among them Joseph, Susanna, Samson, Esther, Joshua, and the people of Israel captive in Egypt. Yet Handel's most popular oratorio, then as now, is Messiah, which draws on passages from the Old and New Testament concerning the idea of a messiah. Handel composed Messiah in only three-and-a-half weeks during the summer of 1741. It was first performed in Dublin, Ireland, the following April as part of a charity benefit, with Handel conducting. Having heard the dress rehearsal, the local press waxed enthusiastic about the new oratorio, saying that it "far surpasses anything of that Nature, which has been performed in this or any other Kingdom." Such a large crowd was expected for the work of the famous Handel that ladies were urged not to wear hoopskirts, and gentlemen were admonished to leave their swords at home. In this way an audience of 700 could be squeezed into a hall possessing only 600 seats!

Pleased with his artistic and financial success in Dublin, Handel took Messiah back to London, made minor alterations, and performed it in the public theater at Covent Garden. In 1750 he again offered Messiah, this time in the chapel of the Foundling Hospital for orphans, and again there was much popular acclaim for Handel, as well as much profit for charity. In time, Handel gave a conducting score and instrumental parts of Messiah to the hospital and paid for an organ there, so that the oratorio might be given annually. The performances of Messiah at the Foundling Hospital did much to convince the public that Handel's oratorios were appropriate for churches and for charitable fund-raisers. As the music historian and friend of

Handel, Charles Burney, said at the time: "[*Messiah*] has fed the hungry, clothed the naked, fostered the orphan, and enriched succeeding managers of Oratorios, more than any single musical production of this or any country."[3] And so it does to the present day.

In a general way, *Messiah* tells the story of the life of Christ. It is divided into three parts (instead of three acts): (1) the prophecy and birth of Christ; (2) his crucifixion, descent into Hell, and resurrection; and (3) the Day of Judgment and the promise of eternal life. Handel usually performed *Messiah* immediately after Easter. Today it is also offered during the season of Advent before Christmas.

Messiah is comprised of fifty-three musical numbers. Nineteen are for chorus, sixteen are solo arias, sixteen are recitatives, and two are purely instrumental pieces. The large number of choruses reflects the importance of the chorus generally in Handel's oratorios. By contrast, while the arias are important, they tend not to be the big *da capo* show pieces heard in Handel's operas. Ornamentation and vocal display was less important in oratorio than opera, and consequently Handel ultimately included only two *da capo* arias in the entire score. Instead, Handel created for *Messiah* a variety of smaller aria forms in which he tried to create a musical shape and mood appropriate for each aria text.

Typical of the simpler text-specific arias in *Messiah* is the lovely "He shall feed his flock," which invokes the image of Christ, the gentle shepherd of his flock, and of shepherds generally. For this calm and comforting text, Handel fashioned appropriately soothing music. Indeed, "He shall feed his flock" is a perfect example of what is called a **pastoral aria,** a slow aria with several distinctive characteristics: parallel thirds that glide mainly in step-wise motion, a lilting rhythm in compound meter, and a harmony that changes slowly and employs many subdominant chords. The tradition of the pastoral in music extends well back into the seventeenth century and includes, among other pieces, Corelli's "Christmas" concerto from his Opus 6. Bach and later composers, among them Beethoven and Schumann, would also compose pastoral works. Thus Handel's aria "He shall feed his flock" is part of a long continuum in music history in which shepherds, and particularly those of Christmas, are supplied with a lilting style of music called the pastoral.

EXAMPLE 38-3

LISTENING CUE

GEORGE FRIDERIC HANDEL   CD 6/1
Messiah (1741)   Anthology, No. 111a
Aria, "He shall feed his flock"

Despite the beauty of its arias, the true glory of *Messiah* is to be found in its choruses. Handel was arguably the finest composer for chorus who ever lived. Nowhere is his choral mastery more evident than in the justly famous "Hallelujah" chorus, which concludes Part II of *Messiah* (Fig. 38-3). Here the multitude shouts for joy, for Christ has been victorious on the cross and has ascended triumphantly to reign in heaven.

The power of the "Hallelujah" chorus is generated by several forces: the rhythmically incisive setting of the word "Hallelujah" makes for an exciting exclamation; the repetition of this word throughout builds a feeling of communal participation in a great dramatic pageant; and a variety of choral styles—unison, chordal, fugal, and chordal and fugal together—creates a kaleidoscope of colors and textures. The music is at once complex and very clear. So moved was King George II when he first heard the great opening chords, as the story goes, that he rose to his feet in admiration, thereby establishing the tradition of the audience standing for the "Hallelujah" chorus—for no one sat while the king stood. With its brilliant writing for trumpets in the bright key of D major, this movement might well serve as a royal coronation march, though in *Messiah*, of course, it is Christ the King who is crowned.

The British Library

❧ FIGURE 38-3

The autograph of the full score of Handel's *Messiah* showing the beginning of the "Hallelujah" chorus.

LISTENING CUE

GEORGE FRIDERIC HANDEL

Messiah (1741)
"Hallelujah" chorus

CD 6/2
Anthology, No. 111b

For the first performance of *Messiah* in 1742, Handel's musical forces were rather diminutive: an orchestra of about twenty (mostly strings) and a chorus of eight choirboys for the soprano and five adult males on each of the alto, tenor, and bass lines. As for the soloists, women sang the alto and soprano solos in *Messiah*, and indeed in all Handel's oratorios. (By contrast, the soprano solos in Bach's religious music were invariably sung by a choirboy.) For the performances of *Messiah* at the Foundling Hospital in London during the 1750s, the orchestra grew to thirty-eight players by the addition of doubling instruments (oboes, bassoons, and horns). Later, for the Handel Commemoration of 1785 in Westminster Abbey, about five hundred performers participated, equally divided between chorus and orchestra. In the course of the next hundred years, the chorus swelled to as many as four thousand, with a balancing orchestra of five hundred.

So too grew Handel's stature in the hearts and minds of the English. When he died in April 1759, he left an enormous estate of 20,000 pounds, much of which he bequeathed to charity. He was buried with full honors in Westminster Abbey, with three thousand persons in attendance. Today a sculpture of the composer holding an aria from *Messiah* stands in the Abbey directly opposite a memorial to another giant of English cultural history, William Shakespeare.

SUMMARY

In some ways the music of George Frideric Handel represents a continuation of the English musical tradition. Henry Purcell and his generation wrote wonderfully expressive choral anthems for the church and brilliant trumpet parts to adorn court festivals, as well as evocative music for the theater. But Handel greatly enriched this tradition. As a world traveler with an unsurpassed ear, he had grown up with the sound of the densely contrapuntal German fugue; when in Rome he absorbed the cohesive harmonic language and well-directed basses of Corelli; and, again in Rome, he embraced the Italianate vocal style of the cantata, opera, and oratorio. By combining these sounds with the English choral tradition, Handel achieved a remarkably rich synthesis of national styles. His oratorios in particular show a melding of English choral traditions with the operatic conventions of aria and recitative. Most important, Handel had a flair for the dramatic gained from a lifetime in the theater. He could seize the emotional core of any text, convert it to musical expression, and maintain it with intensity over long spans of time. The vividness, intensity, and grandeur of Handel's music mark it as a positive, life-affirming force.

KEY TERMS

dance suite	Royal Academy of Music	contralto
French horn	*opera seria*	oratorio
horn fifths	Senesino	pastoral aria

Johann Sebastian Bach: Instrumental Music in Weimar and Cöthen

Johann Sebastian Bach and George Frideric Handel are today the best-known composers of Baroque music. Yet their lives could hardly have been more different. Handel was a man of the world, traveling freely around the European Continent and back and forth to England. Handel had no children, indeed never married. His base of operation was London, a city of a half-million inhabitants. Bach, by contrast, was a devoted father to twenty children and something of a stay-at-home, rarely venturing beyond his familial roots in central Germany. He worked in towns with as few as 3,500 citizens. Handel was a man of the theater, while Bach remained mainly within the precincts of the church.

Yet Bach was keenly attuned to the musical currents of his day, taking great pains to keep in touch with changing musical styles and shape them according to his own intensely rigorous musical intellect. Perhaps more than Handel, Bach used strict constructivist processes to create musical projects of almost superhuman design, such as his Brandenburg Concertos and The Art of Fugue. Whereas Handel wanted his music to sound good, to be heard and enjoyed by all, Bach wanted his music to be good in an almost divinely perfect way; he composed, so he said, "for the greater glory of God alone." By means of intellectual rigor and supreme technical mastery, Bach brought Baroque music to a glorious culmination.[†]

Johann Sebastian Bach came from a long line of musicians who lived and worked in central Germany (Map 39-1). A family tree of this clan includes nearly sixty musical Bachs, extending from the late sixteenth century into the nineteenth. Of these, Johann Sebastian was simply the most talented and industrious. Bach was born in the small town of Eisenach, Germany, in 1685. His father, Ambrosius, directed a town band of five wind players. Bach senior also played the violin, and seems to have taught his son violin, viola, and cello. Young Bach also learned to play the organ, and by the age of fifteen was already composing for that instrument. When Johann Sebastian's parents both died prematurely, he was sent to live with his older brother Johann Christoph in the nearby town of Ohrdruf. There he seems to have learned his trade by secretly copying the works of the masters from a book his brother kept shut away in a cupboard.

As a youth, Johann Sebastian Bach studied music, the humanities, and theology in private Lutheran church schools at Eisenach, Orhdruf, and finally Lüneburg in northern Germany. In all, Bach received twelve years of formal education, more than any other Bach until that time. To pay his way, Bach sang as a choral scholar in various church-school choirs. At Lüneburg, for example, he was a soprano, and then a bass after his voice broke at age fifteen (puberty came later in those earlier centuries). With his formal education completed at the age of seventeen, Bach went forth to make his way in the musical world.

Over the course of the next six years (1702–1708), Bach worked in a number of musical positions, including that of church organist in the small town of Arnstadt (see Map. 39-1). His desire to learn the latest styles resulted in a now-famous story. At age twenty, Bach asked for a leave of absence from his job as organist in Arnstadt

🌿 M A P   3 9 - 1
Central and north Germany in Bach's day.

[†]Like Handel, Bach composed a large number of pieces, more than 1,200. Handel's most important works are vocal compositions and thus are identified simply by their title. Bach, however, wrote a great deal of instrumental music. To avoid confusion among these pieces, twentieth-century musicologists developed a system of grouping his compositions by genre and numbering them. Thus when we buy music by Bach or attend a performance, we usually see an identifying number for the piece in question preceded by the letters **BWV (Bach Werke Verzeichnis),** which is simply German for "Bach Work List." The BWV number for Bach functions much like the "K." numbers used for Mozart's works (see Chapter 47).

to journey to Lübeck, where he could hear the newest organ pieces as well as the famous *Abendmusik* of Dieterich Buxtehude (see Chapter 34). Accordingly, in November 1705, Bach set forth to walk the entire 280-mile distance between Arnstadt and Lübeck. Although his superiors in Arnstadt had given him a leave of a month, Bach walked back into Arnstadt four months after he had left. He was reprimanded not only for truancy but also for the elaborate way he was now playing his chorale preludes on the organ—with so much ornamentation no one could recognize the chorale tune! Evidently, the small town authorities did not like the fancy stuff young Bach had learned from Buxtehude in the big city. Eventually, Bach left Arnstadt and moved on to more promising positions, first in Mühlhausen and then in Weimar.

✸ BACH IN WEIMAR: THE ORGAN MUSIC

During his years in the city of Weimar (1708–1717), Bach wrote most of his great works for organ. In fact, in his day Bach was known more as a virtuoso organist and organ expert than as a composer. At the time, the organ had come to occupy a central place in the religious music of the Lutheran church and in German society generally. In the Lutheran service the organ accompanied the choir and congregation, yet also sounded as a solo instrument, one that could rival a full orchestra in volume and tone color. Moreover, the Germans, then as now, had a tradition of excellence in the manufacture of precision instruments, and they produced pipe organs of the highest quality.

The *Orgelbüchlein*

Among Bach's organ compositions dating from his nine years in Weimar is the **Orgelbüchlein,** a collection of forty-six pieces written mostly between 1708 and 1713. It is called the *Orgelbüchlein* (*Little Organ Book*) because the manuscript measures only 6 x 7 inches. Each of the forty-six pieces is a **chorale prelude,** which, as we have seen (Chapter 34), is an ornamental setting of a pre-existing chorale tune intended to be played on the organ before the singing of the chorale by the full congregation. The performance of the prelude served to recall the chorale tune in the minds of the faithful before they tried to sing it themselves. The title page of the *Orgelbüchlein* suggests that Bach intended to achieve three things with this collection of chorale preludes: (1) to provide the organist with a repertory of pieces to play in church; (2) to show the organist-composer how to construct a chorale prelude on a given tune by providing multiple examples; and (3) to develop the technical facility of the organist by requiring an extensive use of the pedal. In organ music prior to the *Orgelbüchlein*, the bass line could, if the performer wished, be played manually (by the hands) not *pedaliter* (by the feet). Here, in all forty-six pieces, at least one voice must be played by the pedals. Thus users of the *Orgelbüchlein* learned how to coordinate hands and feet, perhaps the most difficult organ technique of all.

Just how challenging a chorale prelude within the *Orgelbüchlein* might be can be seen in "In dulci jubilo" ("In Sweet Jubilation"), a piece intended for Christmas. Originally the melody of "In dulci jubilo" was a Gregorian chant, a hymn sung in Latin in the Roman Catholic Church. In the sixteenth century, the Lutheran Protestants transformed it into a chorale tune by replacing the Latin text with one that combined German and Latin. Even today this jaunty Christmas carol is sung around the world, most often to the English words "Good Christian men rejoice."

The Organ in Bach's Day

The pipe organ, as is well known, makes sounds when air is forced through graduated rows of pipes, usually constructed of metal but sometimes of wood. Pipes of the same type are grouped together and produce a particular sound, and each group of similar-sounding pipes is called a **rank.** Some ranks are made to sound like violins, others like trumpets or horns, and still others like flutes or oboes. Every rank of pipes is activated by pulling out a small wooden knob called a **stop.** A rank of pipes can sound by itself or in combination with other ranks. Thus the fullest sound is made by "pulling out all the stops." The rows, or ranks, of pipes were placed in wooden chests, and one chest usually contained the big pipes for the lowest bass notes. Each of the chests was linked to one or more keyboards at the console of the organ, and a foot (pedal) keyboard was supplied for the bass notes. In Bach's day an assistant was needed to pump the bellows and thereby force air into the pipes, a task nowadays performed by an electrical pump.

Figures 39-1 and 39-2 show the organ at the New Church in Arnstadt, Germany. Dating from the early eighteenth century, it is the only organ Bach himself played that survives to the present day. The organ possesses two manuals and a pedal keyboard, and thus is a mid-size instrument by Bach's standards. A few large north German organs in Bach's time included more than fifty ranks of pipes and four manual keyboards plus one for the feet. One particular virtue of the organ rests in its multiple keyboards, which facilitate playing contrapuntal pieces. By assigning a particular rank of pipes with a distinctive tone color to a particular keyboard, the composer could project three, four, or five individual lines at once, all clearly differentiated from one another by means of their contrasting timbres.

※ FIGURE 39-1

The console of the organ on which Bach played in the New Church at Arnstadt, Germany, now preserved in a local museum. The console with its keyboards served as the "central processor" for the instrument and sent information to the pipes indicating which were to sound.

※ FIGURE 39-2

The pipes of the organ at Arnstadt remain today as they were in Bach's day, although the console of the instrument (Fig. 39-1) with its keyboards has been removed and replaced with a more modern one.

When Bach composed a chorale prelude, he usually placed the tune in the soprano and embellished it, lightly or heavily, with appropriate counterpoint. Here, the melody is indeed in the soprano and Bach does supply counterpoint, but he adds one other important element: canon. In truth, Bach was not the first to set "In dulci jubilo" in canon; earlier German composers had recognized that this melody could easily be set against itself at the distance of a measure because each downbeat is a member of the tonic triad. But Bach was not a man to allow himself to be outdone by any composer. Thus, for his setting of "In dulci jubilo," he created two canons—one between the soprano and bass featuring the chorale melody, and another between the alto and tenor serving as counterpoint against the tune. "In dulci jubilo" is one of the earliest manifestations of Bach's lifelong interest in canon.

EXAMPLE 39-1

At the end of "In dulci jubilo," Bach appends a brief coda in which the parts undulate above a constantly held low note played on the pedal keyboard of the organ. Because of its original association with the pedal of the organ, any such sustained or continually repeated pitch, usually placed in the bass and sounding while the harmonies change around it, is called a **pedal point.** Bach often concludes his keyboard works with such a sustained or repeating bass. Here a pedal point begins in the tenor range and three measures later the left hand adds its own "pedal point" an octave lower.

EXAMPLE 39-2

LISTENING CUE

JOHANN SEBASTIAN BACH
Orgelbüchlein (c1710)
"In dulci jubilo" (BWV 608)

CD 6/3
Anthology, No. 112

Musical symbolism was an important part of Bach's expressive world. In the chorale prelude "In dulci jubilo" he surely chose to include a canon, indeed a double canon, because the text of the original Latin hymn ended with the plea to Christ: "Trahe me post te" ("Lead me after you"). Bach employs a different sort of musical symbolism in another famous chorale prelude from the *Orgelbüchlein*, "Durch Adams Fall ist ganz verderbt" ("Through Adam's Fall All Mankind Fell"). As the chorale tune sounds on high in the soprano, the alto and tenor provide contrapuntal embellishment below. The bass, however, has a different agendum. It falls precipitously in jagged, dissonant sevenths, thereby playing out through music Adam's "fall" into sin.

EXAMPLE 39-3

LISTENING CUE

JOHANN SEBASTIAN BACH
Orgelbüchlein (c1710)
"Durch Adams Fall ist ganz verderbt"
(BWV 637)

CD 6/4
Anthology, No. 113

❧ BACH IN CÖTHEN: CHAMBER AND ORCHESTRAL MUSIC

By 1717 Bach had attained full maturity as a musician. He was also an ambitious man fully aware of his talents and his responsibility to his increasingly large family. To better his station in life, Bach now traveled to the court town of Cöthen (see Map 39-1) and successfully auditioned for the job of director of music. When Bach returned to Weimar to collect his family and possessions, Duke Wilhelm of Weimar had him thrown in jail for a month. The duke was not pleased that his musician had "jumped ship" to another court without ducal permission; musicians before Beethoven were little more than indentured servants. When released from jail on 2 December 1717, Bach fled to the court of Cöthen, where he remained for the next six years (1717–1723).

The position Bach assumed at Cöthen was very much a step up for him. He was appointed **Kapellmeister,** the term used in the Baroque and Classical periods to refer to the chief musician, not just of the chapel, but of the entire court. Cöthen, with a population of only 3,500, was not a big city. Nevertheless, it was ruled by an enlightened prince, Leopold of Anhalt-Cöthen, who loved music, played violin, and sang a passably good bass. Having served primarily as an organist at Weimar, Bach was engaged at Cöthen mainly to compose instrumental music. Indeed, his finest chamber and orchestral music dates from these years.

The Two- and Three-Part Inventions

Early in his career, Bach developed a reputation as a superb teacher. Even in Weimar he had attracted nearly a dozen pupils, some coming from great distances and boarding in the master's home. Not coincidentally, as teaching became an important part of his musical life, Bach began to assemble volumes of pedagogical materials for his pupils to play. The *Orgelbüchlein* was one such musical primer for organists. During the years 1720–1723 he compiled another collection of didactic pieces for keyboard players, which we now call the Two- and Three-Part Inventions (the Three-Part Inventions are also called the Sinfonia). The **Two- and Three-Part Inventions** (1723) are two sets of contrapuntal pieces along the lines of simple fugues. Each collection contains fifteen works and each of these is in a separate key (Bach avoids the keys farthest harmonically from C major). These "mini-fugues" require the player to develop a lyrical playing style and to use all five fingers equally; up to this time keyboardists had neglected the thumb (see Chapters 23 and 27). But Bach had a larger pedagogical plan in mind: having mastered two-voice and then three-voice contrapuntal pieces, the student would progress to even more digitally demanding material, the preludes and fugues of The Well-Tempered Clavier.

The Well-Tempered Clavier

Ever since its creation, The Well-Tempered Clavier (*Das wohltemperirte Clavier* in German) has served as the holy grail for harpsichordists and pianists; it is music of such rarified beauty and technical challenge that mastery of it can be a lifelong quest. **The Well-Tempered Clavier** is a collection of preludes and fugues by Bach in two books, one composed in Cöthen about 1720–1722 and the other in Leipzig during the late 1730s. Each volume contains twenty-four pairs of preludes and fugues arranged by key in ascending order—a prelude and fugue in C major is followed by one in C minor, and in turn by one in C♯ major and then C♯ minor, and so on. In this way all twelve pitches of the octave are supplied with a prelude and fugue in a major and minor key. The title implies that Bach now believed a keyboard instrument could, and indeed should, be tuned to play in all tonalities. Bach was gradually moving from a system of unequal temperament to something close to **equal temperament**—a division of the octave into twelve equal half-steps such as we have on the keyboard today (see Box, p. 349). By "clavier" Bach most likely intended to specify the harpsichord, although a performer in his day might try these pieces on the organ or clavichord as well.

To focus on only one prelude and fugue from The Well-Tempered Clavier is to do an injustice to the great variety of styles and designs throughout the collection. Yet the prelude and fugue in C minor from Book I deserves special attention. The prelude begins with blazing sixteenth notes in perpetual-motion style, giving the impression of a highly skilled player improvising a toccata on the spot. The arpeggiated chords change relentlessly, and the performer must jump with a wing and a prayer in hopes of landing on the right notes to begin each new figural pattern. Thumb and fifth finger in particular get a workout here. Finally, although the prelude is in a minor key, it concludes with a bright-sounding major triad. Such a shift from minor to major at the end of a piece is called a **Picardy third.** Musicologists don't know where or why this term was first used, but Baroque composers frequently ended minor-key pieces with a tonic major chord.

To this prelude Bach joined a companion fugue in C minor, a contrapuntal classic that has been analyzed by many musicians, including Bach himself. It begins with a theme, which in the case of a fugue we call the **subject.** This subject is an energetic one, its lively rhythms reminiscent of Italian instrumental music of the day. Typical of fugal composition, each voice presents the subject in turn in an opening section called the **exposition.** Sounding against this subject from time to time is a unit of thematically distinctive material called the **countersubject,** a counterpoint to the subject (Ex. 39-4). The fugue in C minor is a three-voice fugue (in this case alto, soprano, and bass), so once all three voices have presented the subject the exposition is complete. Next comes a free section, called an **episode,** based on motives derived from the subject. Episodes usually involve melodic sequences and

EXAMPLE 39-4

EXAMPLE 39-5

modulation, and this one carries the tonality by step from the tonic C minor up to the relative major E♭. Thereafter, single statements of the subject in different keys alternate with modulating episodes. The epicenter of this particular fugue is found in the episode at measures 17–19, where Bach composes **invertible counterpoint**; the motive which had been in the bass (A) is moved to the alto and the alto motive (B) is placed in the bass (Ex. 39-5). Notice also that motive B is none other than the original countersubject. Finally, the tonality swings around the circle of fifths before the bass and then soprano return with two statements of the subject in a last affirmation of the tonic key. Bach concludes this keyboard work, once again, with a pedal point and a Picardy third. Because no two fugues are alike, they are difficult to define. But a working definition of the term **fugue** might be as follows: a contrapuntal composition for two, three, four, or five voices, which begins with a presentation of a subject in imitation in each voice (exposition), continues with modulating passages of free counterpoint (episodes) and further appearances of the subject, and ends with a strong affirmation of the tonic key. Below is a visual approximation of how this C-minor fugue by Bach unfolds.

		EPI-SODE		EPI-SODE		EPISODE		EPISODE		EPI-SODE	
EXPOSITION											
S -------			-------			invertible	-------	circle		-------		
A-------				-------		counter-		of				
B		-------				point		fifths		-------	pedal point
1 2 3 4 5	6 7 8	9 10	11 12	13 14	15 16	17 18 19	20 21	22 23 24 25	26 27	28 29	30 31
C minor			E♭ major		G minor			C minor		C minor	

------- statement of the subject

LISTENING CUE

JOHANN SEBASTIAN BACH
The Well-Tempered Clavier (1722)
Prelude and Fugue in C Minor (BWV 847)

CD 6/5–6
Anthology, No. 114

Other Chamber Music

Much of Bach's chamber and orchestral music was written during his years in Cöthen (1717–1723). His position as Kapellmeister required that he compose for, as well as lead, the court orchestra, and that he also provide music for solo performances. In Bach's musical world, solo pieces, works for small ensembles, and even orchestral

Pitch and Tuning in Bach's Day

In Bach's day there was no such thing as standardized pitch. Indeed, the "rule" that concert pitch should be built around an "A" vibrating 440 times per second was not universally mandated until the International Organization for Standardization did so in 1955. The pitch A above middle C was set in Paris in Lully's time (c1675) at about 410 vibrations per second. A tuning fork associated with Handel gives the same A at 422.5. Things were even more variable in Bach's Germany, for here there was one pitch for the organs in church, and another for the instruments of the court or town orchestra. Yet despite the lack of a uniform standard for tuning (A 440, for example), a general trend emerged during the eighteenth century. Tuning slowly evolved from a tuning or temperament with unequal intervals in the various keys (see Musical Interludes 4 and 5) to one of equal temperament with equal intervals.

There were advantages and disadvantages to both the old and new system of tuning. In unequal temperaments, each key had its own distinctive sound because its intervals were slightly different from those belonging to the next key. In most Baroque music, a modulation from the purity of C major to the tension of E major, for example, was a more exciting journey than today. Similarly, a piece in F major sounded very different from one in A major. But the newer equal temperament had its advantages. The composer could modulate through many different keys, indeed all of them, without encountering unpleasant dissonance. Moreover, enharmonic equivalence was now possible; the key of C♯ major sounded exactly like that of D♭ major. Equal temperament was more bland, but more versatile.

In truth, we do not know if Bach's expression "well-tempered" means equal-tempered, or just something very close to equal-tempered. But The Well-Tempered Clavier is an important milestone in the long transition from a scale tuned in unequal intervals to the one tuned in equal intervals that we use today.

---

compositions were considered to be chamber music because all such music was performed in a domestic music room, or chamber (Fig. 39-3).

Among Bach's chamber pieces are a set of six sonatas for violin, another collection of three sonatas for *viola da gamba*, and yet another group of three for flute, all accompanied by obbligato harpsichord. The term **obbligato** (obliged or mandatory) indicates that a composer has written a specific part for an instrument and intends it to be played as written. Apparently, Bach was reluctant to allow other musicians to realize the figured bass parts to his sonatas. Instead, he often wrote out his own demanding keyboard accompaniments. For violinists and cellists, however, Bach's most important chamber music is to be found in his unaccompanied suites, sonatas, and partitas (**partita** is simply a word that Bach used as a synonym for suite). Here the string instrument is entirely alone.

The six unaccompanied violin sonatas and partitas are especially important. They provide violinists today with a basic repertory for both teaching and performance, just as The Well-Tempered Clavier does today for pianists and the six cello suites for cellists, and no self-respecting violinist can be without the set. Bach himself was a violinist, and his son C.P.E. Bach said that even into his old age his father played the instrument "cleanly and penetratingly." Bach's aim in his set of six works for solo violin is to build technique. Among other things, the player must learn to execute double, triple, and even quadruple stops (to play two, three, or four notes almost

FIGURE 39-3

The recently refurbished Crystal Room at the palace of Cöthen where Bach's Brandenburg Concerto No. 5 was first performed.

simultaneously), as well as to maintain several polyphonic lines at once. Bach was determined to show that the violin could play a multi-voice fugue just as effectively as a keyboard instrument, so he made the second movement of each solo sonata a fugue. As Example 39-6 shows, while demonstrating that a violin can play a fugue, Bach also forces the performer to improve technique by stretching to get several notes in tune at once.

EXAMPLE 39-6

The Brandenburg Concertos

Among the concertos Bach composed while in Cöthen is a justly famous set of six called the **Brandenburg Concertos.** Bach's job at Cöthen required him to lead the court orchestra, conducting either from the harpsichord or the first violinist's desk. The Cöthen orchestra consisted of a group of about fifteen specialists, many of whom had come from the area of Berlin (see Map 39-1). In March 1719, Bach himself went to Berlin to pick up a large new harpsichord that Prince Leopold had ordered. While there, he met the Margrave Christian Ludwig of Brandenburg (1677–1734)—Brandenburg is a territory very near Berlin—who expressed an interest in Bach's music. When he returned to Cöthen, Bach assembled a set of six concerti grossi (some written earlier) and eventually sent them to the Margrave with a flowery dedication. Here Bach writes in French, the courtly language of the period, and with a groveling yet *gallant* tone typical of dedications at this time.

> As I [Bach] had the pleasure a couple of years ago of being heard by Your Royal Highness, in accordance with your commands, and observing that you took some delight in the small musical talent that Heaven has granted me, and as, when I took my leave of Your Royal Highness, you did me the honor of requesting that I send you some of my compositions, I have therefore followed your most gracious commands and taken the liberty of discharging my humble obligation to Your Royal Highness with the present concertos which I have adapted to several instruments. I beg you mostly humbly not to judge their imperfections by the standards of that refined and delicate taste in music that everyone knows you to possess, but rather to accept, with benign consideration, the profound respect and most humble devotion that I attempt to show by this means. . . . I desire nothing more than to be employed on occasions more worthy of you and your service, being with unparalleled zeal,
>
> Sire,
> Your Royal Highness's
> most humble and most obedient servant,
>
> Cöthen, 24 March 1721   Jean Sebastien Bach[1]

Most likely, the always-ambitious Bach was angling for a better job. Although no offer of employment was forthcoming from the Margrave, the collection of six concertos still today carries the name "Brandenburg."

In his dedication Bach refers to "the present concertos which I have adapted to several instruments." These words allude to the fact that he designed the Brandenburg Concertos to showcase a variety of orchestral colors. Recall that the concerto grosso consists of a basic orchestra of all players, called the *ripieno* (full) or tutti (all), and from this emerges a small core of soloists, called the *concertino,* to develop and decorate the primary musical themes (see Chapter 33). The various solo groups Bach features in the six Brandenburg Concertos (1721) are as follows.

Key	Movements	Concertino
No. 1 (BWV 1046) F major	[Allegro]-Adagio-Allegro-Minuet	2 horns, 3 oboes, bassoon and *violino piccolo*
No. 2 (BWV 1047) F major	[Allegro]-Andante-Allegro	Trumpet, recorder, oboe, and violin
No. 3 (BWV 1048) G major	[Allegro]-Adagio-Allegro	3 violins, 3 violas, and 3 cellos
No. 4 (BWV 1049) G major	[Allegro]-Andante-Presto	Violin and 2 recorders
No. 5 (BWV 1050) D major	Allegro-Affettuoso-Allegro	Harpsichord, violin, and flute
No. 6 (BWV 1051) B♭ major	[Allegro]-Adagio-Allegro	2 violas, *2 viole da gamba,* and cello

Let us concentrate on Concerto No. 5, for in this work Bach himself surely functioned as the harpsichord soloist during performances at Cöthen. Concerto No. 5 pits the full orchestra against a *concertino,* consisting of harpsichord, violin, and flute. As with most concerti grossi, the first movement is written in ritornello form, a musical plan popularized by Corelli and Vivaldi. In principle, ritornello form demands that the *ripieno* (tutti) play the ritornello while the *concertino* executes either motives derived from the ritornello or free material that complements it. With Bach, however, the separation between ritornello theme and concertino excursion is not as clear-cut as it had been with Corelli and Vivaldi (see Chapter 33). In Bach's more complex design, the distinction between the large ensemble and the small group of soloists is less pronounced. Nonetheless, Bach's ritornello theme is typical of Baroque melodies in three distinctive ways (Ex. 39-7): it is idiomatic to the violin (repeated notes are easy to play on string instruments); it is lengthy and somewhat asymmetrical; and it possesses a driving rhythm that propels the music forward. As the first movement proceeds, the violin and flute gradually fall by the wayside to allow the harpsichord to carry all the solo material. What had started as a concerto grosso has become a showpiece for solo harpsichord. Bach has written, in fact if not in name, the first true solo concerto for keyboard. Only a virtuoso of the highest order can play the extremely difficult passage-work found toward the end of the movement. But Bach was just this sort of keyboard virtuoso. Picture in your mind's eye the orchestra at Cöthen playing in the prince's music room (see Fig. 39-3). At the center of it all was Bach, seated at the large, new harpsichord he had brought from Berlin, and astounding the members of the court with his bravura playing.

EXAMPLE 39-7

LISTENING CUE

JOHANN SEBASTIAN BACH
Brandenburg Concerto No. 5 in D Major
    (BWV 1050; 1721)
First movement

CD 6/7
Anthology, No. 115

 SUMMARY

Johann Sebastian Bach wrote many important vocal works, including some three hundred cantatas for the Lutheran church. But the majority of his nearly 1,100 works are for instruments of one kind or another. In his day Bach was known more as a virtuoso organist than as a composer. Bach also played cello, viola, and violin, and early in his career was hired at a court as a violinist. Throughout his life Bach was also a renowned teacher. Many of his best-known instrumental pieces were conceived of, and are still used today, as sets of instructional works. They intend to develop the technical skills and overall musical understanding of the performer. Among Bach's pedagogical projects are the *Orgelbüchlein* (a series of chorale preludes intended to cover the entire church year), the Two- and Three-Part Inventions, the two books of The Well-Tempered Clavier, the six violin sonatas and partitas, and the six cello suites. Bach's complete understanding of the idiomatic capabilities and distinctive colors of the instruments of the Baroque orchestra can best be seen in his Brandenburg Concertos. In this one collection of six concerti grossi, Bach demonstrates a mastery of virtually every instrumental combination and type of orchestral scoring known in his day.

KEY TERMS

BWV (Bach Werke Verzeichnis)	Two- and Three-Part Inventions	countersubject
Orgelbüchlein	The Well-Tempered Clavier	episode
chorale prelude		invertible counterpoint
rank	equal temperament	fugue
stop	Picardy third	obbligato
pedal point	subject	partita
Kapellmeister	exposition	Brandenburg Concertos

Johann Sebastian Bach: Vocal Music in Leipzig

In the spring of 1723, Bach moved to the city of Leipzig, and there he remained until his death in 1750. Leipzig, with 30,000 inhabitants, was a large German city by the standards of the day, and it boasted an important university where Bach's sons (but not daughters) might enroll. The position that Bach assumed in Leipzig was that of **cantor** (director of church music) at the St. Thomas Church, the largest and most important church in this Lutheran city. While the post of cantor was a prestigious one, the incumbent was nonetheless a civil servant selected by and answerable to the Leipzig town council. Surprisingly, Bach was not the first choice of the city fathers. Only after the well-known composer Georg Philipp Telemann (1681–1767) and the now obscure Christoph Graupner (1683–1760) declined the post, did the members of the town council reluctantly turn to Bach. When he assumed the position in Leipzig, it was understood that Bach would henceforth turn his attention away from instrumental music for the court and would instead concentrate on religious vocal music for the church.

Bach's job in Leipzig was not an easy one. He was required to play the organ at weddings and funerals, teach music and sometimes even Latin grammar to the boys of the choir school of St. Thomas, and superintend the liturgical music of the four principal churches of the city. But by far the most demanding duty of his position as cantor was to provide about a half-hour of new music for the church each Sunday and religious holiday, a total of about sixty days a year. In so doing, Bach brought an important genre of religious music, the Lutheran chorale cantata, to the highest point of its development.

THE LUTHERAN CHORALE CANTATA

When Bach arrived in Leipzig in 1723, he set about composing a cycle of cantatas for the entire church year. In fact, over the next few years he created five such cycles, nearly 300 cantatas in total (although only about two hundred of these survive today). The cantata was the musical high point of the Sunday service. In Bach's time, St. Thomas Church celebrated a Sunday Mass as prescribed two centuries earlier by Martin Luther (1483–1546). Attended by some 2,000 of the faithful, the St. Thomas service began at seven o'clock in the morning and lasted nearly four hours. Following a few introductory chants and prayers, a celebrant read the day's scriptural message from the Gospel. The organist then played a chorale prelude to remind the congregation of the chorale melody of the day and give the instrumentalists an opportunity to tune. At this point, the choir and instrumentalists performed the cantata under Bach's direction. The cantata served as a musical elaboration upon the spiritual theme of the Gospel. Thereafter, a preacher ascended the pulpit (Fig. 40-1) to offer an hour-long sermon discussing the moral and practical implications of this spiritual message. Later that afternoon, the choir and instrumentalists repeated the cantata at a Vespers service at the St. Nicolas Church across town, where an equally large congregation awaited Bach's music.

Typical of the cantatas Bach composed for Leipzig is *Wachet auf, ruft uns die Stimme* (*Awake, A Voice Is Calling*; BWV 140), a work built upon a chorale tune of the same name. A chorale, as we have seen (see Chapter 24), is simply the German version of what most English-speaking communities would call a hymn. *Wachet auf* is a texted chorale tune written in the sixteenth century and widely used by musicians in the Lutheran church before Bach took it up. The structure of the tune is typical of chorale melodies (Ex. 40-1). It is

St. Thomas's Church, Leipzig

FIGURE 40-1

Interior of the St. Thomas Church in the mid nineteenth century, looking across the parishioners' pews toward the high altar. Notice the pulpit on the right from which the sermon would be delivered.

composed of seven phrases that unfold in a pattern **AAB,** specifically **A** (1, 2, 3), **A** (1, 2, 3) **B** (4-7, 3).

EXAMPLE 40-1

A. Awake, a voice is calling
   From the watchmen from high in the tower
   Awake, Jerusalem!
   Midnight is the hour
   They call us with a clarion voice
   Where are the Wise Virgins?

B. Get up, the Bridegroom comes
   Stand up and take your lamps
   Alleluia
   Prepare yourselves
   For the wedding
   You must go forth to meet him!

Because it is based upon a chorale tune, Bach's *Wachet auf* is called a chorale cantata, a genre of music that arose in Germany in the late seventeenth century. The **chorale cantata** is a sacred vocal genre that employs the text and tune of a pre-existing Lutheran chorale in all or several of its movements. *Wachet auf* makes use of a traditional chorale melody during each of its three choral movements, which present the hymn's three textual stanzas in succession. The intervening movements, consisting of recitatives and duet-arias, represent Bach's newly composed settings of the lyrical poems by one of his contemporaries, and use neither the chorale tune nor its text. Thus, Bach creates a formal symmetry, with the chorale-based choral movements at the beginning, middle, and end, flanking each of the recitative-aria pairs and providing a structural framework for the composition as a whole.

Movement:						
1	2	3	4	5	6	7
Chorus	Recitative	Aria (duet)	Chorus	Recitative	Aria (duet)	Chorus
1st stanza			2nd stanza			3rd stanza

Bach was a devoted husband, a loving father to twenty children, and a respected burgher of Leipzig. His cantata *Wachet auf* clearly shows his faith in the religious traditions of his German Lutheran community. Bach composed it in 1731 for a service on a Sunday immediately before Advent (four Sundays before Christmas). The text of the cantata announces the coming of a bridegroom toward his hopeful bride. Christ is the groom. A group of ten virgins represents the bride and, by extension, the entire Christian community. Their story, the Parable of the Wise and Foolish Virgins, is told in the Gospel of St. Matthew (25:1–13); five of the Virgins have brought oil for their lamps and are prepared to meet the coming Christ, but five have not. Both the Gospel and Bach's cantata proclaim this central message: Here

Bach's Choir and Orchestra: Where Were the Ladies?

During the seventeenth century, women frequently appeared as soloists on the operatic stage and occasionally in vocal and instrumental music-making at court. As the eighteenth century progressed, women also began to sing religious music in churches and theaters. But the Lutheran church was a conservative institution in Bach's day. Aside from a few small rural churches where ladies were allowed to appear as "choral adjuncts," women played no role in the performance of Lutheran church music. Ultimately, this traditionalist attitude affected the way the Bach family conducted its business.

When Bach arrived in Leipzig in 1723, he was accompanied by his four children and his second wife, Anna Magdalena Bach (his first wife had died unexpectedly in 1720). Anna Magdalena was a gifted singer who had been employed by the court of Cöthen at a salary almost as great as that of her new husband. But moving to the Lutheran church position in Leipzig forced her to give up her career as a performer. Henceforth, Anna Magdalena would serve as the nucleus of what might be termed "Bach Incorporated"—that industrious group of some dozen or so children, relatives, and students who copied each new Bach cantata and all the necessary parts in preparation for the coming Sunday service. In their quarters next to the St. Thomas Church (Fig. 40-2), Anna Magdalena copied manuscript after manuscript for her husband. She may have assisted him with rehearsals as well.

The actual public performance of a cantata by Bach, however, was an all-male affair. In 1730 Bach stipulated clearly the nature of the orchestra and chorus he required for his sacred vocal music. He drew his instrumentalists from a pool of a dozen string and wind players employed by the town, and these men were supplemented by students from the (all-male) University of Leipzig. Although Bach wanted an orchestra of some twenty players, fifteen seems to have been the norm, and sometimes even fewer were on hand. As to the singers, for the standard four-part choir Bach required at least three singers on each part, though he said he preferred four for a total of sixteen singers. Often, however, many

fewer were actually on hand. All of the vocalists—soloists as well as choral singers—were boys or young men from the St. Thomas choir school or the nearby university. Thus the alto and soprano choral parts in Bach's sacred music were sung by males (young men in falsetto voice and boys), and the difficult soprano solos were executed by a solitary choirboy. Indeed, the ladies never did get a fair hearing.

Bach-Archiv, Leipzig

FIGURE 40-2

Leipzig, the St. Thomas Church (center), and the choir school (left), from an engraving of 1723, the year in which Bach moved to the city. Bach and his large family occupied two floors of the choir school, and it was here that the composing, copying, and rehearsing of his music took place.

in the season of Advent all good citizens of Leipzig should put their spiritual houses in order, for Christ will soon be with them.

The spiritually attuned listener can hear the inexorable march of Christ in the opening movement of cantata *Wachet auf*. Here Bach creates a chorale fantasy that is both dramatic and monumental. First the orchestra announces Christ's arrival by means of a three-part ritornello (Ex. 40-2). The ritornello conveys a feeling of growing anticipation. The increasingly numerous sixteenth notes suggest the urgent movement of the faithful surging forward to meet the coming Christ. Then the ancient chorale melody enters on high in the sopranos; it is the voice of tradition, perhaps the voice of God. In long, steady notes, it enjoins the populace to prepare to receive the Lord. Beneath this the voices of the people—the altos, tenors, and basses—scurry in rapid counterpoint, eager to meet their savior. Lowest of all is the bass of the basso continuo. It moves steadily ahead, mainly in stepwise motion in notes of similar value. This walking bass enhances the meaning of the text, underscoring the steady approach of the Lord. The enormous complexity of the movement, with its dense textural layering and rich symbolism, shows why musicians, then and now, view Bach as the greatest contrapuntalist who ever lived.

EXAMPLE 40-2

LISTENING CUE

JOHANN SEBASTIAN BACH
Cantata BWV 140, *Wachet auf, ruft uns die Stimme* (1731)
Movement 1

CD 6/8

Anthology, No. 116a

Movement 2 is a recitative for tenor solo, a narrator who announces the imminent arrival of Christ, the bridegroom. This is an example of simple recitative because the accompaniment is limited to a basso continuo, featuring in this case the organ and bassoon. Generally speaking, in his sacred vocal works Bach assigns the role of the narrator, or evangelist, to a tenor.

Movement 3 is a lengthy duet for soprano (the Soul) and bass (Christ). In German sacred music of the Baroque period, the role of Christ is traditionally assigned to a bass. Here Bach ornaments the charming soprano-bass duet with a lengthy ritornello played by a **violino piccolo** (a small violin usually tuned a minor third higher than the normal violin).

Movement 4 calls upon the chorale melody once again. Now Bach places the tune (and the second stanza of the chorale text) in long notes in the tenor voice alone. The tenors are the watchmen of Zion who call Jerusalem (Leipzig) to awake. Beneath this chorale the bass plods forward, mostly in unwavering quarter notes. This classic example of a Baroque walking bass again suggests the inevitable coming of Christ. Against the tenor and bass the violins and violas play a hauntingly beautiful ritornello (Ex. 40-3). It is exactly twelve bars long and subdivided into six two-bar groups—an unusually symmetrical construction for Bach. Perhaps because of the symmetrical, lyrical style of the ritornello, this movement has become one of Bach's most beloved compositions. Indeed, it was one of Bach's favorites too, for it was the only cantata movement that he published.[1] All the rest of his Leipzig cantatas were left in handwritten scores at the time of his death.

EXAMPLE 40-3

LISTENING CUE

JOHANN SEBASTIAN BACH
Cantata, *Wachet auf, ruft uns die Stimme*
Movements 2, 3, and 4

CD 6/9–10 and
Book Companion Website (http://schirmer.wadsworth.com/wright_1e)
Anthology, No. 116b-d

Movement 5 is an **accompanied recitative** in which the bass soloist (representing Christ) invites the anguished Soul to find comfort in him. Unlike the tenor's simple recitative (movement 2), this movement features strings providing a lush chordal accompaniment, creating a halo-like effect to surround the words of Christ—another example of musical symbolism in Bach.

Movement 6 is a duet between Christ and the Soul, who are once again represented by the bass and soprano soloists. Bach wrote no operas, and indeed by the time he arrived in 1723 the Leipzig opera house had closed for good. But he frequently went to nearby Dresden (see Map 39-1), where the court sponsored a flourishing opera, one of the best in Europe. In movement 6, Bach comes as close as he ever will to composing an operatic love duet. In fact, the piece is a perfect *da capo* aria of the sort that might be found in a Baroque *opera seria*.

Movement 7 is a four-part harmonization of the chorale tune that sets the third and final stanza of the chorale text. Here the full congregation joined in the singing of the chorale, likely not by reading from a hymnal but by singing the tune from memory. In this concluding movement, all of the instrumental parts double the vocal lines, a technique termed **colla parte** (with the part). Here too all the spiritual energy of Leipzig was united in Bach's simple but expressive harmony.

EXAMPLE 40-4

May glory be sung to you...
The gates are of twelve pearls...

Bach's Four-Part Chorale Harmonizations and Teaching Music Theory Today

Today in colleges, universities, and music conservatories around the world, the study of music theory is grounded in a thorough investigation of four-voice chorale harmonizations by Johann Sebastian Bach. Almost all students majoring in music, for example, study Bach chorales to learn how to write, and thereby understand, proper chord progressions, modulations, and voice leadings. They compose the "missing" three voices (bass, tenor, and alto) below ancient chorale melodies in the style of Bach. Thus the model of Bach, established nearly three hundred years ago, lies at the core of much theory pedagogy today. But would Bach have approved?

Indeed, he would have, for this was precisely the method of teaching Bach himself employed. C.P.E. Bach, the mas-

ter's second son, said this about his father's approach to teaching harmony: "His pupils had to begin their studies by learning pure four-part thorough [figured] bass. From this he went to chorales; first he added the basses to them himself, and they had to invent the alto and the tenor. Then he taught them to devise the basses themselves."[2] Bach also encouraged his students to copy into their notebooks four-part chorale settings from his passions and cantatas (such as, for example, the final movement of the cantata *Wachet auf*). Owing in part to these notebooks of Bach's students, 371 of Bach's chorale settings have been preserved for us to study today. Thus, in a sense, we are all students of Bach.

LISTENING CUE

JOHANN SEBASTIAN BACH
Cantata, *Wachet auf, ruft uns die Stimme*
Movements 5, 6, and 7

CD 6/11–13
Anthology, No. 116e-g

In addition to some three hundred cantatas, Johann Sebastian Bach is said to have composed five passions and a Christmas oratorio, all large-scale works. A **passion** is a musical depiction of Christ's crucifixion as recorded in the Gospels; it is traditionally performed on Good Friday. By Bach's time, a passion had become virtually identical to an oratorio, except that it dealt with just one subject, the death of Christ. Of Bach's five passions, only two survive, the St. John Passion (1724) and the St. Matthew Passion (1727). The former requires about two hours to perform, and the latter two-and-a-half. Perhaps for that reason, members of the Bach family called the St. Matthew setting the "Great Passion." It requires three choirs and two small orchestras, each with a colorful variety of instruments. Many believe the St. Matthew Passion, with no fewer than sixty-eight expressive movements, to be Bach's greatest dramatic work.

BACH'S LATER MUSICAL PROJECTS

By 1730 Bach had tired of the weekly grind of creating new music for the church each Sunday. He did not relinquish his position at the St. Thomas Church, but gave it less time as he turned his attention to other musical activities. In late March 1729, Bach assumed directorship of the Collegium Musicum in Leipzig. A **collegium musicum** was an association of musicians, usually university students, who came together voluntarily to play the latest music before the public in a large café or beer hall. (The name "collegium" is still used today by performing groups in colleges and universities, although now the emphasis is not on a repertory of modern music, but on early music as played on reproductions of historical instruments.) Bach directed the Collegium Musicum of Leipzig, on and off, for at least a dozen years. It provided an opportunity for him to compose and perform orchestral music—concertos and orchestral suites—something that his recent preoccupation with church music in Leipzig had not allowed him to do.

Not only did Bach turn to projects beyond the St. Thomas Church in his last decades but he also looked beyond the city limits of Leipzig. In 1733 he composed a *Kyrie* and *Gloria* for the court in Dresden, which would later serve as the opening movements of his great B-Minor Mass (see below). Another work destined for Dresden at this time is Bach's **Goldberg Variations** (BWV 988), a virtuosic set of thirty variations preceded and concluded by a simple air, the air and each variation based on the same thirty-two-bar harmonic pattern. The collection derives its name from a gifted pupil of Bach, Johann Goldberg, who worked for one of Bach's patrons in Dresden. It seems that the patron was something of an insomniac and asked Bach for music that Goldberg might play to alleviate the tedium of his sleepless nights.

In 1747 Bach undertook his last substantial journey, a trip to Berlin to visit his son, Carl Philipp Emanuel Bach. C.P.E. Bach was employed as a keyboardist at the court of King Frederick the Great of Prussia (1712–1786), who himself was a musical enthusiast, being a skilled flautist. Bach arrived in the evening, when Frederick, as was his custom, was playing chamber music with his court musicians. Immediately the king went to a keyboard to play a melody he had composed, and asked Bach to improvise a fugue on it on the spot. This Bach did in a way such that the king and his courtiers alike "were seized with astonishment," as a newspaper of the day reported. But Bach himself was not satisfied. When he returned home to Leipzig he set about making the royal theme serve as the unifying element, not merely in a single fugue, but in a collection of pieces: a trio sonata, two fugues (called ricercars), and ten puzzle canons. Bach called his royally inspired collection **The Musical Offering** (BWV 1079) and dedicated it to His Majesty with appropriately inflated praise of the king's musical talent. In truth, however, The Musical Offering reveals how the genius of Bach was needed to unlock the full musical potential of the king's original idea.

Bach's other great encyclopedic work is The Art of Fugue, which he began about 1740 and had not quite finished at the time of his death a decade later. **The Art of Fugue** (BWV 1080) is a collection of fugues and canons, all derived from the same subject (Bach's own) and all apparently intended for keyboard. Here we see exemplified almost every contrapuntal technique known to musicians. When published after his death, it consisted of fourteen fugues and four canons, all written in score and most for four voices. Bach intended the final fugue to be a quadruple fugue, but it breaks off shortly after the exposition of the fourth subject. Appropriately, this last subject is built upon the four pitches B♭, A, C, B♮, which in German musical notation spells the word BACH.

The Goldberg Variations, The Musical Offering, and The Art of Fugue demonstrate Bach's focus on large-scale musical projects during the last decade of his life. In each of these he brought one particular form of composition—variation, puzzle canon, or fugue—to a level of excellence that was never surpassed.

B-Minor Mass

Bach's last composition, his **B-Minor Mass** (BWV 232), is perhaps the grandest of all of these large-scale projects, for here he brought the tradition of the Baroque Latin Mass to a glorious culmination. As we have seen, Bach had composed the *Kyrie* and *Gloria* for the court of Catholic Dresden back in 1733. Now, in 1748, in old age and declining health, the master determined to extend the work by adding a *Credo, Sanctus,* and *Agnus,* and thus create a complete setting of the Ordinary of the Mass as sung for centuries in the Roman Catholic Church. For these additional movements, Bach did not compose entirely new music. Instead, he refashioned movements of cantatas and Masses that he had written years before. For example, a *Sanctus* written in 1724 became the opening of the *Sanctus* of the B-Minor Mass; a movement of a cantata of 1714 (*Weinen, Klagen* [*To Whine and Wail*, BWV 12]) was reworked to serve as the "Crucifixus" of the *Credo*. Bach borrowed from this earlier cantata because its subject matter (weeping) was signalled by a descending tetrachordal bass, the Baroque emblem of mourning. The vocal parts of the "Crucifixus" are thus filled with dissonant, painful tritones and augmented seconds, all created in the score by the use of many sharps (but no flats). The sharp, of course, is cruciform or cross-like, in shape; this is the way Bach's musical symbolism works.

EXAMPLE 40-5

Today we may be scandalized that Bach chose to re-use so much previously written material in what would be his last great work. But virtually all composers of the Baroque period engaged in this practice. (Handel was an especially notorious "borrower.") It gave the artist a chance to review an earlier work, revise it, and thereby improve the score. For Bach in particular, this process of musical review provided yet another opportunity to perfect his art, and Bach was nothing if not a perfectionist.

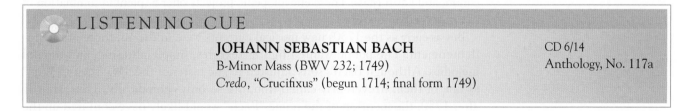

LISTENING CUE

JOHANN SEBASTIAN BACH
B-Minor Mass (BWV 232; 1749)
Credo, "Crucifixus" (begun 1714; final form 1749)

CD 6/14
Anthology, No. 117a

The turn to the relative major at the end of the "Crucifixus" sounds a note of hope to be realized in the next movement, "Et resurrexit" ("And He arose").

The theme of Christ's resurrection now receives an appropriately triumphant setting. With large orchestra and brilliant trumpets sounding in a sprightly triple meter, the music seems to dance joyfully toward heaven. Unlike the "Crucifixus," which was refashioned from much-earlier music, the "Et resurrexit" was apparently newly composed. Indeed, these notes must have been among the last that Bach wrote. Thus what we call the great B-Minor Mass is a compilation of pieces that Bach had composed over the course of three decades. It represents a culmination of all that he had learned about writing sacred music for the church.

LISTENING CUE

JOHANN SEBASTIAN BACH
B-Minor Mass (1749)
Credo, "Et resurrexit" (1749)

CD 6/15
Anthology, No. 117b

Bach's B-Minor Mass is a massive five-movement sacred work that takes some two hours to perform. During the composer's lifetime, the Mass was never heard in its entirety. It was inappropriate for the Lutheran church because it contains portions of the Mass text not used in the Lutheran service; likewise, it was unsuitable for the Catholic liturgy due to its length and the freedoms taken with the text. Nor could it have been sung simply as a concert—concerts of purely religious music as we know them did not exist in Bach's day. Today the B-Minor Mass is performed in concert halls around the world. It is appreciated less as a Catholic Mass and more as a work that transcends denominations. Like Beethoven's Ninth Symphony, Bach's B-Minor Mass is his ecumenical gift to all humanity.

SUMMARY

When Johann Sebastian Bach died during the summer of 1750, apparently of a stroke, he and his music were soon forgotten. With its heavy reliance on traditional chorale tunes and dense counterpoint, his creations were thought to be too old-fashioned and rigid, even pedantic. Yes, Bach's music is often difficult. He was intent on discovering and exploiting the musical potential of every idea, and he took no shortcuts. In so doing, Bach created grand projects that demonstrate the special qualities of almost every musical genre and form except opera—organ prelude, prelude and fugue, solo sonata, concerto grosso, cantata, passion, variation set, puzzle canon, and Latin Mass. These encyclopedic projects offer a splendid summation of music of the Baroque era.

But as early as the 1730s new musical currents were in the air, those of the Enlightenment. The public wanted lighter textures, simple phrasing, and tuneful melodies. Although Bach's sons adjusted to the tastes of the day, "the old Wig," as one of them irreverently called him, did so only sporadically. Thus, shortly after 1750, the mention of the name "Bach" would likely have conjured up the image of one or the other of his fashionable sons, not the great polyphonic master. Yet, a small group of musicians, including Mozart, Beethoven, Schumann, and Mendelssohn, kept the knowledge of Bach's extraordinary music alive. When Mendelssohn performed Bach's St. Matthew Passion in 1829 as part of a centenary commemoration, a "Bach revival" was underway. From that time on, musicians have never ceased to admire Bach's music for its internal integrity, grand design, and superhuman craftsmanship.

KEY TERMS

cantor

chorale cantata

violino piccolo

accompanied recitative

colla parte

passion

collegium musicum

Goldberg Variations

The Musical Offering

The Art of Fugue

B-Minor Mass

NOTES

Abbreviations

History in Documents   *Music in the Western World: A History in Documents*, ed. Piero Weiss and Richard Taruskin (New York, 1984).

JAMS   *Journal of the American Musicological Society*

Letters of Mozart   Emily Anderson, *The Letters of Mozart and His Family*, ed. and trans. Emily Anderson, 3 vols. (London, 1966).

NG   *The New Grove Dictionary of Music and Musicians*, ed. S. Sadie and J. Tyrrell (London, 2001).

PART I

Chapter 1   1. Thomas J. Mathiesen, *Apollo's Lyre: Greek Music and Music Theory in Antiquity and the Middle Ages* (Lincoln, NE, 1999), 145. 2. Anicius Manlius Severinus Boethius, *Fundamentals of Music*, trans. Calvin M. Bower, ed. Claude V. Palisca (New Haven, CT, 1989), Book I, Chapter 1. 3. Aristotle, *Politics*, 8:1340s.

Chapter 2   none

Chapter 3   none

Chapter 4   none

Chapter 5   none

Chapter 6   1. This translation is drawn from Paris, Bibliothèque nationale, fonds français, MS 12473, fol. 15. 2. Translated from Jean Boutière and Irénée-Marcel Cluzel, *Biographies des troubadours; textes provençaux des XIIIe et XIVe siècles*, 2nd ed. (Paris, 1973), 29.

Chapter 7   1. *Hucbald, Guido, and John on Music: Three Medieval Treatises*, trans. Warren Babb, ed. Claude V. Palisca (New Haven, CT 1978), 159.

Chapter 8   1. Edmond de Coussemaker, ed., *Scriptorum de Musica Medii Aevi*, 4 vols. (Paris, 1864–1876; rpt. 1931), I, 342. See also, Jeremy Yudkin, *The Music Treatise of Anonymous IV: A New Translation*, vol. 41 of Musicological Studies and Documents (Rome, 1985), 39.

Chapter 9   1. *The Letters of Abelard and Heloise*, trans. Betty Radice (London, 1974), Letter No. 1, p. 115.

Chapter 10   1. Adapted from Robert F. Hayburn, *Papal Legislation on Sacred Music: 95 A.D. to 1977 A.D.* (Collegeville, MN, 1979), 20–21.

Chapter 11   1. Margaret Bent and Andrew Wathey, "Philippe de Vitry," NG, 26:804. 2. Timothy J. McGee, *Medieval Instrumental Dances* (Bloomington and Indianapolis, 1989), 20. 3. McGee, *Medieval Instrumental Dances*, 26.

Chapter 12   none

Chapter 13   1. Francesco Petrarch, quoted in many translations and many sources including Marcel Frémiot and Charles Pitt, "Avignon," NG, 2:251.

Musical Interlude 1   1. Isidore of Seville, *Etymologies*, as given in *Source Readings in Music History*, ed. Oliver Strunk; rev. ed. Leo Treitler (New York and London, 1998), 149. 2. Jan Herlinger, ed. *Prosdocimus de' Beldomandi: Contrapunctus* (Lincoln, NE, 1984), p. 83 and especially footnote 11.

PART II

Chapter 14   1. Coluccio Salutati, *Le "consulte" e "pratiche" della Repubblica fiorentina* (1403), quoted in part in Michael Levey, *Florence: A Portrait* (Cambridge, MA, 1996), 68. 2. Giovanni Gherardi da Prato, *Il Paradiso degli Alberti*, ed. Antonio Lanza (Rome, 1975), 165. 3. Prato, *Il Paradiso degli Alberti*, 176. 4. *Giovanni Boccaccio's Decameron*, trans. Mark Musa and Peter Bondanella (New York, 1982), 6. 5. *Giovanni Boccaccio's Decameron*, 3.

Chapter 15   1. The correct dimensions of the cathedral of Florence and their symbolic significance are discussed in a splendid article by Marvin Trachtenberg, "Architecture and Music Reunited: A New Reading of Dufay's *Nuper Rosarum Flores* and the Cathedral of Flo-

rence," *Renaissance Quarterly*, 54 (2001): 740–75. 2. Giannozzo Manetti, *Oratio*, cited in Craig Wright, "Dufay's *Nuper Rosarum Flores*, King Solomon's Temple, and the Veneration of the Virgin," JAMS, 47 (1994): 430.

Chapter 16   1. Geraldus Cambrensis, *Descriptio Cambriae* (1198), as given in and adapted from Frederick Sternfeld, *Music from the Middle Ages to the Renaissance* (New York, 1973), 264; also cited in *History in Documents*, 61.

Chapter 17   1. Mathieu d'Escouchy, *Chronique*, quoted in and translated from Jeanne Marix, *Les Musiciens de la cour de Bourgogne au XVe siècle* (Strasbourg, 1937), 41.

Chapter 18   1. Leeman L. Perkins, "Ockeghem," NG, 18:315. 2. Heinrich Glarean, *Dodecachordon* (1547), trans. Clement Miller, 2 vols. (Rome, 1965), II, 284. Glarean, publishing in 1547, identifies the king as Louis XII; the sole musical source (St. Gall, Switzerland, Stiftsarchiv, MS 462), written around 1515, identifies him as Louis XI. The most recent bibliographical discoveries about Josquin suggest that the earlier king (Louis XI) is the royal monotone in question.

Chapter 19   none

PART III

Musical Interlude 2   none

Chapter 20   1. The following discussion draws heavily on part one of Patrick Macey's excellent study, *Bonfire Songs: Savonarola's Musical Legacy* (Oxford, 1998). 2. *The Book of the Courtier: A New Translation*, trans. Charles S. Singleton (Garden City, NJ, 1959), Book II, p. 13.

Chapter 21   1. Patrick Macey, "Josquin," NG, 13:229. 2. Translated from Cosimo Bartoli, *Ragionamenti accademici* (1567); a similar translation can be found in "Josquin," NG, 13:229. 3. Patrick Macey, "Josquin," NG, 13:225. 4. Macey, "Josquin," 13:225. 5. This thesis was first developed in a superb article by Patrick Macey, "Savonarola and the Sixteenth-Century Motet," JAMS, 36 (1983): 422–52. 6. This and the preceding remark are cited in Patrick Macey, "Josquin," in NG, 13:228.

Musical Interlude 3   none

Chapter 22   1. Thoinot Arbeau, *Orchesography*, trans. Mary Steward Evans (New York, 1967), 118–19. 2. Arbeau, *Orchesography*, 121.

Chapter 23   none

Musical Interlude 4   none

Chapter 24   1. Translated from the preface of Walter's *Geistliche Gesangbüchlein* (1524); a similar translation can be found in Carl Schalk, *Music in Early Lutheranism* (St. Louis, 2001), 31.

Chapter 25   1. Lewis Lockwood, ed. *Palestrina: Pope Marcellus Mass* (New York, 1975), 14. 2. Gustave Reese, *Music in the Renaissance* (New York, 1954), 449.

Chapter 26   1. Simon Schama, *A History of Britain* (New York, 2000), 334.

Chapter 27   1. For this and the previous quote, see Craig Monson, "Elizabethan London," in Iain Fenlon, ed., *The Renaissance: From the 1470s to the End of the 16th Century* in the series *Man and Music*, ed. Stanley Sadie (Englewood Cliffs, NJ, 1989), 319, 321. 2. Quoted by Monson, "Elizabethan London," 331. 3. Later in the Fitzwilliam Virginal Book there is an identical setting of this piece with an eighth variation ascribed to John Mundy.

Chapter 28   1. This and the previous quote are found in Anthony Newcomb, *The Madrigal at Ferrara 1579–1597*, 2 vols. (Princeton, 1980), I, 55, 67. 2. This passage has been adapted from the translation of Glenn Watkins given in *Gesualdo, The Man and His Music* (Chapel Hill, 1973), 44–46. 3. This passage is a slight rearrangement of the translation of Gary Tomlinson in *Source Readings in Music History*, ed. Oliver Strunk; rev. ed. Leo Treitler (New York and London, 1998), 528.

PART IV

Chapter 29   none

Chapter 30   1. This translation to Peri's preface of the score of Euridice was kindly provided by Pietro Moretti. 2. The words of Marco da Gagliano (1582-1643) as quoted in *History in Documents,* 176.

Chapter 31   1. Translated from Monteverdi's preface to his eighth book of madrigals as given in the introduction to vol. 8 of G. Francesco Malipiero, ed., *Tutte le opere di Claudio Monteverdi* (Bologna, 1929). 2. *History in Documents,* 185.

Chapter 32   1. Letter of Leopold Mozart of 14 April 1770 as given in *Letters of Mozart,* I, 187.

Chapter 33   1. Michael Talbot, *Vivaldi* (New York, Oxford, Singapore, and Sidney, 1993), 42. 2. Correspondence of Charles de Brosses, translated in H.C. Robbins Landon, *Vivaldi: Voice of the Baroque* (London, 1993), 30. 3. Talbot, *Vivaldi,* 40.

Chapter 34   1. Translated from the preface of Georg Muffat's *Armonico tributo* (Salzburg, 1682). 2. In Froberger's original manuscripts the gigue usually, but not always, precedes the sarabande. Publishers of his music, however, invariably grouped them in the sequence allemande, courante, sarabande, and gigue. It was these posthumous publications that firmly established this as the "standard" order for the dance suite. 3. *The Philosophical Works of Descartes Rendered into English,* by Elizabeth S. Haldane and G.R.T. Ross, 2 vols. (Cambridge, 1973), I, 372, 377. 4. *History in Documents,* 218. 5. Kerala J. Snyder, *Dieterich Buxtehude: Organist in Lübeck* (New York, 1987), 57. 6. Snyder, *Dieterich Buxtehude,* 57–58.

Chapter 35   1. James Anthony, *French Baroque Music from Beaujoyeulx to Rameau* (Portland 1997), 66. 2. Evrard Titon du Tillet, *Second Supplément du Parnasse françois* (Paris, 1755), 791–92. 3. *Dictionnaire universel françois et latin,* 6 vols. (Paris, 1743), I, 1670.

Chapter 36   1. Most fixed-pitched instruments, such as harpsichord and organ, did not use equal temperament in this period, but one kind or another of "mean-tone" temperament which began by adjusting the fifth on C (or perhaps G or F) and proceeding by fifths from there. Thus the keys around C were generally well in tune, but those very far away from them around the circle of fifths, such as F♯, were unpleasantly out of tune. Whether the lute in seventeenth-century France was tuned in mean-tone temperament or equal temperament is not certain. 2. Davitt Moroney, "Prélude non mésuré," *NG,* 20:294. 3. Translated from the French as given in Margery Halford, ed., *L'Art de toucher le clavecin* (Port Washington, NY, 1974), 49.

Musical Interlude 5   1. Handel's letter to Mattheson, cited in Joel Lester, "Recognition of Major and Minor in Germany Music: 1680–1730," *Journal of Music Theory,* 22 (1978): 91–92. 2. Translated from *Traité de l'harmonie* (1722), preface, no page.

Chapter 37   1. An account reported by Sir John Hawkins and reproduced in Michael Burden, *Purcell Remembered* (Portland, OR, 1995), 71–72.

Chapter 38   1. Translated from Johann Mattheson, *Das neu-eröffnete Orchestre* (Hamburg, 1713), 211. 2. H.C. Robins Landon, *Handel and his World* (London, 1984), 88. 3. Charles Burney, *An Account of the Musical Performances in Westminster-Abbey* (New York and London, 1775; rpt. 1979), 27.

Chapter 39   1. *The New Bach Reader,* ed. Hans T. David and Arthur Mendel, rev. Christoph Wolff (New York, 1998), 92–93.

Chapter 40   1. Earlier, when Bach was at Mühlhausen in 1708, the town council sponsored the publication of his Cantata *Gott ist mein König* (BWV 71), but only because the work was in honor of the town council. This was Bach's sole vocal work to be published during his lifetime. 2. *The New Bach Reader,* 399.

BIBLIOGRAPHY

What follows is a brief, preliminary bibliography. Far more comprehensive bibliographies are included in the Student Workbook and Instructor's Manual for *Music in Western Civilization*, and are also available on the Cengage Learning website (where they are updated). These bibliographies cite only works in the English language. Each of the books and articles contains either its own bibliography or copious footnotes that suggest still more useful sources for research. For help in the challenging task of writing about the ephemeral art of music, see the essay "Writing a Research Paper on a Musical Topic" by Sterling Murray that is included in the Workbook.

❁ DICTIONARIES AND ENCYCLOPEDIAS

By far the most useful tool for research in music—both for scholars and students—is **The New Grove Dictionary of Music and Musicians,** 2nd edition (London: Macmillan, 2001). It is available both in a 29-volume printed edition and online (www.grovemusic.com). Many colleges and universities subscribe to the online version, making it accessible to students at many locations on campus and at home. The online version is continually updated, as contemporary scholarship requires. In addition, the online version includes articles from the more specialized *The New Grove Dictionary of Opera* and *The New Grove Dictionary of Jazz*. Almost every subject dealing with classical and popular, Western and non-Western music, can be found in *The New Grove Dictionary*. Each entry is written by a world-renowned scholar and is followed by its own detailed bibliography. For major composers, a complete list of compositions is given, along with the date of publication or first performance, as well as references to scholarly editions in which a specific piece may be found. Other, much smaller but nonetheless useful, reference tools include:

Baker's Biographical Dictionary of Musicians. New York: Schirmer Books, 2001.
The Harvard Biographical Dictionary of Music. Cambridge, MA: Harvard University Press, 1996.
The Harvard Dictionary of Music, 4th ed., ed. Don Randel. Cambridge, MA: Harvard University Press, 2003.
The Norton/Grove Concise Encyclopedia of Music, ed. Stanley Sadie and Alison Lathan. New York and London: Norton, 1988.
The Norton/Grove Dictionary of Women Composers, ed. Julie Anne Sadie and Rhian Samuel. London and New York: MacMillan and Norton, 1994.
The Oxford Companion to Music, ed. Alison Lathan. Oxford: Oxford University Press, 2002.

❁ PRIMARY-SOURCE DOCUMENTS FOR WESTERN MUSIC

Music in the Western World: A History in Documents, ed. Piero Weiss and Richard Taruskin. New York: Schirmer Books, 1984.
Opera: A History in Documents, ed. Piero Weiss. Oxford: Oxford University Press, 2002.
Readings in the History of Musical Performance, ed. Carol MacClintock. Bloomington, IN: Indiana University Press, 1979.
Source Readings in Music History, ed. Oliver Strunk; rev. edition ed. Leo Treitler. New York and London: Norton, 1998.

❁ HISTORICAL SURVEYS OF WESTERN MUSIC

Part I: Antiquity and the Middle Ages

Caldwell, John. *Medieval Music*. Bloomington, IN: Indiana University Press, 1978.
Hoppin, Richard H. *Medieval Music*. New York: Norton, 1978.
Wilson, David Fenwick. *Music of the Middle Ages: Style and Structure*. New York: Schirmer Books, 1990.
Yudkin, Jeremy. *Music in Medieval Europe*. Englewood Cliffs, NJ: Prentice Hall, 1989.

Part II: The Late Middle Ages and Early Renaissance

See later chapters of books listed in Part I, as well as:

Atlas, Allan W. *Renaissance Music: Music in Western Europe, 1400–1600*. New York and London: Norton, 1998.
Brown, Howard Mayer. *Music in the Renaissance*, 2nd ed. (with Louis K. Stein). Saddle River, NJ: Prentice Hall, 1999.
Perkins, Leeman. *Music in the Age of the Renaissance*. New York: Norton, 1999.
Strohm, Reinhard. *The Rise of European Music 1380–1500*. Cambridge: Cambridge University Press, 1993.

Part III: The Late Renaissance

Atlas, Allan W. *Renaissance Music: Music in Western Europe, 1400–1600*. New York and London: Norton, 1998.
Brown, Howard Mayer. *Music in the Renaissance*, 2nd ed. (with Louis K. Stein). Saddle River, NJ: Prentice Hall, 1999.
Carter, Tim. *Music in Late Renaissance and Early Baroque Italy*. London: Batsford, 1992.
Perkins, Leeman. *Music in the Age of the Renaissance*. New York: Norton, 1999.

Part IV: Baroque Music

Buelow, George J. *A History of Baroque Music*. Bloomington, IN: Indiana University Press, 2004.

Hill, John Walter. *Baroque Music: Music in Western Europe, 1580–1750*. New York: Norton, 2005.

Palisca, Claude V. *Baroque Music*, 3rd ed. Englewood Cliffs, NJ: Prentice Hall, 1991.

Schulenberg, David. *Music of the Baroque*. Oxford: Oxford University Press, 2001.

MUSIC JOURNALS

There are hundreds of journals (periodicals containing scholarly articles) dealing with various aspects of the history and performance of Western classical music. Some of these journals regularly publish an index to the articles found in previous issues, but most do not. There are, however, three useful indexes to journals that encompass English as well as foreign-language journals: *Music Index, International Index to Music Periodicals,* and *RILM* (acronym for *Répertoire international de littérature musicale*). All three are available online, usually through a university or college computer network, for a quick search of specific topics. Thus, to find out more about Mozart's *Don Giovanni* or Copland's *Appalachian Spring,* for example, simply go to one of these sites and type in the title in the appropriate search box. *RILM,* perhaps the most useful of the three, often provides helpful abstracts that allow the reader to determine if the article in question will be of use. For dissertations about musical topics, *Dissertations and Theses—Full Text* has not merely abstracts but, as the title states, entire dissertations and theses online (those written after 1997). Finally, more than forty of the most important music journals now also have back issues online through a link called JSTOR (*Journal Storage: The Scholarly Journal Archive*). Most university and college libraries subscribe to this online service.

ONLINE SEARCH ENGINES FOR ARTICLES, DISSERTATIONS, AND THESES ABOUT MUSIC

Music Index (Warren, MI: Harmony Park Press) http://www.hppmusicindex.com

International Index to Music Periodicals (Alexandria, VA: Chadwyck-Healey Inc.) http://iimpft.chadwyck.com/home

RILM (*Répertoire international de littérature musicale*; New York: International Musicological Society) http://www.rilm.org

Dissertations and Theses—Full Texts (Cambridge: ProQuest Company) *http://proquest.umi.com*

JSTOR (*Journal Storage: The Scholarly Journal Archive*; New York: JSTOR) http://www.jstor.org

IMPORTANT ENGLISH LANGUAGE MUSIC JOURNALS

Journal (earlier *Proceedings*) *of the Royal Musical Association* (British, 1874–)

Musical Quarterly (American, 1915–)

Music and Letters (British, 1920–)

Journal (earlier *Bulletin*) *of the American Musicological Society* (American, 1948–)

Ethnomusicology (American, 1953–)

Journal of Music Theory (American, 1957–)

Perspectives of New Music (American, 1963–)

Early Music (British, 1973–)

19-Century Music (American, 1977–)

Music Theory Spectrum (American, 1979–)

Early Music History (British, 1981–)

Journal of Musicology (American, 1981–)

Popular Music (British, 1981–)

American Music (American, 1983–)

CREDITS

GLOSSARY

a cappella: singing without instrumental accompaniment

Abendmusik: an hour-long concert of sacred music with arias and recitatives—something akin to a sacred opera or oratorio; a single religious theme unfolded in music over the course of five late-afternoon performances on the Sundays immediately before and during Advent in the city of Lübeck, Germany

Académie royale de musique: in effect, a French national opera company directly licensed and indirectly financed by the king; it performed in the center of Paris at the Palais Royal

academy: a learned society, sometimes devoted to presenting concerts; in Germany in the eighteenth century the term often referred to a public concert

acciaccatura: a technique of crunching dissonant chords used by Domenico Scarlatti

accompanied recitative: a recitative that features a full orchestral accompaniment; it appears occasionally in the sacred vocal music of Bach, but was used more extensively in the operas of Gluck and later composers.

Aeolian: the first of the four new modes added to the canon of eight medieval church modes by Heinrich Glarean in 1547; first official recognition of the minor mode

aggregate: in twelve-tone composition, a contiguous statement of the twelve notes with none repeated except in an immediate or repetitive context

agréments: French word for ornaments, or embellishments

air de cour: the French term for a simple, strophic song for a single voice or a small group of soloists

Alberti bass: an animation of simple triads brought about by playing the notes successively and in a pattern; a distinctive component of the style of keyboard composer Domenico Alberti (c1710–1746)

allemande: French for the "German" dance and usually the first dance in a Baroque suite; a stately dance in $\frac{4}{4}$ meter at a moderate tempo with upbeat and gracefully interweaving lines that create an improvisatory-like style

alternatim technique: a technique in which the verses of a chant are assigned to alternating performing forces, such as an organ and a choir

Ambrosian chant: a body of chant created by Ambrose (340?–397 C.E.) for the church of Milan in northern Italy

Amen cadence: a final phrase setting the word "Amen"; more specifically, a pla-gal cadence that English composers in particular employed to set "Amen" giving a piece an emphatic conclusion

antecedent phrase: the opening, incomplete-sounding phrase of a melody; often followed by a consequent phrase that brings closure to the melody

anthem: a sacred vocal composition, much like a motet but sung in English, in honor of the Lord or invoking the Lord to preserve and protect the English king or queen

antiphon: in antiphonal singing the short chant sung before and after a psalm and its doxology

antiphonal singing: a method of musical performance in which a divided choir alternately sings back and forth

Aquitanian polyphony: a repertory of about sixty-five pieces of two-voice organum surviving today from various monasteries in Aquitaine in southwestern France

arcicembalo: a sixteenth-century harpsichord constructed in Ferrara, Italy, that had two keyboards, each with three rows of keys

aria: an elaborate, lyrical song for solo voice more florid, more expansive, and more melodious than a recitative or arioso; an aria invariably sets a short poem made up of one or more stanzas

arioso style: an expressive manner of singing somewhere between a recitative and a full-blown aria

Ars antiqua: the music of the thirteenth century characterized by a uniform pace and clear ternary units (as contrasted with the Ars nova of the early fourteenth century)

Ars nova: musical avant garde of the early fourteenth century characterized by duple as well as triple relationships and a wide variety of note values (as contrasted with the Ars antiqua of the thirteenth century)

Ars subtilior: (more subtle art) a style of music exhibited by composers working in Avignon and other parts of southern France and northern Italy during the late fourteenth century; marked by the most subtle, sometimes extreme, rhythmic relationships

Artusi-Monteverdi Controversy: the conflict between Claudio Monteverdi, who composed in a new style inspired by a text-driven approach to musical composition, and Giovanni Maria Artusi, a churchman and conservative music theorist who advocated the older style of music that followed traditional rules of harmony and counterpoint, and who characterized Monteverdi's music as harsh and offensive to the ear

atonal music: twentieth-century harmony lacking consistent tonal center; atonal music normally has no large-scale functional harmonic progressions, uses tones of the full chromatic scale as though structurally equivalent, and emphasizes dissonant chords of any size and intervallic make-up

atonality: see atonal music

aulos: an ancient Greek wind instrument played in pairs that produced a high, clear, penetrating sound

authentic mode: in the eight church modes the authentic is the first of each of the four pairs of modes; each authentic mode has a corresponding lower mode (plagal), but both modes of the pair end on the same final pitch

BACH motive: a motive consisting of the tones B♭ A C B♮ (the musical letters in Bach's name, according to German usage); found in compositions by J.S. Bach himself and many later composers

Bach Revival: a movement originating in Germany in the early nineteenth century by which Bach's entire compositional oeuvre was published and performed

Bach-Abel concerts: a series of public concerts begun in London in 1764 by J.C. Bach (son of J.S.) and another German musician, Carl Abel; the concerts featured the most recent works of Bach and Abel as well as other fashionable composers; continuing for nearly twenty years, they became a model for the public concert series in London and on the Continent

bagatelle: a short instrumental composition

ballad: (1) a narrative poem or its musical setting; (2) a traditional, usually strophic, song that tells a lengthy story; in popular music, a love song in a slow tempo

ballad opera: a type of popular eighteenth-century English musical theater using re-texted ballads (or other popular songs) and spoken dialogue rather than recitative

ballade: one of the three French formes fixes that originated in the Middle Ages; a song always with the form AAB setting a poem with from one to three stanzas, or strophes; employs a lyrical melody accompanied by one or two voices or instruments

ballata: a dance song with a choral refrain; one of the three formes fixes of secular music in trecento Italy

ballet: a theatrical genre made from regulated dancing and mime, accompanied by orchestra

ballet de cour: (court ballet) a type of elaborate ballet with songs and choruses danced at the French royal court from the late sixteenth to the late seventeenth century in which members of the court appeared alongside professional dancers

ballet variations: passages in a ballet featuring soloistic dancing

Baroque: the term used generally to describe the art, architecture, and music of the period 1600–1750

baryton: a *viola da gamba*-like instrument with six strings

bas instruments: (soft instruments) one of the two classifications of instruments in the fifteenth century; constituted no set group but could include recorder, vielle, lute, harp, psaltery, portative organ, and harpsichord, individually or in combination

basse danse: the principal aristocratic dance of court and city during the early Renaissance; a slow and stately dance in which the dancers' feet glided close to the ground

basso continuo: a bass line that provided a never-ending foundation, or "continuous bass," for the melody above; also a small ensemble of usually two instruments that played this support

basso ostinato: a bass line that insistently repeats, note for note

bebop: a style of jazz originating in the 1940s for small improvising ensembles, often in fast tempos

Bebung: German term for the vibrating sound produced by the clavichord technique of holding and "wiggling" a key up and down

Belle époque: (beautiful era) name often given to the years straddling the turn of the twentieth century in France

big band: the dominant medium of jazz during the 1930s and 1940s; big bands typically numbered about fifteen players, divided into a rhythm section (usually piano, bass, guitar, and drums) and choirs of saxophones (doubling on clarinets), trumpets, and trombones

binary form: a structure consisting of two complementary parts, the first moving to a closely related key and the second beginning in that new key but soon returning to the tonic

blue note: a lowered scale degree (usually the third and seventh) in the major mode in blues and other jazz styles

blues: originally an improvised strophic folk song containing a succession of three-line stanzas, each sung to a twelve-measure phrase and using a standard recurrent harmonic progression; the blues form is also applicable to instrumental jazz

blues chorus: a principal subsection of a jazz work in blues form, usually twelve-measures in duration

bolero: Spanish dance in triple meter

boogie woogie: a style of piano blues with a driving ostinato accompaniment

bop: see **bebop**

branle (bransle): a fifteenth- and sixteenth-century group dance

break: in jazz, a sudden and momentary pause during which a player introduces an improvised solo

breve: one of the three basic note values and shapes recognized by Franco of Cologne around 1280 in his classification of musical durations

bridge: see transition

brindisi: a drinking song, often found in nineteenth-century Italian opera

Broadway musical: see musical

broken consort: a mixed ensemble of different types of instruments

burden: the refrain with which an English carol begins and which is repeated after each stanza

Burgundian cadence: (octave-leap cadence) when three voices are present, the contratenor often jumps an octave at a cadence to avoid parallel fifths and dissonances and to fill in the texture of the final chord

Buxheim Organ Book: one of the largest sources of Renaissance organ music; written about 1470, it contains 256 mostly anonymous compositions notated in tablature for organ, almost all of which are arrangements of sacred and secular vocal music

BWV (Bach Werke Verzeichnis): Bach Work List; an identifying system for the works of Johann Sebastian Bach, which functions much like the "K" numbers used for Mozart's works

Byzantine chant: the special dialect of chant developed by the Byzantine Church; it was eventually notated and a body of music theory emerged to explain it

cabaletta: the fast, virtuosic concluding part of an aria or duet, often found in nineteenth-century Italian opera

cabaret: a popular entertainment including songs, skits, and dancing

caccia: a piece involving a musical canon in the upper two voices supported by a slower moving tenor; one of the three *formes fixes* of secular music in trecento Italy

cadenza: a technically demanding, rhapsodic, improvisatory passage for a soloist near the end of a movement

call and response: a style of African-American song alternating phrases between two individuals, or between an individual leader and a group

canon: imitation of a complete subject at a fixed interval and time delay; in a canon (round) the following voice(s) must duplicate exactly the pitches and rhythms of the first, as for example in "Row, row, row your boat"

canonical hours (liturgical offices): a set of eight periods of worship occurring throughout the day and observed in monasteries and convents; first prescribed in the Rule of St. Benedict (c530 C.E.)

canso: the name for a song in southern medieval France, in langue d'oc (occitan)

cantata: the primary genre of vocal chamber music in the Baroque era; it was "something sung" as opposed to a sonata, which was "sounded" on an instrument; in its mature state it consisted of several movements, including one or more arias and recitatives; cantatas can be on secular subjects, but those of J.S. Bach are primarily sacred in content

cantate française: virtually identical to the late seventeenth-century Italian chamber cantata except that it set a French rather than an Italian text

canticle: a particularly lyrical and memorable passage of scripture usually drawn from the New Testament of the Bible

cantiga: a medieval Spanish or Portuguese monophonic song; hundreds were created on subjects of love, epic heroism, and everyday life

cantor: the practitioner who performs music, as distinguished from the *musicus*; in a medieval monastery or nunnery the person specially trained to lead the music of the community who sat with one of the two groups and led the singing

cantrix in a convent, the main female singer and, in effect, the director of the choir

cantus: the highest vocal part in an early polyphonic composition, what would later come to be called the superius and finally the soprano

cantus firmus: a well-established, previously existing melody, be it a sacred chant or a secular song, that usually sounds in long notes and provides a structural framework for a polyphonic composition

cantus firmus Mass: a cyclic Mass in which the five movements of the Ordinary are unified by means of a single cantus firmus

canzona: a freely composed instrumental piece, usually for organ or instrumental ensemble, which imitated the lively rhythms and lightly imitative style of the Parisian chanson

cappella: (1) a building consecrated for religious worship; (2) an organized group of highly trained musicians who sang at the services in such a chapel

cappella pontificia sistina: the pope's private vocal ensemble as it came to be called in the early seventeenth century and that sang in the Sistine Chapel

carnival song: a short, homophonic piece associated with carnival season, the text of which usually deals with everyday life on the streets

carol: a strophic song for one to three voices setting a religious text, usually associated with Christmas

carole: one of two main types of dances of the Middle Ages; a song and dance that often made use of the musical form called strophe plus refrain, in which a series of stanzas would each end with the same refrain; singers and dancers grouped in a circle and a soloist sang each successive strophe of text, while everyone else joined in for the refrain

castrato: an adult male singer who had been castrated as a boy to keep his voice from changing so that it would remain in the soprano or alto register

cauda (pl., caudae): in the vocabulary of the medieval musical theorist, a long melisma on a single syllable; used in a conductus to set off key words

cavatina: in eighteenth- and nineteenth-century Italian opera, an entrance aria; in German opera a simple aria in a slow or moderate tempo

Cecilianism: movement in Catholic Church music in Germany in the nineteenth century that favored the reintroduction of a pure style based on sixteenth-century principles

celesta: a small keyboard instrument on which tones are sounded by hammers striking metal bars

chamber cantata: a cantata performed before a select audience in a private residence; intimate vocal chamber music, principally of the Baroque era

chance music: twentieth-century music in which compositional decisions are made by chance procedures

chanson: the French word for song, monophonic or polyphonic

chansonnier: a book of songs, as created by musicians in the Middle Ages and Renaissance; a collected anthology of chansons

chant: monophonic religious music that is sung in a house of worship

character piece: a short instrumental work (especially for piano or orchestra) that establishes a particular mood

Charleston: a popular dance of the 1920s, fast in tempo with a distinctive asymmetrical rhythm

chekker: original name for the clavichord in England

choir: the eastern end of a cathedral or large church; contained the high altar and was the area in which most music was made; an ensemble of singers

choir festival: special occasion for the performance of choral and orchestral music; especially prominent in Germany and England during the nineteenth and twentieth centuries

choir school: a school that took boys at about the age of six, gave them an education with a strong emphasis on music, especially singing, and prepared them for a lifetime of service within the church

choirbook format: a layout common for writing religious music from the late Middle Ages onward in which the soprano voice was on the upper left, the alto or tenor on bottom left, alto or tenor in upper right, and the bass on the bottom right; contrasted with written music today where all the parts are superimposed on one another

chorale: a monophonic spiritual melody or religious folksong of the Lutheran church, what today is called by many Christian denominations a "hymn"

chorale cantata: a genre of sacred vocal music that employs the text and tune of a pre-existing Lutheran chorale in all or several of its movements

chorale fantasia: a lengthy composition for organ that takes a chorale tune as a point of departure but increasingly gives free rein to the composer's imagination

chorale prelude: an ornamental setting of a pre-existing chorale tune intended to be played on the organ before the singing of the chorale by the full congregation

Choralis Constantinus: a collection of nearly three hundred fifty motet-like compositions of Heinrich Isaac (c1450–1518) setting polyphonically all the Proper chants of the Catholic Mass; the first systematic attempt to provide polyphony for the entire church year since the twelfth century

chord inversion: a revolutionary principal codified by Jean-Philippe Rameau in his *Treatise on Harmony* holding that a triad may have different pitches other than the root in the bass but without changing the identity of the triad

choreographer: in ballet, the creator of the dance steps

chorus: a group of singers performing together; in jazz, a basic phrase in blues

(usually spanning twelve measures), or a refrain in a popular song

chromatic genus: a tetrachord employed by the ancient Greeks consisting of two semi-tones and a minor third

chronos: in ancient Greek musical notation the basic unit of time—a short value

church modes: the eight melodic patterns into which medieval theorists categorized the chants of the church; the four principal ones are Dorian, Phrygian, Lydian, and Mixolydian

ciaconna (chaconne): originally a separate and distinct bass melody, but during the seventeenth century the term came to mean almost any repeating bass pattern of short duration

cimbalom: a Hungarian dulcimer

circle of fifths: an arrangement of the tonic pitches of the twelve major and minor keys by ascending or descending perfect fifths, C-G-D-A etc., for example, which, because of the enharmonic equivalency of F♯ and G♭, ultimately come full circle back to C

clarino register: the very high register of the trumpet; playing in this register was a special technique of Baroque trumpeters that was exploited by Baroque composers

clausula (pl., clausulae): section, phrase, or "musical clause" in a medieval composition

clavecin: French word for harpsichord; the favorite chamber keyboard instrument in the late seventeenth and early eighteenth centuries

clavichord: a keyboard instrument that makes sound when a player depresses a key and thereby pushes a small metal tangent in the shape of a "T" upward to strike a string; the sound produced is very quiet, the softest of any musical instrument

closed ending: the term used in the Middle Ages for what we today call a second ending

coda: the musical section appended to a piece to add extra weight to the end to give it a feeling of conclusion

Codex Calixtinus: manuscript that survives today at the cathedral at Santiago de Compostela, Spain, written around 1150 and once believed to be the work of Pope Calixtus II; contains a service for St. James, which includes twenty polyphonic pieces; important in the history of Western music because it is the first manuscript to ascribe composers' names to particular pieces

colla parte: a technique in which all the instrumental parts double the vocal lines

collegium musicum: an association of musicians in eighteenth-century Germany, consisting usually of university students, who came together voluntarily to play the latest music in a public setting such as a large café or beer hall

color: the melodic unit that serves as a structural backbone in an isorhythmic composition

coloratura: florid figuration assigned to the soprano voice in an opera; also the high female voice capable of singing such a florid part

colossal Baroque: name for the style of large-scale sacred music employing multiple choirs of voices and instruments and sung in largest churches in Rome, Venice, Vienna, and Salzburg

combinatoriality: the capacity of two forms of a twelve-tone row to create multidimensional aggregates

combo: a small jazz ensemble

comic opera: a simple, direct type of musical theater that made use of comic characters, dealt with everyday social issues, and emphasized values more in step with those of the middle class

comping: the playing of accompanimental chords by a pianist or other instrumentalist in jazz

complementary hexachords: two collections of notes, each having six tones, which together contain all tones of the chromatic scale

complete works edition: a musical edition containing the complete oeuvre of a composer

compound melody: a melody made from two or more simultaneous stepwise strands whose tones are touched alternately

conceptual art: a loosely defined movement in art of the 1960s and 1970s in which the artist calls attention to ideas by which the art work is created rather than to traditional artistic objects

concert overture: an orchestral piece in one movement, usually programmatic in content, and intended for concert purposes

Concert spirituel: one of the first and foremost public concert series founded in Paris in 1725; originally formed to give a public hearing to religious music sung in Latin, its repertory soon came to emphasize instrumental symphonies and concertos as well

concert symphony: a three- or four-movement instrumental work projecting the unified sounds of an orchestra; has its origins in the Enlightenment

concertante: a special orchestral style; a concerto-like approach to the use of the orchestra in which individual instruments regularly emerge from the orchestral texture to function as soloists

concerted madrigal: a madrigal in the concertato style with strong contrasts in textures and timbres involving voices and instruments

concerted motet: a motet in the concertato style with strong contrasts in textures and timbres involving voices and instruments

concertino: the small group of solo performers in a concerto grosso

concerto: a purely instrumental piece for ensemble in which one or more soloists both complement and compete with a full orchestra

concerto delle donne: (ensemble of ladies) a group of female singers employed by the duke of Ferrara at the end of the sixteenth century; they constituted the first professional ensemble of women employed by a court

concerto grosso: a concerto in which a larger body of performers, namely the full orchestra (the ripieno, or tutti), contrasts with a smaller group of soloists (the concertino)

concerto-sonata form: a form, originating in the concerto of the Classical period, in which first the orchestra and then the soloist present the primary thematic material; much like sonata form but with two expositions

concrete music: see musique concrète

conductus: an extra-liturgical piece written for one, two, three, or occasionally four voices with texts that are metrical Latin poems arranged in successive stanzas; although not part of the canonical liturgy, most were serious and moralistic in tone; often used to accompany the movement of the clergy from one place to another in and around the church

confraternity: a Christian society of laymen emphasizing religious devotion and charity; in Florence performing laude was an essential part of their fraternal life

Congress of Vienna the meeting called by Emperor Francis I, King of Austria—after Napoleon Bonaparte abdicated his throne and fled France—inviting all the leaders of Europe to meet to redraw the boundaries of their continent and reestablish principles of legitimate rule

consequent phrase: the second phrase of a two-part melodic unit that brings a melody to a point of repose and closure

consort: an ensemble of instruments all of one family

consort song: one of two forms of the solo art song that flourished in England around 1600; the voice is accompanied by a group of independent instruments, usually a consort of viols

contenance angloise: the "English manner" of composition that fifteenth-century Continental musicians admired and adopted, though the exact nature of this style is not known

contrafactum (pl., contrafacta): the transformation of a piece of music from a secular piece to a sacred one, or (less often) from a sacred to a secular one

contralto: a low alto (a low female voice)

contratenor altus the upper of the two contratenor voices (the other being the bass); the medieval equivalent of our alto voice

contratenor bassus: the lower of the two contratenor voices (the other being the alto); the medieval equivalent of our bass voice

conversation books: notebooks used (by Beethoven and others with a hearing impairment) to communicate; one hundred forty of Beethoven's conversation books survive today

cool jazz: a style of jazz of the 1950s characterized by subdued playing and moderate tempos

Coptic chant: the music of the Christian Church of Egypt, which still exists today, passed along for nearly 2000 years entirely by oral tradition

cori spezzati: music for two, three, or four choirs placed in different parts of a building

cornett: a wooden instrument with fingerholes that is played with a mouthpiece and sounds in the soprano range with a tone something like a soft trumpet

Council of Trent: (1545–1563) a congress of bishops and cardinals held at the small town of Trento in the Italian Alps; the institutionalization of the spirit of the Counter-Reformation; its decision regarding music insisted that music must never interfere with the comprehension of the sacred word

counterpoint: from the Latin punctus contra punctum (one note moving against another note); the harmonious opposition of two or more independent musical lines

counterpoint, dissonant: see dissonant counterpoint

Counter-Reformation: the movement that fostered reform in the Roman Church in response to the challenge of the Protestant Reformation

countersubject: in a fugue, a unit of thematically distinctive material that serves as a counterpoint to the subject

countertenor: a male performer who sings in the alto or soprano range in falsetto voice

couplet: a term used in the rondo form of the seventeenth and eighteenth centuries to indicate an intermediate section (episode) distinctly different from the refrain

courante: a lively dance in triple meter characterized by intentional metrical ambiguity created by means of hemiola; one of the four dances typically making up a Baroque dance suite

Credo: a profession of faith formulated as the result of the Council of Nicaea in 325; one of the five parts of the Ordinary of the Mass

crook: a small piece of pipe that could be inserted in a horn if the player needed to change key; it altered the length of tubing within the instrument and consequently its pitch

crumhorn: a capped double-reed wooden instrument with a curving shape; has the range of a tenth and makes a sound like a kazoo

cultural bolshevism: a catch phrase used by Nazi ideologues to condemn art that was considered decadent on account of its association with foreign, Jewish, or Communist influences

cyclic Mass: a Mass in which all of the movements are linked together by a common musical theme; the first was Machaut's *Mass of Our Lady* composed in the mid fourteenth century

cyclicism: the recurrence of melodic ideas (often transformed) throughout a multimovement or multisectional composition

da camera: (of the chamber) a seventeenth-century designation for music that was not intended primarily for the church

da capo aria: an aria in two sections with an obligatory return to and repeat of the first (hence ABA); the reprise was not written out but signaled by the inscription "da capo" meaning "take it from the top"

da chiesa: (of the church) a seventeenth-century designation for music that was intended primarily for the church

dance suite: an ordered set of dances for solo instrument or ensemble, all written in the same key and intended to be performed in a single sitting

development: in sonata form, the middlemost section in which the themes of the exposition are varied or developed in some fashion; it is often the most confrontational and unstable portion of the movement

diabolus in musica: (devil in music) the dissonant, or disagreeable tritone such as F-B

diatonic genus: the basic genus within the ancient Greek musical system; reflects the primary tetrachord spanning the intervals S-T-T

Dies irae: (*Day of Wrath*) an anonymous thirteenth-century sequence; today the most famous of all medieval sequences, one which serves as the sequence of the requiem Mass

discant: a style of music in which the voices move at roughly the same rate and are written in clearly defined modal rhythms (as compared to organum purum)

diseme: in ancient Greek musical notation a long value of time—formed by two chronoi

dissonant counterpoint: term coined by Charles Seeger to refer to counterpoint in which the traditional roles of consonance and dissonance are reversed

dithyramb: in ancient Greece, a wild choral song, mingled with shouts, that honored Dionysus; a term applied today to any poem with these characteristics

divertimento: originally simply a musical diversion, it came to imply a lighter style of music and a five-movement format: fast/minuet and trio/slow/minuet and trio/fast; the term was used interchangeably with serenade

divertissement: (1) a lavishly choreographed diversionary interlude with occasional singing set within French *ballet de cour*; (2) an "entertainment" in an opera or ballet, only loosely connected to its surrounding scenes

Doctrine of Affections: a theory of the Baroque era that held that different musical moods could and should be used to influence the emotions, or affections, of the listeners

dot: following a note, a dot adds fifty percent to the value of the note; this concept entered music history in the early fourteenth century

double escapement action: a piano action in which a hammer falls back only halfway after striking a string, allowing the hammer to restrike more quickly

double leading-tone cadence a cadence with two leading tones in the penultimate chord, one pulling upward to the primary tone of the final chord and the other upward to the fifth degree

double verse structure: a distinctive feature of the sequence; each musical phrase is sung twice to accommodate a pair of verses

doxology: a standard formula of praise to the Holy Trinity

drum set: a collection of percussion instruments in a jazz ensemble that can be wielded by a single player

duplum: second voice in two- three- or four-voice organa

electronic music: works whose sounds are directly realized by a composer using electronic equipment

emancipation of dissonance: term used by Arnold Schoenberg to refer to a phenomenon in modern music by which dissonant chords and intervals are used as though equivalent to consonant ones

empfindsamer Stil: term applied to the hyper-expressivity that affected northern European, and particularly German, arts generally in the second half of the eighteenth century

emulation technique: see parody technique

English cross (false) relation: the simultaneous or adjacent appearance in different voices of two conflicting notes with the same letter name

English discant: a general term for the technique in fifteenth-century English music, both written and improvised, of using parallel 6/3 chords and root position triads in a homorhythmic style

English Madrigal School, The: the name given to the composers who fashioned the great outpouring of English secular music vocal music, mostly madrigals, in London between 1588 and 1627

enharmonic genus: a tetrachord found in ancient Greek music consisting of a major third and two quarter-tones; used for music demanding more subtle variations of pitch than that of the diatonic or chromatic genera

Enlightenment: a philosophical, scientific, and political movement that dominated eighteenth-century thought

ensemble finale: an energetic finish to an operatic act that is sung by a vocal ensemble rather than a soloist

envoi: one or more lines of verse added to the end of a chanson to suggest a leave taking

epic theater: a theatric style, associated with the plays of Bertolt Brecht, that dispels normal theatric illusion and "alienates" the audience from the narrative

episode: a passage in a musical work occurring between other passages that have more central thematic importance (as in a rondo form); in a fugue, a section full of modulation and free counterpoint that is based on motives derived from the subject

equal temperament: a division of the octave into twelve equal half-steps, each with the ratio of approximately 18:17; first advocated by some musicians in the early sixteenth century

estampie: one of two main dance types of the Middle Ages; originally a dance-song in which the dancers also sang a text, usually a poem about love; however, during the thirteenth and fourteenth centuries it evolved into a purely instrumental piece

étude: a study; a work intended to build a player's technique and often also having artistic value

Evensong: the final service of the day in the Anglican religion, an amalgam of Vespers and Compline

exposition: in sonata form the first main section in which the primary thematic material of the movement is presented or exposed; of a fugue, an opening section in which each voice presents the subject in turn

expressionism: a movement in twentieth-century literature and art in which symbolic means are used to explore irrational states of mind and grotesque actions

extended techniques: playing and singing in unusual ways in order to expand the sounds available in a musical work

faburden: a style of English medieval choral music that arose when singers improvised around a given chant placed in the middle voice; it is important because English composers began to incorporate this improvisatory style into their more formal written work

falsobordone: an improvisatory technique used by church singers that originated in Spain and Italy around 1480; at first three voices chanted along with the psalm tone making simple chant sound more splendid; by the seventeenth century, psalm tone and improvisation were abandoned and it became a newly composed piece for four or five voices but with the same simple, chordal style

fantasia: an imaginative composition the exact nature of which depends on the period of origin; in earlier eras these were usually contrapuntal works; later, the term suggested an improvisatory piece in free form, or sometimes pieces incorporating preexisting themes

fauxbourdon: the Continental style related to the English faburden; in fauxbourdon singers of sacred music improvised at pitches a fourth and a sixth below a given plainsong

fête galante: a popular social occasion among the French aristocracy of the eighteenth century

figured bass: a numerical shorthand placed with the bass line that tells the player which unwritten notes to fill in above the written bass note

fill: in jazz, a brief figure added between phrases performed by the principal soloist or singer

fin'amors: the theme of ideal love, an important value in chivalric society, as expressed in the poetry of the troubadours

flat trumpet: a slide trumpet, but one for which the sliding tube extended backward over the player's left shoulder, rather than extending forward from the right; had the capacity to play in minor keys more easily

formalism: in general, emphasis on strict formal principles or patterns in music; more specifically, a pejorative term used in the Soviet Union for music that seemed abstract or difficult, not in tune with the taste of the masses or with Soviet artistic ideology

formes fixes: the three fixed forms—ballade, rondeau, virelai—in which nearly all French secular art songs of the fourteenth and early fifteenth centuries were written

foxtrot: a social dance in $\frac{4}{4}$ time, popular in America in the 1920s

free jazz: a type of jazz of the 1950s and 1960s characterized by the removal or reinterpretation of key, normal harmonic progressions, and familiar jazz forms

French horn: the English term for the instrument that in other languages is simply called a horn; introduced into English ensembles only after 1700

French overture: a distinctive type of instrumental prelude created by the composer Jean-Baptiste Lully; came to be understood as an overture in two sections, the first slow in duple meter with dotted note values, the second fast in triple meter and with light imitation

frottola (pl., frottole): a catch-all word used to describe a polyphonic setting of a wide variety of strophic Italian poetry; the frottola flourished between 1470 and 1530 but had its origins in the improvisatory, solo singing that arose in Italy during the 1400s

fugue: a contrapuntal composition for two, three, four, or five voices, which begins with a presentation of a subject in imitation in each voice (exposition), continues with modulating passages of free counterpoint (episodes) and further appearances of the subject, and ends with a strong affirmation of the tonic key

fuguing tune: a hymn, often composed by American musicians of the eighteenth century, having fugal passages

functional harmony: a theory of harmonic syntax that defines the role of a chord as a point of departure or arrival (a tonic), a secondary point of arrival or moment of harmonic tension (a dominant), or a prefix to a dominant

fusion: a style of popular music that mixes elements of jazz and rock

galant **style:** French term used by music historians (rather than "Enlightenment style") to describe eighteenth-century music that is graceful, light in texture, and generally symmetrical in melodic structure

galliard: a fast leaping dance in triple meter especially popular during the Renaissance

Gallican chant: the Christian music of early-medieval Gaul; it later mixed with chant coming from Rome and that fusion formed the basis of what we call Gregorian chant

gate: in electronic music, a device allowing for shifts in amplitude in an electronic signal; in the music of John Adams a point of modulation from one collection of tones to another

Gebrauchsmusik: (music for use) a term used in the 1920s by Paul Hindemith to designate his compositions for amateurs or for everyday settings; also used by Kurt Weill for music of artistic value that was accessible to a general audience

German flute: what is today called the flute (the transverse flute)

gigue: a fast dance in $\frac{6}{8}$ or $\frac{12}{8}$ with a constant eighth-note pulse that produces a galloping sound; the gigue is sometimes lightly imitative and in the Baroque era was often used to conclude a suite

Gloria: a hymn of praise originating in early Christian times; one of the five parts of the Ordinary of the Mass

Golden Section: the division of a line into two parts such that the ratio of lengths of the smaller to the larger division equals the larger to the whole

Gothic architecture: the style of architecture that emerged in Paris and surrounding territories in the twelfth century; a lighter style than its Romanesque predecessor, it was characterized by greater height, greater light, and an almost obsessive application of repeating geometrical patterns

Gradual: the first of the two melismatic, responsorial chants of the Proper of the Mass that are sung between the *Gloria* and the *Credo*; consists of two parts: a respond and a psalm verse

grand opera: a style of opera originating around 1830 in France characterized by lavish use of chorus and ballet and elaborate spectacle

grand piano: a term that first appeared in England toward the end of the eighteenth century that denoted a large piano with sturdy legs and strings running roughly in the same direction as the keys

graphic notation: in twentieth-century compositions, musical notation that includes unusual graphic designs

Greater Perfect System: the framework of the Greek two-octave scale formed by four tetrachords and the proslambanomenos

Gregorian chant (plainsong): a vast body of monophonic religious music setting Latin texts and intended for use in the Roman Catholic Church; the music sung daily at the eight canonical hours of prayer and at Mass

ground bass: the English term for *basso ostinato*

Guidonian hand: ascribed to Guido of Arezzo that involves a system of using the left hand to inscribe mentally all the notes of the Guidonian scale and thus provide a portable mnemonic aid for the musical staff and the notes set upon it

Gypsy scale: a scale used by Gypsy musicians of the nineteenth and twentieth centuries containing two augmented seconds (such as C D E♭ F♯ G A♭ B C)

hand-crossing: a technique in keyboard playing in which the left hand must cross over the right to create an exciting three-level texture (left hand, right hand, and left over)

hard hexachord: in the Guidonian system, the hexachord—six-note pattern of TTSTT—set on G

Harlem Renaissance: a literary and artistic movement of the 1920s in Harlem (an African-American district in New York City)

harmonics: overtones, or frequencies, that are components of a fundamental tone

Harmonie: German name for an eighteenth-century independent wind band; called thus because winds played mostly harmony and not melody in the symphony of the day

Harmoniemusik: music written for an eighteenth-century *Harmonie*, or independent wind band

harpsichord: a string keyboard instrument that first appeared in the West in the fifteenth century; it utilized a key-jack mechanism to pluck the taut wire strings; during the Baroque era it was the principal keyboard instrument for realizing the basso continuo, but it lost favor as the piano grew in popularity during the second half of the eighteenth century

hautboys: another name for the shawm; the term was in use in England and France in the sixteenth century, and in England was eventually transformed into "oboe"

hauts instruments: (loud instruments) one of the two classifications of instruments in the fifteenth century; included trumpets, sackbuts, shawms, bagpipes, drums, and tambourine

head arrangement: a jazz arrangement rehearsed and memorized by musicians, but not written down

heckelphone: a double-reed woodwind instrument in the bass range sounding as notated

Heiligenstadt Testament: Beethoven's will that he prepared while staying in Heiligenstadt, Austria, in 1802; ostensibly addressed to his two brothers, it is actually an expression of his innermost feelings for all posterity

hexachord: a collection of six pitches

Hoboken (Hob.) number: number by which Josef Haydn's individual works may be identified following the catalogue prepared by the Dutch musicologist Anthony Hoboken

hocket: a contrapuntal technique and a musical genre; it occurs when the sounds of two voices are staggered by the careful placement of rests, thereby creating a highly syncopated piece

Hofkapelle: the group of singers responsible for the religious music at the Hapsburg court of Emperor Maximilian I; they were the center of religious and musical life at the court

horn fifths: a characteristic musical figure assigned to the French horns in which the instruments slide back and forth through sixths, fifths, and thirds, sometimes ornamenting along the way

hot jazz: an intense and exciting style of jazz

hymn: a relatively short chant with a small number of phrases, often four, and a rather narrow vocal range; hymns are invariably strophic, the usual hymn having three or four stanzas

idée fixe: (obsession): term used by Hector Berlioz to describe a recurrent melody in his *Symphonie fantastique*; the *idée fixe* melody symbolizes the beloved in the work's program

imitation: duplication of the notes and rhythms in one voice by a following voice; from the mid fifteenth century onward it became an oft used technique to enliven polyphonic music and sacred polyphonic music in particular

impresario: a manager, as of a ballet or opera company

impressionism: a realistic style of French painting of the late nineteenth century using everyday subjects (especially sea- and landscapes) and emphasizing the effects of sunlight upon colors; used in music to designate the style of Claude Debussy and others composing evocative music partially freed from strict beat and normative harmonic progressions

improvisation: playing or singing without reference to an existing musical composition

indeterminacy: see chance music

indeterminacy of composition: term associated with the composer John Cage by which compositional decisions are largely determined by chance routines; see also chance music and indeterminacy of performance

indeterminacy of performance: term associated with the composer John Cage by which music results from spontaneous decisions made by players, not strictly dictated by a composer; see also chance music

intabulation: a piece of music notated in tablature and specifically for certain solo instruments such as lute or keyboard; an intabulation implies that a preexisting polyphonic vocal piece has been arranged for a single instrument

intermezzo: a musical diversion between the acts of an opera or a play

introduction: a passage at the beginning of a composition or movement that prepares for and is often slower in tempo than the music to come; in nineteenth-century opera, a musical number (usually called an *introduzione*) at the beginning of the first act that is multisectional and composite in medium

Introit: an introductory chant for the entrance of the celebrating clergy; the first item of the Proper of the Mass

inversion: (1) in traditional harmony, the placement of a bass tone into an upper voice; a melody is inverted if its contour is replaced by its mirror image; (2) a tone row in a twelve-tone composition (or set of pitches in freely atonal music) is inverted if each interval separating the notes is replaced by the octave complement—sometimes said to be a "symmetric" inversion

invertible counterpoint: counterpoint carefully written so that the vertical position of two or more voices can be switched without violating the rules of counterpoint or creating undue dissonance

Ionian: added to the canon of eight medieval church modes by Glarean in

1547; first official recognition of the major mode

isorhythm: in isorhythm (same rhythm) a rhythmic pattern is repeated again and again in a line, usually in the tenor voice; a technique introduced by composers in the early fourteenth century

jam session: in jazz, an informal making of music by improvisation

jazz: a collective term for various types of twentieth-century popular music originating among African-American musicians and often involving improvisation; see also swing, hot jazz, free jazz, cool jazz

jazz break: see break

jazz combo: a small jazz ensemble

jazz dance bands: bands of moderate to large size and flexible makeup, freely incorporating jazz idioms, that played for dancing in the period from about 1915 to 1925

jazz standard: see standard

jubilus: the melisma on the final syllable of the word Alleluia; called this because at that moment the full choir and community celebrates with jubilation the redemptive life of Christ

jungle style: a big band style, associated especially with Duke Ellington in the 1920s and 30s, evoking African or primitive musical effects

just tuning: a system in which, in addition to the ratios required by Pythagorean tuning, the major and minor thirds were also tuned according to strict ratios (5:4 and 6:5)

Kapellmeister: chief of music at court; the German equivalent of *maestro di cappella* (chapel master) in Italy

keyboard tablature: a combination of note symbols (for the fast-moving upper part) and pitch-letter names (for the lower parts)

kithara: the largest of all ancient Greek string instruments (an especially large lyre) usually fitted with seven strings and a resonator of wood

Köchel (K) number: an identifying number assigned to each of the works of Mozart, in roughly chronological order, by German botanist and mineralogist Ludwig von Köchel (1800–1877)

kuchka: (handful) the sobriquet given in 1867 to a group of Russian composers living in St. Petersburg: Mily Balakirev (the mentor of the group), Nicolai Rimsky-Korsakov, César Cui, Alexander Borodin, and Modest Mussorgsky; the group is sometimes called "The Five"

Kyrie: an ancient Greek text and the only portion of the traditional Mass not sung in Latin; in this the first section of the Ordinary of the Mass the congregation petitions the Lord for mercy in threefold exclamations

La Guerre des Bouffons: (The War of the Buffoons) a paper war over the relative merits of Italian and French musical style; it raged, on and off, for several years in Paris during the 1750s and centered on the question of what sort of opera was appropriate for the French stage

lament bass: a descending tetrachordal *basso ostinato* employed during the Baroque era as a musical signifier of grief

Landini cadence: the name for a cadential gesture used frequently by Francesco Landini in which he ornamented a cadence by adding a lower neighbor-tone to the upper voice as it moves up to the octave

langue d'oc (occitan): the vernacular language of southern France in the high Middle Ages; the language of the troubadours and trobairitz

langue d'oïl: the vernacular language of northern France in the high Middle Ages; the language of the trouvères

lauda (pl., laude): Italian for a song of praise; a simple, popular sacred song written, not in church Latin but in the local dialect of Italian; from its beginning in the thirteenth century, the lauda had been sung by members of a confraternity

Le nuove musiche: (*The New Music,* 1602) published by Giulio Caccini; an anthology of solo madrigals and strophic solo songs gathered over time, rather than all new music as was implied; the preface contains invaluable information on vocal performance practices of the early Baroque era

leitmotive: a musical motive, normally occurring in the orchestral part of an opera, which symbolizes a character or dramatic entity; associated primarily with the operas of Richard Wagner, and also used by later composers

libretto: the text of an opera or an oratorio written in poetic verse

Lied (pl., Lieder): (song) a German art song or popular song

ligature: in early notation a group of two, three, or four individual notes

lira da braccio: a Renaissance fiddle; a bowed five-string instrument tuned in fifths and played on the shoulder

Lisztomania: Heinrich Heine's term for the emotional effect that Liszt had on his audiences

liturgical drama: a religious play with music intended to be performed as an adjunct to the liturgy, sometimes before Mass

liturgical offices: see canonical hours

liturgy: the collection of prayers, chants, readings, and ritual acts by which the theology of the church, or any organized religion, is practiced

long: one of the three basic note values and shapes recognized by Franco of Cologne around 1280 in his classification of musical durations

lute: a pear-shaped instrument with six sets of strings called courses, as well as frets created with thin strips of leather wrapped around the fingerboard at measured intervals, and a distinctive peg box that turns back at a right angle to the fingerboard; during the sixteenth century the most popular of all musical instruments

lute ayre: one of two forms of the solo art song that flourished in England around 1600; the soloist is accompanied by a lute and possibly a bass instrument such as the *viola da gamba*; a strophic piece that depended on the solo singer to employ the expressive nuances of the voice to make each stanza sound distinctive

lute tablature: a special type of notation for lute music that directs the fingers to stop strings at specific frets so as to produce sounds

lyre: in ancient Greece a medium-sized instrument usually fitted with seven strings of sheep gut and a resonator of turtle shell; plucked with a metal or bone plectrum and used most often to accompany a solo singer

lyricist: the writer of the words of a popular song, especially the songs in a musical

madrigal: (fourteenth century) originally a poem in the vernacular to which music was added for greater emotional effect; having the form AAB, it was one of the three *formes fixes* of secular music in trecento Italy; (sixteenth century) like the frottola, a catch-all term used to describe settings of Italian verse; sixteenth-century madrigals were through composed rather than strophic and employed a variety of textures and compositional techniques

madrigalism: the term for a musical cliché in which the music tries to sound out the meaning of the text, such as a drooping melody that signals a sigh or a dissonance to intensify a "harsh" word

magister cappellae: musician who is leader of the chapel

Mannheim *crescendo*: a gradual increase from very soft to very loud with a repeating figure over a pedal point; a specialty of the highly disciplined orchestra at the court of Mannheim

Mannheim rocket: a triadic theme that bursts forth as a rising arpeggio; another specialty of the highly disciplined orchestra at the court of Mannheim

masque: an elaborate courtly entertainment using music, dance, and drama to portray an allegorical story that shed a favorable light on the royal family

Mass: the central and most important religious service each day in the traditional liturgy of the Roman Catholic Church

Matins: the night office of the canonical hours, required much singing, and on high feasts such as Christmas or Easter, might go on for four hours

mazurka: a triple-time Polish dance

megamusical: a type of musical appearing in the 1980s with large cast and lavish spectacle

melisma: a lengthy vocal phrase setting a single syllable of text

melismatic chant: chants in which there are many notes per syllable of text; Matins, Vespers, and the Mass have the most melismatic chants

mélodie: (melody or song) a French art song of the nineteenth century

melodrama: a musical genre in which spoken text is accompanied by, or alternates with, instrumental music

mensural notation: symbol specific notation developed in the late thirteenth century; the direct ancestor of the system of notation used today (in contrast to modal notation, a contextual notation system used prior to the late thirteenth century)

mensuration canon: a canon in which two voices perform the same music at different rates of speed, the corresponding notes of which grow progressively distant from one another

metamorphoses: changes in form; used by Richard Strauss as the title of his final orchestral tone poem (1945)

metric modulation: a term associated with the composer Elliott Carter designating a proportional change of tempo by which a small division of a beat is regrouped into a new beat so that a new tempo results

Micrologus: (Little Essay) music theory treatise written c1030 by Guido of Arezzo setting forth all that a practicing church musician needed to know to sing the liturgy

micropolyphony: a term associated with the composer György Ligeti designating a texture in which a large number of lines merge into a sound mass

mime: the art of portraying a character or narrative solely by bodily movements and facial gestures

minim: a new short note value recognized by the fourteenth-century theorists of the *Ars nova*; a subdivision of the semibreve

minimalism: a musical style originating in the United States in the 1960s in which works are created by repetition and gradual change enacted upon a minimum of basic materials

Minnesang: (a song of love in old high German) a song created by a Minnesinger

Minnesinger: in the high Middle Ages the name for a German poet-musician writing love songs

minstrel show: a theatric entertainment originating in the United States in the middle of the nineteenth century, containing skits, songs, and dancing, which parodies the language and manners of African Americans

minuet: originally a triple-meter dance that was often added toward the end of the Baroque dance suite; in the Classical period it was invariably written in rounded binary form and coupled with a matching rounded binary movement called a trio

minuet and trio: a pair of movements with each usually constructed in rounded binary form; the trio was often scored for fewer instruments, sometimes only three (thus the name); often served as the third movement of a symphony or piece of chamber music

modal notation: a new type of notation that came into music gradually around 1150–1170 and that allowed composers to specify rhythmic duration as well as pitch; in modal notation the context determines the rhythm as opposed to the modern system of mensural notation in which each sign (note) indicates a specific duration

mode: (*modus*) the division of the long into two or three breves

modernism: in general, a style that departs from traditional norms of musical materials and aesthetic principles in the name of contemporaneity and progress; the term is often encountered in musical criticism of the twentieth century, especially for music arising in its early years and in the decades following World War II

monochord: a ancient device with a single string stretched over a wooden block and anchored at each end; distances were carefully measured on the string to correspond to specific pitches

monody: the overarching term for solo madrigals, solo arias, and solo recitatives written during the early Baroque era

Morning Prayer: the first service of the day in the Anglican religion, an amalgam of Matins and Lauds

motet: (thirteenth century) originally a discant clausula to which sacred words were added; in a motet each of the upper voices declaims its own poetic text that comments on the significance of the single Latin word being sung by the tenor; (later) the term generally used to connote a sacred choral composition, either accompanied by instruments or sung *a cappella*

motet-chanson: (fifteenth century) a hybrid of a motet and a chanson; a genre in which a vernacular text in an upper voice is sung simultaneously with a Latin chant in the tenor

motetus: the second voice (immediately above the tenor) in the thirteenth-century motet

movable type: individual small pieces of metal type cut with the letters of the alphabet or musical symbols that can be arranged to form words or music; once a sheet using the type has been printed the pieces of type can then be "moved"—rearranged to create a completely different page

Mozarabic chant: the old Christian church music as sung by Christians living in Spain under Moslem rule; survives today in more than twenty manuscripts but is nearly impossible to transcribe and perform

multiple cantus firmus Mass: when two or more cantus firmi sound simultaneously or successively in a Mass

multiple stops: on a violin (or other bowed string instruments) playing two or more notes simultaneously as chords

multiple-impression printing: a process for printing musical notation in which the lines of the staff are first printed horizontally across the sheet, then the sheet is pressed a second time to place the notes on the staff, finally a third pressing adds the text, title, composer's name, and any written instructions

murky bass: German name for a rumbling octave bass, created by repeating a bass note in alternating octaves, that became a favorite technique of both Italian and German keyboard composers of the eighteenth century

muses: in ancient Greek mythology, the nine goddesses who attended Apollo and presided over the arts and sciences; root of our word "music"

music drama: a term associated with the operas of Richard Wagner, who rejected the genre term "opera" for his mature works; Wagner preferred the word "drama"—sometimes "music drama"—for his operas to stress their heightened literary value; but in his essay "On the Name 'Music Drama'" (1872) Wagner also rejected this term as misleading

music of the future: a slogan derived from the writings of Richard Wagner that points to a utopian state in which the various arts coalesce into an integrated or "total" work of art

music of the spheres: part of the ancient Greek world-view of music, which held that when the stars and planets rotated in balanced proportions they made heavenly music

Musica enchiriadis (Music Handbook): a music theory treatise that dates from the 890s and is ascribed to Abbot Hoger; it describes a type of polyphonic singing called organum and aimed to teach church singers how to improvise polyphonic music

musica ficta: accidentals not found on the Guidonian scale but that had to be added by medieval performers because, being theoretically "off the scale," they had to be imagined

musica humana: music of the human body—one of the three harmonies Boethius posited as part of his cosmology of music

musica instrumentalis: earthly vocal and instrumental music—one of the three harmonies Boethius posited as part of his cosmology of music

musica mundana: music of the spheres—one of the three harmonies Boethius posited as part of his cosmology of music; the belief that all the universe resonates with music as sounding number

musica reservata: text-sensitive music reserved for a small circle of connoisseurs

musica secreta: (*musica reservata*) progressive chamber music reserved for a small, elite audience; used to describe the performances by the *concerto delle donne* before the ducal family in Ferrara

musical: a form of popular musical theater of the twentieth century, normally with spoken dialogue alternating with songs, dances, ensembles, and choruses; synonymous with musical comedy, musical play, and Broadway musical

musical play: see musical

musicologist: a scholar of music

musicus: as defined by Boethius, the musicologist who studies and understands music; as distinguished from the *cantor*, who is a practitioner

musique concrète: (concrete music) electronic music (q.v.) made from recordings of natural or man-made sounds

mystic chord: a collection of six tones used in the later music of Alexander Scriabin; an example of the mystic chord, placed into a compact scalewise order, is B C D E F♯ G♯

nationalism: in general, the love for or allegiance to a region of birth and its people, culture, and language; in music, nationalism is often expressed by the quotation of folk songs and dances or the use of folk stories

natural hexachord: in the Guidonian system, the hexachord—six-note pattern of TTSTT —set on C

naturalism: a movement in literature of the late nineteenth century that depicts society in an objective and truthful manner

nave: the western end of a cathedral or large church; the public part of the church, which functioned as town hall and civic auditorium as well as a space for religious processions and votive prayers

neoclassical architecture: term for the architecture of the eighteenth century that copied classical Roman qualities of balance, harmonious proportions, and an absence of ornate decoration

neoclassicism: a critic's term designating a dominant musical style of the 1920s through 1940s, especially associated with the music of Igor Stravinsky of that time; characteristics of neoclassical music include parody-like references to earlier music (especially works of Baroque and Classical periods), motoric rhythms, changing meters, a cool and detached tone, modernistic harmony, and an international tone rather than regional allegiances

neumatic chant: chants in which there are three, four, or five notes for each syllable of text

neume: in medieval musical notation, a sign used to delineate single pitches or groups of pitches; originally, around 900 C.E., neumes were just laid out on the parchment above text as a reminder of how it should be sung

New German School: a group of musicians gathering around Franz Liszt in Weimar and supporting the artistic outlook of Liszt and Richard Wagner

new music advisor: a position existing since the 1970s with many American symphony orchestras; the new music advisor typically composes new works for the orchestra and recommends other contemporary compositions

New Orleans style of jazz: a jazz style emerging in New Orleans in the early twentieth century characterized by small bands, an energetic ("hot") style of playing, and group improvisation

Nimrod variation: ninth variation in Edward Elgar's *Enigma* Variations for orchestra; a musical portrait of Elgar's publisher, August Jaeger

nocturne: a type of piano character piece appearing in the nineteenth century distinguished by a dreamy mood, a lyric melody in the right hand, and widely-spaced, arpeggiated chords in the left hand

nota: (Latin for note) a symbol on a line or space representing a single, precise pitch

notes inégales: in which a succession of equal notes moving rapidly up or down the scale are played somewhat unequally, such as "long-short, long-short"

Notre Dame School: the name given by historians to the composers Leoninus, Perotinus, and their colleagues who created a huge musical repertory of more than a thousand pieces during the period 1160–1260 at and around Notre Dame of Paris

number symbolism: a system prevalent during the Middle Ages and Renaissance in which meaning in music was conveyed by the use of numbers representing religious themes and concepts; a composition might have certain structural proportions such as 6:4:2:3 in Dufay's motet that mirror the proportions of the cathedral of Florence

obbligato: indication that a composer has written a specific part for an instrument and intends it to be played as written

obbligato recitative: recitative in which the full orchestra is necessary to the desired effect (also known as accompanied recitative)

oblique motion: motion occurring when one voice repeats or sustains a pitch while another moves away or toward it; used in medieval organum as a way to avoid dissonant tritones

oboe d'amore: an oboe-like instrument in A, slightly lower in range than the oboe; used by J.S. Bach and revived in works by Gustav Mahler and Richard Strauss

occitan: see langue d'oc

occursus: a running together, Guido of Arezzo's term for cadence

octatonic scale: a symmetric scale alternating half and whole steps

ode: a multi-movement hymn of praise to a person or ideal usually lasting about twenty minutes and containing an instrumental introduction, choruses, duets, and solo arias, but no recitative because there is no story

Odhecaton: the first book of polyphonic music printed from movable type; although published in Venice, most of the nearly one-hundred compositions in it were the works of the great northern masters of counterpoint

open ending: the term used in the Middle Ages for what we today call a first ending

opera: a dramatic work, or play, set to music; in opera the lines of the actors and actresses are sung, not spoken, and music, poetry, drama, scenic design, and dance combine to produce a powerful art form

opera buffa: the name for Italian comic opera but which, unlike most other forms of comic opera, uses rapid-fire recitative rather than spoken dialogue

opéra comique: similar to Italian *opera buffa*, has characters from the everyday world, singing in a fresh, natural style, and the dialogue is generally spoken or sometimes delivered in recitative; the principals sing either simple airs or popular melodies

opera seria: serious, not comic, opera; the term is used to designate the heroic, fully sung Italian opera that dominated the stage at the courts of Europe during the eighteenth century

operetta: a genre of light or comic opera with spoken dialogue and traditional operatic numbers originating in the mid nineteenth century

ophicleide: an early nineteenth-century bass brass instrument, forerunner of the tuba

opus dei: "work of the lord"; the services of the canonical hours as referred to in the Rule of St. Benedict

oratorio: a genre of religious music developed in the seventeenth century to satisfy the desire for dramatic music during Lent; a musical setting of a dramatic text in Latin or Italian or, later, other languages that usually elaborates upon an event in the Old Testament; uses the essential processes of opera but without the lavish sets, costumes, or acting

oratory: a prayer hall set aside just for praying, preaching, and devotional singing

Orchésographie: lengthy treatise on dance published by Thoinot Arbeau in 1589; it details all the popular dances of the day with their steps, tells what is in fashion and what is not, and provides unexpected information about performance practices of the day

Ordinary of the Mass: chants of the Mass with unvarying texts that can be sung almost every day of the year; *Kyrie, Gloria, Credo, Sanctus,* and *Agnus dei*

ordre: the term used by François Couperin to designate a group of pieces loosely associated by feeling and key; similar to

what other composers of the Baroque era would call a dance suite

organ Mass: a Mass in which an organ alternates with, or entirely replaces, the choir

organ verset: an independent organ section in an *alternatim* organ Mass; a short piece that replaces a liturgical item otherwise sung by the choir

organum (pl., organa): a type of polyphonic religious music of the Middle Ages; the term came to be used generally to connote all early polyphony of the church

organum purum: florid two-voice organum of medieval Paris continuing the tradition of earlier Aquitanian polyphony in sustained-tone style

ostinato: see *basso ostinato*

overdotting: practice in which a dotted note is made longer than written, while its complementary short note(s) is made shorter

paean: in ancient Greece, a hymn that celebrated the deeds of primary gods such as Zeus or Apollo; today any poetic hymn of praise

pan-consonance: music in which almost every note is a member of a triad or a triadic inversion and not a dissonance

pan-isorhythm: a technique whereby isorhythm is applied to all voices, not just the tenor in an isorhythmic piece

parallel organum: organum in which all voices move in lockstep, up or down, with the intervals between voices remaining the same

paraphrase Mass: a Mass in which the movements are united by a single paraphrased chant

paraphrase motet: a motet that contains a paraphrased chant throughout

paraphrase technique: when a composer takes a preexisting plainsong and embellishes it somewhat, imparting to it a rhythmic profile; the elaborated chant then serves as the basic melodic material for a polyphonic composition

Parisian chanson: a newer (after 1500) style of French chanson in which the rhythm of the text begins to animate the rhythm of the music; almost every note has its own syllable and the duration of that note is often determined by the length or stress of the syllable; subject matter was also more "down to earth" and might include lusty lovers or drinking scenes

parlando-rubato rhythm: term used by Béla Bartók to describe the flexible rhythm of most ancient Hungarian peasant songs

parody technique (emulation technique): when one composer emulates another

by borrowing entire polyphonic sections of an earlier work

part book: a volume that contains the music of one voice part and only one voice part

partita: term used by J.S. Bach as a synonym for suite

partitioning: in twelve-tone music, the distribution of the notes of a tone row into several strands in a texture

partsong: a strophic song with English text intended to be sung by three or four voices in a predominantly homophonic musical style

passacaglia: (1) a musical form involving continuous variations upon a *basso ostinato*, originating in the Baroque period and virtually synonymous with the term chaconne; (2) originally a separate and distinct bass melody but during the seventeenth century it came to mean almost any repeating bass pattern of short duration

passion: a large-scale musical depiction of Christ's crucifixion as recorded in the Gospels; an oratorio on the subject of the passion

pastoral aria: a slow aria with several distinctive characteristics: parallel thirds that glide mainly in step-wise motion, a lilting rhythm in compound meter, and a harmony that changes slowly and employs many subdominant chords

patter-song: the rapid delivery of text on repeated notes

pavane: a slow gliding dance in duple meter performed by couples holding hands; replaced the fifteenth-century *basse danse* as the primary slow dance of the court

pedal point: on the organ, a sustained or continually repeated pitch, usually placed in the bass and sounding while the harmonies change around it

Penitential Psalms: the seven of the one hundred fifty psalms of the Psalter that are especially remorseful in tone and sung in the rites of the Catholic Church surrounding death and burial

pentatonic scale: a scale with five tones per octave; specifically, a scale having the form C D E G A (or a transposition or reordering of these tones); "pentatonic music" makes use of pentatonic scales

pes: (Latin for foot) the English name for a bottom voice that continually repeats throughout a polyphonic composition

phasing: a term associated with composer Steve Reich; a phase piece is one that begins with two sources of sound giving forth an identical ostinato; one sound source gradually pulls ahead, creating a constantly-changing rhythmic interaction with the other source

pianoforte: original name for the piano because, unlike the harpsichord, its mechanism allowed the player to control the force of a blow to the string and thus could play piano or forte

Picardy third: a shift from minor to major in the final chord of a piece

plagal cadence: a IV-I chordal movement with the bass in root position falling down by the interval of a fourth or rising up by a fifth

plagal mode in the eight church modes the plagal is the second of each of the four pairs of modes; plagal means "derived from" and each plagal mode is a fourth below its authentic counterpart; the Dorian mode, for example, has its plagal counterpart in the Hypodorian mode

plainsong: see Gregorian chant

player piano: a piano provided with a mechanical device that "plays" the instrument according to musical instructions entered on a perforated paper roll

point of imitation: a distinctive motive that is sung or played in turn by each voice or instrumental line

pointillism: an artistic style of the late nineteenth century in which dots of color merge into recognizable images in the eye of the viewer; a similar phenomenon occurs in music by modern composers including Anton Webern and Olivier Messiaen in which notes seem isolated and detached from larger context

polychord: a chord made by juxtaposing two familiar harmonies

polymeter: two or more meters sounding simultaneously

polyrhythm: the simultaneous appearance in a musical work of two or more rhythmic patterns or principles of rhythmic organization

polytonality: the simultaneous appearance in a musical work of two or more keys

popular art music: a term coined by Béla Bartók to describe songs composed by nineteenth-century composers, of low artistic value, that had been accepted by the populace as folk songs

portative organ: a small movable instrument that sounded at courtly entertainments, usually to accompany singers rather than dancers

positive organ: a large stationary instrument that began to appear in large numbers in churches in the West shortly after 1300; considered one of the technological wonders of its day, it was usually attached high on the wall in the nave of the church and was the only instrument sanctioned for use in the church

preghiera: a prayer scene, often found in nineteenth-century Italian opera

prelude: a preliminary piece, one that comes immediately before and introduces the main musical event

prepared piano: a piano whose sound is modified by the introduction of mutes and other objects between strings

prima donna: leading lady

prima pratica: a traditional style for church music that is in contrast to the freer writing found in some madrigals of the late sixteenth century; the musical embodiment of the restrained spirit of the Counter-Reformation

program music: instrumental music that explicitly embodies extra-musical content

programmatic symphony: a multimovement symphony that is explicitly programmatic

prolation: (*prolatio*) the division of the semibreve into two or three minims

Proper of the Mass: chants of the Mass whose texts change each day to suit the religious theme, or to honor a particular saint on just that one day

proportions: time signatures often written as fractions that modify the normal value of notes

proslambanomenos: term used by the ancient Greeks to indicate the lowest sounding pitch in their Greater Perfect System

psalm tone: eight simple recitation formulas (simple repeating patterns) to which psalms were chanted

psalmody: act or process of singing the psalms (of the Psalter); done each week during the services of the canonical hours

Psalter: the book of one hundred fifty psalms found in the Old Testament

punctum (pl., puncta): a pair of musical phrases (couplet) usually associated with medieval instrumental music

Pythagorean tuning: a process in which the octaves, fifths, and fourths are tuned in perfect 2:1, 3:2, and 4:3 ratios

quadrivium: the four scientific disciplines of the seven liberal arts—arithmetic, geometry, astronomy, and music— that used number and quantitative reasoning to arrive at the truth

quadruplum: fourth voice in four-voice organa

quattrocento: Italian for what we refer to as "the 1400s"

quodlibet: a genre of music created when several secular tunes are brought together and sound together or in immediate succession

rag see ragtime

ragtime: a style of American popular music, especially found in piano character pieces (called "rags"), in which a syncopated melody is joined to a rhythmically-regular accompaniment

rank: each group of similar sounding pipes in an organ

realism: in Russian music of the nineteenth century a style portraying people objectively and truthfully, often using a melodic style that is close to speech

recapitulation: in sonata form, the return of the first theme and the tonic key following the development; although essentially a revisiting of previous material it is usually by no means an exact repeat

recital: a concert given by a single performer or a small number of musicians

récitatif ordinaire: a style of recitative, developed by French composer Jean-Baptiste Lully, noteworthy for its length, vocal range, and generally dramatic quality

recitation tone: a constantly repeating pitch followed by a mediation or a termination; the recitation tone is the heart of the psalm tone

recitative: a musically heightened speech, often used in an opera, oratorio, or cantata to report dramatic action and advance the plot

reform opera: first created in the 1760s by Christoph Willibald Gluck and Ranieri Calzabigi in an attempt to combine the best features of the Italian and French operatic traditions, to yoke Italian lyricism to the French concern for intense dramatic expression

Reformation: the religious revolution that began as a movement to reform Catholicism and ended with the establishment of Protestantism

release: a contrasting phrase in a popular song refrain

requiem Mass: the burial Mass of the Roman Catholic Church

respond: the opening chant in responsorial singing; usually sung by the full choir, it is followed by a verse sung by a soloist, and is repeated by the full choir

responsorial singing: when the full choir prefaces and responds to the psalm verse, which is sung by a soloist (choral respond, solo verse, choral respond)

retransition: in sonata form, the point near the end of the development where tonal stability returns, often in the form of a dominant pedal point, in preparation for the return of the first theme (in the tonic key) and the beginning of the recapitulation

retrograde: backward in motion, as in twelve-tone music where a tone row is deployed with its tones in reverse order

reverberation time: the time it takes a sound to die out

rhapsody: a type of character piece of the nineteenth century, usually for piano, having no established form or mood

rhythm and blues: a style of American popular songs appearing in the 1940s that use the traditional blues form; forerunner of rock

rhythm section: in jazz, an accompanimental group of instruments

rhythmic imitation: process in which each voice in turn sings the same rhythmic motive, but to melodic motives that differ slightly in pitch

rhythmic modes: simple patterns of repeating rhythms employed in the polyphony created in Paris during the twelfth and thirteenth centuries; modal notation evolved into a system of six rhythmic modes

ricercar: (sixteenth century) an instrumental piece, usually for lute or keyboard, similar in style to the imitative motet; (seventeenth century) Frescobaldi perfected a tightly organized, monothematic ricercar that influenced the later fugal writing of J.S. Bach

rigaudon: a Baroque dance in duple meter

ripieno: the larger ensemble (full orchestra) in a concerto grosso

ripresa: a refrain

Risorgimento: (resurgence) the movement toward Italian political and social unification that began in 1814 and culminated in 1861 when much of Italy was brought together as a single nation under King Victor Emmanuel II

ritornello: a return or refrain

ritornello form: a carefully worked out structure for a concerto grosso, which employs regular reappearances of the ritornello

Robertsbridge Codex: the earliest surviving collection of keyboard music; preserves various pieces typically heard at the French royal court in the mid fourteenth century

rock 'n roll (or rock): a type of popular song, gaining prominence in America in the 1950s, accompanied typically by amplified guitars, drums, and a few other instruments; early rock songs often had the form of a blues, elements of country music, and sexually-suggestive lyrics

rococo: term used to describe the decorative arts and the music of mid eighteenth-century France, with all their lightness, grace and highly ornate surfaces

Roman chant: the dialect of chant sung in the early churches of Rome; the principal repertory from which Gregorian chant would later emerge

romance: in nineteenth-century French music, a simple strophic song

romantic opera: a genre term used by Carl Maria von Weber for certain of his operas and by Richard Wagner for his early operas; the term suggests that the texts stressed mysterious or supernatural elements, as in the contemporary literary genre of the "romance"

Romantic period: a basic period in the history of Western music extending from the early nineteenth to the early twentieth century; although the music of this time is too diverse to admit meaningful generalizations about its style, there is a recurring impulse toward intense expressivity, which often drives the music to free forms expressed through innovative materials

romanticism: the general style of music of the Romantic period

rondeau: (fourteenth and fifteenth centuries) one of the three French *formes fixes* that originated as a dance-song with the troubadours and trouvères; its musical and textual form is ABaAabAB; (seventeenth and eighteenth centuries) a composition based on the alternation of a main theme (refrain) with subsidiary sections called *couplets* to allow musical diversity

rondellus: a distinctly English musical technique in which two or three voices engage in voice exchange, or more correctly, phrase exchange

rondo: one of the main musical forms of the Classical period; a Classical rondo sets a refrain (A) against contrasting material (B, C, or D) to create a pattern such as ABACA, ABACABA, or even ABACADA; it usually projects a playful, exuberant mood, and is often used as the last movement of a sonata or symphony, to bid a happy farewell to the audience

Rossini crescendo: a characteristic feature in operas by Gioachino Rossini in which a long crescendo is accompanied by ever shorter phrases, a thickening of orchestration, and quicker harmonic motions

rota: the English name for a canon that endlessly circles back to the beginning

rotulus: an oblong sheet of paper or parchment on which chansons were inscribed; the sheet music of the late Middle Ages and the Renaissance

Royal Academy of Music: George Frideric Handel's London opera company started in 1719; a publicly held stock company, its principal investor being the king

Russian Revolution: an uprising in the major cities of Russia in 1917 during which Tsar Nicholas II abdicated and power was seized by the Bolshevik political faction

sackbut: a slide trumpet common in the fifteenth and sixteenth centuries; precursor of the modern trombone

sarabande: a slow, stately dance in $\frac{3}{4}$ with a strong accent on the second beat; one of four dances typically found within a Baroque dance suite

Sarum chant: England's special dialect of Gregorian chant; called that from the old Latin name of the cathedral town of Salisbury; melodies and texts were somewhat different from the chant sung on the Continent

scat singing: in jazz, singing on nonsense syllables

scena: a passage of a nineteenth-century opera given largely in recitative and often leading to an aria or duet

scenario: the story outline of a ballet

scene: a passage in an opera or ballet calling to the stage a particular selection of characters

scherzo: (Italian for joke) an exuberant triple-meter dance that frequently replaced the more stately minute as the third movement in symphonies and chamber works of the Classical period; was favored first by Haydn (in his Opus 33 quartets) and then especially by Beethoven in his symphonies

scholasticism: the mode of thinking that rose to prominence at the University of Paris in the thirteenth century; it managed information by constructing chains of hierarchical categories and relationships

Schubertiad: a social gathering organized within the circle of Franz Schubert at which his music was performed

scordatura: tuning a string instrument to something other than standard tuning

seconda pratica: Claudio Monteverdi's term for the new text-driven approach to musical composition that he practiced; it allowed for "deviations" from conventional counterpoint if these moments were inspired by an especially expressive text

semibreve: one of the three basic note shapes recognized by Franco of Cologne around 1280 in his classification of musical durations

semi-opera: a spoken play in which the more exotic, amorous, or even supernatural moments in the story were sung or danced

sequence: a Gregorian chant, sung on high feasts during the Proper of the Mass immediately after the Alleluia, in which successive verses were paired into double verses; the most famous sequence today is the *Dies irae*

serenade: a piece of outdoor music for a small ensemble usually in at least five movements; the term was used interchangeably with divertimento

serialism: a compositional method in which the choice and ordering of elements is governed by a precompositional arrangement or system; see also total serialism

seven liberal arts: a framework of seven intellectual disciplines set forth by Martianus Capella (c435 C.E.) composed of the trivium and the quadrivium

shanty: a sailor's work song

shawm: a double-reed instrument with a loud penetrating tone, used to provide dance music during the Middle Ages and Renaissance; the ancestor of the modern oboe

sideman: in jazz, a section player

Silver Age: (in Russian art) common designation for an artistic period in Russia during the reign of Tsar Nicholas II (1894–1917); a time of changing tastes

simple recitative: a basic form of recitative in operas of the eighteenth and nineteenth centuries: narrative in text, speech-like in melody, and accompanied solely by keyboard or a minimal number of instruments; a recitative accompanied only by a basso continuo

sincopa: the medieval term for syncopation, a temporary shift of the downbeat

sinfonia: (Italian for symphony) a three-section or three-movement instrumental work that might preface an opera or stand alone as an independent concert symphony

single-impression printing: utilizes individual pieces of movable type that are both the note and a small vertical section of the staff; required only one pressing and was thus much more economical than multiple-impression printing

Singspiel: (sung play) a genre of German opera appearing in the eighteenth and nineteenth centuries using a folkish or comic spoken play with musical numbers inserted

Six, The: a critic's sobriquet given in 1920 to a group of six French neoclassical composers: Darius Milhaud, Arthur Honegger, Germaine Tailleferre, Georges Auric, Francis Poulenc, and Louis Durey

skolion: a song setting an aphoristic poem; the primary musical entertainment at an ancient Greek symposium

socialist realism: an officially-approved doctrine guiding the arts in Soviet Russia that promoted a style geared to the understanding of the masses

soft hexachord: in the Guidonian system, the hexachord—six-note pattern of TTSTT—set on F

soggetto cavato: soggetto cavato dale vocali—a cantus firmus extracted from the vowels of a name

solfege: the system of singing different pitches to the syllables "do (ut), re, mi, fa, sol, la, ti (si), do (ut)"

solo concerto: a concerto composed for only one solo instrument

solo sonata: a sonata played by a single melody instrument such as a violin, flute or oboe usually accompanied, in the Baroque era, by a basso continuo

sonata: originally "something sounded" on an instrument as opposed to something sung (a "cantata"); later a multi-movement work for solo instrument or ensemble

sonata form: the most important formal innovation of the Classical period, used by composers most often when writing a fast first movement of a sonata, quartet, or symphony; an expansion of rounded binary form, it consists of an exposition, development, and recapitulation, with optional introduction and coda

sonata-rondo form: a design often found in the finales of symphonies and concertos of the eighteenth and nineteenth centuries that merges elements of sonata and rondo forms

sonatina: a name sometimes used for the easiest and shortest sonatas

song "release": see release

song collection: a group of art songs having a loose connection, such as that coming from a single poet or literary theme

song cycle: a group of songs intended by the composer to be performed as a unit, having definite musical and textual interconnections

Song of Songs: (also called the Song of King Solomon) a particularly lyrical book in the Old Testament of the Bible portions of which have often been set to music over the centuries

song plugger: in the American popular song industry of the early twentieth century, a musician who demonstrated new works for a publisher

sound mass: a basic element in a modern composition made from a conglomerate of tones, lines, and rhythms

Spanish guitar: see *vihuela*

spiccato: designation requiring performers to play in a detached fashion, but not quite as short as *staccato*

spiritual: an American religious song

Sprechgesang: (speech song) a term coined by Arnold Schoenberg to describe the recitational part of his melodrama *Pierrot lunaire* (1912); in *Sprechgesang*, rhythms are notated exactly and pitches are only approximated; a synonym is *Sprechmelodie* (speech melody); the reciter herself is called the *Sprechstimme* (speaking voice); the style was later used in the operas of Alban Berg

square piano: a small box-shape piano with strings running at right angles to the keys, which could be set upon a table or simple stand

standard: in jazz, a popular song that is frequently arranged or used as the basis for improvisation; also called a "jazz standard"

stile antico: the name given to the conservative music emanating from the papal chapel in the seventeenth century

stile concertato: Italian for concerted style; a term broadly used to identify Baroque music marked by grand scale and strong contrast, either between voices and instruments, between separate instrumental ensembles, between separate choral groups, or even between soloist and choir

stile concitato: an agitated style particularly suited to warlike music; Claudio Monteverdi used this term for a new style of music he created that was more direct and insistent than previous martial music

stile rappresentativo: (dramatic or theater style) a type of vocal expression somewhere between song and declaimed speech

stochastic music: a term brought to music from probability theory by the composer Iannis Xenakis to designate works in which individual sonic events are not controlled by the composer, who focuses instead on shaping only their aggregate appearance and behavior

stop: a small wooden knob on an organ that activates a rank of pipes when pulled out

stop time: in jazz, a temporarily simplified rhythm in the accompaniment, which allows for a soloist briefly to improvise

stretta: the climactic section of a number in a nineteenth-century opera, often in a fast tempo; the masculine form *stretto* usually alludes to a passage in a fugue in which a subject is imitated at a shorter than normal time span

stride: a style of ragtime piano playing and composing in which the pianist's left hand moves regularly from chord tones in a low register to harmonies in the middle register

strophe plus refrain: a common musical form in which the strophe, or stanza, is sung by a soloist while all the singers join in with the burden, or refrain

strophic form: a song form in which the music composed for the initial stanza of text is repeated for each additional stanza

strophic variation aria: an aria in which the same melodic and harmonic plan appears, with slight variation, in each successive strophe

Sturm und Drang: (German for "Storm and Stress") as a musical term it refers to a small but significant group of works written around 1770 that are marked by agitated, impassioned writing, such as Mozart's Symphony No. 25 (K. 183) of 1773

style brisé: a modern term for a type of discontinuous texture in which chords are broken apart and notes enter one by one; such a style is inherent in lute music because the sounds of the lute are delicate and quickly evaporate

subject: in a fugue, the theme

substitute clausula: one clausula written in discant style intended to replace another

suite: a musical work that consists of a succession of short pieces, especially dances; also used for a concert work made from excerpts from an opera, ballet, or film score

surrealism: twentieth-century literary and artistic movement that confounds superficial reality or logic in order to evoke unconscious states of mind

sustained-tone organum: organum in which the bottom voice holds a note while the faster-moving top voice embellishes it in a florid fashion

swing: in jazz, a rhythm that drives forward in a triplet pattern; also a style of jazz of the 1930s and 1940s often involving big bands that play in an impulsive and dynamic mood

syllabic chant: chants in which there is usually only one note and only one note for each syllable of text

symmetric inversion: see inversion

symphonic poem: a one-movement programmatic orchestral work; roughly synonymous with tone poem

symphonie concertante: a concerto-like composition of the Classical period with two or more soloists

symposium: in ancient Greece, a tightly organized social gathering of adult male citizens for conversation and entertainment

syncopation: a temporary metric irregularity or dislocation by which beats or divisions of beats do not conform to their normal placement within the meter

syncope: the Renaissance term for a suspension

tablature: directs a performer's fingers to a specific spot on an instrument

tactus: the term used to indicate the beat by music theorists of the Renaissance

Tafelmusik: German name for chamber music, both vocal and instrumental, for the dinner table

talea: a rhythmic pattern, or unit appearing in an isorhythmic composition

tape music: a style of electronic music associated with Vladimir Ussachevsky and Otto Luening in which compositions are recorded and subsequently distorted (especially by reverberating feedback)

temperament: the tuning of intervals in something slightly more or less than strict mathematical ratios

tenor: one of the standard four voice parts; in early medieval polyphony the bottom most voice, often a preexisting chant, upon which the composition is built; called that because in these early works it holds or draws out the notes

Tenorlied: a polyphonic German song in which a preexisting tune is placed in the tenor and two or three other voices enhance it with lightly imitative polyphony

tetrachord: a succession of four pitches

text painting (word painting): the use of striking chord shifts, musical repetition, controlled dissonance, and abrupt textural changes to highlight the meaning of the text; a very popular technique with sixteenth-century madrigal composers

theorbo: a large lute-like instrument with a full octave of additional bass strings descending in a diatonic pattern

third stream: a term coined by the composer Gunther Schuller to describe a musical style merging jazz and classical elements

threnody: a musical lament

through composed: containing new music for every stanza of text, as opposed to strophic form in which the music is repeated for each successive stanza

tibia: Roman name for the aulos

time: (*tempus*) the division of the breve into two or three semibreves

Tin Pan Alley: the art and business of the American popular song of the early twentieth century

tintinnabuli **style:** (bells style) a term coined by the composer Arvo Pärt for a polyphony in which a melodic line is joined to a "bells" line limited to the three tones of the tonic triad

toccata: an instrumental piece, for keyboard or other instruments, requiring the performer to touch the instrument with great technical dexterity; designed to show off the creative spirit of the composer as well as the technical skill of the performer

tombeau: an instrumental piece commemorating someone's death

tonal answer: a following voice that imitates the subject at the interval of a fifth above or fourth below and changes the subject so as to keep the music in the home tonality

tone cluster: a dissonant chord made from sounding all of the tones within a boundary interval

tone poem: a one-movement programmatic work, usually for orchestra, and roughly synonymous with symphonic poem

tone-color melody (*Klangfarbenmelodie*): a term coined by Arnold Schoenberg to designate a melody-like line made from changing tone colors

tonos (pl., tonoi): ancient Greek term for a scale

total serialism: a compositional method in which the choice of most of the principal elements of a composition (including pitches, rhythms, and dynamics) is governed precompositionally by an integrated system or arrangement

total work of art (*Gesamtkunstwerk*): a term used by Richard Wagner to designate a goal for art in which its various branches are merged into a integrated and dramatic whole

tragédie lyrique: the term used to designate French opera in the late seventeenth and eighteenth centuries, which was a fusion of classical French tragedy with traditional French ballet (*ballet de cour*)

transformation of themes: a technique of thematic unity throughout a multisectional work by which one or a few initial themes recur, albeit changed in character

transition (bridge): in sonata form the passage of modulation between the tonic and the new key

treble: the highest of the three voices for which much late-medieval English polyphony was written; evolved in general musical terminology to mean the top part as well as the top clef (G clef), the highest clef in music

trecento: short for *mille trecento*, or the century of the 1300s, in Italian

trio: a composition for three solo instruments; also, a contrasting section of a work originally played by a trio of instruments; in minuets, band marches, and rags, the term refers to a contrasting section or episode, with no implications for medium

trio sonata: comprised a line for two treble instruments (usually two violins) and basso continuo

triplum: third voice in a piece of three- or four-voice organum of the Middle Ages

triseme: a triple unit long value of time in ancient Greek musical notation—formed by three chronoi

trivium: the three verbal disciplines of the seven liberal arts—grammar, logic, and rhetoric—which deal with language, logic, and oratory

trobairitz: a female troubadour (poet-musician)

trope: an addition of music or text, or both, to a preexisting chant; they more fully explain the theology inherent in the chants to which they are added

troubadour: a poet-musician of the courtly art of vernacular sung poetry that developed in the Middle Ages in southern France

trouser role: an opera role designed to be sung by a woman dressed as a man

trouvère: a poet-musician of the courtly art of vernacular sung poetry that developed in northern France during the late twelfth and thirteenth centuries

tuba: Roman name for the trumpet; a long, straight instrument with a cylindrical bore and a bell at the end, which originated with the Etruscans

Turkish music: the noise of Turkish military percussion instruments, which were introduced into Western European music in the eighteenth century during the Turkish Wars; some pianos of the day were equipped with special devices to effect the sounds of "Turkish" music, such as bass drum, cymbals, and the like

twelve-tone composition: a composition in which the twelve tones of the chromatic scale are systematically recirculated; the term usually refers to works using Arnold Schoenberg's "twelve-tone method," formulated in 1923, in which the recirculation of tones is joined to a serialized principle of order

unmeasured prelude: an opening piece without specific indications for rhythmic duration or metrical organization

variation technique: a procedure in which successive statements of a theme are changed or presented in altered musical surroundings

variations: a work, movement of a work, or a form in which an initial theme is subject to a series of modifications or paraphrases; see also ballet variations

vaudeville show: a popular theatric entertainment in America made from acts including dances, songs, and skits

verbal score: a musical composition represented not by conventional musical notation but by verbal instructions to the performers

verismo: (realism) a style of Italian opera appearing in the 1890s in short works in which characters from lower social strata are driven by the passions to violent acts

verse and refrain: a form for popular songs in which each stanza (sometimes only a single stanza) is divided into an introductory passage (the verse) followed by a more tuneful refrain

Vespers: the late-afternoon service, and most important of the eight canonical hours for the history of music; not only were psalms and a hymn sung but also the Magnificat

vida: a brief biographical sketch of a troubadour or trouvère; appears along with a small portrait of the artist in some French chansonniers

vielle: a large five-string fiddle capable of playing the entire Guidonian scale; often provided dance music during the thirteenth and fourteenth centuries

Viennese School: historians' term for composers Haydn, Mozart, Beethoven, and Schubert who capped their careers in Vienna and knew one another personally, however indirectly

vihuela (Spanish guitar): a plucked string instrument with a waisted body, and a long pole-neck that serves as a fingerboard; the direct ancestor of the modern classical guitar

Vingt-quatre violons du roi: twenty-four instruments of the violin family that formed the string core of the French court orchestra under Louis XIV (six violins, twelve violas, and six basse de violons)

viol: a six-string instrument fretted and tuned like the lute and vihuela, but bowed and not plucked; it came in three sizes—treble, tenor, and bass—and was played with the instrument resting on the lap or legs

viola da gamba: Italian name for the bass viol, so called because it was held between each leg (gamba in Italian)

violino: (little viol) original name for the violin

violino piccolo: a small violin usually tuned a minor third higher than the normal violin

virelai: one of the three French formes fixes of the Middle Ages yet more playful than a serious ballade; originated with the troubadours and trouvères as a monophonic dance that involved choral singing; the form is AbbaA

virginal: a diminutive harpsichord possessing a single keyboard with the strings placed at right angles to the keys

vox organalis: (organal voice) one of the two voice parts in an early organum; it is a newly created line added to the preexisting chant

vox principalis: (principal voice) one of the two voice parts in an early organum; it is a preexisting chant that served as a foundation for another newly created line

Wagner tuba: nickname for a tenor-range tuba used by Richard Wagner in his Der Ring des Nibelungen

walking bass: a bass line, especially in jazz, with a predominantly stepwise motion and steady rhythm (for example, entirely quarter or eighth notes)

waltz: a triple-time dance for couples that rose to great popularity in the nineteenth century

whole-tone scale: a scale with six notes per octave separated entirely by whole tones

Winchester Troper: a troper—chant manuscript mainly preserving additions to the liturgy called tropes—dating from c1000 C.E. from a Benedictine Monastery at Winchester, England; shows that the singers had a repertory of about 150 two-voice organa, but the troper was a memory aid and is not a prescriptive document that allows singers today to perform the music with confidence

Wolf's Glen Scene: the finale to Act 2 of Carl Maria von Weber's Der Freischütz, its most striking and most popular scene

WoO numbers: (Werk ohne Opuszahl, or work without opus number) a number given in a catalog of a composer's works designating those pieces lacking a traditional opus number; first used in the 1955 catalog of Beethoven's works compiled by Georg Kinsky and Hans Halm

word painting: see text painting

xylophone: a percussion instrument in which wooden bars are sounded with a mallet

INDEX

A cappella, 205, *See also* Cappella
A chantar m'er song (Beatriz de Dia), 42–43
A l'amara novella recitative (Monteverdi), 245, 247
Abelard, Peter, 53, 62
Abendmusik sacred concert (Buxtehude), 296–297, 342
Academie royale de musique, 303
Accidentals, 98–99
Accompanied recitative, 357
Acrostics, 138
Aeolian (minor) mode, 189
Age of Absolutism, 234, 301
Age of antiquity, 1–17
  ancient Greece
    Baroque music and, 236, 237, 240–242, 256
    ethical power of music, 7
    Euripides, 4, 10
    instruments, 6–7
    music notation, 5–6, 30
    music of the spheres, 8
    music theory, 8–11
    Olympic Games, xxxii, 3
    overview of, 2–3
    Parthenon, xxxii
    philosophers, xxxii, 2–3, 7, 8
    private symposiums, 4–5
    public religious festivals, 3
    Pythagoras, 7–8
    Renaissance music and, 148–149, 186–187
    song types, 3, 5
    summary of, 11–12
    theater music, 4
  ancient Rome, *See also* Roman Empire
    before Christ, 12–13
    Christian chant, 15–16
    instruments, 13
    Jerusalem, 14–15
    music theorists, 13–14
    summary of, 17
  timeline, xxxii-1
Age of Reason, 319
Agincourt Carol (Anonymous), 120–121
Agnus dei chant, 24, 27
Agréments, 314–316
Air de cour, 302
Alfonso the Wise, 46
Allegri, Gregorio, 263–265
Alleluia chant, 24, 27, 55
Allemande, 290
Alternatim technique, 194, 268
Alto voices, 88
Ambrosian chant, 16
Amen cadence, 216
Ancient Greece/Rome. *See* Age of antiquity
Angevin kingdom, 43
Anglican anthems, 214–216
Anglican Church services, 211–212
Anglican Prayer, 211
Anonymous IV, 54, 56, 58
Antiphonal singing, 21
Antiphons, 21–22
Apollo Among the Muses painting (Raphael), 149
Apollo's Lyre: Greek Music and Music Theory in Antiquity (Mathiesen), 5
Apollo, 241
Aquitanian polyphony, 49–50
Arbeau, Thoinot, 175, 182
Arcadelt, Jacques, 155–157

Arcicembalo, 186–187
Aria
  da capo aria, 272
  defined, 246, 247–248
  pastoral aria, 338
Ariosos, 245, 247
Aristotle
  overview of, 3
  quote from *Politics*, 11
  Renaissance and, 148, 149
Armide opera (Lully), 304–306
Ars antiqua, 74, 75
Ars nova, 72–75, 77
Ars subtilior, 93–95
Art of Counterpoint, The (Tinctoris), 187
Art of Fugue, The (J.S Bach), 359
Art of Measured Song (Franco of Cologne), 71–72
Art of Playing the Harpsichord, The (F. Couperin), 314–315
Artusi-Monteverdi controversy, 228–230, 236
As Vesta Was from Latmos Hill Descending madrigal (Weelkes), 220
Athenaeus quote from *Deipnosophistae*, 4–5
Attaingnant, Pierre. *See* Late Renaissance Paris
Augsburg. *See* Late Renaissance Germany
Augustine of Hippo, 13
Aulos, 4, 6, 7
Austria. *See* Baroque music
Authentic mode, 29

B-Minor Mass (J.S. Bach), 360–362
Babylonian Captivity, 90, 128
Bach, Anna Magdalena, 355
Bach, Carl Philipp Emanuel, 349, 358, 359
Bach, Johann Sebastian, 340–363, *See also* Baroque music
  Buxtehude and, 342
  five-finger keyboarding, 346
  Handel vs., 340–341
  instrumental music
    Art of Fugue, The, 359
    Brandenburg Concertos, 350–352
    canons, 134, 343–344
    chamber music, 346–352
    Collegium Musicum and, 358–359
    equal temperament, 347, 349
    Goldberg Variations, 359
    King Frederick and, 359
    Musical Offering, The, 359
    musical symbolism, 345
    organ chorale preludes, 342–345
    Orgelbüchlein, 342–345
    overview of, 346
    preludes and fugues, 346–348
    solo violin sonatas/fugues, 349–350
    summary of, 352
    Two- and Three-Part Inventions, 346
    Well-Tempered Clavier, 312, 346–348
    years in Cöthen, 346–352
    years in Weimar, 342–345
  keyboard tablature and, 178
  life and work, 340–342
  music after his death, 362–363
  portrait of, 232
  summary of, 362
  vocal music in Leipzig
    B-Minor Mass, 360–362
    Lutheran chorale cantatas, 353–358
    overview of, 352–353
    St. John Passion, 358

    St. Matthew Passion, 196, 358
    wives, 355
Balbulus, Notker, 36
Ballad opera, 335–336
Ballade style, 85–86
Ballata form, 106–107
Ballet de cour, 302–303, 304
Bands of wind instruments, 142, 182
Baroque music, 232–363, *See also* Bach, J.S.; Opera
  ancient Greece and, 236, 237, 240–242, 256
  binary form, 280
  characteristics
    basso continuo, 237–238
    chordal harmony, 237–238
    dynamic levels, 239, 254, 260–261
    figured bass notation, 238
    idiomatic writing, 239, 254
    instrumental color, 239
    reflects text emotion, 236
    vocal solos (monody), 237
  concerted style, 251–261
    chamber cantatas, 257–258
    concerted madrigals, 254–256
    concerted motets, 254, 259–261
    cori spezzati choirs, 251–252
    defined, 252–253
    Dresden and, 259–260
    Gabrieli, 253–254, 259
    Monteverdi, 254–256
    St. Mark's Basilica and, 251–255
    Schütz, 259–261
    stile concitato, 255–256
    Strozzi, 256–258
    summary of, 260–261
    Venice and, 251, 252, 258–259
  defined, 234–236
  instrumental, in Germany/Austria, 288–301
    Biber, 291–293
    Buxtehude, 296–298
    chorale fantasias, 298, 299
    chorale preludes, 299, 342–345
    dance suites, 289–291
    emotive power of, 294–296
    Froberger, 289–291
    keyboard sonatas, 294–296
    Kuhnau, 294–296
    organ, north German, 296–298
    organ, south German, 299
    overview of, 288–289
    Pachelbel, 299–300
    program music, 291–292
    scordatura tuning, 292–293
    summary of, 300–301
    violin canon, 300
    violin sonatas, 291–293
  instrumental, in Italy, 274–288
    cadenza in, 285
    characteristics, 236–239
    church/chamber music, 277
    concertos, 283, 284–287
    Corelli, 279–282
    overview of, 274
    Rossi, 278–279
    sinfonias, 283
    sonatas, 277–282, 283
    summary of, 287–288
    symphony orchestras, 276–277
    terminology, 283, 288
    trumpet, Torelli, 282–284
    violin family, 274–276

Vivaldi, 284–287
instrumental, in Paris, 310–319
  agréments, 314–316
  couplets, 317
  Denis Gaultier, 311–313
  Ennemond Gaultier, 311
  François Couperin, 314–318
  French overtures, 304
  harpsichord, 313–318
  Louis Couperin, 313–314
  lute, 310–313
  notes inégales, 315–316
  ordres, 316–318
  ornaments, 314–316
  overdotting, 315–316
  overview of, 310
  rococo style, 316, 318
  rondeau, 317
  style brisé, 312
  summary of, 318–319
  tombeaux, 311–313
  unmeasured preludes, 313–314
  Vingt-quatre violons du roi, 302–303
instruments
  French horn, 333
  harpsichord, 317
  organ, 342, 343
  sackbut, 276
  shawm, 276
  theorbo, 237
  viol, 181, 276
  viola da gamba, 181, 276
  violin family, 181, 274–276
  violino piccolo, 356
London, See also Handel; Purcell
  ballad opera, 335–336
  castrati, 334
  folk music, 327
  ground bass, 325–326
  Handel, 330–340
  masques, 323
  oratorios, 336–337
  overview of, 322–323
  Purcell, 323–330
  semi-opera, 323
music theory
  chord inversion, 321
  circle of fifths, 321
  Doctrine of Affections, 236, 295
  harmony, 237–238, 321
  major/minor tones, 238–239, 319–320
  pitch and tuning, 349
  Rameau, 320–321
  summary of, 322
  terminology, 320
origins of, 234, 236
Paris, See also French opera
  air de cour, 302
  Armide opera, 304–306
  ballet de cour, 302–303, 304
  cantate français, 308–309
  conductor batons, 306
  Jacquet de La Guerre, 307–309
  King Louis XIV and, 232, 301–302
  Lully, 303–307
  religious music, 307
  summary of, 309–310
  tragédie lyrique, 303–307
Picardy third, 347
printing in Venice, 252
religious music in Rome, 262–274
  A. Scarlatti, 272–273

Allegri, 263–265
  cappella pontificia sistina, 263, 265
  Carissimi, 270–271
  chamber cantatas, 272–273
  Christian operas, 270
  colossal Baroque style, 266–267
  da capo arias, 272
  defined, 262–263
  Miserere mei, Deus, 263–265
  oratorios, 270–271
  organ, Frescobaldi, 267–269
  St. Peter's Basilica and, 265–267
  stile antico, 263
  summary of, 273–274
  Tenebrae services, 263
Renaissance music vs., 234, 236–240
  seconda pratica style, 236
  summary of, 239–240
  timeline, 232–233
women
  Anna Magdalena Bach, 355
  Arabella Hunt, 327
  Barbara Strozzi, 256–258
  English theater, 324
  Jacquet de La Guerre, 307–309
  Marie Le Rochois, 305
  Parisian theater, 304, 307
  Venetian orphans, 285–286
Bas instruments, 143
Basilicas, 265
Basiron, Philippe, 132, 136–137
Bass, double, 181, 276
Bass lines
  basso continuo, 237–238
  basso ostinato, 257–258
  chaconne, 258, 317
  figured bass notation, 238
  ground bass, 325–326
  lament bass, 258
  passacaglia, 258
  walking bass, 281
Bass voices, 87–88
Basse dance, 143–144, 174
Bassoon, 182, 185
Battle of Agincourt, 120
Beatriz de Dia, 42–44
Benedictine monasteries/convents. See
  Medieval monasteries
Bernart de Ventadorn, 44–45
Bernini, Gian Lorenzo, 234, 235
Biber, Heinrich, 291–293
Binary form, 280
Binchois, Gilles, 124–127
Black Death
  Avignon, 89
  Florence, 105, 109
  Paris, 168
  Reims, 83
Blanchet the Elder, François, 317
Blow, John, 323
Boccaccio, Giovanni, 107, 109
Boethius, 14, 31, 62
Bologna, Jacopo da, 105–106
Bonfire of the vanities, 152
Book of the Courtier, The (Castiglione), 149, 154
Book of Psalms. See Psalter
Boucher, Louis, 305
Bourgeois, Louis, 201
Bourrée, 290
Braccio, 112
Brandenburg Concertos (J.S Bach), 350–352
Breve notes, 72

Broken consort, 182
Brunelleschi, Filippo, 111
Bull, John, 218
Burden, 120
Burgundian cadence, 127
Burgundy. See Late medieval/early Renaissance
Busnoys, Antoine, 132, 135, 137–138
Buxheim Organ Book, 178
Buxtehude, Dieterich, 296–298, 342
Byrd, William, 214–217, 218, 220
Byzantine chant, 15

Caccia form, 106
Caccini, Giulio, 243–244
Cadence
  Amen (or plagal), 216
  Burgundian, 127
  "Dominant-tonic", 127, 131
  double leading-tone, 99
  Landini, 108–109
Cadenza, 285
Calvin, John, 201
Can vei la lauzeta song (Bernart de Ventadorn),
  44–45
Canaletto, 252
Canonical hours, 19–20
Canons
  caccia, 106
  defined, 92
  Josquin, 136
  J.S. Bach, 134, 343–344, 359
  mensuration canons, 134
  Ockeghem, 133–135
  Pachelbel, 300
  Summer Canon, 116–118
Canso, 42
Cantatas
  cantate français, 308–309, 310
  chamber cantatas, 257–258, 272–273
  chorale cantatas, 354
  defined, 257
Canticles, 22
Cantigas, 46
Cantor, 14, 15, 21, 353
Cantrix, 38
Cantus, 85
Cantus firmus, 130, 139, 141
Cantus firmus Mass, 130, 131
Canzona 5 (Merulo), 184–185
Canzona, 184, 277–278
Capella, Martianus, 13–14
Cappella, 90, See also A cappella
Cappella pontificia sistina, 263, 265
Caravaggio, 260
Carissimi, Giacomo, 270–271
Carnival songs, 151, 152
Carol, 120–121
Carole, 79
Castiglione, Baldassare, 149, 154
Castrato/castrati, 208–209, 334
Cathedrals
  close, 61–62
  Florence, 110–114
  Middle Ages, 53
  Notre Dame of Paris. See Medieval
    polyphony
  Notre Dame of Reims, 82
Cauda/caudae, 65
Cavalli, Francesco, 249, 250
Cellos, 276
Cesti, Antonio, 249–250
Chaconne, 258, 317, See also Passacaglia

Chamber music
  chamber cantatas, 257–258, 272–273
  chamber sonatas, 277
  defined, 277
  J.S. Bach, 346–352
Chansonnier, 42, 125
Chansons, *See also* Medieval music, courtly
    love; Songs
  Binchois, 125–127
  Burgundian cadence in, 127
  Claudin, 169–173
  defined, 42, 125
  motet-chanson, Dufay, 128–129
  Parisian chansons, 168–170, 173
  polyphonic chansons, 124–127
Chant, *See also* Gregorian chant
  Ambrosian, 16
  Byzantine, 15
  Coptic, 15
  defined, 15
  Gallican, 16
  Gregorian, 16
  Mozarabic, 16
  Roman, 15–16
Charlemagne, 20
Chekker, 81
Choir area, 53–54
Choir music, *cori spezzati*, 251–252
Choir schools, 140
Choirbook format, 100
Choral works
  Gabrieli, 253
  polychoral works, 253, 260, 261
  Schütz, 260, 261
Chorale cantatas, 354
Chorale fantasias, 298, 299
Chorale preludes, 299, 342–345, 346
Chorales
  defined, 196
  Isaac, 192, 193
  Luther, 196–198
Choralis Constantinus (Isaac), 192
Chord inversion, 321
Chordal harmony, 237–238
Chords
  hexachords, 32, 33
  monochord device, 9
  tetrachords, 9–10
"Christ Clasping the Cross" painting (El
  Greco), 146
Christian operas, 270
Christine de Pisan, 125, 139
Chromatic genus, 10–11
Chronos/chronoi notation, 5
Church of England, 211
Church modes, 29
Church sonatas, 277
Ciaconna. See Chaconne
Circle of fifths, 321
Clarino register, 182
Claudin de Sermisy, 169–170
Clausula/clausulae, 56, 58
Clavecin, 314, 317
Clavichords, 1, 81, 178
Clementine Chapel, 90
Close, cathedral. *See* Medieval polyphony
Closed endings, 79
Clouet, Jean, 168
Codex Calixtinus, 51
Cold and Raw folksong, 327
Colla part technique, 357
Collegium musicum, 358–359

Color (melodic unit), 78
Colossal Baroque style, 266–267
Communion chant, 24, 27
Concerted style, 251–261, *See also* Baroque
    music
  chamber cantatas, 257–258
  concerted madrigals, 254–256
  concerted motets, 254, 259–261
  cori spezzati choirs, 251–252
  defined, 252–253
  Dresden and, 259–260
  Gabrieli, 253–254, 259
  Monteverdi, 254–256
  St. Mark's and, 251–255
  Schütz, 259–261
  stile concitato, 255–256
  Strozzi, 256–258
  summary of, 260–261
  Venice and, 251, 252, 258–259
Concertino, 286
Concerto delle donne, 224
Concerto grosso, 286–287
Concertos
  defined, 283, 284
  J.S. Bach, 350–352
  solo concertos, 285
  Vivaldi, 286
  word origin, 252
Conductor batons, 306
Conductus, 63–65
Confraternity, 152, 270
Congaudeant Catholici chant (Master Albertus),
  51
Consonance/dissonance, *See also* Harmony
  Middle Ages, 71
  pan-consonance, 122
  Renaissance, 187–188
Consort, 182
Consort songs, 221
Constantinople, fall of, 127–129
Contenance anglois, 122
Contrafactum/contrafacta, 152, 196
Contralto, 334
Contratenors, 87–88
Convents. *See* Medieval monasteries
Conversion of St. Paul painting (Caravaggio),
  260
Coptic chant, 15
Cordier, Baude, 91–93
Cordiforme Chansonnier, 125
Corelli, Arcangelo, 279–282
Cori spezzati, 251–252
Cornett, 143, 182
Coronation Anthems (Handel), 214
Cortona, Pietro da, 235
Cöthen palace, Crystal Room, 349
Council of Trent, 204
Counter-Reformation, 204, 262, *See also* Late
    Renaissance Italy
Counterpoint, *See also* Harmony; Medieval
    polyphony
  age of imitative, 132–133
  invertible, 347
  origins of, 49, 98–99
  Renaissance, 188
  Tinctoris book on, 187
Countersubject, 347
Countertenor, 328
Countess Beatriz de Dia, 42–43
"Country" (folk) music, 121, 327
Couperin, François, 314–318
Couperin, Louis, 313–314

Couplets, 317
Courante, 290
Courtly love. *See* Medieval music, courtly love
Credo chant, 24, 25–26
Cremona, Italy, 275, 276
Cruda Amarilli madrigal (Monteverdi), 228–230
Crumhorn, 182
Cyclic Mass, 87

Da camera sonatas, 277
Da capo arias, 272
Da chiesa sonatas, 277
Dal bel seno d'una stella aria (A. Scarlatti),
  272–273
Dance music, *See also* Dances
  early Renaissance, 142
  late Renaissance, 173–176
  Middle Ages, 80, 81
Dance suites, 183, 289–291, 331–333
Dances
  allemande, 290
  ballet de cour, 302–303, 304
  basse dance, 143–144, 174
  bourrée, 290
  carole, 79
  courante, 290
  estampie, 79, 81
  galliard, 175–176
  gavotte, 290
  gigue, 290
  hornpipe, 290
  minuet, 290
  pavane, 174
  royal dances, 78–80, 81
  sarabande, 290
De institutione musica (Boethius), 1, 14
De Musica (Augustine of Hippo), 1, 13
De Musica (John of St. Gall), 29, 49
De profundis clamavi motet (Lassus), 200
Death of Dido, The (Guercino), 324
Decameron (Boccaccio), 107, 109
Descartes, René, 295
Des Prez, Josquin, *See* Josquin des Prez
D'Este, Isabella, 227–228
Diabolus in musica, 39, 99
Diatonic genus, 10–11
Dic, Christi veritas conductus (Philip the Chan-
  cellor), 65
Dido and Aeneas opera (Purcell), 324–326
Dies irae sequence, 36–38
Diet (or Reichstag), 194
Discant, defined, 56
Discant, English, 118–119
Diseme in Greek notation, 5
Dissonance. *See* Consonance/dissonance
Dithyramb songs, 3
Divertissement, 304
Doctrine of Affections, 236, 295
"Dominant-tonic" cadence, 127, 131
Dots (after notes), 73
Double bass, 181, 276
Double leading-tone cadence, 99
Double verse structure, 36
Douce dames jolie virelai (Machaut), 86–87
Dowland, John, 221–222
Doxology, 21
Dueil angoisseus chanson (Binchois), 125–127
Dufay, Guillaume
  Burgundy, 124–125, 127–131
  Florence, 111–114, 150
  motet-chanson, 128–129
  motets, 111–114

Duke Albrecht V of Bavaria, 199, 201
Duke Hercules of Ferrara, 159–162
Duke Philip the Good, 127–128
Dunstaple, John, 121–123, 131
Duple meter, 73
Duplum, 59
Duration, temporal, 71–72, 97
"Durch Adams Fall ist ganz verderbt" chorale
 prelude (J.S. Bach), 345
Dynamic levels, 239, 254, 260–261, *See also*
 Volume

Ein feste Burg ist unser Gott chorale (Luther),
 196–197, 198
El Greco, 146
El grillo frottola (Josquin), 154–155
El mois d'avril/O quam sancta/Et gaudebit
 (Anonymous motet), 66–68, 74
Eleanor of Aquitane, 43–45
Emperor Maximilian I, 179, 191–192, 194–195
Emulation technique, 208
England, London. *See* Baroque music; Opera
England. *See* Late medieval/early Renaissance;
 Late Renaissance England
English ballad opera, 335–336
English cross (false) relation, 215
English discant, 118–119
English kings. *See* Kings
English Madrigal School, The, 220
English madrigals, 219–220, 221
English psalms, 201–202, 213–214
Enguerran de Marigny, 75–76
Enharmonic genus, 10–11
Envoi, 44
Episodes, 347
Equal temperament, 190, 347, 349
Estampie, 79, 81
Euridice opera (Peri), 240, 241–243
Euripides, 4, 10
Evensong, 211
Exposition, 347
Expression, 97

Faburden, 118–119
Falsobordone, 264
Fantasia for guitar (Fuenllana), 184
Fantasias, chorale, 298, 299
Fantasy on a Theme of Thomas Tallis (Williams),
 214
Fauxbourdon, 119
Feast of Fools, 63
Feast of the Pheasant, 128
Ferrara. *See* Late Renaissance Italy
Figured bass notation, 238
Filli, mirando il cielo madrigal (Caccini),
 243–244
Fin'amors, 42
Fiori musicali organ Mass (Frescobaldi),
 268–269
Fitzwilliam Virginal Book, 218
Flat trumpets, 329
Florence, *See also* Late medieval/early Renais-
 sance; Late Renaissance Italy
 birth of opera, 240–244
 Black Death, 105, 109
 Florentine camerata, 241
Flow my tears lute ayre (Dowland), 221–222
Flutes, 173, 181
Folk music, 121, 327
Formes fixes. See Song forms
Four Seasons, The concertos (Vivaldi), 286

France, Burgundy. *See* Late medieval/early Re-
 naissance
France. *See* Kings; Medieval music; Paris
Franco of Cologne, 71–72
French court. *See* Late medieval/early Renais-
 sance; Medieval music
French *formes fixes. See* Song forms
French psalms, 201
French songs. *See* Chansons; Medieval music,
 courtly love
French *tragédie lyrique, See also* Opera
 ballet de cour, 304
 divertissements, 304
 French overtures, 304
 Lully's *Armide*, 304–306
 overview of, 309–310
 recitatif ordinaire, 304
Frescobaldi, Girolamo, 267–269
Froberger, Johann, 289–291, 313
Frottola/frottole, 153–155
Fugger, Jacob, 195
Fugues
 defined, 347
 solo violin, Bach, 349–350
 Well-Tempered Clavier, Bach, 346–348
Fundamentals of Arithmetic (Boethius), 14
Fundamentals of Music (Boethius), 14, 31, 62

Gabrieli, Giovanni, 253–254, 259
Galilei, Vincenzo, 241
Galliard, 175
Gallican chant, 16
Garrit Gallus/In nova fert/Neuma motet (Vitry),
 77–78
Gaultier, Denis, 311–313
Gaultier, Ennemond, 311
Gavotte, 290
Geistliche Gesangbüchlein (Walter), 197–198
Geneva Psalter, The, 201
German flute, 173, 181
German Lied/Lieder, 192
German *Minnesang*, 46
Germany. *See* Baroque music; Late Renaissance
 Germany
Gervès de Bus, 76
Gesualdo, Carlo, 225–227
Gibbons, Orlando, 218
Giesù, sommo conforto lauda (Savonarola), 153
Gigue, 290
Giulio Cesare opera (Handel), 335–336
Glarean, Heinrich, 135, 164, 189
Gloria hymn in Mass, 25
Gloria polychoral piece (Gabrieli), 253
Glorification of Pope Urban VIII painting (Cor-
 tona), 235
"Glossing", 65–66
Goe from my Window keyboard variations (Mor-
 ley), 218–219
Goldberg Variations (J.S. Bach), 359
Gothic architecture, 52–53
Goupy, Joseph, 331
Gradual chant, 24, 26, 27, 55, 58–60
Grande-Salle in Paris, 75, 78
Great Western Schism, 90
Greater Perfect System, 9–10
Greece, ancient. *See* Age of antiquity
Gregorian chant, *See also* Mass; Medieval
 monasteries; Medieval polyphony
 abstract medium, 37
 antiphonal singing, 21
 antiphons, 21–22
 canonical hours, 19–20

cantors, 21
cantrixes, 38
defined, 16, 20, 27–28
doxologies, 21
England and, 116
Hildegard of Bingen, 38–41
history of, 20–21
how taught, 33–34
hymns, 22
liturgical dramas, 34, 40–41
Magnificat, 20, 22–23
Mass chants, 23–27, 35–38
melismatic chant, 24
neumatic chant, 24
origin of, 16, 17
psalms, 21–22
responsorial singing, 26
syllabic chant, 24
Vespers chants, 21–23
Ground bass, 325–326
Guercino, 324
Guido of Arezzo, 31–33, 48–49, 99
Guidonian hand, 33
Guillaume se va chaufer song joke (Josquin),
 135–136
Gutenburg, Johannes, 165

Hacqueville, Jacqueline de, 138, 139
"Hallelujah" chorus (Handel), 339
Hand as calculator, 33
Handel, George Frideric, 330–340, *See also*
 Baroque music
 caricature of, 331
 castrati and, 334
 Coronation Anthems, 214
 dance suites, 331–333
 Giulio Cesare opera, 335–336
 "Hallelujah" chorus, 339
 Italian opera and, 330–331, 333–336
 J.S. Bach vs., 340–341
 life and work, 330–331
 Messiah oratorio, 337–340
 pastoral arias, 338
 Royal Academy of Music, 333
 Samson oratorio, 271
 summary of, 340
 Water Music, 331–333
Harlequin, 318
Harmony, *See also* Consonance/dissonance;
 Counterpoint; Medieval polyphony
 chord inversion, 321
 chordal harmony, 237–238
 enharmonic genus, 10–11
 modal harmony, 238
Harpsichord music, *See also* Keyboard music
 F. Couperin, 314–318
 L. Couperin, 313–314
Harpsichords, 142, 179, 317
Hass, Johann Wilhelm, 284
Hautboys, 182, *See also* Shawm
Hauts instruments, 142–143
Heinichen, Johann David, 321
Héloise, 62
Hercules of Ferrara, duke, 159–162
Hexachords, 32, 33
Hildegard of Bingen, 38–41
Hocket, 84
Hodie cantandus est nobis Introit trope, 35
Hofhaimer, Paul, 193–194, 195
Hofkapelle singers, 192, 195
Holy Roman Empire. *See* Roman Empire
Hopkins Psalter, Sternhold and, 201–202

Hoquetus David hocket (Machaut), 84
Hor che 'l ciel et la terra madrigal (Monteverdi), 255–256
Horn fifths, 333
Hornpipe, 290
Hospice of Mercy, 285–286
Humanism, musical, 110, 148–149
Hundred Years' War, 83, 131–132, 168
Hunt, Arabella, 327
Hymns, 22

Il bianco e dolce cigno madrigals, 155–158
Il Paradiso (da Prato), 107, 109
Ile de la Cité, 62, 75, *See also* Paris
Imitation
   defined, 132–133, 138, 139
   points of, 205–206
   rhythmic, 207
Improvisation
   English discant, 118–119
   faburden, 118, 119
   falsobordone, 264
   fauxbourdon, 119
   medieval music, 47–49, 96
   Renaissance, 118–119, 171, 173
"In dulci jubilo" chorale prelude (J.S. Bach), 342–345
In ecclesiis motet (Gabrieli), 253–254
Innsbruck, ich muss dich lassen Lied (Isaac), 192–193
Innsbruck. *See* Late Renaissance Germany
Instrumental genres, *See also* Late Renaissance
   arrangement, 171–173, 183
   canzona, 184–185
   dance suite, 183
   fantasia, 184
   intabulation, 171, 183
   overview of, 182
   prelude, 183
   ricercar, 183–184, 269
   summary of, 185
   variation, 183
Instruments
   bas instruments, 143
   hauts instruments, 142–143
   pitch and, 190
   summary of, 185
Instruments, keyboard, *See also* Keyboard music
   arcicembalo, 186–187
   clavichord, 1, 81, 178
   five-finger playing, 346
   harpsichord, 142, 179, 317
   organs
      adding keyboards, 80–81
      allure of, 194
      foot pedals, 342
      pipe/church organs, 178, 296, 343
      portative organs, 81, 178
      positive organs, 81
      stops, 343
   "thumbless" playing, 179, 218
   virginal, 179, 218
Instruments, string, *See also* Lute music
   double bass, 181, 276
   kithara, 6–7
   lira da braccio, 153–154
   lute, 179–180
   lyre, 6
   overview of, 179
   rebec, 46
   theorbo, 237
   vielle, 80

vihuela, 180–181
viol, 181, 276
viola da gamba, 181, 276
violin family, *See also* Violin music
   ballet de cour orchestra, 302–303
   cello, 276
   defined, 181, 276
   scordatura tuning, 292–293
   viola, 276
   violinmakers, 276
   violino piccolo, 356
   violino/violin, 181, 274–276
Instruments, wind
   aulos, 4, 6, 7
   bands of, 142, 182
   bassoon, 182, 185
   cornett, 143, 182
   crumhorn, 182
   flute, 173, 181
   recorder, 181
   sackbut, 142–143, 182, 276
   shawm, 80, 142–143, 182, 276
   tibia, 13
   trombone, 276
   trumpets
      in Baroque era, 282, 284
      ensembles of, 182
      flat trumpets, 329
      music for, 282–284
      overview of, 142–143
      Roman *tuba*, 13
Intabulation, 171, 183
Introit chant, 24, 25
Inversion, chord, 321
Invertible counterpoint, 347
Ionian (major) mode, 189, 238–239, 319–320
Isaac, Heinrich
   basse dance setting, 144
   overview of, 150–151, 164
   polyphonic Lieder, 192–193
Isidore of Seville, 96
Isorhythm, 78
Italian *formes fixes*. *See* Song forms
Italian opera. *See* Opera
Italy, Florence. *See* Florence
Italy. *See* Baroque music; Late Renaissance Italy
Italy, Venice. *See* Venice

Ja nus hons pris ne dira song (Richard the Lionheart), 45
Jacopo da Bologna, 105–106
Jacqueline de Hacqueville, 138, 139
Jacques de Liège, 74
Jacquet de La Guerre, Elizabeth, 307–309
Jacquet, Jean and Claude, 317
Je ne puis vivre ainsy virelai (Busnoys), 138
Je puis trop bien ballade (Machaut), 85–86
Jean des Murs, 72–75
Jephte oratorio (Carissimi), 270–271
Jepthé cantata (Jacquet de La Guerre), 307–309
Jerusalem, 14–15
Jesuits, 262
Joan of Arc, 83, 131
John of St. Gall, 29, 48–49
Josquin des Prez, *See also* Late Renaissance Italy
   after his death, 163–164
   artistic temperament, 164
   canon, 136
   Duke Hercules and, 159–163
   Ferrara and, 158–159
   Florence and, 154–155
   frottola, 154–155

greatness of, 159
illustration of, 159
King Louis XI and, 135–137
leaving Italy, 163
lured to Italy, 150
Luther and, 164
Masses, 136–137, 160–162
Miserere mei, Deus, 162–163
Missa Pange lingua, 136–137
motets, 162–163
soggetto cavato, 160–162
song joke, 135–137
summary of, 164
word painting, 162–163
Jubilus, 27
Just tuning, 189–190

Känler, J.J., 318
Kapellmeister, 259, 346
Keyboard instruments. *See* Instruments, keyboard
Keyboard music
   Attaingnant, 172–173
   five-finger playing, 346
   harpsichord, 313–318
   keyboard tablature, 178
   Kuhnau, 294–296
   Morley, 218–219
   organ
      Bach, 342–345
      Buxheim Organ Book, 178
      Buxtehude, 296–298
      Frescobaldi, 267–269
      Hofhaimer, 194
      north German, 296–298
      organ Mass, 268
      organ versets, 268–269
      pedal points, 344
      south German, 299
   overview of, 179
   "thumbless" playing, 179, 218
   virginal, 218–219
   for women, 218
Kings
   Alfonso the Wise of Spain, 46
   England
      George I, 331, 332
      Henry V, 119–121, 131
      Henry VIII, 210–211
      Richard the Lionheart, 45
      William, and Queen Mary, 322, 326–329
   France
      Charles V, 78, 79, 83–84
      Charles VII, 131–132, 139
      Francis I, 168
      Henry VI, 131
      Louis XI, 132, 135–136, 138
      Louis XIV, 232, 301–302, 303
      overview of, 52
      Philip IV, 75, 76
   Frederick the Great of Prussia, 359
Kithara, 6–7
Kuhnau, Johann, 294–296
Kyrie for Mass, 24, 25, 27
Kyrie trope, 35

La quinte estampie real (Anonymous), 79–80
La Rhétorique des dieux lute suites (D. Gaultier), 311–313
La Spagna dance tune (Isaac), 144
L'Amante Segreto: Voglio morire cantata (Strozzi), 258
Lament bass, 258

Lamentatio sanctae Matris Ecclesiae Constantinopolitanae motet-chanson (Dufay), 128–129
Lamento allemande (Froberger), 290–291
Landini cadence, 108–109
Landini, Francesco, 105, 107–110
Langue d'oc/d'oïl, 42
L'Arlequine character piece (F. Couperin), 318
Lassus, Orlande de, 198–201
Late medieval/early Renaissance, 102–145, *See also* Medieval music; Middle Ages
  Burgundian Low Countries
    basse dance, 143–144
    cantus firmi, 141
    defined, 140
    instruments, 142–143
    Margaret of Austria, 144
    Obrecht, 140–142
    quodlibets, 141
    summary of, 145
  Burgundy court
    Binchois, 124–127
    Burgundian cadence, 127
    cantus firmus, 130, 131
    Constantinople and, 127–129
    defined, 123–124
    Dufay, 124–125
    polyphonic chansons, 124–127
    summary of, 131
  defined, 132–133
  England
    carols, 120–121
    Dunstaple, 121–123
    English discant, 118–119
    faburden, 118–119
    folk music, 121
    Gregorian chant and, 116
    improvisation, 118–119
    King Henry V and, 119–121
    map, 115
    Old Hall Manuscript, 120
    overview of, 115–116
    polyphony, 116, 119, 120–123
    rondellus technique, 116
    Sarum chant, 116
    summary of, 123
    Summer Canon, 116–118
  fauxbourdon, 119
  Florence
    ballata, 106–107
    caccia, 106
    cathedral music, 110–114
    Dufay, 111–114
    Jacopo da Bologna, 105–106
    Landini, 105, 107–110
    madrigals, 105–106
    music theory, 112
    Squarcialupi Codex, 105–107
    summary of, 110, 114–115
    trecento Florence, 104–110
  French court
    acrostics, 138
    Basiron, 136–137
    Busnoys, 135, 137–138
    canons, 133–135, 136
    defined, 131–132
    games/puzzles, 133–136, 138
    imitation, 132–133, 138, 139
    Josquin, 135–136
    Ockeghem, 132–135, 138
    paraphrase technique, 136–137
    summary of, 139
  Germany, 190–191

mixing secular/sacred, 129, 142
musical humanism, 110
number symbolism in, 113
overview of, 102–103
sheet music, 125
timeline, 102–103
women in, 109, 139
Late Renaissance, 146–231, *See also Late Renaissance by location*
  Baroque era vs., 234, 236–240
  future of music, 221
  instrumental genres
    arrangement, 171–173, 183
    canzona, 184–185
    dance, 183
    fantasia, 184
    intabulation, 171, 183
    overview of, 182
    prelude, 183
    ricercar, 183–184
    summary of, 185
    variation, 183
  instrumental music
    improvising, 171, 173
    overview of, 177–178
    reflects text, 148–149, 156–157, 162–163, 230
    vs. vocal music, 177
  instruments
    bas instruments, 143
    hauts instruments, 142–143
    pitch and, 190
    summary of, 185
  instruments, keyboard
    arcicembalo, 186–187
    clavichord, 178
    fingering method, 179, 218
    harpsichord, 142, 179
    organ, 178, 194
    virginal, 179, 218
  instruments, string
    lira da braccio, 153–154
    lute, 179–180
    overview of, 179
    vihuela, 180–181
    viol, 181
    viola da gamba, 181
    violin, 181
  instruments, wind
    bands of, 142, 182
    bassoon, 182, 185
    cornett, 143, 182
    crumhorn, 182
    flute, 173, 181
    recorder, 181
    sackbut, 142–143, 182
    sacred music and, 142, 182
    shawm, 142–143, 182
    trumpet, 142, 182
  music theory
    and analysis, 188–189
    ancient Greece, 148–149, 186–187
    consonance/dissonance, 187–188
    counterpoint, 188
    Glarean, 189
    modes/scales, 188–189
    overview of, 186
    temperaments, 190
    Tinctoris, 187–188
    tunings, 189–190
    Vicentino, 186–187
  musical amateurs appear, 167

musical humanism, 148–149
printing, *See also* Late Renaissance Paris
  Attaingnant in Paris, 166–177
  England and, 217
  Germany and, 191
  Gutenburg invents, 165
  movable type, 165–167
  multiple-impression, 166
  part books, 167, 169
  Petrucci in Venice, 165–166
  polyphonic music, 165
  single-impression, 166–167
  urban business of, 167
Psalter translations, 201–202, 213–214
timeline, 146–147
Late Renaissance England, 210–222
  Amen cadence, 216
  Anglican anthems, 214–216
  Anglican Church services, 211–212
  Byrd, 214–217, 218, 220
  consort songs, 221
  Dowland, 221–222
  English cross relation, 215
  English madrigals, 219–220, 221
  English psalms, 201–202, 213–214
  keyboard music, 218–219
  King Henry VIII, 210–211
  lute ayres, 221–222
  Morley, 218–219
  overview of, 210
  partsongs, 211
  printing, 217, 218
  Queen Elizabeth I
    dancer, 176, 217
    Dowland and, 221
    education of, 212
    madrigals for, 219–220
    musician, 217–218, 219
    portrait of, 212
    religion and, 211–212
  religious music, 211–217
  secular music, 217–222
  solo art songs, 221–222
  summary of, 216–217, 222
  Tallis, 212–214, 217
  variation technique, 218–219
  virginals, 218
  women, 218
Late Renaissance Germany, 191–202
  Augsburg, *See also* Luther
    Augsburg Confession, The, 198
    contrafacta, 196
    German chorales, 196–198
    German Masses, 195–196
    Hofkapelle singers, 195
    Luther, 195–198
    Maximilian I, 194–195
    reformed church, 195–198
    Walter, 197–198
  Holy Roman Empire, 190–191
  Innsbruck
    alternatim technique, 194
    chorale style, 192
    Choralis Constantinus, 192
    Hofhaimer, 193–194
    Hofkapelle singers, 192
    Isaac, 192–193
    Maximilian I, 191–192
    polyphonic Lieder, 192–193
    Proper chants, 192
    Salve, Regina, 194
    Tenorlied, 192

Late Renaissance Germany *(continued)*
　Munich
　　Duke Albrecht V, 199, 201
　　Orlande de Lassus, 198–201
　　Penitential Psalms, 199–201
　overview of, 190–191
　printing, 191
　Reformation, 191, 195–198
　summary of, 202
　Tafelmusik, 199
Late Renaissance Italy, 151–164, 203–209,
　222–231
　Ferrara: Josquin
　　about Ferrara, 158–159
　　about Josquin, 159, 163, 164
　　after his death, 163–164
　　Duke Hercules and, 159–163
　　motets, 162–163
　　soggetto cavato Mass, 160–162
　　summary of, 164
　　word painting, 162–163
　Ferrara: madrigals
　　Gesualdo, 225–227
　　Luzzaschi, 225
　　overview of, 223
　　seconda pratica and, 224–225
　　sung by ladies, 224
　Florence: popular music
　　Arcadelt, 155–157
　　carnival songs, 151, 152
　　frottola, 153–155
　　Josquin des Prez, 154–155
　　lauda, 151–153
　　Lorenzo de' Medici, 150–151, 152
　　madrigals, 155–158
　　quattrocento and, 150
　　Savonarola, 152–153, 162
　　summary of, 158
　Mantua
　　Artusi controversy, 228–230, 236
　　Isabella d'Este and, 227–228
　　Monteverdi madrigals, 228–230
　　overview of, 223, 227
　　seconda pratica and, 228–229, 230
　overview of, 222–223, 230–231
　Rome, Counter-Reformation
　　castrati, 208–209
　　Council of Trent, 204
　　Mass for Pope Marcellus, 204
　　overview of, 203–204
　　Palestrina, 204–209
　　parody (emulation), 208
　　points of imitation, 205–206
　　prima pratica and, 206, 230
　　rhythmic imitation, 207
　　singing *a cappella,* 205
　　Spanish composers, 209
　　summary of, 209
　　text clarity and, 204, 207
　　Tu es Petrus Mass, 208
　　Tu es Petrus motets, 207
　　Victoria, 209
　Venice, printing in, 165–166
Late Renaissance Paris, 166–177
　Claudin, 169–173
　French psalms, 201
　galliards, 175–176
　Parisian chansons, 168–170, 173
　patter-song, 169
　pavanes, 174
　printing by Attaingnant
　　arrangements, 171–173

dance music, 173–176
instrumental vs. vocal music, 177
King Francis I and, 168
lute vs. keyboard music, 179
overview of, 167
part books, 167, 169
polyphonic chansons, 168–170
printing method, 166–167
summary of, 177
Latin Quarter, 62, 168
Lauda/laude, 151–153
Le nouve musiche solos (Caccini), 243, 244
Le Rochois, Marie, 305
Leoninus, 54–58
L'Homme armé tune, 129–131, 135
"Liberal arts", 14
Librettos, 240
Lied/Lieder, 192
Ligature, 57
Lira da braccio, 153–154
Little Book of Spiritual Songs (Walter), 197–198
Liturgical dramas, 34, 40–41
Liturgical offices, 19–20
Liturgies, 14–15
London. *See* Baroque music; Opera
Long notes, 72
Lorenzo de' Medici, 150–151, 152, 153
Lully, Jean-Baptiste, 303–307
Lute music
　arrangements, 171–172
　ayres, 221–222
　D. Gaultier, 311–313
　intabulation, 171
　popularity of, 179–180, 310–311
　tablature, 171, 180
　unmeasured preludes, 313
Lutes, 179–180
Luther, Martin, *See also* Late Renaissance Germany
　Augsburg Confession, 198
　German chorales, 196–198
　German Mass, 195–196
　Josquin and, 164
　Ninety-Five Theses, 195
　overview of, 203
　portrait of, 146
Lutheran chorale cantatas, J.S. Bach, 353–358
Luzzaschi, Luzzasco, 225
Lyres, 6

Ma fin et mon commencement rondeau
　(Machaut), 86
Machaut, Guillaume de, *See also* Medieval music
　Black Death and, 83
　Charles V and, 83–84
　formes fixes and
　　ballade, 85–86
　　defined, 105
　　rondeau, 86, 87
　　virelai, 86–87
　hockets technique, 84
　Hundred Years' War, 83
　Mass of Our Lady, 87–89, 99
　overview of, 82–83
　summary of, 89
Madrigalisms, 157
Madrigals, *See also* Late Renaissance Italy
　Arcadelt, 155–157
　Caccini, 243–244
　concerted madrigals, 254–256
　defined, 105

end of, 107, 221
English madrigals, 219–220, 221
Gesualdo, 225–227
Jacopo da Bologna, 105–106
Luzzaschi, 225
Monteverdi, 228–230, 255–256
Morley, 219–220
overview of, 223
seconda pratica and, 224–225
sung by ladies, 224
Vecchi, 157–158
Magister cappellae, 111
Magnificat, 20, 22–23
Magnus liber organi (Leoninus), 54–55, 66, 68
Major (Ionian) mode, 189, 238–239, 320
Mantua. *See* Late Renaissance Italy
Maps
　ancient Greece, 2
　Angevin kingdom, 43
　Avignon, 89
　Bach's Germany, 341
　Burgundian lands 1477, 124
　Holy Roman Empire c1500, 191
　medieval monasteries c1200, 18
　medieval Paris, 62
　northern Europe 17th c, 289
　Renaissance England, 115
　Renaissance Italy, 104
　Roman Empire, 13
　western Europe 15th c, 124
Margaret of Austria, 144
Marigny, Enguerran de, 75–76
Martianus Capella, 13–14
Masque, 323
Mass, *See also* Gregorian chant
　Christmas Day, 27, 35
　defined, 23
　Ordinary of the
　　Agnus dei, 24, 27
　　Credo, 24, 25–26
　　defined, 24
　　Gloria, 25
　　Ite, missa est, 23, 24, 27
　　Kyrie, 24, 25, 27
　　polyphonic settings, 87–89, 130–131
　　Sanctus, 24, 27
　Proper of the
　　Alleluia, 24, 27, 55
　　Communion, 24, 27
　　defined, 23–24
　　Gradual, 26, 27, 55–56, 59–61
　　Introit, 24, 25
　　Offertory, 24, 27
　　polyphonic settings, 55–56, 59–61, 192
　　Sequences, 24, 34, 36–38
　　tropes added to, 35
Masses
　cantus firmus Mass, 130–131, 141
　cyclic Mass, 87
　L'Homme armé tune use, 129–131, 135
　Mass of Our Lady (Machaut), 87–89, 99
　Mass for Pope Marcellus (Palestrina), 204
　Missa Aeterna Christi munera (Palestrina),
　　205–206
　Missa Hercules dux Ferrarie (Josquin),
　　160–162
　Missa Pange lingua (Josquin), 136–137
　Missa Prolationum (Ockeghem), 134–135
　Missa Salisburgensis (Anonymous), 266–267
　Missa Sub tuum presidium (Obrecht), 141–142
　Missa Tu es Petrus (Palestrina), 208
　organ Mass, 268

paraphrase Mass, 136–137
Requiem Mass, 37
Master Albertus of Paris, 51
Mathiesen, Thomas J., 5
Matins, 19, 20
Mattheson, Johann, 295
Medieval monasteries, 17–41, *See also* Medieval
polyphony, 47–75
defined, 18
Gregorian chant, *See also* Mass
as abstract medium, 37
antiphonal singing, 21
antiphons, 21–22
canonical hours and, 19–20
cantors, 21
cantrixes, 38
defined, 16, 20, 27–28
doxologies, 21
history of, 20–21
how taught, 33–34
hymns, 22
Magnificat, 20, 22–23
Mass chants, 23–27, 35–38
melismatic chant, 24
neumatic chant, 24
origin of, 16, 17
psalms, 21–22
responsorial singing, 26
syllabic chant, 24
Vespers chants, 21–23
Hildegard of Bingen, 38–41
liturgical dramas, 34, 40–41
monks, 17–19, 20
nuns, 17–18, 38–41
overview of, 17–18
Regina Laudis convent, 23
St. Gall monastery, 18–19
theory, 10-13th centuries
chant notation, 30
church modes, 29
Guido of Arezzo, 31–33, 48–49, 99
Guidonian hand, 33
hexachords, 32, 33
John of St. Gall, 29, 48, 49
musical staffs, 30–31
overview of, 28–29
pitch names, 30–31
polyphony/organum, 47–49
solfege, 31–32
summary of, 34
Medieval music, 75–101, *See also* Late
medieval/early Renaissance; Middle Ages
Avignon, France
Ars subtilior, 93–95
canons, 92
Cordier, 91–93
note shapes, 94
papacy and, 89–90
Philippus de Caserta, 93–95
proportions, 94
rhythms, 91, 93, 94–95
summary of, 95
syncopation, 93–94
courtly love, *See also* Chansons
ballade style, 85–86
Eleanor of Aquitaine, 43–45
formes fixes, 84–87, 125, 169
French chansons, 41–46
German *Minnesang,* 46
overview of, 41–42, 84–85, 125
rondeau form, 86, 87
Spanish *cantigas,* 46

summary of, 46
trobairitz, 42–43
troubadours, 42, 43, 44–45
trouvères, 42–43, 45–46
virelai form, 86–87
French courts
first/second endings, 79
instrumental music, 80, 81
instruments, 80–81
isorhythm, 78
overview of, 75
Philippe de Vitry, 76, 77–78
Roman de Fauvel satire, 75–77
royal dances, 78–80
summary of, 81–82
improvisation/oral tradition, 96
Italy, 110–111
Machaut in Reims
Black Death and, 83
Charles V and, 83–84
formes fixes and, 84–87
hockets technique, 84
Hundred Years' War, 83
Mass of Our Lady, 87–89, 99
overview of, 82–83
summary of, 89
number symbolism in, 113
performance elements
accidentals, 98–99
duration and tempo, 97
improvisation vs. composition, 96
ornamentation, 98
overview of, 95–96
pitch, 97
pronunciation, 97
reading scores, 100–101
text underlay, 97–98
volume and expression, 97
women and, 109
Medieval polyphony, 47–75, *See also* Medieval
monasteries
Aquitanian polyphony, 49–50
cathedral close and university
Abelard and Héloïse, 62
conductus, 63–65
defined, 61–62
motets, 65–69
Philip the Chancellor, 63, 65
summary of, 69–70
defined, 47
Notre Dame of Paris
Alleluias, 55
Anonymous IV and, 54, 56, 58
Ars antiqua, 74, 75
choir area, 53–54
floor plan, 60
Graduals, 55–56, 58–61
Leoninus, 54–58
modal notation, 56–57
overview of, xxxii, 53–54
Perotinus, 54, 58–61
photo of, 53
rhythmic modes, 56–58
Ordinary of the Mass, 87–89
organum
defined, 47
improvisation, 47–49
manuscripts of, 49–51
oblique motion in, 48
organum purum, 56
parallel organum, 48
sustained-tone organum, 50

popular urban forms of, 68–69, 70
Proper of the Mass, 55–56, 58–61
summary of, 51–52
theory, 10-12th centuries, 47–49
theory, 13-14th centuries
Ars nova, 72–75, 77, 94, 95
consonance/dissonance, 60, 71, 88
duple meters, 73
Franco of Cologne, 71–72
Jean des Murs, 72–75
mensural notation, 72
meter/time signatures, 73
note values, 72, 73, 94
opposition to, 74
Philippe de Vitry, 72–75
rhythms, 73–74
summary of, 74–75
temporal duration, 71–72
two octaves of, 87–88
Melismatic chant, 24
Mendelssohn, Felix, 198
Mensural notation, 56, 57, 72
Mensuration canons, 134
Messiah oratorio (Handel), 337–340
Meter (time) signatures, 73
Michelangelo
David, 148
Josquin and, 159
Last Judgment, 205
St. Peter's Basilica, 206, 265
Micrologus (Guido of Arezzo), 31, 48
Microtones, 10, 186–187
Middle Ages, *See also* Late medieval/early Re-
naissance; Medieval music
cathedrals, 53
hand as calculator, 33
measuring time, 70–71
overview, xxxii-1, 102, 148
Paris, 52–53, 61–62, 168
Rome, 203
societal groups, 38
timelines, 1, 102–103
women
Beatriz de Dia, 42–43
Christine de Pisan, 125, 139
Decameron and, 109
education of, 109
Eleanor of Aquitane, 43–45
Jacqueline de Hacqueville, 138, 139
Joan of Arc, 83, 131
poets/performers, 139
trobaritz, 42–43
Mielich, Hans, 199
Mighty Fortress is Our God, A chorale (Luther),
196–197
Milán, Luis, 181
Minim notes, 73
Minnesang, 46
Minnesinger, 46
Minor (Aeolian) mode, 189, 238–239, 320
Minuets, 290
Miserere mei, Deus setting
Allegri, 263–265
Josquin, 162–163
Missa. See Masses
Modal harmony, 238
Modal notation, 56–57, 72
Modal scales, 188–189, 319–320
Mode (*modus*), 73
Modes, church, 29, *See also* Scales
Modes, rhythmic, 56–58
Monacha/monachus, 17

Monasteries. *See* Medieval monasteries
Monochord device, 9
Monody, 237, 242, *See also* Solo art songs
Montepellier Codex, 66
Monteverdi, Claudio
　Artusi and, 228–230, 236
　concerted madrigals, 254–256
　madrigals, 228–230
　operas, 244–250
　Orfeo, 244–248
　Poppea, 248–250
Morley, Thomas, 218–219
Morning Prayer, 211
Moro, lasso madrigal (Gesualdo), 226–227
Motets
　Anonymous, 66–69, 74
　concerted motets
　　defined, 254
　　Gabrieli, 253–254
　　Schütz, 259–261
　defined, 65–69
　Dufay, 111–114, 128–129
　Dunstable, 122–123
　isorhythmic, end of, 131
　Josquin, 162–163
　Lassus, 200
　motet-chanson, 128
　Palestrina, 207
　paraphrase motets, 136
　Philippe de Vitry, 77–78
　polychoral motets, 260, 261
Motetus, 66
Movable type, 165
Mozarabic chant, 16
Multiple cantus firmus Mass, 141
Multiple stops, 280
Multiple-impression printing, 166
Munich. *See* Late Renaissance Germany
Muses, 149
Music theory
　10-13th centuries
　　chant notation, 30
　　church modes, 29
　　Guido of Arezzo, 31–33, 48–49, 99
　　Guidonian hand, 33
　　hexachords, 32, 33
　　John of St. Gall, 29, 48, 49
　　musical staffs, 30–31
　　overview of, 28–29
　　pitch names, 30–31
　　polyphony/organum, 47–49
　　solfege, 31–32
　　summary of, 34
　13-14th centuries
　　Ars nova, 72–75, 77, 94, 95
　　consonance/dissonance, 60, 71, 88
　　duple meters, 73
　　Franco of Cologne, 71–72
　　Jean des Murs, 72–75
　　mensural notation, 72
　　meter/time signatures, 73
　　note values, 72, 73, 94
　　opposition to, 74
　　Philippe de Vitry, 72–75
　　polyphony, 71–75
　　rhythms, 73–74
　　summary of, 74–75
　　temporal duration, 71–72
　ancient Greece, 8–11, 148–149
　ancient Rome, 13–14
　Baroque period
　　chord inversion, 321
　　circle of fifths, 321

Doctrine of Affections, 236, 295
　harmony, 237–238, 321
　major/minor modes, 238–239, 319–320
　pitch and tuning, 349
　Rameau, 320–321
　summary of, 322
　terminology, 320
late medieval/early Renaissance, 112
music as science, 8, 14
music of the spheres, 8, 14
Renaissance
　and analysis, 188–189
　ancient Greece, 148–149, 186–187
　consonance/dissonance, 187–188
　counterpoint, 188
　Glarean, 189
　modes/scales, 188–189
　overview of, 186
　temperaments, 190
　Tinctoris, 187–188
　tunings, 189–190
　Vicentino, 186–187
Musica enchiriadis (Abbot Hoger), 47–48
Musica ficta, 99
Musica humana, 14
Musica instrumentalis, 14
Musica mundana, 14
Musica reservata, 201
Musica secreta, 224
Musica transalpine publication, 220
Musical forms. *See* Song forms
Musical games/puzzles/jokes, 133–136, 138
Musical humanism, 110, 148–149
Musical notation
　ancient Greece, 5–6, 30
　chant notation, 30
　evolution of, 6
　figured bass notation, 238
　mensural notation, 56, 57, 72
　modal notation, 56–58, 72
Musical Offering, The (J.S Bach), 359
Musical staffs, 30–31
Musical symbolism, 345
Musicus, 14
"Mystery Sonatas" (Biber), 292–293

Natus ante saecula sequence, 36
Nave, 53
Nepotism, 262
Neumatic chant, 24
Neume, 30–31
Ninety-Five Theses, 195
Non al suo amante madrigal (Jacopo da
　Bologna), 105–106
Nota, 31
Note values/shapes, 72, 73, 94
Notes inégales, 315–316
Notker Balbulus, 36
Notre Dame of Paris. *See* Medieval polyphony
Notre Dame of Reims, 82
Notre Dame School, 60, 61, 68
Number symbolism, 113
Nunneries. *See* Medieval monasteries
Nuper rosarum flores motet (Dufay), 111–114

O Brother, Where Art Thou?, 121
O Lord, make thy servant, Elizabeth anthem
　(Byrd), 214–216
O rubor sanguinis chant (Hildegard of Bingen),
　39–40
Obbligato, 349
Oblique motion, 48
Oboe predecessor. *See* Shawm

Obrecht, Jacob, 140–142
Occursus, 48
Ockeghem, Johannes, 132–135, 138
Octaves, origin, 32
Odhecaton music book, 165–166
Offertory chant, 24, 27
Oh di Betlemme cantata (A. Scarlatti), 272, 273
Old Hall Manuscript, 120
"Old Hundredth" psalm, 201
Olympic Games, xxxii, 3
Omnipotens genitor trope, 27, 35
On parole de batre/A Paris/Frese nouvelle
　(Anonymous motet), 69
Open ending, 79
Opera, *See also* Baroque music
　defined, 240
　French *tragédie lyrique*
　　ballet de cour, 304
　　divertissements, 304
　　French overtures, 304
　　Lully's *Armide*, 304–306
　　overview of, 309–310
　　recitatif ordinaire, 304
　Italian opera, 240–251
　　arias, 246, 247–248
　　ariosos, 245, 247
　　birth of, 240–241
　　Caccini, 243–244
　　castrati, 334
　　Cesti, 249–250
　　Christian operas, 270
　　court to public genre, 248, 250–251
　　Cuzzoni, 334, 336
　　defined, 240
　　Euridice, 241–243
　　Florence and, 240–244
　　Handel and, 330–331, 333–336
　　instrumental toccatas, 244
　　Mantua and, 244–248
　　Marie Le Rochois, 305
　　Monteverdi, 244–250
　　opera seria, 333–335
　　Orfeo, 244–248
　　Peri, 241–243
　　Poppea, 248–250
　　recitatives, 245, 247–248
　　Rome and, 270
　　star singers, 248, 250–251, 334–335
　　stile rappresentativo, 241, 242
　　summary of, 250–251
　　Venice and, 248–250
　　vocal ornamentation, 243–244
　London
　　ballad opera, 335–336
　　Blow's *Venus and Adonis*, 323
　　castrati and, 334
　　Dido and Aeneas, 324–326
　　Giulio Cesare, 335–336
　　Handel, 330–331, 335–336
　　Italian opera, 330–331, 333–336
　　masque, 323
　　Purcell, 324–326
　　semi-opera, 323
　　theater music, 323–324
　　oratorio vs., 336–337
　　pastoral arias, 338
　　then vs. now, 336
Opus dei, 19
Or su, gentili spirti ballata (Landini), 107–110
Oratories, 270
Oratorios, *See also* Baroque music
　Carissimi, 270–271
　defined, 270

Handel, 271, 336–340
  Jephte, 270–271
  Messiah, 337–340
  operas vs., 336–337
  Samson, 271
Orchésographie (Arbeau), 175
Orchestras, 276–277, 302–303
Ordinary of the Mass. *See* Mass
Ordo virtutum drama (Hildegard of Bingen),
  40–41
Ordres, 316–318
Orestes (Euripides), 4, 10
Organ music, *See also* Keyboard music
  Bach, 342–345
  Buxheim Organ Book, 178
  Buxtehude, 296–298
  Frescobaldi, 267–269
  Hofhaimer, 194
  north German, 296–298
  organ Mass, 268
  organ versets, 268–269
  pedal points, 344
  south German, 299
Organs, *See also* Instruments, keyboard
  adding keyboards, 80–81
  allure of, 194
  foot pedals, 342
  pipe/church organs, 178, 296, 343
  portative organs, 81, 178
  positive organs, 81
  stops, 343
Organum. *See* Medieval polyphony
Orgelbuchlein chorale preludes (J.S. Bach),
  342–345, 346
Orientis partibus conductus (Anonymous),
  63–65
Ornamentation
  agréments, 314–316
  Baroque music, 314–315
  medieval music, 98
  vocal, 243–244, 264
Orfeo opera (Monteverdi), 244–248
Orpheus, 181, 241
Overdotting, 315–316
Overtures, French, 304
Oxford University, 102

Pachelbel, Johann, 299–300
Paeans, 3
Palestrina, Giovanni Pierluigi da, 188, 204–205
Pan-consonance, 122
Pan-isorhythmic, 122
Paolini, Pietro, 275
Parallel organum, 48
Paraphrase technique, 136–137
Paris, *See also* Baroque music; Late Renaissance
  Paris
  Black Death, 168
  Grande-Salle, 75, 78
  Ile de la Cité, 62, 75
  Latin Quarter, 62, 168
  map of medieval, 62
  Master Albertus of, 51
  Middle Ages, 52–53, 61–62, 168
  University of, 53, 60, 62–63, 71
Paris, Notre Dame of. *See* Medieval polyphony
Parisian chansons, 168–170, 173
Parker, Matthew, 213–214
Parody (emulation) technique, 208
Pars les bons Gedeons ballade (Caserta), 93–94
Part books, 167
Parthenia (1612) (Byrd, Gibbons, Bull), 218
Parthenon, xxxii

Partita, 349
Partsongs, 211
Passacaglia, 258, *See also* Chaconne
Passions, 358
Pastoral arias, 338
Pastyme with Good Companye partsong (King
  Henry VIII), 210–211
Patter-song, 169
Pavane, 174
Peace of Augsburg, 198
Pedal points, 344
Penitential Psalms. *See* Psalter
Peri, Jacopo, 241–243
Perotinus the Great, 54, 58–61
Pes, 116
Petrarch, Francesco, 89, 102, 105–106, 148,
  155, 255
Petrucci, Ottaviano, 165–167
Philip the Chancellor, 63, 65
Philip the Good, duke, 127–128
Philippe de Vitry, 72–75, 76, 77–78, 90
Philippus de Caserta, 93–95
Philologists, 97
Phrygian tonos, 5, 9–10
Pisan, Christine de, 125, 139
Pitch, 97, 189–190, *See also* Tuning
Pitch names, 30–31
Plagal cadence, 216
Plagal mode, 29
Plainsong. *See* Gregorian chant
Plato, 2–3, 7, 148, 149, 255
Point of imitation, 205–206
Polychoral works, 253, 260, 261
Polymeters, 93
Polyphony, early, *See also* Medieval polyphony
  chansons, 124–127
  England, 116, 119, 120–123
  Lieder, 192–193
  Ordinary of the Mass, 87–89, 130–131
  Penitential Psalms, 200–201
  Proper of the Mass, 55–56, 59–61, 192
Pope John XXII, 74
Poppea opera (Monteverdi), 249–250
Portative organs, 81, 178
Positive organs, 81
Possente spirto aria (Monteverdi), 246–247
Power, Leonel, 120
Prato, Giovanni da, 107, 109
Preludes
  chorale, 299, 342–345
  defined, 183
  unmeasured, 313–314
Prenez sur moi canon (Ockeghem), 133–134
Prima pratica style, 206, 230, 236, 263
Printing. *See* Late Renaissance; Late Renais-
  sance Paris
Program music, 291
Programmatic sonatas, 291–296
Prolation (*prolatio*), 73
Proper of the Mass. *See* Mass
Proportions, 94
Proslambanomenos, 9
Protestant Reformation, 191, 195–198,
  203–204
Psalm settings, Hebrew, 278
Psalm tone, 22
Psalmody, 21
Psalter
  defined, 21, 199
  English translations, 201–202, 213–214
  French translation, 201
  medieval psalms, 21–22
  Penitential Psalm settings

Allegri, 263–265
  Josquin, 162–163
  Lassus, 200–201
  polyphonic, 200–201
Penitential Psalms
  defined, 162, 199
  Protestants and, 199–200
  Psalm 50, 162–163, 263–265
  Protestants and, 201–202
Ptolemy, Claudius, 8, 9–10
Puer natus est nobis Introit, 24–25, 35
Punctum/puncta, 79
"Pur ti miro" aria (Monteverdi), 249–250
Purcell, Henry, *See also* Baroque music
  Dido and Aeneas, 324–326
  odes, 326–328
  opera, 324–326
  Queen Mary and, 329
  summary of, 329–330
  theater music, 323–326
Puritans, 211
Pythagoras, 7–8, 14
Pythagorean tuning, 189

Quadrivium, 14
Quadruplum, 59
Quam pulcra es motet (Dunstaple), 122–123
Quare fremuerunt gentes conductus (Anony-
  mous), 77
Quattrocento, 150
Queen Elizabeth I, *See also* Late Renaissance
  England
  about, 211, 219
  dancer, 176, 217
  Dowland and, 221
  education of, 212
  madrigals for, 219–220
  musician, 217–218, 219
  portrait of, 212
  religion and, 211–212
Queen Mary of England, 322, 326–329
Quodlibets, 141

Rameau, Jean-Philippe, 320–321
Ranks, 343
Raphael, 149
Rebec, 46
Recitation tone, 162–163
Recitative
  accompanied recitative, 357
  aria vs., 247–248
  defined, 245
  recitatif ordinaire, 304
Recorders, 181
Reformation, 191, 195–198, 203–204
Refrains
  burdens, 120
  ritornello, 105
  strophe plus, 120, 121
Reichstag (or Diet), 194
Religious music, *See also* Mass; Motets; Oratorios
  ancient Greece, 3
  Baroque Paris, 307
  Baroque Rome. *See* Baroque music
  early Christian chant, 15–16
  late Renaissance England, 211–217
  Middle Ages. *See* Medieval monasteries; Me-
    dieval polyphony
Renaissance. *See* Late medieval/early Renais-
  sance; Late Renaissance
Requiem Mass, 37
Responsorial singing, 26
Reverberation time, 267

Rhythm
    1200-1300s, 73–74
    isorhythm, 78
    late 1300s, 91, 93, 94–95
    pan-isorhythm, 122
    syncopation, 93–94
Rhythmic imitation, 207
Rhythmic modes, 56–58
Ricercar, 183–184, 269
Richard the Lionheart, 45
Rigaud, Hyacinthe, 301
Ripieno, 286
Ripresa, 107
Ritornello, 105
Ritornello form, 286
Robertsbridge Codex, 81
Rococo style, 316, 318
Roman chant, 15–16
Roman de Fauvel satire (Gervès de Bus), 75–77
Roman Empire, *See also* Age of antiquity
    fall of, 17
    Holy Roman Empire
        Charlemagne, 20
        Charles IV, 78, 79
        Gregorian chant and, 20–21
        map c1500, 191
        overview of, 190
    map of, 13
    papacy to Avignon, 89–90
Rome. *See* Baroque music; Late Renaissance
    Italy
Rondeau form, 86, 87, 317
Rondellus, 116
"*Rosary Sonatas*" (Biber), 292–293
Rossi, Salomone, 278–279
Rota, 116–118, *See also* Canons
Rotulus, 125, 139, 173
Rousseau, Jean-Jacques, 234
Royal Academy of Music, 333
Rule of St. Benedict, 18, 19–20, 21, 22

Sackbut, 142–143, 182, 276
St. Gall
    John of, 29, 48–49
    map, 18
    monastery, 18–19
    Tuotilo of, 35
St. James, 50–51
St. John Passion (J.S. Bach), 358
St. Mark's Basilica, Venice, 251–255
St. Mary's Church, Lübeck, 296–297
St. Matthew Passion (J.S. Bach), 196, 358
St. Peter's Basilica, Rome
    about St. Peter, 206
    colossal Baroque and, 266–267
    defined, 206, 262, 265–266
    Michelangelo and, 206, 265
    photograph of, 234
    and Square, 234
    when built, 203
St. Petronio Basilica, Bologna, 282–283
St. Thomas Church, Leipzig, 353, 355
Salutati, Coluccio, 104
Salve, Regina settings
    keyboard tablature, 178
    for organ, Hofhaimer, 194
    paraphrased chant, Basiron, 137
Sanctus chant, 24, 27
Santiago de Compostela, 50–51
Sarabande, 290
Sarum chant, 116
Satire, musical, 75–77

Saul, Saul, was verfolgst du mich? motet (Schütz), 260–261
Savonarola, Girolamo, 152–153, 162
Scales, *See also* Tones
    ancient Greece, 9–11
    church modes, 29
    major/minor, 189, 238–239, 320
    microtones, 10, 186–187
    modal, 188–189, 319–320
Scarlatti, Alessandro, 272–273
Scholasticism, 71
Schütz, Heinrich, 259–261
Scivias (Hildegard of Bingen), 39
Scordatura tuning, 292–293
Scores
    defined, 100
    in Middle Ages, 100
    number symbolism in, 113
    reading, 100–101
    symbolic scores, 91
Scriptoriums, 19
Seconda pratica style, 224–225, 228–229, 230, 236
Seikilos, 5
Semi-opera, 323
Semibreve notes, 72
Senesino, castrati, 334
Sequence chants, 24, 34, 36–38
Seven liberal arts, 14
Shawm, 80, 142–143, 182, 276
Sheet music (rotulus), 125, 139, 173
Sian galanti di Valenza song (Lorenzo de' Medici), 151
Sincopa, 93–94
Sinfonia, 283, *See also* Symphony
Singing, *See also* Religious music; Songs
    a cappella, 205
    antiphonal singing, 21
    ladies' ensembles, 224–225
    responsorial, 26
Single-impression printing, 166–167
Sistine Chapel
    a cappella Sistina, 205
    cappella pontificia sistina, 263, 265
    defined, 204
    interior, 146, 205
    model for, 90
    photographs, 146, 234
    when built, 203
Skolion, 5
Socrates, 2–3
Soggetto cavato, 160–162
Solfege, 31–32
Solo art songs, 221–222, *See also* Monody; Songs
Solo concertos, 285
Solo lute intabulation, 171
Solo sonatas, 280
Solo violin fugues, 349–350
Sonatas
    Biber, 291–293
    chamber sonatas, 277
    church sonatas, 277
    Corelli, 279–282
    defined, 277–278
    Gabrieli, 254
    Kuhnau, 294–296
    programmatic, 291–296
    Rossi, 278–279
    trio sonatas, 280
Song of the Ass conductus (Anonymous), 63–65
Song forms

French *formes fixes*, *See also* Medieval music, courtly love
    ballade, 85–86
    defined, 84
    end of, 169
    Machaut and, 84–85
    overview of, 125
    rondeau, 86, 87
    virelai, 86–87
Italian *formes fixes*, *See also* Madrigals
    ballata, 106–107
    caccia, 106
    madrigal, 105–106
    strophe plus refrain, 120, 121
    through-composed, 155
Song of Songs, 122
Songs, *See also* Motets; Opera; Oratorios; Singing
    air de cour, 302
    ancient Greece, 3, 5
    Art of Measured Song, 71–72
    Beatriz de Dia, 42–43
    Bernart de Ventadorn, 44–45
    cantate français, 308–309
    carnival songs, 151, 152
    carols, 120–121
    chansons
        Binchois, 125–127
        Burgundian cadence in, 127
        Claudin, 169–173
        defined, 42, 125
        motet-chanson, Dufay, 128–129
        Parisian chansons, 168–170, 173
        polyphonic chansons, 124–127
    consort songs, 221
    courtly love, 41–46, 84–87
    folk songs, 121, 327
    Franco of Cologne and, 71–72
    Jacquet de La Guerre, 307–309
    joke song, Josquin, 135–136
    King Henry VIII, 210–211
    Lied/Lieder, 192
    Little Book of Spiritual Songs, 197–198
    Lorenzo de' Medici, 151
    lute ayres, 221–222
    Minnesang, 46
    partsongs, 211
    patter-song, 169
    Richard the Lionheart, 45
    solo art songs, 221–222
    "swan song", 155
    Walter, 197–198
Songs of Solomon (Rossi), 278
Spanish *cantigas*, 46
Spanish composers, 209
Spanish guitar, *vihuela*, 180–181
Spanish viol, 181
Spiccato, 283
Squarcialupi Codex, 105–107
Staffs, musical, 30–31
Stasimon Chorus, 4, 10
Sternhold and Hopkins Psalter, 201–202, 213
Stile antico, 263
Stile concertato, 252–253, *See also* Concerted style
Stile concitato, 255–256
Stile rappresentativo, 241, 242
Stile recitativo, 245, 247–248
Stops, multiple, 280
Stops, organ, 343
Stradavari, Antonio, 275, 276
String instruments. *See* Instruments, string

Strophe plus refrain form, 120, 121
Strophic variation arias, 246
Strozzi, Barbara, 256–258
Strozzi, Bernardo, 228, 257
Style brisé, 312
Subjects, fugue, 347
Substitute clausula, 58
Suite genre, dance, 183
Suites, 332
Summer Canon (Anonymous), 116–118
Suspension, 188
Sustained-tone organum, 50
"Swan song", 155
Syllabic chant, 24
Symbolic scores, 91
Symbolism, musical, 345
Symbolism, number, 113
Symphonia (Hildegard of Bingen), 39
Symphoniae sacrae motets (Schütz), 260, 261
Symphony orchestra origins, 276–277
Symposiums, 4–5
Syncopation, 93–94
Syncope, 188

Tablature, 171, 178, 180
Tactus, 187
Tafelmusik, 199
Talea, 78
Tallis, Thomas, 212–214, 217
Tant que vivray chanson (Claudin), 169–173
Temperament, defined, 190
Temperament, equal, 190, 347, 349
Temporal duration, 71–72, 97
Tenebrae services, 263
Tenor voices, 56
Tenorlied, 192, 193
Tetrachord, 9–10
Text underlay, 97–98
Text (word) painting, 157, 163, 236
Theater music, *See also* Opera
   ancient Greece, 4
   Purcell, 323–326
Theater, women in English, 324
Theorbo, 237
Thirty Years' War, 259–260
Throne of St. Peter (Bernini), 235
Through-composed form, 155
Tibia, 13
Time, measuring, 70–71
Time (meter) signatures, 73
Time (*tempus*), 73
Timelines
   antiquity/Middle Ages, xxxii-1
   Baroque era, 232–233
   late Middle ages/early Renaissance, 102–103
   late Renaissance, 146–147
Tinctoris, Johannes, 148, 187–188
Toccatas, 244, 268
Tombeaux, 311–313
Tonal answers, 269
Tones, *See also* Scales
   double leading-tone, 99
   microtones, 10, 186–187
   psalm tone, 22
   recitation tone, 162–163
   sustained-tone organum, 50
   tonos/tonoi, 9–11
Torelli, Giacomo, 249
Torelli, Giuseppe, 282–284
Tout par compass suy composés rondeau
   (Cordier), 91–93, 94
Tragédie lyrique. See French *tragédie lyrique*

Treatise on Harmony (Rameau), 321
Treble voice, 119
Trecento, 104
Trio sonatas, 280
Triplum, 59
Triseme in Greek notation, 5
Triumph of Oriana, The madrigals, 219–220
Trivium, 14
Trobairitz, 42–43
Trombone, 13, 276, *See also* Sackbut
Troper, Winchester, 49
Tropes, 27, 34–35, 37, 50
Troubadours, 42, 43, 44–45
Trouvères, 42–43, 45–46
Trumpet music, Torelli, 282–284
Trumpets, *See also* Instruments, wind
   in Baroque era, 282, 284
   ensembles, of, 182
   flat trumpets, 329
   overview of, 142–143
   Roman *tuba,* 13
Tu es Petrus Mass (Palestrina), 208
Tu es Petrus motets (Palestrina), 207
Tu se' morta, mia vita arioso (Monteverdi),
   245–246, 247
Tuba, 13
Tuning, *See also* Pitch
   evolution of, 349
   just tuning, 189–190
   Pythagorean tuning, 189
   scordatura tuning, 292–293
Tuotilo of St. Gall, 35
Two- and Three-Part Inventions (J.S. Bach),
   346

Ubi papa, ibi Roma, 92
Universitas, 62
Universities, 61–62
University, Oxford, 102
University of Paris, 53, 60, 62–63, 71
Unmeasured preludes, 313–314

Variation arias, strophic, 246
Variation genre, 183
Variation technique, 218–219
Vatican, 206
Vaughan Williams, Ralph, 214
Vecchi, Orazio, 157–158
Venice
   concerted style, 251, 252, 258–259
   Italian opera, 248–250
   printing in, 252
   St. Mark's Basilica, 251–255
Venus and Adonis opera (Blow), 323
Versailles, 232, 234, 301–302
Verse structure, double, 36
Versets, organ, 268–269
Vespers, 19, 20, 21–23
Vicentino, Nicola, 186–187
Victoria, Tomás Luis de, 209
Vida, 44
Viderunt omnes Gradual
   defined, 26
   Leoninus, 55–58
   Perotinus, 58–60
   Viderunt Hemanuel trope for, 50
Vielle, 80
Vihuela, 180–181
Vingt-quatre violons du roi orchestra, 302–303
Viol, 181, 276
Viola da gamba, 181, 276
Violin family, *See also* Instruments, string

ballet de cour and, 302–303
   cello, 276
   defined, 181, 276
   scordatura tuning, 292–293
   viola, 276
   violinmakers, 276
   violino piccolo, 356
   violino/violin, 181, 274–276
Violin music
   Bach, 349–350
   Biber, 291–293
   Pachelbel, 300
Virelai form, 86–87
Virginals, 179, 218
Vivaldi, Antonio, 284–287
Vocal ornamentation, 243–244, 264
Vocal religious music. *See* Religious music
Vocal secular music. *See* Madrigals; Opera; Songs
Vocal solos. *See* Monody; Solo art songs
Volta, 176, 217
Volume, 97, 239, *See also* Dynamic levels
Vox principalis/organalis, 48, 49

Wachet auf... chorale cantata (J.S. Bach),
   353–358
Walking bass, 281
Walter, Johann, 197–198
Water Music dance suites (Handel), 331,
   332–333
Well-Tempered Clavier, The (J.S. Bach), 312,
   346–348
Westminster Abbey, 323
Whole Psalter Translated into English Metre, The
   (Parker), 213–214
Wie schön leuchtet der Morgenstern
   chorale fantasia, Buxtehude, 297–298
   chorale prelude, Pachelbel, 299
William and Mary of England, 322, 326–329
Winchester troper, 49
Wind instruments. *See* Instruments, wind
Women, *See also* Queen Elizabeth
   Baroque era
      Anna Magdalena Bach, 355
      Arabella Hunt, 327
      Barbara Strozzi, 256–258
      English theater, 324
      Jacquet de La Guerre, 307–309
      Marie Le Rochois, 305
      Parisian theater, 304, 307
      Venetian orphans, 285–286
   Middle Ages
      Beatriz de Dia, 42–43
      Christine de Pisan, 125, 139
      Decameron and, 109
      education of, 109
      Eleanor of Aquitane, 43–45
      Jacqueline de Hacqueville, 138, 139
      Joan of Arc, 83, 131
      poets/performers, 139
      trobairitz, 42–43
   Renaissance
      Isabella d'Este, 227–228
      keyboard music for, 218
      Margaret of Austria, 144
      vocal ensembles, 224–225
Word (text) painting, 157, 163, 236

Young Man Playing a Violin (Paolini), 275

"Zadok the Priest" anthem (Handel), 214
Zarlino, Gioseffo, 188
Zwolle, Henri Arnaut de, 103, 142